YEATS'S POEMS

YEATS'S POEMS

Edited and annotated by A. Norman Jeffares
with an appendix by Warwick Gould

MACMILLAN
LONDON

This edition first published 1989 by
MACMILLAN LONDON LIMITED
4 Little Essex Street London WC2R 3LF
and Basingstoke

Associated companies in Auckland, Delhi, Dublin, Gaborone, Hamburg, Harare, Hong
Kong, Johannesburg, Kuala Lumpur, Lagos, Manzini, Melbourne, Mexico City, Nairobi,
New York, Singapore and Tokyo

ISBN 978-0-333-51061-2   ISBN 978-1-349-20284-3 (eBook)
DOI 10.1007/978-1-349-20284-3

A Cataloguing in Publication Data record for this title is available from the British Library

Typeset by Wyvern Typesetting Ltd, Bristol

ACKNOWLEDGMENT

The quotations from the work of W. B. Yeats are reprinted by kind permission of
Mr Michael Butler Yeats. The maps in Appendix Two are reproduced by kind
permission of Colin Smythe.

Detail of a portrait of W. B. Yeats by Augustus John,
reproduced by permission of the Tate Gallery, London

CONTENTS

CONTENTS

Introduction

This edition contains the poetry that Yeats wished to preserve. He wrote poetry from his fifteenth year to his seventy-third, poetry that changed as he himself changed and developed. There is the limpid simplicity of Irish local legends and ballads, the sensitive shadowy beauty of the romantic poetry, the increasingly complex symbolism that treated the material of Gaelic mythology, transmuting it into twilight pre-Raphaelite longings. There follows poetry of a more direct, even bitter, kind, concerned with public events, denuded of decoration. Then comes more personal poetry, yet poetry which deals with larger issues. There are more forthright emphases on the body and its demands now, regrets for the physical decay of age when mental powers seemed stronger, the imagination livelier than ever before. And there are the great questionings as illness brought death nearer.

There was a constant process of poetry pulled between ideal and real, between theory and practicality, even between love and hate. Idealistic hopes for an Ireland to be regenerated by awareness of its past mythology, its Gaelic literature, were jostled by the experience of discovering that other minds were not always at one with his own visions. Early failure with his plans to publish Irish books led Yeats to more direct propagandising, in his prose, for the re-creation of an Irish culture, a blend of elements of the Christian present and the pagan past. Though he saw his role as a literary one, he moved into more active political involvements; but his high hopes of unifying different political parties and groups were dashed by experience: the realities of a riot in Dublin in which blood was shed, a life lost, property damaged and the dark submerged forces of the mob surfaced in sinister fashion. Further knowledge of the revolutionary movements which he had thought would support his literary movement led the poet to detach himself from direct political action.

Yeats's idealism for a regenerated Ireland, somewhat battered, now became beaten into a new shape upon the anvil of the Abbey Theatre. To its creation he brought old plans revitalised by Lady Gregory's energy; he wrote verse plays, heroic tragedies about Irish legends, 'helmets, crowns, and swords'. The audience for such drama was not large:

> When we are high and airy hundreds say
> That if we hold that flight they'll leave the place . . .

Instead realistic comedy became popular. That, however, soon posed different problems:

> those same hundreds mock another day
> Because we have made our art of common things.

Oversensitive nationalists were offended by and strenuously objected to the work of J. M. Synge, whose originality Yeats fully recognised: he praised Synge's drama generously and fought fiercely for its right to be staged and to be recognised as great art. After the row over *The Playboy of the Western World* would come battles for Sean O'Casey – and later, with him.

During his period as manager of the Abbey Theatre (1904–10) Yeats had written less poetry. 'All things', he wrote, 'can tempt me from this craft of verse'. In 'Adam's Curse' he had proclaimed the difficulties of that craft:

> A line will take us hours maybe;
> Yet if it does not seem a moment's thought,
> Our stitching and unstitching has been nought.

The craft, however, was again changing. What he wrote in this middle period was stripped of adjectives; he rammed it with verbs and nouns; he charged it with the explosive powder of the rhetoric he had learned from his earlier political activities: his contests on committees, his stirring speeches, his persuasive prose propaganda for a new, culturally revived, intellectually independent Ireland. He had written very effective fiction in the 1890s and the narrative art shown in his short stories was now shaped into narrative poems, *The Old Age of Queen Maeve* and *Baile and Aillinn*. The *Collected Works* of 1908 contained most of Yeats's early and the beginning of his middle period of poetry as well as his verse plays. This sumptuous edition of eight volumes was published when Yeats was forty-three, when

> The fascination of what's difficult
> Has dried the sap out of my veins, and rent
> Spontaneous joy and natural content
> Out of my heart.

His Pegasus seemed harnessed, compelled to the work of a cart-horse, dragged down from its leaping from cloud to cloud on Mount Olympus. Many asked if his career as a poet was over. He had no happiness in his former subjects. 'Under the Moon', written in 1901, had conveyed his unease, his sense of being out of fashion 'Like an old song'. He had changed indeed. No longer the Celt, he was Irish instead; he had left the misty realms of the Celtic Twilight he had created and come out of the moods of the *fin de siècle* into the twentieth century.

This was a harsher world. The practicalities enforced by his work for the Abbey, disgust at the reception given to the work of its creative, individualistic playwrights, as well as rage at the treatment given to Hugh Lane's offer to Dublin of his collection of French Impressionist paintings now provided subject matter for scornful satire. The poems of *Responsibilities* were trained upon Irish targets, the poet's capacity to aim clarified by his capacity to judge the distance Irish patronage had to travel to match that of the Italian Renaissance, when support of art had been so enlightened. His first experience of Italy in 1907 – of Urbino, Ferrara and Ravenna in particular – coming after Dublin's myopic reception of *The Playboy of the Western World* had expanded the horizons of his thought in dramatic fashion. How detached he had become from the nationalist politics of the period emerged in 'Easter, 1916', the poem he wrote on the Easter Rising. When he had met the future revolutionaries he had

> . . . passed with a nod of the head
> Or polite meaningless words,
> Or have lingered awhile and said
> Polite meaningless words,
> And thought before I had done
> Of a mocking tale or a gibe
> To please a companion
> Around the fire at the club,
> Being certain that they and I
> But lived where motley is worn:
> All changed, changed utterly:
> A terrible beauty is born.

Yeats's own life had been changing too. The bachelor who had learned fencing from Ezra Pound in the winters they spent in Stone Cottage in Sussex, who had learned Swedish exercises from Mabel

Dickinson, the mistress from whom he parted after a violent scene in 1913, began to turn his thoughts to marriage. His devotion to Maud Gonne, with whom he fell in love in 1889, his barren unrequited passion for her, had left him childless, with nothing but a book, he wrote bitterly as he approached his forty-ninth year, to prove his blood and that of his ancestors. In writing the first book of his *Autobiographies, Reveries over Childhood and Youth*, he was shaping his own mythology, selecting and emphasising significant moments to present a pattern in his own life, seizing upon events or actions or remarks by others which crystallised his view of them. In the process he stressed his own individuality, stemming from an ancestry of merchants and later members of the professional class (his great-grandfather and his grandfather were Irish country rectors) on his father's side, and of smugglers, traders, sea-captains and ship-owners on his mother's side.

His thought was idiosyncratic. His deep interest in magic and mysticism had been hinted at in some early poems:

> *My rhymes more than their rhyming tell*
> *Of things discovered in the deep,*
> *Where only body's laid asleep.*

In *The Wind Among the Reeds* there are poems which relate to his occultism, but the clearest statements of his own ideas came, more directly, in such poems as 'Ego Dominus Tuus', written in 1915, and 'The Phases of the Moon', finished in 1918, which attempted an ordering of experience, an explanation of human personality in terms of the self and anti-self and the phases of the moon. These were obscure poems. By 1917 he had finished what he called 'a little philosophical book'; originally entitled *An Alphabet*, it became *Per Amica Silentia Lunae*, this Virgilian title containing two parts, 'Anima Hominis' and 'Anima Mundi'. He described it to his father as 'a kind of prose backing' for his poetry, and 'part of a religious system more or less worked out'. He had found that setting it all in order had helped his verse, given him 'a new framework and new patterns'.

When Yeats married in 1917 his wife began automatic writing, and this bred a great confidence in the poet. The communicators were mysterious; they seemed to provide the authority he had yearned for; they gave his poetry a new assurance. He had offered to spend what remained of his life in piecing together and interpreting their messages, their scattered sentences, but was told that they had come to give him metaphors for poetry. He elaborated on this in *A Packet for Ezra Pound*, written in 1928:

> The unknown writer took his theme at first from my just published *Per Amica Silentia Lunae*. I had made a distinction between the perfection that is from a man's combat with himself and that which is from a combat with circumstance, and upon this simple distinction he built up an elaborate classification of men according to their more or less complete expression of one type or the other. He supported his classification by a series of geometrical symbols and put these symbols in an order that answered the question in my essay as to whether some prophet could not prick upon the calendar the birth of a Napoleon or a Christ. A system of symbolism, strange to my wife and myself, certainly awaited expression, and when I asked how long that would take I was told years. Sometimes when my mind strays back to those first days I remember that Browning's Paracelsus did not obtain the secret until he had written his spiritual history at the bidding of his Byzantine teacher, that before initiation Wilhelm Meister read his own history written by another, and I compare my *Per Amica* to these histories.

The subject matter of what became *A Vision* (1925), first published in 1926, and the greatly revised version of 1937 certainly provided an effective scaffolding for Yeats's poetry. He formed through *A Vision*'s ideas a capacity to fuse together apparent contrarieties and contradictions. In doing this he was reverting to ideas in some of his early poems and to his lifelong interest in William Blake. The beauty longed for and evoked in the early verse, but rather brushed aside in his middle period, could now be accommodated, tempered as it was by his experience, by his knowledge of its opposite. Words obeyed his call, and he had much to say with them, based not upon past literature, not upon any illusion that he could reshape his country's spirit to his own pattern nor upon the disillusionment he had brought upon himself in his attempts to reshape it – and he had reshaped it more than he realised – but upon his interpretation of both public and personal life.

Powerfully emotive poetry, technically accomplished in its rhyming, its rhythm, its repetitive patterns (of which 'Byzantium' is such a fine example), matched the accomplishment of ambitions which had come to seem impossible. The unhappy, unsuccessful romantic lover becomes happily married, barren bachelor burgeons as father of daughter and son: the genes of silent, dour, monied Pollexfens and talkative, outgoing, easy-going Yeatses were to continue in their medley of contrariety, their tension of opposites. The rootless man, so frequently travelling between Ireland and England, now owns a medieval tower in the west of Ireland, a fine town house in Merrion Square in Dublin. The youthful revolutionary patriot turned middle-aged sceptic is appointed a Senator of the Irish Free State. And the poet who might have been thought to have ended his career with the publication of his *Collected Works* in 1908 is awarded the Nobel Prize for Literature in 1923, an apt recognition of the full flowering of his gifts into the mode of modernism. It was a late flowering; this was a very different kind of talent from that which had marked his early career. Yet, with a certain reason, he was to declare that he had spent his life saying the same thing in different ways.

What common thread, then, runs through this impressively different poetry? Largely, perhaps, it is a matter of belief or, rather, the endless search for it. Yeats was by nature at once religious and sceptical. He wanted a faith, he wanted to believe, but what was he to believe in? His father's unbelief had a very strong influence on him when he was a child and so the Christianity of his day seemed to be ruled out. His youthful interest in science did not last long; it was replaced by a passion for poetry – stimulated no doubt by the effect on him of Laura Armstrong, a dashing girl for whom he wrote his first verse plays. At the High School he had joined with some friends in inviting an Indian, Mohini Chatterjee, to come from London to discuss his beliefs with them in the Hermetic Society they had formed in Dublin. Yeats was interested in Theosophy, but soon after he joined the Theosophists in London he was asked to resign – the sceptical side of him having wanted proofs. Magic then occupied him; he joined the Order of the Golden Dawn in 1890, and his interest in Rosicrucianism and Cabbalism developed. Study of the occult formed a large part of his life, though he kept it, in general, out of his writing. He wrote to John O'Leary in July 1892 that it was absurd to hold him 'weak' or otherwise because he chose to persist in a study which he had decided four or five years earlier to make, next to his poetry, 'the most important pursuit of my life'. He went on to say that if he had not made magic his constant study he could not have written a single word of his Blake book nor would *The Countess Kathleen* ever have come to exist.

The mystical life is the centre of all that I do and all that I think and all that I write. It holds to my work the same relation that the philosophy of Godwin held to the work of Shelley and I have always considered myself a voice of what I believe to be a greater renaissance – the revolt of the soul against the intellect – now beginning in the world.

He formed the idea of creating an Irish mystical order, an Order of Celtic Mysteries, and for ten years was occupied in devising rituals as well as discovering a philosophy for it. He was deeply involved in the quarrels which broke out in the Order of the Golden Dawn and wrote two privately printed pamphlets about its future. He remained a member (probably until the early 1920s, by which time he was obviously regarded as an elder statesman of the Order), but he returned to an early interest in spiritualism, shunned after a disturbing experience at a seance in Dublin as a young man, the occasion on which he had recited the opening of *Paradise Lost* in lieu of the Lord's Prayer. Now he took to attending seances and consulting various mediums. His attitude to the supernatural was a questioning one and he learned from the Society for Psychical Research to record details of his experiences.

The excitement created by his wife's automatic writing was intensi-fied by the fact that it seemed to offer answers to many of his questionings. Out of it came a system of belief, encompassing human and historical change, which allowed him to face the future – its public as well as its private problems: the threatening loss of civilisation's achievements; the ruin of tradition, of order, all he had come to appreciate so deeply; an apparently approaching decay in values; something of the apocalyptic destruction some of his poems – notably 'The Secret Rose' and 'The Valley of the Black Pig' – had imaged in the 1890s. This was a violent world into which he had brought his children: the future extended now beyond contem-plation of what occurred after the immediacy of an individual's own death.

In Ireland he had seen a model for the world's situation. Those Big Houses which he knew, which had seemed to him centres of culture, were no longer based on land after the British Government passed its Wyndham and Ashbourne Land Acts to buy out the landed estates and sell them to the tenants, thus creating a nation of peasant proprietors. And after the viciousness of the Anglo-Irish war had given way to the Treaty of 1922 which created the Irish Free State there had come the ironic sequel, the anarchy of civil war:

> We are closed in, and the key is turned
> On our uncertainty; somewhere
> A man is killed, or a house burned,
> Yet no clear fact to be discerned.

He viewed the situation clearly if despairingly:

> We had fed the heart on fantasies,
> The heart's grown brutal from the fare;
> More substance in our enmities
> Than in our love . . .

He had reason enough for fearing the irrational violence which, he felt, was gathering force, and he put his feelings about it into 'The Second Coming'. This poem is the most effective encapsulation of *A Vision*'s view of the gyres, the remorseless process of historical change in which an age is the reversal of an age, and the Second Coming undoes all that has been achieved in the centuries of Christian civilisation:

> Things fall apart; the centre cannot hold;
> Mere anarchy is loosed upon the world,
> The blood-dimmed tide is loosed, and everywhere
> The ceremony of innocence is drowned;
> The best lack all conviction, while the worst
> Are full of passionate intensity.

There was not much consolation to be found. The facts seemed brutally clear and had to be faced. Destruction of many ingenious lovely things was nothing new:

> Man is in love and loves what vanishes,
> What more is there to say?

The poet's personal predicament provided some parallels. He had to face increasing 'bodily decrepitude'; various illnesses took their toll of his strength. The 'sixty-year-old smiling public man' was growing old. He had lived intensely and he wanted to continue to do so. But the constant conflict warred on in him, dramatised in 'A Dialogue of Self and Soul' and later sharpened into the stark choice of 'perfection of the life or of the work'.

The work had found temporary solutions to the problems of this particular human life. In his youth Yeats had envisaged escape. The fairy paradises of the other world had beckoned alluringly from the Gaelic legends he read in translation, just as the oral folklore of Sligo (and later that of Galway) offered examples of belief in the supernatural. In *The Wanderings of Oisin* (1889) he had explored his pagan hero's merely temporary immortality, his resistance to St Patrick's admonitions at the end of his escape to the three islands, of the Living, of Victories and of Forgetfulness. They symbolised what man is always seeking: 'infinite feeling, infinite battle, infinite repose'. For himself Yeats created a dream of escape from the lure of women, the imaginings stirred by his senses, from the world of men and its money cares and fears. Remembering Thoreau's *Walden*, homesick for the beauty, timelessness and security of Sligo in the noise, bustle and genteel poverty into which his feckless artist father had landed the family in London, he was stirred by seeing a ball on a jet of water in a shop window in the Strand, turning it into memories of Innisfree. His daydream was of burning out a few years on that island in Lough Gill in Sligo. But the dream was contemporary with the battle for recognition. Not only as a youth did Yeats often seem abstracted in his dreams – a local policeman in Dublin, who had been asking why Yeats went indifferently through clean and muddy places, thought his absence of mind sufficiently explained by the Yeatses' servant telling him that the young man was a poet: 'Oh well, if it is only the poetry that is working in his head' – but always there was also a shrewd awareness that he must avoid his father's lack of will. In his twenties he thought that 'if good or bad luck made his life interesting' he would be a great poet. He must be true to his emotions in his writing; and he had to work hard to get that writing known; yet the pressures of the world must not be allowed to impinge upon the dreams.

There had been another kind of escape as well, into the role of *cavalier serviente* to Maud Gonne, to whom he could only – penniless as he was – offer poetic devotion; though this romantic dream was sanctioned by the hope that, someday, his devotion would be rewarded. It became the fantasy of abstracting Maud Gonne from the world of politics into a world of art. Meeting her had been good luck for his art, bad luck for his life – and yet it was one of the major factors that made it interesting. The idealism was strong:

> O but we dreamed to mend
> Whatever mischief seemed
> To afflict mankind, but now
> That winds of winter blow
> Learn that we were crack-pated when we dreamed.

Writing heroic plays, creating those moments of high tension in which the Gaelic heroes and heroines made their gestures of defiance in the face of despair had been another way of avoiding the unheroic present. Things became different after the years of success (there was even that superbly set realistic play about Swift and his spirit, *The Words upon the Window-pane*): ironically, however, after the freedom gained by marriage, fatherhood, house-ownership, senatorship and the international recognition of his poetic achievement typified by the award of the Nobel Prize, the civil war of body and mind not only continued but intensified. A different kind of escape was demanded now, different from the youthful dreaming he had opposed to the actualities of life. He might try to escape into a world of intellect, of thought: at least its exploration would enrich the poetry. From it he could confront more clearly the difficulties and frustrations arising when an ageing body harboured a youthful mind:

> Why should the imagination of a man
> Long past his prime remember things that are
> Emblematical of love and war?

The imagination was spurred by the sight of 'the young in one another's arms' when it was a time to write his will, to make his soul. True, it could escape from Ireland, 'no country for old men', across the waters to the world of Byzantium as it was envisaged in *A Vision*, and thus mirror Oisin's earlier escape across the water to the Islands of the Other World. But though Yeats momentarily contemplated the attraction of the artificial bird's immortality 'Once out of nature', he had to face the mortal lot: it included more than any escape into a world of unageing intellect:

> I mock Plotinus' thought
> And cry in Plato's teeth,
> Death and life were not
> Till man made up the whole,
> Made lock, stock and barrel
> Out of his bitter soul.

Making up the soul's accounts did not entirely preoccupy him.
There were the great laments for his dead friends. There were the
claims of the body, put in the randy words of Crazy Jane, earthily
opposing the Bishop's focus on Heaven:

> 'A woman can be proud and stiff
> When on love intent;
> But love has pitched his mansion in
> The place of excrement;
> For nothing can be sole or whole
> That has not been rent.'

Love poems looked back, as the great love poems of the middle period,
such as 'No Second Troy', had looked back and simply recorded how
he had loved Maud Gonne, his poetic dreams shattered by her
marriage to John MacBride in 1903. Now, however, they could look
back on that idealised romantic love and balance it with sexuality:

> O but there is wisdom
> In what the sages said;
> But stretch that body for a while
> And lay down that head
> Till I have told the sages
> Where man is comforted.

Despite such defiant gestures, Yeats was constantly aware of the future
as time shrank: what did life hold after this life in which

> Everything that man esteems
> Endures a moment or a day.
> Love's pleasure drives his love away,
> The painter's brush consumes his dreams;
> The herald's cry, the soldier's tread
> Exhaust his glory and his might:
> Whatever flames upon the night
> Man's own resinous heart has fed.

In 'Meru' he thinks civilisation is held together by illusion:

> but man's life is thought,
> And he, despite his terror, cannot cease
> Ravening through century after century,
> Ravening, raging, and uprooting that he may come
> Into the desolation of reality . . .

His sense of despair about the world's future directed such poems as 'Lapis Lazuli' not only into reflecting the increasingly widespread fears of aerial bombing in the 1930s, but into his own offering of a stoic attitude and the idea that true tragedy has its element of gaiety transfiguring dread.

> All men have aimed at, found and lost;
> Black out; Heaven blazing into the head:
> Tragedy wrought to its uttermost.

In 'The Gyres', too, he faced ruin with the laughter of tragic joy; the contradictory cycles of *A Vision* suggest that things will reverse themselves in some later age.

> and all things run
> On that unfashionable gyre again.

Behind all this, behind the bravado that inspired 'The Spur',

> You think it horrible that lust and rage
> Should dance attention upon my old age;
> They were not such a plague when I was young;
> What else have I to spur me into song?

and behind the creative energy of 'An Acre of Grass', where, despite the peace and quiet of Riversdale, the old farmhouse at the foot of the Dublin Mountains into which he had moved in 1932, despite his recognition that

> Neither loose imagination,
> Nor the mill of the mind
> Consuming its rage and bone,
> Can make the truth known

he longs for 'an old man's frenzy'. He wants, impressively at the age of seventy-one, to remake himself; he does not want to be forgotten; he wants 'an old man's eagle mind'. But the poem 'What then?', also set in Riversdale where

> All his happier dreams came true—
> A small old house, wife, daughter, son,
> Grounds where plum and cabbage grew,
> Poets and Wits about him drew . . .

shows what was still at the centre of his thought. The refrain after each stanza, ' *"What then?" sang Plato's ghost. "What then?"* ', alters after the last stanza's statement that the work is done, that he has fulfilled his boyish plan and 'Something to perfection brought'. Now comes the final question: '*But louder sang that ghost, "What then?"* '. This is no new question. Ten years before he died he had meditated upon death while seriously ill at Algeciras:

> Bid imagination run
> Much on the Great Questioner;
> What He can question, what if questioned I
> Can with a fitting confidence reply.

'The Four Ages of Man' of 1934, an intense metaphysical poem compressed tightly into its eight lines, ended

> Now his wars on God begin;
> At stroke of midnight God shall win.

The ultimate question was what was beyond death, beyond the death against which he had made his defiant gestures. There had been a need for *sprezzatura*, an impulsion to strike an attitude of nonchalance, to ruffle

> in a manly pose
> For all his timid heart . . .

And then came the ultimate moment to die, when he could face the fact that he could never know in this world what, if anything, followed death. Yeats's appeal to the imagined seer, to wise old Rocky Voice, comes after he has arranged the life and the work 'in one clear view'; but it is now a question of recognising the ultimate truth; after the questioning of his past actions, amid the myriad uncertainties, there is the one certainty, of death:

> O Rocky Voice,
> Shall we in that great night rejoice?
> What do we know but that we face
> One another in this place?

THE WANDERINGS OF OISIN
1889

'Give me the world if Thou wilt, but grant me an asylum for my affections.' – TULKA

TO
EDWIN J. ELLIS

THE WANDERINGS OF OISIN

BOOK I

S. PATRICK

You who are bent, and bald, and blind,
With a heavy heart and a wandering mind,
Have known three centuries, poets sing,
Of dalliance with a demon thing.

OISIN

Sad to remember, sick with years,
The swift innumerable spears,
The horsemen with their floating hair,
And bowls of barley, honey, and wine,
Those merry couples dancing in tune,
And the white body that lay by mine;
But the tale, though words be lighter than air,
Must live to be old like the wandering moon.

Caoilte, and Conan, and Finn were there,
When we followed a deer with our baying hounds,
With Bran, Sceolan, and Lomair,
And passing the Firbolgs' burial-mounds,
Came to the cairn-heaped grassy hill
Where passionate Maeve is stony-still;
And found on the dove-grey edge of the sea
A pearl-pale, high-born lady, who rode
On a horse with bridle of findrinny;
And like a sunset were her lips,
A stormy sunset on doomed ships;
A citron colour gloomed in her hair,
But down to her feet white vesture flowed,
And with the glimmering crimson glowed
Of many a figured embroidery;

And it was bound with a pearl-pale shell
That wavered like the summer streams,
As her soft bosom rose and fell.

S. PATRICK

You are still wrecked among heathen dreams.

OISIN

'Why do you wind no horn?' she said,
'And every hero droop his head?
The hornless deer is not more sad
That many a peaceful moment had,
More sleek than any granary mouse,
In his own leafy forest house
Among the waving fields of fern:
The hunting of heroes should be glad.'

'O pleasant woman,' answered Finn,
'We think on Oscar's pencilled urn,
And on the heroes lying slain
On Gabhra's raven-covered plain;
But where are your noble kith and kin,
And from what country do you ride?'

'My father and my mother are
Aengus and Edain, my own name
Niamh, and my country far
Beyond the tumbling of this tide.'

'What dream came with you that you came
Through bitter tide on foam-wet feet?
Did your companion wander away
From where the birds of Aengus wing?'

Thereon did she look haughty and sweet:
'I have not yet, war-weary king,
Been spoken of with any man;
Yet now I choose, for these four feet
Ran through the foam and ran to this
That I might have your son to kiss.'

'Were there no better than my son
That you through all that foam should run?'

'I loved no man, though kings besought,
Until the Danaan poets brought
Rhyme that rhymed upon Oisin's name,
And now I am dizzy with the thought
Of all that wisdom and the fame
Of battles broken by his hands,
Of stories builded by his words
That are like coloured Asian birds
At evening in their rainless lands.'

O Patrick, by your brazen bell,
There was no limb of mine but fell
Into a desperate gulph of love!
'You only will I wed,' I cried,
'And I will make a thousand songs,
And set your name all names above,
And captives bound with leathern thongs
Shall kneel and praise you, one by one,
At evening in my western dun.'

'O Oisin, mount by me and ride
To shores by the wash of the tremulous tide,
Where men have heaped no burial-mounds,
And the days pass by like a wayward tune,
Where broken faith has never been known,
And the blushes of first love never have flown;
And there I will give you a hundred hounds;
No mightier creatures bay at the moon;
And a hundred robes of murmuring silk,
And a hundred calves and a hundred sheep
Whose long wool whiter than sea-froth flows,
And a hundred spears and a hundred bows,
And oil and wine and honey and milk,
And always never-anxious sleep;
While a hundred youths, mighty of limb,
But knowing nor tumult nor hate nor strife,
And a hundred ladies, merry as birds,

Who when they dance to a fitful measure
Have a speed like the speed of the salmon herds,
Shall follow your horn and obey your whim,
And you shall know the Danaan leisure;
And Niamh be with you for a wife.'
Then she sighed gently, 'It grows late.
Music and love and sleep await,
Where I would be when the white moon climbs,
The red sun falls and the world grows dim.'

And then I mounted and she bound me
With her triumphing arms around me,
And whispering to herself enwound me;
But when the horse had felt my weight,
He shook himself and neighed three times:
Caoilte, Conan, and Finn came near,
And wept, and raised their lamenting hands,
And bid me stay, with many a tear;
But we rode out from the human lands.

In what far kingdom do you go,
Ah, Fenians, with the shield and bow?
Or are you phantoms white as snow,
Whose lips had life's most prosperous glow?
O you, with whom in sloping valleys,
Or down the dewy forest alleys,
I chased at morn the flying deer,
With whom I hurled the hurrying spear,
And heard the foemen's bucklers rattle,
And broke the heaving ranks of battle!
And Bran, Sceolan, and Lomair,
Where are you with your long rough hair?
You go not where the red deer feeds,
Nor tear the foemen from their steeds.

S. PATRICK

Boast not, nor mourn with drooping head
Companions long accurst and dead,
And hounds for centuries dust and air.

OISIN

We galloped over the glossy sea:
I know not if days passed or hours,
And Niamh sang continually
Danaan songs, and their dewy showers
Of pensive laughter, unhuman sound,
Lulled weariness, and softly round
My human sorrow her white arms wound.
We galloped; now a hornless deer
Passed by us, chased by a phantom hound
All pearly white, save one red ear;
And now a lady rode like the wind
With an apple of gold in her tossing hand;
And a beautiful young man followed behind
With quenchless gaze and fluttering hair.

'Were these two born in the Danaan land,
Or have they breathed the mortal air?'

'Vex them no longer,' Niamh said,
And sighing bowed her gentle head,
And sighing laid the pearly tip
Of one long finger on my lip.

But now the moon like a white rose shone
In the pale west, and the sun's rim sank,
And clouds arrayed their rank on rank
About his fading crimson ball:
The floor of Almhuin's hosting hall
Was not more level than the sea,
As, full of loving fantasy,
And with low murmurs, we rode on,
Where many a trumpet-twisted shell
That in immortal silence sleeps
Dreaming of her own melting hues,
Her golds, her ambers, and her blues,
Pierced with soft light the shallowing deeps.
But now a wandering land breeze came
And a far sound of feathery quires;
It seemed to blow from the dying flame,

They seemed to sing in the smouldering fires.
The horse towards the music raced,
Neighing along the lifeless waste;
Like sooty fingers, many a tree
Rose ever out of the warm sea;
And they were trembling ceaselessly,
As though they all were beating time,
Upon the centre of the sun,
To that low laughing woodland rhyme.
And, now our wandering hours were done,
We cantered to the shore, and knew
The reason of the trembling trees:
Round every branch the song-birds flew,
Or clung thereon like swarming bees;
While round the shore a million stood
Like drops of frozen rainbow light,
And pondered in a soft vain mood
Upon their shadows in the tide,
And told the purple deeps their pride,
And murmured snatches of delight;
And on the shores were many boats
With bending sterns and bending bows,
And carven figures on their prows
Of bitterns, and fish-eating stoats,
And swans with their exultant throats:
And where the wood and waters meet
We tied the horse in a leafy clump,
And Niamh blew three merry notes
Out of a little silver trump;
And then an answering whispering flew
Over the bare and woody land,
A whisper of impetuous feet,
And ever nearer, nearer grew;
And from the woods rushed out a band
Of men and ladies, hand in hand,
And singing, singing all together;
Their brows were white as fragrant milk,
Their cloaks made out of yellow silk,
And trimmed with many a crimson feather;

And when they saw the cloak I wore
Was dim with mire of a mortal shore,
They fingered it and gazed on me
And laughed like murmurs of the sea;
But Niamh with a swift distress
Bid them away and hold their peace;
And when they heard her voice they ran
And knelt there, every girl and man,
And kissed, as they would never cease,
Her pearl-pale hand and the hem of her dress.
She bade them bring us to the hall
Where Aengus dreams, from sun to sun,
A Druid dream of the end of days
When the stars are to wane and the world be done.

They led us by long and shadowy ways
Where drops of dew in myriads fall,
And tangled creepers every hour
Blossom in some new crimson flower,
And once a sudden laughter sprang
From all their lips, and once they sang
Together, while the dark woods rang,
And made in all their distant parts,
With boom of bees in honey-marts,
A rumour of delighted hearts.
And once a lady by my side
Gave me a harp, and bid me sing,
And touch the laughing silver string;
But when I sang of human joy
A sorrow wrapped each merry face,
And, Patrick! by your beard, they wept,
Until one came, a tearful boy;
'A sadder creature never stept
Than this strange human bard,' he cried;
And caught the silver harp away,
And, weeping over the white strings, hurled
It down in a leaf-hid, hollow place
That kept dim waters from the sky;
And each one said, with a long, long sigh,

'O saddest harp in all the world,
Sleep there till the moon and the stars die!'

And now, still sad, we came to where
A beautiful young man dreamed within
A house of wattles, clay, and skin;
One hand upheld his beardless chin,
And one a sceptre flashing out
Wild flames of red and gold and blue,
Like to a merry wandering rout
Of dancers leaping in the air;
And men and ladies knelt them there
And showed their eyes with teardrops dim,
And with low murmurs prayed to him,
And kissed the sceptre with red lips,
And touched it with their finger-tips.

He held that flashing sceptre up.
'Joy drowns the twilight in the dew,
And fills with stars night's purple cup,
And wakes the sluggard seeds of corn,
And stirs the young kid's budding horn,
And makes the infant ferns unwrap,
And for the peewit paints his cap,
And rolls along the unwieldy sun,
And makes the little planets run:
And if joy were not on the earth,
There were an end of change and birth,
And Earth and Heaven and Hell would die,
And in some gloomy barrow lie
Folded like a frozen fly;
Then mock at Death and Time with glances
And wavering arms and wandering dances.

'Men's hearts of old were drops of flame
That from the saffron morning came,
Or drops of silver joy that fell
Out of the moon's pale twisted shell;
But now hearts cry that hearts are slaves,
And toss and turn in narrow caves;

But here there is nor law nor rule,
Nor have hands held a weary tool;
And here there is nor Change nor Death,
But only kind and merry breath,
For joy is God and God is joy.'
With one long glance for girl and boy
And the pale blossom of the moon,
He fell into a Druid swoon.

And in a wild and sudden dance
We mocked at Time and Fate and Chance
And swept out of the wattled hall
And came to where the dewdrops fall
Among the foamdrops of the sea,
And there we hushed the revelry;
And, gathering on our brows a frown,
Bent all our swaying bodies down,
And to the waves that glimmer by
That sloping green De Danaan sod
Sang, 'God is joy and joy is God,
And things that have grown sad are wicked,
And things that fear the dawn of the morrow
Or the grey wandering osprey Sorrow.'

We danced to where in the winding thicket
The damask roses, bloom on bloom,
Like crimson meteors hang in the gloom,
And bending over them softly said,
Bending over them in the dance,
With a swift and friendly glance
From dewy eyes: 'Upon the dead
Fall the leaves of other roses,
On the dead dim earth encloses:
But never, never on our graves,
Heaped beside the glimmering waves,
Shall fall the leaves of damask roses.
For neither Death nor Change comes near us,
And all listless hours fear us,
And we fear no dawning morrow,
Nor the grey wandering osprey Sorrow.'

The dance wound through the windless woods;
The ever-summered solitudes;
Until the tossing arms grew still
Upon the woody central hill;
And, gathered in a panting band,
We flung on high each waving hand,
And sang unto the starry broods.
In our raised eyes there flashed a glow
Of milky brightness to and fro
As thus our song arose: 'You stars,
Across your wandering ruby cars
Shake the loose reins: you slaves of God,
He rules you with an iron rod,
He holds you with an iron bond,
Each one woven to the other,
Each one woven to his brother
Like bubbles in a frozen pond;
But we in a lonely land abide
Unchainable as the dim tide,
With hearts that know nor law nor rule,
And hands that hold no wearisome tool,
Folded in love that fears no morrow,
Nor the grey wandering osprey Sorrow.'

O Patrick! for a hundred years
I chased upon that woody shore
The deer, the badger, and the boar.
O Patrick! for a hundred years
At evening on the glimmering sands,
Beside the piled-up hunting spears,
These now outworn and withered hands
Wrestled among the island bands.
O Patrick! for a hundred years
We went a-fishing in long boats
With bending sterns and bending bows,
And carven figures on their prows
Of bitterns and fish-eating stoats.
O Patrick! for a hundred years
The gentle Niamh was my wife;

But now two things devour my life;
The things that most of all I hate:
Fasting and prayers.

S. PATRICK

Tell on.

OISIN

　　　　　　　　Yes, yes,
For these were ancient Oisin's fate
Loosed long ago from Heaven's gate,
For his last days to lie in wait.

When one day by the tide I stood,
I found in that forgetfulness
Of dreamy foam a staff of wood
From some dead warrior's broken lance:
I turned it in my hands; the stains
Of war were on it, and I wept,
Remembering how the Fenians stept
Along the blood-bedabbled plains,
Equal to good or grievous chance:
Thereon young Niamh softly came
And caught my hands, but spake no word
Save only many times my name,
In murmurs, like a frighted bird.
We passed by woods, and lawns of clover,
And found the horse and bridled him,
For we knew well the old was over.
I heard one say, 'His eyes grow dim
With all the ancient sorrow of men';
And wrapped in dreams rode out again
With hoofs of the pale findrinny
Over the glimmering purple sea.
Under the golden evening light,
The Immortals moved among the fountains
By rivers and the woods' old night;
Some danced like shadows on the mountains,

Some wandered ever hand in hand;
Or sat in dreams on the pale strand,
Each forehead like an obscure star
Bent down above each hookèd knee,
And sang, and with a dreamy gaze
Watched where the sun in a saffron blaze
Was slumbering half in the sea-ways;
And, as they sang, the painted birds
Kept time with their bright wings and feet;
Like drops of honey came their words,
But fainter than a young lamb's bleat.

'An old man stirs the fire to a blaze,
In the house of a child, of a friend, of a brother.
He has over-lingered his welcome; the days,
Grown desolate, whisper and sigh to each other;
He hears the storm in the chimney above,
And bends to the fire and shakes with the cold,
While his heart still dreams of battle and love,
And the cry of the hounds on the hills of old.

'But we are apart in the grassy places,
Where care cannot trouble the least of our days,
Or the softness of youth be gone from our faces,
Or love's first tenderness die in our gaze.
The hare grows old as she plays in the sun
And gazes around her with eyes of brightness;
Before the swift things that she dreamed of were done
She limps along in an aged whiteness;
A storm of birds in the Asian trees
Like tulips in the air a-winging,
And the gentle waves of the summer seas,
That raise their heads and wander singing,
Must murmur at last, "Unjust, unjust";
And "My speed is a weariness," falters the mouse,
And the kingfisher turns to a ball of dust,
And the roof falls in of his tunnelled house.
But the love-dew dims our eyes till the day
When God shall come from the sea with a sigh

And bid the stars drop down from the sky,
And the moon like a pale rose wither away.'

BOOK II

Now, man of croziers, shadows called our names
And then away, away, like whirling flames;
And now fled by, mist-covered, without sound,
The youth and lady and the deer and hound;
'Gaze no more on the phantoms,' Niamh said,
And kissed my eyes, and, swaying her bright head
And her bright body, sang of faery and man
Before God was or my old line began;
Wars shadowy, vast, exultant; faeries of old
Who wedded men with rings of Druid gold;
And how those lovers never turn their eyes
Upon the life that fades and flickers and dies,
Yet love and kiss on dim shores far away
Rolled round with music of the sighing spray:
Yet sang no more as when, like a brown bee
That has drunk full, she crossed the misty sea
With me in her white arms a hundred years
Before this day; for now the fall of tears
Troubled her song.
                        I do not know if days
Or hours passed by, yet hold the morning rays
Shone many times among the glimmering flowers
Woven into her hair, before dark towers
Rose in the darkness, and the white surf gleamed
About them; and the horse of Faery screamed
And shivered, knowing the Isle of Many Fears,
Nor ceased until white Niamh stroked his ears
And named him by sweet names.
                                        A foaming tide
Whitened afar with surge, fan-formed and wide,
Burst from a great door marred by many a blow
From mace and sword and pole-axe, long ago

When gods and giants warred. We rode between
The seaweed-covered pillars; and the green
And surging phosphorus alone gave light
On our dark pathway, till a countless flight
Of moonlit steps glimmered; and left and right
Dark statues glimmered over the pale tide
Upon dark thrones. Between the lids of one
The imaged meteors had flashed and run
And had disported in the stilly jet,
And the fixed stars had dawned and shone and set,
Since God made Time and Death and Sleep: the other
Stretched his long arm to where, a misty smother,
The stream churned, churned, and churned – his lips apart,
As though he told his never-slumbering heart
Of every foamdrop on its misty way.
Tying the horse to his vast foot that lay
Half in the unvesselled sea, we climbed the stair
And climbed so long, I thought the last steps were
Hung from the morning star; when these mild words
Fanned the delighted air like wings of birds:
'My brothers spring out of their beds at morn,
A-murmur like young partridge: with loud horn
They chase the noontide deer;
And when the dew-drowned stars hang in the air
Look to long fishing-lines, or point and pare
An ashen hunting spear.
O sigh, O fluttering sigh, be kind to me;
Flutter along the froth lips of the sea,
And shores the froth lips wet:
And stay a little while, and bid them weep:
Ah, touch their blue-veined eyelids if they sleep,
And shake their coverlet.
When you have told how I weep endlessly,
Flutter along the froth lips of the sea
And home to me again,
And in the shadow of my hair lie hid,
And tell me that you found a man unbid,
The saddest of all men.'

A lady with soft eyes like funeral tapers,
And face that seemed wrought out of moonlit vapours,
And a sad mouth, that fear made tremulous
As any ruddy moth, looked down on us;
And she with a wave-rusted chain was tied
To two old eagles, full of ancient pride,
That with dim eyeballs stood on either side.
Few feathers were on their dishevelled wings,
For their dim minds were with the ancient things.

'I bring deliverance,' pearl-pale Niamh said.

'Neither the living, nor the unlabouring dead,
Nor the high gods who never lived, may fight
My enemy and hope; demons for fright
Jabber and scream about him in the night;
For he is strong and crafty as the seas
That sprang under the Seven Hazel Trees,
And I must needs endure and hate and weep,
Until the gods and demons drop asleep,
Hearing Aedh touch the mournful strings of gold.'

'Is he so dreadful?'
                    'Be not over-bold,
But fly while still you may.'

                              And thereon I:
'This demon shall be battered till he die,
And his loose bulk be thrown in the loud tide.'

'Flee from him,' pearl-pale Niamh weeping cried,
'For all men flee the demons'; but moved not
My angry king-remembering soul one jot.
There was no mightier soul of Heber's line;
Now it is old and mouse-like. For a sign
I burst the chain: still earless, nerveless, blind,
Wrapped in the things of the unhuman mind,
In some dim memory or ancient mood,
Still earless, nerveless, blind, the eagles stood.

And then we climbed the stair to a high door;
A hundred horsemen on the basalt floor

Beneath had paced content: we held our way
And stood within: clothed in a misty ray
I saw a foam-white seagull drift and float
Under the roof, and with a straining throat
Shouted, and hailed him: he hung there a star,
For no man's cry shall ever mount so far;
Not even your God could have thrown down that hall;
Stabling His unloosed lightnings in their stall,
He had sat down and sighed with cumbered heart,
As though His hour were come.

       We sought the part
That was most distant from the door; green slime
Made the way slippery, and time on time
Showed prints of sea-born scales, while down through it
The captive's journeys to and fro were writ
Like a small river, and where feet touched came
A momentary gleam of phosphorus flame.
Under the deepest shadows of the hall
That woman found a ring hung on the wall,
And in the ring a torch, and with its flare
Making a world about her in the air,
Passed under the dim doorway, out of sight,
And came again, holding a second light
Burning between her fingers, and in mine
Laid it and sighed: I held a sword whose shine
No centuries could dim, and a word ran
Thereon in Ogham letters, 'Manannan';
That sea-god's name, who in a deep content
Sprang dripping, and, with captive demons sent
Out of the sevenfold seas, built the dark hall
Rooted in foam and clouds, and cried to all
The mightier masters of a mightier race;
And at his cry there came no milk-pale face
Under a crown of thorns and dark with blood,
But only exultant faces.
      Niamh stood
With bowed head, trembling when the white blade shone,
But she whose hours of tenderness were gone

Had neither hope nor fear. I bade them hide
Under the shadows till the tumults died
Of the loud-crashing and earth-shaking fight,
Lest they should look upon some dreadful sight;
And thrust the torch between the slimy flags.
A dome made out of endless carven jags,
Where shadowy face flowed into shadowy face,
Looked down on me; and in the self-same place
I waited hour by hour, and the high dome,
Windowless, pillarless, multitudinous home
Of faces, waited; and the leisured gaze
Was loaded with the memory of days
Buried and mighty. When through the great door
The dawn came in, and glimmered on the floor
With a pale light, I journeyed round the hall
And found a door deep sunken in the wall,
The least of doors; beyond on a dim plain
A little runnel made a bubbling strain,
And on the runnel's stony and bare edge
A dusky demon dry as a withered sedge
Swayed, crooning to himself an unknown tongue:
In a sad revelry he sang and swung
Bacchant and mournful, passing to and fro
His hand along the runnel's side, as though
The flowers still grew there: far on the sea's waste
Shaking and waving, vapour vapour chased,
While high frail cloudlets, fed with a green light,
Like drifts of leaves, immovable and bright,
Hung in the passionate dawn. He slowly turned:
A demon's leisure: eyes, first white, now burned
Like wings of kingfishers; and he arose
Barking. We trampled up and down with blows
Of sword and brazen battle-axe, while day
Gave to high noon and noon to night gave way;
And when he knew the sword of Manannan
Amid the shades of night, he changed and ran
Through many shapes; I lunged at the smooth throat
Of a great eel; it changed, and I but smote
A fir-tree roaring in its leafless top;

And thereupon I drew the livid chop
Of a drowned dripping body to my breast;
Horror from horror grew; but when the west
Had surged up in a plumy fire, I drave
Through heart and spine; and cast him in the wave
Lest Niamh shudder.

              Full of hope and dread
Those two came carrying wine and meat and bread,
And healed my wounds with unguents out of flowers
That feed white moths by some De Danaan shrine;
Then in that hall, lit by the dim sea-shine,
We lay on skins of otters, and drank wine,
Brewed by the sea-gods, from huge cups that lay
Upon the lips of sea-gods in their day;
And then on heaped-up skins of otters slept.
And when the sun once more in saffron stept,
Rolling his flagrant wheel out of the deep,
We sang the loves and angers without sleep,
And all the exultant labours of the strong.
But now the lying clerics murder song
With barren words and flatteries of the weak.
In what land do the powerless turn the beak
Of ravening Sorrow, or the hand of Wrath?
For all your croziers, they have left the path
And wander in the storms and clinging snows,
Hopeless for ever: ancient Oisin knows,
For he is weak and poor and blind, and lies
On the anvil of the world.

S. PATRICK

              Be still: the skies
Are choked with thunder, lightning, and fierce wind,
For God has heard, and speaks His angry mind;
Go cast your body on the stones and pray,
For He has wrought midnight and dawn and day.

OISIN

Saint, do you weep? I hear amid the thunder
The Fenian horses; armour torn asunder;
Laughter and cries. The armies clash and shock,
And now the daylight-darkening ravens flock.
Cease, cease, O mournful, laughing Fenian horn!

We feasted for three days. On the fourth morn
I found, dropping sea-foam on the wide stair,
And hung with slime, and whispering in his hair,
That demon dull and unsubduable;
And once more to a day-long battle fell,
And at the sundown threw him in the surge,
To lie until the fourth morn saw emerge
His new-healed shape; and for a hundred years
So warred, so feasted, with nor dreams nor fears,
Nor languor nor fatigue: an endless feast,
An endless war.

　　　　　The hundred years had ceased;
I stood upon the stair: the surges bore
A beech-bough to me, and my heart grew sore,
Remembering how I had stood by white-haired Finn
Under a beech at Almhuin and heard the thin
Outcry of bats.

　　　　　And then young Niamh came
Holding that horse, and sadly called my name;
I mounted, and we passed over the lone
And drifting greyness, while this monotone,
Surly and distant, mixed inseparably
Into the clangour of the wind and sea.

'I hear my soul drop down into decay,
And Manannan's dark tower, stone after stone,
Gather sea-slime and fall the seaward way,
And the moon goad the waters night and day,
That all be overthrown.

'But till the moon has taken all, I wage
War on the mightiest men under the skies,
And they have fallen or fled, age after age.
Light is man's love, and lighter is man's rage;
His purpose drifts and dies.'

And then lost Niamh murmured, 'Love, we go
To the Island of Forgetfulness, for lo!
The Islands of Dancing and of Victories
Are empty of all power.'

                  'And which of these
Is the Island of Content?'

                       'None know,' she said;
And on my bosom laid her weeping head.

BOOK III

Fled foam underneath us, and round us, a wandering and milky
   smoke,
High as the saddle-girth, covering away from our glances the tide;
And those that fled, and that followed, from the foam-pale
   distance broke;
The immortal desire of Immortals we saw in their faces, and
   sighed.

I mused on the chase with the Fenians, and Bran, Sceolan, Lomair,
And never a song sang Niamh, and over my finger-tips
Came now the sliding of tears and sweeping of mist-cold hair,
And now the warmth of sighs, and after the quiver of lips.

Were we days long or hours long in riding, when, rolled in a
   grisly peace,
An isle lay level before us, with dripping hazel and oak?
And we stood on a sea's edge we saw not; for whiter than new-
   washed fleece
Fled foam underneath us, and round us, a wandering and milky
   smoke.

And we rode on the plains of the sea's edge; the sea's edge barren
   and grey,
Grey sand on the green of the grasses and over the dripping trees,
Dripping and doubling landward, as though they would hasten
   away,
Like an army of old men longing for rest from the moan of the
   seas.

But the trees grew taller and closer, immense in their wrinkling
   bark;
Dropping; a murmurous dropping; old silence and that one sound;
For no live creatures lived there, no weasels moved in the dark:
Long sighs arose in our spirits, beneath us bubbled the ground.

And the ears of the horse went sinking away in the hollow night,
For, as drift from a sailor slow drowning the gleams of the world
   and the sun,
Ceased on our hands and our faces, on hazel and oak leaf, the
   light,
And the stars were blotted above us, and the whole of the world
   was one.

Till the horse gave a whinny; for, cumbrous with stems of the
   hazel and oak,
A valley flowed down from his hoofs, and there in the long grass
   lay,
Under the starlight and shadow, a monstrous slumbering folk,
Their naked and gleaming bodies poured out and heaped in the
   way.

And by them were arrow and war-axe, arrow and shield and
   blade;
And dew-blanched horns, in whose hollow a child of three years
   old
Could sleep on a couch of rushes, and all inwrought and inlaid,
And more comely than man can make them with bronze and silver
   and gold.

And each of the huge white creatures was huger than fourscore
   men;
The tops of their ears were feathered, their hands were the claws
   of birds,

And, shaking the plumes of the grasses and the leaves of the mural
  glen,
The breathing came from those bodies, long warless, grown
  whiter than curds.

The wood was so spacious above them, that He who has stars for
  His flocks
Could fondle the leaves with His fingers, nor go from His dew-
  cumbered skies;
So long were they sleeping, the owls had builded their nests in
  their locks,
Filling the fibrous dimness with long generations of eyes.

And over the limbs and the valley the slow owls wandered and
  came,
Now in a place of star-fire, and now in a shadow-place wide;
And the chief of the huge white creatures, his knees in the soft
  star-flame,
Lay loose in a place of shadow: we drew the reins by his side.

Golden the nails of his bird-claws, flung loosely along the dim
  ground;
In one was a branch soft-shining with bells more many than sighs
In midst of an old man's bosom; owls ruffling and pacing around
Sidled their bodies against him, filling the shade with their eyes.

And my gaze was thronged with the sleepers; no, not since the
  world began,
In realms where the handsome were many, nor in glamours by
  demons flung,
Have faces alive with such beauty been known to the salt eye of
  man,
Yet weary with passions that faded when the sevenfold seas were
  young.

And I gazed on the bell-branch, sleep's forebear, far sung by the
  Sennachies.
I saw how those slumberers, grown weary, there camping in
  grasses deep,

Of wars with the wide world and pacing the shores of the
   wandering seas,
Laid hands on the bell-branch and swayed it, and fed of unhuman
   sleep.

Snatching the horn of Niamh, I blew a long lingering note.
Came sound from those monstrous sleepers, a sound like the
   stirring of flies.
He, shaking the fold of his lips, and heaving the pillar of his
   throat,
Watched me with mournful wonder out of the wells of his eyes.

I cried, 'Come out of the shadow, king of the nails of gold!
And tell of your goodly household and the goodly works of your
   hands,
That we may muse in the starlight and talk of the battles of old;
Your questioner, Oisin, is worthy, he comes from the Fenian
   lands.'

Half open his eyes were, and held me, dull with the smoke of their
   dreams;
His lips moved slowly in answer, no answer out of them came;
Then he swayed in his fingers the bell-branch, slow dropping a
   sound in faint streams
Softer than snow-flakes in April and piercing the marrow like
   flame.

Wrapt in the wave of that music, with weariness more than of
   earth,
The moil of my centuries filled me; and gone like a sea-covered
   stone
Were the memories of the whole of my sorrow and the memories
   of the whole of my mirth,
And a softness came from the starlight and filled me full to the
   bone.

In the roots of the grasses, the sorrels, I laid my body as low;
And the pearl-pale Niamh lay by me, her brow on the midst of
   my breast;

And the horse was gone in the distance, and years after years 'gan
  flow;
Square leaves of the ivy moved over us, binding us down to our
  rest.

And, man of the many white croziers, a century there I forgot
How the fetlocks drip blood in the battle, when the fallen on fallen
  lie rolled;
How the falconer follows the falcon in the weeds of the heron's
  plot,
And the name of the demon whose hammer made Conchubar's
  sword-blade of old.

And, man of the many white croziers, a century there I forgot
That the spear-shaft is made out of ashwood, the shield out of
  osier and hide;
How the hammers spring on the anvil, on the spearhead's burning
  spot;
How the slow, blue-eyed oxen of Finn low sadly at evening tide.

But in dreams, mild man of the croziers, driving the dust with
  their throngs,
Moved round me, of seamen or landsmen, all who are winter tales;
Came by me the kings of the Red Branch, with roaring of laughter
  and songs,
Or moved as they moved once, love-making or piercing the
  tempest with sails.

Came Blanaid, Mac Nessa, tall Fergus who feastward of old time
  slunk,
Cook Barach, the traitor; and warward, the spittle on his beard
  never dry,
Dark Balor, as old as a forest, car-borne, his mighty head sunk
Helpless, men lifting the lids of his weary and death-making eye.

And by me, in soft red raiment, the Fenians moved in loud
  streams,
And Grania, walking and smiling, sewed with her needle of bone.
So lived I and lived not, so wrought I and wrought not, with
  creatures of dreams,
In a long iron sleep, as a fish in the water goes dumb as a stone.

At times our slumber was lightened. When the sun was on silver
  or gold;
When brushed with the wings of the owls, in the dimness they
  love going by;
When a glow-worm was green on a grass-leaf, lured from his lair
  in the mould;
Half wakening, we lifted our eyelids, and gazed on the grass with
  a sigh.

So watched I when, man of the croziers, at the heel of a century
  fell,
Weak, in the midst of the meadow, from his miles in the midst of
  the air,
A starling like them that forgathered 'neath a moon waking white
  as a shell
When the Fenians made foray at morning with Bran, Sceolan,
  Lomair.

I awoke: the strange horse without summons out of the distance
  ran,
Thrusting his nose to my shoulder; he knew in his bosom deep
That once more moved in my bosom the ancient sadness of man,
And that I would leave the Immortals, their dimness, their dews
  dropping sleep.

O had you seen beautiful Niamh grow white as the waters are
  white,
Lord of the croziers, you even had lifted your hands and wept:
But, the bird in my fingers, I mounted, remembering alone that
  delight
Of twilight and slumber were gone, and that hoofs impatiently
  stept.

I cried, 'O Niamh! O white one! if only a twelve-houred day,
I must gaze on the beard of Finn, and move where the old men
  and young
In the Fenians' dwellings of wattle lean on the chessboards and
  play,
Ah, sweet to me now were even bald Conan's slanderous tongue!

'Like me were some galley forsaken far off in Meridian isle,
Remembering its long-oared companions, sails turning to
    threadbare rags;
No more to crawl on the seas with long oars mile after mile,
But to be amid shooting of flies and flowering of rushes and flags.'

Their motionless eyeballs of spirits grown mild with mysterious
    thought,
Watched her those seamless faces from the valley's glimmering
    girth;
As she murmured, 'O wandering Oisin, the strength of the bell-
    branch is naught,
For there moves alive in your fingers the fluttering sadness of
    earth.

'Then go through the lands in the saddle and see what the mortals
    do,
And softly come to your Niamh over the tops of the tide;
But weep for your Niamh, O Oisin, weep; for if only your shoe
Brush lightly as haymouse earth's pebbles, you will come no more
    to my side.

'O flaming lion of the world, O when will you turn to your rest?'
I saw from a distant saddle; from the earth she made her moan:
'I would die like a small withered leaf in the autumn, for breast
    unto breast
We shall mingle no more, nor our gazes empty their sweetness
    lone

'In the isles of the farthest seas where only the spirits come.
Were the winds less soft than the breath of a pigeon who sleeps on
    her nest,
Nor lost in the star-fires and odours the sound of the sea's vague
    drum?
O flaming lion of the world, O when will you turn to your rest?'

The wailing grew distant; I rode by the woods of the wrinkling
    bark,
Where ever is murmurous dropping, old silence and that one
    sound;
For no live creatures live there, no weasels move in the dark;
In a reverie forgetful of all things, over the bubbling ground.

And I rode by the plains of the sea's edge, where all is barren and
grey,
Grey sand on the green of the grasses and over the dripping trees,
Dripping and doubling landward, as though they would hasten
away,
Like an army of old men longing for rest from the moan of the
seas.

And the winds made the sands on the sea's edge turning and
turning go,
As my mind made the names of the Fenians. Far from the hazel
and oak,
I rode away on the surges, where, high as the saddle-bow,
Fled foam underneath me, and round me, a wandering and milky
smoke.

Long fled the foam-flakes around me, the winds fled out of the
vast,
Snatching the bird in secret; nor knew I, embosomed apart,
When they froze the cloth on my body like armour riveted fast,
For Remembrance, lifting her leanness, keened in the gates of my
heart.

Till, fattening the winds of the morning, an odour of new-mown
hay
Came, and my forehead fell low, and my tears like berries fell
down;
Later a sound came, half lost in the sound of a shore far away,
From the great grass-barnacle calling, and later the shore-weeds
brown.

If I were as I once was, the strong hoofs crushing the sand and the
shells,
Coming out of the sea as the dawn comes, a chaunt of love on my
lips,
Not coughing, my head on my knees, and praying, and wroth
with the bells,
I would leave no saint's head on his body from Rachlin to Bera of
ships.

Making way from the kindling surges, I rode on a bridle-path
Much wondering to see upon all hands, of wattles and woodwork
    made,
Your bell-mounted churches, and guardless the sacred cairn and
    the rath,
And a small and a feeble populace stooping with mattock and
    spade,

Or weeding or ploughing with faces a-shining with much-toil wet;
While in this place and that place, with bodies unglorious, their
    chieftains stood,
Awaiting in patience the straw-death, croziered one, caught in
    your net:
Went the laughter of scorn from my mouth like the roaring of
    wind in a wood.

And because I went by them so huge and so speedy with eyes so
    bright,
Came after the hard gaze of youth, or an old man lifted his head:
And I rode and I rode, and I cried out, 'The Fenians hunt wolves
    in the night,
So sleep thee by daytime.' A voice cried, 'The Fenians a long time
    are dead.'

A whitebeard stood hushed on the pathway, the flesh of his face as
    dried grass,
And in folds round his eyes and his mouth, he sad as a child
    without milk;
And the dreams of the islands were gone, and I knew how men
    sorrow and pass,
And their hound, and their horse, and their love, and their eyes
    that glimmer like silk.

And wrapping my face in my hair, I murmured, 'In old age they
    ceased';
And my tears were larger than berries, and I murmured, 'Where
    white clouds lie spread
On Crevroe or broad Knockfefin, with many of old they feast
On the floors of the gods.' He cried, 'No, the gods a long time are
    dead.'

And lonely and longing for Niamh, I shivered and turned me
   about,
The heart in me longing to leap like a grasshopper into her heart;
I turned and rode to the westward, and followed the sea's old shout
Till I saw where Maeve lies sleeping till starlight and midnight part.

And there at the foot of the mountain, two carried a sack full of
   sand,
They bore it with staggering and sweating, but fell with their
   burden at length.
Leaning down from the gem-studded saddle, I flung it five yards
   with my hand,
With a sob for men waxing so weakly, a sob for the Fenians' old
   strength.

The rest you have heard of, O croziered man; how, when divided
   the girth,
I fell on the path, and the horse went away like a summer fly;
And my years three hundred fell on me, and I rose, and walked on
   the earth,
A creeping old man, full of sleep, with the spittle on his beard
   never dry.

How the men of the sand-sack showed me a church with its belfry
   in air;
Sorry place, where for swing of the war-axe in my dim eyes the
   crozier gleams;
What place have Caoilte and Conan, and Bran, Sceolan, Lomair?
Speak, you too are old with your memories, an old man
   surrounded with dreams.

S. PATRICK

Where the flesh of the footsole clingeth on the burning stones is
   their place;
Where the demons whip them with wires on the burning stones of
   wide Hell,
Watching the blessèd ones move far off, and the smile on God's
   face,
Between them a gateway of brass, and the howl of the angels who
   fell.

OISIN

Put the staff in my hands; for I go to the Fenians, O cleric, to
    chaunt
The war-songs that roused them of old; they will rise, making
    clouds with their breath,
Innumerable, singing, exultant; the clay underneath them shall
    pant,
And demons be broken in pieces, and trampled beneath them in
    death.

And demons afraid in their darkness; deep horror of eyes and of
    wings,
Afraid, their ears on the earth laid, shall listen and rise up and
    weep;
Hearing the shaking of shields and the quiver of stretched
    bowstrings,
Hearing Hell loud with a murmur, as shouting and mocking we
    sweep.

We will tear out the flaming stones, and batter the gateway of
    brass
And enter, and none sayeth 'No' when there enters the strongly
    armed guest;
Make clean as a broom cleans, and march on as oxen move over
    young grass;
Then feast, making converse of wars, and of old wounds, and turn
    to our rest.

S. PATRICK

On the flaming stones, without refuge, the limbs of the Fenians are
    tost;
None war on the masters of Hell, who could break up the world
    in their rage;
But kneel and wear out the flags and pray for your soul that is lost
Through the demon love of its youth and its godless and
    passionate age.

OISIN

Ah me! to be shaken with coughing and broken with old age and
　pain,
Without laughter, a show unto children, alone with remembrance
　and fear;
All emptied of purple hours as a beggar's cloak in the rain,
As a hay-cock out on the flood, or a wolf sucked under a weir.

It were sad to gaze on the blessèd and no man I loved of old there;
I throw down the chain of small stones! when life in my body has
　ceased,
I will go to Caoilte, and Conan, and Bran, Sceolan, Lomair,
And dwell in the house of the Fenians, be they in flames or at
　feast.

CROSSWAYS
1889

'*The stars are threshed, and the souls are threshed from their husks.*' –
WILLIAM BLAKE

TO
A.E.

CROSSWAYS

The Song of the Happy Shepherd

The woods of Arcady are dead,
And over is their antique joy;
Of old the world on dreaming fed;
Grey Truth is now her painted toy;
Yet still she turns her restless head:
But O, sick children of the world,
Of all the many changing things
In dreary dancing past us whirled,
To the cracked tune that Chronos sings,
Words alone are certain good.
Where are now the warring kings,
Word be-mockers? – By the Rood,
Where are now the warring kings?
An idle word is now their glory,
By the stammering schoolboy said,
Reading some entangled story:
The kings of the old time are dead;
The wandering earth herself may be
Only a sudden flaming word,
In clanging space a moment heard,
Troubling the endless reverie.

Then nowise worship dusty deeds,
Nor seek, for this is also sooth,
To hunger fiercely after truth,
Lest all thy toiling only breeds
New dreams, new dreams; there is no truth
Saving in thine own heart. Seek, then,
No learning from the starry men,
Who follow with the optic glass
The whirling ways of stars that pass –
Seek, then, for this is also sooth,

No word of theirs – the cold star-bane
Has cloven and rent their hearts in twain,
And dead is all their human truth.
Go gather by the humming sea
Some twisted, echo-harbouring shell,
And to its lips thy story tell,
And they thy comforters will be,
Rewording in melodious guile
Thy fretful words a little while,
Till they shall singing fade in ruth
And die a pearly brotherhood;
For words alone are certain good:
Sing, then, for this is also sooth.

I must be gone: there is a grave
Where daffodil and lily wave,
And I would please the hapless faun,
Buried under the sleepy ground,
With mirthful songs before the dawn.
His shouting days with mirth were crowned;
And still I dream he treads the lawn,
Walking ghostly in the dew,
Pierced by my glad singing through,
My songs of old earth's dreamy youth:
But ah! she dreams not now; dream thou!
For fair are poppies on the brow:
Dream, dream, for this is also sooth.

The Sad Shepherd

There was a man whom Sorrow named his friend,
And he, of his high comrade Sorrow dreaming,
Went walking with slow steps along the gleaming
And humming sands, where windy surges wend:
And he called loudly to the stars to bend
From their pale thrones and comfort him, but they
Among themselves laugh on and sing alway:

And then the man whom Sorrow named his friend
Cried out, *Dim sea, hear my most piteous story!*
The sea swept on and cried her old cry still,
Rolling along in dreams from hill to hill.
He fled the persecution of her glory
And, in a far-off, gentle valley stopping,
Cried all his story to the dewdrops glistening.
But naught they heard, for they are always listening,
The dewdrops, for the sound of their own dropping.
And then the man whom Sorrow named his friend
Sought once again the shore, and found a shell,
And thought, *I will my heavy story tell*
Till my own words, re-echoing, shall send
Their sadness through a hollow, pearly heart;
And my own tale again for me shall sing,
And my own whispering words be comforting,
And lo! my ancient burden may depart.
Then he sang softly nigh the pearly rim;
But the sad dweller by the sea-ways lone
Changed all he sang to inarticulate moan
Among her wildering whirls, forgetting him.

The Cloak, the Boat, and the Shoes

'What do you make so fair and bright?'

'I make the cloak of Sorrow:
O lovely to see in all men's sight
Shall be the cloak of Sorrow,
In all men's sight.'

'What do you build with sails for flight?'

'I build a boat for Sorrow:
O swift on the seas all day and night
Saileth the rover Sorrow,
All day and night.'

'What do you weave with wool so white?'

'I weave the shoes of Sorrow:
Soundless shall be the footfall light
In all men's ears of Sorrow,
Sudden and light.'

Anashuya and Vijaya

A little Indian temple in the Golden Age. Around it a garden; around that the forest. ANASHUYA, *the young priestess, kneeling within the temple.*

ANASHUYA

Send peace on all the lands and flickering corn. –
O may tranquillity walk by his elbow
When wandering in the forest, if he love
No other. – Hear, and may the indolent flocks
Be plentiful. – And if he love another,
May panthers end him. – Hear, and load our king
With wisdom hour by hour. – May we two stand,
When we are dead, beyond the setting suns,
A little from the other shades apart,
With mingling hair, and play upon one lute.

VIJAYA [*entering and throwing a lily at her*]

Hail! hail, my Anashuya.

ANASHUYA

                No: be still.
I, priestess of this temple, offer up
Prayers for the land.

VIJAYA

I will wait here, Amrita.

ANASHUYA

By mighty Brahma's ever-rustling robe,
Who is Amrita? Sorrow of all sorrows!
Another fills your mind.

VIJAYA

My mother's name.

ANASHUYA [*sings, coming out of the temple*]

A sad, sad thought went by me slowly:
Sigh, O you little stars! O sigh and shake your blue apparel!
The sad, sad thought has gone from me now wholly:
Sing, O you little stars! O sing and raise your rapturous carol
To mighty Brahma, he who made you many as the sands,
And laid you on the gates of evening with his quiet hands.

[*Sits down on the steps of the temple.*]

Vijaya, I have brought my evening rice;
The sun has laid his chin on the grey wood,
Weary, with all his poppies gathered round him.

VIJAYA

The hour when Kama, full of sleepy laughter,
Rises, and showers abroad his fragrant arrows,
Piercing the twilight with their murmuring barbs.

ANASHUYA

See how the sacred old flamingoes come,
Painting with shadow all the marble steps:
Aged and wise, they seek their wonted perches
Within the temple, devious walking, made
To wander by their melancholy minds.
Yon tall one eyes my supper; chase him away,
Far, far away. I named him after you.
He is a famous fisher; hour by hour
He ruffles with his bill the minnowed streams.
Ah! there he snaps my rice. I told you so.

Now cuff him off. He's off! A kiss for you,
Because you saved my rice. Have you no thanks?

VIJAYA [*sings*]

Sing you of her, O first few stars,
Whom Brahma, touching with his finger, praises, for you hold
The van of wandering quiet; ere you be too calm and old,
Sing, turning in your cars,
Sing, till you raise your hands and sigh, and from your car-heads peer,
With all your whirling hair, and drop many an azure tear.

ANASHUYA

What know the pilots of the stars of tears?

VIJAYA

Their faces are all worn, and in their eyes
Flashes the fire of sadness, for they see
The icicles that famish all the North,
Where men lie frozen in the glimmering snow;
And in the flaming forests cower the lion
And lioness, with all their whimpering cubs;
And, ever pacing on the verge of things,
The phantom, Beauty, in a mist of tears;
While we alone have round us woven woods,
And feel the softness of each other's hand,
Amrita, while ——

ANASHUYA [*going away from him*]

Ah me! you love another,
[*Bursting into tears.*]
And may some sudden dreadful ill befall her!

VIJAYA

I loved another; now I love no other.
Among the mouldering of ancient woods
You live, and on the village border she,
With her old father the blind wood-cutter;
I saw her standing in her door but now.

ANASHUYA

Vijaya, swear to love her never more.

VIJAYA

Ay, ay.

ANASHUYA

> Swear by the parents of the gods,
> Dread oath, who dwell on sacred Himalay,
> On the far Golden Peak; enormous shapes,
> Who still were old when the great sea was young;
> On their vast faces mystery and dreams;
> Their hair along the mountains rolled and filled
> From year to year by the unnumbered nests
> Of aweless birds, and round their stirless feet
> The joyous flocks of deer and antelope,
> Who never hear the unforgiving hound.
> Swear!

VIJAYA

By the parents of the gods, I swear.

ANASHUYA [*sings*]

I have forgiven, O new star!
Maybe you have not heard of us, you have come forth so newly,
You hunter of the fields afar!
Ah, you will know my loved one by his hunter's arrows truly,
Shoot on him shafts of quietness, that he may ever keep
A lonely laughter, and may kiss his hands to me in sleep.

Farewell, Vijaya. Nay, no word, no word;
I, priestess of this temple, offer up
Prayers for the land.

[VIJAYA goes.]

> O Brahma, guard in sleep
The merry lambs and the complacent kine,
The flies below the leaves, and the young mice

In the tree roots, and all the sacred flocks
Of red flamingoes; and my love, Vijaya;
And may no restless fay with fidget finger
Trouble his sleeping: give him dreams of me.

The Indian upon God

I passed along the water's edge below the humid trees,
My spirit rocked in evening light, the rushes round my knees,
My spirit rocked in sleep and sighs; and saw the moorfowl pace
All dripping on a grassy slope, and saw them cease to chase
Each other round in circles, and heard the eldest speak:
Who holds the world between His bill and made us strong or weak
Is an undying moorfowl, and He lives beyond the sky.
The rains are from His dripping wing, the moonbeams from His eye.
I passed a little further on and heard a lotus talk:
Who made the world and ruleth it, He hangeth on a stalk,
For I am in His image made, and all this tinkling tide
Is but a sliding drop of rain between His petals wide.
A little way within the gloom a roebuck raised his eyes
Brimful of starlight, and he said: *The Stamper of the Skies,*
He is a gentle roebuck; for how else, I pray, could He
Conceive a thing so sad and soft, a gentle thing like me?
I passed a little further on and heard a peacock say:
Who made the grass and made the worms and made my feathers gay,
He is a monstrous peacock, and He waveth all the night
His languid tail above us, lit with myriad spots of light.

The Indian to His Love

The island dreams under the dawn
And great boughs drop tranquillity;
The peahens dance on a smooth lawn,
A parrot sways upon a tree,
Raging at his own image in the enamelled sea.

Here we will moor our lonely ship
And wander ever with woven hands,
Murmuring softly lip to lip,
Along the grass, along the sands,
Murmuring how far away are the unquiet lands:

How we alone of mortals are
Hid under quiet boughs apart,
While our love grows an Indian star,
A meteor of the burning heart,
One with the tide that gleams, the wings that gleam and dart,

The heavy boughs, the burnished dove
That moans and sighs a hundred days:
How when we die our shades will rove,
When eve has hushed the feathered ways,
With vapoury footsole by the water's drowsy blaze.

The Falling of the Leaves

Autumn is over the long leaves that love us,
And over the mice in the barley sheaves;
Yellow the leaves of the rowan above us,
And yellow the wet wild-strawberry leaves.

The hour of the waning of love has beset us,
And weary and worn are our sad souls now;
Let us part, ere the season of passion forget us,
With a kiss and a tear on thy drooping brow.

Ephemera

'Your eyes that once were never weary of mine
Are bowed in sorrow under pendulous lids,
Because our love is waning.'

        And then she:
'Although our love is waning, let us stand
By the lone border of the lake once more,
Together in that hour of gentleness
When the poor tired child, Passion, falls asleep.
How far away the stars seem, and how far
Is our first kiss, and ah, how old my heart!'
Pensive they paced along the faded leaves,
While slowly he whose hand held hers, replied:
'Passion has often worn our wandering hearts.'

The woods were round them, and the yellow leaves
Fell like faint meteors in the gloom, and once
A rabbit old and lame limped down the path;
Autumn was over him: and now they stood
On the lone border of the lake once more:
Turning, he saw that she had thrust dead leaves
Gathered in silence, dewy as her eyes,
In bosom and hair.

        'Ah, do not mourn,' he said,
'That we are tired, for other loves await us;
Hate on and love through unrepining hours.
Before us lies eternity; our souls
Are love, and a continual farewell.'

The Madness of King Goll

I sat on cushioned otter-skin:
My word was law from Ith to Emain,
And shook at Invar Amargin
The hearts of the world-troubling seamen,
And drove tumult and war away
From girl and boy and man and beast;
The fields grew fatter day by day,
The wild fowl of the air increased;
And every ancient Ollave said,
While he bent down his fading head,
'He drives away the Northern cold.'
They will not hush, the leaves a-flutter round me, the beech leaves old.

I sat and mused and drank sweet wine;
A herdsman came from inland valleys,
Crying, the pirates drove his swine
To fill their dark-beaked hollow galleys.
I called my battle-breaking men
And my loud brazen battle-cars
From rolling vale and rivery glen;
And under the blinking of the stars
Fell on the pirates by the deep,
And hurled them in the gulph of sleep:
These hands won many a torque of gold.
They will not hush, the leaves a-flutter round me, the beech leaves old.

But slowly, as I shouting slew
And trampled in the bubbling mire,
In my most secret spirit grew
A whirling and a wandering fire:
I stood: keen stars above me shone,
Around me shone keen eyes of men:
I laughed aloud and hurried on
By rocky shore and rushy fen;
I laughed because birds fluttered by,
And starlight gleamed, and clouds flew high,

And rushes waved and waters rolled.
They will not hush, the leaves a-flutter round me, the beech leaves old.

And now I wander in the woods
When summer gluts the golden bees,
Or in autumnal solitudes
Arise the leopard-coloured trees;
Or when along the wintry strands
The cormorants shiver on their rocks;
I wander on, and wave my hands,
And sing, and shake my heavy locks.
The grey wolf knows me; by one ear
I lead along the woodland deer;
The hares run by me growing bold.
They will not hush, the leaves a-flutter round me, the beech leaves old.

I came upon a little town
That slumbered in the harvest moon,
And passed a-tiptoe up and down,
Murmuring, to a fitful tune,
How I have followed, night and day,
A tramping of tremendous feet,
And saw where this old tympan lay
Deserted on a doorway seat,
And bore it to the woods with me;
Of some inhuman misery
Our married voices wildly trolled.
They will not hush, the leaves a-flutter round me, the beech leaves old.

I sang how, when day's toil is done,
Orchil shakes out her long dark hair
That hides away the dying sun
And sheds faint odours through the air:
When my hand passed from wire to wire
It quenched, with sound like falling dew,
The whirling and the wandering fire;
But lift a mournful ulalu,
For the kind wires are torn and still,
And I must wander wood and hill
Through summer's heat and winter's cold.
They will not hush, the leaves a-flutter round me, the beech leaves old.

The Stolen Child

Where dips the rocky highland
Of Sleuth Wood in the lake,
There lies a leafy island
Where flapping herons wake
The drowsy water-rats;
There we've hid our faery vats,
Full of berries
And of reddest stolen cherries.
Come away, O human child!
To the waters and the wild
With a faery, hand in hand,
For the world's more full of weeping than you can understand.

Where the wave of moonlight glosses
The dim grey sands with light,
Far off by furthest Rosses
We foot it all the night,
Weaving olden dances,
Mingling hands and mingling glances
Till the moon has taken flight;
To and fro we leap
And chase the frothy bubbles,
While the world is full of troubles
And is anxious in its sleep.
Come away, O human child!
To the waters and the wild
With a faery, hand in hand,
For the world's more full of weeping than you can understand.

Where the wandering water gushes
From the hills above Glen-Car,
In pools among the rushes
That scarce could bathe a star,
We seek for slumbering trout
And whispering in their ears
Give them unquiet dreams;
Leaning softly out

From ferns that drop their tears
Over the young streams.
Come away, O human child!
To the waters and the wild
With a faery, hand in hand,
For the world's more full of weeping than you can understand.

Away with us he's going,
The solemn-eyed:
He'll hear no more the lowing
Of the calves on the warm hillside
Or the kettle on the hob
Sing peace into his breast,
Or see the brown mice bob
Round and round the oatmeal-chest.
For he comes, the human child,
To the waters and the wild
With a faery, hand in hand,
From a world more full of weeping than he can understand.

To an Isle in the Water

Shy one, shy one,
Shy one of my heart,
She moves in the firelight
Pensively apart.

She carries in the dishes,
And lays them in a row.
To an isle in the water
With her would I go.

She carries in the candles,
And lights the curtained room,
Shy in the doorway
And shy in the gloom;

And shy as a rabbit,
Helpful and shy.
To an isle in the water
With her would I fly.

Down by the Salley Gardens

Down by the salley gardens my love and I did meet;
She passed the salley gardens with little snow-white feet.
She bid me take love easy, as the leaves grow on the tree;
But I, being young and foolish, with her would not agree.

In a field by the river my love and I did stand,
And on my leaning shoulder she laid her snow-white hand.
She bid me take life easy, as the grass grows on the weirs;
But I was young and foolish, and now am full of tears.

The Meditation of the Old Fisherman

You waves, though you dance by my feet like children at play,
Though you glow and you glance, though you purr and you dart;
In the Junes that were warmer than these are, the waves were
    more gay,
When I was a boy with never a crack in my heart.

The herring are not in the tides as they were of old;
My sorrow! for many a creak gave the creel in the cart
That carried the take to Sligo town to be sold,
When I was a boy with never a crack in my heart.

And ah, you proud maiden, you are not so fair when his oar
Is heard on the water, as they were, the proud and apart,
Who paced in the eve by the nets on the pebbly shore,
When I was a boy with never a crack in my heart.

The Ballad of Father O'Hart

Good Father John O'Hart
In penal days rode out
To a shoneen who had free lands
And his own snipe and trout.

In trust took he John's lands;
Sleiveens were all his race;
And he gave them as dowers to his daughters,
And they married beyond their place.

But Father John went up,
And Father John went down;
And he wore small holes in his shoes,
And he wore large holes in his gown.

All loved him, only the shoneen,
Whom the devils have by the hair,
From the wives, and the cats, and the children,
To the birds in the white of the air.

The birds, for he opened their cages
As he went up and down;
And he said with a smile, 'Have peace now';
And he went his way with a frown.

But if when anyone died
Came keeners hoarser than rooks,
He bade them give over their keening;
For he was a man of books.

And these were the works of John,
When, weeping score by score,
People came into Coloony;
For he'd died at ninety-four.

There was no human keening;
The birds from Knocknarea
And the world round Knocknashee
Came keening in that day.

The young birds and old birds
Came flying, heavy and sad;
Keening in from Tiraragh,
Keening from Ballinafad;

Keening from Inishmurray,
Nor stayed for bite or sup;
This way were all reproved
Who dig old customs up.

The Ballad of Moll Magee

Come round me, little childer;
There, don't fling stones at me
Because I mutter as I go;
But pity Moll Magee.

My man was a poor fisher
With shore lines in the say;
My work was saltin' herrings
The whole of the long day.

And sometimes from the saltin' shed
I scarce could drag my feet,
Under the blessed moonlight,
Along the pebbly street.

I'd always been but weakly,
And my baby was just born;
A neighbour minded her by day,
I minded her till morn.

I lay upon my baby;
Ye little childer dear,
I looked on my cold baby
When the morn grew frosty and clear.

A weary woman sleeps so hard!
My man grew red and pale,
And gave me money, and bade me go
To my own place, Kinsale.

He drove me out and shut the door,
And gave his curse to me;
I went away in silence,
No neighbour could I see.

The windows and the doors were shut,
One star shone faint and green,
The little straws were turnin' round
Across the bare boreen.

I went away in silence:
Beyond old Martin's byre
I saw a kindly neighbour
Blowin' her mornin' fire.

She drew from me my story –
My money's all used up,
And still, with pityin', scornin' eye,
She gives me bite and sup.

She says my man will surely come,
And fetch me home agin;
But always, as I'm movin' round,
Without doors or within,

Pilin' the wood or pilin' the turf,
Or goin' to the well,
I'm thinkin' of my baby
And keenin' to mysel'.

And sometimes I am sure she knows
When, openin' wide His door,
God lights the stars, His candles,
And looks upon the poor.

So now, ye little childer,
Ye won't fling stones at me;
But gather with your shinin' looks
And pity Moll Magee.

The Ballad of the Foxhunter

'Lay me in a cushioned chair;
Carry me, ye four,
With cushions here and cushions there,
To see the world once more.

'To stable and to kennel go;
Bring what is there to bring;
Lead my Lollard to and fro,
Or gently in a ring.

'Put the chair upon the grass:
Bring Rody and his hounds,
That I may contented pass
From these earthly bounds.'

His eyelids droop, his head falls low,
His old eyes cloud with dreams;
The sun upon all things that grow
Falls in sleepy streams.

Brown Lollard treads upon the lawn,
And to the armchair goes,
And now the old man's dreams are gone,
He smooths the long brown nose.

And now moves many a pleasant tongue
Upon his wasted hands,
For leading aged hounds and young
The huntsman near him stands.

'Huntsman Rody, blow the horn,
Make the hills reply.'
The huntsman loosens on the morn
A gay wandering cry.

Fire is in the old man's eyes,
His fingers move and sway,
And when the wandering music dies
They hear him feebly say,

'Huntsman Rody, blow the horn,
Make the hills reply.'
'I cannot blow upon my horn,
I can but weep and sigh.'

Servants round his cushioned place
Are with new sorrow wrung;
Hounds are gazing on his face,
Aged hounds and young.

One blind hound only lies apart
On the sun-smitten grass;
He holds deep commune with his heart:
The moments pass and pass;

The blind hound with a mournful din
Lifts slow his wintry head;
The servants bear the body in;
The hounds wail for the dead.

THE ROSE
1893

'Sero te amavi, Pulchritudo tam antiqua et tam nova! Sero te amavi.' –
S. AUGUSTINE

TO
LIONEL JOHNSON

THE ROSE

To the Rose upon the Rood of Time

Red Rose, proud Rose, sad Rose of all my days!
Come near me, while I sing the ancient ways:
Cuchulain battling with the bitter tide;
The Druid, grey, wood-nurtured, quiet-eyed,
Who cast round Fergus dreams, and ruin untold;
And thine own sadness, whereof stars, grown old
In dancing silver-sandalled on the sea,
Sing in their high and lonely melody.
Come near, that no more blinded by man's fate,
I find under the boughs of love and hate,
In all poor foolish things that live a day,
Eternal beauty wandering on her way.

Come near, come near, come near – Ah, leave me still
A little space for the rose-breath to fill!
Lest I no more hear common things that crave;
The weak worm hiding down in its small cave,
The field-mouse running by me in the grass,
And heavy mortal hopes that toil and pass;
But seek alone to hear the strange things said
By God to the bright hearts of those long dead,
And learn to chaunt a tongue men do not know.
Come near; I would, before my time to go,
Sing of old Eire and the ancient ways:
Red Rose, proud Rose, sad Rose of all my days.

Fergus and the Druid

FERGUS

This whole day have I followed in the rocks,
And you have changed and flowed from shape to shape,
First as a raven on whose ancient wings
Scarcely a feather lingered, then you seemed
A weasel moving on from stone to stone,
And now at last you wear a human shape,
A thin grey man half lost in gathering night.

DRUID

What would you, king of the proud Red Branch kings?

FERGUS

This would I say, most wise of living souls:
Young subtle Conchubar sat close by me
When I gave judgment, and his words were wise,
And what to me was burden without end,
To him seemed easy, so I laid the crown
Upon his head to cast away my sorrow.

DRUID

What would you, king of the proud Red Branch kings?

FERGUS

A king and proud! and that is my despair.
I feast amid my people on the hill,
And pace the woods, and drive my chariot-wheels
In the white border of the murmuring sea;
And still I feel the crown upon my head.

DRUID

What would you, Fergus?

FERGUS

Be no more a king
But learn the dreaming wisdom that is yours.

DRUID

Look on my thin grey hair and hollow cheeks
And on these hands that may not lift the sword,
This body trembling like a wind-blown reed.
No woman's loved me, no man sought my help.

FERGUS

A king is but a foolish labourer
Who wastes his blood to be another's dream.

DRUID

Take, if you must, this little bag of dreams;
Unloose the cord, and they will wrap you round.

FERGUS

I see my life go drifting like a river
From change to change; I have been many things –
A green drop in the surge, a gleam of light
Upon a sword, a fir-tree on a hill,
An old slave grinding at a heavy quern,
A king sitting upon a chair of gold –
And all these things were wonderful and great;
But now I have grown nothing, knowing all.
Ah! Druid, Druid, how great webs of sorrow
Lay hidden in the small slate-coloured thing!

Cuchulain's Fight with the Sea

A man came slowly from the setting sun,
To Emer, raddling raiment in her dun,
And said, 'I am that swineherd whom you bid
Go watch the road between the wood and tide,
But now I have no need to watch it more.'

Then Emer cast the web upon the floor,
And raising arms all raddled with the dye,
Parted her lips with a loud sudden cry.

That swineherd stared upon her face and said,
'No man alive, no man among the dead,
Has won the gold his cars of battle bring.'

'But if your master comes home triumphing
Why must you blench and shake from root to crown?'

Thereon he shook the more and cast him down
Upon the web-heaped floor, and cried his word:
'With him is one sweet-throated like a bird.'

'You dare me to my face,' and thereupon
She smote with raddled fist, and where her son
Herded the cattle came with stumbling feet,
And cried with angry voice, 'It is not meet
To idle life away, a common herd.'

'I have long waited, mother, for that word:
But wherefore now?'

                'There is a man to die;
You have the heaviest arm under the sky.'

'Whether under its daylight or its stars
My father stands amid his battle-cars.'

'But you have grown to be the taller man.'

'Yet somewhere under starlight or the sun
My father stands.'

'Aged, worn out with wars
On foot, on horseback or in battle-cars.'

'I only ask what way my journey lies,
For He who made you bitter made you wise.'

'The Red Branch camp in a great company
Between wood's rim and the horses of the sea.
Go there, and light a camp-fire at wood's rim;
But tell your name and lineage to him
Whose blade compels, and wait till they have found
Some feasting man that the same oath has bound.'

Among those feasting men Cuchulain dwelt,
And his young sweetheart close beside him knelt,
Stared on the mournful wonder of his eyes,
Even as Spring upon the ancient skies,
And pondered on the glory of his days;
And all around the harp-string told his praise,
And Conchubar, the Red Branch king of kings,
With his own fingers touched the brazen strings.

At last Cuchulain spake, 'Some man has made
His evening fire amid the leafy shade.
I have often heard him singing to and fro,
I have often heard the sweet sound of his bow.
Seek out what man he is.'

                 One went and came.
'He bade me let all know he gives his name
At the sword-point, and waits till we have found
Some feasting man that the same oath has bound.'

Cuchulain cried, 'I am the only man
Of all this host so bound from childhood on.'

After short fighting in the leafy shade,
He spake to the young man, 'Is there no maid
Who loves you, no white arms to wrap you round,
Or do you long for the dim sleepy ground,
That you have come and dared me to my face?'

'The dooms of men are in God's hidden place.'

'Your head a while seemed like a woman's head
That I loved once.'

                       Again the fighting sped,
But now the war-rage in Cuchulain woke,
And through that new blade's guard the old blade broke,
And pierced him.
                'Speak before your breath is done.'

'Cuchulain I, mighty Cuchulain's son.'

'I put you from your pain. I can no more.'

While day its burden on to evening bore,
With head bowed on his knees Cuchulain stayed;
Then Conchubar sent that sweet-throated maid,
And she, to win him, his grey hair caressed;
In vain her arms, in vain her soft white breast.
Then Conchubar, the subtlest of all men,
Ranking his Druids round him ten by ten,
Spake thus: 'Cuchulain will dwell there and brood
For three days more in dreadful quietude,
And then arise, and raving slay us all.
Chaunt in his ear delusions magical,
That he may fight the horses of the sea.'
The Druids took them to their mystery,
And chaunted for three days.

                     Cuchulain stirred,
Stared on the horses of the sea, and heard
The cars of battle and his own name cried;
And fought with the invulnerable tide.

The Rose of the World

Who dreamed that beauty passes like a dream?
For these red lips, with all their mournful pride,
Mournful that no new wonder may betide,
Troy passed away in one high funeral gleam,
And Usna's children died.

We and the labouring world are passing by:
Amid men's souls, that waver and give place
Like the pale waters in their wintry race,
Under the passing stars, foam of the sky,
Lives on this lonely face.

Bow down, archangels, in your dim abode:
Before you were, or any hearts to beat,
Weary and kind one lingered by His seat;
He made the world to be a grassy road
Before her wandering feet.

The Rose of Peace

If Michael, leader of God's host
When Heaven and Hell are met,
Looked down on you from Heaven's door-post
He would his deeds forget.

Brooding no more upon God's wars
In his divine homestead,
He would go weave out of the stars
A chaplet for your head.

And all folk seeing him bow down,
And white stars tell your praise,
Would come at last to God's great town,
Led on by gentle ways;

And God would bid His warfare cease,
Saying all things were well;
And softly make a rosy peace,
A peace of Heaven with Hell.

The Rose of Battle

Rose of all Roses, Rose of all the World!
The tall thought-woven sails, that flap unfurled
Above the tide of hours, trouble the air,
And God's bell buoyed to be the water's care;
While hushed from fear, or loud with hope, a band
With blown, spray-dabbled hair gather at hand.
Turn if you may from battles never done,
I call, as they go by me one by one,
Danger no refuge holds, and war no peace,
For him who hears love sing and never cease,
Beside her clean-swept hearth, her quiet shade:
But gather all for whom no love hath made
A woven silence, or but came to cast
A song into the air, and singing passed
To smile on the pale dawn; and gather you
Who have sought more than is in rain or dew,
Or in the sun and moon, or on the earth,
Or sighs amid the wandering, starry mirth,
Or comes in laughter from the sea's sad lips,
And wage God's battles in the long grey ships.
The sad, the lonely, the insatiable,
To these Old Night shall all her mystery tell;
God's bell has claimed them by the little cry
Of their sad hearts, that may not live nor die.

Rose of all Roses, Rose of all the World!
You, too, have come where the dim tides are hurled
Upon the wharves of sorrow, and heard ring
The bell that calls us on; the sweet far thing.

Beauty grown sad with its eternity
Made you of us, and of the dim grey sea.
Our long ships loose thought-woven sails and wait,
For God has bid them share an equal fate;
And when at last, defeated in His wars,
They have gone down under the same white stars,
We shall no longer hear the little cry
Of our sad hearts, that may not live nor die.

A Faery Song

*Sung by the people of Faery over Diarmuid and Grania, in their bridal
sleep under a Cromlech.*

We who are old, old and gay,
O so old!
Thousands of years, thousands of years,
If all were told:

Give to these children, new from the world,
Silence and love;
And the long dew-dropping hours of the night,
And the stars above:

Give to these children, new from the world,
Rest far from men.
Is anything better, anything better?
Tell us it then:

Us who are old, old and gay,
O so old!
Thousands of years, thousands of years,
If all were told.

The Lake Isle of Innisfree

I will arise and go now, and go to Innisfree,
And a small cabin build there, of clay and wattles made:
Nine bean-rows will I have there, a hive for the honey-bee,
And live alone in the bee-loud glade.

And I shall have some peace there, for peace comes dropping slow,
Dropping from the veils of the morning to where the cricket sings;
There midnight's all a glimmer, and noon a purple glow,
And evening full of the linnet's wings.

I will arise and go now, for always night and day
I hear lake water lapping with low sounds by the shore;
While I stand on the roadway, or on the pavements grey,
I hear it in the deep heart's core.

A Cradle Song

The angels are stooping
Above your bed;
They weary of trooping
With the whimpering dead.

God's laughing in Heaven
To see you so good;
The Sailing Seven
Are gay with His mood.

I sigh that kiss you,
For I must own
That I shall miss you
When you have grown.

The Pity of Love

A pity beyond all telling
Is hid in the heart of love:
The folk who are buying and selling,
The clouds on their journey above,
The cold wet winds ever blowing,
And the shadowy hazel grove
Where mouse-grey waters are flowing,
Threaten the head that I love.

The Sorrow of Love

The brawling of a sparrow in the eaves,
The brilliant moon and all the milky sky,
And all that famous harmony of leaves,
Had blotted out man's image and his cry.

A girl arose that had red mournful lips
And seemed the greatness of the world in tears,
Doomed like Odysseus and the labouring ships
And proud as Priam murdered with his peers;

Arose, and on the instant clamorous eaves,
A climbing moon upon an empty sky,
And all that lamentation of the leaves,
Could but compose man's image and his cry.

When You are Old

When you are old and grey and full of sleep,
And nodding by the fire, take down this book,
And slowly read, and dream of the soft look
Your eyes had once, and of their shadows deep;

How many loved your moments of glad grace,
And loved your beauty with love false or true,
But one man loved the pilgrim soul in you,
And loved the sorrows of your changing face;

And bending down beside the glowing bars,
Murmur, a little sadly, how Love fled
And paced upon the mountains overhead
And hid his face amid a crowd of stars.

The White Birds

I would that we were, my beloved, white birds on the foam of the
    sea!
We tire of the flame of the meteor, before it can fade and flee;
And the flame of the blue star of twilight, hung low on the rim of
    the sky,
Has awaked in our hearts, my beloved, a sadness that may not die.

A weariness comes from those dreamers, dew-dabbled, the lily and
    rose;
Ah, dream not of them, my beloved, the flame of the meteor that
    goes,
Or the flame of the blue star that lingers hung low in the fall of
    the dew:
For I would we were changed to white birds on the wandering
    foam: I and you!

I am haunted by numberless islands, and many a Danaan shore,
Where Time would surely forget us, and Sorrow come near us no
  more;
Soon far from the rose and the lily and fret of the flames would we
  be,
Were we only white birds, my beloved, buoyed out on the foam
  of the sea!

A Dream of Death

I dreamed that one had died in a strange place
Near no accustomed hand;
And they had nailed the boards above her face,
The peasants of that land,
Wondering to lay her in that solitude,
And raised above her mound
A cross they had made out of two bits of wood,
And planted cypress round;
And left her to the indifferent stars above
Until I carved these words:
She was more beautiful than thy first love,
But now lies under boards.

The Countess Cathleen in Paradise

All the heavy days are over;
Leave the body's coloured pride
Underneath the grass and clover,
With the feet laid side by side.

Bathed in flaming founts of duty
She'll not ask a haughty dress;
Carry all that mournful beauty
To the scented oaken press.

Did the kiss of Mother Mary
Put that music in her face?
Yet she goes with footstep wary,
Full of earth's old timid grace.

'Mong the feet of angels seven
What a dancer glimmering!
All the heavens bow down to Heaven,
Flame to flame and wing to wing.

Who Goes with Fergus?

Who will go drive with Fergus now,
And pierce the deep wood's woven shade,
And dance upon the level shore?
Young man, lift up your russet brow,
And lift your tender eyelids, maid,
And brood on hopes and fear no more.

And no more turn aside and brood
Upon love's bitter mystery;
For Fergus rules the brazen cars,
And rules the shadows of the wood,
And the white breast of the dim sea
And all dishevelled wandering stars.

The Man who Dreamed of Faeryland

He stood among a crowd at Drumahair;
His heart hung all upon a silken dress,
And he had known at last some tenderness,
Before earth took him to her stony care;
But when a man poured fish into a pile,
It seemed they raised their little silver heads,
And sang what gold morning or evening sheds
Upon a woven world-forgotten isle
Where people love beside the ravelled seas;
That Time can never mar a lover's vows
Under that woven changeless roof of boughs:
The singing shook him out of his new ease.

He wandered by the sands of Lissadell;
His mind ran all on money cares and fears,
And he had known at last some prudent years
Before they heaped his grave under the hill;
But while he passed before a plashy place,
A lug-worm with its grey and muddy mouth
Sang that somewhere to north or west or south
There dwelt a gay, exulting, gentle race
Under the golden or the silver skies;
That if a dancer stayed his hungry foot
It seemed the sun and moon were in the fruit:
And at that singing he was no more wise.

He mused beside the well of Scanavin,
He mused upon his mockers: without fail
His sudden vengeance were a country tale,
When earthy night had drunk his body in;
But one small knot-grass growing by the pool
Sang where – unnecessary cruel voice –
Old silence bids its chosen race rejoice,
Whatever ravelled waters rise and fall
Or stormy silver fret the gold of day,
And midnight there enfold them like a fleece

And lover there by lover be at peace.
The tale drove his fine angry mood away.

He slept under the hill of Lugnagall;
And might have known at last unhaunted sleep
Under that cold and vapour-turbaned steep,
Now that the earth had taken man and all:
Did not the worms that spired about his bones
Proclaim with that unwearied, reedy cry
That God has laid His fingers on the sky,
That from those fingers glittering summer runs
Upon the dancer by the dreamless wave.
Why should those lovers that no lovers miss
Dream, until God burn Nature with a kiss?
The man has found no comfort in the grave.

The Dedication to a Book of Stories selected from the Irish Novelists

There was a green branch hung with many a bell
When her own people ruled this tragic Eire;
And from its murmuring greenness, calm of Faery,
A Druid kindness, on all hearers fell.

It charmed away the merchant from his guile,
And turned the farmer's memory from his cattle,
And hushed in sleep the roaring ranks of battle:
And all grew friendly for a little while.

Ah, Exiles wandering over lands and seas,
And planning, plotting always that some morrow
May set a stone upon ancestral Sorrow!
I also bear a bell-branch full of ease.

I tore it from green boughs winds tore and tossed
Until the sap of summer had grown weary!
I tore it from the barren boughs of Eire,
That country where a man can be so crossed;

Can be so battered, badgered and destroyed
That he's a loveless man: gay bells bring laughter
That shakes a mouldering cobweb from the rafter;
And yet the saddest chimes are best enjoyed.

Gay bells or sad, they bring you memories
Of half-forgotten innocent old places:
We and our bitterness have left no traces
On Munster grass and Connemara skies.

The Lamentation of the Old Pensioner

Although I shelter from the rain
Under a broken tree,
My chair was nearest to the fire
In every company
That talked of love or politics,
Ere Time transfigured me.

Though lads are making pikes again
For some conspiracy,
And crazy rascals rage their fill
At human tyranny,
My contemplations are of Time
That has transfigured me.

There's not a woman turns her face
Upon a broken tree,
And yet the beauties that I loved
Are in my memory;
I spit into the face of Time
That has transfigured me.

The Ballad of Father Gilligan

The old priest Peter Gilligan
Was weary night and day;
For half his flock were in their beds,
Or under green sods lay.

Once, while he nodded on a chair,
At the moth-hour of eve,
Another poor man sent for him,
And he began to grieve.

'I have no rest, nor joy, nor peace,
For people die and die';
And after cried he, 'God forgive!
My body spake, not I!'

He knelt, and leaning on the chair
He prayed and fell asleep;
And the moth-hour went from the fields,
And stars began to peep.

They slowly into millions grew,
And leaves shook in the wind;
And God covered the world with shade,
And whispered to mankind.

Upon the time of sparrow-chirp
When the moths came once more,
The old priest Peter Gilligan
Stood upright on the floor.

'Mavrone, mavrone! the man has died
While I slept on the chair';
He roused his horse out of its sleep,
And rode with little care.

He rode now as he never rode,
By rocky lane and fen;
The sick man's wife opened the door:
'Father! you come again!'

'And is the poor man dead?' he cried.
'He died an hour ago.'
The old priest Peter Gilligan
In grief swayed to and fro.

'When you were gone, he turned and died
As merry as a bird.'
The old priest Peter Gilligan
He knelt him at that word.

'He Who hath made the night of stars
For souls who tire and bleed,
Sent one of His great angels down
To help me in my need.

'He Who is wrapped in purple robes,
With planets in His care,
Had pity on the least of things
Asleep upon a chair.'

The Two Trees

Beloved, gaze in thine own heart,
The holy tree is growing there;
From joy the holy branches start,
And all the trembling flowers they bear.
The changing colours of its fruit
Have dowered the stars with merry light;
The surety of its hidden root
Has planted quiet in the night;
The shaking of its leafy head
Has given the waves their melody,
And made my lips and music wed,
Murmuring a wizard song for thee.
There the Loves a circle go,
The flaming circle of our days,
Gyring, spiring to and fro
In those great ignorant leafy ways;

Remembering all that shaken hair
And how the wingèd sandals dart,
Thine eyes grow full of tender care:
Beloved, gaze in thine own heart.

Gaze no more in the bitter glass
The demons, with their subtle guile,
Lift up before us when they pass,
Or only gaze a little while;
For there a fatal image grows
That the stormy night receives,
Roots half hidden under snows,
Broken boughs and blackened leaves.
For all things turn to barrenness
In the dim glass the demons hold,
The glass of outer weariness,
Made when God slept in times of old.
There, through the broken branches, go
The ravens of unresting thought;
Flying, crying, to and fro,
Cruel claw and hungry throat,
Or else they stand and sniff the wind,
And shake their ragged wings; alas!
Thy tender eyes grow all unkind:
Gaze no more in the bitter glass.

To Some I have Talked with by the Fire

While I wrought out these fitful Danaan rhymes,
My heart would brim with dreams about the times
When we bent down above the fading coals
And talked of the dark folk who live in souls
Of passionate men, like bats in the dead trees;
And of the wayward twilight companies
Who sigh with mingled sorrow and content,
Because their blossoming dreams have never bent

Under the fruit of evil and of good:
And of the embattled flaming multitude
Who rise, wing above wing, flame above flame,
And, like a storm, cry the Ineffable Name,
And with the clashing of their sword-blades make
A rapturous music, till the morning break
And the white hush end all but the loud beat
Of their long wings, the flash of their white feet.

To Ireland in the Coming Times

Know, that I would accounted be
True brother of a company
That sang, to sweeten Ireland's wrong,
Ballad and story, rann and song;
Nor be I any less of them,
Because the red-rose-bordered hem
Of her, whose history began
Before God made the angelic clan,
Trails all about the written page.
When Time began to rant and rage
The measure of her flying feet
Made Ireland's heart begin to beat;
And Time bade all his candles flare
To light a measure here and there;
And may the thoughts of Ireland brood
Upon a measured quietude.

Nor may I less be counted one
With Davis, Mangan, Ferguson,
Because, to him who ponders well,
My rhymes more than their rhyming tell
Of things discovered in the deep,
Where only body's laid asleep.
For the elemental creatures go
About my table to and fro,

That hurry from unmeasured mind
To rant and rage in flood and wind;
Yet he who treads in measured ways
May surely barter gaze for gaze.
Man ever journeys on with them
After the red-rose-bordered hem.
Ah, faeries, dancing under the moon,
A Druid land, a Druid tune!

While still I may, I write for you
The love I lived, the dream I knew.
From our birthday, until we die,
Is but the winking of an eye;
And we, our singing and our love,
What measurer Time has lit above,
And all benighted things that go
About my table to and fro,
Are passing on to where may be,
In truth's consuming ecstasy,
No place for love and dream at all;
For God goes by with white footfall.
I cast my heart into my rhymes,
That you, in the dim coming times,
May know how my heart went with them
After the red-rose-bordered hem.

THE WIND AMONG
THE REEDS
1899

THE WIND AMONG THE REEDS

The Hosting of the Sidhe

The host is riding from Knocknarea
And over the grave of Clooth-na-Bare;
Caoilte tossing his burning hair,
And Niamh calling *Away, come away:*
Empty your heart of its mortal dream.
The winds awaken, the leaves whirl round,
Our cheeks are pale, our hair is unbound,
Our breasts are heaving, our eyes are agleam,
Our arms are waving, our lips are apart;
And if any gaze on our rushing band,
We come between him and the deed of his hand,
We come between him and the hope of his heart.
The host is rushing 'twixt night and day,
And where is there hope or deed as fair?
Caoilte tossing his burning hair,
And Niamh calling *Away, come away.*

The Everlasting Voices

O sweet everlasting Voices, be still;
Go to the guards of the heavenly fold
And bid them wander obeying your will,
Flame under flame, till Time be no more;
Have you not heard that our hearts are old,
That you call in birds, in wind on the hill,
In shaken boughs, in tide on the shore?
O sweet everlasting Voices, be still.

The Moods

Time drops in decay,
Like a candle burnt out,
And the mountains and woods
Have their day, have their day;
What one in the rout
Of the fire-born moods
Has fallen away?

The Lover tells of the Rose in his Heart

All things uncomely and broken, all things worn out and old,
The cry of a child by the roadway, the creak of a lumbering cart,
The heavy steps of the ploughman, splashing the wintry mould,
Are wronging your image that blossoms a rose in the deeps of my
    heart.

The wrong of unshapely things is a wrong too great to be told;
I hunger to build them anew and sit on a green knoll apart,
With the earth and the sky and the water, re-made, like a casket of
    gold
For my dreams of your image that blossoms a rose in the deeps of
    my heart.

The Host of the Air

O'Driscoll drove with a song
The wild duck and the drake
From the tall and the tufted reeds
Of the drear Hart Lake.

And he saw how the reeds grew dark
At the coming of night-tide,
And dreamed of the long dim hair
Of Bridget his bride.

He heard while he sang and dreamed
A piper piping away,
And never was piping so sad,
And never was piping so gay.

And he saw young men and young girls
Who danced on a level place,
And Bridget his bride among them,
With a sad and a gay face.

The dancers crowded about him
And many a sweet thing said,
And a young man brought him red wine
And a young girl white bread.

But Bridget drew him by the sleeve
Away from the merry bands,
To old men playing at cards
With a twinkling of ancient hands.

The bread and the wine had a doom,
For these were the host of the air;
He sat and played in a dream
Of her long dim hair.

He played with the merry old men
And thought not of evil chance,
Until one bore Bridget his bride
Away from the merry dance.

He bore her away in his arms,
The handsomest young man there,
And his neck and his breast and his arms
Were drowned in her long dim hair.

O'Driscoll scattered the cards
And out of his dream awoke:
Old men and young men and young girls
Were gone like a drifting smoke;

But he heard high up in the air
A piper piping away,
And never was piping so sad,
And never was piping so gay.

The Fish

Although you hide in the ebb and flow
Of the pale tide when the moon has set,
The people of coming days will know
About the casting out of my net,

And how you have leaped times out of mind
Over the little silver cords,
And think that you were hard and unkind,
And blame you with many bitter words.

The Unappeasable Host

The Danaan children laugh, in cradles of wrought gold,
And clap their hands together, and half close their eyes,
For they will ride the North when the ger-eagle flies,
With heavy whitening wings, and a heart fallen cold:
I kiss my wailing child and press it to my breast,
And hear the narrow graves calling my child and me.
Desolate winds that cry over the wandering sea;
Desolate winds that hover in the flaming West;
Desolate winds that beat the doors of Heaven, and beat
The doors of Hell and blow there many a whimpering ghost;
O heart the winds have shaken, the unappeasable host
Is comelier than candles at Mother Mary's feet.

Into the Twilight

Out-worn heart, in a time out-worn,
Come clear of the nets of wrong and right;
Laugh, heart, again in the grey twilight,
Sigh, heart, again in the dew of the morn.

Your mother Eire is always young,
Dew ever shining and twilight grey;
Though hope fall from you and love decay,
Burning in fires of a slanderous tongue.

Come, heart, where hill is heaped upon hill:
For there the mystical brotherhood
Of sun and moon and hollow and wood
And river and stream work out their will;

And God stands winding His lonely horn,
And time and the world are ever in flight;
And love is less kind than the grey twilight,
And hope is less dear than the dew of the morn.

The Song of Wandering Aengus

I went out to the hazel wood,
Because a fire was in my head,
And cut and peeled a hazel wand,
And hooked a berry to a thread;
And when white moths were on the wing,
And moth-like stars were flickering out,
I dropped the berry in a stream
And caught a little silver trout.

When I had laid it on the floor
I went to blow the fire aflame,
But something rustled on the floor,
And some one called me by my name:

It had become a glimmering girl
With apple blossom in her hair
Who called me by my name and ran
And faded through the brightening air.

Though I am old with wandering
Through hollow lands and hilly lands,
I will find out where she has gone,
And kiss her lips and take her hands;
And walk among long dappled grass,
And pluck till time and times are done
The silver apples of the moon,
The golden apples of the sun.

The Song of the Old Mother

I rise in the dawn, and I kneel and blow
Till the seed of the fire flicker and glow;
And then I must scrub and bake and sweep
Till stars are beginning to blink and peep;
And the young lie long and dream in their bed
Of the matching of ribbons for bosom and head,
And their day goes over in idleness,
And they sigh if the wind but lift a tress:
While I must work because I am old,
And the seed of the fire gets feeble and cold.

The Heart of the Woman

O what to me the little room
That was brimmed up with prayer and rest;
He bade me out into the gloom,
And my breast lies upon his breast.

O what to me my mother's care,
The house where I was safe and warm;
The shadowy blossom of my hair
Will hide us from the bitter storm.

O hiding hair and dewy eyes,
I am no more with life and death,
My heart upon his warm heart lies,
My breath is mixed into his breath.

The Lover mourns for the Loss of Love

Pale brows, still hands and dim hair,
I had a beautiful friend
And dreamed that the old despair
Would end in love in the end:
She looked in my heart one day
And saw your image was there;
She has gone weeping away.

He mourns for the Change that has come upon him and his Beloved, and longs for the End of the World

Do you not hear me calling, white deer with no horns?
I have been changed to a hound with one red ear;
I have been in the Path of Stones and the Wood of Thorns,
For somebody hid hatred and hope and desire and fear
Under my feet that they follow you night and day.
A man with a hazel wand came without sound;
He changed me suddenly; I was looking another way;
And now my calling is but the calling of a hound;

And Time and Birth and Change are hurrying by.
I would that the Boar without bristles had come from the West
And had rooted the sun and moon and stars out of the sky
And lay in the darkness, grunting, and turning to his rest.

He bids his Beloved be at Peace

I hear the Shadowy Horses, their long manes a-shake,
Their hoofs heavy with tumult, their eyes glimmering white;
The North unfolds above them clinging, creeping night,
The East her hidden joy before the morning break,
The West weeps in pale dew and sighs passing away,
The South is pouring down roses of crimson fire:
O vanity of Sleep, Hope, Dream, endless Desire,
The Horses of Disaster plunge in the heavy clay:
Beloved, let your eyes half close, and your heart beat
Over my heart, and your hair fall over my breast,
Drowning love's lonely hour in deep twilight of rest,
And hiding their tossing manes and their tumultuous feet.

He reproves the Curlew

O Curlew, cry no more in the air,
Or only to the water in the West;
Because your crying brings to my mind
Passion-dimmed eyes and long heavy hair
That was shaken out over my breast:
There is enough evil in the crying of wind.

He remembers Forgotten Beauty

When my arms wrap you round I press
My heart upon the loveliness
That has long faded from the world;
The jewelled crowns that kings have hurled
In shadowy pools, when armies fled;
The love-tales wrought with silken thread
By dreaming ladies upon cloth
That has made fat the murderous moth;
The roses that of old time were
Woven by ladies in their hair,
The dew-cold lilies ladies bore
Through many a sacred corridor
Where such grey clouds of incense rose
That only God's eyes did not close:
For that pale breast and lingering hand
Come from a more dream-heavy land,
A more dream-heavy hour than this;
And when you sigh from kiss to kiss
I hear white Beauty sighing, too,
For hours when all must fade like dew,
But flame on flame, and deep on deep,
Throne over throne where in half sleep,
Their swords upon their iron knees,
Brood her high lonely mysteries.

A Poet to his Beloved

I bring you with reverent hands
The books of my numberless dreams,
White woman that passion has worn
As the tide wears the dove-grey sands,
And with heart more old than the horn
That is brimmed from the pale fire of time:
White woman with numberless dreams,
I bring you my passionate rhyme.

He gives his Beloved certain Rhymes

Fasten your hair with a golden pin,
And bind up every wandering tress;
I bade my heart build these poor rhymes:
It worked at them, day out, day in,
Building a sorrowful loveliness
Out of the battles of old times.

You need but lift a pearl-pale hand,
And bind up your long hair and sigh;
And all men's hearts must burn and beat;
And candle-like foam on the dim sand,
And stars climbing the dew-dropping sky,
Live but to light your passing feet.

To his Heart, bidding it have no Fear

Be you still, be you still, trembling heart;
Remember the wisdom out of the old days:
Him who trembles before the flame and the flood,
And the winds that blow through the starry ways,
Let the starry winds and the flame and the flood
Cover over and hide, for he has no part
With the lonely, majestical multitude.

The Cap and Bells

The jester walked in the garden:
The garden had fallen still;
He bade his soul rise upward
And stand on her window-sill.

It rose in a straight blue garment,
When owls began to call:
It had grown wise-tongued by thinking
Of a quiet and light footfall;

But the young queen would not listen;
She rose in her pale night-gown;
She drew in the heavy casement
And pushed the latches down.

He bade his heart go to her,
When the owls called out no more;
In a red and quivering garment
It sang to her through the door.

It had grown sweet-tongued by dreaming
Of a flutter of flower-like hair;
But she took up her fan from the table
And waved it off on the air.

'I have cap and bells,' he pondered,
'I will send them to her and die';
And when the morning whitened
He left them where she went by.

She laid them upon her bosom,
Under a cloud of her hair,
And her red lips sang them a love-song
Till stars grew out of the air.

She opened her door and her window,
And the heart and the soul came through,
To her right hand came the red one,
To her left hand came the blue.

They set up a noise like crickets,
A chattering wise and sweet,
And her hair was a folded flower
And the quiet of love in her feet.

The Valley of the Black Pig

The dews drop slowly and dreams gather: unknown spears
Suddenly hurtle before my dream-awakened eyes,
And then the clash of fallen horsemen and the cries
Of unknown perishing armies beat about my ears.
We who still labour by the cromlech on the shore,
The grey cairn on the hill, when day sinks drowned in dew,
Being weary of the world's empires, bow down to you,
Master of the still stars and of the flaming door.

The Lover asks Forgiveness because of his Many Moods

If this importunate heart trouble your peace
With words lighter than air,
Or hopes that in mere hoping flicker and cease;
Crumple the rose in your hair;
And cover your lips with odorous twilight and say,
'O Hearts of wind-blown flame!
O Winds, older than changing of night and day,
That murmuring and longing came
From marble cities loud with tabors of old
In dove-grey faery lands;
From battle-banners, fold upon purple fold,
Queens wrought with glimmering hands;
That saw young Niamh hover with love-lorn face
Above the wandering tide;
And lingered in the hidden desolate place
Where the last Phoenix died,
And wrapped the flames above his holy head;
And still murmur and long:
O Piteous Hearts, changing till change be dead
In a tumultuous song':
And cover the pale blossoms of your breast
With your dim heavy hair,
And trouble with a sigh for all things longing for rest
The odorous twilight there.

He tells of a Valley full of Lovers

I dreamed that I stood in a valley, and amid sighs,
For happy lovers passed two by two where I stood;
And I dreamed my lost love came stealthily out of the wood
With her cloud-pale eyelids falling on dream-dimmed eyes:
I cried in my dream, *O women, bid the young men lay*
Their heads on your knees, and drown their eyes with your hair,
Or remembering hers they will find no other face fair
Till all the valleys of the world have been withered away.

He tells of the Perfect Beauty

O cloud-pale eyelids, dream-dimmed eyes,
The poets labouring all their days
To build a perfect beauty in rhyme
Are overthrown by a woman's gaze
And by the unlabouring brood of the skies:
And therefore my heart will bow, when dew
Is dropping sleep, until God burn time,
Before the unlabouring stars and you.

He hears the Cry of the Sedge

I wander by the edge
Of this desolate lake
Where wind cries in the sedge:
Until the axle break
That keeps the stars in their round,
And hands hurl in the deep
The banners of East and West,
And the girdle of light is unbound,
Your breast will not lie by the breast
Of your beloved in sleep.

He thinks of those who have Spoken Evil of his Beloved

Half close your eyelids, loosen your hair,
And dream about the great and their pride;
They have spoken against you everywhere,
But weigh this song with the great and their pride;
I made it out of a mouthful of air,
Their children's children shall say they have lied.

The Blessed

Cumhal called out, bending his head,
Till Dathi came and stood,
With a blink in his eyes, at the cave-mouth,
Between the wind and the wood.

And Cumhal said, bending his knees,
'I have come by the windy way
To gather the half of your blessedness
And learn to pray when you pray.

'I can bring you salmon out of the streams
And heron out of the skies.'
But Dathi folded his hands and smiled
With the secrets of God in his eyes.

And Cumhal saw like a drifting smoke
All manner of blessed souls,
Women and children, young men with books,
And old men with croziers and stoles.

'Praise God and God's Mother,' Dathi said,
'For God and God's Mother have sent
The blessedest souls that walk in the world
To fill your heart with content.'

'And which is the blessedest,' Cumhal said,
'Where all are comely and good?
Is it these that with golden thuribles
Are singing about the wood?'

'My eyes are blinking,' Dathi said,
'With the secrets of God half blind,
But I can see where the wind goes
And follow the way of the wind;

'And blessedness goes where the wind goes,
And when it is gone we are dead;
I see the blessedest soul in the world
And he nods a drunken head.

'O blessedness comes in the night and the day
And whither the wise heart knows;
And one has seen in the redness of wine
The Incorruptible Rose,

'That drowsily drops faint leaves on him
And the sweetness of desire,
While time and the world are ebbing away
In twilights of dew and of fire.'

The Secret Rose

Far-off, most secret, and inviolate Rose,
Enfold me in my hour of hours; where those
Who sought thee in the Holy Sepulchre,
Or in the wine-vat, dwell beyond the stir
And tumult of defeated dreams; and deep
Among pale eyelids, heavy with the sleep
Men have named beauty. Thy great leaves enfold
The ancient beards, the helms of ruby and gold
Of the crowned Magi; and the king whose eyes
Saw the Pierced Hands and Rood of elder rise

In Druid vapour and make the torches dim;
Till vain frenzy awoke and he died; and him
Who met Fand walking among flaming dew
By a grey shore where the wind never blew,
And lost the world and Emer for a kiss;
And him who drove the gods out of their liss,
And till a hundred morns had flowered red
Feasted, and wept the barrows of his dead;
And the proud dreaming king who flung the crown
And sorrow away, and calling bard and clown
Dwelt among wine-stained wanderers in deep woods;
And him who sold tillage, and house, and goods,
And sought through lands and islands numberless years,
Until he found, with laughter and with tears,
A woman of so shining loveliness
That men threshed corn at midnight by a tress,
A little stolen tress. I, too, await
The hour of thy great wind of love and hate.
When shall the stars be blown about the sky,
Like the sparks blown out of a smithy, and die?
Surely thine hour has come, thy great wind blows,
Far-off, most secret, and inviolate Rose?

Maid Quiet

Where has Maid Quiet gone to,
Nodding her russet hood?
The winds that awakened the stars
Are blowing through my blood.
O how could I be so calm
When she rose up to depart?
Now words that called up the lightning
Are hurtling through my heart.

The Travail of Passion

When the flaming lute-thronged angelic door is wide
When an immortal passion breathes in mortal clay;
Our hearts endure the scourge, the plaited thorns, the way
Crowded with bitter faces, the wounds in palm and side,
The vinegar-heavy sponge, the flowers by Kedron stream;
We will bend down and loosen our hair over you,
That it may drop faint perfume, and be heavy with dew,
Lilies of death-pale hope, roses of passionate dream.

The Lover pleads with his Friend for Old Friends

Though you are in your shining days,
Voices among the crowd
And new friends busy with your praise,
Be not unkind or proud,
But think about old friends the most:
Time's bitter flood will rise,
Your beauty perish and be lost
For all eyes but these eyes.

The Lover speaks to the Hearers of his Songs in Coming Days

O women, kneeling by your altar-rails long hence,
When songs I wove for my beloved hide the prayer,
And smoke from this dead heart drifts through the violet air
And covers away the smoke of myrrh and frankincense;

Bend down and pray for all that sin I wove in song,
Till the Attorney for Lost Souls cry her sweet cry,
And call to my beloved and me: 'No longer fly
Amid the hovering, piteous, penitential throng.'

The Poet pleads with the Elemental Powers

The Powers whose name and shape no living creature knows
Have pulled the Immortal Rose;
And though the Seven Lights bowed in their dance and wept,
The Polar Dragon slept,
His heavy rings uncoiled from glimmering deep to deep:
When will he wake from sleep?

Great Powers of falling wave and wind and windy fire,
With your harmonious choir
Encircle her I love and sing her into peace,
That my old care may cease;
Unfold your flaming wings and cover out of sight
The nets of day and night.

Dim Powers of drowsy thought, let her no longer be
Like the pale cup of the sea,
When winds have gathered and sun and moon burned dim
Above its cloudy rim;
But let a gentle silence wrought with music flow
Whither her footsteps go.

He wishes his Beloved were Dead

Were you but lying cold and dead,
And lights were paling out of the West,
You would come hither, and bend your head,
And I would lay my head on your breast;

And you would murmur tender words,
Forgiving me, because you were dead:
Nor would you rise and hasten away,
Though you have the will of the wild birds,
But know your hair was bound and wound
About the stars and moon and sun:
O would, beloved, that you lay
Under the dock-leaves in the ground,
While lights were paling one by one.

He wishes for the Cloths of Heaven

Had I the heavens' embroidered cloths,
Enwrought with golden and silver light,
The blue and the dim and the dark cloths
Of night and light and the half-light,
I would spread the cloths under your feet:
But I, being poor, have only my dreams;
I have spread my dreams under your feet;
Tread softly because you tread on my dreams.

He thinks of his Past Greatness when a Part of the Constellations of Heaven

I have drunk ale from the Country of the Young
And weep because I know all things now:
I have been a hazel-tree, and they hung
The Pilot Star and the Crooked Plough
Among my leaves in times out of mind:
I became a rush that horses tread:
I became a man, a hater of the wind,
Knowing one, out of all things, alone, that his head

May not lie on the breast nor his lips on the hair
Of the woman that he loves, until he dies.
O beast of the wilderness, bird of the air,
Must I endure your amorous cries?

The Fiddler of Dooney

When I play on my fiddle in Dooney,
Folk dance like a wave of the sea;
My cousin is priest in Kilvarnet,
My brother in Mocharabuiee.

I passed my brother and cousin:
They read in their books of prayer;
I read in my book of songs
I bought at the Sligo fair.

When we come at the end of time
To Peter sitting in state,
He will smile on the three old spirits,
But call me first through the gate;

For the good are always the merry,
Save by an evil chance,
And the merry love the fiddle,
And the merry love to dance:

And when the folk there spy me,
They will all come up to me,
With 'Here is the fiddler of Dooney!'
And dance like a wave of the sea.

THE OLD AGE OF
QUEEN MAEVE
1903

THE OLD AGE OF QUEEN MAEVE

A certain poet in outlandish clothes
Gathered a crowd in some Byzantine lane,
Talked of his country and its people, sang
To some stringed instrument none there had seen,
A wall behind his back, over his head
A latticed window. His glance went up at times
As though one listened there, and his voice sank
Or let its meaning mix into the strings.

Maeve the Great Queen was pacing to and fro,
Between the walls covered with beaten bronze,
In her high house at Cruachan; the long hearth,
Flickering with ash and hazel, but half showed
Where the tired horse-boys lay upon the rushes,
Or on the benches underneath the walls,
In comfortable sleep; all living slept
But that great queen, who more than half the night
Had paced from door to fire and fire to door.
Though now in her old age, in her young age
She had been beautiful in that old way
That's all but gone; for the proud heart is gone,
And the fool heart of the counting-house fears all
But soft beauty and indolent desire.
She could have called over the rim of the world
Whatever woman's lover had hit her fancy,
And yet had been great-bodied and great-limbed,
Fashioned to be the mother of strong children;
And she'd had lucky eyes and a high heart,
And wisdom that caught fire like the dried flax,
At need, and made her beautiful and fierce,
Sudden and laughing.
               O unquiet heart,
Why do you praise another, praising her,
As if there were no tale but your own tale

Worth knitting to a measure of sweet sound?
Have I not bid you tell of that great queen
Who has been buried some two thousand years?

When night was at its deepest, a wild goose
Cried from the porter's lodge, and with long clamour
Shook the ale-horns and shields upon their hooks;
But the horse-boys slept on, as though some power
Had filled the house with Druid heaviness;
And wondering who of the many-changing Sidhe
Had come as in the old times to counsel her,
Maeve walked, yet with slow footfall, being old,
To that small chamber by the outer gate.
The porter slept, although he sat upright
With still and stony limbs and open eyes.
Maeve waited, and when that ear-piercing noise
Broke from his parted lips and broke again,
She laid a hand on either of his shoulders,
And shook him wide awake, and bid him say
Who of the wandering many-changing ones
Had troubled his sleep. But all he had to say
Was that, the air being heavy and the dogs
More still than they had been for a good month,
He had fallen asleep, and, though he had dreamed nothing,
He could remember when he had had fine dreams.
It was before the time of the great war
Over the White-Horned Bull and the Brown Bull.

She turned away; he turned again to sleep
That no god troubled now, and, wondering
What matters were afoot among the Sidhe,
Maeve walked through that great hall, and with a sigh
Lifted the curtain of her sleeping-room,
Remembering that she too had seemed divine
To many thousand eyes, and to her own
One that the generations had long waited
That work too difficult for mortal hands
Might be accomplished. Bunching the curtain up
She saw her husband Ailell sleeping there,
And thought of days when he'd had a straight body,

And of that famous Fergus, Nessa's husband,
Who had been the lover of her middle life.

Suddenly Ailell spoke out of his sleep,
And not with his own voice or a man's voice,
But with the burning, live, unshaken voice
Of those that, it may be, can never age.
He said, 'High Queen of Cruachan and Magh Ai,
A king of the Great Plain would speak with you.'
And with glad voice Maeve answered him, 'What king
Of the far-wandering shadows has come to me
As in the old days when they would come and go
About my threshold to counsel and to help?'
The parted lips replied, 'I seek your help,
For I am Aengus, and I am crossed in love.'
'How may a mortal whose life gutters out
Help them that wander with hand clasping hand,
Their haughty images that cannot wither,
For all their beauty's like a hollow dream,
Mirrored in streams that neither hail nor rain
Nor the cold North has troubled?'
                              He replied,
'I am from those rivers and I bid you call
The children of the Maines out of sleep,
And set them digging under Bual's hill.
We shadows, while they uproot his earthy house,
Will overthrow his shadows and carry off
Caer, his blue-eyed daughter that I love.
I helped your fathers when they built these walls,
And I would have your help in my great need,
Queen of high Cruachan.'
                              'I obey your will
With speedy feet and a most thankful heart:
For you have been, O Aengus of the birds,
Our giver of good counsel and good luck.'
And with a groan, as if the mortal breath
Could but awaken sadly upon lips
That happier breath had moved, her husband turned
Face downward, tossing in a troubled sleep;

But Maeve, and not with a slow feeble foot,
Came to the threshold of the painted house
Where her grandchildren slept, and cried aloud,
Until the pillared dark began to stir
With shouting and the clang of unhooked arms.
She told them of the many-changing ones;
And all that night, and all through the next day
To middle night, they dug into the hill.
At middle night great cats with silver claws,
Bodies of shadow and blind eyes like pearls,
Came up out of the hole, and red-eared hounds
With long white bodies came out of the air
Suddenly, and ran at them and harried them.

The Maines' children dropped their spades, and stood
With quaking joints and terror-stricken faces,
Till Maeve called out, 'These are but common men.
The Maines' children have not dropped their spades
Because Earth, crazy for its broken power,
Casts up a show and the winds answer it
With holy shadows.' Her high heart was glad,
And when the uproar ran along the grass
She followed with light footfall in the midst,
Till it died out where an old thorn-tree stood.

Friend of these many years, you too had stood
With equal courage in that whirling rout;
For you, although you've not her wandering heart,
Have all that greatness, and not hers alone,
For there is no high story about queens
In any ancient book but tells of you;
And when I've heard how they grew old and died,
Or fell into unhappiness, I've said,
'She will grow old and die, and she has wept!'
And when I'd write it out anew, the words,
Half crazy with the thought, She too has wept!
Outrun the measure.
                          I'd tell of that great queen
Who stood amid a silence by the thorn
Until two lovers came out of the air

With bodies made out of soft fire. The one,
About whose face birds wagged their fiery wings,
Said, 'Aengus and his sweetheart give their thanks
To Maeve and to Maeve's household, owing all
In owing them the bride-bed that gives peace.'
Then Maeve: 'O Aengus, Master of all lovers,
A thousand years ago you held high talk
With the first kings of many-pillared Cruachan.
O when will you grow weary?'
                                        They had vanished;
But out of the dark air over her head there came
A murmur of soft words and meeting lips.

BAILE AND AILLINN
1903

BAILE AND AILLINN

ARGUMENT. *Baile and Aillinn were lovers, but Aengus, the Master of Love,
wishing them to be happy in his own land among the dead, told to each a
story of the other's death, so that their hearts were broken and they died.*

I hardly hear the curlew cry,
Nor the grey rush when the wind is high,
Before my thoughts begin to run
On the heir of Ulad, Buan's son,
Baile, who had the honey mouth;
And that mild woman of the south,
Aillinn, who was King Lugaidh's heir.
Their love was never drowned in care
Of this or that thing, nor grew cold
Because their bodies had grown old.
Being forbid to marry on earth,
They blossomed to immortal mirth.

About the time when Christ was born,
When the long wars for the White Horn
And the Brown Bull had not yet come,
Young Baile Honey-Mouth, whom some
Called rather Baile Little-Land,
Rode out of Emain with a band
Of harpers and young men; and they
Imagined, as they struck the way
To many-pastured Muirthemne,
That all things fell out happily,
And there, for all that fools had said,
Baile and Aillinn would be wed.

They found an old man running there:
He had ragged long grass-coloured hair;
He had knees that stuck out of his hose;
He had puddle-water in his shoes;

He had half a cloak to keep him dry,
Although he had a squirrel's eye.

O wandering birds and rushy beds,
You put such folly in our heads
With all this crying in the wind,
No common love is to our mind,
And our poor Kate or Nan is less
Than any whose unhappiness
Awoke the harp-strings long ago.
Yet they that know all things but know
That all this life can give us is
A child's laughter, a woman's kiss.
Who was it put so great a scorn
In the grey reeds that night and morn
Are trodden and broken by the herds,
And in the light bodies of birds
The north wind tumbles to and fro
And pinches among hail and snow?

That runner said: 'I am from the south;
I run to Baile Honey-Mouth,
To tell him how the girl Aillinn
Rode from the country of her kin,
And old and young men rode with her:
For all that country had been astir
If anybody half as fair
Had chosen a husband anywhere
But where it could see her every day.
When they had ridden a little way
An old man caught the horse's head
With: "You must home again, and wed
With somebody in your own land."
A young man cried and kissed her hand,
"O lady, wed with one of us";
And when no face grew piteous
For any gentle thing she spake,
She fell and died of the heart-break.'

Because a lover's heart's worn out,
Being tumbled and blown about

By its own blind imagining,
And will believe that anything
That is bad enough to be true, is true,
Baile's heart was broken in two;
And he, being laid upon green boughs,
Was carried to the goodly house
Where the Hound of Ulad sat before
The brazen pillars of his door,
His face bowed low to weep the end
Of the harper's daughter and her friend.
For although years had passed away
He always wept them on that day,
For on that day they had been betrayed;
And now that Honey-Mouth is laid
Under a cairn of sleepy stone
Before his eyes, he has tears for none,
Although he is carrying stone, but two
For whom the cairn's but heaped anew.

We hold, because our memory is
So full of that thing and of this,
That out of sight is out of mind.
But the grey rush under the wind
And the grey bird with crooked bill
Have such long memories that they still
Remember Deirdre and her man;
And when we walk with Kate or Nan
About the windy water-side,
Our hearts can hear the voices chide.
How could we be so soon content,
Who know the way that Naoise went?
And they have news of Deirdre's eyes,
Who being lovely was so wise —
Ah! wise, my heart knows well how wise.

Now had that old gaunt crafty one,
Gathering his cloak about him, run
Where Aillinn rode with waiting-maids,
Who amid leafy lights and shades

Dreamed of the hands that would unlace
Their bodices in some dim place
When they had come to the marriage-bed;
And harpers, pacing with high head
As though their music were enough
To make the savage heart of love
Grow gentle without sorrowing,
Imagining and pondering
Heaven knows what calamity;

'Another's hurried off,' cried he,
'From heat and cold and wind and wave;
They have heaped the stones above his grave
In Muirthemne, and over it
In changeless Ogham letters writ –
Baile, that was of Rury's seed.
But the gods long ago decreed
No waiting-maid should ever spread
Baile and Aillinn's marriage-bed,
For they should clip and clip again
Where wild bees hive on the Great Plain.
Therefore it is but little news
That put this hurry in my shoes.'

Then seeing that he scarce had spoke
Before her love-worn heart had broke,
He ran and laughed until he came
To that high hill the herdsmen name
The Hill Seat of Laighen, because
Some god or king had made the laws
That held the land together there,
In old times among the clouds of the air.

That old man climbed; the day grew dim;
Two swans came flying up to him,
Linked by a gold chain each to each,
And with low murmuring laughing speech
Alighted on the windy grass.
They knew him: his changed body was
Tall, proud and ruddy, and light wings
Were hovering over the harp-strings

That Edain, Midhir's wife, had wove
In the hid place, being crazed by love.

What shall I call them? fish that swim,
Scale rubbing scale where light is dim
By a broad water-lily leaf;
Or mice in the one wheaten sheaf
Forgotten at the threshing-place;
Or birds lost in the one clear space
Of morning light in a dim sky;
Or, it may be, the eyelids of one eye,
Or the door-pillars of one house,
Or two sweet blossoming apple-boughs
That have one shadow on the ground;
Or the two strings that made one sound
Where that wise harper's finger ran.
For this young girl and this young man
Have happiness without an end,
Because they have made so good a friend.

They know all wonders, for they pass
The towery gates of Gorias,
And Findrias and Falias,
And long-forgotten Murias,
Among the giant kings whose hoard,
Cauldron and spear and stone and sword,
Was robbed before earth gave the wheat;
Wandering from broken street to street
They come where some huge watcher is,
And tremble with their love and kiss.

They know undying things, for they
Wander where earth withers away,
Though nothing troubles the great streams
But light from the pale stars, and gleams
From the holy orchards, where there is none
But fruit that is of precious stone,
Or apples of the sun and moon.

What were our praise to them? They eat
Quiet's wild heart, like daily meat;

Who when night thickens are afloat
On dappled skins in a glass boat,
Far out under a windless sky;
While over them birds of Aengus fly,
And over the tiller and the prow,
And waving white wings to and fro
Awaken wanderings of light air
To stir their coverlet and their hair.

And poets found, old writers say,
A yew-tree where his body lay;
But a wild apple hid the grass
With its sweet blossom where hers was;
And being in good heart, because
A better time had come again
After the deaths of many men,
And that long fighting at the ford,
They wrote on tablets of thin board,
Made of the apple and the yew,
All the love stories that they knew.

Let rush and bird cry out their fill
Of the harper's daughter if they will,
Beloved, I am not afraid of her.
She is not wiser nor lovelier,
And you are more high of heart than she,
For all her wanderings over-sea;
But I'd have bird and rush forget
Those other two; for never yet
Has lover lived, but longed to wive
Like them that are no more alive.

IN THE SEVEN WOODS
1904

IN THE SEVEN WOODS

In the Seven Woods

I have heard the pigeons of the Seven Woods
Make their faint thunder, and the garden bees
Hum in the lime-tree flowers; and put away
The unavailing outcries and the old bitterness
That empty the heart. I have forgot awhile
Tara uprooted, and new commonness
Upon the throne and crying about the streets
And hanging its paper flowers from post to post,
Because it is alone of all things happy.
I am contented, for I know that Quiet
Wanders laughing and eating her wild heart
Among pigeons and bees, while that Great Archer,
Who but awaits His hour to shoot, still hangs
A cloudy quiver over Pairc-na-lee.

The Arrow

I thought of your beauty, and this arrow,
Made out of a wild thought, is in my marrow.
There's no man may look upon her, no man,
As when newly grown to be a woman,
Tall and noble but with face and bosom
Delicate in colour as apple blossom.
This beauty's kinder, yet for a reason
I could weep that the old is out of season.

The Folly of Being Comforted

One that is ever kind said yesterday:
'Your well-belovèd's hair has threads of grey,
And little shadows come about her eyes;
Time can but make it easier to be wise
Though now it seems impossible, and so
All that you need is patience.'
                              Heart cries, 'No,
I have not a crumb of comfort, not a grain.
Time can but make her beauty over again:
Because of that great nobleness of hers
The fire that stirs about her, when she stirs,
Burns but more clearly. O she had not these ways
When all the wild summer was in her gaze.'

O heart! O heart! if she'd but turn her head,
You'd know the folly of being comforted.

Old Memory

O thought, fly to her when the end of day
Awakens an old memory, and say,
'Your strength, that is so lofty and fierce and kind,
It might call up a new age, calling to mind
The queens that were imagined long ago,
Is but half yours: he kneaded in the dough
Through the long years of youth, and who would have thought
It all, and more than it all, would come to naught,
And that dear words meant nothing?' But enough,
For when we have blamed the wind we can blame love;
Or, if there needs be more, be nothing said
That would be harsh for children that have strayed.

Never Give all the Heart

Never give all the heart, for love
Will hardly seem worth thinking of
To passionate women if it seem
Certain, and they never dream
That it fades out from kiss to kiss;
For everything that's lovely is
But a brief, dreamy, kind delight.
O never give the heart outright,
For they, for all smooth lips can say,
Have given their hearts up to the play.
And who could play it well enough
If deaf and dumb and blind with love?
He that made this knows all the cost,
For he gave all his heart and lost.

The Withering of the Boughs

I cried when the moon was murmuring to the birds:
'Let peewit call and curlew cry where they will,
I long for your merry and tender and pitiful words,
For the roads are unending, and there is no place to my mind.'
The honey-pale moon lay low on the sleepy hill,
And I fell asleep upon lonely Echtge of streams.
No boughs have withered because of the wintry wind;
The boughs have withered because I have told them my dreams.

I know of the leafy paths that the witches take
Who come with their crowns of pearl and their spindles of wool,
And their secret smile, out of the depths of the lake;
I know where a dim moon drifts, where the Danaan kind
Wind and unwind their dances when the light grows cool
On the island lawns, their feet where the pale foam gleams.
No boughs have withered because of the wintry wind;
The boughs have withered because I have told them my dreams.

I know of the sleepy country, where swans fly round
Coupled with golden chains, and sing as they fly.
A king and a queen are wandering there, and the sound
Has made them so happy and hopeless, so deaf and so blind
With wisdom, they wander till all the years have gone by;
I know, and the curlew and peewit on Echtge of streams.
No boughs have withered because of the wintry wind;
The boughs have withered because I have told them my dreams.

Adam's Curse

We sat together at one summer's end,
That beautiful mild woman, your close friend,
And you and I, and talked of poetry.
I said: 'A line will take us hours maybe;
Yet if it does not seem a moment's thought,
Our stitching and unstitching has been naught.
Better go down upon your marrow-bones
And scrub a kitchen pavement, or break stones
Like an old pauper, in all kinds of weather;
For to articulate sweet sounds together
Is to work harder than all these, and yet
Be thought an idler by the noisy set
Of bankers, schoolmasters, and clergymen
The martyrs call the world.'

                              And thereupon
That beautiful mild woman for whose sake
There's many a one shall find out all heartache
On finding that her voice is sweet and low
Replied: 'To be born woman is to know –
Although they do not talk of it at school –
That we must labour to be beautiful.'

I said: 'It's certain there is no fine thing
Since Adam's fall but needs much labouring.
There have been lovers who thought love should be
So much compounded of high courtesy

That they would sigh and quote with learned looks
Precedents out of beautiful old books;
Yet now it seems an idle trade enough.'

We sat grown quiet at the name of love;
We saw the last embers of daylight die,
And in the trembling blue-green of the sky
A moon, worn as if it had been a shell
Washed by time's waters as they rose and fell
About the stars and broke in days and years.

I had a thought for no one's but your ears:
That you were beautiful, and that I strove
To love you in the old high way of love;
That it had all seemed happy, and yet we'd grown
As weary-hearted as that hollow moon.

Red Hanrahan's Song about Ireland

The old brown thorn-trees break in two high over Cummen
   Strand,
Under a bitter black wind that blows from the left hand;
Our courage breaks like an old tree in a black wind and dies,
But we have hidden in our hearts the flame out of the eyes
Of Cathleen, the daughter of Houlihan.

The wind has bundled up the clouds high over Knocknarea,
And thrown the thunder on the stones for all that Maeve can say.
Angers that are like noisy clouds have set our hearts abeat;
But we have all bent low and low and kissed the quiet feet
Of Cathleen, the daughter of Houlihan.

The yellow pool has overflowed high up on Clooth-na-Bare,
For the wet winds are blowing out of the clinging air;
Like heavy flooded waters our bodies and our blood;
But purer than a tall candle before the Holy Rood
Is Cathleen, the daughter of Houlihan.

The Old Men Admiring Themselves in the Water

I heard the old, old men say,
'Everything alters,
And one by one we drop away.'
They had hands like claws, and their knees
Were twisted like the old thorn-trees
By the waters.
I heard the old, old men say,
'All that's beautiful drifts away
Like the waters.'

Under the Moon

I have no happiness in dreaming of Brycelinde,
Nor Avalon the grass-green hollow, nor Joyous Isle,
Where one found Lancelot crazed and hid him for a while;
Nor Ulad, when Naoise had thrown a sail upon the wind;
Nor lands that seem too dim to be burdens on the heart:
Land-under-Wave, where out of the moon's light and the sun's
Seven old sisters wind the threads of the long-lived ones,
Land-of-the-Tower, where Aengus has thrown the gates apart,
And Wood-of-Wonders, where one kills an ox at dawn,
To find it when night falls laid on a golden bier.
Therein are many queens like Branwen and Guinevere;
And Niamh and Laban and Fand, who could change to an otter or
    fawn,
And the wood-woman, whose lover was changed to a blue-eyed
    hawk;
And whether I go in my dreams by woodland, or dun, or shore,
Or on the unpeopled waves with kings to pull at the oar,
I hear the harp-string praise them, or hear their mournful talk.

Because of something told under the famished horn
Of the hunter's moon, that hung between the night and the day,
To dream of women whose beauty was folded in dismay,
Even in an old story, is a burden not to be borne.

The Ragged Wood

O hurry where by water among the trees
The delicate-stepping stag and his lady sigh,
When they have but looked upon their images –
Would none had ever loved but you and I!

Or have you heard that sliding silver-shoed
Pale silver-proud queen-woman of the sky,
When the sun looked out of his golden hood? –
O that none ever loved but you and I!

O hurry to the ragged wood, for there
I will drive all those lovers out and cry –
O my share of the world, O yellow hair!
No one has ever loved but you and I.

O Do Not Love Too Long

Sweetheart, do not love too long:
I loved long and long,
And grew to be out of fashion
Like an old song.

All through the years of our youth
Neither could have known
Their own thought from the other's,
We were so much at one.

But O, in a minute she changed –
O do not love too long,
Or you will grow out of fashion
Like an old song.

The Players ask for a Blessing on the Psalteries and on Themselves

THREE VOICES [TOGETHER]

Hurry to bless the hands that play,
The mouths that speak, the notes and strings,
O masters of the glittering town!
O! lay the shrilly trumpet down,
Though drunken with the flags that sway
Over the ramparts and the towers,
And with the waving of your wings.

FIRST VOICE

Maybe they linger by the way.
One gathers up his purple gown;
One leans and mutters by the wall –
He dreads the weight of mortal hours.

SECOND VOICE

O no, O no! they hurry down
Like plovers that have heard the call.

THIRD VOICE

O kinsmen of the Three in One,
O kinsmen, bless the hands that play.
The notes they waken shall live on
When all this heavy history's done;
Our hands, our hands must ebb away.

THREE VOICES [TOGETHER]

The proud and careless notes live on,
But bless our hands that ebb away.

The Happy Townland

There's many a strong farmer
Whose heart would break in two,
If he could see the townland
That we are riding to;
Boughs have their fruit and blossom
At all times of the year;
Rivers are running over
With red beer and brown beer.
An old man plays the bagpipes
In a golden and silver wood;
Queens, their eyes blue like the ice,
Are dancing in a crowd.

The little fox he murmured,
'O what of the world's bane?'
The sun was laughing sweetly,
The moon plucked at my rein;
But the little red fox murmured,
'O do not pluck at his rein,
He is riding to the townland
That is the world's bane.'

When their hearts are so high
That they would come to blows,
They unhook their heavy swords
From golden and silver boughs;
But all that are killed in battle
Awaken to life again.
It is lucky that their story
Is not known among men,

For O, the strong farmers
That would let the spade lie,
Their hearts would be like a cup
That somebody had drunk dry.

The little fox he murmured,
'O what of the world's bane?'
The sun was laughing sweetly,
The moon plucked at my rein;
But the little red fox murmured,
'O do not pluck at his rein,
He is riding to the townland
That is the world's bane.'

Michael will unhook his trumpet
From a bough overhead,
And blow a little noise
When the supper has been spread.
Gabriel will come from the water
With a fish-tail, and talk
Of wonders that have happened
On wet roads where men walk,
And lift up an old horn
Of hammered silver, and drink
Till he has fallen asleep
Upon the starry brink.

The little fox he murmured,
'O what of the world's bane?'
The sun was laughing sweetly,
The moon plucked at my rein;
But the little red fox murmured,
'O do not pluck at his rein,
He is riding to the townland
That is the world's bane.'

THE SHADOWY WATERS
A Dramatic Poem
1906

[Introductory Lines]

I walked among the seven woods of Coole:
Shan-walla, where a willow-bordered pond
Gathers the wild duck from the winter dawn;
Shady Kyle-dortha; sunnier Kyle-na-no,
Where many hundred squirrels are as happy
As though they had been hidden by green boughs
Where old age cannot find them; Pairc-na-lee,
Where hazel and ash and privet blind the paths;
Dim Pairc-na-carraig, where the wild bees fling
Their sudden fragrances on the green air;
Dim Pairc-na-tarav, where enchanted eyes
Have seen immortal, mild, proud shadows walk;
Dim Inchy wood, that hides badger and fox
And marten-cat, and borders that old wood
Wise Biddy Early called the wicked wood:
Seven odours, seven murmurs, seven woods.
I had not eyes like those enchanted eyes,
Yet dreamed that beings happier than men
Moved round me in the shadows, and at night
My dreams were cloven by voices and by fires;
And the images I have woven in this story
Of Forgael and Dectora and the empty waters
Moved round me in the voices and the fires,
And more I may not write of, for they that cleave
The waters of sleep can make a chattering tongue
Heavy like stone, their wisdom being half silence.
How shall I name you, immortal, mild, proud shadows?
I only know that all we know comes from you,
And that you come from Eden on flying feet.
Is Eden far away, or do you hide
From human thought, as hares and mice and coneys
That run before the reaping-hook and lie
In the last ridge of the barley? Do our woods
And winds and ponds cover more quiet woods,
More shining winds, more star-glimmering ponds?

Is Eden out of time and out of space?
And do you gather about us when pale light
Shining on water and fallen among leaves,
And winds blowing from flowers, and whirr of feathers
And the green quiet, have uplifted the heart?

I have made this poem for you, that men may read it
Before they read of Forgael and Dectora,
As men in the old times, before the harps began,
Poured out wine for the high invisible ones.

The Harp of Aengus

Edain came out of Midhir's hill, and lay
Beside young Aengus in his tower of glass,
Where time is drowned in odour-laden winds
And Druid moons, and murmuring of boughs,
And sleepy boughs, and boughs where apples made
Of opal and ruby and pale chrysolite
Awake unsleeping fires; and wove seven strings,
Sweet with all music, out of his long hair,
Because her hands had been made wild by love.
When Midhir's wife had changed her to a fly,
He made a harp with Druid apple-wood
That she among her winds might know he wept;
And from that hour he has watched over none
But faithful lovers.

PERSONS IN THE POEM

FORGAEL
AIBRIC
SAILORS
DECTORA

THE SHADOWY WATERS

The deck of an ancient ship. At the right of the stage is the mast, with a large square sail hiding a great deal of the sky and sea on that side. The tiller is at the left of the stage; it is a long oar coming through an opening in the bulwark. The deck rises in a series of steps behind the tiller, and the stern of the ship curves overhead. When the play opens there are four persons upon the deck. AIBRIC *stands by the tiller.* FORGAEL *sleeps upon the raised portion of the deck towards the front of the stage. Two* SAILORS *are standing near to the mast, on which a harp is hanging.*

FIRST SAILOR

Has he not led us into these waste seas
For long enough?

SECOND SAILOR

Aye, long and long enough.

FIRST SAILOR

We have not come upon a shore or ship
These dozen weeks.

SECOND SAILOR

And I had thought to make
A good round sum upon this cruise, and turn –
For I am getting on in life – to something
That has less ups and downs than robbery.

FIRST SAILOR

I am so tired of being bachelor
I could give all my heart to that Red Moll
That had but the one eye.

SECOND SAILOR

Can no bewitchment
Transform these rascal billows into women
That I may drown myself?

FIRST SAILOR

Better steer home,
Whether he will or no; and better still
To take him while he sleeps and carry him
And drop him from the gunnel.

SECOND SAILOR

I dare not do it.
Were't not that there is magic in his harp,
I would be of your mind; but when he plays it
Strange creatures flutter up before one's eyes,
Or cry about one's ears.

FIRST SAILOR

Nothing to fear.

SECOND SAILOR

Do you remember when we sank that galley
At the full moon?

FIRST SAILOR

He played all through the night.

SECOND SAILOR

Until the moon had set; and when I looked
Where the dead drifted, I could see a bird
Like a grey gull upon the breast of each.
While I was looking they rose hurriedly,
And after circling with strange cries awhile
Flew westward; and many a time since then
I've heard a rustling overhead in the wind.

FIRST SAILOR

I saw them on that night as well as you.
But when I had eaten and drunk myself asleep
My courage came again.

SECOND SAILOR

But that's not all.
The other night, while he was playing it,
A beautiful young man and girl came up
In a white breaking wave; they had the look
O those that are alive for ever and ever.

FIRST SAILOR

I saw them, too, one night. Forgael was playing,
And they were listening there beyond the sail.
He could not see them, but I held out my hands
To grasp the woman.

SECOND SAILOR

You have dared to touch her?

FIRST SAILOR

O she was but a shadow, and slipped from me.

SECOND SAILOR

But were you not afraid?

FIRST SAILOR

Why should I fear?

SECOND SAILOR

'Twas Aengus and Edain, the wandering lovers,
To whom all lovers pray.

FIRST SAILOR

But what of that?
A shadow does not carry sword or spear.

SECOND SAILOR

My mother told me that there is not one
Of the Ever-living half so dangerous
As that wild Aengus. Long before her day
He carried Edain off from a king's house,
And hid her among fruits of jewel-stone
And in a tower of glass, and from that day
Has hated every man that's not in love,
And has been dangerous to him.

FIRST SAILOR

I have heard
He does not hate seafarers as he hates
Peaceable men that shut the wind away,
And keep to the one weary marriage-bed.

SECOND SAILOR

I think that he has Forgael in his net,
And drags him through the sea.

FIRST SAILOR

Well, net or none,
I'd drown him while we have the chance to do it.

SECOND SAILOR

It's certain I'd sleep easier o' nights
If he were dead; but who will be our captain,
Judge of the stars, and find a course for us?

FIRST SAILOR

I've thought of that. We must have Aibric with us,
For he can judge the stars as well as Forgael.

[*Going towards* AIBRIC.

Become our captain, Aibric. I am resolved
To make an end of Forgael while he sleeps.
There's not a man but will be glad of it
When it is over, nor one to grumble at us.

AIBRIC

You have taken pay and made your bargain for it.

FIRST SAILOR

What good is there in this hard way of living,
Unless we drain more flagons in a year
And kiss more lips than lasting peaceable men
In their long lives? Will you be of our troop
And take the captain's share of everything
And bring us into populous seas again?

AIBRIC

Be of your troop! Aibric be one of you
And Forgael in the other scale! kill Forgael,
And he my master from my childhood up!
If you will draw that sword out of its scabbard
I'll give my answer.

FIRST SAILOR

   You have awakened him.
          [*To* SECOND SAILOR.
We'd better go, for we have lost this chance.
           [*They go out.*

FORGAEL

Have the birds passed us? I could hear your voice,
But there were others.

AIBRIC

   I have seen nothing pass.

FORGAEL

You're certain of it? I never wake from sleep
But that I am afraid they may have passed,
For they're my only pilots. If I lost them
Straying too far into the north or south,
I'd never come upon the happiness
That has been promised me. I have not seen them
These many days; and yet there must be many
Dying at every moment in the world,
And flying towards their peace.

AIBRIC

                              Put by these thoughts,
And listen to me for a while. The sailors
Are plotting for your death.

FORGAEL

                              Have I not given
More riches than they ever hoped to find?
And now they will not follow, while I seek
The only riches that have hit my fancy.

AIBRIC

What riches can you find in this waste sea
Where no ship sails, where nothing that's alive
Has ever come but those man-headed birds,
Knowing it for the world's end?

FORGAEL

                              Where the world ends
The mind is made unchanging, for it finds
Miracle, ecstasy, the impossible hope,
The flagstone under all, the fire of fires,
The roots of the world.

AIBRIC

Shadows before now
Have driven travellers mad for their own sport.

FORGAEL

Do you, too, doubt me? Have you joined their plot?

AIBRIC

No, no, do not say that. You know right well
That I will never lift a hand against you.

FORGAEL

Why should you be more faithful than the rest,
Being as doubtful?

AIBRIC

I have called you master
Too many years to lift a hand against you.

FORGAEL

Maybe it is but natural to doubt me.
You've never known, I'd lay a wager on it,
A melancholy that a cup of wine,
A lucky battle, or a woman's kiss
Could not amend.

AIBRIC

I have good spirits enough.

FORGAEL

If you will give me all your mind awhile –
All, all, the very bottom of the bowl –
I'll show you that I am made differently,
That nothing can amend it but these waters,
Where I am rid of life – the events of the world –

What do you call it? – that old promise-breaker,
The cozening fortune-teller that comes whispering,
'You will have all you have wished for when you have earned
Land for your children or money in a pot.'
And when we have it we are no happier,
Because of that old draught under the door,
Or creaky shoes. And at the end of all
How are we better off than Seaghan the fool,
That never did a hand's turn? Aibric! Aibric!
We have fallen in the dreams the Ever-living
Breathe on the burnished mirror of the world
And then smooth out with ivory hands and sigh,
And find their laughter sweeter to the taste
For that brief sighing.

AIBRIC

If you had loved some woman –

FORGAEL

You say that also? You have heard the voices,
For that is what they say – all, all the shadows –
Aengus and Edain, those passionate wanderers,
And all the others; but it must be love
As they have known it. Now the secret's out;
For it is love that I am seeking for,
But of a beautiful, unheard-of kind
That is not in the world.

AIBRIC

And yet the world
Has beautiful women to please every man.

FORGAEL

But he that gets their love after the fashion
Loves in brief longing and deceiving hope
And bodily tenderness, and finds that even
The bed of love, that in the imagination

Had seemed to be the giver of all peace,
Is no more than a wine-cup in the tasting,
And as soon finished.

AIBRIC

All that ever loved
Have loved that way – there is no other way.

FORGAEL

Yet never have two lovers kissed but they
Believed there was some other near at hand,
And almost wept because they could not find it.

AIBRIC

When they have twenty years; in middle life
They take a kiss for what a kiss is worth,
And let the dream go by.

FORGAEL

It's not a dream,
But the reality that makes our passion
As a lamp shadow – no – no lamp, the sun.
What the world's million lips are thirsting for
Must be substantial somewhere.

AIBRIC

I have heard the Druids
Mutter such things as they awake from trance.
It may be that the Ever-living know it –
No mortal can.

FORGAEL

Yes; if they give us help.

AIBRIC

They are besotting you as they besot
The crazy herdsman that will tell his fellows
That he has been all night upon the hills,
Riding to hurley, or in the battle-host
With the Ever-living.

FORGAEL

                    What if he speak the truth,
And for a dozen hours have been a part
Of that more powerful life?

AIBRIC

                    His wife knows better.
Has she not seen him lying like a log,
Or fumbling in a dream about the house?
And if she hear him mutter of wild riders,
She knows that it was but the cart-horse coughing
That set him to the fancy.

FORGAEL

                    All would be well
Could we but give us wholly to the dreams,
And get into their world that to the sense
Is shadow, and not linger wretchedly
Among substantial things; for it is dreams
That lift us to the flowing, changing world
That the heart longs for. What is love itself,
Even though it be the lightest of light love,
But dreams that hurry from beyond the world
To make low laughter more than meat and drink,
Though it but set us sighing? Fellow-wanderer,
Could we but mix ourselves into a dream,
Not in its image on the mirror!

AIBRIC

While
We're in the body that's impossible.

FORGAEL

And yet I cannot think they're leading me
To death; for they that promised to me love
As those that can outlive the moon have known it,
Had the world's total life gathered up, it seemed,
Into their shining limbs – I've had great teachers.
Aengus and Edain ran up out of the wave –
You'd never doubt that it was life they promised
Had you looked on them face to face as I did,
With so red lips, and running on such feet,
And having such wide-open, shining eyes.

AIBRIC

It's certain they are leading you to death.
None but the dead, or those that never lived,
Can know that ecstasy. Forgael! Forgael!
They have made you follow the man-headed birds,
And you have told me that their journey lies
Towards the country of the dead.

FORGAEL

What matter
If I am going to my death? – for there,
Or somewhere, I shall find the love they have promised.
That much is certain. I shall find a woman,
One of the Ever-living, as I think –
One of the Laughing People – and she and I
Shall light upon a place in the world's core,
Where passion grows to be a changeless thing,
Like charmèd apples made of chrysoprase,
Or chrysoberyl, or beryl, or chrysolite;
And there, in juggleries of sight and sense,
Become one movement, energy, delight,
Until the overburthened moon is dead.

[*A number of* SAILORS *enter hurriedly*]

FIRST SAILOR

Look there! there in the mist! a ship of spice!
And we are almost on her!

SECOND SAILOR

     We had not known
But for the ambergris and sandalwood.

FIRST SAILOR

No; but opoponax and cinnamon.

FORGAEL [*taking the tiller from* AIBRIC]

The Ever-living have kept my bargain for me,
And paid you on the nail.

AIBRIC

     Take up that rope
To make her fast while we are plundering her.

FIRST SAILOR

There is a king and queen upon her deck,
And where there is one woman there'll be others.

AIBRIC

Speak lower, or they'll hear.

FIRST SAILOR

     They cannot hear;
They are too busy with each other. Look!
He has stooped down and kissed her on the lips.

SECOND SAILOR

When she finds out we have better men aboard
She may not be too sorry in the end.

FIRST SAILOR

She will be like a wild cat; for these queens
Care more about the kegs of silver and gold
And the high fame that come to them in marriage,
Than a strong body and a ready hand.

SECOND SAILOR

There's nobody is natural but a robber,
And that is why the world totters about
Upon its bandy legs.

AIBRIC

Run at them now,
And overpower the crew while yet asleep!

[*The* SAILORS *go out.*
[*Voices and the clashing of swords are heard from the other ship, which
cannot be seen because of the sail.*

A VOICE

Armed men have come upon us! O I am slain!

ANOTHER VOICE

Wake all below!

ANOTHER VOICE

Why have you broken our sleep?

FIRST VOICE

Armed men have come upon us! O I am slain!

FORGAEL [*who has remained at the tiller*]

There! there they come! Gull, gannet, or diver,
But with a man's head, or a fair woman's,
They hover over the masthead awhile
To wait their friends; but when their friends have come

They'll fly upon that secret way of theirs.
One – and one – a couple – five together;
And I will hear them talking in a minute.
Yes, voices! but I do not catch the words.
Now I can hear. There's one of them that says,
'How light we are, now we are changed to birds!'
Another answers, 'Maybe we shall find
Our heart's desire now that we are so light.'
And then one asks another how he died,
And says, 'A sword-blade pierced me in my sleep.'
And now they all wheel suddenly and fly
To the other side, and higher in the air.
And now a laggard with a woman's head
Comes crying, 'I have run upon the sword.
I have fled to my beloved in the air,
In the waste of the high air, that we may wander
Among the windy meadows of the dawn.'
But why are they still waiting? why are they
Circling and circling over the masthead?
What power that is more mighty than desire
To hurry to their hidden happiness
Withholds them now? Have the Ever-living Ones
A meaning in that circling overhead?
But what's the meaning? [*He cries out.*] Why do you linger there?
Why linger? Run to your desire,
Are you not happy wingèd bodies now?

                                    [*His voice sinks again.*

Being too busy in the air and the high air,
They cannot hear my voice; but what's the meaning?

                    [*The* SAILORS *have returned.* DECTORA *is with them.*

FORGAEL [*turning and seeing her*]

Why are you standing with your eyes upon me?
You are not the world's core. O no, no, no!
That cannot be the meaning of the birds.
You are not its core. My teeth are in the world,
But have not bitten yet.

DECTORA

I am a queen,
And ask for satisfaction upon these
Who have slain my husband and laid hands upon me.
[*Breaking loose from the* SAILORS *who are holding her.*
Let go my hands!

FORGAEL

Why do you cast a shadow?
Where do you come from? Who brought you to this place?
They would not send me one that casts a shadow.

DECTORA

Would that the storm that overthrew my ships,
And drowned the treasures of nine conquered nations,
And blew me hither to my lasting sorrow,
Had drowned me also. But, being yet alive,
I ask a fitting punishment for all
That raised their hands against him.

FORGAEL

There are some
That weigh and measure all in these waste seas –
They that have all the wisdom that's in life,
And all that prophesying images
Made of dim gold rave out in secret tombs;
They have it that the plans of kings and queens
Are dust on the moth's wing; that nothing matters
But laughter and tears – laughter, laughter, and tears;
That every man should carry his own soul
Upon his shoulders.

DECTORA

You've nothing but wild words,
And I would know if you will give me vengeance.

FORGAEL

When she finds out I will not let her go –
When she knows that.

DECTORA

                    What is it that you are muttering –
That you'll not let me go? I am a queen.

FORGAEL

Although you are more beautiful than any,
I almost long that it were possible;
But if I were to put you on that ship,
With sailors that were sworn to do your will,
And you had spread a sail for home, a wind
Would rise of a sudden, or a wave so huge
It had washed among the stars and put them out,
And beat the bulwark of your ship on mine,
Until you stood before me on the deck –
As now.

DECTORA

            Does wandering in these desolate seas
And listening to the cry of wind and wave
Bring madness?

FORGAEL

        Queen, I am not mad.

DECTORA

                                Yet say
That unimaginable storms of wind and wave
Would rise against me.

FORGAEL

            No, I am not mad –
If it be not that hearing messages

From lasting watchers, that outlive the moon,
At the most quiet midnight is to be stricken.

DECTORA

And did those watchers bid you take me captive?

FORGAEL

Both you and I are taken in the net.
It was their hands that plucked the winds awake
And blew you hither; and their mouths have promised
I shall have love in their immortal fashion;
And for this end they gave me my old harp
That is more mighty than the sun and moon,
Or than the shivering casting-net of the stars,
That none might take you from me.

DECTORA [*first trembling back from the mast
where the harp is, and then laughing*]

For a moment
Your raving of a message and a harp
More mighty than the stars half troubled me,
But all that's raving. Who is there can compel
The daughter and the granddaughter of kings
To be his bedfellow?

FORGAEL

Until your lips
Have called me their beloved, I'll not kiss them.

DECTORA

My husband and my king died at my feet,
And yet you talk of love.

FORGAEL

The movement of time
Is shaken in these seas, and what one does

One moment has no might upon the moment
That follows after.

DECTORA

I understand you now.
You have a Druid craft of wicked sound
Wrung from the cold women of the sea –
A magic that can call a demon up,
Until my body give you kiss for kiss.

FORGAEL

Your soul shall give the kiss.

DECTORA

I am not afraid,
While there's a rope to run into a noose
Or wave to drown. But I have done with words,
And I would have you look into my face
And know that it is fearless.

FORGAEL

Do what you will,
For neither I nor you can break a mesh
Of the great golden net that is about us.

DECTORA

There's nothing in the world that's worth a fear.
[*She passes* FORGAEL *and stands for a moment looking into his face.*
I have good reason for that thought.
[*She runs suddenly on to the raised part of the po*
And now
I can put fear away as a queen should.
[*She mounts on to the bulwark and turns towards* FORGA
Fool, fool! Although you have looked into my face
You do not see my purpose. I shall have gone
Before a hand can touch me.

FORGAEL [*folding his arms*]

My hands are still;
The Ever-living hold us. Do what you will,
You cannot leap out of the golden net.

FIRST SAILOR

No need to drown, for, if you will pardon us
And measure out a course and bring us home,
We'll put this man to death.

DECTORA

I promise it.

FIRST SAILOR

There is none to take his side.

AIBRIC

I am on his side.
I'll strike a blow for him to give him time
To cast his dreams away.
[AIBRIC *goes in front of* FORGAEL *with drawn sword.* FORGAEL *takes
the harp.*

FIRST SAILOR

No other 'll do it.
[*The* SAILORS *throw* AIBRIC *on one side. He falls and lies upon the deck.
They lift their swords to strike* FORGAEL, *who is about to play the harp. The
stage begins to darken. The* SAILORS *hesitate in fear.*

SECOND SAILOR

He has put a sudden darkness over the moon.

DECTORA

Nine swords with handles of rhinoceros horn
To him that strikes him first!

FIRST SAILOR

I will strike him first.

[*He goes close up to* FORGAEL *with his sword lifted.*
[*Shrinking back.*] He has caught the crescent moon out of the sky,
And carries it between us.

SECOND SAILOR

Holy fire
To burn us to the marrow if we strike.

DECTORA

I'll give a golden galley full of fruit,
That has the heady flavour of new wine,
To him that wounds him to the death.

FIRST SAILOR

I'll do it.
For all his spells will vanish when he dies,
Having their life in him.

SECOND SAILOR

Though it be the moon
That he is holding up between us there,
I will strike at him.

THE OTHERS

And I! And I! And I!

[FORGAEL *plays the harp.*

FIRST SAILOR [*falling into a dream suddenly*]

But you were saying there is somebody
Upon that other ship we are to wake.
You did not know what brought him to his end,
But it was sudden.

SECOND SAILOR

You are in the right;
I had forgotten that we must go wake him.

DECTORA

He has flung a Druid spell upon the air,
And set you dreaming.

SECOND SAILOR

How can we have a wake
When we have neither brown nor yellow ale?

FIRST SAILOR

I saw a flagon of brown ale aboard her.

THIRD SAILOR

How can we raise the keen that do not know
What name to call him by?

FIRST SAILOR

Come to his ship.
His name will come into our thoughts in a minute.
I know that he died a thousand years ago,
And has not yet been waked.

SECOND SAILOR [*beginning to keen*]

Ohone! O! O! O!
The yew-bough has been broken into two,
And all the birds are scattered.

ALL THE SAILORS

O! O! O! O!
[*They go out keening.*

DECTORA

Protect me now, gods that my people swear by.
[AIBRIC *has risen from the deck where he had fallen. He has begun looking for his sword as if in a dream.*

AIBRIC

Where is my sword that fell out of my hand
When I first heard the news? Ah, there it is!
[*He goes dreamily towards the sword, but* DECTORA *runs at it and takes it up before he can reach it.*

AIBRIC [*sleepily*]

Queen, give it me.

DECTORA

No, I have need of it.

AIBRIC

Why do you need a sword? But you may keep it.
Now that he's dead I have no need of it,
For everything is gone.

A SAILOR [*calling from the other ship*]

Come hither, Aibric,
And tell me who it is that we are waking.

AIBRIC [*half to* DECTORA, *half to himself*]

What name had that dead king? Arthur of Britain?
No, no – not Arthur. I remember now.
It was golden-armed Iollan, and he died
Broken-hearted, having lost his queen
Through wicked spells. That is not all the tale,
For he was killed. O! O! O! O! O! O!
For golden-armed Iollan has been killed.
[*He goes out.*

[*While he has been speaking, and through part of what follows, one hears the wailing of the* SAILORS *from the other ship.* DECTORA *stands with the sword lifted in front of* FORGAEL.

DECTORA

I will end all your magic on the instant.
[*Her voice becomes dreamy, and she lowers the sword slowly, and finally lets it fall. She spreads out her hair. She takes off her crown and lays it upon the deck.*

This sword is to lie beside him in the grave.
It was in all his battles. I will spread my hair,
And wring my hands, and wail him bitterly,
For I have heard that he was proud and laughing,
Blue-eyed, and a quick runner on bare feet,
And that he died a thousand years ago.
O! O! O! O!

[FORGAEL *changes the tune.*

But no, that is not it.
I knew him well, and while I heard him laughing
They killed him at my feet. O! O! O! O!
For golden-armed Iollan that I loved.
But what is it that made me say I loved him?
It was that harper put it in my thoughts,
But it is true. Why did they run upon him,
And beat the golden helmet with their swords?

FORGAEL

Do you not know me, lady? I am he
That you are weeping for.

DECTORA

No, for he is dead.
O! O! O! O! for golden-armed Iollan.

FORGAEL

It was so given out, but I will prove
That the grave-diggers in a dreamy frenzy

Have buried nothing but my golden arms.
Listen to that low-laughing string of the moon
And you will recollect my face and voice,
For you have listened to me playing it
These thousand years.

[*He starts up, listening to the birds. The harp slips from his hands, and remains leaning against the bulwarks behind him.*

What are the birds at there?
Why are they all a-flutter of a sudden?
What are you calling out above the mast?
If railing and reproach and mockery
Because I have awakened her to love
By magic strings, I'll make this answer to it:
Being driven on by voices and by dreams
That were clear messages from the Ever-living,
I have done right. What could I but obey?
And yet you make a clamour of reproach.

DECTORA [*laughing*]

Why, it's a wonder out of reckoning
That I should keen him from the full of the moon
To the horn, and he be hale and hearty.

FORGAEL

How have I wronged her now that she is merry?
But no, no, no! your cry is not against me.
You know the counsels of the Ever-living,
And all that tossing of your wings is joy,
And all that murmuring's but a marriage-song;
But if it be reproach, I answer this:
There is not one among you that made love
By any other means. You call it passion,
Consideration, generosity;
But it was all deceit, and flattery
To win a woman in her own despite,
For love is war, and there is hatred in it;
And if you say that she came willingly —

DECTORA

Why do you turn away and hide your face,
That I would look upon for ever?

FORGAEL

My grief!

DECTORA

Have I not loved you for a thousand years?

FORGAEL

I never have been golden-armed Iollan.

DECTORA

I do not understand. I know your face
Better than my own hands.

FORGAEL

I have deceived you
Out of all reckoning.

DECTORA

Is it not true
That you were born a thousand years ago,
In islands where the children of Aengus wind
In happy dances under a windy moon,
And that you'll bring me there?

FORGAEL

I have deceived you;
I have deceived you utterly.

DECTORA

How can that be?
Is it that though your eyes are full of love

Some other woman has a claim on you,
And I've but half?

FORGAEL

O no!

DECTORA

                    And if there is,
If there be half a hundred more, what matter?
I'll never give another thought to it;
No, no, nor half a thought; but do not speak.
Women are hard and proud and stubborn-hearted,
Their heads being turned with praise and flattery;
And that is why their lovers are afraid
To tell them a plain story.

FORGAEL

                        That's not the story;
But I have done so great a wrong against you,
There is no measure that it would not burst.
I will confess it all.

DECTORA

                    What do I care,
Now that my body has begun to dream,
And you have grown to be a burning sod
In the imagination and intellect?
If something that's most fabulous were true –
If you had taken me by magic spells,
And killed a lover or husband at my feet –
I would not let you speak, for I would know
That it was yesterday and not to-day
I loved him; I would cover up my ears,
As I am doing now. [*A pause.*] Why do you weep?

FORGAEL

I weep because I've nothing for your eyes
But desolate waters and a battered ship.

DECTORA

O why do you not lift your eyes to mine?

FORGAEL

I weep – I weep because bare night's above,
And not a roof of ivory and gold.

DECTORA

I would grow jealous of the ivory roof,
And strike the golden pillars with my hands.
I would that there was nothing in the world
But my beloved – that night and day had perished,
And all that is and all that is to be,
All that is not the meeting of our lips.

FORGAEL

You turn away. Why do you turn away?
Am I to fear the waves, or is the moon
My enemy?

DECTORA

I looked upon the moon,
Longing to knead and pull it into shape
That I might lay it on your head as a crown.
But now it is your thoughts that wander away,
For you are looking at the sea. Do you not know
How great a wrong it is to let one's thought
Wander a moment when one is in love?
[*He has moved away. She follows him. He is looking out over the sea,
shading his eyes.*
Why are you looking at the sea?

FORGAEL

Look there!

DECTORA

What is there but a troop of ash-grey birds
That fly into the west?

FORGAEL

But listen, listen!

DECTORA

What is there but the crying of the birds?

FORGAEL

If you'll but listen closely to that crying
You'll hear them calling out to one another
With human voices.

DECTORA

O I can hear them now.
What are they? Unto what country do they fly?

FORGAEL

To unimaginable happiness.
They have been circling over our heads in the air,
But now that they have taken to the road
We have to follow, for they are our pilots;
And though they're but the colour of grey ash,
They're crying out, could you but hear their words,
'There is a country at the end of the world
Where no child's born but to outlive the moon.'
[*The* SAILORS *come in with* AIBRIC. *They are in great excitement.*

FIRST SAILOR

The hold is full of treasure.

SECOND SAILOR

Full to the hatches.

FIRST SAILOR

Treasure on treasure.

THIRD SAILOR

Boxes of precious spice.

FIRST SAILOR

Ivory images with amethyst eyes.

THIRD SAILOR

Dragons with eyes of ruby.

FIRST SAILOR

The whole ship
Flashes as if it were a net of herrings.

THIRD SAILOR

Let's home; I'd give some rubies to a woman.

SECOND SAILOR

There's somebody I'd give the amethyst eyes to.

AIBRIC [*silencing them with a gesture*]

We would return to our own country, Forgael,
For we have found a treasure that's so great
Imagination cannot reckon it.
And having lit upon this woman there,
What more have you to look for on the seas?

FORGAEL

I cannot – I am going on to the end.
As for this woman, I think she is coming with me.

AIBRIC

The Ever-living have made you mad; but no,
It was this woman in her woman's vengeance
That drove you to it, and I fool enough
To fancy that she'd bring you home again.
'Twas you that egged him to it, for you know
That he is being driven to his death.

DECTORA

That is not true, for he has promised me
An unimaginable happiness.

AIBRIC

And if that happiness be more than dreams,
More than the froth, the feather, the dust-whirl,
The crazy nothing that I think it is,
It shall be in the country of the dead,
If there be such a country.

DECTORA

                              No, not there,
But in some island where the life of the world
Leaps upward, as if all the streams o' the world
Had run into one fountain.

AIBRIC

                              Speak to him.
He knows that he is taking you to death;
Speak – he will not deny it.

DECTORA

                              Is that true?

FORGAEL

I do not know for certain, but I know
That I have the best of pilots.

AIBRIC

> Shadows, illusions,
> That the Shape-changers, the Ever-laughing Ones,
> The Immortal Mockers have cast into his mind,
> Or called before his eyes.

DECTORA

> O carry me
> To some sure country, some familiar place.
> Have we not everything that life can give
> In having one another?

FORGAEL

> How could I rest
> If I refused the messengers and pilots
> With all those sights and all that crying out?

DECTORA

> But I will cover up your eyes and ears,
> That you may never hear the cry of the birds,
> Or look upon them.

FORGAEL

> Were they but lowlier
> I'd do your will, but they are too high – too high.

DECTORA

> Being too high, their heady prophecies
> But harry us with hopes that come to nothing,
> Because we are not proud, imperishable,
> Alone and winged.

FORGAEL

> Our love shall be like theirs
> When we have put their changeless image on.

DECTORA

I am a woman, I die at every breath.

AIBRIC

Let the birds scatter, for the tree is broken,
And there's no help in words. [*To the* SAILORS] To the other ship,
And I will follow you and cut the rope
When I have said farewell to this man here,
For neither I nor any living man
Will look upon his face again.   [*The* SAILORS *go out.*

FORGAEL [*to* DECTORA]

                    Go with him,
For he will shelter you and bring you home.

AIBRIC [*taking* FORGAEL'S *hand*]

I'll do it for his sake.

DECTORA

                    No. Take this sword
And cut the rope, for I go on with Forgael.

AIBRIC [*half falling into the keen*]

The yew-bough has been broken into two,
And all the birds are scattered – O! O! O!
Farewell! farewell!

                                        [*He goes out.*

DECTORA

                    The sword is in the rope –
The rope's in two – it falls into the sea,
It whirls into the foam. O ancient worm,
Dragon that loved the world and held us to it,
You are broken, you are broken. The world drifts away,
And I am left alone with my beloved,

Who cannot put me from his sight for ever.
We are alone for ever, and I laugh,
Forgael, because you cannot put me from you.
The mist has covered the heavens, and you and I
Shall be alone for ever. We two – this crown –
I half remember. It has been in my dreams.
Bend lower, O king, that I may crown you with it.
O flower of the branch, O bird among the leaves,
O silver fish that my two hands have taken
Out of the running stream, O morning star,
Trembling in the blue heavens like a white fawn
Upon the misty border of the wood,
Bend lower, that I may cover you with my hair,
For we will gaze upon this world no longer.

FORGAEL [*gathering* DECTORA'S *hair about him*]

Beloved, having dragged the net about us,
And knitted mesh to mesh, we grow immortal;
And that old harp awakens of itself
To cry aloud to the grey birds, and dreams,
That have had dreams for father, live in us.

FROM
'THE GREEN HELMET
AND OTHER POEMS'
1910

FROM
'THE GREEN HELMET AND
OTHER POEMS'

His Dream

I swayed upon the gaudy stern
The butt-end of a steering-oar,
And saw wherever I could turn
A crowd upon a shore.

And though I would have hushed the crowd,
There was no mother's son but said,
'What is the figure in a shroud
Upon a gaudy bed?'

And after running at the brim
Cried out upon that thing beneath
– It had such dignity of limb –
By the sweet name of Death.

Though I'd my finger on my lip,
What could I but take up the song?
And running crowd and gaudy ship
Cried out the whole night long,

Crying amid the glittering sea,
Naming it with ecstatic breath,
Because it had such dignity,
By the sweet name of Death.

A Woman Homer Sung

If any man drew near
When I was young,
I thought, 'He holds her dear,'
And shook with hate and fear.
But O! 'twas bitter wrong
If he could pass her by
With an indifferent eye.

Whereon I wrote and wrought,
And now, being grey,
I dream that I have brought
To such a pitch my thought
That coming time can say,
'He shadowed in a glass
What thing her body was.'

For she had fiery blood
When I was young,
And trod so sweetly proud
As 'twere upon a cloud,
A woman Homer sung,
That life and letters seem
But an heroic dream.

Words

I had this thought a while ago,
'My darling cannot understand
What I have done, or what would do
In this blind bitter land.'

And I grew weary of the sun
Until my thoughts cleared up again,
Remembering that the best I have done
Was done to make it plain;

That every year I have cried, 'At length
My darling understands it all,
Because I have come into my strength,
And words obey my call';

That had she done so who can say
What would have shaken from the sieve?
I might have thrown poor words away
And been content to live.

No Second Troy

Why should I blame her that she filled my days
With misery, or that she would of late
Have taught to ignorant men most violent ways,
Or hurled the little streets upon the great,
Had they but courage equal to desire?
What could have made her peaceful with a mind
That nobleness made simple as a fire,
With beauty like a tightened bow, a kind
That is not natural in an age like this,
Being high and solitary and most stern?
Why, what could she have done, being what she is?
Was there another Troy for her to burn?

Reconciliation

Some may have blamed you that you took away
The verses that could move them on the day
When, the ears being deafened, the sight of the eyes blind
With lightning, you went from me, and I could find
Nothing to make a song about but kings,
Helmets, and swords, and half-forgotten things
That were memories of you – but now
We'll out, for the world lives as long ago;

And while we're in our laughing, weeping fit,
Hurl helmets, crowns, and swords into the pit.
But, dear, cling close to me; since you were gone,
My barren thoughts have chilled me to the bone.

King and No King

'Would it were anything but merely voice!'
The No King cried who after that was King,
Because he had not heard of anything
That balanced with a word is more than noise;
Yet Old Romance being kind, let him prevail
Somewhere or somehow that I have forgot,
Though he'd but cannon – Whereas we that had thought
To have lit upon as clean and sweet a tale
Have been defeated by that pledge you gave
In momentary anger long ago;
And I that have not your faith, how shall I know
That in the blinding light beyond the grave
We'll find so good a thing as that we have lost?
The hourly kindness, the day's common speech,
The habitual content of each with each
When neither soul nor body has been crossed.

Peace

Ah, that Time could touch a form
That could show what Homer's age
Bred to be a hero's wage.
'Were not all her life but storm,
Would not painters paint a form

Of such noble lines,' I said,
'Such a delicate high head,
All that sternness amid charm,
All that sweetness amid strength?'
Ah, but peace that comes at length,
Came when Time had touched her form.

Against Unworthy Praise

O heart, be at peace, because
Nor knave nor dolt can break
What's not for their applause,
Being for a woman's sake.
Enough if the work has seemed,
So did she your strength renew,
A dream that a lion had dreamed
Till the wilderness cried aloud,
A secret between you two,
Between the proud and the proud.

What, still you would have their praise!
But here's a haughtier text,
The labyrinth of her days
That her own strangeness perplexed;
And how what her dreaming gave
Earned slander, ingratitude,
From self-same dolt and knave;
Aye, and worse wrong than these.
Yet she, singing upon her road,
Half lion, half child, is at peace.

The Fascination of What's Difficult

The fascination of what's difficult
Has dried the sap out of my veins, and rent
Spontaneous joy and natural content
Out of my heart. There's something ails our colt
That must, as if it had not holy blood
Nor on Olympus leaped from cloud to cloud,
Shiver under the lash, strain, sweat and jolt
As though it dragged road metal. My curse on plays
That have to be set up in fifty ways,
On the day's war with every knave and dolt,
Theatre business, management of men.
I swear before the dawn comes round again
I'll find the stable and pull out the bolt.

A Drinking Song

Wine comes in at the mouth
And love comes in at the eye;
That's all we shall know for truth
Before we grow old and die.
I lift the glass to my mouth,
I look at you, and I sigh.

The Coming of Wisdom with Time

Though leaves are many, the root is one;
Through all the lying days of my youth
I swayed my leaves and flowers in the sun;
Now I may wither into the truth.

On hearing that the Students of our New University have joined the Agitation against Immoral Literature

Where, where but here have Pride and Truth,
That long to give themselves for wage,
To shake their wicked sides at youth
Restraining reckless middle-age?

To a Poet, who would have me Praise certain Bad Poets, Imitators of His and Mine

You say, as I have often given tongue
In praise of what another's said or sung,
'Twere politic to do the like by these;
But was there ever dog that praised his fleas?

The Mask

'Put off that mask of burning gold
With emerald eyes.'
'O no, my dear, you make so bold
To find if hearts be wild and wise,
And yet not cold.'

'I would but find what's there to find,
Love or deceit.'
'It was the mask engaged your mind,
And after set your heart to beat,
Not what's behind.'

'But lest you are my enemy,
I must enquire.'
'O no, my dear, let all that be;
What matter, so there is but fire
In you, in me?'

Upon a House shaken by the Land Agitation

How should the world be luckier if this house,
Where passion and precision have been one
Time out of mind, became too ruinous
To breed the lidless eye that loves the sun?
And the sweet laughing eagle thoughts that grow
Where wings have memory of wings, and all
That comes of the best knit to the best? Although
Mean roof-trees were the sturdier for its fall,
How should their luck run high enough to reach
The gifts that govern men, and after these
To gradual Time's last gift, a written speech
Wrought of high laughter, loveliness and ease?

At the Abbey Theatre

(Imitated from Ronsard)

Dear Craoibhin Aoibhin, look into our case.
When we are high and airy hundreds say
That if we hold that flight they'll leave the place,
While those same hundreds mock another day
Because we have made our art of common things,
So bitterly, you'd dream they longed to look
All their lives through into some drift of wings.
You've dandled them and fed them from the book

And know them to the bone; impart to us –
We'll keep the secret – a new trick to please.
Is there a bridle for this Proteus
That turns and changes like his draughty seas?
Or is there none, most popular of men,
But when they mock us, that we mock again?

These are the Clouds

These are the clouds about the fallen sun,
The majesty that shuts his burning eye:
The weak lay hand on what the strong has done,
Till that be tumbled that was lifted high
And discord follow upon unison,
And all things at one common level lie.
And therefore, friend, if your great race were run
And these things came, so much the more thereby
Have you made greatness your companion,
Although it be for children that you sigh:
These are the clouds about the fallen sun,
The majesty that shuts his burning eye.

At Galway Races

There where the course is,
Delight makes all of the one mind,
The riders upon the galloping horses,
The crowd that closes in behind:
We, too, had good attendance once,
Hearers and hearteners of the work;
Aye, horsemen for companions,
Before the merchant and the clerk

Breathed on the world with timid breath.
Sing on: somewhere at some new moon,
We'll learn that sleeping is not death,
Hearing the whole earth change its tune,
Its flesh being wild, and it again
Crying aloud as the racecourse is,
And we find hearteners among men
That ride upon horses.

A Friend's Illness

Sickness brought me this
Thought, in that scale of his:
Why should I be dismayed
Though flame had burned the whole
World, as it were a coal,
Now I have seen it weighed
Against a soul?

All Things can Tempt me

All things can tempt me from this craft of verse:
One time it was a woman's face, or worse –
The seeming needs of my fool-driven land;
Now nothing but comes readier to the hand
Than this accustomed toil. When I was young,
I had not given a penny for a song
Did not the poet sing it with such airs
That one believed he had a sword upstairs;
Yet would be now, could I but have my wish,
Colder and dumber and deafer than a fish.

Brown Penny

I whispered, 'I am too young,'
And then, 'I am old enough';
Wherefore I threw a penny
To find out if I might love.
'Go and love, go and love, young man,
If the lady be young and fair.'
Ah, penny, brown penny, brown penny,
I am looped in the loops of her hair.

O love is the crooked thing,
There is nobody wise enough
To find out all that is in it,
For he would be thinking of love
Till the stars had run away
And the shadows eaten the moon.
Ah, penny, brown penny, brown penny,
One cannot begin it too soon.

RESPONSIBILITIES
1914

'In dreams begins responsibility.'

Old Play

*'How am I fallen from myself, for a long time now
I have not seen the Prince of Chang in my dreams.'*

KHOUNG–FOU–TSEU

[*Introductory Rhymes*]

Pardon, old fathers, if you still remain
Somewhere in ear-shot for the story's end,
Old Dublin merchant 'free of the ten and four'
Or trading out of Galway into Spain;
Old country scholar, Robert Emmet's friend,
A hundred-year-old memory to the poor;
Merchant and scholar who have left me blood
That has not passed through any huckster's loin,
Soldiers that gave, whatever die was cast:
A Butler or an Armstrong that withstood
Beside the brackish waters of the Boyne
James and his Irish when the Dutchman crossed;
Old merchant skipper that leaped overboard
After a ragged hat in Biscay Bay;
You most of all, silent and fierce old man,
Because the daily spectacle that stirred
My fancy, and set my boyish lips to say,
'Only the wasteful virtues earn the sun';
Pardon that for a barren passion's sake,
Although I have come close on forty-nine,
I have no child, I have nothing but a book,
Nothing but that to prove your blood and mine.

RESPONSIBILITIES

The Grey Rock

Poets with whom I learned my trade,
Companions of the Cheshire Cheese,
Here's an old story I've re-made,
Imagining 'twould better please
Your ears than stories now in fashion,
Though you may think I waste my breath
Pretending that there can be passion
That has more life in it than death,
And though at bottling of your wine
Old wholesome Goban had no say;
The moral's yours because it's mine.

When cups went round at close of day –
Is not that how good stories run? –
The gods were sitting at the board
In their great house at Slievenamon.
They sang a drowsy song, or snored,
For all were full of wine and meat.
The smoky torches made a glare
On metal Goban 'd hammered at,
On old deep silver rolling there
Or on some still unemptied cup
That he, when frenzy stirred his thews,
Had hammered out on mountain top
To hold the sacred stuff he brews
That only gods may buy of him.

Now from that juice that made them wise
All those had lifted up the dim
Imaginations of their eyes,
For one that was like woman made
Before their sleepy eyelids ran
And trembling with her passion said,

'Come out and dig for a dead man,
Who's burrowing somewhere in the ground,
And mock him to his face and then
Hollo him on with horse and hound,
For he is the worst of all dead men.'

We should be dazed and terror-struck,
If we but saw in dreams that room,
Those wine-drenched eyes, and curse our luck
That emptied all our days to come.
I knew a woman none could please,
Because she dreamed when but a child
Of men and women made like these;
And after, when her blood ran wild,
Had ravelled her own story out,
And said, 'In two or in three years
I needs must marry some poor lout,'
And having said it, burst in tears.

Since, tavern comrades, you have died,
Maybe your images have stood,
Mere bone and muscle thrown aside,
Before that roomful or as good.
You had to face your ends when young –
'Twas wine or women, or some curse –
But never made a poorer song
That you might have a heavier purse,
Nor gave loud service to a cause
That you might have a troop of friends.
You kept the Muses' sterner laws,
And unrepenting faced your ends,
And therefore earned the right – and yet
Dowson and Johnson most I praise –
To troop with those the world's forgot,
And copy their proud steady gaze.

'The Danish troop was driven out
Between the dawn and dusk,' she said;
'Although the event was long in doubt,
Although the King of Ireland's dead

And half the kings, before sundown
All was accomplished.

                'When this day
Murrough, the King of Ireland's son,
Foot after foot was giving way,
He and his best troops back to back
Had perished there, but the Danes ran,
Stricken with panic from the attack,
The shouting of an unseen man;
And being thankful Murrough found,
Led by a footsole dipped in blood
That had made prints upon the ground,
Where by old thorn-trees that man stood;
And though when he gazed here and there,
He had but gazed on thorn-trees, spoke,
"Who is the friend that seems but air
And yet could give so fine a stroke?"
Thereon a young man met his eye,
Who said, "Because she held me in
Her love, and would not have me die,
Rock-nurtured Aoife took a pin,
And pushing it into my shirt,
Promised that for a pin's sake
No man should see to do me hurt;
But there it's gone; I will not take
The fortune that had been my shame
Seeing, King's son, what wounds you have."
'Twas roundly spoke, but when night came
He had betrayed me to his grave,
For he and the King's son were dead.
I'd promised him two hundred years,
And when for all I'd done or said –
And these immortal eyes shed tears –
He claimed his country's need was most,
I'd saved his life, yet for the sake
Of a new friend he has turned a ghost.
What does he care if my heart break?
I call for spade and horse and hound

That we may harry him.' Thereon
She cast herself upon the ground
And rent her clothes and made her moan:
'Why are they faithless when their might
Is from the holy shades that rove
The grey rock and the windy light?
Why should the faithfullest heart most love
The bitter sweetness of false faces?
Why must the lasting love what passes,
Why are the gods by men betrayed?'

But thereon every god stood up
With a slow smile and without sound,
And stretching forth his arm and cup
To where she moaned upon the ground,
Suddenly drenched her to the skin;
And she with Goban's wine adrip,
No more remembering what had been,
Stared at the gods with laughing lip.

I have kept my faith, though faith was tried,
To that rock-born, rock-wandering foot,
And the world's altered since you died,
And I am in no good repute
With the loud host before the sea,
That think sword-strokes were better meant
Than lover's music — let that be,
So that the wandering foot's content.

The Two Kings

King Eochaid came at sundown to a wood
Westward of Tara. Hurrying to his queen
He had outridden his war-wasted men
That with empounded cattle trod the mire,
And where beech trees had mixed a pale green light
With the ground-ivy's blue, he saw a stag
Whiter than curds, its eyes the tint of the sea.

Because it stood upon his path and seemed
More hands in height than any stag in the world
He sat with tightened rein and loosened mouth
Upon his trembling horse, then drove the spur;
But the stag stooped and ran at him, and passed,
Rending the horse's flank. King Eochaid reeled,
Then drew his sword to hold its levelled point
Against the stag. When horn and steel were met
The horn resounded as though it had been silver,
A sweet, miraculous, terrifying sound.
Horn locked in sword, they tugged and struggled there
As though a stag and unicorn were met
Among the African Mountains of the Moon,
Until at last the double horns, drawn backward,
Butted below the single and so pierced
The entrails of the horse. Dropping his sword
King Eochaid seized the horns in his strong hands
And stared into the sea-green eye, and so
Hither and thither to and fro they trod
Till all the place was beaten into mire.
The strong thigh and the agile thigh were met,
The hands that gathered up the might of the world,
And hoof and horn that had sucked in their speed
Amid the elaborate wilderness of the air.
Through bush they plunged and over ivied root,
And where the stone struck fire, while in the leaves
A squirrel whinnied and a bird screamed out;
But when at last he forced those sinewy flanks
Against a beech-bole, he threw down the beast
And knelt above it with drawn knife. On the instant
It vanished like a shadow, and a cry
So mournful that it seemed the cry of one
Who had lost some unimaginable treasure
Wandered between the blue and the green leaf
And climbed into the air, crumbling away,
Till all had seemed a shadow or a vision
But for the trodden mire, the pool of blood,
The disembowelled horse.
                              King Eochaid ran

Toward peopled Tara, nor stood to draw his breath
Until he came before the painted wall,
The posts of polished yew, circled with bronze,
Of the great door; but though the hanging lamps
Showed their faint light through the unshuttered windows,
Nor door, nor mouth, nor slipper made a noise,
Nor on the ancient beaten paths, that wound
From well-side or from plough-land, was there noise;
Nor had there been the noise of living thing
Before him or behind, but that far off
On the horizon edge bellowed the herds.
Knowing that silence brings no good to kings,
And mocks returning victory, he passed
Between the pillars with a beating heart
And saw where in the midst of the great hall
Pale-faced, alone upon a bench, Edain
Sat upright with a sword before her feet.
Her hands on either side had gripped the bench,
Her eyes were cold and steady, her lips tight.
Some passion had made her stone. Hearing a foot
She started and then knew whose foot it was;
But when he thought to take her in his arms
She motioned him afar, and rose and spoke:
'I have sent among the fields or to the woods
The fighting-men and servants of this house,
For I would have your judgment upon one
Who is self-accused. If she be innocent
She would not look in any known man's face
Till judgment has been given, and if guilty,
Would never look again on known man's face.'
And at these words he paled, as she had paled,
Knowing that he should find upon her lips
The meaning of that monstrous day.
                                        Then she:
'You brought me where your brother Ardan sat
Always in his one seat, and bid me care him
Through that strange illness that had fixed him there,
And should he die to heap his burial-mound
And carve his name in Ogham.' Eochaid said,

'He lives?' 'He lives and is a healthy man.'
'While I have him and you it matters little
What man you have lost, what evil you have found.'
'I bid them make his bed under this roof
And carried him his food with my own hands,
And so the weeks passed by. But when I said,
"What is this trouble?" he would answer nothing,
Though always at my words his trouble grew;
And I but asked the more, till he cried out,
Weary of many questions: "There are things
That make the heart akin to the dumb stone."
Then I replied, "Although you hide a secret,
Hopeless and dear, or terrible to think on,
Speak it, that I may send through the wide world
For medicine." Thereon he cried aloud,
"Day after day you question me, and I,
Because there is such a storm amid my thoughts
I shall be carried in the gust, command,
Forbid, beseech and waste my breath." Then I:
"Although the thing that you have hid were evil,
The speaking of it could be no great wrong,
And evil must it be, if done 'twere worse
Than mound and stone that keep all virtue in,
And loosen on us dreams that waste our life,
Shadows and shows that can but turn the brain."
But finding him still silent I stooped down
And whispering that none but he should hear,
Said, "If a woman has put this on you,
My men, whether it please her or displease,
And though they have to cross the Loughlan waters
And take her in the middle of armed men,
Shall make her look upon her handiwork,
That she may quench the rick she has fired; and though
She may have worn silk clothes, or worn a crown,
She'll not be proud, knowing within her heart
That our sufficient portion of the world
Is that we give, although it be brief giving,
Happiness to children and to men."
Then he, driven by his thought beyond his thought,

And speaking what he would not though he would,
Sighed, "You, even you yourself, could work the cure!"
And at those words I rose and I went out
And for nine days he had food from other hands,
And for nine days my mind went whirling round
The one disastrous zodiac, muttering
That the immedicable mound's beyond
Our questioning, beyond our pity even.
But when nine days had gone I stood again
Before his chair and bending down my head
I bade him go when all his household slept
To an old empty woodman's house that's hidden
Westward of Tara, among the hazel-trees –
For hope would give his limbs the power – and await
A friend that could, he had told her, work his cure
And would be no harsh friend.
                              When night had deepened,
I groped my way from beech to hazel wood,
Found that old house, a sputtering torch within,
And stretched out sleeping on a pile of skins
Ardan, and though I called to him and tried
To shake him out of sleep, I could not rouse him.
I waited till the night was on the turn,
Then fearing that some labourer, on his way
To plough or pasture-land, might see me there,
Went out.
             Among the ivy-covered rocks,
As on the blue light of a sword, a man
Who had unnatural majesty, and eyes
Like the eyes of some great kite scouring the woods,
Stood on my path. Trembling from head to foot
I gazed at him like grouse upon a kite;
But with a voice that had unnatural music,
"A weary wooing and a long," he said,
"Speaking of love through other lips and looking
Under the eyelids of another, for it was my craft
That put a passion in the sleeper there,
And when I had got my will and drawn you here,
Where I may speak to you alone, my craft

Sucked up the passion out of him again
And left mere sleep. He'll wake when the sun wakes,
Push out his vigorous limbs and rub his eyes,
And wonder what has ailed him these twelve months."
I cowered back upon the wall in terror,
But that sweet-sounding voice ran on: "Woman,
I was your husband when you rode the air,
Danced in the whirling foam and in the dust,
In days you have not kept in memory,
Being betrayed into a cradle, and I come
That I may claim you as my wife again."
I was no longer terrified – his voice
Had half awakened some old memory –
Yet answered him, "I am King Eochaid's wife
And with him have found every happiness
Women can find." With a most masterful voice,
That made the body seem as it were a string
Under a bow, he cried, "What happiness
Can lovers have that know their happiness
Must end at the dumb stone? But where we build
Our sudden palaces in the still air
Pleasure itself can bring no weariness,
Nor can time waste the cheek, nor is there foot
That has grown weary of the whirling dance,
Nor an unlaughing mouth, but mine that mourns,
Among those mouths that sing their sweethearts' praise,
Your empty bed." "How should I love," I answered,
"Were it not that when the dawn has lit my bed
And shown my husband sleeping there, I have sighed,
'Your strength and nobleness will pass away'.
Or how should love be worth its pains were it not
That when he has fallen asleep within my arms,
Being wearied out, I love in man the child?
What can they know of love that do not know
She builds her nest upon a narrow ledge
Above a windy precipice?" Then he:
"Seeing that when you come to the deathbed
You must return, whether you would or no,
This human life blotted from memory,

Why must I live some thirty, forty years,
Alone with all this useless happiness?"
Thereon he seized me in his arms, but I
Thrust him away with both my hands and cried,
"Never will I believe there is any change
Can blot out of my memory this life
Sweetened by death, but if I could believe,
That were a double hunger in my lips
For what is doubly brief."
                    And now the shape
My hands were pressed to vanished suddenly.
I staggered, but a beech tree stayed my fall,
And clinging to it I could hear the cocks
Crow upon Tara.'
                King Eochaid bowed his head
And thanked her for her kindness to his brother,
For that she promised, and for that refused.
Thereon the bellowing of the empounded herds
Rose round the walls, and through the bronze-ringed door
Jostled and shouted those war-wasted men,
And in the midst King Eochaid's brother stood,
And bade all welcome, being ignorant.

To a Wealthy Man who promised a Second Subscription to the Dublin Municipal Gallery if it were proved the People wanted Pictures

You gave, but will not give again
Until enough of Paudeen's pence
By Biddy's halfpennies have lain
To be 'some sort of evidence',
Before you'll put your guineas down,
That things it were a pride to give
Are what the blind and ignorant town
Imagines best to make it thrive.

What cared Duke Ercole, that bid
His mummers to the market-place,
What th' onion-sellers thought or did
So that his Plautus set the pace
For the Italian comedies?
And Guidobaldo, when he made
That grammar school of courtesies
Where wit and beauty learned their trade
Upon Urbino's windy hill,
Had sent no runners to and fro
That he might learn the shepherds' will.
And when they drove out Cosimo,
Indifferent how the rancour ran,
He gave the hours they had set free
To Michelozzo's latest plan
For the San Marco Library,
Whence turbulent Italy should draw
Delight in Art whose end is peace,
In logic and in natural law
By sucking at the dugs of Greece.

Your open hand but shows our loss,
For he knew better how to live.
Let Paudeens play at pitch and toss,
Look up in the sun's eye and give
What the exultant heart calls good
That some new day may breed the best
Because you gave, not what they would,
But the right twigs for an eagle's nest!

September 1913

What need you, being come to sense,
But fumble in a greasy till
And add the halfpence to the pence
And prayer to shivering prayer, until
You have dried the marrow from the bone?
For men were born to pray and save:
Romantic Ireland's dead and gone,
It's with O'Leary in the grave.

Yet they were of a different kind,
The names that stilled your childish play,
They have gone about the world like wind,
But little time had they to pray
For whom the hangman's rope was spun,
And what, God help us, could they save?
Romantic Ireland's dead and gone,
It's with O'Leary in the grave.

Was it for this the wild geese spread
The grey wing upon every tide;
For this that all that blood was shed,
For this Edward Fitzgerald died,
And Robert Emmet and Wolfe Tone,
All that delirium of the brave?
Romantic Ireland's dead and gone,
It's with O'Leary in the grave.

Yet could we turn the years again,
And call those exiles as they were
In all their loneliness and pain,
You'd cry, 'Some woman's yellow hair
Has maddened every mother's son':
They weighed so lightly what they gave.
But let them be, they're dead and gone,
They're with O'Leary in the grave.

To a Friend whose Work has come to Nothing

Now all the truth is out,
Be secret and take defeat
From any brazen throat,
For how can you compete,
Being honour bred, with one
Who, were it proved he lies,
Were neither shamed in his own
Nor in his neighbours' eyes?
Bred to a harder thing
Than Triumph, turn away
And like a laughing string
Whereon mad fingers play
Amid a place of stone,
Be secret and exult,
Because of all things known
That is most difficult.

Paudeen

Indignant at the fumbling wits, the obscure spite
Of our old Paudeen in his shop, I stumbled blind
Among the stones and thorn-trees, under morning light;
Until a curlew cried and in the luminous wind
A curlew answered; and suddenly thereupon I thought
That on the lonely height where all are in God's eye,
There cannot be, confusion of our sound forgot,
A single soul that lacks a sweet crystalline cry.

To a Shade

If you have revisited the town, thin Shade,
Whether to look upon your monument
(I wonder if the builder has been paid)
Or happier-thoughted when the day is spent
To drink of that salt breath out of the sea
When grey gulls flit about instead of men,
And the gaunt houses put on majesty:
Let these content you and be gone again;
For they are at their old tricks yet.
                              A man
Of your own passionate serving kind who had brought
In his full hands what, had they only known,
Had given their children's children loftier thought,
Sweeter emotion, working in their veins
Like gentle blood, has been driven from the place,
And insult heaped upon him for his pains,
And for his open-handedness, disgrace;
Your enemy, an old foul mouth, had set
The pack upon him.
                        Go, unquiet wanderer,
And gather the Glasnevin coverlet
About your head till the dust stops your ear,
The time for you to taste of that salt breath
And listen at the corners has not come;
You had enough of sorrow before death –
Away, away! You are safer in the tomb.

When Helen Lived

We have cried in our despair
That men desert,
For some trivial affair
Or noisy, insolent sport,
Beauty that we have won
From bitterest hours;
Yet we, had we walked within
Those topless towers
Where Helen walked with her boy,
Had given but as the rest
Of the men and women of Troy,
A word and a jest.

On those that hated 'The Playboy of the Western World', 1907

Once, when midnight smote the air,
Eunuchs ran through Hell and met
On every crowded street to stare
Upon great Juan riding by:
Even like these to rail and sweat
Staring upon his sinewy thigh.

The Three Beggars

'Though to my feathers in the wet,
I have stood here from break of day,
I have not found a thing to eat,
For only rubbish comes my way.
Am I to live on lebeen-lone?'
Muttered the old crane of Gort.
'For all my pains on lebeen-lone?'

King Guaire walked amid his court
The palace-yard and river-side
And there to three old beggars said,
'You that have wandered far and wide
Can ravel out what's in my head.
Do men who least desire get most,
Or get the most who most desire?'
A beggar said, 'They get the most
Whom man or devil cannot tire,
And what could make their muscles taut
Unless desire had made them so?'
But Guaire laughed with secret thought,
'If that be true as it seems true,
One of you three is a rich man,
For he shall have a thousand pounds
Who is first asleep, if but he can
Sleep before the third noon sounds.'
And thereon, merry as a bird
With his old thoughts, King Guaire went
From river-side and palace-yard
And left them to their argument.
'And if I win,' one beggar said,
'Though I am old I shall persuade
A pretty girl to share my bed';
The second: 'I shall learn a trade';
The third: 'I'll hurry to the course
Among the other gentlemen,
And lay it all upon a horse';
The second: 'I have thought again:

A farmer has more dignity.'
One to another sighed and cried:
The exorbitant dreams of beggary,
That idleness had borne to pride,
Sang through their teeth from noon to noon;
And when the second twilight brought
The frenzy of the beggars' moon
None closed his blood-shot eyes but sought
To keep his fellows from their sleep;
All shouted till their anger grew
And they were whirling in a heap.

They mauled and bit the whole night through;
They mauled and bit till the day shone;
They mauled and bit through all that day
And till another night had gone,
Or if they made a moment's stay
They sat upon their heels to rail,
And when old Guaire came and stood
Before the three to end this tale,
They were commingling lice and blood.
'Time's up,' he cried, and all the three
With blood-shot eyes upon him stared.
'Time's up,' he cried, and all the three
Fell down upon the dust and snored.

'Maybe I shall be lucky yet,
Now they are silent,' said the crane.
'Though to my feathers in the wet
I've stood as I were made of stone
And seen the rubbish run about,
It's certain there are trout somewhere
And maybe I shall take a trout
If but I do not seem to care.'

The Three Hermits

Three old hermits took the air
By a cold and desolate sea,
First was muttering a prayer,
Second rummaged for a flea;
On a windy stone, the third,
Giddy with his hundredth year,
Sang unnoticed like a bird:
'Though the Door of Death is near
And what waits behind the door,
Three times in a single day
I, though upright on the shore,
Fall asleep when I should pray.'
So the first, but now the second:
'We're but given what we have earned
When all thoughts and deeds are reckoned,
So it's plain to be discerned
That the shades of holy men
Who have failed, being weak of will,
Pass the Door of Birth again,
And are plagued by crowds, until
They've the passion to escape.'
Moaned the other, 'They are thrown
Into some most fearful shape.'
But the second mocked his moan:
'They are not changed to anything,
Having loved God once, but maybe
To a poet or a king
Or a witty lovely lady.'
While he'd rummaged rags and hair,
Caught and cracked his flea, the third,
Giddy with his hundredth year,
Sang unnoticed like a bird.

Beggar to Beggar Cried

'Time to put off the world and go somewhere
And find my health again in the sea air,'
Beggar to beggar cried, being frenzy-struck,
'And make my soul before my pate is bare.'

'And get a comfortable wife and house
To rid me of the devil in my shoes,'
Beggar to beggar cried, being frenzy-struck,
'And the worse devil that is between my thighs.'

'And though I'd marry with a comely lass,
She need not be too comely – let it pass,'
Beggar to beggar cried, being frenzy-struck,
'But there's a devil in a looking-glass.'

'Nor should she be too rich, because the rich
Are driven by wealth as beggars by the itch,'
Beggar to beggar cried, being frenzy-struck,
'And cannot have a humorous happy speech.'

'And there I'll grow respected at my ease,
And hear amid the garden's nightly peace,'
Beggar to beggar cried, being frenzy-struck,
'The wind-blown clamour of the barnacle-geese.'

Running to Paradise

As I came over Windy Gap
They threw a halfpenny into my cap,
For I am running to Paradise;
And all that I need do is to wish
And somebody puts his hand in the dish
To throw me a bit of salted fish:
And there the king is but as the beggar.

My brother Mourteen is worn out
With skelping his big brawling lout,
And I am running to Paradise;
A poor life, do what he can,
And though he keep a dog and a gun,
A serving-maid and a serving-man:
And there the king is but as the beggar.

Poor men have grown to be rich men,
And rich men grown to be poor again,
And I am running to Paradise;
And many a darling wit's grown dull
That tossed a bare heel when at school,
Now it has filled an old sock full:
And there the king is but as the beggar.

The wind is old and still at play
While I must hurry upon my way,
For I am running to Paradise;
Yet never have I lit on a friend
To take my fancy like the wind
That nobody can buy or bind:
And there the king is but as the beggar.

The Hour before Dawn

A cursing rogue with a merry face,
A bundle of rags upon a crutch,
Stumbled upon that windy place
Called Cruachan, and it was as much
As the one sturdy leg could do
To keep him upright while he cursed.
He had counted, where long years ago
Queen Maeve's nine Maines had been nursed,
A pair of lapwings, one old sheep,
And not a house to the plain's edge,
When close to his right hand a heap
Of grey stones and a rocky ledge

Reminded him that he could make,
If he but shifted a few stones,
A shelter till the daylight broke.

But while he fumbled with the stones
They toppled over; 'Were it not
I have a lucky wooden shin
I had been hurt'; and toppling brought
Before his eyes, where stones had been,
A dark deep hollow in the rock.
He gave a gasp and thought to have fled,
Being certain it was no right rock
Because an ancient history said
Hell Mouth lay open near that place,
And yet stood still, because inside
A great lad with a beery face
Had tucked himself away beside
A ladle and a tub of beer,
And snored, no phantom by his look.
So with a laugh at his own fear
He crawled into that pleasant nook.

'Night grows uneasy near the dawn
Till even I sleep light; but who
Has tired of his own company?
What one of Maeve's nine brawling sons
Sick of his grave has wakened me?
But let him keep his grave for once
That I may find the sleep I have lost.'

'What care I if you sleep or wake?
But I'll have no man call me ghost.'

'Say what you please, but from daybreak
I'll sleep another century.'

'And I will talk before I sleep
And drink before I talk.'
                              And he
Had dipped the wooden ladle deep
Into the sleeper's tub of beer
Had not the sleeper started up.

'Before you have dipped it in the beer
I dragged from Goban's mountain-top
I'll have assurance that you are able
To value beer; no half-legged fool
Shall dip his nose into my ladle
Merely for stumbling on this hole
In the bad hour before the dawn.'

'Why, beer is only beer.'
                                             'But say
"I'll sleep until the winter's gone,
Or maybe to Midsummer Day,"
And drink, and you will sleep that length.'

'I'd like to sleep till winter's gone
Or till the sun is in his strength.
This blast has chilled me to the bone.'

'I had no better plan at first.
I thought to wait for that or this;
Maybe the weather was accursed
Or I had no woman there to kiss;
So slept for half a year or so;
But year by year I found that less
Gave me such pleasure I'd forgo
Even a half-hour's nothingness,
And when at one year's end I found
I had not waked a single minute,
I chose this burrow under ground.
I'll sleep away all time within it:
My sleep were now nine centuries
But for those mornings when I find
The lapwing at their foolish cries
And the sheep bleating at the wind
As when I also played the fool.'

The beggar in a rage began
Upon his hunkers in the hole,
'It's plain that you are no right man
To mock at everything I love
As if it were not worth the doing.

I'd have a merry life enough
If a good Easter wind were blowing,
And though the winter wind is bad
I should not be too down in the mouth
For anything you did or said
If but this wind were in the south.'

'You cry aloud, O would 'twere spring
Or that the wind would shift a point,
And do not know that you would bring,
If time were suppler in the joint,
Neither the spring nor the south wind
But the hour when you shall pass away
And leave no smoking wick behind,
For all life longs for the Last Day
And there's no man but cocks his ear
To know when Michael's trumpet cries
That flesh and bone may disappear,
And souls as if they were but sighs,
And there be nothing but God left;
But I alone being blessèd keep
Like some old rabbit to my cleft
And wait Him in a drunken sleep.'
He dipped his ladle in the tub
And drank and yawned and stretched him out,
The other shouted, 'You would rob
My life of every pleasant thought
And every comfortable thing,
And so take that and that.' Thereon
He gave him a great pummelling,
But might have pummelled at a stone
For all the sleeper knew or cared;
And after heaped up stone on stone,
And then, grown weary, prayed and cursed
And heaped up stone on stone again,
And prayed and cursed and cursed and fled
From Maeve and all that juggling plain,
Nor gave God thanks till overhead
The clouds were brightening with the dawn.

A Song from 'The Player Queen'

My mother dandled me and sang,
'How young it is, how young!'
And made a golden cradle
That on a willow swung.

'He went away,' my mother sang,
'When I was brought to bed,'
And all the while her needle pulled
The gold and silver thread.

She pulled the thread and bit the thread
And made a golden gown,
And wept because she had dreamt that I
Was born to wear a crown.

'When she was got,' my mother sang,
'I heard a sea-mew cry,
And saw a flake of the yellow foam
That dropped upon my thigh.'

How therefore could she help but braid
The gold into my hair,
And dream that I should carry
The golden top of care?

The Realists

Hope that you may understand!
What can books of men that wive
In a dragon-guarded land,
Paintings of the dolphin-drawn
Sea-nymphs in their pearly wagons
Do, but awake a hope to live
That had gone
With the dragons?

I

The Witch

Toil and grow rich,
What's that but to lie
With a foul witch
And after, drained dry,
To be brought
To the chamber where
Lies one long sought
With despair?

II

The Peacock

What's riches to him
That has made a great peacock
With the pride of his eye?
The wind-beaten, stone-grey,
And desolate Three Rock
Would nourish his whim.
Live he or die
Amid wet rocks and heather,
His ghost will be gay
Adding feather to feather
For the pride of his eye.

The Mountain Tomb

Pour wine and dance if manhood still have pride,
Bring roses if the rose be yet in bloom;
The cataract smokes upon the mountain side,
Our Father Rosicross is in his tomb.

Pull down the blinds, bring fiddle and clarionet
That there be no foot silent in the room
Nor mouth from kissing, nor from wine unwet;
Our Father Rosicross is in his tomb.

In vain, in vain; the cataract still cries;
The everlasting taper lights the gloom;
All wisdom shut into his onyx eyes,
Our Father Rosicross sleeps in his tomb.

I

To a Child Dancing in the Wind

Dance there upon the shore;
What need have you to care
For wind or water's roar?
And tumble out your hair
That the salt drops have wet;
Being young you have not known
The fool's triumph, nor yet
Love lost as soon as won,
Nor the best labourer dead
And all the sheaves to bind.
What need have you to dread
The monstrous crying of wind?

II

Two Years Later

Has no one said those daring
Kind eyes should be more learn'd?
Or warned you how despairing
The moths are when they are burned?
I could have warned you; but you are young,
So we speak a different tongue.

O you will take whatever's offered
And dream that all the world's a friend,
Suffer as your mother suffered,
Be as broken in the end.
But I am old and you are young,
And I speak a barbarous tongue.

A Memory of Youth

The moments passed as at a play;
I had the wisdom love brings forth;
I had my share of mother-wit,
And yet for all that I could say,
And though I had her praise for it,
A cloud blown from the cut-throat North
Suddenly hid Love's moon away.

Believing every word I said,
I praised her body and her mind
Till pride had made her eyes grow bright,
And pleasure made her cheeks grow red,
And vanity her footfall light,
Yet we, for all that praise, could find
Nothing but darkness overhead.

We sat as silent as a stone,
We knew, though she'd not said a word,
That even the best of love must die,
And had been savagely undone
Were it not that Love upon the cry
Of a most ridiculous little bird
Tore from the clouds his marvellous moon.

Fallen Majesty

Although crowds gathered once if she but showed her face,
And even old men's eyes grew dim, this hand alone,
Like some last courtier at a gypsy camping-place
Babbling of fallen majesty, records what's gone.

The lineaments, a heart that laughter has made sweet,
These, these remain, but I record what's gone. A crowd
Will gather, and not know it walks the very street
Whereon a thing once walked that seemed a burning cloud.

Friends

Now must I these three praise –
Three women that have wrought
What joy is in my days:
One because no thought,
Nor those unpassing cares,
No, not in these fifteen
Many-times-troubled years,
Could ever come between
Mind and delighted mind;
And one because her hand
Had strength that could unbind
What none can understand,

What none can have and thrive,
Youth's dreamy load, till she
So changed me that I live
Labouring in ecstasy.
And what of her that took
All till my youth was gone
With scarce a pitying look?
How could I praise that one?
When day begins to break
I count my good and bad,
Being wakeful for her sake,
Remembering what she had,
What eagle look still shows,
While up from my heart's root
So great a sweetness flows
I shake from head to foot.

The Cold Heaven

Suddenly I saw the cold and rook-delighting heaven
That seemed as though ice burned and was but the more ice,
And thereupon imagination and heart were driven
So wild that every casual thought of that and this
Vanished, and left but memories, that should be out of season
With the hot blood of youth, of love crossed long ago;
And I took all the blame out of all sense and reason,
Until I cried and trembled and rocked to and fro,
Riddled with light. Ah! when the ghost begins to quicken,
Confusion of the death-bed over, is it sent
Out naked on the roads, as the books say, and stricken
By the injustice of the skies for punishment?

That the Night Come

She lived in storm and strife,
Her soul had such desire
For what proud death may bring
That it could not endure
The common good of life,
But lived as 'twere a king
That packed his marriage day
With banneret and pennon,
Trumpet and kettledrum,
And the outrageous cannon,
To bundle time away
That the night come.

An Appointment

Being out of heart with government
I took a broken root to fling
Where the proud, wayward squirrel went,
Taking delight that he could spring;
And he, with that low whinnying sound
That is like laughter, sprang again
And so to the other tree at a bound.
Nor the tame will, nor timid brain,
Nor heavy knitting of the brow
Bred that fierce tooth and cleanly limb
And threw him up to laugh on the bough;
No government appointed him.

The Magi

Now as at all times I can see in the mind's eye,
In their stiff, painted clothes, the pale unsatisfied ones
Appear and disappear in the blue depth of the sky
With all their ancient faces like rain-beaten stones,
And all their helms of silver hovering side by side,
And all their eyes still fixed, hoping to find once more,
Being by Calvary's turbulence unsatisfied,
The uncontrollable mystery on the bestial floor.

The Dolls

A doll in the doll-maker's house
Looks at the cradle and bawls:
'That is an insult to us.'
But the oldest of all the dolls,
Who had seen, being kept for show,
Generations of his sort,
Out-screams the whole shelf: 'Although
There's not a man can report
Evil of this place,
The man and the woman bring
Hither, to our disgrace,
A noisy and filthy thing.'
Hearing him groan and stretch
The doll-maker's wife is aware
Her husband has heard the wretch,
And crouched by the arm of his chair,
She murmurs into his ear,
Head upon shoulder leant:
'My dear, my dear, O dear,
It was an accident.'

A Coat

I made my song a coat
Covered with embroideries
Out of old mythologies
From heel to throat;
But the fools caught it,
Wore it in the world's eyes
As though they'd wrought it.
Song, let them take it,
For there's more enterprise
In walking naked.

[Closing Rhymes]

While I, from that reed-throated whisperer
Who comes at need, although not now as once
A clear articulation in the air,
But inwardly, surmise companions
Beyond the fling of the dull ass's hoof
– Ben Jonson's phrase – and find when June is come
At Kyle-na-no under that ancient roof
A sterner conscience and a friendlier home,
I can forgive even that wrong of wrongs,
Those undreamt accidents that have made me
– Seeing that Fame has perished this long while,
Being but a part of ancient ceremony –
Notorious, till all my priceless things
Are but a post the passing dogs defile.

THE WILD SWANS AT COOLE
1919

THE WILD SWANS AT COOLE

The Wild Swans at Coole

The trees are in their autumn beauty,
The woodland paths are dry,
Under the October twilight the water
Mirrors a still sky;
Upon the brimming water among the stones
Are nine-and-fifty swans.

The nineteenth autumn has come upon me
Since I first made my count;
I saw, before I had well finished,
All suddenly mount
And scatter wheeling in great broken rings
Upon their clamorous wings.

I have looked upon those brilliant creatures,
And now my heart is sore.
All's changed since I, hearing at twilight,
The first time on this shore,
The bell-beat of their wings above my head,
Trod with a lighter tread.

Unwearied still, lover by lover,
They paddle in the cold
Companionable streams or climb the air;
Their hearts have not grown old;
Passion or conquest, wander where they will,
Attend upon them still.

But now they drift on the still water,
Mysterious, beautiful;
Among what rushes will they build,
By what lake's edge or pool
Delight men's eyes when I awake some day
To find they have flown away?

In Memory of Major Robert Gregory

I

Now that we're almost settled in our house
I'll name the friends that cannot sup with us
Beside a fire of turf in th' ancient tower,
And having talked to some late hour
Climb up the narrow winding stair to bed:
Discoverers of forgotten truth
Or mere companions of my youth,
All, all are in my thoughts to-night being dead.

II

Always we'd have the new friend meet the old
And we are hurt if either friend seem cold,
And there is salt to lengthen out the smart
In the affections of our heart,
And quarrels are blown up upon that head;
But not a friend that I would bring
This night can set us quarrelling,
For all that come into my mind are dead.

III

Lionel Johnson comes the first to mind,
That loved his learning better than mankind,
Though courteous to the worst; much falling he
Brooded upon sanctity
Till all his Greek and Latin learning seemed
A long blast upon the horn that brought
A little nearer to his thought
A measureless consummation that he dreamed.

IV

And that enquiring man John Synge comes next,
That dying chose the living world for text

And never could have rested in the tomb
But that, long travelling, he had come
Towards nightfall upon certain set apart
In a most desolate stony place,
Towards nightfall upon a race
Passionate and simple like his heart.

V

And then I think of old George Pollexfen,
In muscular youth well known to Mayo men
For horsemanship at meets or at racecourses,
That could have shown how pure-bred horses
And solid men, for all their passion, live
But as the outrageous stars incline
By opposition, square and trine;
Having grown sluggish and contemplative.

VI

They were my close companions many a year,
A portion of my mind and life, as it were,
And now their breathless faces seem to look
Out of some old picture-book;
I am accustomed to their lack of breath,
But not that my dear friend's dear son,
Our Sidney and our perfect man,
Could share in that discourtesy of death.

VII

For all things the delighted eye now sees
Were loved by him: the old storm-broken trees
That cast their shadows upon road and bridge;
The tower set on the stream's edge;
The ford where drinking cattle make a stir
Nightly, and startled by that sound
The water-hen must change her ground;
He might have been your heartiest welcomer.

VIII

When with the Galway foxhounds he would ride
From Castle Taylor to the Roxborough side
Or Esserkelly plain, few kept his pace;
At Mooneen he had leaped a place
So perilous that half the astonished meet
Had shut their eyes; and where was it
He rode a race without a bit?
And yet his mind outran the horses' feet.

IX

We dreamed that a great painter had been born
To cold Clare rock and Galway rock and thorn,
To that stern colour and that delicate line
That are our secret discipline
Wherein the gazing heart doubles her might.
Soldier, scholar, horseman, he,
And yet he had the intensity
To have published all to be a world's delight.

X

What other could so well have counselled us
In all lovely intricacies of a house
As he that practised or that understood
All work in metal or in wood,
In moulded plaster or in carven stone?
Soldier, scholar, horeseman, he,
And all he did done perfectly
As though he had but that one trade alone.

XI

Some burn damp faggots, others may consume
The entire combustible world in one small room
As though dried straw, and if we turn about
The bare chimney is gone black out

Because the work had finished in that flare.
Soldier, scholar, horseman, he,
As 'twere all life's epitome.
What made us dream that he could comb grey hair?

XII

I had thought, seeing how bitter is that wind
That shakes the shutter, to have brought to mind
All those that manhood tried, or childhood loved
Or boyish intellect approved,
With some appropriate commentary on each;
Until imagination brought
A fitter welcome; but a thought
Of that late death took all my heart for speech.

An Irish Airman Foresees his Death

I know that I shall meet my fate
Somewhere among the clouds above;
Those that I fight I do not hate,
Those that I guard I do not love;
My country is Kiltartan Cross,
My countrymen Kiltartan's poor,
No likely end could bring them loss
Or leave them happier than before.
Nor law, nor duty bade me fight,
Nor public men, nor cheering crowds,
A lonely impulse of delight
Drove to this tumult in the clouds;
I balanced all, brought all to mind,
The years to come seemed waste of breath,
A waste of breath the years behind
In balance with this life, this death.

Men Improve with the Years

I am worn out with dreams;
A weather-worn, marble triton
Among the streams;
And all day long I look
Upon this lady's beauty
As though I had found in a book
A pictured beauty,
Pleased to have filled the eyes
Or the discerning ears,
Delighted to be but wise,
For men improve with the years;
And yet, and yet,
Is this my dream, or the truth?
O would that we had met
When I had my burning youth!
But I grow old among dreams,
A weather-worn, marble triton
Among the streams.

The Collar-Bone of a Hare

Would I could cast a sail on the water
Where many a king has gone
And many a king's daughter,
And alight at the comely trees and the lawn,
The playing upon pipes and the dancing,
And learn that the best thing is
To change my loves while dancing
And pay but a kiss for a kiss.

I would find by the edge of that water
The collar-bone of a hare
Worn thin by the lapping of water,
And pierce it through with a gimlet, and stare
At the old bitter world where they marry in churches,
And laugh over the untroubled water
At all who marry in churches,
Through the white thin bone of a hare.

Under the Round Tower

'Although I'd lie lapped up in linen
A deal I'd sweat and little earn
If I should live as live the neighbours,'
Cried the beggar, Billy Byrne;
'Stretch bones till the daylight come
On great-grandfather's battered tomb.'

Upon a grey old battered tombstone
In Glendalough beside the stream,
Where the O'Byrnes and Byrnes are buried,
He stretched his bones and fell in a dream
Of sun and moon that a good hour
Bellowed and pranced in the round tower;

Of golden king and silver lady,
Bellowing up and bellowing round,
Till toes mastered a sweet measure,
Mouth mastered a sweet sound,
Prancing round and prancing up
Until they pranced upon the top.

That golden king and that wild lady
Sang till stars began to fade,
Hands gripped in hands, toes close together,
Hair spread on the wind they made;
That lady and that golden king
Could like a brace of blackbirds sing.

'It's certain that my luck is broken,'
That rambling jailbird Billy said;
'Before nightfall I'll pick a pocket
And snug it in a feather-bed.
I cannot find the peace of home
On great-grandfather's battered tomb.'

Solomon to Sheba

Sang Solomon to Sheba,
And kissed her dusky face,
'All day long from mid-day
We have talked in the one place,
All day long from shadowless noon
We have gone round and round
In the narrow theme of love
Like an old horse in a pound.'

To Solomon sang Sheba,
Planted on his knees,
'If you had broached a matter
That might the learned please,
You had before the sun had thrown
Our shadows on the ground
Discovered that my thoughts, not it,
Are but a narrow pound.'

Sang Solomon to Sheba,
And kissed her Arab eyes,
'There's not a man or woman
Born under the skies
Dare match in learning with us two,
And all day long we have found
There's not a thing but love can make
The world a narrow pound.'

The Living Beauty

I bade, because the wick and oil are spent
And frozen are the channels of the blood,
My discontented heart to draw content
From beauty that is cast out of a mould
In bronze, or that in dazzling marble appears,
Appears, but when we have gone is gone again,
Being more indifferent to our solitude
Than 'twere an apparition. O heart, we are old;
The living beauty is for younger men:
We cannot pay its tribute of wild tears.

A Song

I thought no more was needed
Youth to prolong
Than dumb-bell and foil
To keep the body young.
O who could have foretold
That the heart grows old?

Though I have many words,
What woman's satisfied,
I am no longer faint
Because at her side?
O who could have foretold
That the heart grows old?

I have not lost desire
But the heart that I had;
I thought 'twould burn my body
Laid on the death-bed,
For who could have foretold
That the heart grows old?

To a Young Beauty

Dear fellow-artist, why so free
With every sort of company,
With every Jack and Jill?
Choose your companions from the best;
Who draws a bucket with the rest
Soon topples down the hill.

You may, that mirror for a school,
Be passionate, not bountiful
As common beauties may,
Who were not born to keep in trim
With old Ezekiel's cherubim
But those of Beauvarlet.

I know what wages beauty gives,
How hard a life her servant lives,
Yet praise the winters gone:
There is not a fool can call me friend,
And I may dine at journey's end
With Landor and with Donne.

To a Young Girl

My dear, my dear, I know
More than another
What makes your heart beat so;
Not even your own mother
Can know it as I know,
Who broke my heart for her
When the wild thought,
That she denies
And has forgot,
Set all her blood astir
And glittered in her eyes.

The Scholars

Bald heads forgetful of their sins,
Old, learned, respectable bald heads
Edit and annotate the lines
That young men, tossing on their beds,
Rhymed out in love's despair
To flatter beauty's ignorant ear.

All shuffle there; all cough in ink;
All wear the carpet with their shoes;
All think what other people think;
All know the man their neighbour knows.
Lord, what would they say
Did their Catullus walk that way?

Tom O'Roughley

'Though logic-choppers rule the town,
And every man and maid and boy
Has marked a distant object down,
An aimless joy is a pure joy,'
Or so did Tom O'Roughley say
That saw the surges running by,
'And wisdom is a butterfly
And not a gloomy bird of prey.

'If little planned is little sinned
But little need the grave distress.
What's dying but a second wind?
How but in zig-zag wantonness
Could trumpeter Michael be so brave?'
Or something of that sort he said,
'And if my dearest friend were dead
I'd dance a measure on his grave.'

Shepherd and Goatherd

SHEPHERD

That cry's from the first cuckoo of the year.
I wished before it ceased.

GOATHERD

         Nor bird nor beast
Could make me wish for anything this day,
Being old, but that the old alone might die,
And that would be against God's Providence.
Let the young wish. But what has brought you here?
Never until this moment have we met
Where my goats browse on the scarce grass or leap
From stone to stone.

SHEPHERD

         I am looking for strayed sheep;
Something has troubled me and in my trouble
I let them stray. I thought of rhyme alone,
For rhyme can beat a measure out of trouble
And make the daylight sweet once more; but when
I had driven every rhyme into its place
The sheep had gone from theirs.

GOATHERD

         I know right well
What turned so good a shepherd from his charge.

SHEPHERD

He that was best in every country sport
And every country craft, and of us all
Most courteous to slow age and hasty youth,
Is dead.

GOATHERD

The boy that brings my griddle-cake
Brought the bare news.

SHEPHERD

He had thrown the crook away
And died in the great war beyond the sea.

GOATHERD

He had often played his pipes among my hills,
And when he played it was their loneliness,
The exultation of their stone, that cried
Under his fingers.

SHEPHERD

I had it from his mother,
And his own flock was browsing at the door.

GOATHERD

How does she bear her grief? There is not a shepherd
But grows more gentle when he speaks her name,
Remembering kindness done, and how can I,
That found when I had neither goat nor grazing
New welcome and old wisdom at her fire
Till winter blasts were gone, but speak of her
Even before his children and his wife?

SHEPHERD

She goes about her house erect and calm
Between the pantry and the linen-chest,
Or else at meadow or at grazing overlooks
Her labouring men, as though her darling lived,
But for her grandson now; there is no change
But such as I have seen upon her face
Watching our shepherd sports at harvest-time
When her son's turn was over.

GOATHERD

Sing your song.
I too have rhymed my reveries, but youth
Is hot to show whatever it has found,
And till that's done can neither work nor wait.
Old goatherds and old goats, if in all else
Youth can excel them in accomplishment,
Are learned in waiting.

SHEPHERD

You cannot but have seen
That he alone had gathered up no gear,
Set carpenters to work on no wide table,
On no long bench nor lofty milking-shed
As others will, when first they take possession,
But left the house as in his father's time
As though he knew himself, as it were, a cuckoo,
No settled man. And now that he is gone
There's nothing of him left but half a score
Of sorrowful, austere, sweet, lofty pipe tunes.

GOATHERD

You have put the thought in rhyme.

SHEPHERD

I worked all day,
And when 'twas done so little had I done
That maybe 'I am sorry' in plain prose
Had sounded better to your mountain fancy.

[*He sings.*

    'Like the speckled bird that steers
    Thousands of leagues oversea,
    And runs or a while half-flies
    On his yellow legs through our meadows,
    He stayed for a while; and we
    Had scarcely accustomed our ears

To his speech at the break of day,
Had scarcely accustomed our eyes
To his shape at the rinsing-pool
Among the evening shadows,
When he vanished from ears and eyes.
I might have wished on the day
He came, but man is a fool.'

GOATHERD

You sing as always of the natural life,
And I that made like music in my youth
Hearing it now have sighed for that young man
And certain lost companions of my own.

SHEPHERD

They say that on your barren mountain ridge
You have measured out the road that the soul treads
When it has vanished from our natural eyes;
That you have talked with apparitions.

GOATHERD

                                        Indeed
My daily thoughts since the first stupor of youth
Have found the path my goats' feet cannot find.

SHEPHERD

Sing, for it may be that your thoughts have plucked
Some medicable herb to make our grief
Less bitter.

GOATHERD

        They have brought me from that ridge
Seed-pods and flowers that are not all wild poppy.

                                        [*Sings.*

'He grows younger every second
That were all his birthdays reckoned
Much too solemn seemed;
Because of what he had dreamed,
Or the ambitions that he served,
Much too solemn and reserved.
Jaunting, journeying
To his own dayspring,
He unpacks the loaded pern
Of all 'twas pain or joy to learn,
Of all that he had made.
The outrageous war shall fade;
At some old winding whitethorn root
He'll practise on the shepherd's flute,
Or on the close-cropped grass
Court his shepherd lass,
Or put his heart into some game
Till daytime, playtime seem the same;
Knowledge he shall unwind
Through victories of the mind,
Till, clambering at the cradle-side,
He dreams himself his mother's pride,
All knowledge lost in trance
Of sweeter ignorance.'

SHEPHERD

When I have shut these ewes and this old ram
Into the fold, we'll to the woods and there
Cut out our rhymes on strips of new-torn bark
But put no name and leave them at her door.
To know the mountain and the valley have grieved
May be a quiet thought to wife and mother,
And children when they spring up shoulder-high.

Lines Written in Dejection

When have I last looked on
The round green eyes and the long wavering bodies
Of the dark leopards of the moon?
All the wild witches, those most noble ladies,
For all their broom-sticks and their tears,
Their angry tears, are gone.
The holy centaurs of the hills are vanished;
I have nothing but the embittered sun;
Banished heroic mother moon and vanished,
And now that I have come to fifty years
I must endure the timid sun.

The Dawn

I would be ignorant as the dawn
That has looked down
On that old queen measuring a town
With the pin of a brooch,
Or on the withered men that saw
From their pedantic Babylon
The careless planets in their courses,
The stars fade out where the moon comes,
And took their tablets and did sums;
I would be ignorant as the dawn
That merely stood, rocking the glittering coach
Above the cloudy shoulders of the horses;
I would be – for no knowledge is worth a straw –
Ignorant and wanton as the dawn.

On Woman

May God be praised for woman
That gives up all her mind,
A man may find in no man
A friendship of her kind
That covers all he has brought
As with her flesh and bone,
Nor quarrels with a thought
Because it is not her own.

Though pedantry denies,
It's plain the Bible means
That Solomon grew wise
While talking with his queens,
Yet never could, although
They say he counted grass,
Count all the praises due
When Sheba was his lass,
When she the iron wrought, or
When from the smithy fire
It shuddered in the water:
Harshness of their desire
That made them stretch and yawn,
Pleasure that comes with sleep,
Shudder that made them one.
What else He give or keep
God grant me – no, not here,
For I am not so bold
To hope a thing so dear
Now I am growing old,
But when, if the tale's true,
The Pestle of the moon
That pounds up all anew
Brings me to birth again –
To find what once I had
And know what once I have known,
Until I am driven mad,

Sleep driven from my bed,
By tenderness and care,
Pity, an aching head,
Gnashing of teeth, despair;
And all because of some one
Perverse creature of chance,
And live like Solomon
That Sheba led a dance.

The Fisherman

Although I can see him still,
The freckled man who goes
To a grey place on a hill
In grey Connemara clothes
At dawn to cast his flies,
It's long since I began
To call up to the eyes
This wise and simple man.
All day I'd looked in the face
What I had hoped 'twould be
To write for my own race
And the reality;
The living men that I hate,
The dead man that I loved,
The craven man in his seat,
The insolent unreproved,
And no knave brought to book
Who has won a drunken cheer,
The witty man and his joke
Aimed at the commonest ear,
The clever man who cries
The catch-cries of the clown,
The beating down of the wise
And great Art beaten down.

Maybe a twelvemonth since
Suddenly I began,
In scorn of this audience,
Imagining a man,
And his sun-freckled face,
And grey Connemara cloth,
Climbing up to a place
Where stone is dark under froth,
And the down-turn of his wrist
When the flies drop in the stream;
A man who does not exist,
A man who is but a dream;
And cried, 'Before I am old
I shall have written him one
Poem maybe as cold
And passionate as the dawn.'

The Hawk

'Call down the hawk from the air;
Let him be hooded or caged
Till the yellow eye has grown mild,
For larder and spit are bare,
The old cook enraged,
The scullion gone wild.'

'I will not be clapped in a hood,
Nor a cage, nor alight upon wrist,
Now I have learnt to be proud
Hovering over the wood
In the broken mist
Or tumbling cloud.'

'What tumbling cloud did you cleave,
Yellow-eyed hawk of the mind,
Last evening? that I, who had sat
Dumbfounded before a knave,
Should give to my friend
A pretence of wit.'

Memory

One had a lovely face,
And two or three had charm,
But charm and face were in vain
Because the mountain grass
Cannot but keep the form
Where the mountain hare has lain.

Her Praise

She is foremost of those that I would hear praised.
I have gone about the house, gone up and down
As a man does who has published a new book,
Or a young girl dressed out in her new gown,
And though I have turned the talk by hook or crook
Until her praise should be the uppermost theme,
A woman spoke of some new tale she had read,
A man confusedly in a half dream
As though some other name ran in his head.
She is foremost of those that I would hear praised.
I will talk no more of books or the long war
But walk by the dry thorn until I have found
Some beggar sheltering from the wind, and there
Manage the talk until her name come round.
If there be rags enough he will know her name
And be well pleased remembering it, for in the old days,
Though she had young men's praise and old men's blame,
Among the poor both old and young gave her praise.

The People

'What have I earned for all that work,' I said,
'For all that I have done at my own charge?
The daily spite of this unmannerly town,
Where who has served the most is most defamed,
The reputation of his lifetime lost
Between the night and morning. I might have lived,
And you know well how great the longing has been,
Where every day my footfall should have lit
In the green shadow of Ferrara wall;
Or climbed among the images of the past –
The unperturbed and courtly images –
Evening and morning, the steep street of Urbino
To where the Duchess and her people talked
The stately midnight through until they stood
In their great window looking at the dawn;
I might have had no friend that could not mix
Courtesy and passion into one like those
That saw the wicks grow yellow in the dawn;
I might have used the one substantial right
My trade allows: chosen my company,
And chosen what scenery had pleased me best.'
Thereon my phoenix answered in reproof,
'The drunkards, pilferers of public funds,
All the dishonest crowd I had driven away,
When my luck changed and they dared meet my face,
Crawled from obscurity, and set upon me
Those I had served and some that I had fed;
Yet never have I, now nor any time,
Complained of the people.'

                     All I could reply
Was: 'You, that have not lived in thought but deed,
Can have the purity of a natural force,
But I, whose virtues are the definitions
Of the analytic mind, can neither close

The eye of the mind nor keep my tongue from speech.'
And yet, because my heart leaped at her words,
I was abashed, and now they come to mind
After nine years, I sink my head abashed.

His Phoenix

There is a queen in China, or maybe it's in Spain,
And birthdays and holidays such praises can be heard
Of her unblemished lineaments, a whiteness with no stain,
That she might be that sprightly girl trodden by a bird;
And there's a score of duchesses, surpassing womankind,
Or who have found a painter to make them so for pay
And smooth out stain and blemish with the elegance of his mind:
I knew a phoenix in my youth, so let them have their day.

The young men every night applaud their Gaby's laughing eye,
And Ruth St. Denis had more charm although she had poor luck;
From nineteen hundred nine or ten, Pavlova's had the cry,
And there's a player in the States who gathers up her cloak
And flings herself out of the room when Juliet would be bride
With all a woman's passion, a child's imperious way,
And there are – but no matter if there are scores beside:
I knew a phoenix in my youth, so let them have their day.

There's Margaret and Marjorie and Dorothy and Nan,
A Daphne and a Mary who live in privacy;
One's had her fill of lovers, another's had but one,
Another boasts, 'I pick and choose and have but two or three.'
If head and limb have beauty and the instep's high and light
They can spread out what sail they please for all I have to say,
Be but the breakers of men's hearts or engines of delight:
I knew a phoenix in my youth, so let them have their day.

There'll be that crowd, that barbarous crowd, through all the
    centuries,
And who can say but some young belle may walk and talk men
    wild

Who is my beauty's equal, though that my heart denies,
But not the exact likeness, the simplicity of a child,
And that proud look as though she had gazed into the burning
    sun,
And all the shapely body no tittle gone astray.
I mourn for that most lonely thing; and yet God's will be done:
I knew a phoenix in my youth, so let them have their day.

A Thought from Propertius

She might, so noble from head
To great shapely knees
The long flowing line,
Have walked to the altar
Through the holy images
At Pallas Athene's side,
Or been fit spoil for a centaur
Drunk with the unmixed wine.

Broken Dreams

There is grey in your hair.
Young men no longer suddenly catch their breath
When you are passing;
But maybe some old gaffer mutters a blessing
Because it was your prayer
Recovered him upon the bed of death.
For your sole sake – that all heart's ache have known,
And given to others all heart's ache,
From meagre girlhood's putting on
Burdensome beauty – for your sole sake
Heaven has put away the stroke of her doom,
So great her portion in that peace you make
By merely walking in a room.

Your beauty can but leave among us
Vague memories, nothing but memories.
A young man when the old men are done talking
Will say to an old man, 'Tell me of that lady
The poet stubborn with his passion sang us
When age might well have chilled his blood.'

Vague memories, nothing but memories,
But in the grave all, all, shall be renewed.
The certainty that I shall see that lady
Leaning or standing or walking
In the first loveliness of womanhood,
And with the fervour of my youthful eyes,
Has set me muttering like a fool.

You are more beautiful than any one,
And yet your body had a flaw:
Your small hands were not beautiful,
And I am afraid that you will run
And paddle to the wrist
In that mysterious, always brimming lake
Where those that have obeyed the holy law
Paddle and are perfect. Leave unchanged
The hands that I have kissed,
For old sake's sake.

The last stroke of midnight dies.
All day in the one chair
From dream to dream and rhyme to rhyme I have ranged
In rambling talk with an image of air:
Vague memories, nothing but memories.

A Deep-sworn Vow

Others because you did not keep
That deep-sworn vow have been friends of mine;
Yet always when I look death in the face,
When I clamber to the heights of sleep,
Or when I grow excited with wine,
Suddenly I meet your face.

Presences

This night has been so strange that it seemed
As if the hair stood up on my head.
From going-down of the sun I have dreamed
That women laughing, or timid or wild,
In rustle of lace or silken stuff,
Climbed up my creaking stair. They had read
All I had rhymed of that monstrous thing
Returned and yet unrequited love.
They stood in the door and stood between
My great wood lectern and the fire
Till I could hear their hearts beating:
One is a harlot, and one a child
That never looked upon man with desire,
And one, it may be, a queen.

The Balloon of the Mind

Hands, do what you're bid:
Bring the balloon of the mind
That bellies and drags in the wind
Into its narrow shed.

To a Squirrel at Kyle-na-no

Come play with me;
Why should you run
Through the shaking tree
As though I'd a gun
To strike you dead?
When all I would do
Is to scratch your head
And let you go.

On being asked for a War Poem

I think it better that in times like these
A poet's mouth be silent, for in truth
We have no gift to set a statesman right;
He has had enough of meddling who can please
A young girl in the indolence of her youth,
Or an old man upon a winter's night.

In Memory of Alfred Pollexfen

Five-and-twenty years have gone
Since old William Pollexfen
Laid his strong bones down in death
By his wife Elizabeth
In the grey stone tomb he made.
And after twenty years they laid
In that tomb by him and her
His son George, the astrologer;
And Masons drove from miles away
To scatter the Acacia spray

Upon a melancholy man
Who had ended where his breath began.
Many a son and daughter lies
Far from the customary skies,
The Mall and Eades's grammar school,
In London or in Liverpool;
But where is laid the sailor John
That so many lands had known,
Quiet lands or unquiet seas
Where the Indians trade or Japanese?
He never found his rest ashore,
Moping for one voyage more.
Where have they laid the sailor John?
And yesterday the youngest son,
A humorous, unambitious man,
Was buried near the astrologer,
Yesterday in the tenth year
Since he who had been contented long,
A nobody in a great throng,
Decided he would journey home,
Now that his fiftieth year had come,
And 'Mr. Alfred' be again
Upon the lips of common men
Who carried in their memory
His childhood and his family.
At all these death-beds women heard
A visionary white sea-bird
Lamenting that a man should die;
And with that cry I have raised my cry.

Upon a Dying Lady

I

HER COURTESY

With the old kindness, the old distinguished grace,
She lies, her lovely piteous head amid dull red hair
Propped upon pillows, rouge on the pallor of her face.
She would not have us sad because she is lying there,
And when she meets our gaze her eyes are laughter-lit,
Her speech a wicked tale that we may vie with her,
Matching our broken-hearted wit against her wit,
Thinking of saints and of Petronius Arbiter.

II

CERTAIN ARTISTS BRING HER DOLLS AND DRAWINGS

Bring where our Beauty lies
A new modelled doll, or drawing,
With a friend's or an enemy's
Features, or maybe showing
Her features when a tress
Of dull red hair was flowing
Over some silken dress
Cut in the Turkish fashion,
Or, it may be, like a boy's.
We have given the world our passion,
We have naught for death but toys.

III

SHE TURNS THE DOLLS' FACES TO THE WALL

Because to-day is some religious festival
They had a priest say Mass, and even the Japanese,
Heel up and weight on toe, must face the wall
– Pedant in passion, learned in old courtesies,
Vehement and witty she had seemed – ; the Venetian lady
Who had seemed to glide to some intrigue in her red shoes,

Her domino, her panniered skirt copied from Longhi;
The meditative critic; all are on their toes,
Even our Beauty with her Turkish trousers on.
Because the priest must have like every dog his day
Or keep us all awake with baying at the moon,
We and our dolls being but the world were best away.

IV

THE END OF DAY

She is playing like a child
And penance is the play,
Fantastical and wild
Because the end of day
Shows her that some one soon
Will come from the house, and say —
Though play is but half done —
'Come in and leave the play.'

V

HER RACE

She has not grown uncivil
As narrow natures would
And called the pleasures evil.
Happier days thought good;
She knows herself a woman,
No red and white of a face,
Or rank, raised from a common
Unreckonable race;
And how should her heart fail her
Or sickness break her will
With her dead brother's valour
For an example still?

VI

HER COURAGE

When her soul flies to the predestined dancing-place
(I have no speech but symbol, the pagan speech I made
Amid the dreams of youth) let her come face to face,
Amid that first astonishment, with Grania's shade,
All but the terrors of the woodland flight forgot
That made her Diarmuid dear, and some old cardinal
Pacing with half-closed eyelids in a sunny spot
Who had murmured of Giorgione at his latest breath –
Aye, and Achilles, Timor, Babar, Barhaim, all
Who have lived in joy and laughed into the face of Death.

VII

HER FRIENDS BRING HER A CHRISTMAS TREE

Pardon, great enemy,
Without an angry thought
We've carried in our tree,
And here and there have bought
Till all the boughs are gay,
And she may look from the bed
On pretty things that may
Please a fantastic head.
Give her a little grace,
What if a laughing eye
Have looked into your face?
It is about to die.

Ego Dominus Tuus

HIC

On the grey sand beside the shallow stream
Under your old wind-beaten tower, where still
A lamp burns on beside the open book
That Michael Robartes left, you walk in the moon,
And, though you have passed the best of life, still trace,
Enthralled by the unconquerable delusion,
Magical shapes.

ILLE

        By the help of an image
I call to my own opposite, summon all
That I have handled least, least looked upon.

HIC

And I would find myself and not an image.

ILLE

That is our modern hope, and by its light
We have lit upon the gentle, sensitive mind
And lost the old nonchalance of the hand;
Whether we have chosen chisel, pen or brush,
We are but critics, or but half create,
Timid, entangled, empty and abashed,
Lacking the countenance of our friends.

HIC

                  And yet
The chief imagination of Christendom,
Dante Alighieri, so utterly found himself
That he has made that hollow face of his
More plain to the mind's eye than any face
But that of Christ.

ILLE

And did he find himself
Or was the hunger that had made it hollow
A hunger for the apple on the bough
Most out of reach? and is that spectral image
The man that Lapo and that Guido knew?
I think he fashioned from his opposite
An image that might have been a stony face
Staring upon a Bedouin's horse-hair roof
From doored and windowed cliff, or half upturned
Among the coarse grass and the camel-dung.
He set his chisel to the hardest stone.
Being mocked by Guido for his lecherous life,
Derided and deriding, driven out
To climb that stair and eat that bitter bread,
He found the unpersuadable justice, he found
The most exalted lady loved by a man.

HIC

Yet surely there are men who have made their art
Out of no tragic war, lovers of life,
Impulsive men that look for happiness
And sing when they have found it.

ILLE

No, not sing,
For those that love the world serve it in action,
Grow rich, popular and full of influence,
And should they paint or write, still it is action:
The struggle of the fly in marmalade.
The rhetorician would deceive his neighbours,
The sentimentalist himself; while art
Is but a vision of reality.
What portion in the world can the artist have
Who has awakened from the common dream
But dissipation and despair?

H I C

And yet
No one denies to Keats love of the world;
Remember his deliberate happiness.

I L L E

His art is happy, but who knows his mind?
I see a schoolboy when I think of him,
With face and nose pressed to a sweet-shop window,
For certainly he sank into his grave
His senses and his heart unsatisfied,
And made – being poor, ailing and ignorant,
Shut out from all the luxury of the world,
The coarse-bred son of a livery-stable keeper –
Luxuriant song.

H I C

Why should you leave the lamp
Burning alone beside an open book,
And trace these characters upon the sands?
A style is found by sedentary toil
And by the imitation of great masters.

I L L E

Because I seek an image, not a book.
Those men that in their writings are most wise
Own nothing but their blind, stupefied hearts.
I call to the mysterious one who yet
Shall walk the wet sands by the edge of the stream
And look most like me, being indeed my double,
And prove of all imaginable things
The most unlike, being my anti-self,
And, standing by these characters, disclose
All that I seek; and whisper it as though
He were afraid the birds, who cry aloud
Their momentary cries before it is dawn,
Would carry it away to blasphemous men.

A Prayer on going into my House

God grant a blessing on this tower and cottage
And on my heirs, if all remain unspoiled,
No table or chair or stool not simple enough
For shepherd lads in Galilee; and grant
That I myself for portions of the year
May handle nothing and set eyes on nothing
But what the great and passionate have used
Throughout so many varying centuries
We take it for the norm; yet should I dream
Sinbad the sailor's brought a painted chest,
Or image, from beyond the Loadstone Mountain,
That dream is a norm; and should some limb of the Devil
Destroy the view by cutting down an ash
That shades the road, or setting up a cottage
Planned in a government office, shorten his life,
Manacle his soul upon the Red Sea bottom.

The Phases of the Moon

An old man cocked his ear upon a bridge;
He and his friend, their faces to the South,
Had trod the uneven road. Their boots were soiled,
Their Connemara cloth worn out of shape;
They had kept a steady pace as though their beds,
Despite a dwindling and late-risen moon,
Were distant still. An old man cocked his ear.

AHERNE

What made that sound?

ROBARTES

                    A rat or water-hen
Splashed, or an otter slid into the stream.
We are on the bridge; that shadow is the tower,
And the light proves that he is reading still.
He has found, after the manner of his kind,
Mere images; chosen this place to live in
Because, it may be, of the candle-light
From the far tower where Milton's Platonist
Sat late, or Shelley's visionary prince:
The lonely light that Samuel Palmer engraved,
An image of mysterious wisdom won by toil;
And now he seeks in book or manuscript
What he shall never find.

AHERNE

                         Why should not you
Who know it all ring at his door, and speak
Just truth enough to show that his whole life
Will scarcely find for him a broken crust
Of all those truths that are your daily bread;
And when you have spoken take the roads again?

ROBARTES

He wrote of me in that extravagant style
He had learnt from Pater, and to round his tale
Said I was dead; and dead I choose to be.

AHERNE

Sing me the changes of the moon once more;
True song, though speech: 'mine author sung it me.'

ROBARTES

Twenty-and-eight the phases of the moon,
The full and the moon's dark and all the crescents,
Twenty-and-eight, and yet but six-and-twenty

The cradles that a man must needs be rocked in:
For there's no human life at the full or the dark.
From the first crescent to the half, the dream
But summons to adventure and the man
Is always happy like a bird or a beast;
But while the moon is rounding towards the full
He follows whatever whim's most difficult
Among whims not impossible, and though scarred,
As with the cat-o'-nine-tails of the mind,
His body moulded from within his body
Grows comelier. Eleven pass, and then
Athene takes Achilles by the hair,
Hector is in the dust, Nietzsche is born,
Because the hero's crescent is the twelfth.
And yet, twice born, twice buried, grow he must,
Before the full moon, helpless as a worm.
The thirteenth moon but sets the soul at war
In its own being, and when that war's begun
There is no muscle in the arm; and after,
Under the frenzy of the fourteenth moon,
The soul begins to tremble into stillness,
To die into the labyrinth of itself!

AHERNE

Sing out the song; sing to the end, and sing
The strange reward of all that discipline.

ROBARTES

All thought becomes an image and the soul
Becomes a body: that body and that soul
Too perfect at the full to lie in a cradle,
Too lonely for the traffic of the world:
Body and soul cast out and cast away
Beyond the visible world.

AHERNE

All dreams of the soul
End in a beautiful man's or woman's body.

ROBARTES

Have you not always known it?

AHERNE

                                    The song will have it
That those that we have loved got their long fingers
From death, and wounds, or on Sinai's top,
Or from some bloody whip in their own hands.
They ran from cradle to cradle till at last
Their beauty dropped out of the loneliness
Of body and soul.

ROBARTES

The lover's heart knows that.

AHERNE

It must be that the terror in their eyes
Is memory or foreknowledge of the hour
When all is fed with light and heaven is bare.

ROBARTES

When the moon's full those creatures of the full
Are met on the waste hills by countrymen
Who shudder and hurry by: body and soul
Estranged amid the strangeness of themselves,
Caught up in contemplation, the mind's eye
Fixed upon images that once were thought;
For separate, perfect, and immovable
Images can break the solitude
Of lovely, satisfied, indifferent eyes.

And thereupon with aged, high-pitched voice
Aherne laughed, thinking of the man within,
His sleepless candle and laborious pen.

ROBARTES

And after that the crumbling of the moon.
The soul remembering its loneliness
Shudders in many cradles; all is changed,
It would be the world's servant, and as it serves,
Choosing whatever task's most difficult
Among tasks not impossible, it takes
Upon the body and upon the soul
The coarseness of the drudge.

AHERNE

                                        Before the full
It sought itself and afterwards the world.

ROBARTES

Because you are forgotten, half out of life,
And never wrote a book, your thought is clear.
Reformer, merchant, statesman, learned man,
Dutiful husband, honest wife by turn,
Cradle upon cradle, and all in flight and all
Deformed because there is no deformity
But saves us from a dream.

AHERNE

                                And what of those
That the last servile crescent has set free?

ROBARTES

Because all dark, like those that are all light,
They are cast beyond the verge, and in a cloud,
Crying to one another like the bats;
And having no desire they cannot tell
What's good or bad, or what it is to triumph
At the perfection of one's own obedience;
And yet they speak what's blown into the mind;
Deformed beyond deformity, unformed,

Insipid as the dough before it is baked,
They change their bodies at a word.

AHERNE

                    And then?

ROBARTES

When all the dough has been so kneaded up
That it can take what form cook Nature fancies
The first thin crescent is wheeled round once more.

AHERNE

But the escape; the song's not finished yet.

ROBARTES

Hunchback and Saint and Fool are the last crescents.
The burning bow that once could shoot an arrow
Out of the up and down, the wagon-wheel
Of beauty's cruelty and wisdom's chatter –
Out of that raving tide – is drawn betwixt
Deformity of body and of mind.

AHERNE

Were not our beds far off I'd ring the bell,
Stand under the rough roof-timbers of the hall
Beside the castle door, where all is stark
Austerity, a place set out for wisdom
That he will never find; I'd play a part;
He would never know me after all these years
But take me for some drunken countryman;
I'd stand and mutter there until he caught
'Hunchback and Saint and Fool,' and that they came
Under the three last crescents of the moon,
And then I'd stagger out. He'd crack his wits
Day after day, yet never find the meaning.

And then he laughed to think that what seemed hard
Should be so simple – a bat rose from the hazels
And circled round him with its squeaky cry,
The light in the tower window was put out.

The Cat and the Moon

The cat went here and there
And the moon spun round like a top,
And the nearest kin of the moon,
The creeping cat, looked up.
Black Minnaloushe stared at the moon,
For, wander and wail as he would,
The pure cold light in the sky
Troubled his animal blood.
Minnaloushe runs in the grass
Lifting his delicate feet.
Do you dance, Minnaloushe, do you dance?
When two close kindred meet,
What better than call a dance?
Maybe the moon may learn,
Tired of that courtly fashion,
A new dance turn.
Minnaloushe creeps through the grass
From moonlit place to place,
The sacred moon overhead
Has taken a new phase.
Does Minnaloushe know that his pupils
Will pass from change to change,
And that from round to crescent,
From crescent to round they range?
Minnaloushe creeps through the grass
Alone, important and wise,
And lifts to the changing moon
His changing eyes.

The Saint and the Hunchback

HUNCHBACK

Stand up and lift your hand and bless
A man that finds great bitterness
In thinking of his lost renown.
A Roman Caesar is held down
Under this hump.

SAINT

        God tries each man
According to a different plan.
I shall not cease to bless because
I lay about me with the taws
That night and morning I may thrash
Greek Alexander from my flesh,
Augustus Caesar, and after these
That great rogue Alcibiades.

HUNCHBACK

To all that in your flesh have stood
And blessed, I give my gratitude,
Honoured by all in their degrees,
But most to Alcibiades.

Two Songs of a Fool

I

A speckled cat and a tame hare
Eat at my hearthstone
And sleep there;
And both look up to me alone
For learning and defence
As I look up to Providence.

I start out of my sleep to think
Some day I may forget
Their food and drink;
Or, the house door left unshut,
The hare may run till it's found
The horn's sweet note and the tooth of the hound.

I bear a burden that might well try
Men that do all by rule,
And what can I
That am a wandering-witted fool
But pray to God that He ease
My great responsibilities?

II

I slept on my three-legged stool by the fire,
The speckled cat slept on my knee;
We never thought to enquire
Where the brown hare might be,
And whether the door were shut.
Who knows how she drank the wind
Stretched up on two legs from the mat,
Before she had settled her mind
To drum with her heel and to leap?
Had I but awakened from sleep
And called her name, she had heard,
It may be, and had not stirred,
That now, it may be, has found
The horn's sweet note and the tooth of the hound.

Another Song of a Fool

This great purple butterfly,
In the prison of my hands,
Has a learning in his eye
Not a poor fool understands.

Once he lived a schoolmaster
With a stark, denying look;
A string of scholars went in fear
Of his great birch and his great book.

Like the clangour of a bell,
Sweet and harsh, harsh and sweet,
That is how he learnt so well
To take the roses for his meat.

The Double Vision of Michael Robartes

I

On the grey rock of Cashel the mind's eye
Has called up the cold spirits that are born
When the old moon is vanished from the sky
And the new still hides her horn.

Under blank eyes and fingers never still
The particular is pounded till it is man.
When had I my own will?
O not since life began.

Constrained, arraigned, baffled, bent and unbent
By these wire-jointed jaws and limbs of wood,
Themselves obedient,
Knowing not evil and good;

Obedient to some hidden magical breath.
They do not even feel, so abstract are they,
So dead beyond our death,
Triumph that we obey.

II

On the grey rock of Cashel I suddenly saw
A Sphinx with woman breast and lion paw,
A Buddha, hand at rest,
Hand lifted up that blest;

And right between these two a girl at play
That, it may be, had danced her life away,
For now being dead it seemed
That she of dancing dreamed.

Although I saw it all in the mind's eye
There can be nothing solider till I die;
I saw by the moon's light
Now at its fifteenth night.

One lashed her tail; her eyes lit by the moon
Gazed upon all things known, all things unknown,
In triumph of intellect
With motionless head erect.

That other's moonlit eyeballs never moved,
Being fixed on all things loved, all things unloved,
Yet little peace he had,
For those that love are sad.

O little did they care who danced between,
And little she by whom her dance was seen
So she had outdanced thought.
Body perfection brought,

For what but eye and ear silence the mind
With the minute particulars of mankind?
Mind moved yet seemed to stop
As 'twere a spinning-top.

In contemplation had those three so wrought
Upon a moment, and so stretched it out
That they, time overthrown,
Were dead yet flesh and bone.

III

I knew that I had seen, had seen at last
That girl my unremembering nights hold fast
Or else my dreams that fly
If I should rub an eye,

And yet in flying fling into my meat
A crazy juice that makes the pulses beat
As though I had been undone
By Homer's Paragon

Who never gave the burning town a thought;
To such a pitch of folly I am brought,
Being caught between the pull
Of the dark moon and the full,

The commonness of thought and images
That have the frenzy of our western seas.
Thereon I made my moan,
And after kissed a stone,

And after that arranged it in a song
Seeing that I, ignorant for so long,
Had been rewarded thus
In Cormac's ruined house.

MICHAEL ROBARTES
AND THE DANCER
1921

MICHAEL ROBARTES
AND THE DANCER

Michael Robartes and the Dancer

HE

Opinion is not worth a rush;
In this altar-piece the knight,
Who grips his long spear so to push
That dragon through the fading light,
Loved the lady; and it's plain
The half-dead dragon was her thought,
That every morning rose again
And dug its claws and shrieked and fought.
Could the impossible come to pass
She would have time to turn her eyes,
Her lover thought, upon the glass
And on the instant would grow wise.

SHE

You mean they argued.

HE

          Put it so;
But bear in mind your lover's wage
Is what your looking-glass can show,
And that he will turn green with rage
At all that is not pictured there.

SHE

May I not put myself to college?

HE

Go pluck Athene by the hair;
For what mere book can grant a knowledge
With an impassioned gravity
Appropriate to that beating breast,
That vigorous thigh, that dreaming eye?
And may the Devil take the rest.

SHE

And must no beautiful woman be
Learned like a man?

HE

                    Paul Veronese
And all his sacred company
Imagined bodies all their days
By the lagoon you love so much,
For proud, soft, ceremonious proof
That all must come to sight and touch;
While Michael Angelo's Sistine roof,
His 'Morning' and his 'Night' disclose
How sinew that has been pulled tight,
Or it may be loosened in repose,
Can rule by supernatural right
Yet be but sinew.

SHE

                    I have heard said
There is great danger in the body.

HE

Did God in portioning wine and bread
Give man His thought or His mere body?

SHE

My wretched dragon is perplexed.

HE

I have principles to prove me right.
It follows from this Latin text
That blest souls are not composite,
And that all beautiful women may
Live in uncomposite blessedness,
And lead us to the like – if they
Will banish every thought, unless
The lineaments that please their view
When the long looking-glass is full,
Even from the foot-sole think it too.

SHE

They say such different things at school.

Solomon and the Witch

And thus declared that Arab lady:
'Last night, where under the wild moon
On grassy mattress I had laid me,
Within my arms great Solomon,
I suddenly cried out in a strange tongue
Not his, not mine.'
                    Who understood
Whatever has been said, sighed, sung,
Howled, miau-d, barked, brayed, belled, yelled, cried, crowed,
Thereon replied: 'A cockerel
Crew from a blossoming apple bough
Three hundred years before the Fall,
And never crew again till now,
And would not now but that he thought,
Chance being at one with Choice at last,
All that the brigand apple brought
And this foul world were dead at last.

He that crowed out eternity
Thought to have crowed it in again.
For though love has a spider's eye
To find out some appropriate pain –
Aye, though all passion's in the glance –
For every nerve, and tests a lover
With cruelties of Choice and Chance;
And when at last that murder's over
Maybe the bride-bed brings despair,
For each an imagined image brings
And finds a real image there;
Yet the world ends when these two things,
Though several, are a single light,
When oil and wick are burned in one;
Therefore a blessed moon last night
Gave Sheba to her Solomon.'

'Yet the world stays.'
                              'If that be so,
Your cockerel found us in the wrong
Although he thought it worth a crow.
Maybe an image is too strong
Or maybe is not strong enough.'

'The night has fallen; not a sound
In the forbidden sacred grove
Unless a petal hit the ground,
Nor any human sight within it
But the crushed grass where we have lain;
And the moon is wilder every minute.
O! Solomon! let us try again.'

An Image from a Past Life

HE

Never until this night have I been stirred.
The elaborate starlight throws a reflection
On the dark stream,
Till all the eddies gleam;
And thereupon there comes that scream
From terrified, invisible beast or bird:
Image of poignant recollection.

SHE

An image of my heart that is smitten through
Out of all likelihood, or reason,
And when at last,
Youth's bitterness being past,
I had thought that all my days were cast
Amid most lovely places; smitten as though
It had not learned its lesson.

HE

Why have you laid your hands upon my eyes?
What can have suddenly alarmed you
Whereon 'twere best
My eyes should never rest?
What is there but the slowly fading west,
The river imaging the flashing skies,
All that to this moment charmed you?

SHE

A sweetheart from another life floats there
As though she had been forced to linger
From vague distress
Or arrogant loveliness,
Merely to loosen out a tress
Among the starry eddies of her hair
Upon the paleness of a finger.

HE

But why should you grow suddenly afraid
And start – I at your shoulder –
Imagining
That any night could bring
An image up, or anything
Even to eyes that beauty had driven mad,
But images to make me fonder?

SHE

Now she has thrown her arms above her head;
Whether she threw them up to flout me,
Or but to find,
Now that no fingers bind,
That her hair streams upon the wind,
I do not know, that know I am afraid
Of the hovering thing night brought me.

Under Saturn

Do not because this day I have grown saturnine
Imagine that lost love, inseparable from my thought
Because I have no other youth, can make me pine;
For how should I forget the wisdom that you brought,
The comfort that you made? Although my wits have gone
On a fantastic ride, my horse's flanks are spurred
By childish memories of an old cross Pollexfen,
And of a Middleton, whose name you never heard,
And of a red-haired Yeats whose looks, although he died
Before my time, seem like a vivid memory.
You heard that labouring man who had served my people. He said
Upon the open road, near to the Sligo quay –
No, no, not said, but cried it out – 'You have come again,
And surely after twenty years it was time to come.'
I am thinking of a child's vow sworn in vain
Never to leave that valley his fathers called their home.

Easter 1916

I have met them at close of day
Coming with vivid faces
From counter or desk among grey
Eighteenth-century houses.
I have passed with a nod of the head
Or polite meaningless words,
Or have lingered awhile and said
Polite meaningless words,
And thought before I had done
Of a mocking tale or a gibe
To please a companion
Around the fire at the club,
Being certain that they and I
But lived where motley is worn:
All changed, changed utterly:
A terrible beauty is born.

That woman's days were spent
In ignorant good-will,
Her nights in argument
Until her voice grew shrill.
What voice more sweet than hers
When, young and beautiful,
She rode to harriers?
This man had kept a school
And rode our wingèd horse;
This other his helper and friend
Was coming into his force;
He might have won fame in the end,
So sensitive his nature seemed,
So daring and sweet his thought.
This other man I had dreamed
A drunken, vainglorious lout.
He had done most bitter wrong
To some who are near my heart,
Yet I number him in the song;
He, too, has resigned his part

In the casual comedy;
He, too, has been changed in his turn,
Transformed utterly:
A terrible beauty is born.

Hearts with one purpose alone
Through summer and winter seem
Enchanted to a stone
To trouble the living stream.
The horse that comes from the road,
The rider, the birds that range
From cloud to tumbling cloud,
Minute by minute they change;
A shadow of cloud on the stream
Changes minute by minute;
A horse-hoof slides on the brim,
And a horse plashes within it;
The long-legged moor-hens dive,
And hens to moor-cocks call;
Minute by minute they live:
The stone's in the midst of all.

Too long a sacrifice
Can make a stone of the heart.
O when may it suffice?
That is Heaven's part, our part
To murmur name upon name,
As a mother names her child
When sleep at last has come
On limbs that had run wild.
What is it but nightfall?
No, no, not night but death;
Was it needless death after all?
For England may keep faith
For all that is done and said.
We know their dream; enough
To know they dreamed and are dead;
And what if excess of love
Bewildered them till they died?
I write it out in a verse –

MacDonagh and MacBride
And Connolly and Pearse
Now and in time to be,
Wherever green is worn,
Are changed, changed utterly:
A terrible beauty is born.

Sixteen Dead Men

O but we talked at large before
The sixteen men were shot,
But who can talk of give and take,
What should be and what not
While those dead men are loitering there
To stir the boiling pot?

You say that we should still the land
Till Germany's overcome;
But who is there to argue that
Now Pearse is deaf and dumb?
And is their logic to outweigh
MacDonagh's bony thumb?

How could you dream they'd listen
That have an ear alone
For those new comrades they have found,
Lord Edward and Wolfe Tone,
Or meddle with our give and take
That converse bone to bone?

The Rose Tree

'O words are lightly spoken,'
Said Pearse to Connolly,
'Maybe a breath of politic words
Has withered our Rose Tree;
Or maybe but a wind that blows
Across the bitter sea.'

'It needs to be but watered,'
James Connolly replied,
'To make the green come out again
And spread on every side,
And shake the blossom from the bud
To be the garden's pride.'

'But where can we draw water,'
Said Pearse to Connolly,
'When all the wells are parched away?
O plain as plain can be
There's nothing but our own red blood
Can make a right Rose Tree.'

On a Political Prisoner

She that but little patience knew,
From childhood on, had now so much
A grey gull lost its fear and flew
Down to her cell and there alit,
And there endured her fingers' touch
And from her fingers ate its bit.

Did she in touching that lone wing
Recall the years before her mind
Became a bitter, an abstract thing,

Her thought some popular enmity:
Blind and leader of the blind
Drinking the foul ditch where they lie?

When long ago I saw her ride
Under Ben Bulben to the meet,
The beauty of her country-side
With all youth's lonely wildness stirred,
She seemed to have grown clean and sweet
Like any rock-bred, sea-borne bird:

Sea-borne, or balanced on the air
When first it sprang out of the nest
Upon some lofty rock to stare
Upon the cloudy canopy,
While under its storm-beaten breast
Cried out the hollows of the sea.

The Leaders of the Crowd

They must to keep their certainty accuse
All that are different of a base intent;
Pull down established honour; hawk for news
Whatever their loose fantasy invent
And murmur it with bated breath, as though
The abounding gutter had been Helicon
Or calumny a song. How can they know
Truth flourishes where the student's lamp has shone,
And there alone, that have no solitude?
So the crowd come they care not what may come.
They have loud music, hope every day renewed
And heartier loves; that lamp is from the tomb.

Towards Break of Day

Was it the double of my dream
The woman that by me lay
Dreamed, or did we halve a dream
Under the first cold gleam of day?

I thought: 'There is a waterfall
Upon Ben Bulben side
That all my childhood counted dear;
Were I to travel far and wide
I could not find a thing so dear.'
My memories had magnified
So many times childish delight.

I would have touched it like a child
But knew my finger could but have touched
Cold stone and water. I grew wild,
Even accusing Heaven because
It had set down among its laws:
Nothing that we love over-much
Is ponderable to our touch.

I dreamed towards break of day,
The cold blown spray in my nostril.
But she that beside me lay
Had watched in bitterer sleep
The marvellous stag of Arthur,
That lofty white stag, leap
From mountain steep to steep.

Demon and Beast

For certain minutes at the least
That crafty demon and that loud beast
That plague me day and night
Ran out of my sight;
Though I had long perned in the gyre,
Between my hatred and desire,
I saw my freedom won
And all laugh in the sun.

The glittering eyes in a death's head
Of old Luke Wadding's portrait said
Welcome, and the Ormondes all
Nodded upon the wall,
And even Strafford smiled as though
It made him happier to know
I understood his plan.
Now that the loud beast ran
There was no portrait in the Gallery
But beckoned to sweet company,
For all men's thoughts grew clear
Being dear as mine are dear.

But soon a tear-drop started up,
For aimless joy had made me stop
Beside the little lake
To watch a white gull take
A bit of bread thrown up into the air;
Now gyring down and perning there
He splashed where an absurd
Portly green-pated bird
Shook off the water from his back;
Being no more demoniac
A stupid happy creature
Could rouse my whole nature.

Yet I am certain as can be
That every natural victory

Belongs to beast or demon,
That never yet had freeman
Right mastery of natural things,
And that mere growing old, that brings
Chilled blood, this sweetness brought;
Yet have no dearer thought
Than that I may find out a way
To make it linger half a day.

O what a sweetness strayed
Through barren Thebaid,
Or by the Mareotic sea
When that exultant Anthony
And twice a thousand more
Starved upon the shore
And withered to a bag of bones!
What had the Caesars but their thrones?

The Second Coming

Turning and turning in the widening gyre
The falcon cannot hear the falconer;
Things fall apart; the centre cannot hold;
Mere anarchy is loosed upon the world,
The blood-dimmed tide is loosed, and everywhere
The ceremony of innocence is drowned;
The best lack all conviction, while the worst
Are full of passionate intensity.

Surely some revelation is at hand;
Surely the Second Coming is at hand.
The Second Coming! Hardly are those words out
When a vast image out of *Spiritus Mundi*
Troubles my sight: somewhere in sands of the desert
A shape with lion body and the head of a man,
A gaze blank and pitiless as the sun,
Is moving its slow thighs, while all about it

Reel shadows of the indignant desert birds.
The darkness drops again; but now I know
That twenty centuries of stony sleep
Were vexed to nightmare by a rocking cradle,
And what rough beast, its hour come round at last,
Slouches towards Bethlehem to be born?

A Prayer for my Daughter

Once more the storm is howling, and half hid
Under this cradle-hood and coverlid
My child sleeps on. There is no obstacle
But Gregory's wood and one bare hill
Whereby the haystack- and roof-levelling wind,
Bred on the Atlantic, can be stayed;
And for an hour I have walked and prayed
Because of the great gloom that is in my mind.

I have walked and prayed for this young child an hour
And heard the sea-wind scream upon the tower,
And under the arches of the bridge, and scream
In the elms above the flooded stream;
Imagining in excited reverie
That the future years had come,
Dancing to a frenzied drum,
Out of the murderous innocence of the sea.

May she be granted beauty and yet not
Beauty to make a stranger's eye distraught,
Or hers before a looking-glass, for such,
Being made beautiful overmuch,
Consider beauty a sufficient end,
Lose natural kindness and maybe
The heart-revealing intimacy
That chooses right, and never find a friend.

Helen being chosen found life flat and dull
And later had much trouble from a fool,
While that great Queen, that rose out of the spray,
Being fatherless could have her way
Yet chose a bandy-leggèd smith for man.
It's certain that fine women eat
A crazy salad with their meat
Whereby the Horn of Plenty is undone.

In courtesy I'd have her chiefly learned;
Hearts are not had as a gift but hearts are earned
By those that are not entirely beautiful;
Yet many, that have played the fool
For beauty's very self, has charm made wise,
And many a poor man that has roved,
Loved and thought himself beloved,
From a glad kindness cannot take his eyes.

May she become a flourishing hidden tree
That all her thoughts may like the linnet be,
And have no business but dispensing round
Their magnanimities of sound,
Nor but in merriment begin a chase,
Nor but in merriment a quarrel.
O may she live like some green laurel
Rooted in one dear perpetual place.

My mind, because the minds that I have loved,
The sort of beauty that I have approved,
Prosper but little, has dried up of late,
Yet knows that to be choked with hate
May well be of all evil chances chief.
If there's no hatred in a mind
Assault and battery of the wind
Can never tear the linnet from the leaf.

An intellectual hatred is the worst,
So let her think opinions are accursed.
Have I not seen the loveliest woman born
Out of the mouth of Plenty's horn,

Because of her opinionated mind
Barter that horn and every good
By quiet natures understood
For an old bellows full of angry wind?

Considering that, all hatred driven hence,
The soul recovers radical innocence
And learns at last that it is self-delighting,
Self-appeasing, self-affrighting,
And that its own sweet will is Heaven's will;
She can, though every face should scowl
And every windy quarter howl
Or every bellows burst, be happy still.

And may her bridegroom bring her to a house
Where all's accustomed, ceremonious;
For arrogance and hatred are the wares
Peddled in the thoroughfares.
How but in custom and in ceremony
Are innocence and beauty born?
Ceremony's a name for the rich horn,
And custom for the spreading laurel tree.

A Meditation in Time of War

For one throb of the artery,
While on that old grey stone I sat
Under the old wind-broken tree,
I knew that One is animate,
Mankind inanimate phantasy.

To be Carved on a Stone at Thoor Ballylee

I, the poet William Yeats,
With old mill boards and sea-green slates,
And smithy work from the Gort forge,
Restored this tower for my wife George;
And may these characters remain
When all is ruin once again.

THE TOWER
1928

THE TOWER

Sailing to Byzantium

I

That is no country for old men. The young
In one another's arms, birds in the trees
– Those dying generations – at their song,
The salmon-falls, the mackerel-crowded seas,
Fish, flesh, or fowl, commend all summer long
Whatever is begotten, born, and dies.
Caught in that sensual music all neglect
Monuments of unageing intellect.

II

An aged man is but a paltry thing,
A tattered coat upon a stick, unless
Soul clap its hands and sing, and louder sing
For every tatter in its mortal dress,
Nor is there singing school but studying
Monuments of its own magnificence;
And therefore I have sailed the seas and come
To the holy city of Byzantium.

III

O sages standing in God's holy fire
As in the gold mosaic of a wall,
Come from the holy fire, perne in a gyre,
And be the singing-masters of my soul.
Consume my heart away; sick with desire
And fastened to a dying animal
It knows not what it is; and gather me
Into the artifice of eternity.

IV

Once out of nature I shall never take
My bodily form from any natural thing,
But such a form as Grecian goldsmiths make
Of hammered gold and gold enamelling
To keep a drowsy Emperor awake;
Or set upon a golden bough to sing
To lords and ladies of Byzantium
Of what is past, or passing, or to come.

The Tower

I

What shall I do with this absurdity –
O heart, O troubled heart – this caricature,
Decrepit age that has been tied to me
As to a dog's tail?
                          Never had I more
Excited, passionate, fantastical
Imagination, nor an ear and eye
That more expected the impossible –
No, not in boyhood when with rod and fly,
Or the humbler worm, I climbed Ben Bulben's back
And had the livelong summer day to spend.
It seems that I must bid the Muse go pack,
Choose Plato and Plotinus for a friend
Until imagination, ear and eye,
Can be content with argument and deal
In abstract things; or be derided by
A sort of battered kettle at the heel.

II

I pace upon the battlements and stare
On the foundations of a house, or where
Tree, like a sooty finger, starts from the earth;
And send imagination forth

Under the day's declining beam, and call
Images and memories
From ruin or from ancient trees,
For I would ask a question of them all.

Beyond that ridge lived Mrs. French, and once
When every silver candlestick or sconce
Lit up the dark mahogany and the wine,
A serving-man, that could divine
That most respected lady's every wish,
Ran and with the garden shears
Clipped an insolent farmer's ears
And brought them in a little covered dish.

Some few remembered still when I was young
A peasant girl commended by a song,
Who'd lived somewhere upon that rocky place,
And praised the colour of her face,
And had the greater joy in praising her,
Remembering that, if walked she there,
Farmers jostled at the fair
So great a glory did the song confer.

And certain men, being maddened by those rhymes,
Or else by toasting her a score of times,
Rose from the table and declared it right
To test their fancy by their sight;
But they mistook the brightness of the moon
For the prosaic light of day –
Music had driven their wits astray –
And one was drowned in the great bog of Cloone.

Strange, but the man who made the song was blind;
Yet, now I have considered it, I find
That nothing strange; the tragedy began
With Homer that was a blind man,
And Helen has all living hearts betrayed.
O may the moon and sunlight seem
One inextricable beam,
For if I triumph I must make men mad.

And I myself created Hanrahan
And drove him drunk or sober through the dawn
From somewhere in the neighbouring cottages.
Caught by an old man's juggleries
He stumbled, tumbled, fumbled to and fro
And had but broken knees for hire
And horrible splendour of desire;
I thought it all out twenty years ago:

Good fellows shuffled cards in an old bawn;
And when that ancient ruffian's turn was on
He so bewitched the cards under his thumb
That all but the one card became
A pack of hounds and not a pack of cards,
And that he changed into a hare.
Hanrahan rose in frenzy there
And followed up those baying creatures towards –

O towards I have forgotten what – enough!
I must recall a man that neither love
Nor music nor an enemy's clipped ear
Could, he was so harried, cheer;
A figure that has grown so fabulous
There's not a neighbour left to say
When he finished his dog's day:
An ancient bankrupt master of this house.

Before that ruin came, for centuries,
Rough men-at-arms, cross-gartered to the knees
Or shod in iron, climbed the narrow stairs,
And certain men-at-arms there were
Whose images, in the Great Memory stored,
Come with loud cry and panting breast
To break upon a sleeper's rest
While their great wooden dice beat on the board.

As I would question all, come all who can;
Come old, necessitous, half-mounted man;
And bring beauty's blind rambling celebrant;
The red man the juggler sent

Through God-forsaken meadows; Mrs. French,
Gifted with so fine an ear;
The man drowned in a bog's mire,
When mocking Muses chose the country wench.

Did all old men and women, rich and poor,
Who trod upon these rocks or passed this door,
Whether in public or in secret rage
As I do now against old age?
But I have found an answer in those eyes
That are impatient to be gone;
Go therefore; but leave Hanrahan,
For I need all his mighty memories.

Old lecher with a love on every wind,
Bring up out of that deep considering mind
All that you have discovered in the grave,
For it is certain that you have
Reckoned up every unforeknown, unseeing
Plunge, lured by a softening eye,
Or by a touch or a sigh,
Into the labyrinth of another's being;

Does the imagination dwell the most
Upon a woman won or woman lost?
If on the lost, admit you turned aside
From a great labyrinth out of pride,
Cowardice, some silly over-subtle thought
Or anything called conscience once;
And that if memory recur, the sun's
Under eclipse and the day blotted out.

III

It is time that I wrote my will;
I choose upstanding men
That climb the streams until
The fountain leap, and at dawn
Drop their cast at the side
Of dripping stone; I declare

They shall inherit my pride,
The pride of people that were
Bound neither to Cause nor to State,
Neither to slaves that were spat on,
Nor to the tyrants that spat,
The people of Burke and of Grattan
That gave, though free to refuse –
Pride, like that of the morn,
When the headlong light is loose,
Or that of the fabulous horn,
Or that of the sudden shower
When all streams are dry,
Or that of the hour
When the swan must fix his eye
Upon a fading gleam,
Float out upon a long
Last reach of glittering stream
And there sing his last song.
And I declare my faith:
I mock Plotinus' thought
And cry in Plato's teeth,
Death and life were not
Till man made up the whole,
Made lock, stock and barrel
Out of his bitter soul,
Aye, sun and moon and star, all,
And further add to that
That, being dead, we rise,
Dream and so create
Translunar Paradise.
I have prepared my peace
With learned Italian things
And the proud stones of Greece,
Poet's imaginings
And memories of love,
Memories of the words of women,
All those things whereof
Man makes a superhuman
Mirror-resembling dream.

As at the loophole there
The daws chatter and scream,
And drop twigs layer upon layer.
When they have mounted up,
The mother bird will rest
On their hollow top,
And so warm her wild nest.

I leave both faith and pride
To young upstanding men
Climbing the mountain-side,
That under bursting dawn
They may drop a fly;
Being of that metal made
Till it was broken by
This sedentary trade.

Now shall I make my soul,
Compelling it to study
In a learned school
Till the wreck of body,
Slow decay of blood,
Testy delirium
Or dull decrepitude,
Or what worse evil come –
The death of friends, or death
Of every brilliant eye
That made a catch in the breath –
Seem but the clouds of the sky
When the horizon fades,
Or a bird's sleepy cry
Among the deepening shades.

Meditations in Time of Civil War

I

ANCESTRAL HOUSES

Surely among a rich man's flowering lawns,
Amid the rustle of his planted hills,
Life overflows without ambitious pains;
And rains down life until the basin spills,
And mounts more dizzy high the more it rains
As though to choose whatever shape it wills
And never stoop to a mechanical
Or servile shape, at others' beck and call.

Mere dreams, mere dreams! Yet Homer had not sung
Had he not found it certain beyond dreams
That out of life's own self-delight had sprung
The abounding glittering jet; though now it seems
As if some marvellous empty sea-shell flung
Out of the obscure dark of the rich streams,
And not a fountain, were the symbol which
Shadows the inherited glory of the rich.

Some violent bitter man, some powerful man
Called architect and artist in, that they,
Bitter and violent men, might rear in stone
The sweetness that all longed for night and day,
The gentleness none there had ever known;
But when the master's buried mice can play,
And maybe the great-grandson of that house,
For all its bronze and marble, 's but a mouse.

O what if gardens where the peacock strays
With delicate feet upon old terraces,
Or else all Juno from an urn displays
Before the indifferent garden deities;
O what if levelled lawns and gravelled ways
Where slippered Contemplation finds his ease
And Childhood a delight for every sense,
But take our greatness with our violence?

What if the glory of escutcheoned doors,
And buildings that a haughtier age designed,
The pacing to and fro on polished floors
Amid great chambers and long galleries, lined
With famous portraits of our ancestors;
What if those things the greatest of mankind
Consider most to magnify, or to bless,
But take our greatness with our bitterness?

II

MY HOUSE

An ancient bridge, and a more ancient tower,
A farmhouse that is sheltered by its wall,
An acre of stony ground,
Where the symbolic rose can break in flower,
Old ragged elms, old thorns innumerable,
The sound of the rain or sound
Of every wind that blows;
The stilted water-hen
Crossing stream again
Scared by the splashing of a dozen cows;

A winding stair, a chamber arched with stone,
A grey stone fireplace with an open hearth,
A candle and written page.
Il Penseroso's Platonist toiled on
In some like chamber, shadowing forth
How the daemonic rage
Imagined everything.
Benighted travellers
From markets and from fairs
Have seen his midnight candle glimmering.

Two men have founded here. A man-at-arms
Gathered a score of horse and spent his days
In this tumultuous spot,
Where through long wars and sudden night alarms
His dwindling score and he seemed castaways
Forgetting and forgot;

And I, that after me
My bodily heirs may find,
To exalt a lonely mind,
Befitting emblems of adversity.

III
MY TABLE

Two heavy trestles, and a board
Where Sato's gift, a changeless sword,
By pen and paper lies,
That it may moralise
My days out of their aimlessness.
A bit of an embroidered dress
Covers its wooden sheath.
Chaucer had not drawn breath
When it was forged. In Sato's house,
Curved like new moon, moon-luminous,
It lay five hundred years.
Yet if no change appears
No moon; only an aching heart
Conceives a changeless work of art.
Our learned men have urged
That when and where 'twas forged
A marvellous accomplishment,
In painting or in pottery, went
From father unto son
And through the centuries ran
And seemed unchanging like the sword.
Soul's beauty being most adored,
Men and their business took
The soul's unchanging look;
For the most rich inheritor,
Knowing that none could pass Heaven's door
That loved inferior art,
Had such an aching heart
That he, although a country's talk
For silken clothes and stately walk,
Had waking wits; it seemed
Juno's peacock screamed.

IV

MY DESCENDANTS

Having inherited a vigorous mind
From my old fathers, I must nourish dreams
And leave a woman and a man behind
As vigorous of mind, and yet it seems
Life scarce can cast a fragrance on the wind,
Scarce spread a glory to the morning beams,
But the torn petals strew the garden plot;
And there's but common greenness after that.

And what if my descendants lose the flower
Through natural declension of the soul,
Through too much business with the passing hour,
Through too much play, or marriage with a fool?
May this laborious stair and this stark tower
Become a roofless ruin that the owl
May build in the cracked masonry and cry
Her desolation to the desolate sky.

The Primum Mobile that fashioned us
Has made the very owls in circles move;
And I, that count myself most prosperous,
Seeing that love and friendship are enough,
For an old neighbour's friendship chose the house
And decked and altered it for a girl's love,
And know whatever flourish and decline
These stones remain their monument and mine.

V

THE ROAD AT MY DOOR

An affable Irregular,
A heavily-built Falstaffian man,
Comes cracking jokes of civil war
As though to die by gunshot were
The finest play under the sun.

A brown Lieutenant and his men,
Half dressed in national uniform,
Stand at my door, and I complain
Of the foul weather, hail and rain,
A pear tree broken by the storm.

I count those feathered balls of soot
The moor-hen guides upon the stream,
To silence the envy in my thought;
And turn towards my chamber, caught
In the cold snows of a dream.

VI

THE STARE'S NEST BY MY WINDOW

The bees build in the crevices
Of loosening masonry, and there
The mother birds bring grubs and flies.
My wall is loosening; honey-bees,
Come build in the empty house of the stare.

We are closed in, and the key is turned
On our uncertainty; somewhere
A man is killed, or a house burned,
Yet no clear fact to be discerned:
Come build in the empty house of the stare.

A barricade of stone or of wood;
Some fourteen days of civil war;
Last night they trundled down the road
That dead young soldier in his blood:
Come build in the empty house of the stare.

We had fed the heart on fantasies,
The heart's grown brutal from the fare;
More substance in our enmities
Than in our love; O honey-bees,
Come build in the empty house of the stare.

VII

I SEE PHANTOMS OF HATRED AND OF THE HEART'S FULLNESS AND OF THE COMING EMPTINESS

I climb to the tower-top and lean upon broken stone,
A mist that is like blown snow is sweeping over all,
Valley, river, and elms, under the light of a moon
That seems unlike itself, that seems unchangeable,
A glittering sword out of the east. A puff of wind
And those white glimmering fragments of the mist sweep by.
Frenzies bewilder, reveries perturb the mind;
Monstrous familiar images swim to the mind's eye.

'Vengeance upon the murderers,' the cry goes up,
'Vengeance for Jacques Molay.' In cloud-pale rags, or in lace,
The rage-driven, rage-tormented, and rage-hungry troop,
Trooper belabouring trooper, biting at arm or at face,
Plunges towards nothing, arms and fingers spreading wide
For the embrace of nothing; and I, my wits astray
Because of all that senseless tumult, all but cried
For vengeance on the murderers of Jacques Molay.

Their legs long, delicate and slender, aquamarine their eyes,
Magical unicorns bear ladies on their backs.
The ladies close their musing eyes. No prophecies,
Remembered out of Babylonian almanacs,
Have closed the ladies' eyes, their minds are but a pool
Where even longing drowns under its own excess;
Nothing but stillness can remain when hearts are full
Of their own sweetness, bodies of their loveliness.

The cloud-pale unicorns, the eyes of aquamarine,
The quivering half-closed eyelids, the rags of cloud or of lace,
Or eyes that rage has brightened, arms it has made lean,
Give place to an indifferent multitude, give place
To brazen hawks. Nor self-delighting reverie,
Nor hate of what's to come, nor pity for what's gone,
Nothing but grip of claw, and the eye's complacency,
The innumerable clanging wings that have put out the moon.

I turn away and shut the door, and on the stair
Wonder how many times I could have proved my worth
In something that all others understand or share;
But O! ambitious heart, had such a proof drawn forth
A company of friends, a conscience set at ease,
It had but made us pine the more. The abstract joy,
The half-read wisdom of daemonic images,
Suffice the ageing man as once the growing boy.

Nineteen Hundred and Nineteen

I

Many ingenious lovely things are gone
That seemed sheer miracle to the multitude,
Protected from the circle of the moon
That pitches common things about. There stood
Amid the ornamental bronze and stone
An ancient image made of olive wood –
And gone are Phidias' famous ivories
And all the golden grasshoppers and bees.

We too had many pretty toys when young:
A law indifferent to blame or praise,
To bribe or threat; habits that made old wrong
Melt down, as it were wax in the sun's rays;
Public opinion ripening for so long
We thought it would outlive all future days.
O what fine thought we had because we thought
That the worst rogues and rascals had died out.

All teeth were drawn, all ancient tricks unlearned,
And a great army but a showy thing;
What matter that no cannon had been turned
Into a ploughshare! Parliament and king
Thought that unless a little powder burned
The trumpeters might burst with trumpeting
And yet it lack all glory; and perchance
The guardsmen's drowsy chargers would not prance.

Now days are dragon-ridden, the nightmare
Rides upon sleep: a drunken soldiery
Can leave the mother, murdered at her door,
To crawl in her own blood, and go scot-free;
The night can sweat with terror as before
We pieced our thoughts into philosophy,
And planned to bring the world under a rule,
Who are but weasels fighting in a hole.

He who can read the signs nor sink unmanned
Into the half-deceit of some intoxicant
From shallow wits; who knows no work can stand,
Whether health, wealth or peace of mind were spent
On master-work of intellect or hand,
No honour leave its mighty monument,
Has but one comfort left: all triumph would
But break upon his ghostly solitude.

But is there any comfort to be found?
Man is in love and loves what vanishes,
What more is there to say? That country round
None dared admit, if such a thought were his,
Incendiary or bigot could be found
To burn that stump on the Acropolis,
Or break in bits the famous ivories
Or traffic in the grasshoppers or bees.

II

When Loie Fuller's Chinese dancers enwound
A shining web, a floating ribbon of cloth,
It seemed that a dragon of air
Had fallen among dancers, had whirled them round
Or hurried them off on its own furious path;
So the Platonic Year
Whirls out new right and wrong,
Whirls in the old instead;
All men are dancers and their tread
Goes to the barbarous clangour of a gong.

III

Some moralist or mythological poet
Compares the solitary soul to a swan;
I am satisfied with that,
Satisfied if a troubled mirror show it,
Before that brief gleam of its life be gone,
An image of its state;
The wings half spread for flight,
The breast thrust out in pride
Whether to play, or to ride
Those winds that clamour of approaching night.

A man in his own secret meditation
Is lost amid the labyrinth that he has made
In art or politics;
Some Platonist affirms that in the station
Where we should cast off body and trade
The ancient habit sticks,
And that if our works could
But vanish with our breath
That were a lucky death,
For triumph can but mar our solitude.

The swan has leaped into the desolate heaven:
That image can bring wildness, bring a rage
To end all things, to end
What my laborious life imagined, even
The half-imagined, the half-written page;
O but we dreamed to mend
Whatever mischief seemed
To afflict mankind, but now
That winds of winter blow
Learn that we were crack-pated when we dreamed

IV

We, who seven years ago
Talked of honour and of truth,
Shriek with pleasure if we show
The weasel's twist, the weasel's tooth.

V

Come let us mock at the great
That had such burdens on the mind
And toiled so hard and late
To leave some monument behind,
Nor thought of the levelling wind.

Come let us mock at the wise;
With all those calendars whereon
They fixed old aching eyes,
They never saw how seasons run,
And now but gape at the sun.

Come let us mock at the good
That fancied goodness might be gay,
And sick of solitude
Might proclaim a holiday:
Wind shrieked – and where are they?

Mock mockers after that
That would not lift a hand maybe
To help good, wise or great
To bar that foul storm out, for we
Traffic in mockery.

VI

Violence upon the roads: violence of horses;
Some few have handsome riders, are garlanded
On delicate sensitive ear or tossing mane,
But wearied running round and round in their courses
All break and vanish, and evil gathers head:
Herodias' daughters have returned again,
A sudden blast of dusty wind and after
Thunder of feet, tumult of images,
Their purpose in the labyrinth of the wind;
And should some crazy hand dare touch a daughter
All turn with amorous cries, or angry cries,
According to the wind, for all are blind.

But now wind drops, dust settles; thereupon
There lurches past, his great eyes without thought
Under the shadow of stupid straw-pale locks,
That insolent fiend Robert Artisson
To whom the love-lorn Lady Kyteler brought
Bronzed peacock feathers, red combs of her cocks.

The Wheel

Through winter-time we call on spring,
And through the spring on summer call,
And when abounding hedges ring
Declare that winter's best of all;
And after that there's nothing good
Because the spring-time has not come –
Nor know that what disturbs our blood
Is but its longing for the tomb.

Youth and Age

Much did I rage when young,
Being by the world oppressed,
But now with flattering tongue
It speeds the parting guest.

The New Faces

If you, that have grown old, were the first dead,
Neither catalpa tree nor scented lime
Should hear my living feet, nor would I tread
Where we wrought that shall break the teeth of Time.

Let the new faces play what tricks they will
In the old rooms; night can outbalance day,
Our shadows rove the garden gravel still,
The living seem more shadowy than they.

A Prayer for my Son

Bid a strong ghost stand at the head
That my Michael may sleep sound,
Nor cry, nor turn in the bed
Till his morning meal come round;
And may departing twilight keep
All dread afar till morning's back,
That his mother may not lack
Her fill of sleep.

Bid the ghost have sword in fist:
Some there are, for I avow
Such devilish things exist,
Who have planned his murder, for they know
Of some most haughty deed or thought
That waits upon his future days,
And would through hatred of the bays
Bring that to nought.

Though You can fashion everything
From nothing every day, and teach
The morning stars to sing,
You have lacked articulate speech
To tell Your simplest want, and known,
Wailing upon a woman's knee,
All of that worst ignominy
Of flesh and bone;

And when through all the town there ran
The servants of Your enemy,
A woman and a man,
Unless the Holy Writings lie,

Hurried through the smooth and rough
And through the fertile and waste,
Protecting, till the danger past,
With human love.

Two Songs from a Play

I

I saw a staring virgin stand
Where holy Dionysus died,
And tear the heart out of his side,
And lay the heart upon her hand
And bear that beating heart away;
And then did all the Muses sing
Of Magnus Annus at the spring,
As though God's death were but a play.

Another Troy must rise and set,
Another lineage feed the crow,
Another Argo's painted prow
Drive to a flashier bauble yet.
The Roman Empire stood appalled:
It dropped the reins of peace and war
When that fierce virgin and her Star
Out of the fabulous darkness called.

II

In pity for man's darkening thought
He walked that room and issued thence
In Galilean turbulence;
The Babylonian starlight brought
A fabulous, formless darkness in;
Odour of blood when Christ was slain
Made all Platonic tolerance vain
And vain all Doric discipline.

Everything that man esteems
Endures a moment or a day.
Love's pleasure drives his love away,
The painter's brush consumes his dreams;
The herald's cry, the soldier's tread
Exhaust his glory and his might:
Whatever flames upon the night
Man's own resinous heart has fed.

Fragments

I

Locke sank into a swoon;
The Garden died;
God took the spinning-jenny
Out of his side.

II

Where got I that truth?
Out of a medium's mouth,
Out of nothing it came,
Out of the forest loam,
Out of dark night where lay
The crowns of Nineveh.

Wisdom

The true faith discovered was
When painted panel, statuary,
Glass-mosaic, window-glass,
Amended what was told awry

By some peasant gospeller;
Swept the sawdust from the floor
Of that working-carpenter.
Miracle had its playtime where
In damask clothed and on a seat
Chryselephantine, cedar-boarded,
His majestic Mother sat
Stitching at a purple hoarded
That He might be nobly breeched
In starry towers of Babylon
Noah's freshet never reached.
King Abundance got Him on
Innocence; and Wisdom He.
That cognomen sounded best
Considering what wild infancy
Drove horror from His Mother's breast.

Leda and the Swan

A sudden blow: the great wings beating still
Above the staggering girl, her thighs caressed
By the dark webs, her nape caught in his bill,
He holds her helpless breast upon his breast.

How can those terrified vague fingers push
The feathered glory from her loosening thighs?
And how can body, laid in that white rush,
But feel the strange heart beating where it lies?

A shudder in the loins engenders there
The broken wall, the burning roof and tower
And Agamemnon dead.
                              Being so caught up,
So mastered by the brute blood of the air,
Did she put on his knowledge with his power
Before the indifferent beak could let her drop?

On a Picture of a Black Centaur
by Edmund Dulac

Your hooves have stamped at the black margin of the wood,
Even where horrible green parrots call and swing.
My works are all stamped down into the sultry mud.
I knew that horse-play, knew it for a murderous thing.
What wholesome sun has ripened is wholesome food to eat,
And that alone; yet I, being driven half insane
Because of some green wing, gathered old mummy wheat
In the mad abstract dark and ground it grain by grain
And after baked it slowly in an oven; but now
I bring full-flavoured wine out of a barrel found
Where seven Ephesian topers slept and never knew
When Alexander's empire passed, they slept so sound.
Stretch out your limbs and sleep a long Saturnian sleep;
I have loved you better than my soul for all my words,
And there is none so fit to keep a watch and keep
Unwearied eyes upon those horrible green birds.

Among School Children

I

I walk through the long schoolroom questioning;
A kind old nun in a white hood replies;
The children learn to cipher and to sing,
To study reading-books and history,
To cut and sew, be neat in everything
In the best modern way – the children's eyes
In momentary wonder stare upon
A sixty-year-old smiling public man.

II

I dream of a Ledaean body, bent
Above a sinking fire, a tale that she
Told of a harsh reproof, or trivial event
That changed some childish day to tragedy –
Told, and it seemed that our two natures blent
Into a sphere from youthful sympathy,
Or else, to alter Plato's parable,
Into the yolk and white of the one shell.

III

And thinking of that fit of grief or rage
I look upon one child or t'other there
And wonder if she stood so at that age –
For even daughters of the swan can share
Something of every paddler's heritage –
And had that colour upon cheek or hair,
And thereupon my heart is driven wild:
She stands before me as a living child.

IV

Her present image floats into the mind –
Did Quattrocento finger fashion it
Hollow of cheek as though it drank the wind
And took a mess of shadows for its meat?
And I though never of Ledaean kind
Had pretty plumage once – enough of that,
Better to smile on all that smile, and show
There is a comfortable kind of old scarecrow.

V

What youthful mother, a shape upon her lap
Honey of generation had betrayed,
And that must sleep, shriek, struggle to escape
As recollection or the drug decide,

Would think her son, did she but see that shape
With sixty or more winters on its head,
A compensation for the pang of his birth,
Or the uncertainty of his setting forth?

VI

Plato thought nature but a spume that plays
Upon a ghostly paradigm of things;
Solider Aristotle played the taws
Upon the bottom of a king of kings;
World-famous golden-thighed Pythagoras
Fingered upon a fiddle-stick or strings
What a star sang and careless Muses heard:
Old clothes upon old sticks to scare a bird.

VII

Both nuns and mothers worship images,
But those the candles light are not as those
That animate a mother's reveries,
But keep a marble or a bronze repose.
And yet they too break hearts – O Presences
That passion, piety or affection knows,
And that all heavenly glory symbolise –
O self-born mockers of man's enterprise;

VIII

Labour is blossoming or dancing where
The body is not bruised to pleasure soul,
Nor beauty born out of its own despair,
Nor blear-eyed wisdom out of midnight oil.
O chestnut tree, great rooted blossomer,
Are you the leaf, the blossom or the bole?
O body swayed to music, O brightening glance,
How can we know the dancer from the dance?

Colonus' Praise
(From 'Oedipus at Colonus')

CHORUS

Come praise Colonus' horses, and come praise
The wine-dark of the wood's intricacies,
The nightingale that deafens daylight there,
If daylight ever visit where,
Unvisited by tempest or by sun,
Immortal ladies tread the ground
Dizzy with harmonious sound,
Semele's lad a gay companion.

And yonder in the gymnasts' garden thrives
The self-sown, self-begotten shape that gives
Athenian intellect its mastery,
Even the grey-leaved olive-tree
Miracle-bred out of the living stone;
Nor accident of peace nor war
Shall wither that old marvel, for
The great grey-eyed Athene stares thereon.

Who comes into this country, and has come
Where golden crocus and narcissus bloom,
Where the Great Mother, mourning for her daughter
And beauty-drunken by the water
Glittering among grey-leaved olive-trees,
Has plucked a flower and sung her loss;
Who finds abounding Cephisus
Has found the loveliest spectacle there is.

Because this country has a pious mind
And so remembers that when all mankind
But trod the road, or splashed about the shore,
Poseidon gave it bit and oar,
Every Colonus lad or lass discourses
Of that oar and of that bit;
Summer and winter, day and night,
Of horses and horses of the sea, white horses.

The Fool by the Roadside

When all works that have
From cradle run to grave
From grave to cradle run instead;
When thoughts that a fool
Has wound upon a spool
Are but loose thread, are but loose thread;

When cradle and spool are past
And I mere shade at last
Coagulate of stuff
Transparent like the wind,
I think that I may find
A faithful love, a faithful love.

Owen Aherne and his Dancers

I

A strange thing surely that my Heart, when love had come
   unsought
Upon the Norman upland or in that poplar shade,
Should find no burden but itself and yet should be worn out.
It could not bear that burden and therefore it went mad.

The south wind brought it longing, and the east wind despair,
The west wind made it pitiful, and the north wind afraid.
It feared to give its love a hurt with all the tempest there;
It feared the hurt that she could give and therefore it went mad.

I can exchange opinion with any neighbouring mind,
I have as healthy flesh and blood as any rhymer's had,
But O! my Heart could bear no more when the upland caught the
   wind;
I ran, I ran, from my love's side because my Heart went mad.

II

The Heart behind its rib laughed out. 'You have called me mad,' it
      said,
'Because I made you turn away and run from that young child;
How could she mate with fifty years that was so wildly bred?
Let the cage bird and the cage bird mate and the wild bird mate in
      the wild.'

'You but imagine lies all day, O murderer,' I replied.
'And all those lies have but one end, poor wretches to betray;
I did not find in any cage the woman at my side.
O but her heart would break to learn my thoughts are far away.'

'Speak all your mind,' my Heart sang out, 'speak all your mind;
      who cares,
Now that your tongue cannot persuade the child till she mistake
Her childish gratitude for love and match your fifty years?
O let her choose a young man now and all for his wild sake.'

A Man Young and Old

I

FIRST LOVE

Though nurtured like the sailing moon
In beauty's murderous brood,
She walked awhile and blushed awhile
And on my pathway stood
Until I thought her body bore
A heart of flesh and blood.

But since I laid a hand thereon
And found a heart of stone
I have attempted many things
And not a thing is done,

For every hand is lunatic
That travels on the moon.

She smiled and that transfigured me
And left me but a lout,
Maundering here, and maundering there,
Emptier of thought
Than the heavenly circuit of its stars
When the moon sails out.

II

HUMAN DIGNITY

Like the moon her kindness is,
If kindness I may call
What has no comprehension in't,
But is the same for all
As though my sorrow were a scene
Upon a painted wall.

So like a bit of stone I lie
Under a broken tree.
I could recover if I shrieked
My heart's agony
To passing bird, but I am dumb
From human dignity.

III

THE MERMAID

A mermaid found a swimming lad,
Picked him for her own,
Pressed her body to his body,
Laughed; and plunging down
Forgot in cruel happiness
That even lovers drown.

IV

THE DEATH OF THE HARE

I have pointed out the yelling pack,
The hare leap to the wood,
And when I pass a compliment
Rejoice as lover should
At the drooping of an eye,
At the mantling of the blood.

Then suddenly my heart is wrung
By her distracted air
And I remember wildness lost
And after, swept from there,
Am set down standing in the wood
At the death of the hare.

V

THE EMPTY CUP

A crazy man that found a cup,
When all but dead of thirst,
Hardly dared to wet his mouth
Imagining, moon-accursed,
That another mouthful
And his beating heart would burst.
October last I found it too
But found it dry as bone,
And for that reason am I crazed
And my sleep is gone.

VI

HIS MEMORIES

We should be hidden from their eyes,
Being but holy shows
And bodies broken like a thorn
Whereon the bleak north blows,

To think of buried Hector
And that none living knows.

The women take so little stock
In what I do or say
They'd sooner leave their cosseting
To hear a jackass bray;
My arms are like the twisted thorn
And yet there beauty lay;

The first of all the tribe lay there
And did such pleasure take –
She who had brought great Hector down
And put all Troy to wreck –
That she cried into this ear,
'Strike me if I shriek.'

VII

THE FRIENDS OF HIS YOUTH

Laughter not time destroyed my voice
And put that crack in it,
And when the moon's pot-bellied
I get a laughing fit,
For that old Madge comes down the lane,
A stone upon her breast,
And a cloak wrapped about the stone,
And she can get no rest
With singing hush and hush-a-bye;
She that has been wild
And barren as a breaking wave
Thinks that the stone's a child.

And Peter that had great affairs
And was a pushing man
Shrieks, 'I am King of the Peacocks,'
And perches on a stone;
And then I laugh till tears run down
And the heart thumps at my side,
Remembering that her shriek was love
And that he shrieks from pride.

VIII

SUMMER AND SPRING

We sat under an old thorn-tree
And talked away the night,
Told all that had been said or done
Since first we saw the light,
And when we talked of growing up
Knew that we'd halved a soul
And fell the one in t'other's arms
That we might make it whole;
Then Peter had a murdering look,
For it seemed that he and she
Had spoken of their childish days
Under that very tree.
O what a bursting out there was,
And what a blossoming,
When we had all the summer-time
And she had all the spring!

IX

THE SECRETS OF THE OLD

I have old women's secrets now
That had those of the young;
Madge tells me what I dared not think
When my blood was strong,
And what had drowned a lover once
Sounds like an old song.

Though Margery is stricken dumb
If thrown in Madge's way,
We three make up a solitude;
For none alive to-day
Can know the stories that we know
Or say the things we say:

How such a man pleased women most
Of all that are gone,
How such a pair loved many years
And such a pair but one,
Stories of the bed of straw
Or the bed of down.

X

HIS WILDNESS

O bid me mount and sail up there
Amid the cloudy wrack,
For Peg and Meg and Paris' love
That had so straight a back,
Are gone away, and some that stay
Have changed their silk for sack.

Were I but there and none to hear
I'd have a peacock cry,
For that is natural to a man
That lives in memory,
Being all alone I'd nurse a stone
And sing it lullaby.

X I

FROM 'OEDIPUS AT COLONUS'

Endure what life God gives and ask no longer span;
Cease to remember the delights of youth, travel-wearied aged
    man;
Delight becomes death-longing if all longing else be vain.

Even from that delight memory treasures so,
Death, despair, division of families, all entanglements of mankind
    grow,
As that old wandering beggar and these God-hated children know.

In the long echoing street the laughing dancers throng,
The bride is carried to the bridegroom's chamber through
    torchlight and tumultuous song;
I celebrate the silent kiss that ends short life or long.

Never to have lived is best, ancient writers say;
Never to have drawn the breath of life, never to have looked into
    the eye of day;
The second best's a gay goodnight and quickly turn away.

The Three Monuments

They hold their public meetings where
Our most renownèd patriots stand,
One among the birds of the air,
A stumpier on either hand;
And all the popular statesmen say
That purity built up the State
And after kept it from decay;
Admonish us to cling to that
And let all base ambition be,
For intellect would make us proud
And pride bring in impurity:
The three old rascals laugh aloud.

The Gift of Harun Al-Rashid

Kusta ben Luka is my name, I write
To Abd Al-Rabban; fellow-roysterer once,
Now the good Caliph's learned Treasurer,
And for no ear but his.

                              Carry this letter
Through the great gallery of the Treasure House
Where banners of the Caliphs hang, night-coloured
But brilliant as the night's embroidery,
And wait war's music; pass the little gallery;
Pass books of learning from Byzantium
Written in gold upon a purple stain,
And pause at last, I was about to say,
At the great book of Sappho's song; but no,
For should you leave my letter there, a boy's
Love-lorn, indifferent hands might come upon it
And let it fall unnoticed to the floor.
Pause at the Treatise of Parmenides
And hide it there, for Caliphs to world's end
Must keep that perfect, as they keep her song,
So great its fame.
                              When fitting time has passed
The parchment will disclose to some learned man
A mystery that else had found no chronicler
But the wild Bedouin. Though I approve
Those wanderers that welcomed in their tents
What great Harun Al-Rashid, occupied
With Persian embassy or Grecian war,
Must needs neglect, I cannot hide the truth
That wandering in a desert, featureless
As air under a wing, can give birds' wit.
In after time they will speak much of me
And speak but fantasy. Recall the year
When our beloved Caliph put to death
His Vizir Jaffer for an unknown reason:
'If but the shirt upon my body knew it
I'd tear it off and throw it in the fire.'
That speech was all that the town knew, but he
Seemed for a while to have grown young again;
Seemed so on purpose, muttered Jaffer's friends,
That none might know that he was conscience-struck –
But that's a traitor's thought. Enough for me
That in the early summer of the year
The mightiest of the princes of the world

Came to the least considered of his courtiers;
Sat down upon the fountain's marble edge,
One hand amid the goldfish in the pool;
And thereupon a colloquy took place
That I commend to all the chroniclers
To show how violent great hearts can lose
Their bitterness and find the honeycomb.

'I have brought a slender bride into the house;
You know the saying, "Change the bride with spring,"
And she and I, being sunk in happiness,
Cannot endure to think you tread these paths,
When evening stirs the jasmine bough, and yet
Are brideless.'
                    'I am falling into years.'

'But such as you and I do not seem old
Like men who live by habit. Every day
I ride with falcon to the river's edge
Or carry the ringed mail upon my back,
Or court a woman; neither enemy,
Game-bird, nor woman does the same thing twice;
And so a hunter carries in the eye
A mimicry of youth. Can poet's thought
That springs from body and in body falls
Like this pure jet, now lost amid blue sky,
Now bathing lily leaf and fish's scale,
Be mimicry?'
                    'What matter if our souls
Are nearer to the surface of the body
Than souls that start no game and turn no rhyme!
The soul's own youth and not the body's youth
Shows through our lineaments. My candle's bright,
My lantern is too loyal not to show
That it was made in your great father's reign.'

'And yet the jasmine season warms our blood.'

'Great prince, forgive the freedom of my speech:
You think that love has seasons, and you think
That if the spring bear off what the spring gave
The heart need suffer no defeat; but I
Who have accepted the Byzantine faith,
That seems unnatural to Arabian minds,
Think when I choose a bride I choose for ever;
And if her eye should not grow bright for mine
Or brighten only for some younger eye,
My heart could never turn from daily ruin,
Nor find a remedy.'
     'But what if I
Have lit upon a woman who so shares
Your thirst for those old crabbed mysteries,
So strains to look beyond our life, an eye
That never knew that strain would scarce seem bright,
And yet herself can seem youth's very fountain,
Being all brimmed with life?'
      'Were it but true
I would have found the best that life can give,
Companionship in those mysterious things
That make a man's soul or a woman's soul
Itself and not some other soul.'
      'That love
Must needs be in this life and in what follows
Unchanging and at peace, and it is right
Every philosopher should praise that love.
But I being none can praise its opposite.
It makes my passion stronger but to think
Like passion stirs the peacock and his mate,
The wild stag and the doe; that mouth to mouth
Is a man's mockery of the changeless soul.'

And thereupon his bounty gave what now
Can shake more blossom from autumnal chill
Than all my bursting springtime knew. A girl
Perched in some window of her mother's house
Had watched my daily passage to and fro;
Had heard impossible history of my past;

Imagined some impossible history
Lived at my side; thought time's disfiguring touch
Gave but more reason for a woman's care.
Yet was it love of me, or was it love
Of the stark mystery that has dazed my sight,
Perplexed her fantasy and planned her care?
Or did the torchlight of that mystery
Pick out my features in such light and shade
Two contemplating passions chose one theme
Through sheer bewilderment? She had not paced
The garden paths, nor counted up the rooms,
Before she had spread a book upon her knees
And asked about the pictures or the text;
And often those first days I saw her stare
On old dry writing in a learned tongue,
On old dry faggots that could never please
The extravagance of spring; or move a hand
As if that writing or the figured page
Were some dear cheek.
                              Upon a moonless night
I sat where I could watch her sleeping form,
And wrote by candle-light; but her form moved,
And fearing that my light disturbed her sleep
I rose that I might screen it with a cloth.
I heard her voice, 'Turn that I may expound
What's bowed your shoulder and made pale your cheek';
And saw her sitting upright on the bed;
Or was it she that spoke or some great Djinn?
I say that a Djinn spoke. A livelong hour
She seemed the learned man and I the child;
Truths without father came, truths that no book
Of all the uncounted books that I have read,
Nor thought out of her mind or mine begot,
Self-born, high-born, and solitary truths,
Those terrible implacable straight lines
Drawn through the wandering vegetative dream,
Even those truths that when my bones are dust
Must drive the Arabian host.

                                      The voice grew still,
And she lay down upon her bed and slept,
But woke at the first gleam of day, rose up
And swept the house and sang about her work
In childish ignorance of all that passed.
A dozen nights of natural sleep, and then
When the full moon swam to its greatest height
She rose, and with her eyes shut fast in sleep
Walked through the house. Unnoticed and unfelt
I wrapped her in a hooded cloak, and she,
Half running, dropped at the first ridge of the desert
And there marked out those emblems on the sand
That day by day I study and marvel at,
With her white finger. I led her home asleep
And once again she rose and swept the house
In childish ignorance of all that passed.
Even to-day, after some seven years
When maybe thrice in every moon her mouth
Murmured the wisdom of the desert Djinns,
She keeps that ignorance, nor has she now
That first unnatural interest in my books.
It seems enough that I am there; and yet,
Old fellow-student, whose most patient ear
Heard all the anxiety of my passionate youth,
It seems I must buy knowledge with my peace.
What if she lose her ignorance and so
Dream that I love her only for the voice,
That every gift and every word of praise
Is but a payment for that midnight voice
That is to age what milk is to a child?
Were she to lose her love, because she had lost
Her confidence in mine, or even lose
Its first simplicity, love, voice and all,
All my fine feathers would be plucked away
And I left shivering. The voice has drawn
A quality of wisdom from her love's
Particular quality. The signs and shapes;
All those abstractions that you fancied were
From the great Treatise of Parmenides;

All, all those gyres and cubes and midnight things
Are but a new expression of her body
Drunk with the bitter sweetness of her youth.
And now my utmost mystery is out.
A woman's beauty is a storm-tossed banner;
Under it wisdom stands, and I alone –
Of all Arabia's lovers I alone –
Nor dazzled by the embroidery, nor lost
In the confusion of its night-dark folds,
Can hear the armed man speak.

All Souls' Night

EPILOGUE TO 'A VISION'

Midnight has come, and the great Christ Church Bell
And many a lesser bell sound through the room;
And it is All Souls' Night,
And two long glasses brimmed with muscatel
Bubble upon the table. A ghost may come;
For it is a ghost's right,
His element is so fine
Being sharpened by his death,
To drink from the wine-breath
While our gross palates drink from the whole wine.

I need some mind that, if the cannon sound
From every quarter of the world, can stay
Wound in mind's pondering
As mummies in the mummy-cloth are wound;
Because I have a marvellous thing to say,
A certain marvellous thing
None but the living mock,
Though not for sober ear;
It may be all that hear
Should laugh and weep an hour upon the clock.

Horton's the first I call. He loved strange thought
And knew that sweet extremity of pride
That's called platonic love,
And that to such a pitch of passion wrought
Nothing could bring him, when his lady died,
Anodyne for his love.
Words were but wasted breath;
One dear hope had he:
The inclemency
Of that or the next winter would be death.

Two thoughts were so mixed up I could not tell
Whether of her or God he thought the most,
But think that his mind's eye,
When upward turned, on one sole image fell;
And that a slight companionable ghost,
Wild with divinity,
Had so lit up the whole
Immense miraculous house
The Bible promised us,
It seemed a gold-fish swimming in a bowl.

On Florence Emery I call the next,
Who finding the first wrinkles on a face
Admired and beautiful,
And knowing that the future would be vexed
With 'minished beauty, multiplied commonplace,
Preferred to teach a school
Away from neighbour or friend,
Among dark skins, and there
Permit foul years to wear
Hidden from eyesight to the unnoticed end.

Before that end much had she ravelled out
From a discourse in figurative speech
By some learned Indian
On the soul's journey. How it is whirled about,
Wherever the orbit of the moon can reach,
Until it plunge into the sun;

And there, free and yet fast,
Being both Chance and Choice,
Forget its broken toys
And sink into its own delight at last.

And I call up MacGregor from the grave,
For in my first hard springtime we were friends,
Although of late estranged.
I thought him half a lunatic, half knave,
And told him so, but friendship never ends,
And what if mind seem changed,
And it seem changed with the mind,
When thoughts rise up unbid
On generous things that he did
And I grow half contented to be blind!

He had much industry at setting out,
Much boisterous courage, before loneliness
Had driven him crazed;
For meditations upon unknown thought
Make human intercourse grow less and less;
They are neither paid nor praised.
But he'd object to the host,
The glass because my glass;
A ghost-lover he was
And may have grown more arrogant being a ghost.

But names are nothing. What matter who it be,
So that his elements have grown so fine
The fume of muscatel
Can give his sharpened palate ecstasy.
No living man can drink from the whole wine.
I have mummy truths to tell
Whereat the living mock,
Though not for sober ear,
For maybe all that hear
Should laugh and weep an hour upon the clock.

Such thought – such thought have I that hold it tight
Till meditation master all its parts,

Nothing can stay my glance
Until that glance run in the world's despite
To where the damned have howled away their hearts,
And where the blessed dance;
Such thought, that in it bound
I need no other thing,
Wound in mind's wandering
As mummies in the mummy-cloth are wound.

THE WINDING STAIR
AND OTHER POEMS
1933

THE WINDING STAIR
AND OTHER POEMS

In Memory of Eva Gore-Booth
and Con Markiewicz

The light of evening, Lissadell,
Great windows open to the south,
Two girls in silk kimonos, both
Beautiful, one a gazelle.
But a raving autumn shears
Blossom from the summer's wreath;
The older is condemned to death,
Pardoned, drags out lonely years
Conspiring among the ignorant.
I know not what the younger dreams –
Some vague Utopia – and she seems,
When withered old and skeleton-gaunt,
An image of such politics.
Many a time I think to seek
One or the other out and speak
Of that old Georgian mansion, mix
Pictures of the mind, recall
That table and the talk of youth,
Two girls in silk kimonos, both
Beautiful, one a gazelle.

Dear shadows, now you know it all,
All the folly of a fight
With a common wrong or right.
The innocent and the beautiful
Have no enemy but time;
Arise and bid me strike a match
And strike another till time catch;
Should the conflagration climb,

Run till all the sages know.
We the great gazebo built,
They convicted us of guilt;
Bid me strike a match and blow.

Death

Nor dread nor hope attend
A dying animal;
A man awaits his end
Dreading and hoping all;
Many times he died,
Many times rose again.
A great man in his pride
Confronting murderous men
Casts derision upon
Supersession of breath;
He knows death to the bone –
Man has created death.

A Dialogue of Self and Soul

I

MY SOUL

I summon to the winding ancient stair;
Set all your mind upon the steep ascent,
Upon the broken, crumbling battlement,
Upon the breathless starlit air,
Upon the star that marks the hidden pole;
Fix every wandering thought upon
That quarter where all thought is done:
Who can distinguish darkness from the soul?

MY SELF

The consecrated blade upon my knees
Is Sato's ancient blade, still as it was,
Still razor-keen, still like a looking-glass
Unspotted by the centuries;
That flowering, silken, old embroidery, torn
From some court-lady's dress and round
The wooden scabbard bound and wound,
Can, tattered, still protect, faded adorn.

MY SOUL

Why should the imagination of a man
Long past his prime remember things that are
Emblematical of love and war?
Think of ancestral night that can,
If but imagination scorn the earth
And intellect its wandering
To this and that and t'other thing,
Deliver from the crime of death and birth.

MY SELF

Montashigi, third of his family, fashioned it
Five hundred years ago, about it lie
Flowers from I know not what embroidery –
Heart's purple – and all these I set
For emblems of the day against the tower
Emblematical of the night,
And claim as by a soldier's right
A charter to commit the crime once more.

MY SOUL

Such fullness in that quarter overflows
And falls into the basin of the mind
That man is stricken deaf and dumb and blind,
For intellect no longer knows

Is from the *Ought*, or *Knower* from the *Known* –
That is to say, ascends to Heaven;
Only the dead can be forgiven;
But when I think of that my tongue's a stone.

II

MY SELF

A living man is blind and drinks his drop.
What matter if the ditches are impure?
What matter if I live it all once more?
Endure that toil of growing up;
The ignominy of boyhood; the distress
Of boyhood changing into man;
The unfinished man and his pain
Brought face to face with his own clumsiness;

The finished man among his enemies? –
How in the name of Heaven can he escape
That defiling and disfigured shape
The mirror of malicious eyes
Casts upon his eyes until at last
He thinks that shape must be his shape?
And what's the good of an escape
If honour find him in the wintry blast?

I am content to live it all again
And yet again, if it be life to pitch
Into the frog-spawn of a blind man's ditch,
A blind man battering blind men;
Or into that most fecund ditch of all,
The folly that man does
Or must suffer, if he woos
A proud woman not kindred of his soul.

I am content to follow to its source
Every event in action or in thought;
Measure the lot; forgive myself the lot!
When such as I cast out remorse

So great a sweetness flows into the breast
We must laugh and we must sing,
We are blest by everything,
Everything we look upon is blest.

Blood and the Moon

I

Blessed be this place,
More blessed still this tower;
A bloody, arrogant power
Rose out of the race
Uttering, mastering it,
Rose like these walls from these
Storm-beaten cottages –
In mockery I have set
A powerful emblem up,
And sing it rhyme upon rhyme
In mockery of a time
Half dead at the top.

II

Alexandria's was a beacon tower, and Babylon's
An image of the moving heavens, a log-book of the sun's journey
and the moon's;
And Shelley had his towers, thought's crowned powers he called
them once.

I declare this tower is my symbol; I declare
This winding, gyring, spiring treadmill of a stair is my ancestral
stair;
That Goldsmith and the Dean, Berkeley and Burke have travelled
there.

Swift beating on his breast in sibylline frenzy blind
Because the heart in his blood-sodden breast had dragged him
    down into mankind,
Goldsmith deliberately sipping at the honey-pot of his mind,

And haughtier-headed Burke that proved the State a tree,
That this unconquerable labyrinth of the birds, century after
    century,
Cast but dead leaves to mathematical equality;

And God-appointed Berkeley that proved all things a dream,
That this pragmatical, preposterous pig of a world, its farrow that
    so solid seem,
Must vanish on the instant if the mind but change its theme;

Saeva Indignatio and the labourer's hire,
The strength that gives our blood and state magnanimity of its
    own desire;
Everything that is not God consumed with intellectual fire.

III

The purity of the unclouded moon
Has flung its arrowy shaft upon the floor.
Seven centuries have passed and it is pure,
The blood of innocence has left no stain.
There, on blood-saturated ground, have stood
Soldier, assassin, executioner,
Whether for daily pittance or in blind fear
Or out of abstract hatred, and shed blood,
But could not cast a single jet thereon.
Odour of blood on the ancestral stair!
And we that have shed none must gather there
And clamour in drunken frenzy for the moon.

IV

Upon the dusty, glittering windows cling,
And seem to cling upon the moonlit skies,
Tortoiseshell butterflies, peacock butterflies,
A couple of night-moths are on the wing.

Is every modern nation like the tower,
Half dead at the top? No matter what I said,
For wisdom is the property of the dead,
A something incompatible with life; and power,
Like everything that has the stain of blood,
A property of the living; but no stain
Can come upon the visage of the moon
When it has looked in glory from a cloud.

Oil and Blood

In tombs of gold and lapis lazuli
Bodies of holy men and women exude
Miraculous oil, odour of violet.

But under heavy loads of trampled clay
Lie bodies of the vampires full of blood;
Their shrouds are bloody and their lips are wet.

Veronica's Napkin

The Heavenly Circuit; Berenice's Hair;
Tent-pole of Eden; the tent's drapery;
Symbolical glory of the earth and air!
The Father and His angelic hierarchy
That made the magnitude and glory there
Stood in the circuit of a needle's eye.

Some found a different pole, and where it stood
A pattern on a napkin dipped in blood.

Symbols

A storm-beaten old watch-tower,
A blind hermit rings the hour.

All-destroying sword-blade still
Carried by the wandering fool.

Gold-sewn silk on the sword-blade,
Beauty and fool together laid.

Spilt Milk

We that have done and thought,
That have thought and done,
Must ramble, and thin out
Like milk spilt on a stone.

The Nineteenth Century and After

Though the great song return no more
There's keen delight in what we have:
The rattle of pebbles on the shore
Under the receding wave.

Statistics

'Those Platonists are a curse,' he said,
'God's fire upon the wane,
A diagram hung there instead,
More women born than men.'

Three Movements

Shakespearean fish swam the sea, far away from land;
Romantic fish swam in nets coming to the hand;
What are all those fish that lie gasping on the strand?

The Seven Sages

THE FIRST

My great-grandfather spoke to Edmund Burke
In Grattan's house.

THE SECOND

    My great-grandfather shared
A pot-house bench with Oliver Goldsmith once.

THE THIRD

My great-grandfather's father talked of music,
Drank tar-water with the Bishop of Cloyne.

THE FOURTH

But mine saw Stella once.

THE FIFTH

     Whence came our thought?

THE SIXTH

From four great minds that hated Whiggery.

THE FIFTH

Burke was a Whig.

THE SIXTH

Whether they knew or not,
Goldsmith and Burke, Swift and the Bishop of Cloyne
All hated Whiggery; but what is Whiggery?
A levelling, rancorous, rational sort of mind
That never looked out of the eye of a saint
Or out of drunkard's eye.

THE SEVENTH

All's Whiggery now,
But we old men are massed against the world.

THE FIRST

American colonies, Ireland, France and India
Harried, and Burke's great melody against it.

THE SECOND

Oliver Goldsmith sang what he had seen,
Roads full of beggars, cattle in the fields,
But never saw the trefoil stained with blood,
The avenging leaf those fields raised up against it.

THE FOURTH

The tomb of Swift wears it away.

THE THIRD

A voice
Soft as the rustle of a reed from Cloyne
That gathers volume; now a thunder-clap.

THE SIXTH

What schooling had these four?

             They walked the roads
Mimicking what they heard, as children mimic;
They understood that wisdom comes of beggary.

The Crazed Moon

Crazed through much child-bearing
The moon is staggering in the sky;
Moon-struck by the despairing
Glances of her wandering eye
We grope, and grope in vain,
For children born of her pain.

Children dazed or dead!
When she in all her virginal pride
First trod on the mountain's head
What stir ran through the countryside
Where every foot obeyed her glance!
What manhood led the dance!

Fly-catchers of the moon,
Our hands are blenched, our fingers seem
But slender needles of bone;
Blenched by that malicious dream
They are spread wide that each
May rend what comes in reach.

Coole Park, 1929

I meditate upon a swallow's flight,
Upon an aged woman and her house,
A sycamore and lime-tree lost in night
Although that western cloud is luminous,

Great works constructed there in nature's spite
For scholars and for poets after us,
Thoughts long knitted into a single thought,
A dance-like glory that those walls begot.

There Hyde before he had beaten into prose
That noble blade the Muses buckled on,
There one that ruffled in a manly pose
For all his timid heart, there that slow man,
That meditative man, John Synge, and those
Impetuous men, Shawe-Taylor and Hugh Lane,
Found pride established in humility,
A scene well set and excellent company.

They came like swallows and like swallows went,
And yet a woman's powerful character
Could keep a swallow to its first intent;
And half a dozen in formation there,
That seemed to whirl upon a compass-point,
Found certainty upon the dreaming air,
The intellectual sweetness of those lines
That cut through time or cross it withershins.

Here, traveller, scholar, poet, take your stand
When all those rooms and passages are gone,
When nettles wave upon a shapeless mound
And saplings root among the broken stone,
And dedicate – eyes bent upon the ground,
Back turned upon the brightness of the sun
And all the sensuality of the shade –
A moment's memory to that laurelled head.

Coole and Ballylee, 1931

Under my window-ledge the waters race,
Otters below and moor-hens on the top,
Run for a mile undimmed in Heaven's face
Then darkening through 'dark' Raftery's 'cellar' drop,

Run underground, rise in a rocky place
In Coole demesne, and there to finish up
Spread to a lake and drop into a hole.
What's water but the generated soul?

Upon the border of that lake's a wood
Now all dry sticks under a wintry sun,
And in a copse of beeches there I stood,
For Nature's pulled her tragic buskin on
And all the rant's a mirror of my mood:
At sudden thunder of the mounting swan
I turned about and looked where branches break
The glittering reaches of the flooded lake.

Another emblem there! That stormy white
But seems a concentration of the sky;
And, like the soul, it sails into the sight
And in the morning's gone, no man knows why;
And is so lovely that it sets to right
What knowledge or its lack had set awry,
So arrogantly pure, a child might think
It can be murdered with a spot of ink.

Sound of a stick upon the floor, a sound
From somebody that toils from chair to chair;
Beloved books that famous hands have bound,
Old marble heads, old pictures everywhere;
Great rooms where travelled men and children found
Content or joy; a last inheritor
Where none has reigned that lacked a name and fame
Or out of folly into folly came.

A spot whereon the founders lived and died
Seemed once more dear than life; ancestral trees,
Or gardens rich in memory glorified
Marriages, alliances and families,
And every bride's ambition satisfied.
Where fashion or mere fantasy decrees
We shift about – all that great glory spent –
Like some poor Arab tribesman and his tent.

We were the last romantics – chose for theme
Traditional sanctity and loveliness;
Whatever's written in what poets name
The book of the people; whatever most can bless
The mind of man or elevate a rhyme;
But all is changed, that high horse riderless,
Though mounted in that saddle Homer rode
Where the swan drifts upon a darkening flood.

For Anne Gregory

'Never shall a young man,
Thrown into despair
By those great honey-coloured
Ramparts at your ear,
Love you for yourself alone
And not your yellow hair.'

'But I can get a hair-dye
And set such colour there,
Brown, or black, or carrot,
That young men in despair
May love me for myself alone
And not my yellow hair.'

'I heard an old religious man
But yesternight declare
That he had found a text to prove
That only God, my dear,
Could love you for yourself alone
And not your yellow hair.'

Swift's Epitaph

Swift has sailed into his rest;
Savage indignation there
Cannot lacerate his breast.
Imitate him if you dare,
World-besotted traveller; he
Served human liberty.

At Algeciras – A Meditation upon Death

The heron-billed pale cattle-birds
That feed on some foul parasite
Of the Moroccan flocks and herds
Cross the narrow Straits to light
In the rich midnight of the garden trees
Till the dawn break upon those mingled seas.

Often at evening when a boy
Would I carry to a friend –
Hoping more substantial joy
Did an older mind commend –
Not such as are in Newton's metaphor,
But actual shells of Rosses' level shore.

Greater glory in the sun,
An evening chill upon the air,
Bid imagination run
Much on the Great Questioner;
What He can question, what if questioned I
Can with a fitting confidence reply.

The Choice

The intellect of man is forced to choose
Perfection of the life, or of the work,
And if it take the second must refuse
A heavenly mansion, raging in the dark.
When all that story's finished, what's the news?
In luck or out the toil has left its mark:
That old perplexity an empty purse,
Or the day's vanity, the night's remorse.

Mohini Chatterjee

I asked if I should pray,
But the Brahmin said,
'Pray for nothing, say
Every night in bed,
"I have been a king,
I have been a slave,
Nor is there anything,
Fool, rascal, knave,
That I have not been,
And yet upon my breast
A myriad heads have lain." '

That he might set at rest
A boy's turbulent days
Mohini Chatterjee
Spoke these, or words like these.
I add in commentary,
'Old lovers yet may have
All that time denied –
Grave is heaped on grave
That they be satisfied –

Over the blackened earth
The old troops parade,
Birth is heaped on birth
That such cannonade
May thunder time away,
Birth-hour and death-hour meet,
Or, as great sages say,
Men dance on deathless feet.'

Byzantium

The unpurged images of day recede;
The Emperor's drunken soldiery are abed;
Night resonance recedes, night-walkers' song
After great cathedral gong;
A starlit or a moonlit dome disdains
All that man is,
All mere complexities,
The fury and the mire of human veins.

Before me floats an image, man or shade,
Shade more than man, more image than a shade;
For Hades' bobbin bound in mummy-cloth
May unwind the winding path;
A mouth that has no moisture and no breath
Breathless mouths may summon;
I hail the superhuman;
I call it death-in-life and life-in-death.

Miracle, bird or golden handiwork,
More miracle than bird or handiwork,
Planted on the star-lit golden bough,
Can like the cocks of Hades crow,
Or, by the moon embittered, scorn aloud
In glory of changeless metal
Common bird or petal
And all complexities of mire or blood.

At midnight on the Emperor's pavement flit
Flames that no faggot feeds, nor steel has lit,
Nor storm disturbs, flames begotten of flame,
Where blood-begotten spirits come
And all complexities of fury leave,
Dying into a dance,
An agony of trance,
An agony of flame that cannot singe a sleeve.

Astraddle on the dolphin's mire and blood,
Spirit after spirit! The smithies break the flood,
The golden smithies of the Emperor!
Marbles of the dancing floor
Break bitter furies of complexity,
Those images that yet
Fresh images beget,
That dolphin-torn, that gong-tormented sea.

The Mother of God

The threefold terror of love; a fallen flare
Through the hollow of an ear;
Wings beating about the room;
The terror of all terrors that I bore
The Heavens in my womb.

Had I not found content among the shows
Every common woman knows,
Chimney corner, garden walk,
Or rocky cistern where we tread the clothes
And gather all the talk?

What is this flesh I purchased with my pains,
This fallen star my milk sustains,
This love that makes my heart's blood stop
Or strikes a sudden chill into my bones
And bids my hair stand up?

Vacillation

I

Between extremities
Man runs his course;
A brand, or flaming breath,
Comes to destroy
All those antinomies
Of day and night;
The body calls it death,
The heart remorse.
But if these be right
What is joy?

II

A tree there is that from its topmost bough
Is half all glittering flame and half all green
Abounding foliage moistened with the dew;
And half is half and yet is all the scene;
And half and half consume what they renew,
And he that Attis' image hangs between
That staring fury and the blind lush leaf
May know not what he knows, but knows not grief.

III

Get all the gold and silver that you can,
Satisfy ambition, or animate
The trivial days and ram them with the sun,
And yet upon these maxims meditate:
All women dote upon an idle man
Although their children need a rich estate;
No man has ever lived that had enough
Of children's gratitude or woman's love.

No longer in Lethean foliage caught
Begin the preparation for your death
And from the fortieth winter by that thought
Test every work of intellect or faith,
And everything that your own hands have wrought,
And call those works extravagance of breath
That are not suited for such men as come
Proud, open-eyed and laughing to the tomb.

IV

My fiftieth year had come and gone,
I sat, a solitary man,
In a crowded London shop,
An open book and empty cup
On the marble table-top.

While on the shop and street I gazed
My body of a sudden blazed;
And twenty minutes more or less
It seemed, so great my happiness,
That I was blessèd and could bless.

V

Although the summer sunlight gild
Cloudy leafage of the sky,
Or wintry moonlight sink the field
In storm-scattered intricacy,
I cannot look thereon,
Responsibility so weighs me down.

Things said or done long years ago,
Or things I did not do or say
But thought that I might say or do,
Weigh me down, and not a day
But something is recalled,
My conscience or my vanity appalled.

VI

A rivery field spread out below,
An odour of the new-mown hay
In his nostrils, the great lord of Chou
Cried, casting off the mountain snow,
'Let all things pass away.'

Wheels by milk-white asses drawn
Where Babylon or Nineveh
Rose; some conqueror drew rein
And cried to battle-weary men,
'Let all things pass away.'

From man's blood-sodden heart are sprung
Those branches of the night and day
Where the gaudy moon is hung.
What's the meaning of all song?
'Let all things pass away.'

VII

THE SOUL

Seek out reality, leave things that seem.

THE HEART

What, be a singer born and lack a theme?

THE SOUL

Isaiah's coal, what more can man desire?

THE HEART

Struck dumb in the simplicity of fire!

THE SOUL

Look on that fire, salvation walks within.

THE HEART

What theme had Homer but original sin?

VIII

Must we part, Von Hügel, though much alike, for we
Accept the miracles of the saints and honour sanctity?
The body of Saint Teresa lies undecayed in tomb,
Bathed in miraculous oil, sweet odours from it come,
Healing from its lettered slab. Those self-same hands perchance
Eternalised the body of a modern saint that once
Had scooped out Pharaoh's mummy. I – though heart might find
    relief
Did I become a Christian man and choose for my belief
What seems most welcome in the tomb – play a predestined part.
Homer is my example and his unchristened heart.
The lion and the honeycomb, what has Scripture said?
So get you gone, Von Hügel, though with blessings on your head.

Quarrel in Old Age

Where had her sweetness gone?
What fanatics invent
In this blind bitter town,
Fantasy or incident
Not worth thinking of,
Put her in a rage.
I had forgiven enough
That had forgiven old age.

All lives that has lived;
So much is certain;
Old sages were not deceived:
Somewhere beyond the curtain
Of distorting days
Lives that lonely thing
That shone before these eyes
Targeted, trod like Spring.

The Results of Thought

Acquaintance; companion;
One dear brilliant woman;
The best-endowed, the elect,
All by their youth undone,
All, all, by that inhuman
Bitter glory wrecked.

But I have straightened out
Ruin, wreck and wrack;
I toiled long years and at length
Came to so deep a thought
I can summon back
All their wholesome strength.

What images are these
That turn dull-eyed away,
Or shift Time's filthy load,
Straighten aged knees,
Hesitate or stay?
What heads shake or nod?

Gratitude to the Unknown Instructors

What they undertook to do
They brought to pass;
All things hang like a drop of dew
Upon a blade of grass.

Remorse for Intemperate Speech

I ranted to the knave and fool,
But outgrew that school,
Would transform the part,
Fit audience found, but cannot rule
My fanatic heart.

I sought my betters: though in each
Fine manners, liberal speech,
Turn hatred into sport,
Nothing said or done can reach
My fanatic heart.

Out of Ireland have we come.
Great hatred, little room,
Maimed us at the start.
I carry from my mother's womb
A fanatic heart.

Stream and Sun at Glendalough

Through intricate motions ran
Stream and gliding sun
And all my heart seemed gay:
Some stupid thing that I had done
Made my attention stray.

Repentance keeps my heart impure;
But what am I that dare
Fancy that I can
Better conduct myself or have more
Sense than a common man?

What motion of the sun or stream
Or eyelid shot the gleam
That pierced my body through?
What made me live like these that seem
Self-born, born anew?

Words for Music Perhaps

I

CRAZY JANE AND THE BISHOP

Bring me to the blasted oak
That I, midnight upon the stroke,
(*All find safety in the tomb.*)
May call down curses on his head
Because of my dear Jack that's dead.
Coxcomb was the least he said:
The solid man and the coxcomb.

Nor was he Bishop when his ban
Banished Jack the Journeyman,
(*All find safety in the tomb.*)
Nor so much as parish priest,
Yet he, an old book in his fist,
Cried that we lived like beast and beast:
The solid man and the coxcomb.

The Bishop has a skin, God knows,
Wrinkled like the foot of a goose,
(*All find safety in the tomb.*)
Nor can he hide in holy black
The heron's hunch upon his back,
But a birch-tree stood my Jack:
The solid man and the coxcomb.

Jack had my virginity,
And bids me to the oak, for he
(*All find safety in the tomb.*)
Wanders out into the night
And there is shelter under it,
But should that other come, I spit:
The solid man and the coxcomb.

II

CRAZY JANE REPROVED

I care not what the sailors say:
All those dreadful thunder-stones,
All that storm that blots the day
Can but show that Heaven yawns;
Great Europa played the fool
That changed a lover for a bull.
Fol de rol, fol de rol.

To round that shell's elaborate whorl,
Adorning every secret track
With the delicate mother-of-pearl,
Made the joints of Heaven crack:
So never hang your heart upon
A roaring, ranting journeyman.
Fol de rol, fol de rol.

III

CRAZY JANE ON THE DAY OF JUDGMENT

'Love is all
Unsatisfied
That cannot take the whole
Body and soul';
And that is what Jane said.

'Take the sour
If you take me,
I can scoff and lour
And scold for an hour.'
'That's certainly the case,' said he.

'Naked I lay,
The grass my bed;
Naked and hidden away,
That black day';
And that is what Jane said.

'What can be shown?
What true love be?
All could be known or shown
If Time were but gone.'
'That's certainly the case,' said he.

IV

CRAZY JANE AND JACK THE JOURNEYMAN

I know, although when looks meet
I tremble to the bone,
The more I leave the door unlatched
The sooner love is gone,
For love is but a skein unwound
Between the dark and dawn.

A lonely ghost the ghost is
That to God shall come;
I – love's skein upon the ground,
My body in the tomb –
Shall leap into the light lost
In my mother's womb.

But were I left to lie alone
In an empty bed,
The skein so bound us ghost to ghost
When he turned his head
Passing on the road that night,
Mine must walk when dead.

V

CRAZY JANE ON GOD

That lover of a night
Came when he would,
Went in the dawning light
Whether I would or no;
Men come, men go:
All things remain in God.

Banners choke the sky;
Men-at-arms tread;
Armoured horses neigh
Where the great battle was
In the narrow pass:
All things remain in God.

Before their eyes a house
That from childhood stood
Uninhabited, ruinous,
Suddenly lit up
From door to top:
All things remain in God.

I had wild Jack for a lover;
Though like a road
That men pass over
My body makes no moan
But sings on:
All things remain in God.

VI

CRAZY JANE TALKS WITH THE BISHOP

I met the Bishop on the road
And much said he and I.
'Those breasts are flat and fallen now,
Those veins must soon be dry;
Live in a heavenly mansion,
Not in some foul sty.'

'Fair and foul are near of kin,
And fair needs foul,' I cried.
'My friends are gone, but that's a truth
Nor grave nor bed denied,
Learned in bodily lowliness
And in the heart's pride.

'A woman can be proud and stiff
When on love intent;
But Love has pitched his mansion in
The place of excrement;
For nothing can be sole or whole
That has not been rent.'

VII

CRAZY JANE GROWN OLD LOOKS AT THE DANCERS

I found that ivory image there
Dancing with her chosen youth,
But when he wound her coal-black hair
As though to strangle her, no scream
Or bodily movement did I dare,
Eyes under eyelids did so gleam;
Love is like the lion's tooth.

When she, and though some said she played
I said that she had danced heart's truth,
Drew a knife to strike him dead,
I could but leave him to his fate;
For no matter what is said
They had all that had their hate;
Love is like the lion's tooth.

Did he die or did she die?
Seemed to die or died they both?
God be with the times when I
Cared not a thraneen for what chanced
So that I had the limbs to try
Such a dance as there was danced –
Love is like the lion's tooth.

VIII

GIRL'S SONG

I went out alone
To sing a song or two,
My fancy on a man,
And you know who.

Another came in sight
That on a stick relied
To hold himself upright;
I sat and cried.

And that was all my song –
When everything is told,
Saw I an old man young
Or young man old?

IX

YOUNG MAN'S SONG

'She will change,' I cried,
'Into a withered crone.'
The heart in my side,
That so still had lain,
In noble rage replied
And beat upon the bone:

'Uplift those eyes and throw
Those glances unafraid:
She would as bravely show
Did all the fabric fade;
No withered crone I saw
Before the world was made.'

Abashed by that report,
For the heart cannot lie,
I knelt in the dirt.
And all shall bend the knee
To my offended heart
Until it pardon me.

X

HER ANXIETY

Earth in beauty dressed
Awaits returning spring.
All true love must die,
Alter at the best
Into some lesser thing.
Prove that I lie.

Such body lovers have,
Such exacting breath,
That they touch or sigh.
Every touch they give,
Love is nearer death.
Prove that I lie.

XI

HIS CONFIDENCE

Undying love to buy
I wrote upon
The corners of this eye
All wrongs done.
What payment were enough
For undying love?

I broke my heart in two
So hard I struck.
What matter? for I know
That out of rock,
Out of a desolate source,
Love leaps upon its course.

XII

LOVE'S LONELINESS

Old fathers, great-grandfathers,
Rise as kindred should.
If ever lover's loneliness
Came where you stood,
Pray that Heaven protect us
That protect your blood.

The mountain throws a shadow,
Thin is the moon's horn;
What did we remember
Under the ragged thorn?
Dread has followed longing,
And our hearts are torn.

XIII

HER DREAM

I dreamed as in my bed I lay,
All night's fathomless wisdom come,
That I had shorn my locks away
And laid them on Love's lettered tomb;
But something bore them out of sight
In a great tumult of the air,
And after nailed upon the night
Berenice's burning hair.

XIV

HIS BARGAIN

Who talks of Plato's spindle;
What set it whirling round?
Eternity may dwindle,
Time is unwound,
Dan and Jerry Lout
Change their loves about.

However they may take it,
Before the thread began
I made, and may not break it
When the last thread has run,
A bargain with that hair
And all the windings there.

XV

THREE THINGS

'O cruel Death, give three things back,'
Sang a bone upon the shore;
'A child found all a child can lack,
Whether of pleasure or of rest,
Upon the abundance of my breast':
A bone wave-whitened and dried in the wind.

'Three dear things that women know,'
Sang a bone upon the shore;
'A man if I but held him so
When my body was alive
Found all the pleasure that life gave':
A bone wave-whitened and dried in the wind.

'The third thing that I think of yet,'
Sang a bone upon the shore;
'Is that morning when I met
Face to face my rightful man
And did after stretch and yawn':
A bone wave-whitened and dried in the wind.

XVI

LULLABY

Beloved, may your sleep be sound
That have found it where you fed.
What were all the world's alarms
To mighty Paris when he found
Sleep upon a golden bed
That first dawn in Helen's arms?

Sleep, beloved, such a sleep
As did that wild Tristram know
When, the potion's work being done,
Roe could run or doe could leap
Under oak and beechen bough,
Roe could leap or doe could run;

Such a sleep and sound as fell
Upon Eurotas' grassy bank
When the holy bird, that there
Accomplished his predestined will,
From the limbs of Leda sank
But not from her protecting care.

XVII

AFTER LONG SILENCE

Speech after long silence; it is right,
All other lovers being estranged or dead,
Unfriendly lamplight hid under its shade,
The curtains drawn upon unfriendly night,
That we descant and yet again descant
Upon the supreme theme of Art and Song:
Bodily decrepitude is wisdom; young
We loved each other and were ignorant.

XVIII

MAD AS THE MIST AND SNOW

Bolt and bar the shutter,
For the foul winds blow:
Our minds are at their best this night,
And I seem to know
That everything outside us is
Mad as the mist and snow.

Horace there by Homer stands,
Plato stands below,
And here is Tully's open page.

How many years ago
Were you and I unlettered lads
Mad as the mist and snow?

You ask what makes me sigh, old friend,
What makes me shudder so?
I shudder and I sigh to think
That even Cicero
And many-minded Homer were
Mad as the mist and snow.

XIX

THOSE DANCING DAYS ARE GONE

Come, let me sing into your ear;
Those dancing days are gone,
All that silk and satin gear;
Crouch upon a stone,
Wrapping that foul body up
In as foul a rag:
I carry the sun in a golden cup,
The moon in a silver bag.

Curse as you may I sing it through;
What matter if the knave
That the most could pleasure you,
The children that he gave,
Are somewhere sleeping like a top
Under a marble flag?
I carry the sun in a golden cup,
The moon in a silver bag.

I thought it out this very day,
Noon upon the clock,
A man may put pretence away
Who leans upon a stick,
May sing, and sing until he drop,
Whether to maid or hag:
I carry the sun in a golden cup,
The moon in a silver bag.

XX

'I AM OF IRELAND'

'I am of Ireland,
And the Holy Land of Ireland,
And time runs on,' cried she.
'Come out of charity,
Come dance with me in Ireland.'

One man, one man alone
In that outlandish gear,
One solitary man
Of all that rambled there
Had turned his stately head.
'That is a long way off,
And time runs on,' he said,
'And the night grows rough.'

'I am of Ireland,
And the Holy Land of Ireland,
And time runs on,' cried she.
'Come out of charity,
And dance with me in Ireland.'

'The fiddlers are all thumbs,
Or the fiddle-string accursed,
The drums and the kettledrums
And the trumpets all are burst,
And the trombone,' cried he,
'The trumpet and trombone,'
And cocked a malicious eye,
'But time runs on, runs on.'

'I am of Ireland,
And the Holy Land of Ireland,
And time runs on,' cried she.
'Come out of charity,
And dance with me in Ireland.'

XXI

THE DANCER AT CRUACHAN AND CRO-PATRICK

I, proclaiming that there is
Among birds or beasts or men
One that is perfect or at peace,
Danced on Cruachan's windy plain,
Upon Cro-Patrick sang aloud;
All that could run or leap or swim
Whether in wood, water or cloud,
Acclaiming, proclaiming, declaiming Him.

XXII

TOM THE LUNATIC

Sang old Tom the lunatic
That sleeps under the canopy:
'What change has put my thoughts astray
And eyes that had so keen a sight?
What has turned to smoking wick
Nature's pure unchanging light?

'Huddon and Duddon and Daniel O'Leary,
Holy Joe, the beggar-man,
Wenching, drinking, still remain
Or sing a penance on the road;
Something made these eyeballs weary
That blinked and saw them in a shroud.

'Whatever stands in field or flood,
Bird, beast, fish or man,
Mare or stallion, cock or hen,
Stands in God's unchanging eye
In all the vigour of its blood;
In that faith I live or die.'

XXIII

TOM AT CRUACHAN

On Cruachan's plain slept he
That must sing in a rhyme
What most could shake his soul:
'The stallion Eternity
Mounted the mare of Time,
'Gat the foal of the world.'

XXIV

OLD TOM AGAIN

Things out of perfection sail,
And all their swelling canvas wear,
Nor shall the self-begotten fail
Though fantastic men suppose
Building-yard and stormy shore,
Winding-sheet and swaddling-clothes.

XXV

THE DELPHIC ORACLE UPON PLOTINUS

Behold that great Plotinus swim,
Buffeted by such seas;
Bland Rhadamanthus beckons him,
But the Golden Race looks dim,
Salt blood blocks his eyes.

Scattered on the level grass
Or winding through the grove
Plato there and Minos pass,
There stately Pythagoras
And all the choir of Love.

A Woman Young and Old

I

FATHER AND CHILD

She hears me strike the board and say
That she is under ban
Of all good men and women,
Being mentioned with a man
That has the worst of all bad names;
And thereupon replies
That his hair is beautiful,
Cold as the March wind his eyes.

II

BEFORE THE WORLD WAS MADE

If I make the lashes dark
And the eyes more bright
And the lips more scarlet,
Or ask if all be right
From mirror after mirror,
No vanity's displayed:
I'm looking for the face I had
Before the world was made.

What if I look upon a man
As though on my beloved,
And my blood be cold the while
And my heart unmoved?
Why should he think me cruel
Or that he is betrayed?
I'd have him love the thing that was
Before the world was made.

III

A FIRST CONFESSION

I admit the briar
Entangled in my hair
Did not injure me;
My blenching and trembling,
Nothing but dissembling,
Nothing but coquetry.

I long for truth, and yet
I cannot stay from that
My better self disowns,
For a man's attention
Brings such satisfaction
To the craving in my bones.

Brightness that I pull back
From the Zodiac,
Why those questioning eyes
That are fixed upon me?
What can they do but shun me
If empty night replies?

IV

HER TRIUMPH

I did the dragon's will until you came
Because I had fancied love a casual
Improvisation, or a settled game
That followed if I let the kerchief fall:
Those deeds were best that gave the minute wings
And heavenly music if they gave it wit;
And then you stood among the dragon-rings.
I mocked, being crazy, but you mastered it
And broke the chain and set my ankles free,
Saint George or else a pagan Perseus;
And now we stare astonished at the sea,
And a miraculous strange bird shrieks at us.

V

CONSOLATION

O but there is wisdom
In what the sages said;
But stretch that body for a while
And lay down that head
Till I have told the sages
Where man is comforted.

How could passion run so deep
Had I never thought
That the crime of being born
Blackens all our lot?
But where the crime's committed
The crime can be forgot.

VI

CHOSEN

The lot of love is chosen. I learnt that much
Struggling for an image on the track
Of the whirling Zodiac.
Scarce did he my body touch,
Scarce sank he from the west
Or found a subterranean rest
On the maternal midnight of my breast
Before I had marked him on his northern way,
And seemed to stand although in bed I lay.

I struggled with the horror of daybreak,
I chose it for my lot! If questioned on
My utmost pleasure with a man
By some new-married bride, I take
That stillness for a theme
Where his heart my heart did seem
And both adrift on the miraculous stream
Where – wrote a learned astrologer –
The Zodiac is changed into a sphere.

VII

PARTING

HE

Dear, I must be gone
While night shuts the eyes
Of the household spies;
That song announces dawn.

SHE

No, night's bird and love's
Bids all true lovers rest,
While his loud song reproves
The murderous stealth of day.

HE

Daylight already flies
From mountain crest to crest.

SHE

That light is from the moon.

HE

That bird . . .

SHE

Let him sing on,
I offer to love's play
My dark declivities.

VIII

HER VISION IN THE WOOD

Dry timber under that rich foliage,
At wine-dark midnight in the sacred wood,
Too old for a man's love I stood in rage
Imagining men. Imagining that I could

A greater with a lesser pang assuage
Or but to find if withered vein ran blood,
I tore my body that its wine might cover
Whatever could recall the lip of lover.

And after that I held my fingers up,
Stared at the wine-dark nail, or dark that ran
Down every withered finger from the top;
But the dark changed to red, and torches shone,
And deafening music shook the leaves; a troop
Shouldered a litter with a wounded man,
Or smote upon the string and to the sound
Sang of the beast that gave the fatal wound.

All stately women moving to a song
With loosened hair or foreheads grief-distraught,
It seemed a Quattrocento painter's throng,
A thoughtless image of Mantegna's thought –
Why should they think that are for ever young?
Till suddenly in grief's contagion caught,
I stared upon his blood-bedabbled breast
And sang my malediction with the rest.

That thing all blood and mire, that beast-torn wreck,
Half turned and fixed a glazing eye on mine,
And, though love's bitter-sweet had all come back,
Those bodies from a picture or a coin
Nor saw my body fall nor heard it shriek,
Nor knew, drunken with singing as with wine,
That they had brought no fabulous symbol there
But my heart's victim and its torturer.

IX

A LAST CONFESSION

What lively lad most pleasured me
Of all that with me lay?
I answer that I gave my soul
And loved in misery,
But had great pleasure with a lad
That I loved bodily.

Flinging from his arms I laughed
To think his passion such
He fancied that I gave a soul
Did but our bodies touch,
And laughed upon his breast to think
Beast gave beast as much.

I gave what other women gave
That stepped out of their clothes,
But when this soul, its body off,
Naked to naked goes,
He it has found shall find therein
What none other knows,

And give his own and take his own
And rule in his own right;
And though it loved in misery
Close and cling so tight,
There's not a bird of day that dare
Extinguish that delight.

X

MEETING

Hidden by old age awhile
In masker's cloak and hood,
Each hating what the other loved,
Face to face we stood:
'That I have met with such,' said he,
'Bodes me little good.'

'Let others boast their fill,' said I,
'But never dare to boast
That such as I had such a man
For lover in the past;
Say that of living men I hate
Such a man the most.'

'A loony'd boast of such a love,'
He in his rage declared:
But such as he for such as me –
Could we both discard
This beggarly habiliment –
Had found a sweeter word.

XI

FROM THE 'ANTIGONE'

Overcome – O bitter sweetness,
Inhabitant of the soft cheek of a girl –
The rich man and his affairs,
The fat flocks and the fields' fatness,
Mariners, rough harvesters;
Overcome Gods upon Parnassus;

Overcome the Empyrean; hurl
Heaven and Earth out of their places,
That in the same calamity
Brother and brother, friend and friend,
Family and family,
City and city may contend,
By that great glory driven wild.

Pray I will and sing I must,
And yet I weep – Oedipus' child
Descends into the loveless dust.

FROM
'A FULL MOON IN MARCH'
1935

FROM
'A FULL MOON IN MARCH'

Parnell's Funeral

I

Under the Great Comedian's tomb the crowd.
A bundle of tempestuous cloud is blown
About the sky; where that is clear of cloud
Brightness remains; a brighter star shoots down;
What shudders run through all that animal blood?
What is this sacrifice? Can someone there
Recall the Cretan barb that pierced a star?

Rich foliage that the starlight glittered through,
A frenzied crowd, and where the branches sprang
A beautiful seated boy; a sacred bow;
A woman, and an arrow on a string;
A pierced boy, image of a star laid low.
That woman, the Great Mother imaging,
Cut out his heart. Some master of design
Stamped boy and tree upon Sicilian coin.

An age is the reversal of an age:
When strangers murdered Emmet, Fitzgerald, Tone,
We lived like men that watch a painted stage.
What matter for the scene, the scene once gone:
It had not touched our lives. But popular rage,
Hysterica passio dragged this quarry down.
None shared our guilt; nor did we play a part
Upon a painted stage when we devoured his heart.

Come, fix upon me that accusing eye.
I thirst for accusation. All that was sung,

All that was said in Ireland is a lie
Bred out of the contagion of the throng,
Saving the rhyme rats hear before they die.
Leave nothing but the nothings that belong
To this bare soul, let all men judge that can
Whether it be an animal or a man.

II

The rest I pass, one sentence I unsay.
Had de Valéra eaten Parnell's heart
No loose-lipped demagogue had won the day,
No civil rancour torn the land apart.

Had Cosgrave eaten Parnell's heart, the land's
Imagination had been satisfied,
Or lacking that, government in such hands,
O'Higgins its sole statesman had not died.

Had even O'Duffy – but I name no more –
Their school a crowd, his master solitude;
Through Jonathan Swift's dark grove he passed, and there
Plucked bitter wisdom that enriched his blood.

Three Songs to the Same Tune

I

Grandfather sang it under the gallows:
'Hear, gentlemen, ladies, and all mankind:
Money is good and a girl might be better,
But good strong blows are delights to the mind.'
There, standing on the cart,
He sang it from his heart.

Those fanatics all that we do would undo;
Down the fanatic, down the clown;
Down, down, hammer them down,
Down to the tune of O'Donnell Abu.

'A girl I had, but she followed another,
Money I had, and it went in the night,
Strong drink I had, and it brought me to sorrow,
But a good strong cause and blows are delight.'
All there caught up the tune:
'On, on, my darling man'.

Those fanatics all that we do would undo;
Down the fanatic, down the clown;
Down, down, hammer them down,
Down to the tune of O'Donnell Abu.

'Money is good and a girl might be better,
No matter what happens and who takes the fall,
But a good strong cause' – the rope gave a jerk there,
No more sang he, for his throat was too small;
But he kicked before he died,
He did it out of pride.

Those fanatics all that we do would undo;
Down the fanatic, down the clown;
Down, down, hammer them down,
Down to the tune of O'Donnell Abu.

II

Justify all those renowned generations;
They left their bodies to fatten the wolves,
They left their homesteads to fatten the foxes,
Fled to far countries, or sheltered themselves
In cavern, crevice, hole,
Defending Ireland's soul.

'Drown all the dogs,' said the fierce young woman,
'They killed my goose and a cat.
Drown, drown in the water-butt,
Drown all the dogs,' said the fierce young woman.

Justify all those renowned generations,
Justify all that have sunk in their blood,
Justify all that have died on the scaffold,
Justify all that have fled, that have stood,

Stood or have marched the night long
Singing, singing a song.

'Drown all the dogs,' said the fierce young woman,
'They killed my goose and a cat.
Drown, drown in the water-butt,
Drown all the dogs,' said the fierce young woman.

Fail, and that history turns into rubbish,
All that great past to a trouble of fools;
Those that come after shall mock at O'Donnell,
Mock at the memory of both O'Neills,
Mock Emmet, mock Parnell:
All the renown that fell.

'Drown all the dogs,' said the fierce young woman,
'They killed my goose and a cat.
Drown, drown in the water-butt,
Drown all the dogs,' said the fierce young woman.

III

The soldier takes pride in saluting his Captain,
The devotee proffers a knee to his Lord,
Some back a mare thrown from a thoroughbred,
Troy backed its Helen; Troy died and adored;
Great nations blossom above;
A slave bows down to a slave.

'Who'd care to dig 'em,' said the old, old man,
'Those six feet marked in chalk?
Much I talk, more I walk;
Time I were buried,' said the old, old man.

When nations are empty up there at the top,
When order has weakened or faction is strong,
Time for us all to pick out a good tune,
Take to the roads and go marching along.
March, march – How does it run? –
O any old words to a tune.

'Who'd care to dig 'em,' said the old, old man,
'Those six feet marked in chalk?
Much I talk, more I walk;
Time I were buried,' said the old, old man.

Soldiers take pride in saluting their Captain,
Where are the captains that govern mankind?
What happens a tree that has nothing within it?
O marching wind, O a blast of the wind,
Marching, marching along.
March, march, lift up the song:

'Who'd care to dig 'em,' said the old, old man,
'Those six feet marked in chalk?
Much I talk, more I walk;
Time I were buried,' said the old, old man.

Alternative Song for the Severed Head in
'The King of the Great Clock Tower'

Saddle and ride, I heard a man say,
Out of Ben Bulben and Knocknarea,
What says the Clock in the Great Clock Tower?
All those tragic characters ride
But turn from Rosses' crawling tide,
The meet's upon the mountain-side.
A slow low note and an iron bell.

What brought them there so far from their home,
Cuchulain that fought night long with the foam,
What says the Clock in the Great Clock Tower?
Niamh that rode on it; lad and lass
That sat so still and played at the chess?
What but heroic wantonness?
A slow low note and an iron bell.

Aleel, his Countess; Hanrahan
That seemed but a wild wenching man;
What says the Clock in the Great Clock Tower?
And all alone comes riding there
The King that could make his people stare,
Because he had feathers instead of hair.
A slow low note and an iron bell.

Two Songs Rewritten for the Tune's Sake

I

My Paistin Finn is my sole desire,
And I am shrunken to skin and bone,
For all my heart has had for its hire
Is what I can whistle alone and alone.
          Oro, oro!
To-morrow night I will break down the door.

What is the good of a man and he
Alone and alone, with a speckled shin?
I would that I drank with my love on my knee,
Between two barrels at the inn.
          Oro, oro!
To-morrow night I will break down the door.

Alone and alone nine nights I lay
Between two bushes under the rain;
I thought to have whistled her down that way,
I whistled and whistled and whistled in vain.
          Oro, oro!
To-morrow night I will break down the door.

II

I would that I were an old beggar
Rolling a blind pearl eye,
For he cannot see my lady
Go gallivanting by;

A dreary, dreepy beggar
Without a friend on the earth
But a thieving rascally cur –
O a beggar blind from his birth;

Or anything else but a rhymer
Without a thing in his head
But rhymes for a beautiful lady,
He rhyming alone in his bed.

A Prayer for Old Age

God guard me from those thoughts men think
In the mind alone;
He that sings a lasting song
Thinks in a marrow-bone;

From all that makes a wise old man
That can be praised of all;
O what am I that I should not seem
For the song's sake a fool?

I pray – for fashion's word is out
And prayer comes round again –
That I may seem, though I die old,
A foolish, passionate man.

Church and State

Here is fresh matter, poet,
Matter for old age meet;
Might of the Church and the State,
Their mobs put under their feet.
O but heart's wine shall run pure,
Mind's bread grow sweet.

That were a cowardly song,
Wander in dreams no more;
What if the Church and the State
Are the mob that howls at the door!
Wine shall run thick to the end,
Bread taste sour.

Supernatural Songs

I

RIBH AT THE TOMB OF BAILE AND AILLINN

Because you have found me in the pitch-dark night
With open book you ask me what I do.
Mark and digest my tale, carry it afar
To those that never saw this tonsured head
Nor heard this voice that ninety years have cracked.
Of Baile and Aillinn you need not speak,
All know their tale, all know what leaf and twig,
What juncture of the apple and the yew,
Surmount their bones; but speak what none have heard.

The miracle that gave them such a death
Transfigured to pure substance what had once
Been bone and sinew; when such bodies join
There is no touching here, nor touching there,
Nor straining joy, but whole is joined to whole;
For the intercourse of angels is a light
Where for its moment both seem lost, consumed.

Here in the pitch-dark atmosphere above
The trembling of the apple and the yew,
Here on the anniversary of their death,
The anniversary of their first embrace,
Those lovers, purified by tragedy,
Hurry into each other's arms; these eyes,
By water, herb and solitary prayer

Made aquiline, are open to that light.
Though somewhat broken by the leaves, that light
Lies in a circle on the grass; therein
I turn the pages of my holy book.

II

RIBH DENOUNCES PATRICK

An abstract Greek absurdity has crazed the man –
Recall that masculine Trinity. Man, woman, child (a daughter or a
son),
That's how all natural or supernatural stories run.

Natural and supernatural with the self-same ring are wed.
As man, as beast, as an ephemeral fly begets, Godhead begets
Godhead,
For things below are copies, the Great Smaragdine Tablet said.

Yet all must copy copies, all increase their kind;
When the conflagration of their passion sinks, damped by the body
or the mind,
That juggling nature mounts, her coil in their embraces twined.

The mirror-scalèd serpent is multiplicity,
But all that run in couples, on earth, in flood or air, share God that
is but three,
And could beget or bear themselves could they but love as He.

III

RIBH IN ECSTASY

What matter that you understood no word!
Doubtless I spoke or sang what I had heard
In broken sentences. My soul had found
All happiness in its own cause or ground.
Godhead on Godhead in sexual spasm begot
Godhead. Some shadow fell. My soul forgot
Those amorous cries that out of quiet come
And must the common round of day resume.

IV

THERE

There all the barrel-hoops are knit,
There all the serpent-tails are bit,
There all the gyres converge in one,
There all the planets drop in the Sun.

V

RIBH CONSIDERS CHRISTIAN LOVE INSUFFICIENT

Why should I seek for love or study it?
It is of God and passes human wit.
I study hatred with great diligence,
For that's a passion in my own control,
A sort of besom that can clear the soul
Of everything that is not mind or sense.

Why do I hate man, woman or event?
That is a light my jealous soul has sent.
From terror and deception freed it can
Discover impurities, can show at last
How soul may walk when all such things are past,
How soul could walk before such things began.

Then my delivered soul herself shall learn
A darker knowledge and in hatred turn
From every thought of God mankind has had.
Thought is a garment and the soul's a bride
That cannot in that trash and tinsel hide:
Hatred of God may bring the soul to God.

At stroke of midnight soul cannot endure
A bodily or mental furniture.
What can she take until her Master give!
Where can she look until He make the show!
What can she know until He bid her know!
How can she live till in her blood He live!

VI

HE AND SHE

As the moon sidles up
Must she sidle up,
As trips the scared moon
Away must she trip:
'His light had struck me blind
Dared I stop'.

She sings as the moon sings:
'I am I, am I;
The greater grows my light
The further that I fly'.
All creation shivers
With that sweet cry.

VII

WHAT MAGIC DRUM?

He holds him from desire, all but stops his breathing lest
Primordial Motherhood forsake his limbs, the child no longer rest,
Drinking joy as it were milk upon his breast.

Through light-obliterating garden foliage what magic drum?
Down limb and breast or down that glimmering belly move his
    mouth and sinewy tongue.
What from the forest came? What beast has licked its young?

VIII

WHENCE HAD THEY COME?

Eternity is passion, girl or boy
Cry at the onset of their sexual joy
'For ever and for ever'; then awake
Ignorant what Dramatis Personae spake;
A passion-driven exultant man sings out
Sentences that he has never thought;

The Flagellant lashes those submissive loins
Ignorant what that dramatist enjoins,
What master made the lash. Whence had they come,
The hand and lash that beat down frigid Rome?
What sacred drama through her body heaved
When world-transforming Charlemagne was conceived?

IX

THE FOUR AGES OF MAN

He with body waged a fight,
But body won; it walks upright.

Then he struggled with the heart;
Innocence and peace depart.

Then he struggled with the mind;
His proud heart he left behind.

Now his wars on God begin;
At stroke of midnight God shall win.

X

CONJUNCTIONS

If Jupiter and Saturn meet,
What a crop of mummy wheat!

The sword's a cross; thereon He died:
On breast of Mars the goddess sighed.

XI

A NEEDLE'S EYE

All the stream that's roaring by
Came out of a needle's eye;
Things unborn, things that are gone,
From needle's eye still goad it on.

XII

MERU

Civilisation is hooped together, brought
Under a rule, under the semblance of peace
By manifold illusion; but man's life is thought,
And he, despite his terror, cannot cease
Ravening through century after century,
Ravening, raging, and uprooting that he may come
Into the desolation of reality:
Egypt and Greece, good-bye, and good-bye, Rome!
Hermits upon Mount Meru or Everest,
Caverned in night under the drifted snow,
Or where that snow and winter's dreadful blast
Beat down upon their naked bodies, know
That day brings round the night, that before dawn
His glory and his monuments are gone.

NEW POEMS
1938

NEW POEMS

The Gyres

The gyres! the gyres! Old Rocky Face, look forth;
Things thought too long can be no longer thought,
For beauty dies of beauty, worth of worth,
And ancient lineaments are blotted out.
Irrational streams of blood are staining earth;
Empedocles has thrown all things about;
Hector is dead and there's a light in Troy;
We that look on but laugh in tragic joy.

What matter though numb nightmare ride on top,
And blood and mire the sensitive body stain?
What matter? Heave no sigh, let no tear drop,
A greater, a more gracious time has gone;
For painted forms or boxes of make-up
In ancient tombs I sighed, but not again;
What matter? Out of cavern comes a voice,
And all it knows is that one word 'Rejoice!'

Conduct and work grow coarse, and coarse the soul,
What matter? Those that Rocky Face holds dear,
Lovers of horses and of women, shall,
From marble of a broken sepulchre,
Or dark betwixt the polecat and the owl,
Or any rich, dark nothing disinter
The workman, noble and saint, and all things run
On that unfashionable gyre again.

Lapis Lazuli

(For Harry Clifton)

I have heard that hysterical women say
They are sick of the palette and fiddle-bow,
Of poets that are always gay,
For everybody knows or else should know
That if nothing drastic is done
Aeroplane and Zeppelin will come out,
Pitch like King Billy bomb-balls in
Until the town lie beaten flat.

All perform their tragic play,
There struts Hamlet, there is Lear,
That's Ophelia, that Cordelia;
Yet they, should the last scene be there,
The great stage curtain about to drop,
If worthy their prominent part in the play,
Do not break up their lines to weep.
They know that Hamlet and Lear are gay;
Gaiety transfiguring all that dread.
All men have aimed at, found and lost;
Black out; Heaven blazing into the head:
Tragedy wrought to its uttermost.
Though Hamlet rambles and Lear rages,
And all the drop-scenes drop at once
Upon a hundred thousand stages,
It cannot grow by an inch or an ounce.

On their own feet they came, or on shipboard,
Camel-back, horse-back, ass-back, mule-back,
Old civilisations put to the sword.
Then they and their wisdom went to rack:
No handiwork of Callimachus,
Who handled marble as if it were bronze,
Made draperies that seemed to rise
When sea-wind swept the corner, stands;

His long lamp-chimney shaped like the stem
Of a slender palm, stood but a day;
All things fall and are built again,
And those that build them again are gay.

Two Chinamen, behind them a third,
Are carved in lapis lazuli,
Over them flies a long-legged bird,
A symbol of longevity;
The third, doubtless a serving-man,
Carries a musical instrument.

Every discoloration of the stone,
Every accidental crack or dent,
Seems a water-course or an avalanche,
Or lofty slope where it still snows
Though doubtless plum or cherry-branch
Sweetens the little half-way house
Those Chinamen climb towards, and I
Delight to imagine them seated there;
There, on the mountain and the sky,
On all the tragic scene they stare.
One asks for mournful melodies;
Accomplished fingers begin to play.
Their eyes mid many wrinkles, their eyes,
Their ancient, glittering eyes, are gay.

Imitated from the Japanese

A most astonishing thing –
Seventy years have I lived;

(Hurrah for the flowers of Spring,
For Spring is here again.)

Seventy years have I lived
No ragged beggar-man,
Seventy years have I lived,
Seventy years man and boy,
And never have I danced for joy.

Sweet Dancer

The girl goes dancing there
On the leaf-sown, new-mown, smooth
Grass plot of the garden;
Escaped from bitter youth,
Escaped out of her crowd,
Or out of her black cloud.
Ah, dancer, ah, sweet dancer!

If strange men come from the house
To lead her away, do not say
That she is happy being crazy;
Lead them gently astray;
Let her finish her dance,
Let her finish her dance.
Ah, dancer, ah, sweet dancer!

The Three Bushes

*(An incident from the 'Historia mei Temporis' of the
Abbé Michel de Bourdeille)*

Said lady once to lover,
'None can rely upon
A love that lacks its proper food;
And if your love were gone
How could you sing those songs of love?
I should be blamed, young man.
    O my dear, O my dear.

'Have no lit candles in your room,'
That lovely lady said,
'That I at midnight by the clock
May creep into your bed,
For if I saw myself creep in
I think I should drop dead.'
    O my dear, O my dear.

'I love a man in secret,
Dear chambermaid,' said she.
'I know that I must drop down dead
If he stop loving me,
Yet what could I but drop down dead
If I lost my chastity?'
        O my dear, O my dear.

'So you must lie beside him
And let him think me there,
And maybe we are all the same
Where no candles are,
And maybe we are all the same
That strip the body bare.'
        O my dear, O my dear.

But no dogs barked, and midnights chimed,
And through the chime she'd say,
'That was a lucky thought of mine,
My lover looked so gay';
But heaved a sigh if the chambermaid
Looked half asleep all day.
        O my dear, O my dear.

'No, not another song,' said he,
'Because my lady came
A year ago for the first time
At midnight to my room,
And I must lie between the sheets
When the clock begins to chime.'
        O my dear, O my dear.

'A laughing, crying, sacred song,
A leching song,' they said.
Did ever men hear such a song?
No, but that day they did.
Did ever man ride such a race?
No, not until he rode.
        O my dear, O my dear.

But when his horse had put its hoof
Into a rabbit-hole
He dropped upon his head and died.
His lady saw it all
And dropped and died thereon, for she
Loved him with her soul.
            O my dear, O my dear.

The chambermaid lived long, and took
Their graves into her charge,
And there two bushes planted
That when they had grown large
Seemed sprung from but a single root
So did their roses merge.
            O my dear, O my dear.

When she was old and dying,
The priest came where she was;
She made a full confession.
Long looked he in her face,
And O he was a good man
And understood her case.
            O my dear, O my dear.

He bade them take and bury her
Beside her lady's man,
And set a rose-tree on her grave,
And now none living can,
When they have plucked a rose there,
Know where its roots began.
            O my dear, O my dear.

The Lady's First Song

I turn round
Like a dumb beast in a show,
Neither know what I am
Nor where I go,

My language beaten
Into one name;
I am in love
And that is my shame.
What hurts the soul
My soul adores,
No better than a beast
Upon all fours.

The Lady's Second Song

What sort of man is coming
To lie between your feet?
What matter, we are but women.
Wash; make your body sweet;
I have cupboards of dried fragrance,
I can strew the sheet.
 The Lord have mercy upon us.

He shall love my soul as though
Body were not at all,
He shall love your body
Untroubled by the soul,
Love cram love's two divisions
Yet keep his substance whole.
 The Lord have mercy upon us.

Soul must learn a love that is
Proper to my breast,
Limbs a love in common
With every noble beast.
If soul may look and body touch,
Which is the more blest?
 The Lord have mercy upon us.

The Lady's Third Song

When you and my true lover meet
And he plays tunes between your feet,
Speak no evil of the soul,
Nor think that body is the whole,
For I that am his daylight lady
Know worse evil of the body;
But in honour split his love
Till either neither have enough,
That I may hear if we should kiss
A contrapuntal serpent hiss,
You, should hand explore a thigh,
All the labouring heavens sigh.

The Lover's Song

Bird sighs for the air,
Thought for I know not where,
For the womb the seed sighs.
Now sinks the same rest
On mind, on nest,
On straining thighs.

The Chambermaid's First Song

How came this ranger
Now sunk in rest,
Stranger with stranger,
On my cold breast?

What's left to sigh for?
Strange night has come;
God's love has hidden him
Out of all harm,
Pleasure has made him
Weak as a worm.

The Chambermaid's Second Song

From pleasure of the bed,
Dull as a worm,
His rod and its butting head
Limp as a worm,
His spirit that has fled
Blind as a worm.

An Acre of Grass

Picture and book remain,
An acre of green grass
For air and exercise,
Now strength of body goes;
Midnight, an old house
Where nothing stirs but a mouse.

My temptation is quiet.
Here at life's end
Neither loose imagination,
Nor the mill of the mind
Consuming its rag and bone,
Can make the truth known.

Grant me an old man's frenzy,
Myself must I remake
Till I am Timon and Lear
Or that William Blake
Who beat upon the wall
Till Truth obeyed his call;

A mind Michael Angelo knew
That can pierce the clouds,
Or inspired by frenzy
Shake the dead in their shrouds;
Forgotten else by mankind,
An old man's eagle mind.

What Then?

His chosen comrades thought at school
He must grow a famous man;
He thought the same and lived by rule,
All his twenties crammed with toil;
'What then?' sang Plato's ghost. 'What then?'

Everything he wrote was read,
After certain years he won
Sufficient money for his need,
Friends that have been friends indeed;
'What then?' sang Plato's ghost. 'What then?'

All his happier dreams came true –
A small old house, wife, daughter, son,
Grounds where plum and cabbage grew,
Poets and Wits about him drew;
'What then?' sang Plato's ghost. 'What then?'

'The work is done,' grown old he thought,
'According to my boyish plan;
Let the fools rage, I swerved in naught,
Something to perfection brought';
But louder sang that ghost, 'What then?'

Beautiful Lofty Things

Beautiful lofty things: O'Leary's noble head;
My father upon the Abbey stage, before him a raging crowd:
'This Land of Saints,' and then as the applause died out,
'Of plaster Saints'; his beautiful mischievous head thrown back.
Standish O'Grady supporting himself between the tables
Speaking to a drunken audience high nonsensical words;
Augusta Gregory seated at her great ormolu table,
Her eightieth winter approaching: 'Yesterday he threatened my
    life.
I told him that nightly from six to seven I sat at this table,
The blinds drawn up'; Maud Gonne at Howth station waiting a
    train,
Pallas Athene in that straight back and arrogant head:
All the Olympians; a thing never known again.

A Crazed Girl

That crazed girl improvising her music,
Her poetry, dancing upon the shore,
Her soul in division from itself
Climbing, falling she knew not where,
Hiding amid the cargo of a steamship,
Her knee-cap broken, that girl I declare
A beautiful lofty thing, or a thing
Heroically lost, heroically found.

No matter what disaster occurred
She stood in desperate music wound,
Wound, wound, and she made in her triumph
Where the bales and the baskets lay
No common intelligible sound
But sang, 'O sea-starved, hungry sea.'

To Dorothy Wellesley

Stretch towards the moonless midnight of the trees,
As though that hand could reach to where they stand,
And they but famous old upholsteries
Delightful to the touch; tighten that hand
As though to draw them closer yet.
                             Rammed full
Of that most sensuous silence of the night
(For since the horizon's bought strange dogs are still)
Climb to your chamber full of books and wait,
No books upon the knee, and no one there
But a Great Dane that cannot bay the moon
And now lies sunk in sleep.
                        What climbs the stair?
Nothing that common women ponder on
If you are worth my hope! Neither Content
Nor satisfied Conscience, but that great family
Some ancient famous authors misrepresent,
The Proud Furies each with her torch on high.

The Curse of Cromwell

You ask what I have found, and far and wide I go:
Nothing but Cromwell's house and Cromwell's murderous crew,
The lovers and the dancers are beaten into the clay,
And the tall men and the swordsmen and the horsemen, where are
    they?
And there is an old beggar wandering in his pride –
His fathers served their fathers before Christ was crucified.
                O what of that, O what of that,
                What is there left to say?

All neighbourly content and easy talk are gone,
But there's no good complaining, for money's rant is on.

He that's mounting up must on his neighbour mount,
And we and all the Muses are things of no account.
They have schooling of their own, but I pass their schooling by,
What can they know that we know that know the time to die?
      O what of that, O what of that,
      What is there left to say?

But there's another knowledge that my heart destroys,
As the fox in the old fable destroyed the Spartan boy's,
Because it proves that things both can and cannot be;
That the swordsmen and the ladies can still keep company,
Can pay the poet for a verse and hear the fiddle sound,
That I am still their servant though all are underground.
      O what of that, O what of that,
      What is there left to say?

I came on a great house in the middle of the night,
Its open lighted doorway and its windows all alight,
And all my friends were there and made me welcome too;
But I woke in an old ruin that the winds howled through;
And when I pay attention I must out and walk
Among the dogs and horses that understand my talk.
      O what of that, O what of that,
      What is there left to say?

Roger Casement

(After reading 'The Forged Casement Diaries'
by Dr. Maloney)

I say that Roger Casement
Did what he had to do.
He died upon the gallows,
But that is nothing new.

Afraid they might be beaten
Before the bench of Time,
They turned a trick by forgery
And blackened his good name.

A perjurer stood ready
To prove their forgery true;
They gave it out to all the world,
And that is something new;

For Spring-Rice had to whisper it,
Being their Ambassador,
And then the speakers got it
And writers by the score.

Come Tom and Dick, come all the troop
That cried it far and wide,
Come from the forger and his desk,
Desert the perjurer's side;

Come speak your bit in public
That some amends be made
To this most gallant gentleman
That is in quicklime laid.

The Ghost of Roger Casement

O what has made that sudden noise?
What on the threshold stands?
It never crossed the sea because
John Bull and the sea are friends;
But this is not the old sea
Nor this the old seashore.
What gave that roar of mockery,
That roar in the sea's roar?
The ghost of Roger Casement
Is beating on the door.

John Bull has stood for Parliament,
A dog must have his day,
The country thinks no end of him,
For he knows how to say,

At a beanfeast or a banquet,
That all must hang their trust
Upon the British Empire,
Upon the Church of Christ.
The ghost of Roger Casement
Is beating on the door.

John Bull has gone to India
And all must pay him heed,
For histories are there to prove
That none of another breed
Has had a like inheritance,
Or sucked such milk as he,
And there's no luck about a house
If it lack honesty.
The ghost of Roger Casement
Is beating on the door.

I poked about a village church
And found his family tomb
And copied out what I could read
In that religious gloom;
Found many a famous man there;
But fame and virtue rot.
Draw round, beloved and bitter men,
Draw round and raise a shout;
The ghost of Roger Casement
Is beating on the door.

The O'Rahilly

Sing of the O'Rahilly,
Do not deny his right;
Sing a 'the' before his name;
Allow that he, despite

All those learned historians,
Established it for good;
He wrote out that word himself,
He christened himself with blood.
                    How goes the weather?

Sing of the O'Rahilly
That had such little sense
He told Pearse and Connolly
He'd gone to great expense
Keeping all the Kerry men
Out of that crazy fight;
That he might be there himself
Had travelled half the night.
                    How goes the weather?

'Am I such a craven that
I should not get the word
But for what some travelling man
Had heard I had not heard?'
Then on Pearse and Connolly
He fixed a bitter look:
'Because I helped to wind the clock
I come to hear it strike.'
                    How goes the weather?

What remains to sing about
But of the death he met
Stretched under a doorway
Somewhere off Henry Street;
They that found him found upon
The door above his head
'Here died the O'Rahilly.
R.I.P.' writ in blood.
                    How goes the weather?

Come Gather Round Me, Parnellites

Come gather round me, Parnellites,
And praise our chosen man;
Stand upright on your legs awhile,
Stand upright while you can,
For soon we lie where he is laid,
And he is underground;
Come fill up all those glasses
And pass the bottle round.

And here's a cogent reason,
And I have many more,
He fought the might of England
And saved the Irish poor,
Whatever good a farmer's got
He brought it all to pass;
And here's another reason,
That Parnell loved a lass.

And here's a final reason,
He was of such a kind
Every man that sings a song
Keeps Parnell in his mind,
For Parnell was a proud man,
No prouder trod the ground,
And a proud man's a lovely man,
So pass the bottle round.

The Bishops and the Party
That tragic story made,
A husband that had sold his wife
And after that betrayed;
But stories that live longest
Are sung above the glass,
And Parnell loved his country,
And Parnell loved his lass.

The Wild Old Wicked Man

'Because I am mad about women
I am mad about the hills,'
Said that wild old wicked man
Who travels where God wills.
'Not to die on the straw at home,
Those hands to close these eyes,
That is all I ask, my dear,
From the old man in the skies.
          Daybreak and a candle-end.

'Kind are all your words, my dear,
Do not the rest withhold.
Who can know the year, my dear,
When an old man's blood grows cold?
I have what no young man can have
Because he loves too much.
Words I have that can pierce the heart,
But what can he do but touch?'
          Daybreak and a candle-end.

Then said she to that wild old man,
His stout stick under his hand,
'Love to give or to withhold
Is not at my command.
I gave it all to an older man:
That old man in the skies.
Hands that are busy with His beads
Can never close those eyes.'
          Daybreak and a candle-end.

'Go your ways, O go your ways,
I choose another mark,
Girls down on the seashore
Who understand the dark;

Bawdy talk for the fishermen;
A dance for the fisher-lads;
When dark hangs upon the water
They turn down their beds.
Daybreak and a candle-end.

'A young man in the dark am I,
But a wild old man in the light,
That can make a cat laugh, or
Can touch by mother wit
Things hid in their marrow–bones
From time long passed away,
Hid from all those warty lads
That by their bodies lay.
Daybreak and a candle-end.

'All men live in suffering,
I know as few can know,
Whether they take the upper road
Or stay content on the low,
Rower bent in his row-boat
Or weaver bent at his loom,
Horseman erect upon horseback
Or child hid in the womb.
Daybreak and a candle-end.

'That some stream of lightning
From the old man in the skies
Can burn out that suffering
No right-taught man denies.
But a coarse old man am I,
I choose the second-best,
I forget it all awhile
Upon a woman's breast.'
Daybreak and a candle-end.

The Great Day

Hurrah for revolution and more cannon-shot!
A beggar upon horseback lashes a beggar on foot.
Hurrah for revolution and cannon come again!
The beggars have changed places, but the lash goes on.

Parnell

Parnell came down the road, he said to a cheering man:
'Ireland shall get her freedom and you still break stone.'

What Was Lost

I sing what was lost and dread what was won,
I walk in a battle fought over again,
My king a lost king, and lost soldiers my men;
Feet to the Rising and Setting may run,
They always beat on the same small stone.

The Spur

You think it horrible that lust and rage
Should dance attention upon my old age;
They were not such a plague when I was young;
What else have I to spur me into song?

A Drunken Man's Praise of Sobriety

Come swish around, my pretty punk,
And keep me dancing still
That I may stay a sober man
Although I drink my fill.
Sobriety is a jewel
That I do much adore;
And therefore keep me dancing
Though drunkards lie and snore.
O mind your feet, O mind your feet,
Keep dancing like a wave,
And under every dancer
A dead man in his grave.
No ups and downs, my pretty,
A mermaid, not a punk;
A drunkard is a dead man,
And all dead men are drunk.

The Pilgrim

I fasted for some forty days on bread and buttermilk,
For passing round the bottle with girls in rags or silk,
In country shawl or Paris cloak, had put my wits astray,
And what's the good of women, for all that they can say
Is fol de rol de rolly O.

Round Lough Derg's holy island I went upon the stones,
I prayed at all the Stations upon my marrow-bones,
And there I found an old man, and though I prayed all day
And that old man beside me, nothing would he say
But fol de rol de rolly O.

All know that all the dead in the world about that place are stuck,
And that should mother seek her son she'd have but little luck
Because the fires of Purgatory have ate their shapes away;
I swear to God I questioned them, and all they had to say
Was fol de rol de rolly O.

A great black ragged bird appeared when I was in the boat;
Some twenty feet from tip to tip had it stretched rightly out,
With flopping and with flapping it made a great display,
But I never stopped to question, what could the boatman say
But fol de rol de rolly O.

Now I am in the public-house and lean upon the wall,
So come in rags or come in silk, in cloak or country shawl,
And come with learned lovers or with what men you may,
For I can put the whole lot down, and all I have to say
Is fol de rol de rolly O.

Colonel Martin

I

The Colonel went out sailing,
He spoke with Turk and Jew,
With Christian and with Infidel,
For all tongues he knew.
'O what's a wifeless man?' said he,
And he came sailing home.
He rose the latch and went upstairs
And found an empty room.
The Colonel went out sailing.

II

'I kept her much in the country
And she was much alone,
And though she may be there,' he said,
'She may be in the town.

She may be all alone there,
For who can say?' he said.
'I think that I shall find her
In a young man's bed.'
The Colonel went out sailing.

III

The Colonel met a pedlar,
Agreed their clothes to swop,
And bought the grandest jewelry
In a Galway shop,
Instead of thread and needle
Put jewelry in the pack,
Bound a thong about his hand,
Hitched it on his back.
The Colonel went out sailing.

IV

The Colonel knocked on the rich man's door,
'I am sorry,' said the maid,
'My mistress cannot see these things,
But she is still abed,
And never have I looked upon
Jewelry so grand.'
'Take all to your mistress,'
And he laid them on her hand.
The Colonel went out sailing.

V

And he went in and she went on
And both climbed up the stair,
And O he was a clever man,
For he his slippers wore.
And when they came to the top stair
He ran on ahead,
His wife he found and the rich man
In the comfort of a bed.
The Colonel went out sailing.

VI

The Judge at the Assize Court,
When he heard that story told,
Awarded him for damages
Three kegs of gold.
The Colonel said to Tom his man,
'Harness an ass and cart,
Carry the gold about the town,
Throw it in every part.'
The Colonel went out sailing.

VII

And there at all street-corners
A man with a pistol stood,
And the rich man had paid them well
To shoot the Colonel dead;
But they threw down their pistols
And all men heard them swear
That they could never shoot a man
Did all that for the poor.
The Colonel went out sailing.

VIII

'And did you keep no gold, Tom?
You had three kegs,' said he.
'I never thought of that, Sir.'
'Then want before you die.'
And want he did; for my own grand-dad
Saw the story's end,
And Tom make out a living
From the seaweed on the strand.
The Colonel went out sailing.

A Model for the Laureate

On thrones from China to Peru
All sorts of kings have sat
That men and women of all sorts
Proclaimed both good and great;
And what's the odds if such as these
For reason of the State
Should keep their lovers waiting,
   Keep their lovers waiting?

Some boast of beggar-kings and kings
Of rascals black and white
That rule because a strong right arm
Puts all men in a fright,
And drunk or sober live at ease
Where none gainsay their right,
And keep their lovers waiting,
   Keep their lovers waiting.

The Muse is mute when public men
Applaud a modern throne:
Those cheers that can be bought or sold,
That office fools have run,
That waxen seal, that signature,
For things like these what decent man
Would keep his lover waiting,
   Keep his lover waiting?

The Old Stone Cross

A statesman is an easy man,
He tells his lies by rote;
A journalist makes up his lies
And takes you by the throat;

So stay at home and drink your beer
And let the neighbours vote,
    Said the man in the golden breastplate
    Under the old stone Cross.

Because this age and the next age
Engender in the ditch,
No man can know a happy man
From any passing wretch;
If Folly link with Elegance
No man knows which is which,
    Said the man in the golden breastplate
    Under the old stone Cross.

But actors lacking music
Do most excite my spleen,
They say it is more human
To shuffle, grunt and groan,
Not knowing what unearthly stuff
Rounds a mighty scene,
    Said the man in the golden breastplate
    Under the old stone Cross.

The Spirit Medium

Poetry, music, I have loved, and yet
Because of those new dead
That come into my soul and escape
Confusion of the bed,
Or those begotten or unbegotten
Perning in a band,
I bend my body to the spade
Or grope with a dirty hand.

Or those begotten or unbegotten,
For I would not recall
Some that being unbegotten
Are not individual,

But copy some one action,
Moulding it of dust or sand,
I bend my body to the spade
Or grope with a dirty hand.

An old ghost's thoughts are lightning,
To follow is to die;
Poetry and music I have banished,
But the stupidity
Of root, shoot, blossom or clay
Makes no demand.
I bend my body to the spade
Or grope with a dirty hand.

Those Images

What if I bade you leave
The cavern of the mind?
There's better exercise
In the sunlight and wind.

I never bade you go
To Moscow or to Rome.
Renounce that drudgery,
Call the Muses home.

Seek those images
That constitute the wild,
The lion and the virgin,
The harlot and the child.

Find in middle air
An eagle on the wing,
Recognise the five
That make the Muses sing.

The Municipal Gallery Revisited

I

Around me the images of thirty years:
An ambush; pilgrims at the water-side;
Casement upon trial, half hidden by the bars,
Guarded; Griffith staring in hysterical pride;
Kevin O'Higgins' countenance that wears
A gentle questioning look that cannot hide
A soul incapable of remorse or rest;
A revolutionary soldier kneeling to be blessed;

II

An Abbot or Archbishop with an upraised hand
Blessing the Tricolour. 'This is not,' I say,
'The dead Ireland of my youth, but an Ireland
The poets have imagined, terrible and gay.'
Before a woman's portrait suddenly I stand,
Beautiful and gentle in her Venetian way.
I met her all but fifty years ago
For twenty minutes in some studio.

III

Heart-smitten with emotion I sink down,
My heart recovering with covered eyes;
Wherever I had looked I had looked upon
My permanent or impermanent images:
Augusta Gregory's son; her sister's son,
Hugh Lane, 'onlie begetter' of all these;
Hazel Lavery living and dying, that tale
As though some ballad-singer had sung it all;

IV

Mancini's portrait of Augusta Gregory,
'Greatest since Rembrandt,' according to John Synge;
A great ebullient portrait certainly;
But where is the brush that could show anything
Of all that pride and that humility?
And I am in despair that time may bring
Approved patterns of women or of men
But not that selfsame excellence again.

V

My mediaeval knees lack health until they bend,
But in that woman, in that household where
Honour had lived so long, all lacking found.
Childless I thought, 'My children may find here
Deep-rooted things,' but never foresaw its end,
And now that end has come I have not wept;
No fox can foul the lair the badger swept –

VI

(An image out of Spenser and the common tongue).
John Synge, I and Augusta Gregory, thought
All that we did, all that we said or sang
Must come from contact with the soil, from that
Contact everything Antaeus-like grew strong.
We three alone in modern times had brought
Everything down to that sole test again,
Dream of the noble and the beggar-man.

VII

And here's John Synge himself, that rooted man,
'Forgetting human words,' a grave deep face.
You that would judge me, do not judge alone
This book or that, come to this hallowed place

Where my friends' portraits hang and look thereon;
Ireland's history in their lineaments trace;
Think where man's glory most begins and ends,
And say my glory was I had such friends.

Are You Content?

I call on those that call me son,
Grandson, or great-grandson,
On uncles, aunts, great-uncles or great-aunts,
To judge what I have done.
Have I, that put it into words,
Spoilt what old loins have sent?
Eyes spiritualised by death can judge,
I cannot, but I am not content.

He that in Sligo at Drumcliff
Set up the old stone Cross,
That red-headed rector in County Down,
A good man on a horse,
Sandymount Corbets, that notable man
Old William Pollexfen,
The smuggler Middleton, Butlers far back,
Half legendary men.

Infirm and aged I might stay
In some good company,
I who have always hated work,
Smiling at the sea,
Or demonstrate in my own life
What Robert Browning meant
By an old hunter talking with Gods;
But I am not content.

[POEMS FROM 'ON THE BOILER']
1939

[POEMS FROM 'ON THE BOILER']

[*Why should not Old Men be Mad?*]

Why should not old men be mad?
Some have known a likely lad
That had a sound fly-fisher's wrist
Turn to a drunken journalist;
A girl that knew all Dante once
Live to bear children to a dunce;
A Helen of social welfare dream,
Climb on a wagonette to scream.
Some think it a matter of course that chance
Should starve good men and bad advance,
That if their neighbours figured plain,
As though upon a lighted screen,
No single story would they find
Of an unbroken happy mind,
A finish worthy of the start.
Young men know nothing of this sort,
Observant old men know it well;
And when they know what old books tell,
And that no better can be had,
Know why an old man should be mad.

[*Crazy Jane on the Mountain*]

I am tired of cursing the Bishop,
(Said Crazy Jane)
Nine books or nine hats
Would not make him a man.

I have found something worse
To meditate on.
A King had some beautiful cousins,
But where are they gone?
Battered to death in a cellar,
And he stuck to his throne.
Last night I lay on the mountain,
(Said Crazy Jane)
There in a two-horsed carriage
That on two wheels ran
Great-bladdered Emer sat,
Her violent man
Cuchulain sat at her side;
Thereupon,
Propped upon my two knees,
I kissed a stone;
I lay stretched out in the dirt
And I cried tears down.

[*The Statesman's Holiday*]

I lived among great houses,
Riches drove out rank,
Base drove out the better blood,
And mind and body shrank.
No Oscar ruled the table,
But I'd a troop of friends
That knowing better talk had gone
Talked of odds and ends.
Some knew what ailed the world
But never said a thing,
So I have picked a better trade
And night and morning sing:
Tall dames go walking in grass-green Avalon.

Am I a great Lord Chancellor
That slept upon the Sack?
Commanding officer that tore
The khaki from his back?
Or am I de Valéra,
Or the King of Greece,
Or the man that made the motors?
Ach, call me what you please!
Here's a Montenegrin lute,
And its old sole string
Makes me sweet music
And I delight to sing:
Tall dames go walking in grass-green Avalon.

With boys and girls about him,
With any sort of clothes,
With a hat out of fashion,
With old patched shoes,
With a ragged bandit cloak,
With an eye like a hawk,
With a stiff straight back,
With a strutting turkey walk,
With a bag full of pennies,
With a monkey on a chain,
With a great cock's feather,
With an old foul tune.
Tall dames go walking in grass-green Avalon.

[LAST POEMS]
1938–1939

[LAST POEMS]

Under Ben Bulben

I

Swear by what the sages spoke
Round the Mareotic Lake
That the Witch of Atlas knew,
Spoke and set the cocks a-crow.

Swear by those horsemen, by those women
Complexion and form prove superhuman,
That pale, long-visaged company
That air in immortality
Completeness of their passions won;
Now they ride the wintry dawn
Where Ben Bulben sets the scene.

Here's the gist of what they mean.

II

Many times man lives and dies
Between his two eternities,
That of race and that of soul,
And ancient Ireland knew it all.
Whether man die in his bed
Or the rifle knocks him dead,
A brief parting from those dear
Is the worst man has to fear.

Though grave-diggers' toil is long,
Sharp their spades, their muscles strong,
They but thrust their buried men
Back in the human mind again.

III

You that Mitchel's prayer have heard,
'Send war in our time, O Lord!'
Know that when all words are said
And a man is fighting mad,
Something drops from eyes long blind,
He completes his partial mind,
For an instant stands at ease,
Laughs aloud, his heart at peace.
Even the wisest man grows tense
With some sort of violence
Before he can accomplish fate,
Know his work or choose his mate.

IV

Poet and sculptor, do the work,
Nor let the modish painter shirk
What his great forefathers did,
Bring the soul of man to God,
Make him fill the cradles right.

Measurement began our might:
Forms a stark Egyptian thought,
Forms that gentler Phidias wrought.

Michael Angelo left a proof
On the Sistine Chapel roof,
Where but half-awakened Adam
Can disturb globe-trotting Madam
Till her bowels are in heat,
Proof that there's a purpose set
Before the secret working mind:
Profane perfection of mankind.

Quattrocento put in paint
On backgrounds for a God or Saint
Gardens where a soul's at ease;
Where everything that meets the eye,
Flowers and grass and cloudless sky,

Resemble forms that are or seem
When sleepers wake and yet still dream,
And when it's vanished still declare,
With only bed and bedstead there,
That heavens had opened.
                              Gyres run on;
When that greater dream had gone
Calvert and Wilson, Blake and Claude,
Prepared a rest for the people of God,
Palmer's phrase, but after that
Confusion fell upon our thought.

V

Irish poets, learn your trade,
Sing whatever is well made,
Scorn the sort now growing up
All out of shape from toe to top,
Their unremembering hearts and heads
Base-born products of base beds.
Sing the peasantry, and then
Hard-riding country gentlemen,
The holiness of monks, and after
Porter-drinkers' randy laughter;
Sing the lords and ladies gay
That were beaten into the clay
Through seven heroic centuries;
Cast your mind on other days
That we in coming days may be
Still the indomitable Irishry.

VI

Under bare Ben Bulben's head
In Drumcliff churchyard Yeats is laid.
An ancestor was rector there
Long years ago, a church stands near,
By the road an ancient cross.
No marble, no conventional phrase;

On limestone quarried near the spot
By his command these words are cut:
        Cast a cold eye
        On life, on death.
        Horseman, pass by!

Three Songs to the One Burden

I

The Roaring Tinker if you like,
But Mannion is my name,
And I beat up the common sort
And think it is no shame.
The common breeds the common,
A lout begets a lout,
So when I take on half a score
I knock their heads about.

From mountain to mountain ride the fierce horsemen.

All Mannions come from Manannan,
Though rich on every shore
He never lay behind four walls
He had such character,
Nor ever made an iron red
Nor soldered pot or pan;
His roaring and his ranting
Best please a wandering man.

From mountain to mountain ride the fierce horsemen.

Could Crazy Jane put off old age
And ranting time renew,
Could that old god rise up again
We'd drink a can or two,

And out and lay our leadership
On country and on town,
Throw likely couples into bed
And knock the others down.

From mountain to mountain ride the fierce horsemen.

II

My name is Henry Middleton,
I have a small demesne,
A small forgotten house that's set
On a storm-bitten green.
I scrub its floors and make my bed,
I cook and change my plate,
The post and garden-boy alone
Have keys to my old gate.

From mountain to mountain ride the fierce horsemen.

Though I have locked my gate on them,
I pity all the young,
I know what devil's trade they learn
From those they live among,
Their drink, their pitch-and-toss by day,
Their robbery by night;
The wisdom of the people's gone,
How can the young go straight?

From mountain to mountain ride the fierce horsemen.

When every Sunday afternoon
On the Green Lands I walk
And wear a coat in fashion,
Memories of the talk
Of henwives and of queer old men
Brace me and make me strong;
There's not a pilot on the perch
Knows I have lived so long.

From mountain to mountain ride the fierce horsemen.

III

Come gather round me, players all:
Come praise Nineteen-Sixteen,
Those from the pit and gallery
Or from the painted scene
That fought in the Post Office
Or round the City Hall,
Praise every man that came again,
Praise every man that fell.

From mountain to mountain ride the fierce horsemen.

Who was the first man shot that day?
The player Connolly,
Close to the City Hall he died;
Carriage and voice had he;
He lacked those years that go with skill,
But later might have been
A famous, a brilliant figure
Before the painted scene.

From mountain to mountain ride the fierce horsemen.

Some had no thought of victory
But had gone out to die
That Ireland's mind be greater,
Her heart mount up on high;
And yet who knows what's yet to come?
For Patrick Pearse had said
That in every generation
Must Ireland's blood be shed.

From mountain to mountain ride the fierce horsemen.

The Black Tower

Say that the men of the old black tower,
Though they but feed as the goatherd feeds,
Their money spent, their wine gone sour,
Lack nothing that a soldier needs,
That all are oath-bound men:
Those banners come not in.

There in the tomb stand the dead upright,
But winds come up from the shore:
They shake when the winds roar,
Old bones upon the mountain shake.

Those banners come to bribe or threaten,
Or whisper that a man's a fool
Who, when his own right king's forgotten,
Cares what king sets up his rule.
If he died long ago
Why do you dread us so?

There in the tomb drops the faint moonlight,
But wind comes up from the shore:
They shake when the winds roar,
Old bones upon the mountain shake.

The tower's old cook that must climb and clamber
Catching small birds in the dew of the morn
When we hale men lie stretched in slumber
Swears that he hears the king's great horn.
But he's a lying hound:
Stand we on guard oath-bound!

There in the tomb the dark grows blacker,
But wind comes up from the shore:
They shake when the winds roar,
Old bones upon the mountain shake.

Cuchulain Comforted

A man that had six mortal wounds, a man
Violent and famous, strode among the dead;
Eyes stared out of the branches and were gone.

Then certain Shrouds that muttered head to head
Came and were gone. He leant upon a tree
As though to meditate on wounds and blood.

A Shroud that seemed to have authority
Among those bird-like things came, and let fall
A bundle of linen. Shrouds by two and three

Came creeping up because the man was still.
And thereupon that linen-carrier said:
'Your life can grow much sweeter if you will

'Obey our ancient rule and make a shroud;
Mainly because of what we only know
The rattle of those arms makes us afraid.

'We thread the needles' eyes, and all we do
All must together do.' That done, the man
Took up the nearest and began to sew.

'Now must we sing and sing the best we can,
But first you must be told our character:
Convicted cowards all, by kindred slain

'Or driven from home and left to die in fear.'
They sang, but had nor human tunes nor words,
Though all was done in common as before;

They had changed their throats and had the throats of birds.

Three Marching Songs

I

Remember all those renowned generations,
They left their bodies to fatten the wolves,
They left their homesteads to fatten the foxes,
Fled to far countries, or sheltered themselves
In cavern, crevice, or hole,
Defending Ireland's soul.

Be still, be still, what can be said?
My father sang that song,
But time amends old wrong,
All that is finished, let it fade.

Remember all those renowned generations,
Remember all that have sunk in their blood,
Remember all that have died on the scaffold,
Remember all that have fled, that have stood,
Stood, took death like a tune
On an old tambourine.

Be still, be still, what can be said?
My father sang that song,
But time amends old wrong,
And all that's finished, let it fade.

Fail, and that history turns into rubbish,
All that great past to a trouble of fools;
Those that come after shall mock at O'Donnell,
Mock at the memory of both O'Neills,
Mock Emmet, mock Parnell,
All the renown that fell.

Be still, be still, what can be said?
My father sang that song,
But time amends old wrong,
And all that's finished, let it fade.

II

The soldier takes pride in saluting his Captain,
The devotee proffers a knee to his Lord,
Some back a mare thrown from a thoroughbred,
Troy backed its Helen; Troy died and adored;
Great nations blossom above;
A slave bows down to a slave.

What marches through the mountain pass?
No, no, my son, not yet;
That is an airy spot,
And no man knows what treads the grass.

We know what rascal might has defiled,
The lofty innocence that it has slain,
We were not born in the peasant's cot
Where men forgive if the belly gain.
More dread the life that we live,
How can the mind forgive?

What marches down the mountain pass?
No, no, my son, not yet;
That is an airy spot,
And no man knows what treads the grass.

What if there's nothing up there at the top?
Where are the captains that govern mankind?
What tears down a tree that has nothing within it?
A blast of the wind, O a marching wind,
March wind, and any old tune,
March, march, and how does it run?

What marches down the mountain pass?
No, no, my son, not yet;
That is an airy spot,
And no man knows what treads the grass.

III

Grandfather sang it under the gallows:
'Hear, gentlemen, ladies, and all mankind:
Money is good and a girl might be better,
But good strong blows are delights to the mind.'
There, standing on the cart,
He sang it from his heart.

Robbers had taken his old tambourine,
But he took down the moon
And rattled out a tune;
Robbers had taken his old tambourine.

'A girl I had, but she followed another,
Money I had, and it went in the night,
Strong drink I had, and it brought me to sorrow,
But a good strong cause and blows are delight.'
All there caught up the tune:
'On, on, my darling man.'

Robbers had taken his old tambourine,
But he took down the moon
And rattled out a tune;
Robbers had taken his old tambourine.

'Money is good and a girl might be better,
No matter what happens and who takes the fall,
But a good strong cause' – the rope gave a jerk there,
No more sang he, for his throat was too small;
But he kicked before he died,
He did it out of pride.

Robbers had taken his old tambourine,
But he took down the moon
And rattled out a tune;
Robbers had taken his old tambourine.

In Tara's Halls

A man I praise that once in Tara's Halls
Said to the woman on his knees, 'Lie still.
My hundredth year is at an end. I think
That something is about to happen, I think
That the adventure of old age begins.
To many women I have said, "Lie still,"
And given everything a woman needs,
A roof, good clothes, passion, love perhaps,
But never asked for love; should I ask that,
I shall be old indeed.'
                              Thereon the man
Went to the Sacred House and stood between
The golden plough and harrow and spoke aloud
That all attendants and the casual crowd might hear.
'God I have loved, but should I ask return
Of God or woman, the time were come to die.'
He bade, his hundred and first year at end,
Diggers and carpenters make grave and coffin;
Saw that the grave was deep, the coffin sound,
Summoned the generations of his house,
Lay in the coffin, stopped his breath and died.

The Statues

Pythagoras planned it. Why did the people stare?
His numbers, though they moved or seemed to move
In marble or in bronze, lacked character.
But boys and girls, pale from the imagined love
Of solitary beds, knew what they were,
That passion could bring character enough,
And pressed at midnight in some public place
Live lips upon a plummet-measured face.

No! Greater than Pythagoras, for the men
That with a mallet or a chisel modelled these
Calculations that look but casual flesh, put down
All Asiatic vague immensities,
And not the banks of oars that swam upon
The many-headed foam at Salamis.
Europe put off that foam when Phidias
Gave women dreams and dreams their looking-glass.

One image crossed the many-headed, sat
Under the tropic shade, grew round and slow,
No Hamlet thin from eating flies, a fat
Dreamer of the Middle Ages. Empty eyeballs knew
That knowledge increases unreality, that
Mirror on mirror mirrored is all the show.
When gong and conch declare the hour to bless
Grimalkin crawls to Buddha's emptiness.

When Pearse summoned Cuchulain to his side,
What stalked through the Post Office? What intellect,
What calculation, number, measurement, replied?
We Irish, born into that ancient sect
But thrown upon this filthy modern tide
And by its formless spawning fury wrecked,
Climb to our proper dark, that we may trace
The lineaments of a plummet-measured face.

News for the Delphic Oracle

I

There all the golden codgers lay,
There the silver dew,
And the great water sighed for love,
And the wind sighed too.

Man-picker Niamh leant and sighed
By Oisin on the grass;
There sighed amid his choir of love
Tall Pythagoras.
Plotinus came and looked about,
The salt-flakes on his breast,
And having stretched and yawned awhile
Lay sighing like the rest.

II

Straddling each a dolphin's back
And steadied by a fin,
Those Innocents re-live their death,
Their wounds open again.
The ecstatic waters laugh because
Their cries are sweet and strange,
Through their ancestral patterns dance,
And the brute dolphins plunge
Until, in some cliff-sheltered bay
Where wades the choir of love
Proffering its sacred laurel crowns,
They pitch their burdens off.

III

Slim adolescence that a nymph has stripped,
Peleus on Thetis stares.
Her limbs are delicate as an eyelid,
Love has blinded him with tears;
But Thetis' belly listens.
Down the mountain walls
From where Pan's cavern is
Intolerable music falls.
Foul goat-head, brutal arm appear,
Belly, shoulder, bum,
Flash fishlike; nymphs and satyrs
Copulate in the foam.

Long-legged Fly

That civilisation may not sink,
Its great battle lost,
Quiet the dog, tether the pony
To a distant post;
Our master Caesar is in the tent
Where the maps are spread,
His eyes fixed upon nothing,
A hand under his head.

Like a long-legged fly upon the stream
His mind moves upon silence.

That the topless towers be burnt
And men recall that face,
Move most gently if move you must
In this lonely place.
She thinks, part woman, three parts a child,
That nobody looks; her feet
Practise a tinker shuffle
Picked up on a street.

Like a long-legged fly upon the stream
Her mind moves upon silence.

That girls at puberty may find
The first Adam in their thought,
Shut the door of the Pope's chapel,
Keep those children out.
There on that scaffolding reclines
Michael Angelo.
With no more sound than the mice make
His hand moves to and fro.

Like a long-legged fly upon the stream
His mind moves upon silence.

A Bronze Head

Here at right of the entrance this bronze head,
Human, superhuman, a bird's round eye,
Everything else withered and mummy-dead.
What great tomb-haunter sweeps the distant sky
(Something may linger there though all else die;)
And finds there nothing to make its terror less
Hysterica passio of its own emptiness?

No dark tomb-haunter once; her form all full
As though with magnanimity of light,
Yet a most gentle woman; who can tell
Which of her forms has shown her substance right?
Or maybe substance can be composite,
Profound McTaggart thought so, and in a breath
A mouthful held the extreme of life and death.

But even at the starting-post, all sleek and new,
I saw the wildness in her and I thought
A vision of terror that it must live through
Had shattered her soul. Propinquity had brought
Imagination to that pitch where it casts out
All that is not itself: I had grown wild
And wandered murmuring everywhere, 'My child, my child!'

Or else I thought her supernatural;
As though a sterner eye looked through her eye
On this foul world in its decline and fall;
On gangling stocks grown great, great stocks run dry,
Ancestral pearls all pitched into a sty,
Heroic reverie mocked by clown and knave,
And wondered what was left for massacre to save.

A Stick of Incense

Whence did all that fury come?
From empty tomb or Virgin womb?
Saint Joseph thought the world would melt
But liked the way his finger smelt.

Hound Voice

Because we love bare hills and stunted trees
And were the last to choose the settled ground,
Its boredom of the desk or of the spade, because
So many years companioned by a hound,
Our voices carry; and though slumber-bound,
Some few half wake and half renew their choice,
Give tongue, proclaim their hidden name – 'Hound Voice.'

The women that I picked spoke sweet and low
And yet gave tongue. 'Hound Voices' were they all.
We picked each other from afar and knew
What hour of terror comes to test the soul,
And in that terror's name obeyed the call,
And understood, what none have understood,
Those images that waken in the blood.

Some day we shall get up before the dawn
And find our ancient hounds before the door,
And wide awake know that the hunt is on;
Stumbling upon the blood-dark track once more,
Then stumbling to the kill beside the shore;
Then cleaning out and bandaging of wounds,
And chants of victory amid the encircling hounds.

John Kinsella's Lament for Mrs. Mary Moore

A bloody and a sudden end,
    Gunshot or a noose,
For Death who takes what man would keep,
    Leaves what man would lose.
He might have had my sister,
    My cousins by the score,
But nothing satisfied the fool
    But my dear Mary Moore,
None other knows what pleasures man
    At table or in bed.
What shall I do for pretty girls
    Now my old bawd is dead?

Though stiff to strike a bargain,
    Like an old Jew man,
Her bargain struck we laughed and talked
    And emptied many a can;
And O! but she had stories,
    Though not for the priest's ear,
To keep the soul of man alive,
    Banish age and care,
And being old she put a skin
    On everything she said.
What shall I do for pretty girls
    Now my old bawd is dead?

The priests have got a book that says
    But for Adam's sin
Eden's Garden would be there
    And I there within.
No expectation fails there,
    No pleasing habit ends,
No man grows old, no girl grows cold,
    But friends walk by friends.

Who quarrels over halfpennies
    That plucks the trees for bread?
What shall I do for pretty girls
    Now my old bawd is dead?

High Talk

Processions that lack high stilts have nothing that catches the eye.
What if my great-granddad had a pair that were twenty foot high,
And mine were but fifteen foot, no modern stalks upon higher,
Some rogue of the world stole them to patch up a fence or a fire.
Because piebald ponies, led bears, caged lions, make but poor
  shows,
Because children demand Daddy-long-legs upon his timber toes,
Because women in the upper storeys demand a face at the pane,
That patching old heels they may shriek, I take to chisel and plane.

Malachi Stilt-Jack am I, whatever I learned has run wild,
From collar to collar, from stilt to stilt, from father to child.
All metaphor, Malachi, stilts and all. A barnacle goose
Far up in the stretches of night; night splits and the dawn breaks
  loose.
I, through the terrible novelty of light, stalk on, stalk on;
Those great sea-horses bare their teeth and laugh at the dawn.

The Apparitions

Because there is safety in derision
I talked about an apparition,
I took no trouble to convince,
Or seem plausible to a man of sense,

Distrustful of that popular eye
Whether it be bold or sly.
Fifteen apparitions have I seen;
The worst a coat upon a coat-hanger.

I have found nothing half so good
As my long-planned half solitude,
Where I can sit up half the night
With some friend that has the wit
Not to allow his looks to tell
When I am unintelligible.
Fifteen apparitions have I seen;
The worst a coat upon a coat-hanger.

When a man grows old his joy
Grows more deep day after day,
His empty heart is full at length,
But he has need of all that strength
Because of the increasing Night
That opens her mystery and fright.
Fifteen apparitions have I seen;
The worst a coat upon a coat-hanger.

A Nativity

What woman hugs her infant there?
Another star has shot an ear.

What made the drapery glisten so?
Not a man but Delacroix.

What made the ceiling waterproof?
Landor's tarpaulin on the roof.

What brushes fly and moth aside?
Irving and his plume of pride.

What hurries out the knave and dolt?
Talma and his thunderbolt.

Why is the woman terror-struck?
Can there be mercy in that look?

Man and the Echo

MAN

In a cleft that's christened Alt
Under broken stone I halt
At the bottom of a pit
That broad noon has never lit,
And shout a secret to the stone.
All that I have said and done,
Now that I am old and ill,
Turns into a question till
I lie awake night after night
And never get the answers right.
Did that play of mine send out
Certain men the English shot?
Did words of mine put too great strain
On that woman's reeling brain?
Could my spoken words have checked
That whereby a house lay wrecked?
And all seems evil until I
Sleepless would lie down and die.

ECHO

Lie down and die.

MAN

       That were to shirk
The spiritual intellect's great work,

And shirk it in vain. There is no release
In a bodkin or disease,
Nor can there be work so great
As that which cleans man's dirty slate.
While man can still his body keep
Wine or love drug him to sleep,
Waking he thanks the Lord that he
Has body and its stupidity,
But body gone he sleeps no more,
And till his intellect grows sure
That all's arranged in one clear view,
Pursues the thoughts that I pursue,
Then stands in judgment on his soul,
And, all work done, dismisses all
Out of intellect and sight
And sinks at last into the night.

ECHO

Into the night.

MAN

        O Rocky Voice,
Shall we in that great night rejoice?
What do we know but that we face
One another in this place?
But hush, for I have lost the theme,
Its joy or night seem but a dream;
Up there some hawk or owl has struck,
Dropping out of sky or rock,
A stricken rabbit is crying out,
And its cry distracts my thought.

The Circus Animals' Desertion

I

I sought a theme and sought for it in vain,
I sought it daily for six weeks or so.
Maybe at last, being but a broken man,
I must be satisfied with my heart, although
Winter and summer till old age began
My circus animals were all on show,
Those stilted boys, that burnished chariot,
Lion and woman and the Lord knows what.

II

What can I but enumerate old themes?
First that sea-rider Oisin led by the nose
Through three enchanted islands, allegorical dreams,
Vain gaiety, vain battle, vain repose,
Themes of the embittered heart, or so it seems,
That might adorn old songs or courtly shows;
But what cared I that set him on to ride,
I, starved for the bosom of his faery bride?

And then a counter-truth filled out its play,
The Countess Cathleen was the name I gave it;
She, pity-crazed, had given her soul away,
But masterful Heaven had intervened to save it.
I thought my dear must her own soul destroy,
So did fanaticism and hate enslave it,
And this brought forth a dream and soon enough
This dream itself had all my thought and love.

And when the Fool and Blind Man stole the bread
Cuchulain fought the ungovernable sea;
Heart-mysteries there, and yet when all is said
It was the dream itself enchanted me:
Character isolated by a deed
To engross the present and dominate memory.

Players and painted stage took all my love,
And not those things that they were emblems of.

III

Those masterful images because complete
Grew in pure mind, but out of what began?
A mound of refuse or the sweepings of a street,
Old kettles, old bottles, and a broken can,
Old iron, old bones, old rags, that raving slut
Who keeps the till. Now that my ladder's gone,
I must lie down where all the ladders start,
In the foul rag-and-bone shop of the heart.

Politics

*'In our time the destiny of man presents its
meanings in political terms.'* – THOMAS MANN

How can I, that girl standing there,
My attention fix
On Roman or on Russian
Or on Spanish politics?
Yet here's a travelled man that knows
What he talks about,
And there's a politician
That has read and thought,
And maybe what they say is true
Of war and war's alarms,
But O that I were young again
And held her in my arms.

NOTES, APPENDICES, BIBLIOGRAPHY, INDEX

Abbreviations

BOOKS BY YEATS

A	*Autobiographies* (1955)
ASTP	*A Speech and Two Poems* (1937)
AV(A)	*A Vision* (1925)
AV(B)	*A Vision* (1937)
B	*A Broadside* (various dates)
BS	*The Bounty of Sweden* (1925)
CATM	*The Cat and the Moon and Certain Poems* (1924)
CDE	Copy for Dublin Edition
CK	*The Countess Kathleen and Various Legends and Lyrics* (1982). (In *Poems* (1895) and subsequent printings the spelling *Countess Cathleen* was used)
CP	*Collected Poems* (1933; 2nd edn, with later poems added, 1950). References are to the second edition unless otherwise stated
CPl	*Collected Plays* (1934; 2nd edn, with additional plays, 1952)
CT	*The Celtic Twilight* (1893)
CT (1902)	*The Celtic Twilight* (1902)
CW	*Collected Works* (1908)
DP	*Dramatis Personae* (Dublin, 1935; London, 1936). The latter edition includes *Estrangement, The Death of Synge* and *The Bounty of Sweden*
DWL	*Letters on Poetry from W. B. Yeats to Dorothy Wellesley* (1940; reissued 1964). References are to the 1964 reissue
E	*Explorations* (1962)
E (1937)	*Essays* (1937)
E & I	*Essays and Introductions* (1961)

EPS	*Early Poems and Stories* (1925)
FFT	*Fairy and Folk Tales of the Irish Peasantry* (1888)
FMM	*A Full Moon in March* (1935)
HRHRC	Harry Ransom Humanities Research Center, Austin, Texas
ISW	*In the Seven Woods* (1903)
KGCT	*The King of the Great Clock Tower* (1934)
L(K)	*Letters*, ed. John Kelly (1986)
L(W)	*Letters*, ed. Allan Wade (1954)
LKT	*Letters to Katharine Tynan*, ed. Roger McHugh (1953)
LPP	*Last Poems & Plays* (1940)
LPTP	*Last Poems and Two Plays* (1939)
M	*Mythologies* (1959)
MRD	*Michael Robartes and the Dancer* (1921)
MS	*Memoirs*, ed. Denis Donoghue (1972)
NP	*New Poems* (1938)
OB	*October Blast* (1927)
OTB	*On the Boiler* (1939)
P (1895)	*Poems* (1895)
P (1949)	*The Poems of W. B. Yeats* (2 vols., 1949)
P (1899–1905)	*Poems (1899–1905)* (1906)
PASL	*Per Amica Silentia Lunae* (1918)
PEP	*A Packet for Ezra Pound* (1929)
PMLA	*Publications of the Modern Language Association*
PNE	*The Poems: A New Edition*, ed. Richard J. Finneran (1984)
PPV	*Plays in Prose and Verse* (1922)
PR	*The Poems Revised* (1989)
P:SS	*Poems: Second Series* (1909)
PW	*Poetical Works*, 2 vols. (1906; 1907)
PWD	*Poems Written in Discouragement* (1913)

RIT	*Representative Irish Tales* (2 vols., 1891)
ROP	*Responsibilities and Other Poems* (1916)
RPP	*Responsibilities: Poems and a Play* (1914)
SPF	*Seven Poems and a Fragment* (1922)
SSY	*The Senate Speeches of W. B. Yeats*, ed. Donald R. Pearce (1960)
TGH	*The Green Helmet and Other Poems* (1910/1911/1912)
TSR	*The Secret Rose* (1897)
TSR (1927)	*Stories of Red Hanrahan and The Secret Rose* (1927)
TT	*The Tower* (1928)
TWO	*The Wanderings of Oisin and Other Poems* (1889)
TWS	*The Winding Stair* (1929)
TWSOP	*The Winding Stair and Other Poems* (1933)
UP	*Uncollected Prose by W. B. Yeats*, I, ed. John P. Frayne (1970); II, ed. John P. Frayne and Colton Johnson (1975)
VE	*The Variorum Edition of the Poems of W. B. Yeats*, ed. Peter Allt and Russell K. Alspach (1957)
VPl	*The Variorum Edition of the Plays of W. B. Yeats*, ed. Russell K. Alspach (1966)
W & B	*Wheels and Butterflies* (1934)
WMP	*Words for Music Perhaps and Other Poems* (1932)
WO	*The Wanderings of Oisin*
WR	*The Wind Among the Reeds* (1899)
WSC	*The Wild Swans at Coole* (1917)
WWP	*The Words upon the Window-pane* (1934)
Y & TSM	*W. B. Yeats and T. Sturge Moore. Their Correspondence 1901–1937*, ed. Ursula Bridge (1953)

OTHER BOOKS

AB	*A Broad Sheet* (1902)
ACE	Hugh Kenner, *A Colder Eye. The Modern Irish Writers* (1983)

BY	*A Bibliography of the Writings of W. B. Yeats*, ed. Allan Wade, 3rd edn (1958)
BL	J. Stallworthy, *Between the Lines* (1963)
C	Lady Gregory, *Coole* (1931)
COM	Lady Gregory, *Cuchulain of Muirthemne* (1902)
ED	Richard Ellmann, *Eminent Domain* (1967)
EPY	Patty Gurd, *The Early Poetry of William Butler Yeats* (1916)
EYP	Richard J. Finneran, *Editing Yeats's Poems* (1983)
EYPR	Richard J. Finneran, *Editing Yeats's Poems: a Reconsideration* (1989)
GFM	Lady Gregory, *Gods and Fighting Men* (1904)
HG	*An Honoured Guest*, ed. Denis Donoghue and J. R. Mulryne (1965)
HI	Edmund Curtis, *A History of Ireland* (1936)
HS	C. M. Bowra, *The Heritage of Symbolism* (1943)
ICL	Birgit Bjersby, *The Interpretation of the Cuchulain Legend in the Works of W. B. Yeats* (1950)
IER	*In Excited Reverie*, ed. A. Norman Jeffares and K. G. W. Cross (1965)
IP	D. J. Gordon, *W. B. Yeats, Images of a Poet* (1961)
IY	Richard Ellmann, *The Identity of Yeats* (1954)
LCH	John Rhys, *Lectures on the Origin and Growth of Religion as Illustrated by Celtic Heathendom* (1888)
LT	T. R. Henn, *The Lonely Tower* (1950; rev. edn 1965). References are to the 1965 edition
LTHS	John Butler Yeats, *Letters to his Son W. B. Yeats and others* (1944)
McG	James McGarry, *Place Names in the Writings of William Butler Yeats* (1976)
MFLI	Jeremiah Curtin, *Myths and Folk-Lore in Ireland* (1890)
MGLE	Nancy Cardozo, *Maud Gonne Lucky Eyes and a High Heart* (1979)

MLD	John Rees Moore, *Masks of Love and Death* (1971)
MYAV	George Mills Harper, *The Making of Yeats's A Vision* (2 vols., 1987)
NC	A. Norman Jeffares, *A New Commentary on the Poems of W. B. Yeats* (1984)
PYP	George Brandon Saul, *Prolegomena to the Study of Yeats's Poems* (1957)
RG	John Unterecker, *A Reader's Guide to W. B. Yeats* (1959)
RI	Frank Kermode, *Romantic Image* (1957)
S & S	Thomas R. Whitaker, *Swan and Shadow: Yeats's Dialogue with History* (1964)
SBRC	*The Second Book of the Rhymers' Club* (1894)
SQ	Maud Gonne MacBride, *A Servant of the Queen* (1938)
TCA	A. Norman Jeffares, *The Circus Animals. Essays on W. B. Yeats* (1970)
TD	Leonard E. Nathan, *The Tragic Drama of W. B. Yeats* (1965)
TLT	Margot Ruddock, *The Lemon Tree* (1937)
TM	Peter Ure, *Towards a Mythology* (1946)
WBY	J. M. Hone, *W. B. Yeats 1865–1939* (1942; rev. edn 1962). References are to the 1962 edition
WMA	Giorgio Melchiori, *The Whole Mystery of Art* (1960)
Y	Harold Bloom, *Yeats* (1970)
YANB	A. Norman Jeffares, *Yeats. A New Biography* (1988)
Y & GI	Donald T. Torchiana, *Yeats and Georgian Ireland* (1966)
Y & T	F. A. C. Wilson, *W. B. Yeats and Tradition* (1958)
YASAC	David R. Clark, *Yeats at Songs and Choruses* (1983)
YCE	*W. B. Yeats 1865–1939 Centenary Essays*, ed. D. E. S. Maxwell and S. B. Bushrui (1965)
YCI	B. Rajan, *W. B. Yeats. A Critical Introduction* (1965)
YI	F. A. C. Wilson, *Yeats's Iconography* (1960)
Y:M & M	Richard Ellmann, *Yeats: the Man and the Masks* (1948; rev. edn 1961). References are to the 1948 edition

Y:M & P   A. Norman Jeffares, *Yeats: Man and Poet* (1949; rev. edn 1962). References are to the 1962 edition

YP & T   A. G. Stock, *W. B. Yeats His Poetry and Thought* (1961, rev. edn 1964). References are to the 1964 edition

YTLP   Thomas Parkinson, *W. B. Yeats: the Later Poetry* (1964)

YTDR   David R. Clark, *W. B. Yeats and the Theatre of Desolate Reality* (1965)

YTP   Peter Ure, *Yeats the Playwright* (1963)

YUIT   Sheila O'Sullivan, 'W. B. Yeats's Use of Irish Oral and Literary Tradition', *Heritage: Essays and Studies* presented to Seumas O'Duilearga, ed. Bo Almqvist and others (1975), pp. 266–79. Also included in *Béaloideas* [Journal of the Folklore of Ireland Society], 39–41, 1971–3 [1975], pp. 266–79

YV   Helen Hennessy Vendler, *Yeats's Vision and the Later Plays* (1963)

YVP   S. B. Bushrui, *Yeats's Verse-Plays: The Revisions 1900–1910* (1965)

YW   Curtis Bradford, *Yeats at Work* (1965)

JOURNALS

AM   *Atlantic Monthly*

BR   *British Review*

CA   *Catholic Anthology*

D   *The Dome*

DL   *The Dial*

DUR   *Dublin University Review*

EH   *Evening Herald*

ER   *English Review*

FR   *Fortnightly Review*

HW   *Harper's Weekly*

II   *The Irish Independent*

IM   *Irish Monthly*

IP	*The Irish Press*
IR	*Irish Review*
IT	*The Irish Times*
LH	*The Leisure Hour*
LL	*Life and Letters*
LM	*London Mercury*
LR	*London Review*
MCM	*McClure's Magazine*
MLN	*Modern Language Notes*
MR	*Monthly Review*
N & Q	*Notes & Queries*
NO	*National Observer*
NR	*New Republic*
NS	*New Statesman*
P(Ch)	*Poetry* (Chicago)
RES	*Review of English Studies*
S	*The Savoy*
SEN	*The Senate*
SKT	*The Sketch*
SO	*Scots Observer*
SP	*The Spectator*
SR	*Saturday Review*
TB	*The Bookman*
TBR	*The British Review*
TC	*The Criterion*
TG	*The Gael*
TIR	*The Irish Review*
TLR	*The Little Review*
TN(L)	*The Nation* (London)
TN(NY)	*The Nation* (New York)
TNR	*The New Republic*

TS	*The Speaker*
TSN	*The Shanachie*
TSS	*The Smart Set*
TYB	*The Yellow Book*
UI	*United Ireland*

NOTE

Throughout the Notes section, the following abbreviations are used:

dc: date of composition

fp: date and place of first publication

Notes

THE WANDERINGS OF OISIN

dc: begun 1886, finished Nov. 1887   *fp*: WO   Epigraph: so far no source has been discovered for this quotation, which Yeats may have invented. See *NC*, 375   Dedication: Edwin J. Ellis (1848–1916), painter and friend of Yeats's father, John Butler Yeats (1846–1922), collaborated with Yeats in editing *The Works of William Blake, Poetic, Symbolic and Critical* (3 vols., 1893). Ellis is described in *M* and *A*. Yeats wrote that the greater number of poems in *P* (1895), including *The Wanderings of Oisin*, were founded on Irish tradition.

> That poem endeavoured to set forth the impress left on my imagination by the pre-Christian cycle of legends. The Christian cycle being mainly concerned with contending moods and moral motives needed, I thought, a dramatic vehicle. The tumultuous and heroic Pagan cycle, on the other hand, having to do with vast and shadowy activities and with the great impersonal emotions, expressed itself naturally – or so I imagined – in epic and epic–lyric measures. No epic method seemed sufficiently minute and subtle for the one, and no dramatic method elastic and all-containing enough for the other.
>   Ireland having a huge body of tradition behind her in the depths of time, will probably draw her deepest literary inspiration from this double fountainhead if she ever, as is the hope of all her children, make for herself a great distinctive poetic literature. She has already many moving songs and ballads which are quite her own. 'The Countess Kathleen,' like 'The Wanderings of Oisin,' is an attempt to unite a more ample method to feeling not less national, Celtic, and distinctive.

In his notes Yeats commented that the poem

> is founded upon the Middle Irish dialogues of Saint Patrick and Oisin and a certain Gaelic poem of the last century. The events it describes, like the events in most of the poems in this volume, are supposed to have taken place rather in the indefinite period, made up of many periods, described by the folk-tales, than in any particular century; it therefore, like the later Fenian stories themselves, mixes much that is mediaeval with much that is ancient. The Gaelic poems do not make Oisin go to more than one island, but a story in *Silva Gadelica* describes 'four paradises,' an island to the north, an island to the west, an island to the south, and Adam's paradise in the east.

The poem's Gaelic sources were *Oisin i dTir na nOg* ('The Lay of Oisin in the Land of Youth') and *Agallamh na Senorach* ('The Colloquy of the Ancients'); see notes below on *a hornless deer . . . young man*, p. 486. See Giles W. L. Telfer, *Yeats's Idea of the Gael* (1965). Yeats revised the poem extensively, see *VE*, 1–63

p. 5, Book I   S. *Patrick*: Patrick (c. 385–c. 461), patron saint of
Ireland, was captured in Britain by Irish slave raiders, escaped after six
years' slavery and became a monk in France. Ordained a bishop, he
returned to Ireland in AD 432 as a missionary, converting various chiefs and
preaching to the High King, Leary, at Tara. After twenty years' missionary work he fixed his see in Armagh   *Oisin*: son of Finn and Saeva (of
the Sidhe (see Glossary)); his name (spelt 'Usheen' in some earlier
versions) means the little fawn. Yeats described Finn as the poet of the
Fenian cycle of legend (as Fergus was of the Red Branch cycle). These
Fenian legends centred on the mythological deeds of Finn MacCumhaill
(MacCool) and his warriors, the Fianna, thought to have been a body of
infantry; they were prominent in the reign of Cormac MacArt, reputedly
Finn's father-in-law; they are thought to have been put down in the Battle
of Gabhra (AD 297). The legends – tales and ballads – seem to have been
composed in the 12th century according to MS evidence, though some
may have been composed as early as the 8th century   *Caoilte*: Caoilte
MacRonain, Finn's favourite warrior. See Standish James O'Grady,
History of Ireland: Critical and Philosophical (1881), I, 324–5, 354, and
Eugene O'Curry, 'The Fate of the Children of Tuireann', *Atlantis* (1863),
4, 231–3, and *On the Manners and Customs of the Ancient Irish* (1873), III, 366.
He appeared to Finn when the King was lost in a forest, 'a flaming man that
he might lead him in the darkness'. When the King enquired who he was,
he replied, 'I am your candlestick' (notes to *WR*). He appears, 'tossing his
burning hair', in 'The Hosting of the Sidhe', p. 89, and in 'The Secret
Rose', p. 104, where he 'drove the gods out of their liss' when almost all
his companions were dead after the Battle of Gabhra. See notes on these
poems, pp. 506 and 518   *Conan*: Conan Mail ('the Bald Headed' or 'the
Crop Headed'), a braggart Fenian warrior described in *P* (1895) as the
Thersites of the Fenian cycle (in Greek legend Thersites, the ugliest and
most evil-tongued of the Greeks fighting in the Trojan war, was killed by
Achilles when he mocked him)   *Finn*: see note above on *Oisin*, p. 484.
Yeats described Finn as 'a very famous hero, and chief of the heroes of
Ireland in his time' (*P* (1895); rev. edn 1899)   *Bran, Sceolan and Lomair*:
Bran and Sceolan were Finn's cousins, his aunt Uirne having been
transformed to a hound while pregnant. Lomair was another of Finn's
hounds   *Firbolgs' burial-mounds*: the Firbolgs were supposedly pre-
historic invaders of Ireland, a short, dark, plebeian people. Yeats described
them as an early race 'who warred mainly upon the Fomorians, or
Fomoroh, before the coming of the Tuatha de Danaan' (*P* (1895)). He
added that certain of their kings, killed at the battle of Southern Moytura,
were supposed to be buried at Ballisodare, Co. Sligo (including Eochaid
MacEirc, buried 'where he fell', according to H. d'Arbois de Jubainville,
The Irish Mythological Cycle and Celtic Mythology, tr. Richard Irvine Best
(1903), 93: 'It is by their graves that Usheen [Oisin] and his companions
rode'). The Fomoroh (Fomorians), Yeats commented in *P* (1895), were

powers of death and darkness, cold and evil who came from the north ('Northern cold' in 'The Madness of King Goll', p. 51). He commented that Fomoroh

> means from under the sea and is the name of the gods of night and death and cold. The Fomoroh were misshapen and had now the heads of goats and bulls, and now but one leg, and one arm that came out of the middle of their breasts. They were ancestors of the evil faeries and, according to one Gaelic writer, of all misshapen persons, the giants and the leprechauns are expressly mentioned as of the Fomoroh. [P (1895)]

In pagan Irish mythology the Fomorians were demons; in the *Book of Invasions*, however, they are described as pirates attacking early settlers in Ireland. The Tuatha de Danaan, the tribes of the goddess Danu (spelt Dana by Yeats), were traditionally masters of magic. Yeats described them as

> the Race of the Gods of Dana. Dana was the mother of all the ancient Gods of Ireland. They were the powers of light and life and warmth, and did battle with the Fomoroh, or powers of night and death and cold. Robbed of offerings and honour, they have gradually dwindled in the popular imagination until they have become the faeries. [P (1895)]

'According to mythology' (P (1895)) they were conquered by the three sons of the invader Milesius, Heber, Heremon and Ir. The Milesians were traditionally thought to have come from Spain and invaded Ireland about the time of Alexander the Great   *cairn-heaped grassy hill . . . Maeve is stony-still*: Knocknarea, mountain in Co. Sligo, 'round cairn-headed', the 'Hill of the Executions', with a cairn on its summit where Queen Maeve is supposed to be buried. A Queen of Connaught, she invaded Ulster in the Cattle Raid of Cooley, the central story of the Red Branch cycle of tales told in the *Tain Bo Cualgne*. The mountain is also called the Hill of the King, the last pagan King of Ireland, Eoghan Bel, being buried upright there, with his spear. While he remained there it was thought no northerners could ever defeat Connaught; later his body was disinterred by the Ui Neill, who buried it face downwards at Lough Gill. Some MS tradition, however, holds that Maeve was buried at Cruachan in Co. Roscommon, capital of Connaught, named after Maeve's mother Cruacha. See Yeats's notes on 'The Hosting of the Sidhe', p. 506   *a pearl-pale, high-born lady*: Niamh, daughter of Aengus and Edain (see note on them below), described as a child of the Shee (Sidhe) in the version of the poem in P (1895)   *findrinny*: (Irish, *findruine*), an alloy, described by Yeats as a kind of red bronze (P (1895)) and a kind of white bronze (P (1895); rev. edn 1899); the latter description is probably correct   *Oscar's pencilled urn*: Oscar was Oisin's son, killed in the Battle of Gabhra. The 'pencilled urn' echoes Sir Samuel Ferguson's 'Aideen's Grave': 'A cup of bodkin pencill'd clay/Holds Oscar'   *Gabhra*: near Garristown, north Co. Dublin, where the Fianna were almost wiped out in AD 284   *Aengus and Edain*: Aengus was the Celtic god of love, beauty, youth and poetry, who reigned in Tir na nOg, the Country of the Young. Edain or Etain (Adene in some versions of the poem) was a legendary queen 'who went away and lived among the Shee' (*P* (1895)); she was lured away by Meder (Midhir), King of the Shee (*P* (1895); rev. edn 1899). Yeats's 'The Two Kings' (p. 202) tells of Midhir's wooing her through King Eochaid's brother Ardan. In *Tochmarc Etaine* ('The Wooing of Etain') Aengus is foster-son to Midhir for whom he obtains Etain (Edain) as a wife. Fuamnach, Midhir's previous wife, turns Etain into a fly which takes refuge with Aengus. He kept her in a house of glass, where Yeats imagined her weaving harp strings out of his hair (*fn* to *Baile and Aillinn* (1903)). See notes on 'The Harp of Aengus', p. 531   *Niamh*: her name means brightness, brilliance, beauty   *the birds of Aengus*: the kisses of Aengus turned into four birds, and flew around his head   *Danaan poets*: see note above on *Firbolgs' burial-mounds*, p. 484   *brazen bell*: St Patrick is reputed to have introduced oblong bells made of iron into Ireland. See *EPY*, 53   *Fenians*: see note above on *Oisin*, p. 484   *a hornless deer . . . young man*: this passage is derived from Michael Comyn, 'The Lay of Oisin in the Land of Youth', tr. Brian O'Looney, *Transactions of the Ossianic Society* (1859), IV, 21–5, 117–18, 249, and David Comyn, *Gaelic Union Publications* (1880). See notes on 'He mourns for . . . End of the World', p. 512   *Almhuin*: the Hill of Allen, Co. Kildare, headquarters of the Fianna and home of Finn, where he brought Grainne (Grania) after the death of Diarmuid on Ben Bulben (see note below on *Grania*, p. 488)   *Aengus . . . A Druid dream*: the Druids were pagan priests, seers and healers in Gaelic Ireland; here their ability as seers is suggested   *this strange human bard*: Oisin's difference from the dwellers in Tir na nOg, the Land of the Young, is emphasised

p. 17, Book II   *man of croziers*: St Patrick   *the Seven Hazel Trees*: Yeats's note reads:

> There was once a well overshadowed by seven sacred hazel trees, in the midst of Ireland. A certain lady plucked their fruit, and seven rivers arose out of the land and swept her away. In my poems this is the source of all the waters of this world, which are therefore sevenfold [*P* (1895)]

Patty Gurd, *EPY*, 55, suggests the legend is derived from the nine hazel trees of the Wisdom of the Tuatha de Danaan. Ancient Irish poets believed there were fountains at the heads of Ireland's main rivers over which nine hazels grew; the red nuts they produced fell on the water and were eaten by salmon; as a result the salmon had red spots on their bellies and anyone who ate them would gain the sublimest poetic intellect. *PNE* cites John O'Donovan's translation of *Cormac's Glossary*, ed. Whitley Stokes (1868), 35, as a source   *Aedh . . . strings of gold*: Aedh (Irish for Hugh), the Irish god of death. Yeats remarked that all who heard his harp died; he was one of the two gods who appeared to the hero Cuchulain before his death (*P*

(1895)). Yeats's source was 'the bardic tale'; he read it in Standish James O'Grady, *History of Ireland* (1878–80), II, 39, where Aedh's harp is described as pure gold; not even the gods can resist its power and Aedh, the strongest of the gods, sings sweetly, suggesting things unknown, beauty beyond beauty, and visions of bliss   *Heber's line*: a son of Milesius, Heber was supposed to have ruled over southern Ireland after the Milesian invasion. Yeats called him and his brother Heremon the ancestors of 'the merely human inhabitants of Ireland' (*P* (1895))   *That woman*: the lady rescued by Oisin from her chain between the eagles   *Ogham letters*: Ogham is an ancient Irish script, an alphabet of twenty characters (represented by a straight line with shorter straight lines carved or drawn at angles to it) dating back to the 3rd century, usually found in stone inscriptions   *'Manannan'*: Manannan MacLir, Irish god of the sea, who had two famous swords. Lear (genitive, *Lir*), his father, was the sea or ocean   *milk-pale face*: of Jesus Christ (cf. Swinburne, 'To Proserpine': 'Thou hast conquered, O pale Galilean')   *crown of thorns*: see Matthew 27:29 and John 19:2   *many shapes*: shape-changing occurs frequently in Irish mythology and legend   *Those two*: Niamh and the lady released from her chain by Oisin   *De Danaan*: see note above on *Firbolgs' burial-mounds*, p. 484

p. 24, Book III   *owls had builded their nests*: perhaps an echo of the image of 'the parents of the Gods', used in 'Anashuya and Vijaya', p. 44, whose hair was filled by the nests of 'aweless birds'   *bell-branch*: 'a legendary branch whose shaking cast all men into a gentle sleep' (*P* (1895))   *Sennachies*: (Irish, *Seanchai*) story-tellers, persons who recite ancient lore   *king*: early editions read 'cann', a chieftain   *moil*: to toil or drudge   *the demon*: Culann, a smith who made sword, spear and shield for Conchubar MacNessa, King of Ulster, one of the major figures in the Red Branch cycle of tales   *Blanaid*: wife of the King of Munster in the Red Branch cycle, in love with Cuchulain, one of the Ulster heroes; 'the heroine of a beautiful and sad story told by Keating' (*P* (1895)). Geoffrey Keating (*c.* 1570–*c.* 1650), author of a *History of Ireland*, used 'The Death of Cu-Roi Mac Daire' (now available in R. I. Best's translation, *Eriu* (1905), 2, 20–35), in which Curaoi, son of Daire, helped Cuchulain to sack Manainn and claimed Blanaid, daughter of the Lord of Manainn as his prize; he carried her off when Cuchulain refused. Later she conspired with Cuchulain to kill Curaoi, whose murder was avenged by his harper Feircheirtne, who leapt off a high rock with her, killing himself as well as her   *Mac Nessa*: Conchubar, King of Ulster, son of Nessa   *Fergus . . . Cook Barach*: Fergus, Conchubar's stepfather, who gave up his throne to Conchubar, was under *geasa* (a kind of *tabu*, an imperative) never to refuse an invitation to a feast. He was invited by Barach (on Conchubar's orders) to a feast when acting as safe-conduct, bringing back to Ulster Deirdre and the sons of Usna (who were murdered by Conchubar's men

when Fergus was – unwillingly – away from them at Barach's feast).
Deirdre, intended as Conchubar's bride, had run away to Scotland with
Naoise, a son of Usna, one of Conchubar's warriors; his brothers Ainle
and Ardan, accompanied them. See also notes on 'To the Rose of the
World', p. 498   *Dark Balor*: a Fomorian king, described by Yeats as 'the
Irish Chimaera, the leader of the hosts of darkness at the great battle of
good and evil, life and death, light and darkness, which was fought out on
the strands of Moytura, near Sligo' (P (1895))   *Grania*: Yeats took his
account from Standish Hayes O'Grady, *Transactions of the Ossianic Society*
(1857), 3, the only version in which Grania returns to Finn. Yeats described
her as a beautiful woman,

> who fled with Dermot to escape from the love of aged Finn. She fled from place to
> place over Ireland, but at last Dermot [Diarmuid] was killed at Sligo upon the
> seaward point of Ben Bulben, and Finn won her love and brought her, leaning
> upon his neck, into the assembly of the Fenians, who burst into inextinguishable
> laughter. [P (1895)]

In the tale *The Pursuit of Diarmuid and Grania*, Finn, an ageing widower,
decides to marry Grania, daughter of Cormac MacArt; she, however,
prefers a younger man, and, having drugged the other banqueters at her
betrothal feast, offers herself to Diarmuid and Oisin. Both refuse, but she
puts Diarmuid under *geasa* (see notes above on *Fergus . . . Cook Barach*,
p. 487) to elope with her that night. He does so unwillingly. They are
pursued by Finn and the Fianna (who try to protect the lovers from Finn)
and Diarmuid is eventually killed by treachery   *Meridian isle*: an island
in the middle of the earth   *keened*: uttered the keen, a wail of lamentation for the dead (Irish, *caoinim*, I wail)   *Rachlin*: Rathlin, an island off
the coast of Co. Antrim   *Bera of ships*: possibly a place near Dunboy,
but Beare Island, Bantry Bay, Co. Cork, seems more likely. Beare Island is
named after Beara, a legendary Spanish princess who married Eoghan
Mor, the King of Munster who forced Conn (Cetchathach, the Hundred
Fighter, or, of the Hundred Battles) to divide Ireland into two parts. From
'Rachlin to Bera' implies the length of Ireland   *rath*: an Irish fort   *the
straw-death*: death in bed   *Crevroe or broad Knockfefin*: Patric Colum
described Crevroe and Knockfefin as two small townlands in Co. Sligo.
McG, 38, however, suggests Crevroe is *Craobh Ruadh* (Irish, Red Branch),
the building in which the Red Branch heroes lived at Emain Macha (near
Armagh) and Knockfefin may be *Cnoc Femein* (the Hill of Femen), *Sliabh
na mBan Femen* (the Mountain of the Women of Femen), now known as
Slievenamon, Co. Tipperary, being a fairy palace named *Sid ar Femen*, the
home of Bodb-Derg, son of Dagda, in which the Sidhe enchanted Finn
MacCool   *where Maeve lies*: Knocknarea (see note on *cairn-heaped grassy
hill*, p. 485)   *burning stones of wide Hell*: Yeats wrote that

> In the older Irish books Hell is always cold, and this is probably because the
> Fomoroh, or evil powers, ruled over the north and the winter. Christianity

adopted as far as possible the Pagan symbolism in Ireland as elsewhere, and Irish poets, when they became Christian, did not cease to speak of 'the cold flagstone of Hell'. The folk-tales and Keating in his description of Hell, make use, however, of the ordinary fire symbolism. [*P* (1895)]

There does not appear to be a mention of hell in Keating, but *PNE* cites references to 'cold hell'; the 'flagstones of pain' occur in *Fenian Poems*, ed. John O'Daly (1859), IV, 15, 119, 45 *hay-cock out on the flood*: cf. William Morris's 'The Haystack in the Floods' *chain of small stones*: a rosary. Oisin is rejecting Christianity in this gesture

CROSSWAYS

This heading was first given to a group of poems in *P* (1895) most of which were taken from *TWO* (the exceptions being 'The Ballad of Father O'Hart' and 'The Ballad of the Foxhunter', written at the same time but published later). The title *Crossways* indicated that Yeats had been trying 'many pathways'. See Yeats's note, dated 1925:

> Many of the poems in *Crossways*, certainly those upon Indian subjects or upon shepherds and fauns, must have been written before I was twenty, for from the moment when I began *The Wanderings of Oisin*, which I did at that age, I believe, my subject-matter became Irish. Every time I have reprinted them I have considered the leaving out of most, and then remembered an old school friend who has some of them by heart, for no better reason, as I think, than that they remind him of his own youth. The little Indian dramatic scene was meant to be the first scene of a play about a man loved by two women, who had the one soul between them, the one woman waking when the other slept, and knowing but daylight as the other only night. It came into my head when I saw a man at Rosses Point carrying two salmon. 'One man with two souls,' I said, and added, 'O no, two people with one soul.' I am now once more in *A Vision* busy with that thought, the antitheses of day and of night and of moon and of sun.

Dedication: A. E. (shortened from Aeon), the pen-name of Yeats's friend George William Russell (1867–1935), mystic, poet, painter, editor of the *Irish Homestead* (1906–23) and the *Irish Statesman* (1923–30) *Epigraph*: from Blake's 'Night the Ninth being The Last Judgement', *Vala, or the Four Zoas*. In *The Works of William Blake*, ed. E. J. Ellis and W. B. Yeats (1893), III, 131, the line reads 'And all the Nations were threshed out, & the stars thresh'd from their husks'

p. 41, 'The Song of the Happy Shepherd' *dc*: 1885 *fp*: *DUR*, Oct. 1885 *Arcady*: Arcadia in the Peloponnesus, in southern Greece, a pastoral paradise in Greek literature. Yeats may have got his ideas about Arcadia from reading Edmund Spenser *Grey Truth*: the poem elevates poetic tradition, 'what had been believed in all countries and periods' (*A*, 78; see also *A*, 116). Yeats did not believe in 'starting all over afresh and only believing what one could prove'. He had grown to hate science (*A*,

82). Hugh Kenner, *A Colder Eye. The Modern Irish Writers* (1983), 95, suggests Truth inheres in a toy, 'a wheel kept spinning by a thumb-driven plunger', a little tin wheel painted in seven colours which blurs into grey 'as Newton prescribed'   *Chronos*: Greek for time, Kronos or Cronos, one of the Titans in Greek legend, was a son of Uranus (Heaven) and Ge (Earth) who succeeded his father as ruler of the universe; he was later overthrown by his own son Zeus. (The Roman god Saturn was later identified with Kronos.) The Greek word for time, Χρόνος, was later used for Kronos, who thus became associated with the concept of time   *the Rood*: the cross on which Jesus Christ was crucified   *Word be-mockers*: the warring kings, the men of action, whose memory lives on in the words of the poets, the dreamers   *sooth*: truth   *starry men*: astronomers   *optic glass*: telescope. This echoes Milton's description in *Paradise Lost*, I, 286–91, of Galileo's use of the telescope   *shell*: the happy shepherd's fretful words are reworded by the shell, but the sad shepherd's words in 'The Sad Shepherd', p. 42, are changed to an inarticulate moan   *Rewording*: a better reading, originally in *P* (1895), than the 'Rewarding' of other editions; probably an uncorrected misprint *poppies*: poppies possess narcotic properties

p. 42, 'The Sad Shepherd'   *dc*: 1885   *fp*: *DUR*, Oct. 1886   This poem was originally entitled 'Miserrimus' (Latin, the most miserable one)   *shell*: see notes on 'The Happy Shepherd' above   *sad dweller*: the shell

p. 43, 'The Cloak, the Boat, and the Shoes'   *fp*: *DUR*, March 1885   The poem, then entitled 'Voices', was included in Yeats's *The Island of Statues*, 'an Arcadian play in imitation of Edmund Spenser' (*DUR*, March 1885); it opens act 2, scene 3. In early printings it is sung by six voices in turn; they are the 'guardian sprights' (later 'sprites') of the flowers

p. 44, 'Anashuya and Vijaya'   *dc*: 1887 (thus in *P* (1895))   *fp*: *WO*   The poem, originally entitled 'Jealousy', is founded on Yeats's reading of *Śakuntalā*, a Sanskrit drama by Kalidāsa (*fl.* AD 450), tr. Monier Williams. It was intended to be the first scene of a play about a man loved by two women who had 'the one soul between them, the one woman waking when the other slept, and knowing but daylight as the other only night'. Yeats got the idea when seeing a man in Sligo carrying two salmon. See notes above on *Crossways*, p. 489   *Anashuya*: a character in *Śakuntalā*; in Hindu mythology a daughter of Daksha   *Vijaya*: the name means victorious   *Golden Age*: in various traditions the earliest age of man, a peaceful and happy period   *Brahma*: the supreme Hindu god, creator of the universe   *Amrita*: in Hindu mythology the word means the drink of the gods, the elixir of immortality   *Kama*: the Hindu god of love. Yeats annotated him as the 'Indian Cupid' in *WO*, as the 'Indian Eros' in *P* (1895)   *the parents of the gods*: Ellmann, *Y: M & M*, 71, suggested they were Koot-Hoomi and Morya, masters of Madame Blavatsky, the founder of the Theosophical Society (of which Yeats was a member from 1888–90); he wrote of her in *A*, 173–82. *PNE*, however, suggests Kásyapa 'depicted in Hinduism as a great progenitor'; he and Aditi were the parents of Agni, son of Heaven and Earth   *Golden Peak*: Hemakūta, a sacred mountain to the north of the Himalayas, sometimes identified with the mountain Kailāsa   *nests of aweless birds*: George Russell told of Yeats having a collection of tales about Madame Blavatsky's masters who lived in the Himalayas; their beards grew and grew and lay upon the mountain sides, birds building their nests in them. Yeats remembered that his nurse used to tell him that herons built their nests in old men's beards (*E & I*, 101). Cf. note on '*owls . . . nests*', *WO*, p. 487

p. 48, 'The Indian upon God'   *dc*: 1886   *fp*: *DUR*, Oct. 1886   Originally entitled 'From the Book of Kauri the Indian – Section V. On the Nature of God'; in *TWO* this became 'Kanva the Indian upon God'. This poem may, like 'The Indian to His Love', have been stimulated by the Brahmin Mohini Chatterjee (1858–1936), who visited Dublin in 1885

p. 49, 'The Indian to His Love'   *dc*: 1886   *fp*: *DUR*, Dec. 1886   *The peahens dance*: Yeats replied to a critic, who complained that peahens do not dance, that 'they dance through the whole of Indian poetry'. He added that he could find many such dancings if he had *Kalidāsa* (see notes on 'Anashuya and Vijaya', p. 490) by him: 'The wild peahen dances or all Indian poets lie.'

p. 49, 'The Falling of the Leaves'   *fp*: *TWO*   Yeats remarked that sometimes one composes poetry to a remembered air, and this poem was composed to 'a traditional air', though, he added, he 'could not tell that air or any other on another's lips' (*E & I*, 21). He was tone deaf, and often composed poems by repeating the words aloud in a form of chant (see *A*, 532–3)

p. 50, 'Ephemera'   *dc*: 1884   *fp*: *TWO* with the title 'Ephemera. An Autumn Idyll'   *other loves*: the idea of reincarnation appears in Yeats's poetry; both Mohini Chatterjee and George Russell believed in it, but Yeats was sceptical: 'Ought I not to say "The whole doctrine of the reincarnation of the soul is hypothetic; it is the most plausible of the explanations of the world but can we say more than that?" '

p. 51, 'The Madness of King Goll'   *dc*: 1884   *fp*: *LH*, Sept. 1887   The title was altered: 'King Goll. An Irish Legend' of 1887 became 'King Goll (*Third Century*)', in *Poems and Ballads of Young Ireland*

(1888), then 'King Goll (Third Century)' in *TWO*. It was frequently revised by Yeats (see *VE*, 81-6), who gave as his source Eugene O'Curry, *Lectures on the Manuscript Materials of Ancient Irish History* (2nd edn 1878), where O'Curry used an 18th- or 19th-century version of 'The Battle of Ventry'; he makes Gall the fifteen-year-old son of the King of Ulster. In a 15th-century version of the tale, Gall dies bravely in battle. Yeats, however, used O'Curry's variant in which Goll or Gall,

> having reached the battle with extreme eagerness, his excitement soon increased to frenzy, and after having performed astounding deeds of valour he fled in a state of derangement from the scene of the slaughter, and never stopped until he plunged into the wild seclusion of a deep glen far up the country. This glen has ever since been called Glen-na-Gealt, or the Glen of the Lunatics, and it is even to this day believed in the south that all the lunatics of Erin would resort to this spot if they were allowed to be free. [*LH*, Sept. 1887]

Yeats located the valley in Cork (usually it is placed in Antrim), where 'all the madmen in Ireland would gather were they free, so mighty a spell did he cast over that valley' (*P* (1895)). Later versions of the legend seem to introduce the element of madness from tales of Mad Sweeney (Irish, *Suibhne Geilt*), a king who took to the woods in frenzy after the Battle of Moira (Irish, *Magh Rath*) in AD 637. The poems he is said to have composed in his madness are collected in *Sweeney's Frenzy* (Irish, *Buile Shuibhne*)   *Ith*: possibly the Plain of Corn (Irish, *Magh Itha*) near Raphoe, Co. Donegal, said to be named after Ith, one of the Milesian invaders   *Emain*: the capital and chief town of the Red Branch kings. Their deeds are the subject of the Red Branch cycle of Irish sagas, probably transmitted orally in the 7th or 8th centuries and incorporated in manuscripts between the 11th and 15th centuries. The ruins of Emain Macha can be seen some miles south-west of Armagh. The name means the Twins of Macha (a horse goddess)   *Invar Amargin*: Amergin's Estuary (Irish, *Inber Amergin*), the mouth of the River Avoca in Co. Wicklow, named after a druid of Conchubar who appears in the Red Branch cycle; he was tutor to the young Cuchulain (see Glossary) and was thought to be one of the sons of Mil or Milesius by Scota   *world-troubling seamen*: probably Fomorians, demons or evil spirits in Irish mythology; see note on *Firbolgs' burial-mounds*, *WO*, p. 484   *Ollave*: an Irish poet (Irish, *ollamh*) of the highest order, the *Filidh*, hereditary keepers of the lore and learning of Ireland   *Northern cold*: see note on *Firbolgs' burial-mounds*, *WO*, p. 484   *tympan*: in the original version of the poem a harp, but here a stringed instrument played on with a fiddle-bow; Yeats probably derived it from Eugene O'Curry, *On the Manners and Customs of the Ancient Irish* (1893)   *Orchil*: a Fomorian sorceress, described as a great sorceress and a queen or ruler of the underworld in Standish O'Grady, *The Coming of Cuchulain: A Romance of the Heroic Age* (1894), Yeats's likely source; in *P* (1895) he said he had forgotten whatever he 'may once have known about her' *ulalu*: Irish cry or exclamation, usually of mourning, but sometimes of amazement or wonder, sometimes spelled 'ululu'

p. 53, 'The Stolen Child' *fp: IM*, Dec. 1886 The places mentioned are around Sligo, as Yeats explained in *FFT* (1888): 'Further Rosses is a very noted fairy locality. There is here a little point of rocks where, if anyone falls asleep, there is danger of their waking silly, the faeries having carried off their souls.' See also *M*, 88–9 *Sleuth Wood*: a wood (Irish, *sliv*, a slope) locally known as Slish or Slesh Wood (from Irish, *slis/slios*, sloped) on the south of Lough Gill, south-east of Sligo *Come away, O human child*: Yeats wrote to Katharine Tynan in March 1888 that this chorus summed up his poetry, 'not the poetry of insight and knowledge' which he hoped 'some day' to write, 'but of longing and complaint – the cry of the heart against necessity' (*L*(K), 54). The poem marks a shift from Arcadian and Indian scenes, and at this point Yeats decided he should only use Irish scenery in his poetry in future (*E & I*, 203) *Rosses*: Rosses Point, a seaside village north-west of Sligo where the Garavogue river meets the sea *Glen-Car*: the Valley of the Standing Monumental Stone, north-east of Sligo (see Glossary). Here Glen-Car probably stands for the lake; there is also a spectacular waterfall there

p. 54, 'To an Isle in the Water' *fp: TWO* Yeats regarded this poem in March 1892 as more obviously Irish than his recent love poetry; he wrote thus to Katharine Tynan (*L*(K), 288), who included it (and 'An Old Song Re-sung', later 'Down by the Salley Gardens', p. 55) in her anthology *Irish Love-Songs* (1892)

p. 55, 'Down by the Salley Gardens' *dc*: 1888 (see *L*(W), 86, *L*(K), 97) *fp: TWO*. Yeats originally entitled this poem 'An Old Song Re-sung' in *TWO*, a footnote explaining it as an attempt to reconstruct an old song 'from three lines imperfectly remembered by an old peasant woman in the village of Ballysodare, Sligo, who often sings them to herself'. There are two theories about its source. Colm O'Lochlainn, *Anglo-Irish Song Writers* (1950), 17, suggested a Sligo ballad, 'Going to Mass last Sunday my True Love passed me by'. H. E. Shields, however, argues in 'Yeats and the "Salley Gardens" ', *Hermathena* CI, autumn 1965, 22–6, that the source is an Anglo-Irish broadside ballad, 'The Rambling Boys of Pleasure', of which he gives several versions. The poet's son Michael B. Yeats, 'W. B. Yeats and Irish Folk Song', *Southern Folklore Quarterly* 30, 2 June 1966, 158, gives the text of an MS version in the P. J. McCall Ballad Collection in the National Library of Ireland, which contains some images used in the poem *salley*: willow

p. 55, 'The Meditations of the Old Fisherman' *dc*: June 1886 *fp*: *IM*, Oct. 1886 Yeats commented that the poem was founded upon 'some things a fisherman said to me when out fishing in Sligo Bay' (*P* (1895)). Elsewhere the fisherman is described as 'a not very old fisherman at Rosses Point'   *creel*: wicker basket

p. 56, 'The Ballad of Father O'Hart'   *fp*: *Irish Minstrelsy*, ed. H. Halliday Sparling (1888)   First entitled 'The Priest of Coloony', in *CK* the title became 'Father O'Hart'   *Father John O'Hart*: in *FFT* Yeats explained Coloony (see Glossary) as a few miles south of the town of Sligo, where Father O'Hart lived in the last century. The poem records tradition; no one who held the stolen land had prospered and it had changed owners many times. The notes in *FFT* expand this information. Father O'Rorke (*d.* 1739) was priest of the parishes of Ballysodare and Kilvarnet, in which the village of Coloony was situated; Yeats's information about him came from T. F. O'Rorke, *History, Antiquities and Present State of the Parishes of Ballysodare and Kilvarnet* (1878), IV, Section 2. Yeats records a saying of the priest, who forbade his parishioners to keen (Irish, *caoinim*, I wail; the keen or wail is uttered by mourners at wakes and funerals)   *penal days*: after the victories of William of Orange in Ireland the Irish parliament enacted a series of measures against Catholics from 1695 to 1727, which violated the spirit and letter of the Treaty of Limerick of 1691; they were repealed in 1829   *shoneen*: someone who affects English ways (Irish, *Seon* is John, hence John Bull, an Englishman). Yeats footnoted the word as 'upstart'; his notes amplified this into *shoneen*, being the diminutive of *shone* (Irish, *seon*):

> There are two Irish names for John – one is *Shone*, the other is *Shawn* (Irish, Seaghan). Shone is the 'grandest' of the two, and is applied to the gentry. Hence *Shoneen* means 'a little gentry John', and is applied to upstarts and 'big' farmers, who ape the rank of gentlemen. [*FFT*]

(In Irish *Shawn* is actually *Sean*, Seaghan being an archaic form of the word)   *in trust . . . John's lands*: Yeats described the incident in *CK* as one of those

> that occurred sometimes, though but rarely, during the time of the penal laws. Catholics, who were forbidden to own landed property, evaded the law by giving some honest Protestant nominal possession of their estates. There are cases on record in which poor men were nominal owners of unnumbered acres

Sleiveens: mean fellows, rogues (probably from Irish *sliabh*, a mountain)   *only*: except   *Knocknarea*: see note on '*cairn-heaped . . . hill*', *WO*, p. 485   *Knocknashee*: probably Knocknashee Common or a round hill near Achonry in the Barony of Leyny, Co. Sligo (see Glossary). (There is also a Knocknashee near Boyle, Co. Roscommon)   *Tiraragh*: probably Teeraree (Irish, *tir a rig*), a townland in Kilmorgan parish, Co. Sligo   *Ballinafad*: a village in Aughanagh parish, on the Sligo road near Boyle; the name means the Mouth of the Long Ford (Irish, *Bel an-atha-*

fada)   *Inishmurray*: an island off the Sligo coast near Streedagh Point; now uninhabited, it is named after St Muireadhach, a Bishop of Killala

p. 57, 'The Ballad of Moll Magee'   *fp*: probably *TG*, 1887 (see *B*, 20)   Yeats commented that the poem was derived from a sermon preached in the chapel at Howth (*PW*, II, 1907). The Yeats family lived at Howth, then a fishing village with a large harbour, from autumn 1881 to spring 1884. It is on the northern side of the headland and peninsula forming the northern arm of Dublin Bay (see Glossary)   *say*: sea   *saltin' herrings . . . saltin' shed*: Howth herrings were caught by a local fishing fleet; the salting sheds lined one of the harbour piers   *Kinsale*: fishing port in Co. Cork (see Glossary)   *boreen*: (Irish, *boithrin*) a lane, a narrow road   *keenin'*: see notes on 'The Ballad of Father O'Hart', p. 494   *she*: the dead child

p. 59, 'The Ballad of the Foxhunter'   *fp*: *East and West*, Nov. 1889   Originally entitled 'The Ballad of the Old Fox-Hunter', the second printing, *UI*, 28 May 1892, added after the title '(an incident from Kickham's *Knocknagow*)'. Yeats's note suggested that this incident in the novel *Knocknagow* (pp. 491–4) was probably a transcript from Tipperary tradition. C. J. Kickham (1826–82) also wrote ballads. A Fenian, he was sentenced to fourteen years' penal servitude in 1865, but released after four years   *Lollard*: the name of the horse; in other versions of the poem (*UI*, 28 May 1892, and *EPS*) he is called Dermot   *Rody*: the huntsman in *Knocknagow*

THE ROSE

The Rose was a heading first used in *P* (1895) for a group of poems taken from *CK*. Yeats wrote in 1925:

> . . . *The Rose* was part of my second book, *The Countess Kathleen and Various Legends and Lyrics*, 1892, and I notice upon reading these poems for the first time for several years that the quality symbolised as The Rose differs from the Intellectual Beauty of Shelley and of Spenser in that I have imagined it as suffering with man and not as something pursued and seen from afar. It must have been a thought of my generation, for I remember the mystical painter Horton [William Thomas Horton (1864–1919), an Irvingite who produced mystical drawings for *S* in 1896] whose work had little of his personal charm and real strangeness, writing me these words, 'I met your beloved in Russell Square, and she was weeping,' by which he meant that he had seen a vision of my neglected soul.

The poems in *The Rose* were printed because in them Yeats had found, he believed, 'the only pathway whereon he can hope to see with his own eyes the Eternal Rose of Beauty and Peace' (*P* (1895))   *Epigraph*: St Augustine, *Confessions*, X, 27: 'Too late I loved you Beauty so old and so

new. Too late I loved you.'   *Dedication*: Lionel Johnson (1867–1902),
English poet and critic, author of two books of poems, *Poems* (1895) and
Ireland (1897). Yeats and he were friends and fellow members of the
Rhymers' Club. See *A*, 164 f.

p. 65, 'To the Rose upon the Rood of Time'   *fp: CK*   *Red Rose*:
roses are decorative in Yeats's early poetry but by 1891 he is using them as
an increasingly complex symbol. In *CK* he wrote that the Rose is a
favourite symbol with the Irish poets:

> It has given a name to more than one poem, both Gaelic and English, and is used,
> not merely in love poems, but in addresses to Ireland as in De Vere's [Aubrey De
> Vere (1788–1846)] line 'The little black rose shall be red at last' and in Mangan's
> [James Clarence Mangan (1803–49)] 'Dark Rosaleen'. I do not, of course, use it in
> this latter sense.

Rose was the name of a girl with black hair in Irish patriotic poetry (Irish,
Roisin Dubh, Dark Rosaleen) who personified Ireland. Yeats also alluded to
the use of the Rose symbol in religious poems, 'like the old Gaelic which
speaks of "the Rose of Friday" meaning the Rose of Austerity'. The Rose
symbolises spiritual and eternal beauty. It was a central symbol in the
Order of the Golden Dawn, the occult society or Rosicrucian order into
which Yeats was initiated on 7 March 1890 by MacGregor Mathers (1854–
1918), author of the *Kabbalah Unveiled*. He is described in 'All Souls'
Night', p. 340 (see notes, p. 593), and *A*, 182–3. From Mathers and the
Rosicrucian rituals Yeats learned of the conjunction of the Rose (with four
leaves) and the Cross, making a fifth element, a mystic marriage; the Rose
possessed feminine sexual elements, the Cross masculine; the Rose was the
flower that bloomed on the Sacrifice of the Cross. Yeats wrote (*L*(W), 592)
that he studied the mystic tradition from 1887 onwards, reading such
authors as Valentin Andrea (Johannes Valentine Andreae or Andreas
(1586–1654), a German mystic and theologian, whom he probably met in
A. E. Waite, *The Real History of the Rosicrucians* (1887)). He thought for a
time that he

> could rhyme of love, calling it *The Rose*, because of the Rose's double meaning; of
> a fisherman who had 'never a crack' in his heart; of an old woman complaining of
> the idleness of the young, or of some cheerful fiddler, all those things that 'popular
> poets' write of, but that I must some day – on that day when the gates began to
> open – become difficult or obscure. With a rhythm that still echoed Morris I
> prayed to the Red Rose, to Intellectual Beauty. [*A*, 25]

The Rose also symbolised Maud Gonne (1866–1953), the daughter of a
colonel in the British army, who had independent means and had
attempted a career as an actress. Illness – she had a tendency to tuberculosis
– caused her to abandon the stage and she then took up Irish nationalism.
She was tall and beautiful, and Yeats fell in love with her when they met in

January 1889, when he was twenty-three. His love was hopeless; he never meant to speak of love to her: 'What wife could she make,' I thought, 'what share could she have in the life of a student?' (*MS*, 42). He first proposed to her in 1891 and continued to do so at intervals until her marriage in 1903   *Cuchulain . . . bitter tide*: the Hound of Culain, a hero of the Red Branch cycle whose name Yeats spelled as Cuhoollin and Cuchullin, and commented that his name is pronounced Cuhoolin. Originally Setanta, he was called the Hound of Culain because as a boy he killed Culain's hound and offered to take its place. In *The Tragical Death of Con Laech* he kills his own son (see 'Cuchulain's Fight with the Sea', p. 68, and the plays *On Baile's Strand* and *The Only Jealousy of Emer*). Yeats remarked that he founded his poem on a West of Ireland legend in Jeremiah Curtin, *MFLI*, but added that the bardic tale of Cuchulain's death was very different   *The Druid*: see notes on *A Druid dream*, *WO*, p. 486   *Fergus*: see notes *WO*, p. 487, and 'Fergus and the Druid' below. The story of his being tricked out of his crown by Ness, mother of Conchubar, is told in *The Book of Leinster* (tr. Whitley Stokes, *Eriu*, IV, 22)   *bright hearts*: Yeats commented that he 'did not remember' what he meant by 'the bright hearts' but a little later he wrote of spirits 'with mirrors in their hearts' (*A*, 255)   *chaunt a tongue men do not know*: 'chaunt' was spelt 'chant' in *CK*. The line means that Yeats intends to incorporate his knowledge of the occult and of symbolism into his poetry and re-create the old mythology of Ireland and infuse new life into it   *Eire*: (Irish, Ireland) originally the name of a queen of the tribes of the goddess Dana, subsequently Tuatha de Danaan. See notes on *WO*, p. 485

p. 66, 'Fergus and the Druid'   *fp*: *NO*, 21 May 1892   *Fergus*: see notes on *WO* and 'To the Rose upon the Rood of Time', pp. 487 and 496. Yeats's source for the legend was Sir Samuel Ferguson, 'The Abdication of Fergus MacRoy' (who after his abdication 'lived out his days feasting and fighting, and hunting' (*WR*))   *shape to shape*: see notes on *many shapes*, *WO*, p. 487   *Druid*: see notes on *A Druid dream*, *WO*, p. 486   *Red Branch kings*: The Red Branch heroes served Conchubar, King of Ulster, at his court, Emain Macha   *Conchubar*: Yeats also spelled his name Conhor, Conchobar and Concobar. The central figure in *The Fate of the Children of Usna*, he succeeded his stepfather Fergus as King of Ulster through the trickery of Ness, his own mother. See also notes on *WO*, p. 487   *quern*: apparatus for grinding corn, usually made of two circular stones, the upper turned by hand   *slate-coloured thing*: the little bag of dreams ('slate-coloured' in early versions of the poem)

p. 68, 'Cuchulain's Fight with the Sea'   *fp*: *UI*, 11 June 1892   *Emer*: Emer (Emir in the original version) of Borda, who was the daughter of Forgael, and Cuchulain's wife. This poem derives from Jeremiah Curtin, *MFLI*, from oral tradition and from a 9th-century tale in

The Yellow Book of Lecan. In the last, Cuchulain's son, Conlaech, is by Aoife, with whom Cuchulain had an affair (when he was having advanced training in warfare with Scathach, an Amazon). Yeats may here have confused Emer and Aoife   *raddling*: dying with red ochre   *dun*: fortress   *swineherd*: he announced himself as 'Aileel, the swineherd' in the original version, later spelt Aleel   *one sweet-throated*: Eithne Inguba, Cuchulain's young mistress   *her son*: Cuchulain, son of Cuchulain, called Finmole in the original version and in *P* (1895, 1924)   *herd*: herds-man   *The Red Branch*: Conchubar and his army   *Conchubar*: see notes on 'Fergus and the Druid', p. 497   *sweet-throated maid*: Eithne Inguba

p. 71, 'The Rose of the World'   *fp*: *NO*, 2 Jan. 1892 with the title 'Rosa Mundi'   The poem was written to Maud Gonne   *Troy passed away*: Yeats identified Maud Gonne with Helen of Troy (particularly in poems written between 1903 and 1914) and with Deirdre. Troy was the Trojan city destroyed by the Greeks after a ten-year siege; they besieged it because Helen, wife of King Menelaus of Sparta, had been abducted by Paris, one of the sons of Priam, King of Troy   *Usna's children*: Deirdre, daughter of King Conchubar's storyteller, prophesied that she would bring great suffering on Ulster. She was saved from death at the hands of the Ulstermen by Conchubar declaring she was to be brought up to be his Queen. Isolated, in the charge of an old nurse, Lavarcham, she fell in love with Naoise, one of Conchubar's Red Branch heroes. See notes on *WO*, p. 487. Cathbad the Druid, who had used spells to achieve the capture of Deirdre and the sons of Usna, subsequently cursed Conchubar (who had broken promises not to kill the captives) and Emania, a curse worked out in the tale of the *Tain Bo Cualgne*. In *P* (1895) Yeats refers to 'Deirdre's Lament for the Sons of Usnach' by Sir Samuel Ferguson, included in his *Lays of the Western Gael and Other Poems* (1864). In one version of the legend Deirdre stabs herself. In another she is forced to live with Conchubar for a year; he intends to hand her on to Owen, who had killed Naoise, but she kills herself by leaping from a chariot in which both men were travelling with her   *Weary and kind . . . a grassy road*: originally the poem consisted of the first two stanzas only; the third was added after Yeats and Maud Gonne had returned from walking in the Dublin Mountains. He was worried by her being exhausted after walking on rough mountain roads. 'Weary and kind' refers to her; the 'grassy road' to the world of human experience. See comment on her in notes on 'To the Rose upon the Rood of Time', p. 496

p. 71, 'The Rose of Peace'   *fp*: *NO*, 13 Feb. 1892, originally entitled 'The Peace of the Rose'   *Michael*: the archangel who overcomes Satan   *deeds*: probably a remembrance of Milton's *Paradise Lost*, which recounts the war between God and Satan   *Heaven with Hell*: a Swedenborgian idea (Yeats read several books by the Swedish mystic

Emanuel Swedenborg (1688–1772), including *Arcana Coelestia* (1749–56), *Diarium Spirituale* (1845) and *Principia* (1845)), though he may also have been thinking of Blake's *The Marriage of Heaven and Hell* (see *E*, 44)

p. 72, 'The Rose of Battle'   *fp*: *CK*   The original title was 'They went forth to the Battle but they always fell'   *Rose*: see notes on *The Rose*, p. 495, and 'To the Rose upon the Rood of Time', p. 496

p. 73, 'A Faery Song'   *fp*: *NO*, 12 Sept. 1891   *Subtitle*: earlier versions state that the song was sung by 'the good people' over an author, Michael Dwyer, and his bride, who had escaped into the mountains (Michael Dwyer was a rebel leader in Co. Wicklow in the 1798 rebellion). *The Pursuit of Diarmuid and Grania* is part of the Fenian cycle of tales (see notes on *WO*, p. 484)   *Cromlech*: a prehistoric stone construction, usually one large stone supported by several upright stones; they are sometimes known in Ireland as the beds of Diarmuid and Grania, used by them in their flight from Finn   *these children*: the lovers Diarmuid and Grania. See also Yeats's story 'Hanrahan's Vision' (*M*, 246–52)

p. 74, 'The Lake Isle of Innisfree'   *dc*: Dec. 1888   *fp*: *NO*, 13 Dec. 1890   The poem was written in London, at 3 Blenheim Road, Bedford Park, where Yeats lived with his family from 24 March 1888 to October 1895. Cf. a passage in his novel *John Sherman* (1891):

> Delayed by a crush in the Strand, he heard a faint trickling of water near by; it came from a shop window where a little water-jet balanced a wooden ball upon its point. The sound suggested a cataract with a long Gaelic name, that leaped crying into the gate of the winds at Ballagh. . . . He was set dreaming a whole day by walking down one Sunday morning to the borders of the Thames a few hundred yards from his house – and looking at the osier-covered Chiswick eyot. It made him remember an old day-dream of his. The source of the river that passed his garden at home was a certain wood-bordered and islanded lake, whither in childhood he had often gone blackberrying. At the further end was a little islet called Innisfree. Its rocky centre, covered with many bushes, rose some forty feet above the lake. Often when life and its difficulties had seemed to him like the lessons of some elder boy given to a younger by mistake, it had seemed good to dream of going away to that islet and building a wooden hut there and burning a few years out rowing to and fro fishing, or lying on the island slopes by day, and listening at night to the ripple of the water and the quivering of the bushes – full always of unknown creatures – and going out at morning to see the island's edge marked by the feet of birds.

Later he described how

> when walking through Fleet Street very homesick I heard a little tinkle of water and saw a fountain in a shop-window which balanced a little ball upon its jet, and began to remember lake water. From the sudden remembrance came my poem *Innisfree*, my first lyric with anything in its rhythm of my own music. I had begun

to loosen rhythm as an escape from rhetoric and from that emotion of the crowd rhetoric brings, but I only understood vaguely and occasionally that I must for my special purpose use nothing but the common syntax. A couple of years later I would not have written that first line with its conventional archaism – 'Arise and go' – nor the inversion in the last stanza. [*A*, 153]

The poem was influenced by the American author Henry Thoreau (1817–62), from whose *Walden* Yeats's father had read to him; he knew Katharine Tynan's poem 'Thoreau at Walden' and had planned in his teens

to live some day in a cottage on a little island called Innisfree, and Innisfree was opposite Slish Wood. . . . I thought that having conquered bodily desire and the inclination of my mind toward women and love, I should live, as Thoreau lived, seeking wisdom. There was a story in the county history [William Gregory Wood-Martin, *History of Sligo* (1882)] of a tree that had once grown upon that island guarded by some terrible monster and borne the food of the gods. A young girl pined for the fruit and told her lover to kill the monster and carry the fruit away. He did as he had been told, but tasted the fruit; and when he reached the mainland where she waited for him, he was dying of its powerful virtue. And from sorrow and remorse she too ate of it and died. I do not remember whether I chose the island because of its beauty or for the story's sake, but I was twenty-two or three before I gave up the dream. [*A*, 71–2]

I will arise: an echo of the parable of the prodigal son in Luke 15:18: 'I will arise and go to my father'   *Innisfree*: Heather Island, situated in Lough Gill in Co. Sligo (see Glossary). See *M*, 101, 171. One of the island's attractions for Yeats was its association with local legend and folklore. See *NC*, 30, and Russell K. Alspach, *Yeats and Innisfree* (1965)   *night and day*: cf. the cleansing of the unclean spirits in Mark 5:5: 'And always, night and day, he was in the mountains'   *heart's core*: possibly an echo of Shelley's *Adonais*, l.192: 'thy heart's core'

p. 74, 'A Cradle Song'   *dc*: Jan. 1890, *fp*: *SO*, 19 April 1890   Early versions had the epigraph '*Cloth yani me von gilli beg,/'N heur ve thu more a creena*'. '*Cloth*' was altered to '*Coth*' in *CK*. These lines, the chorus of a Gaelic lullaby sung by an old nurse, were included in Gerald Griffin's (1803–40) novel *The Collegians* (1829), Ch. XXXII, in phonetic spelling:

> Gilli beg le m'onum thu!
> Gilli beg le m'chree!
> Coth yani me von gilli beg,
> 'N heur ve thu more a creena.

Griffin translated the lines as:

> My soul's little darling you are!
> My heart's little darling
> What will I do without my little darling
> When you're grown up and old.

Yeats told Katharine Tynan that the last two lines of his poem were suggested by this song (*L*(K), 209)   *The Sailing Seven*: the planets. *PNE* suggests, however, the seven stars of the Pleiades

p. 75, 'The Pity of Love'   *fp*: *CK*   The poem is written to Maud Gonne; see notes on 'To the Rose upon the Rood of Time', p. 496

p. 75, 'The Sorrow of Love'   *dc*: Oct. 1891. *fp*: *CK*   This poem was considerably altered. It is described in *EPS* (1925) as one of several 'altogether new' poems produced by rewriting. See *VE*, 119, for the different versions   *A girl arose*: presumably Helen of Troy, but the poem celebrates Maud Gonne (see notes on 'To the Rose upon the Rood of Time', p. 496)   *Odysseus*: in Greek legend the son of Laertes, King of the island of Ithaca. Odysseus was married to Penelope and took part in the siege of Troy (see notes on 'The Rose of the World', p. 496) taking nearly ten years to return to Ithaca after the sack of Troy. His adventures and return are told in Homer's *Odyssey*   *Priam*: son of Laomedon and last King of Troy. He had many children by his wife Hecuba, among them Hector, Paris and Cassandra. He was killed by Neoptolemus, son of Achilles, after the fall of Troy

p. 76, 'When You are Old'   *dc*: 21 Oct. 1891   *fp*: *CK*   The poem is written to Maud Gonne and is founded upon (but is not a translation of) a sonnet by Pierre de Ronsard (1524–85), 'Quand Vous Serez Bien Vieille', *Sonnets pour Hélène*, II (1578)

p. 76, 'The White Birds'   *fp*: *NO*, 7 May 1892   The first printing had a note after the title '(*The birds of fairyland are said to be white as snow. The Danaan Islands are the islands of the fairies*)'. In *CK* Yeats commented 'The Danaan shore is, of course, *Tier-nan-oge*, or fairy-land'. (Irish, *Tir na nOg*, the Land of the Young, a paradise where mortals could share the everlasting youth of the fairies (*FFT*, 323).) Yeats wrote the poem to Maud Gonne, who had been walking with him on the cliffs at Howth (see notes on 'The Ballad of Moll Magee', p. 495) the day after he had first proposed to her and been rejected. They were resting when two seagulls flew overhead and out to sea. She told him that if she were to have the choice of being any bird she would prefer to be a seagull above all, and 'in three days he sent me the poem with its gentle theme, "I would we were my beloved, white birds on the foam of the sea" '   *meteor . . . flee*: meteors are not seen for long by an onlooker   *blue star*: Venus   *the lily and rose*: the lily is a masculine symbol, the rose feminine   *Danaan shore*: see note on title of poem above, and notes on *WO*, p. 484

p. 77, 'A Dream of Death'   *fp*: *NO*, 12 Dec. 1891   Its first title was 'An Epitaph'   *one*: Maud Gonne, then in France recovering from

extreme fatigue caused by her activities in aid of victims of evictions in
Donegal, where there was a famine. She was getting steadily better and
was greatly amused 'when Willie Yeats sent me a poem, my epitaph he had
written with much feeling' (*SQ*, 147)   *strange place*: the south of France,
where Maud Gonne was recuperating   *thy first love*: probably Laura
Armstrong, a red-headed cousin with whom Yeats fell in love when the
Yeatses were living in Howth (see notes on 'The Ballad of Moll Magee',
p. 495). He described her later as having a 'wild dash of half insane genius',
and as having 'wakened him from the metallic sleep of science' and set him
writing his first play (*L*(K), 155). He commented that he did not tell her he
was in love, because she was engaged:

> she had chosen me for her confidant and I learned all about her quarrels with her
> lover. Several times he broke the engagement off, and she fell ill, and friends had
> to make peace. . . . I wrote her some bad poems and had more than one sleepless
> night through anger with her betrothed [*A*, 76]

p. 77, 'The Countess Cathleen in Paradise'   *fp*: *NO*, 31 Oct.
1891   The title, initially 'Kathleen', was altered to 'Song' in *CK*. The
song is from scene 5 of *The Countess Kathleen* (Yeats spelt the name
'Cathleen' in *P* (1895) and after). In *P* (1895) it was entitled 'A Dream of a
Blessed Spirit'. The title was altered to the present form because, Yeats
remarked in 1926, he had rewritten it so much it was 'almost a new poem'
(*P* (1895); rcv. edn 1927). The play, initially written to convince Maud
Gonne that he could write for a public audience, was founded on *The
Countess Kathleen O'Shea* (see *FFT*, 232–5). The Countess's sad resolve to
aid her famine-struck people parallels Maud Gonne's desire to help
starving and evicted peasants in Donegal (see notes on 'A Dream of Death',
p. 501). The poet Kevin (later named Aleel) in the play is like Yeats, who
was attempting to persuade Maud Gonne to marry him and give up
politics. Yeats stated that the chief poem in the volume, the play, was an
attempt to mingle personal thought and feeling with the beliefs and
customs of Christian Ireland, whereas his earlier book, *The Wanderings of
Oisin*, had tried to record the effect on his imagination of the pre-Christian
cycle of Irish legends. He hoped Ireland, with her vast body of tradition
rooted in the past, would be inspired by the 'double fountainhead' of the
Christian and pagan cycles and make 'a great distinctive poetic literature'
(see Preface to *CK*)   *Mother Mary*: the Virgin Mary, mother of Jesus
Christ   *angels seven*: a Rossetti-like detail; the original version read 'And
her guides are angels seven', reminiscent of 'The Blessed Damozel': 'She
had three lilies in her hand,/And the stars in her hair were seven.'

p. 78, 'Who Goes with Fergus?'   *fp*: *CK*   This is a lyric in the
second scene of the play *The Countess Cathleen*   *Fergus*: see notes on
'Fergus and the Druid', p. 497   *the brazen cars*: Fergus now uses chariots

for his peaceful purposes, exploring the woods, a place of escape from the world's cares

p. 79, 'The Man who Dreamed of Faeryland'   *fp: NO*, 7 Feb. 1891   *Drumahair*: a village in Co. Leitrim on the River Bonnet, which flows into Lough Gill. See Glossary   *world-forgotten isle*: reminiscent of the first island paradise to which Niamh brought Oisin in *WO*, II. Cf. George Mills Harper, *Yeats's Quest for Eden* (1965), 302–5   *Lissadell*: Lissadell, Co. Sligo, home of the Gore-Booth family since the early 18th century. Lissadell, the house, was built in 1832–4. See Glossary   *money cares and fears*: through lack of funds Yeats spent many summers in Sligo as a young man, sometimes with his maternal grandparents, William and Elizabeth Pollexfen, and, later, with his uncle George Pollexfen   *hill*: see note below on *the hill of Lugnagall*   *golden or the silver skies*: solar and lunar principles when fused are an alchemical emblem of perfection. Yeats used gold and silver as symbols in several later poems, and an idea of blessedness was built up through the repetition. Cf. 'The Song of Wandering Aengus', p. 93, 'He wishes for the Cloths of Heaven', p. 108, 'The Happy Townland', p. 137, 'Under the Round Tower', p. 239, 'The Tower', p. 302, and 'Those Dancing Days are Gone', p. 381   *a dancer*: a symbol of fairyland and blessedness, repeated four lines from the end of the poem. Cf. 'To a Child Dancing in the Wind', p. 224, 'The Double Vision of Michael Robartes', p. 276, 'Among School Children', p. 323, and 'News for the Delphic Oracle', p. 461   *sun and moon*: see note on *golden or the silver skies* above   *well of Scanavin*: there is a well at Scanavin, near Colloney, Co. Sligo. Scanavin is also the name of a small townland in Co. Sligo (see Glossary)   *silver fret the gold*: see note on *golden or the silver skies* above   *the hill of Lugnagall*: Lugnagall is a townland in the Glen-Car Valley in Co. Sligo (see Glossary). Yeats set his story 'The Curse of the Fires and of the Shadows' there. It was a modified version of a poem 'The Protestants' Leap', published in *TG*, 19 Nov. 1887, a dramatic monologue in which a surviving Cromwellian trooper tells how a Catholic Irish guide led his companions over a precipice to their deaths, he having escaped because his horse fell before the edge of the chasm. In the prose tale, five Puritan troopers who had attacked an abbey are led by a piper to their deaths over the brink of the abyss called Lugnagall. Six horses sprang over it, but five screams were heard and five men and five horses crashed at the foot of the rocks (*M*, 177–83). In a note to 'The Protestants' Leap', Yeats described Lug-na-Gal as 'a very grey cliff overlooking that Glen-Car lake where Diarmuid and Grania (see notes on *WO*, p. 488) had once a cranoque (where the remnants were found some years back)'   *spired*: pointed upwards, assumed the shape of a spire   *God burn Nature*: Yeats used this idea of God burning time in several poems. Cf. 'He tells of the Perfect Beauty', p. 108, and 'In Memory of Eva Gore-Booth and Con Markiewicz', p. 347

p. 80, 'The Dedication to a Book of Stories selected from the Irish Novelists'   *fp*: *RIT*   The poem was originally entitled 'Dedication'   *green branch*: see note on *bell-branch*, *WO*, p. 487   *Eire*: Irish, Ireland; spelt 'Eri' in early version. See notes on 'To the Rose upon the Rood of Time', p. 496   *Munster . . . Connemara*: Munster is the southernmost of Ireland's four provinces. Connemara is an area in Co. Galway, the western border of which is on the Atlantic. See Glossary

p. 81, 'The Lamentation of the Old Pensioner'   *fp*: *SO*, 15 Nov. 1890   The poem was drastically rewritten. Notes in *CK* call it 'little more than a translation of the very words of an old Wicklow peasant'. It is founded upon a conversation Yeats's friend George Russell had on the Two Rock Mountain, Co. Dublin, in 1890 and recounted to Yeats on his return to Dublin. Russell (1867–1935) appears as X in Yeats's story 'A Visionary' (*CT*, 23). See *NC*, 37, and *M*, 13 ff. Russell's unpublished autobiography records this incident:

> [The old peasant] was hugging his body as if there were none other in the world but himself that would hold it with familiar hands and he was talking to himself, and his grief seemed so great he must speak . . . He stepped before me [and said]: 'Over those hills I wandered forty years ago. Nobody but myself knows what happened under the thorn tree forty years ago. The fret is on me!' [See Peter Kuch, 'A Few Twigs from the Wild Bird's Nest', *Yeats the European*, ed. A. Norman Jeffares (1989), 103]

p. 82, 'The Ballad of Father Gilligan'   *fp*: *SO*, 5 July 1890   The title of the first version was 'Father Gilligan/A Legend told by the people of Castleisland, Kerry'. The ballad was written to a modification of the air 'A Fine Old English Gentleman' (*E & I*, 21)   *Mavrone*: a cry of grief (Irish, *mo bhron*). In the version in *The Book of the Rhymers' Club* (1892) 'Ochone, ochone!' (a similar cry) is substituted

p. 83, 'The Two Trees'   *fp*: *CK*   *The holy tree*: the Sephirotic tree of the Kabalah and the Tree of Knowledge, of Life, of Imagination. The poem can be understood without a knowledge of its esoteric sources; they do, however, add to its meaning. Ellmann (*IY*, 76) says the Sephirotic tree has two aspects, one benign, the other malign:

> On one side are the *Sephiroth*, on the other the dead *Qlippoth*. Since the Kabbalists consider man to be a microcosm, the double-natured tree is a picture both of the universe and of the human mind, whose faculties, even the lowest, can work for good or ill. Yeats can therefore write,

> > Beloved, gaze in thine own heart,
> > The holy tree is growing there . . .

and at the same time warn her not to look in 'the bitter glass', where the tree appears in its reverse aspect:

> For there a fatal image grows,
> With broken boughs and blackened leaves,
> And roots half-hidden under snows
> Driven by a storm that ever grieves

[The line 'With . . . leaves' is taken from editions from *P* (1895) to *EPS*]

Kermode suggests Blake as a source, who saw Art as the 'Tree of Life' and Science as the 'Tree of Death'. Yeats, Kermode thinks, is trying to incorporate in 'The Two Trees' ideas in 'Blake's Illustrations to Dante', that the good tree is desire and divine energy, the bad morality and nature, the fallen world, selfhood and abstraction (*RI*, 96). Yeats wrote that Blake held that the kingdom that was passing was

> the kingdom of the Tree of Knowledge; the kingdom that was coming was the Kingdom of the Tree of Life: men who ate from the Tree of Knowledge wasted their days in anger against one another, and in taking one another captive in great nets; men who sought their food among the green leaves of the Tree of Life condemned none but the unimaginative and the idle, and those that forget that even love and death and old age are imaginative art [*E & I*, 130]

Kermode sees the holy tree of the poem as the Tree of Life, inhabited by love growing in the heart of a woman who does not think. If she does so, she breaks her beauty, bartering it for argument, for the abstract, for the Tree of the Fall, something shown in the lines: 'Gaze no more in the bitter glass . . .'. In an essay Yeats described a young woman who thought, in her normal state, that the apple of Eve was the kind bought in a grocer's shop but, in trance, saw the Tree of Life with souls moving in its branches instead of sap, and the fowls of the air among its leaves, with a white fowl wearing a crown on the highest bough. When Yeats returned home he took up a translation of *The Book of Concealed Mystery*, in MacGregor Mathers's book *The Kabbalah Unveiled*, and when he cut the pages he came on this passage 'The Tree . . . is the Tree of the Knowledge of Good and Evil . . . in its branches the birds lodge and build their nests, the souls and the angels have their place' (*E & I*, 44)   *a circle go*: Yeats described the Tree of Life as a geometrical figure made up of ten circles or spheres called Sephiroth, joined by straight lines, and added that once men must have thought of it as like 'some great tree covered with its fruit and foliage', but that it must have lost its natural form at some period (*A*, 375)   *ignorant*: a virtue here, compared to the 'unresting thought' of the second part of the poem   *The demons*: perhaps the demons of abstract thought, likely to ambush the soul on its way to truth   *a fatal image*: the Tree of Knowledge as opposed to that of Life. See *E & I*, 130

p. 84, 'To Some I have Talked with by the Fire'   *fp*: *TB*, May 1895   The original printing supplied a subtitle: (*The Dedication of a new book of verse*)   *Danaan*: see notes on *WO*, p. 484

p. 85, 'To Ireland in the Coming Times'   *fp*: CK   The title was
originally 'Apologia addressed to Ireland in the Coming Days'. The poem
defends the obscurity caused by 'a passion for the symbolism of the
magical rose' which had 'saddened' Yeats's friends. It justifies Yeats's
attitude to literature in the struggle for Irish independence; it is also a love
poem to Maud Gonne, asserting that his kind of patriotism is no less
important than that of earlier, more obviously patriotic writers   *rann*: a
verse of a poem in Irish, not the whole poem   *red-rose-bordered*: see notes
on *The Rose*, p. 495, and 'To the Rose upon the Rood of Time',
p. 496   *Davis, Mangan, Ferguson*: Thomas Osborne Davis (1814–45)
founded the *Nation* in 1842 and was leader of the Young Ireland Party. He
wrote poems and prose of a popular patriotic kind, and the *Nation* had a
considerable influence in shaping nationalist ideas in Ireland in the latter
part of the 19th century. James Clarence Mangan (1803–49), a romantic
Irish poet and essayist who wrote prolifically for the magazines and
journals of his period, sometimes translating, sometimes adapting Irish
and German material. Sir Samuel Ferguson (1810–86), an Irish lawyer,
poet and antiquary, translated Gaelic legends in a masculine manner and
was much admired for going 'back to the Irish cycle' by the youthful
Yeats, whose first published prose was 'The Poetry of Sir Samuel
Ferguson', *Irish Fireside*, 9 Oct. 1886   *more than their rhyming tell*: Yeats
wants to re-create the old mythology by infusing new life into it; his
interest in the occult and in symbolism added mystery to his material, and
would go beyond nationality. But he wants to be seen as belonging to the
Irish tradition; his esoteric interests are not to diminish his patriotic
reputation, they add to his poems because they 'more than their rhyming
tell' to those who realise their hidden meanings   *Druid*: see notes on
WO, p. 486

THE WIND AMONG THE REEDS

This volume, published in 1899, was introduced in *CW* with Yeats's
explanation that he had so meditated on the images that had come to him
when he was writing *Ballads and Lyrics*, *The Rose* and *The Wanderings of
Oisin*, and other images from Irish folklore that they had become true
symbols. When awake, though more often in sleep, he had moments of
vision which he described as a state very unlike dreaming, 'where these
images took upon themselves what seemed an independent life and became
a part of a mystic language, which seemed always as if it would bring me
some 'strange revelation'. The full notes of *WR* are contained in *VE*, 800–2
(for Yeats's notes on individual poems, see *VE*, 803–14), and *NC*, 42–4.

p. 89, 'The Hosting of the Sidhe'   *dc*: 29 Aug. 1893   *fp*: NO, 7
Oct. 1893, entitled 'The Faery Host'   *Sidhe . . . Knocknarea . . . Clooth-
na-Bare*: see Yeats's condensed note on the poem (dated 1899–1906):

The gods of ancient Ireland, the Tuatha de Danaan, or the Tribes of the goddess Dana, or the Sidhe, from Aes Sidhe, or Sluagh Sidhe, the people of the Faery Hills, as these words are usually explained, still ride the country as of old. Sidhe is also Gaelic for wind, and certainly the Sidhe have much to do with the wind. They journey in whirling wind, the winds that were called the dance of the daughters of Herodias in the Middle Ages, Herodias doubtless taking the place of some old goddess. When old countrypeople see the leaves whirling on the road they bless themselves, because they believe the Sidhe to be passing by. Knocknarea is in Sligo, and the countrypeople say that Maeve, still a great queen of the western Sidhe, is buried in the cairn of stones upon it. I have written of Clooth-na-Bare in *The Celtic Twilight* [his footnote read 'Doubtless Clooth-na-Bare should be Cailleac Beare, which would mean the old Woman Beare. Beare or Bere or Verah or Dera or Dhera was a very famous person, perhaps the Mother of the Gods herself. Standish O'Grady found her, as he thinks, frequenting Lough Leath, or the Grey Lake on a mountain of the Fews. Perhaps Lough Ia is my mishearing or the story-teller's mispronunciation of Lough Leath, for there are many Lough Leaths']. She 'went all over the world, seeking a lake deep enough to drown her faery life, of which she had grown weary, leaping from hill to hill, and setting up a cairn of stones wherever her feet lighted, until, at last, she found the deepest water in the world in little Lough Ia, on the top of the bird mountain, in Sligo.' I forget, now, where I heard this story, but it may have been from a priest at Coolooney.

Caoilte: see notes on *WO*, p. 484. Yeats said that he did not remember where he had read the story; he had, 'maybe, half forgotten it'. Sheila O'Sullivan (*YUIT*, 271) suggests his source was Standish James O'Grady, *History of Ireland Critical and Philosophical* (1881), 354, and thinks that O'Grady was quoting *The Dean of Lismore's Book*, ed. Rev. Thomas McLaughlan (1862), 62–72   *Niamh*: the fairy who spirits Oisin away for three hundred years. See notes on *WO*, p. 486   *between him and the deed . . . and the hope of his heart*: cf. 'The Everlasting Voices', p. 89, and 'To his Heart, bidding it have no Fear', p. 99. Human reason, Yeats wrote in his diary in 1930, cannot reconcile his conceptions – one of reality as a congeries of beings, another of reality as a single being – which alternate in emotion and history. He saw himself as driven to a moment when he realised himself 'as unique and free or to a moment which is the surrender to God of all that I am'. There were, he thought, historical cycles when one or the other conception prevailed; a cycle was approaching where everything would be as particular and concrete as human intensity would permit. He had tried 'to sing that approach' in this poem and the two linked to it, and 'almost understood' his intention. But again and again 'with remorse, a sense of defeat' he had failed, when he wanted to write 'of God, [had] written coldly and conventionally'. Could the two impulses, both part of truth, he wondered, be reconciled, 'or if one or the other could prevail, all life would cease' (*E*, 305)

p. 89, 'The Everlasting Voices'   *dc*: 29 Aug. 1895   *fp*: *NR*, Jan. 1896, with the title 'Everlasting Voices'   *everlasting Voices . . . tide*:

Hanrahan (see notes on 'He reproves the Curlew', p. 514), hears faint joyful voices when he is dying, and is told that it is the voice of one who has come looking for him, that 'you are mine until the whole world is burned out like a candle that is spent'. This is 'one of the lasting people, of the lasting unwearied Voices that make my dwelling in the broken and the dying and those that have lost their wits' (*M*, 260). In *CT* Yeats recorded his seeming to hear a voice of lamentation out of the Golden Age which told him that the world was once perfect and kindly, and existed thus 'but buried like a mass of roses under many spadefuls of earth'. In it the fairies and more innocent spirits dwelt, lamenting over the fallen world of humans; their lamentations are in the wind-tossed reeds, the song of birds, the moan of the waves, and the cry of the fiddle. It said, he added, that if only those who live in the Golden Age could die, 'we might be happy, for the sad voices would be still; but they must sing and we must weep until the eternal gates swing open' (*M*, 104–5)

p. 90, 'The Moods', *fp*: *TB*, Aug. 1893   An essay of 1895, 'The Moods', acts as an explanation of the poem's purpose:

> Literature differs from explanatory and scientific writing in being wrought about a mood, or a community of moods, as the body is wrought about an invisible soul; and if it uses argument, theory, erudition, observation, and seems to grow hot in assertion or denial, it does so merely to make us partakers at the banquet of the moods. It seems to me that these moods are the labourers and messengers of the Ruler of All, the gods of ancient days still dwelling on their secret Olympus, the angels of more modern days ascending and descending upon their shining ladder; and that argument, theory, erudition, observation, are merely what Blake called 'little devils who fight for themselves,' illusions of our visible passing life, who must be made to serve the moods, or we have no part in eternity. Everything that can be seen, touched, measured, explained, understood, argued over, is to the imaginative artist nothing more than a means, for he belongs to the invisible life, and delivers its ever new and ever ancient revelation. We hear much of his need for the restraints of reason, but the only restraint he can obey is the mysterious instinct that has made him an artist, and that teaches him to discover immortal moods in mortal desires, an undecaying hope in our trivial ambitions, a divine love in sexual passion. [*E & I*, 195]

candle burnt out . . . woods: In Yeats's story 'The Death of Hanrahan' there is a parallel passage:

> I am young, I am young; look upon me, mountains; look upon me, perishing woods, for my body will be shining like the white waters when you have been hurried away. You and the whole race of men, and the race of the beasts, and the race of the fish, and the winged race, are dropping like a candle that is nearly burned out. . . . [*M*, 254]

Have their day: Yeats's story 'Rosa Alchemica' illustrates these lines with the picture given to six students in a book of alchemical doctrines. If they were to imagine the semblance of a living being it was at once possessed by a wandering soul going hither and thither working good or evil, until the moment of its death had come:

> If you would give forms to the evil powers, it went on, you were to make them ugly, thrusting out a lip with the thirsts of life, or breaking the proportions of a body with the burdens of life; but the divine powers would only appear in beautiful shapes, which are but, as it were, shapes trembling out of existence, folding up into a timeless ecstasy, drifting with half-shut eyes into a sleepy stillness. The bodiless souls who descended into these forms were what men called the moods; and worked all great changes in the world; for just as the magician or the artist could call them when he would, so they could call out of the mind of the magician or the artist, or if they were demons, out of the mind of the mad or the ignoble, what shape they would, and through its voice and its gestures pour themselves out upon the world. In this way all great events were accomplished; a mood, a divinity or a demon, first descending like a faint sigh into men's minds and then changing their thoughts and their actions until hair that was yellow had grown black, or hair that was black had grown yellow, and empires moved their border, as though they were but drifts of leaves. [*M*, 285]

fire-born moods: Yeats, distinguishing between terrestrial reality and the condition of fire, wrote that in the condition of fire 'is all music and all rest' (*M*, 357)   *fallen away*: Yeats quoted the present poem (see also the later 'A Meditation in Time of War', p. 297) after this passage in his essay 'Anima Mundi':

> All power is from the terrestrial condition, for there all opposites meet and there only is the extreme of choice possible, full freedom. And there the heterogeneous is, and evil, for evil is the strain one upon another of opposites; but in the condition of fire is all music and all rest. Between is the condition of air where images have but a borrowed life, that of memory or that reflected upon them when they symbolise colours and intensities of fire: the place of shades who are 'in the whirl of those who are fading . . .'
> After so many rhythmic beats the soul must cease to desire its images, and can, as it were, close its eyes.
> When all sequence comes to an end, time comes to an end and the soul puts on the rhythmic or spiritual body or luminous body and contemplates all the events of its memory [cf. 'Man and the Echo', p. 469, where Yeats contemplates events in his life, arranges all in one clear view, 'Then stands in judgment on his soul'] and every possible impulse in an eternal possession of itself in one single moment. That condition is alone animate, all the rest is fantasy, and from thence come all the passions and, some have held, the very heat of the body. [*M*, 356–7]

p. 90, 'The Lover tells of the Rose in his Heart'   *fp*: *NO*, 12 Nov. 1892, with the title 'The Rose in my Heart'. In *WR* the title is 'Aedh tells of the Rose in his Heart'. Notes to *WR* explain that Aedh, the Irish god of death, Hanrahan (see notes on 'He reproves the Curlew', p. 514) and Michael Robartes (another invented character, a visionary, a magician, founded upon George Russell and MacGregor Mathers) were personages in *TSR*. He was using them more as 'principles of the mind' than as actual personages; only students of the magical tradition would understand him

when he said that Michael Robartes was fire reflected in water, Aedh fire
burning by itself   *your image*: Maud Gonne's

p. 90, 'The Host of the Air'   *fp*: TB, Nov. 1893 with the title 'The
Stolen Bride'. After the title came this note:

> I heard the story on which this ballad is founded from an old woman at
> Balesodare, Sligo. She repeated me a Gaelic poem on the subject, and then
> translated it to me. I have always regretted not having taken down her words, and
> as some amends for not having done so, have made this ballad. Any one who
> tastes fairy food or drink is glamoured and stolen by the fairies. This is why
> Bridget sets O'Driscoll to play cards. 'The folk of the air' is a Gaelic name for the
> fairies.

A later note in *WR* added that in the ballad the husband 'found the keeners
[see notes on 'The Ballad of Father O'Hart', p. 494] keening his wife when
he got to his house; and knew that she was dead'   *Title*: The host (folk)
of the air are fairies. Cf. Yeats's note in *WR*:

> Some writers distinguish between the Sluagh Gaoith [*PNE* points out that this
> should be Gaoithe], the host of the air, and Sluagh Sidhe, the host of the Sidhe,
> and describe the host of the air of a peculiar malignancy. Dr Joyce says, 'of all the
> different kinds of goblins . . . air demons were most dreaded by the people. They
> lived among clouds, and mists, and rocks, and hated the human race with the
> utmost malignity.' ['Fergus O'Mara and the Demons', *Good and Pleasant Reading*
> (1892), which Yeats included in *Irish Fairy Tales* (1892).] A very old Arann charm,
> which contains the words 'Send God, by his strength, between us and the host of
> the Sidhe, between us and the host of the air', seems also to distinguish among
> them. I am inclined, however, to think that the distinction came in with
> Christianity and its belief about the prince of the air [Satan], for the host of the
> Sidhe, as I have already explained, are closely associated with the wind.

See also notes on 'The Hosting of the Sidhe', p. 506   *Hart Lake*: a lake
high up in the Ox Mountains, 6 or 7 miles west of Ballisodare, Co.
Sligo   *his bride*: the Sidhe 'are said to steal brides just after their marriage
and sometimes in a blast of wind' (*WR*)   *gone like a drifting smoke*: in
'Kidnappers', the melting away of the jolly company of fairies that a young
man had met with his bride, whom they had stolen, shows him that they
were faeries (*M*, 73 ff.)

p. 92, 'The Fish'   *fp*: *Cornish Magazine*, Dec. 1898, with the title
'Bressel the Fisherman', altered in *WR* to 'Breasel the Fisherman'

p. 92, 'The Unappeasable Host'   *fp*: S, April 1896, with the title
'Two Poems concerning Peasant Visionaries' (the other poem being 'The
Valley of the Black Pig', p. 100). This poem had the title 'A Cradle Song'
in *WR*   *Danaan children*: the Tuatha de Danaan. See notes on *WO*,
p. 484   *the North*: presumably the North wind. Yeats associated the
North with night and sleep elsewhere; he commented that the wind was 'a

symbol of vague desires and hopes, not merely because the Sidhe are in the wind, or because the wind bloweth as it listeth but because wind and spirit and vague desire haνε been associated everywhere' (*WR*)   *ger-eagle*: geier-eagle (gier-eagle) used in the Bible (Authorised Version) to translate the Hebrew word *raham*, a kind of vulture. Cf. Leviticus 11:18 and Deuteronomy 14:17   *flaming West*: Yeats associated the West with dreaming things, fading things, as it was the place of sunset   *Mother Mary*: the Virgin Mary, mother of Christ

p. 93, 'Into the Twilight'   *dc*: 31 June [?1893]   *fp*: *NO*, 29 July 1893, with the title 'The Celtic Twilight'; it was given its final title in *CT*   *Eire*: see notes on 'To the Rose upon the Rood of Time', p. 496

p. 93, 'The Song of Wandering Aengus'   *dc*: 31 June [?1897]   *fp*: *The Sketch*, 4 Aug. 1897, with the title 'A Mad Song'   Yeats wrote that the tribes of the goddess Danu (the Tuatha de Danaan) can take all shapes, those in the waters often taking the shape of fish (*WR*). The poem was suggested to him, he added, by a Greek folksong, identified by R. K. Alspach, 'The Songs of Yeats', *Modern Language Notes*, lxi, 395–400, as Lucy Garnett's 'The Three Fishes', *Greek Folk Poesy* (1896), which Yeats reviewed in *TB*, Oct., 1896; Alspach also suggested that Samuel Lover's (1797–1868) 'The White Trout', included in Yeats's *FFT*, could have contributed. Yeats thought the folk belief of Greece very like that of Ireland and, when he wrote the poem, was 'thinking of Ireland, and of the spirits that are in Ireland'   *I*: The man 'with a hazel wand' in 'He mourns for . . . End of the World', p. 95, 'may well have been Aengus, the Master of Love' (*P* (1895)); the speaker here may be the god, though the poet himself seems more likely (the poem is in part about Maud Gonne's effect on him)   *hazel wood . . . berry*: Sheila O'Sullivan, *YUIT*, 268, suggests that the imagery of the first stanza comes from Standish Hayes O'Grady's edition of the story of Diarmuid and Grainne (Grania), *Transactions of the Ossianic Society*, III (1857), 78–81. A youth tells the two lovers (see notes on *WO*, p. 488) he is seeking a lord to serve; in reality he is Aengus. He gives them food, going into a wood, plucking a long rod and putting a holly berry upon a hook and catching a trout   *glimmering girl . . . apple blossom*: Yeats associated Maud Gonne with apple blossom; at his first meeting with her in 1889

she passed before a window and rearranged a spray of flowers in a vase. Twelve years after I put this impression into verse ('She pulled down the pale blossoms') [from 'The Arrow' as it was published in *ISW*: 'Blossom pale, she pulled down the pale blossom/At the moth hour and hid it in her bosom.'] I felt in the presence of a great generosity and courage and a mind without rest, and when she and all the singing birds had gone, my melancholy was not the mere melancholy of love. I had what I thought was a clairvoyant perception but was, I can see now, but an obvious deduction of an awaiting immediate disaster [*MS*, 42]

He also wrote of her complexion being 'luminous, like that of apple-blossom through which the light falls, and I remember her standing that first day by a great heap of such blossoms in the window' (*A*, 123)   *silver apples . . . golden apples*: see notes on 'The Man who Dreamed of Faeryland', p. 503. Sheila O'Sullivan suggests that the image of sun and moon may come from Lady Wilde, *Ancient Cures, Charms and Usages* (1890), 101–2, which describes two balls representing sun and moon, covered in gold and silver paper respectively, and suspended within a hoop wreathed with rowan and marsh marigold, carried in Mayday processions in Ireland (*YUIT*, 270)

p. 94, 'The Song of the Old Mother'   *fp*: *TB*, April 1894   Yeats later described this, 'an old woman complaining of the idleness of the young', as one of the poems that 'popular poets' write (*A*, 254)   *seed of the fire*: Yeats's note glossed this as an Irish phrase 'for the little fragment of burning turf [peat] and hot ashes which remains in the hearth from the night before'

p. 94, 'The Heart of the Woman'   *dc*: 1894   *fp*: *The Speaker*, 21 July 1894, untitled and included in a story 'Those Who Live in the Storm', reprinted as 'The Rose of Shadow', *TSR*

p. 95, 'The Lover mourns for the Loss of Love'   *fp*: *D*, May 1898, with the title 'Aodh to Dectora/Three Songs' (the others were 'He hears the Cry of the Sedge', p. 102, and 'He thinks of those who have Spoken Evil of his Beloved', p. 103)   The poem describes a sad moment in Yeats's relationship with Olivia Shakespear, whom he met in 1894 and with whom he had his first affair in 1896 (see notes on 'Friends', p. 549). See *Y:M & P*, 100–3, and *YANB*, 78–9, 82–4, 101–2, and see *M*, 72, 85–9   *beautiful friend*: Mrs Shakespear   *your image*: Maud Gonne's. See *M*, 89, and *YANB*, 101–2

p. 95, 'He mourns for the Change that has come upon him and his Beloved, and longs for the End of the World'   *dc*: [? June 1897]   *fp*: *D*, June, 1897, with the title 'The Desire of Man and Woman'. In *WR* it became 'Mongan laments the Change that has . . .'. Mongan, 'in the old Celtic poetry, is a famous wizard and king who remembers his passed lives' (note, *D*, Oct., 1897)   *white deer . . . one red ear*: Yeats's note of 1899 read:

> My deer and hound are properly related to the deer and hound that flicker in and out of the various tellings of the Arthurian legends, leading different knights upon adventures, and to the hounds and to the hornless deer at the beginning of, I think, all tellings of Oisin's journey to the country of the young. The hound is certainly related to the Hounds of Annwoyn or of Hades, who are white, and have red ears, and were heard, and are, perhaps, still heard by Welsh peasants, following some

flying thing in the night winds; and is probably related to the hounds that Irish countrypeople believe will awake and seize the souls of the dead if you lament them too loudly or too soon. An old woman told a friend and myself that she saw what she thought were white birds, flying over an enchanted place, but found, when she got near, that they had dogs' heads; and I do not doubt that my hound and these dog-headed birds are of the same family. I got my hound and deer out of a last-century Gaelic poem about Oisin's journey to the country of the young. After the hunting of the hornless deer, that leads him to the seashore, and while he is riding over the sea with Niamh, he sees amid the waters – I have not the Gaelic poem by me, and describe it from memory – a young man following a girl who has a golden apple, and afterwards a hound with one red ear following a deer with no horns. This hound and this deer seem plain images of the desire of the man 'which is for the woman,' and 'the desire of the woman which is for the desire of the man,' and of all desires that are as these. I have read them in this way in *The Wanderings of Oisin*, and have made my lover sigh because he has seen in their faces 'the immortal desire of Immortals.'

The man in my poem who has a hazel wand may have been Aengus, Master of Love; and I have made the Boar without bristles come out of the West, because the place of sunset was in Ireland, as in other countries, a place of symbolic darkness and death.

Cf. the description in *WO* of the Land of Youth, p. 9:

> We galloped; now a hornless deer
> Passed by us, chased by a phantom hound
> All pearly white, save one red ear . . .

The image probably comes from Michael Comyn's 'The Lay of Oisin in the Land of Youth':

> A hornless fawn leaping nimbly
> A red-eared white dog,
> Urging it boldly in the chase.

See notes on *WO*, p. 486   *A man . . . hazel wand*: probably Aengus, the Irish god of love   *the Boar without bristles*: see Yeats's note on 'The Valley of the Black Pig':

> If one reads Professor Rhys' *Celtic Heathendom* by the light of Professor Frazer's *Golden Bough*, and puts together what one finds there about the boar that killed Diarmuid, and other old Celtic boars and sows, one sees that the battle is mythological, and that the Pig it is named from must be a type of cold and winter doing battle with the summer, or of death battling with life. For the purposes of poetry, at any rate, I think it a symbol of the darkness that will destroy the world.

Here Yeats refers to Irish prophecies or visions of a great battle to be fought in the Valley of the Black Pig, which would rout Ireland's enemies (see notes on 'The Valley of the Black Pig', p. 516)   *the West*: see notes on 'The Unappeasable Host', p. 510, and cf. ll. 1–5 of 'He bids his Beloved be at Peace', p. 96, 'He reproves the Curlew', p. 96, and 'He wishes his Beloved were Dead', p. 107

p. 96, 'He bids his Beloved be at Peace'   *dc*: 24 Sept. 1895   *fp*: *S*, Jan. 1896, with the title 'Two Love Poems. The Shadowy Horses; Michael Robartes bids his Beloved be at Peace'. For Robartes see notes on 'The Lover tells of the Rose in his Heart', p. 509. Yeats commented:

> November, the old beginning of winter, or of the victory of the Fomor [see notes on *WO*, p. 484], or powers of death, and dismay, and cold, and darkness, is associated by the Irish people with the horse-shaped Pucas [see *FFT*, 94, for a description of pucas as solitary faeries and of their shapes], who are now mischievous spirits, but were once Fomorian divinities. I think that they may have some connection with the horses of Mannannan [god of the sea], who reigned over the country of the dead, where the Fomorian Tethra [a king of the Fomorians, whom older stories make a ruler of Tir-na-nOg] reigned also; and the horses of Mannannan, though they could cross the land as easily as the sea, are constantly associated with the waves. Some neo-platonist, I forget who [*PNE* suggests Thomas Taylor (1758–1835), writing of the sea in *A Dissertation on the Eleusinian and Bacchic Mysteries* (1790), p. 165, as perpetually rolling without admitting any period of repose], describes the sea as a symbol of the drifting indefinite bitterness of life, and I believe there is like symbolism intended in the many Irish voyages to the islands of enchantment, or that there was, at any rate, in the mythology out of which these stories have been shaped. I follow much Irish and other mythology, and the magical tradition, in associating the North with night and sleep, and the East, the place of sunrise, with hope, and the South, the place of the sun when at its height, with passion and desire, and the West, the place of sunset, with fading and dreaming things. [*WR*]

The North: Yeats described the Fomoroh (see notes on *WO*, p. 484), as being of the North and of winter   *Beloved*: The poem was written to Olivia Shakespear. See notes on 'The Lover mourns for the Loss of Love', p. 512   *your hair fall over my breast*: cf. l. 6 of 'The Travail of Passion', p. 106, also written to Mrs Shakespear

p. 96, 'He reproves the Curlew'   *fp*: *S*, Nov. 1896, with the title 'Windlestraws I. O'Sullivan Rua to the Curlew', which became 'Hanrahan reproves the Curlew' in *WR*. The name Hanrahan Yeats saw 'over a shop, or rather part of it over a shop in a Galway village – but there were many poets like him in the eighteenth century in Ireland'. Hanrahan is probably modelled on the Irish poet Eoghan Ruadh O'Suilleabhan (1748–84), whose wandering life as soldier, sailor, labourer, schoolmaster and poet is mirrored in his poems, edited in 1907 by Father Padraig O'Duinnin. He served in the navy and army and died of fever after being wounded in a brawl. He appears in Yeats's *Stories of Red Hanrahan* (1904) and *The Secret Rose* (1907)   *water in the West*: see notes on 'The Unappeasable Host', p. 510, and Yeats's note on 'He bids his Beloved be at Peace' above   *wind*: a symbol of vague hopes and desires

p. 97, 'He remembers Forgotten Beauty'   *fp*: S, July 1896, with the title 'O'Sullivan Rua to Mary Lavell', which became 'Michael Robartes remembers Forgotten Beauty' in *WR*. For Robartes, see notes on 'The Lover tells of the Rose in his Heart', p. 509

p. 98, 'A Poet to his Beloved'   *dc*: 1895   *fp*: SEN, March 1896, with the title 'O'Sullivan the Red to Mary Lavell II', which became 'A Poet to his Beloved' in *WR*

p. 98, 'He gives his Beloved certain Rhymes'   *dc*: 1895   *fp*: S, Jan. 1896, untitled, appearing in a story 'The Binding of the Hair'. In *WR* it was entitled 'Aedh gives his Beloved Certain Rhymes' (see notes on 'The Lover tells of the Rose in his Heart', p. 509)   Yeats stated that the story (as it appeared in that first edition of *TSR*) was based on some old Gaelic legend:

> A certain man swears to sing the praise of a certain woman, his head is cut off and the head sings [reminiscent of the story of the horse Fallada in Grimm's *Fairy Tales*]. A poem of mine called 'He Gives His Beloved Certain Rhymes' was the song of the head.

Hone (*WBY*, 123) thought the poem was addressed to 'Diana Vernon' (Mrs Shakespear, see notes on 'The Lover mourns for the Loss of Love', p. 512) but it is more likely to have been written to Maud Gonne

p. 99, 'To his Heart, bidding it have no Fear'   *fp*: S, Nov. 1896, with the title 'Windlestraws II Out of the Old Days'; the present title was used in *WR*   *the flame and the flood*: a phrase from the initiation ritual of the Order of the Golden Dawn. Cf. Virginia Moore, *The Unicorn* (1954), 139

p. 99, 'The Cap and Bells'   *dc*: 1893   *fp*: NO, 17 March 1894, with the title 'Cap and Bell'. Yeats commented:

> I dreamed this story exactly as I have written it, and dreamed another long dream after it, trying to make out its meaning, and whether I was to write it in prose or verse. The first dream was more a vision than a dream, for it was beautiful and coherent, and gave me the sense of illumination and exaltation that one gets from visions, while the second dream was confused and meaningless. The poem has always meant a great deal to me, though, as is the way with symbolic poems, it has not always meant quite the same thing. Blake would have said 'The authors are in eternity' [Blake letter, 6 July 1803, to Thomas Butts about *Milton*: '. . . I dare not pretend to be any other than the secretary; the authors are in eternity'; cf. *The Works of William Blake*, ed. E. J. Ellis and W. B. Yeats (1893), I, vii, and Alexander Gilchrist, *Life of William Blake* (1880), I, 187] and I am quite sure they can only be questioned in dreams. [*WR*]

his soul: the jester offers the lady his soul and heart; she is not affected by either but by his cap and bells. Yeats later said this poem was the way to

win a lady, while 'He wishes for the Cloths of Heaven', p. 108, was the
way to lose one   *cap and bells*: Yeats wrote of a man trying to bring
before his mind's eye an image of Aengus, the Irish god of love and beauty,
who changed four of his kisses into birds. Suddenly 'the image of a man
with cap and bells rushed before his mind's eye and grew vivid and spoke
and called itself "Aengus' Messenger" ' (*M*, 115)

p. 100, 'The Valley of the Black Pig'   *fp*: *S*, April 1896, with the title
'Two Poems concerning Peasant Visionaries. The Valley of the Black Pig'
(the companion poem was 'A Cradle Song', later 'The Unappeasable
Host', p. 92). Yeats's note read:

> The Irish peasantry have for generations comforted themselves, in their mis-
> fortunes, with visions of a great battle, to be fought in a mysterious valley called,
> 'The Valley of the Black Pig', and to break at last the power of their enemies. A
> few years ago, in the barony of Lisadell, in county Sligo, an old man would fall
> entranced upon the ground from time to time, and rave out a description of the
> battle . . .

A note dated 1899–1906 continues:

> . . . and a man in Sligo has told me that it will be so great a battle that the horses
> shall go up to their fetlocks in blood, and that their girths, when it is over, will rot
> from their bellies for lack of a hand to unbuckle them.

The note ends in a manner similar to that cited in notes on 'He mourns for
. . . End of the World', p. 512. The note in *WR* links peasant beliefs and
stories with the work of anthropologists (see *NC*, 59–61); Yeats had been
reading John Rhys, *Lectures on the Origin and Growth of Religion as Illustrated
by Celtic Heathendom* (2nd edn 1892), and Sir James Frazer's *The Golden
Bough: A Study in Comparative Religion* (1890). As a result he thought that
the battle was mythological. The bristleless boar had killed Diarmuid (see
notes on *WO*, p. 488) on the western end of Ben Bulben in Co. Sligo;
Misroide MacDatha's son, whose carving brought on a great battle; the
sow of Welsh November rhymes (here he cited Rhys, *Celtic Heathendom*);
the boar that killed Adonis; the boar that killed Attis and the pig embodiment of Typhon (here he cited Frazer's *The Golden Bough*). The pig was a
corn genius; but pigs and boars became types of evil, the enemies of the
gods they had once typified. So, Yeats argued, the pig became the Black
Pig, a type of cold and of winter, which warred against the summer. He
believed it was a symbol of the darkness that would destroy the gods and
the world (see notes on 'He mourns for . . . End of the World', p. 512). He
compared this prophesied battle with three other battles: one the Sidhe (see
Glossary) are said to fight when someone is being taken from them, a battle
they fight in November for the harvest, and the battle fought by the Tuatha
de Danaan with the Fomor (see Glossary and notes on *WO*, p. 484) at
Moytura (Irish, the towery plain; it overlooks Lough Arrow, Co. Sligo).
He linked these battles together, suggesting that

the battle between the Tribes of the goddess Danu, the powers of light, and warmth, and fruitfulness, and goodness, and the Fomor, the powers of darkness, and cold, and barrenness, and badness upon the Towery Plain, was the establishment of the habitable world, the rout of the ancestral darkness; that the battle among the Sidhe for the harvest is the annual battle of summer and winter; that the battle among the Sidhe at a man's death is the battle between the manifest world and the ancestral darkness at the end of all things; and that all these battles are one, the battle of all things with shadowy decay. Once a symbolism has possessed the imagination of large numbers of men, it becomes, as I believe, an embodiment of disembodied powers, and repeats itself in dreams and visions, age after age. [*WR*]

He wrote the poem because of 'some talk of MacGregor Mathers' (see notes on 'To the Rose upon the Rood of Time', p. 496, 'The Two Trees', p. 504, and 'All Souls Night', p. 593). In 1893 or 1894 Mathers had prophesied the imminence of vast wars (*A*, 336); Yeats wrote in 1902 that when he discussed the Battle of the Black Pig with a Sligo countrywoman she thought of a battle between Ireland and England, but he of an Armageddon which would 'quench all things in ancestral Darkness again' (*M*, 111)   *cromlech*: see notes on 'A Faery Song', p. 499   *grey cairn*: probably a reference to Maeve's grave on Knocknarea; see notes on *WO*, p. 485

p. 101, 'The Lover asks Forgiveness because of his Many Moods'   *dc*: 23 Aug. 1895   *fp*: *SR*, 2 Nov. 1895, with the title 'The Twilight of Forgiveness', altered to 'Michael Robartes asks Forgiveness because of his many Moods' in *WR*; see notes on 'The Lover tells of the Rose in his Heart', p. 509   *O Winds*: Yeats commented that he used the wind as a symbol of vague desires and hopes 'not merely because the Sidhe [see Glossary] are in the wind, or because the wind bloweth as it listeth, but because wind and spirit and vague desire have been associated everywhere'   *tabors*: small drums   *Niamh*: see notes on *WO*, p. 486   *Phoenix*: a mythical bird, supposedly the only one of its kind: it lived for 500–600 years in the Arabian desert, burnt itself to death on a funeral pyre but emerged with renewed youth to live another cycle

p. 102, 'He tells of a Valley full of Lovers'   *fp*: *SR*, 9 Jan. 1897, with the title 'The Valley of Lovers', altered to 'Aedh tells . . . Lovers' in *WR*; see notes on 'The Lover tells of the Rose in his Heart', p. 509

p. 102, 'He tells of the Perfect Beauty'   *dc*: Dec. 1895   *fp*: *SEN*, March 1896, with the title 'O'Sullivan The Red to Mary Lavell', became 'Aedh tells . . . Beauty' in *WR*; see notes on 'The Lover tells of the Rose in his Heart', p. 509   *brood of the skies*: the stars   *God burn time*: see notes on 'the Man who Dreamed of Faeryland', p. 503

p. 102, 'He hears the Cry of the Sedge'   *fp*: *D*, May 1898, with the title 'Aodh to Dectora/Three Songs/I', altered to 'Aedh hears the Cry of the Sedge'; see notes on 'The Lover tells of the Rose in his Heart', p. 509   Yeats's note on *The Rose* indicates that he put the Tree of Life into several poems, linking it with the pole of the heavens (an imaginary line around which the heavens were thought to revolve); he 'made it an axle-tree in "Aedh hears the Cry of the Sedge", for this was an ancient way of representing it' [*WR*]   *lake*: possibly Coole Lake, in Co. Galway. Yeats wrote the poem to Maud Gonne at a time of great stress, when he was 'tortured with sexual desire and disappointed love. Often as I walked in the woods at Coole it would have been a relief to have screamed aloud' (*MS*, 125). He met Lady Gregory in 1894, and made his first long visit to her house, Coole Park, in 1897: from then on he spent many summers there   *sedge*: probably a deliberate echo of Keats's 'La Belle Dame Sans Merci', 'the sedge is withered from the lake'   *banners of East and West*: see notes on 'To his Heart, bidding it have no Fear', p. 515

p. 103, 'He thinks of those who have Spoken Evil of his Beloved'   *fp*: *D*, May 1898, with the title 'Aodh to Dectora/Three Songs/3'; see notes on 'The Lover tells of the Rose in his Heart', p. 509   *a mouthful of air*: a description of fairies, 'nations of gay creatures, having no souls; nothing in their bright bodies but a mouthful of sweet air' ('Tales from the Twilight', *SO*, 1 March 1890)

p. 103, 'The Blessed'   *fp*: *TYB*, April 1897   *Cumhal*: 'Cumhal the King' in earlier versions   *Dathi*: 'Dathi the Blessed' in earlier versions   *The Incorruptible Rose*: see notes on *The Rose*, p. 495, and on 'To the Rose upon the Rood of Time', p. 496

p. 104, 'The Secret Rose'   *fp*: *S*, Sept. 1896, with the title 'O'Sullivan Rua to the Secret Rose', which became 'To the Secret Rose' in *TSR*, then 'The Secret Rose' in *WR*   Yeats commented:

I find that I have unintentionally changed the old story of Conchobar's death. [Conchubar was King of Ulster in the Red Branch cycle of tales.] He did not see the crucifix in a vision, but was told about it. He had been struck by a ball, made of the dried brain of a dead enemy, and hurled out of a sling; and this ball had been left in his head, and his head had been mended, the Book of Leinster [now in Trinity College Dublin, part of a manuscript miscellany of nearly 1000 pieces of different kinds. Yeats may have read this part of it in Eugene O'Curry, *Lectures on the Manuscript Material of Ancient Ireland*, 2nd edn 1878, 637–43] says, with thread of gold because his hair was like gold. Keating, a writer of the time of Elizabeth [Geoffrey Keating (*c.* 1570–1650), author of the *History of Ireland*, begun *c.* 1620, completed 1634], says: 'In that state did he remain seven years, until the Friday on which Christ was crucified, according to some historians; and when he saw the unusual changes of the creation and the eclipse of the sun and the moon at its full, he asked of Bucrach, a Leinster Druid, who was along with him, what was it that brought that unusual change upon the planets of Heaven and Earth. "Jesus Christ, the son of God," said the Druid, "who is now being crucified by the Jews." "That is a pity," said Conchobar; "were I in his presence I would kill those who were putting him to death." And with that he brought out his sword, and rushed at a woody grove which was convenient to him, and began to cut and fell it; and what he said was, that if he were among the Jews that was the usage he would give them, and from the excessiveness of his fury which seized upon him, the ball started out of his head, and some of the brain came after it, and in that way he died. The wood of Lanshraigh, in Feara Rois, is the name by which that shrubby wood is called.' [The source is the Irish Texts Society edn of Keating, *History of Ireland* (1902–14), II, 203.]

I have imagined Cuchullain [see note on 'To the Rose upon the Rood of Time', p. 496] meeting Fand 'walking among flaming dew'. [See Standish O'Grady, *History of Ireland* (1879–80), II, 73, or his *History of Ireland: Critical and Philosophical* (1881), 107.] The story of their love is one of the most beautiful of our old tales. Two birds, bound one to another with a chain of gold, came to a lake side where Cuchullain and the host of Uladh was encamped, and sang so sweetly that all the host fell into a magic sleep. Presently they took the shape of two beautiful women, and cast a magical weakness upon Cuchullain, in which he lay for a year. At the year's end an Aengus, who was probably Aengus the master of love, one of the greatest of the children of the goddess Danu, came and sat upon his bedside, and sang how Fand, the wife of Mannannan, the master of the sea, and of the islands of the dead, loved him; and that if he would come into the country of the gods, where there was wine and gold and silver, Fand, and Laban her sister, would heal him of his magical weakness. In 'Mortal Help' Cuchullain went to the country of the gods, and, after being for a month the lover of Fand [see *M*, 9], made her a promise to meet her at a place called 'the Yew at the Strand's End,' and came back to the earth. Emer, his mortal wife, won his love again, and Mannannan came to 'the Yew at the Strand's End', and carried Fand away. When Cuchullain saw her going, his love for her fell upon him again, and he went mad, and wandered among the mountains without food or drink, until he was at last cured by a Druid drink of forgetfulness.

I have founded the man 'who drove the gods out of their Liss,' or fort, upon something I have read about Caolte [Caoilte] after the battle of Gabra, when almost all his companions were killed, driving the gods out of their Liss, either at Osraighe, now Ossory, or at Eas Ruaidh, now Asseroe, a waterfall at Ballyshannon, where Ilbreac, one of the children of the goddess Danu, had a Liss. [Probably Yeats learned about Caolte MacRonan from Standish O'Grady, *History of Ireland: Critical and Philosophical* (1881) 324–5 and 353, and from Eugene O'Curry's commentary on 'The Fate of the Children of Tuireann', *Atlantis* (1863), 4, 231–3, and his *On the Manners and Customs of the Ancient Irish* (1873), III, 366.] I am writing away from most of my books, and have not been able to find the passage; but I certainly read it somewhere. But maybe I only read it in Mr Standish O'Grady, who has a fine imagination, for I find no such story in Lady Gregory's book. [This sentence added in *CW*.]

I have founded 'the proud dreaming king' upon Fergus, the son of Roigh, the legendary poet of 'the quest of the bull of Cualg[n]e,' as he is in the ancient story of Deirdre, and in modern poems by Ferguson. ['The Abdication of Fergus Mac Roy', *Lays of the Western Gael, and Other Poems* (1864). Yeats had also used

Standish O'Grady, *History of Ireland*, II, 249–50, as a source (*CW* 1).] He married Nessa, and Ferguson makes him tell how she took him 'captive in a single look'.

> 'I am but an empty shade,
> Far from life and passion laid;
> Yet does sweet remembrance thrill
> All my shadowy being still.'

Presently, because of his great love, he gave up his throne to Conchobar, her son by another, and lived out his days feasting, and fighting, and hunting. [In the Irish legend Fergus agreed to give up his throne for a year to Conchubar, the son of Ness; she so influenced the chiefs that they refused to allow Fergus to reclaim the kingship when the year was up.] His promise never to refuse a feast from a certain comrade, and the mischief that came by his promise, and the vengeance he took afterwards, are a principal theme of the poets. I have explained my imagination of him in 'Fergus and the Druid,' and in a little song in the second act of 'The Countess Kathleen' ['Who Goes with Fergus', p. 78].

I have founded him 'who sold tillage, and house, and goods,' upon something in 'The Red Pony,' a folk tale in Mr Larmine's *West Irish Folk Tales* [*and Romances* (1893), 212 ff.]. A young man 'saw a light before him on the high road. When he came as far, there was an open box on the road, and a light coming up out of it. He took up the box. There was a lock of hair in it. Presently he had to go to become the servant of a king for his living. There were eleven boys. When they were going out into the stable at ten o'clock, each of them took a light but he. He took no candle at all with him. Each of them went into his own stable. When he went into his stable he opened the box. He left it in a hole in the wall. The light was great. It was twice as much as in the other stables. The king hears of it, and makes him show him the box. The king says, 'You must go and bring me the woman to whom the hair belongs.' In the end, the young man, and not the king, marries the woman. [*WR*]

Rose: see notes on 'To the Rose upon the Rood of Time', p. 496   *thee . . . Sepulchre*: Jesus Christ . . . his tomb in Jerusalem   *wine-vat*: possibly a reference to the followers of Bacchus   *great leaves*: the Rosicrucian emblem of the four-leaved rose   *Magi*: the three wise men who came from the east to attend Christ's birth, bringing gifts of gold, frankincense and myrrh   *the king*: Conchubar, King of Ulster   *Pierced Hands and Rood*: Christ's hands and the Cross on which he was crucified   *Fand*: the wife of Manannan MacLir, god of the sea   *liss*: (Irish, *lios*) a mound inhabited by supernatural beings (also an enclosed space)   *Emer*: Cuchulain's wife; see Yeats's note, p. 519   *him who drove*: Caoilte MacRonan; see Yeats's note above   *proud dreaming king*: Fergus, Conchubar's predecessor   *him who sold*: see Yeats's note above   *A woman . . . loveliness*: the poem was written to Maud Gonne   *thy great wind*: probably the end of the world. See note on 'He mourns for . . . End of the World', p. 512. When he wrote this poem, Yeats was planning an Irish Order of Mysteries; he thought there was a need for mystical rites, a ritual system of meditation and evocation, through which perception of the spirit, the divine would be reunited with natural beauty. He wanted to turn

Irish places of beauty or legendary association into holy symbols, to unite what he called the 'radical truths' of Christianity to those of a more ancient world (*M*, 123–4, and *A*, 254)

p. 105, 'Maid Quiet'   *fp*: *NO*, 24 Dec. 1892, untitled, included in a story 'The Twisting of the Rope'; it was entitled 'O'Sullivan the Red upon his Wanderings' in *NR*, Aug. 1897, a title which became 'Hanrahan laments because of his Wanderings' in *WR*, 'Hanrahan' altered to 'The Lover' in *PW* I. (For Hanrahan, see notes on 'He reproves the Curlew', p. 514.) The poem was cut (from twelve lines to eight) and given its present title in *CW* I. Yeats commented on 'He mourns for . . . End of the World' that when Cuchulain hunted the enchanted deer of Slieve Fuad (the mountain now called The Fews, 'Gulleon's place of pride' in the original version of the poem, 'fabled to be Hanrahan's tomb' and place of worship, Gulleon being Cullain, a god of the underworld) he was the sun pursuing clouds or cold or darkness. In this poem, Yeats made Hanrahan long for the day 'when they, fragments of ancestral darkness, will overthrow the world'

p. 106, 'The Travail of Passion'   *fp*: *S*, Jan. 1896, entitled 'Two Love Poems. The Travail of Passion'   The poem was written to Olivia Shakespear. See notes on 'The Lover mourns for the Loss of Love', p. 512   *the scourge . . . heavy sponge*: this Biblical imagery condensed the Crucifixion and death of Jesus Christ   *Kedron*: the brook flowing between Jerusalem and the Mount of Olives, which it suggests as part of the Crucifixion imagery

p. 106, 'The Lover pleads with his Friend for Old Friends'   *fp*: *SR*, 24 July 1897, entitled 'The Poet . . . Friends'   *your shining days*: Maud Gonne was at the peak of her political career, addressing many public meetings in 1897 and 1898 in the cause of the '98 Centennial Association (Yeats was president of the British and French branches), formed to commemorate the 1798 Rebellion and its leader Wolfe Tone

p. 106, 'The Lover speaks to the Hearers of his Songs in Coming Days'   *dc*: Nov. 1895   *fp*: *NR*, April 1896, then untitled and included in a story of 'The Vision of O'Sullivan the Red'. It was entitled 'Hanrahan speaks to the Lovers of his Songs in Coming Days' in *WR*; see notes on 'He reproves the Curlew', p. 514   *Attorney for Lost Souls*: the Virgin Mary (in early versions 'Maurya [later "Mary"] of the wounded heart')

p. 107, 'The Poet pleads with the Elemental Powers'   *fp*: *TB*, Oct. 1892, entitled 'A Mystical Prayer to the Masters of the Elements, Michael, Gabriel and Raphael'. In the version in *SBRC*, 'Finvarra Feacra, and

Caolte' replaced 'Michael, Gabriel, and Raphael' in the title, which became 'Aodh pleads . . . Powers' in *WR*; see notes on 'The Lover tells of the Rose in his Heart', p. 509   *The Powers*: W. Y. Tindall, *Forces in Modern British Literature* (1947), 243, thought them Madame Blavatsky's elemental spirits (see notes on 'Anashuya and Vijaya', p. 490); Saul (*PYP*, 75) drew on *M*, 171, to suggest beings who dwell 'in the waters and among the hazels and oak trees', and Henn (*LT*, 252) thought the first stanza was a Rosicrucian or Hermetic image. The poem's original title suggests that the three Masters of the Elements correspond to the Great Powers of wave, wind and fire in l. 7   *the Immortal Rose*: the Rosicrucian symbol (see notes on 'To the Rose upon the Rood of Time', p. 496), here probably the Rose of Ideal Beauty   *Seven Lights*: the seven stars of the Great Bear   *The Polar Dragon*: the constellation of the Dragon. Yeats commented that the Great Bear and the constellation of the Dragon 'in certain old mythologies' encircle the Tree of Life (see notes on 'The Two Trees', p. 504), 'on which is here imagined the Rose of the Ideal Beauty growing before it was cast into the world' (note, *D*, Dec. 1898). Ellmann drew attention to the cover of *TSR* in which the serpent's folds encircle the trunk of the Tree of Life as if it were the 'Guardian of the Rose'. He pointed out that in Kabbalism this serpent

> is the serpent of Nature in its benign aspects, and the occultist is said to follow the serpent's winding path upwards through many initiations, corresponding to each of the *Sephiroth*, until he reaches the top of the tree. Since in the poem the polar dragon sleeps, like earth in the 'Introduction' to Blake's *Songs of Experience*, the meaning seems to be that the natural world has become uncoiled or detached from beauty [*IY* 78]

her I love: Maud Gonne

p. 107, 'He wishes his Beloved were Dead'   *fp*: *SKT*, 9 Feb. 1898, entitled 'Aodh to Dectora' (altered to 'Aedh' in *WR*; see notes on 'The Lover tells of the Rose in his Heart', p. 509)   This poem develops 'A Dream of Death', p. 77, written when Maud Gonne was in France convalescing from an illness

p. 108, 'He wishes for the Cloths of Heaven'   *fp*: *WR*, entitled 'Aedh wishes . . . Heaven' (see notes on 'The Lover tells of the Rose in his Heart', p. 509)   See notes on 'The Cap and Bells', p. 515

p. 108, 'He thinks of his Past Greatness when a Part of the Constellations of Heaven'   *fp*: *D*, Oct. 1898, entitled 'Song of Mongan'; the title became 'Mongan thinks of his Past Greatness' in *WR*   Yeats's note (*D*, Oct. 1898), read:

> Mongan, in the old Celtic poetry, is a famous wizard and king, who remembers his passed lives. 'The Country of the Young' is a name in the Celtic poetry for the

country of the gods and of the happy dead. The hazel tree was the Irish tree of Life or of Knowledge, and in Ireland it was doubtless, as elsewhere, the tree of the heavens [see notes on 'The Two Trees', p. 504, and on title of 'He hears the Cry of the Sedge', p. 518]. The Crooked Plough and the Pilot Star are translations of the Gaelic names of the Plough and the Pole Star [see Yeats's note on 'He hears the Cry of the Sedge', p. 518]

the woman that he loves: probably a reference to the 'spiritual' marriage between Maud Gonne and Yeats, agreed to in 1898. Maud had told him she had 'a horror and terror of physical love'. See *MS*, 131–4, and *YANB*, 111–13

   p. 109, 'The Fiddler of Dooney'   *dc*: Nov. 1892   *fp*: *TB*, Dec. 1892   *Dooney*: Dooney Rock on the shore of Lough Gill, Co. Sligo. See Glossary   *Kilvarnet*: a townland near Ballinacarrow, Co. Sligo. See Glossary   *Mocharabuiee*: the line was originally 'My cousin of Rosnaree', subsequently altered in *WR*. Mrs W. B. Yeats added a footnote to *CP* (1950) that the word was 'pronounced as if spelt "Mockrabwee" '. See Glossary   *Sligo fair*: Sligo, the town in north-west Ireland where Yeats's maternal grandparents, the Pollexfens, lived, as well as various Yeats relatives, descendants of the Rev. John Yeats, Rector of Drumcliff, Co. Sligo. (See notes on '[Introductory Rhymes]', p. 539, and on 'Under Ben Bulben', p. 632.) Yeats spent much time there as a child and as a young man (see Appendix One, p. 667)   *Peter*: St Peter, Keeper of the Gate of Heaven   *wave of the sea*: T. R. Henn (*LT*, 305) compared this line to Shakespeare, *A Winter's Tale*, act 4, scene 5, 'When you do dance, I wish you/A wave o' the sea'

THE OLD AGE OF QUEEN MAEVE

fp: *FR*, April 1903. The first eight lines were added in *CP* (1933)   *Maeve the Great Queen*: see notes on *WO*, p. 485   *Cruachan*: Maeve's palace at Cruachan, Co. Roscommon, where the action of the Irish epic tale the *Tain Bo Cualgne* begins and ends. Yeats commented that it was pronounced 'as if spelt Crockan in modern Gaelic'   *praising her*: Maud Gonne has been pictured in the foregoing description of Maeve   *Druid*: here magical; see notes on *WO*, p. 486   *many-changing Sidhe*: see notes on 'The Hosting of the Sidhe', p. 506   *the great war . . . Bull*: In the Prelude, the 'Pillow Talk' added in the 11th century to the *Tain Bo Cualgne*, Maeve invades Ulster in order to capture the Brown Bull of Cooley, enraged that her white-horned bull had gone over to her husband's herds   *Ailell*: Maeve's husband   *Fergus*: see notes on *WO*, p. 487   *Magh Ai*: a plain in Co. Roscommon   *Great Plain*: the great plain of the Other World. Yeats described it as the Land of the Dead and the Happy, also called 'The Land of the Living Heart', and 'many beautiful names besides'   *Aengus*: the Irish god of love   *the children of the Maines*: usually thought to be the seven or eight children of Maeve and

Ailell. Her grandchildren, however, are mentioned (l.109) and may be the children of Maeve's son Maines, married to Ferbe and killed by Conchubar   *Bual's hill* . . . *Caer*: Ethal Anbual from the Sidhe of Connaught was the father of Caer   *Aengus of the birds*: four birds made from his kisses fluttered overhead   *Friend . . . many years*: Maud Gonne, whom Yeats first met in January 1889   *that great queen*: Maeve

BAILE AND AILLINN

dc: this 'half lyrical half narrative poem' was 'just finished' on 11 Aug. 1901   *fp*: *MR*, July 1902   *Ulad*: Ulster, the northern province of Ireland   *Buan's son, Baile*: Buan was an Ulster goddess, wife of Mesgedra, a King of Leinster. (See Sir Samuel Ferguson, 'Mesgedra', *Poems* (1880), 32, and Eleanor Hull, *The Cuchulain Saga in Irish Literature* (1898), 94   *Aillinn*: daughter and heir of Lugaidh, son of Curoi (Curaoi) Mac Daire, a King of Munster. In the *Tain Bo Cualgne* he refrained from attacking Cuchulain (see notes on 'To the Rose upon the Rood of Time, p. 496) after seeing that he had been badly wounded in his fight with Ferdiad at the Yellow Ford   *the long wars*: those described in the *Tain Bo Cualgne*   *Honey-Mouth* . . . *Little-Land*: he was 'sweet-spoken' and had little land. See Lady Gregory, *COM*, 305   *Emain*: Emain Macha, Armagh, capital of Ulster   *Muirthemne*: a plain in Co. Louth (named after Muirthemne, son of Breogan, a Milesian leader), the site of the main fight in the *Tain Bo Cualgne*. Cuchulain came from there   *there*: Baile and Aillinn were to be married at Rosnaree, on the River Boyne   *there*: Saul, *PYP*, 184, glosses this as Dundalk (Irish, *Dun Dealgan*)   *the Hound of Ulad*: Cuchulain, the Hound of Ulster (Irish, *Uladh*), also known as the Hound of Culann (see notes on 'To the Rose upon the Rood of Time, p. 496)   *the harper's daughter and her friend*: Deirdre, daughter of Felimid, Conchubar's storyteller, and Naoise, son of Usna, her lover   *betrayed*: see notes on *WO*, p. 487   *Deirdre and her man*: Deirdre, earlier referred to as 'the harper's daughter', and Naoise. See notes on 'The Rose of the World', p. 498   *Ogham letters*: see notes on *WO*, p. 487   *of Rury's seed*: Baile was of the race of Rudraige, a term used for Ulster heroes other than Cuchulain, who were traced back to Ir, son of Mil. See Lady Gregory, *COM*, 305   *the Great Plain*: see notes on *The Old Age of Queen Maeve*, p. 523   *Hill Seat of Laighen*: a hill fort (Irish, *Dunn Ailinne* or *Ailann*), seat of the Kings of Leinster on the Dublin–Kildare border near Kilcullen in the Knockline Mountains   *Two swans*: the lovers Baile and Aillinn changed into swans by Aengus. See notes on 'The Withering of the Boughs', p. 527   *his changed body*: the old man (cf. ll. 25, 47, 100, 113 and 134) reveals himself to be Aengus   *Edain, Midhir's wife*: for Edain (or Etain) see notes on *WO*, p. 485, 'The Harp of Aengus', p. 531, and 'The Two Kings', p. 541   *two* . . . *apple boughs*: cf. 'Ribh at the Tomb of Baile and Aillinn', p. 412   *Gorias, and Findrias and Falias, . . . Murias*:

mysterious cities of learning, whence the Tuatha de Danaan came to Ireland   *Cauldron and spear and stone and sword*: the four talismans of the Tuatha de Danaan – the spear (Lugh's), the stone (the *Lia Fail*, or Stone of Destiny, brought to Scotland by Irish invaders in the 5th century, moved to England by Edward I, and called the Stone of Scone), the cauldron (the Dagda's) and the sword (Lugh's) – were found in the four cities   *apples of the sun and moon*: see notes on 'The Man who Dreamed of Faeryland', p. 503, and on 'The Song of Wandering Aengus', p. 511   *Quiet's wild heart*: cf. similar personification in 'Maid Quiet', p. 105   *glass boat*: *EPY*, 79, suggests this may derive from Bonwick, *Irish Druids and Old Irish Religion* (1894), 293   *birds of Aengus*: see notes on *The Old Age of Queen Maeve*, p. 524   *a yew-tree . . . wild apple*: cf. 'Ribh at the Tomb of Baile and Aillinn', p. 402   *fighting at the ford*: the fight, described in the *Tain Bo Cualgne*, between Cuchulain and his friend Ferdiad   *Beloved*: Maud Gonne

IN THE SEVEN WOODS

This was the first work published by the Dun Emer Press, founded by Yeats's sister Elizabeth Corbet (Lollie) Yeats in 1903; it later became the Cuala Press. Some of the poems in this volume, Yeats remarked, he had made when

> walking about among the Seven Woods [at Coole Park, Co. Galway], before the big wind of nineteeen hundred and three blew down so many trees, & troubled the wild creatures, & changed the look of things; and I thought out there a good part of the play which follows [*On Baile's Strand*]. The first shape of it came to me in a dream, but it changed much in the making, foreshadowing, it may be, a change that may bring a less dream-burdened will into my verses. [*ISW*]

p. 129, 'In the Seven Woods'   *dc*: Aug. 1902   *fp*: *ISW*   Title: the seven woods were in Coole Park and are named in '[Introductory Lines]', p. 143; see notes on that poem, p. 531, for meanings of their Irish names   *Tara uprooted*: the Hill of Tara in Co. Meath, traditionally the seat of the ancient Irish kings (see Glossary). Douglas Hyde, George Moore and Yeats wrote to *The Times*, 27 June 1902, drawing attention to the fact that labourers were excavating the site of the ancient royal duns and houses 'apparently that the sect [the British Israelites] which believes the English to be descended from the ten tribes [of Israel] may find the Ark of the Covenant'. The excavation was stopped   *new commonness*: the coronation of Edward VII and Alexandra   *paper flowers*: street decorations in Dublin celebrating the coronation   *Quiet*: cf. 'Maid Quiet', p. 105   *Great Archer*: *PYP*, 77, glosses this as Sagittarius, a hint of some revelation to come   *Pairc-na-lee*: one of the seven woods of Coole; see note above on *Title*

p. 129, 'The Arrow'   *dc*: 1901   *fp*: *ISW*   *your beauty*: Maud

Gonne's   *this arrow*: this may have a Blakean meaning. In *The Works of William Blake* (3 vols., 1893), Yeats and Ellis commented on these lines of Blake's preface to *Milton*:

> Bring me my bow of burning gold:
> Bring me my arrows of desire:
> Bring me my spear: O Clouds unfold!
> Bring me my chariot of fire.

that the bow had a sexual symbolism, the arrow was desire, the spear male potency and the chariot joy   *apple blossom*: associated with Yeats's memories of his first meeting with Maud in January 1889. See notes on 'The Song of Wandering Aengus', p. 511

p. 130, 'The Folly of Being Comforted'   *fp*: TS, 11 Jan. 1902   *One that is ever kind*: possibly Lady Gregory   *Your well-belovèd's hair*: Maud Gonne's hair

p. 130, 'Old Memory'   *dc*: Nov. or Dec. (probably the third week) 1903   *fp*: *Wayfarer's Love*, ed. the Duchess of Sutherland (1904)   *her*: Maud Gonne   *queens . . . imagined long ago*: Yeats thought there was an element in Maud Gonne's beauty that moved minds full of old Gaelic poems and stories; she looked as if she had lived in some ancient civilisation where superiority of mind or body were part of public ceremonial, part 'in some way the crowd's creation'. He recorded the effect of her beauty backed by her great stature (she was about six feet tall); her face

> like the face of some Greek statue, showed little thought, her whole body seemed a master-work of long labouring thought as though a Scopas [architect and sculptor, *fl.* 430 BC; he made the mausoleum raised to her husband by Artemisia, one of the Seven Wonders of the ancient world] had measured and calculated, consorted with Egyptian sages and mathematicians out of Babylon that he might outface even Artemisia's sepulchral image with a living norm' [*A*, 364]

he kneaded: a reference to Yeats's work for the Irish literary movement – and his hopes of persuading Maud Gonne to abandon politics and marry him   *the long years*: he first met Maud Gonne in January 1889, when he was twenty-three   *come to naught*: Maud Gonne married Major John MacBride in Paris in February 1903; it came as a great shock to Yeats

p. 131, 'Never Give all the Heart'   *fp*: MCM, Dec. 1905   *Never give*: cf. Blake's 'Love's Secret':

> Never seek to tell thy love
> Love that never told can be;
> For the gentle wind doth more
> Silently, invisibly.

I told my love, I told my love,
I told her all my heart,
Trembling, cold, in ghastly fears
Ah! she did depart!

deaf . . . love: Yeats's hopeless passion for Maud Gonne   *and lost*: a reference to Maud Gonne's marriage; see notes on 'Old Memory', p. 526

p. 131, 'The Withering of the Boughs'   *fp*: *TS*, Aug. 1900, with the title 'Echtge of the Streams'   *Echtge*: a mountain range in Co. Galway and Co. Clare (see Glossary). Echtge was a goddess of the Tuatha de Danaan, given this area of country as her dowry   *No boughs . . . my dreams*: Yeats commented that Irish stories tell that, as fruits, vegetables, trees or plants decay on earth, they ripen among the faeries, that dreams lose their wisdom when the sap rises in the trees, and that 'our dreams can make the trees wither' (*M*, 116)   *Danaan*: see note on *WO*, p. 484   *swans . . . golden chains*: the lovers Baile and Aillinn were told separately by Aengus, the god of love, that the other was dead, for he wished them to be happy in his land among the dead. They died of broken hearts at the news, and took the shape of swans 'Linked by a gold chain each to each', the shape that 'other enchanted lovers took before them in the old stories'   *A king and a queen*: Baile and Aillinn

p. 132, 'Adam's Curse'   *dc*: probably May 1901   *fp*: *MR*, Dec. 1902   *That beautiful mild woman*: Maud Gonne's sister, Mrs Kathleen Pilcher   *And you and I*: Maud Gonne and Yeats   *talked of poetry*: see *SQ*, 328–30, for the poem's inspiration   *A line . . . a moment's thought*: Corinna Salvadori, *Yeats and Castiglione* (1965), 83–4, considers that these lines – which proclaim the need for poetry, despite the work that goes to its composition and finishing, to seem nonchalant, a spontaneous improvisation – convey the quality of *sprezzatura* praised by Castiglione in *The Courtier* (see notes on 'The People', p. 560)   *labour to be beautiful*: Maud Gonne told how:

> I saw Willie Yeats looking critically at me and he told Kathleen he liked her dress and that she was looking younger than ever. It was on that occasion Kathleen remarked that it was hard work being beautiful which Willie turned into his poem 'Adam's Curse' [*SQ*]

Yeats praised 'the discipline of the looking-glass' as heroic (*E & I*, 270); cf. 'To a Young Beauty', p. 242, and 'Michael Robartes and the Dancer', p. 281   *Adam's fall*: see Genesis 3: 1–6   *high courtesy*: Yeats thought true love a discipline requiring wisdom; see notes on 'Solomon to Sheba', p. 555

p. 133, 'Red Hanrahan's Song about Ireland'   *fp*: *NO*, 4 Aug. 1894, untitled, included in the story 'Kathleen-ny-Houlihan'. In *TSR* the title was 'Kathleen the Daughter of Hoolihan and Hanrahan the Red'; this became 'The Song of Red Hanrahan' in *ISW*; the present title was first used in *PW* I (1906). The poem was considerably altered; for these variations, see *VE*, 206–8. The poem may owe something to James Clarence Mangan, 'Kathleen-ny-Houlahan', in *Irish Minstrelsy*, ed. H. Halliday Sparling (1888), 141   *Title*: for Hanrahan see notes on 'He reproves the Curlew', p. 514   *Cummen Strand*: the southern shore of the estuary, to the north-west of Sligo, on the road to Strandhill (Irish, *Caimin*, the little common)   *left hand*: the left hand is often considered unlucky in Ireland   *Cathleen, the daughter of Houlihan*: Cathleen symbolised Ireland. Maud Gonne (who regarded this as her favourite Yeats poem; it was written to her) played the role of Cathleen in Yeats's play *Cathleen ni Houlihan* (1902), which greatly affected Dublin audiences in 1902. Cf. 'Man and the Echo', p. 469: 'Did that play of mine send out/Certain men the English shot?' Maud played the part 'very finely, and her great height made Cathleen seem a divine being fallen into our mortal infirmity' (Appendix 2 of *Cathleen ni Houlihan*). See *VPl*, 233. The play's subject was Ireland 'and its struggle for independence' (*UI*, 5 May 1902)   *Knock-narea*: mountain overlooking Sligo. See Glossary   *stones . . . Maeve*: Maeve's supposed burial place is the cairn on the top of Knocknarea. See notes on *WO*, p. 485   *Clooth-na-Bare*: Lough Ia, Co. Sligo. See notes on 'The Hosting of the Sidhe', p. 506   *Holy Rood*: the cross on which Jesus Christ was crucified

p. 134, 'The Old Men Admiring Themselves in the Water'   *dc*: before 20 Nov. 1902   *fp*: *Pall Mall Magazine*, Jan. 1903

p. 134, 'Under the Moon'   *fp*: *TS*, 15 June 1901   *Brycelinde*: the forest of Broceliande in Brittany where Merlin was bewitched by Viviane   *Avalon*: a mythical land, like the Isles of the Blessed, where the virtuous went after death. Cf. Sir Thomas Malory, *La Morte d'Arthur*, VIII, ch. 27; XII, ch. 7, 29, and see Yeats's mocking treatment of it in '[The Statesman's Holiday]', p. 444   *Joyous Isle . . . Lancelot*: this place occurs in the Agravain portion of the prose Vulgate *Lancelot* (see *PYP*, 80). Lancelot, an Arthurian knight, was the lover of Arthur's Queen Guinevere. Finding Arthur dead he sought the Queen, to discover that she had taken the veil. He then became a priest and guarded Arthur's grave. When he died he was carried to Joyous Gard   *crazed . . . hid him*: Lancelot lived in the Joyous Isle with Elayne after her friend Dame Brysen had cured him of madness; Elayne's father, King Pelles, gave them the Castle of Blyaunt to live in   *Ulad*: Ulster, the northern province of Ireland   *Naoise*: see notes on *WO*, p. 487   *Land-under-Wave*: (Irish, *Tir-fa-Thonn*) the enchanted underworld beneath the sea   *Seven old sisters*: possibly the planets but more likely the Pleiades, in Greek mythology the seven daughters of Atlas   *Land-of-the-Tower*: *PNE* suggests this may be Tory Island (Irish, *Toraigh*, a place of towers) in Co. Donegal; this argument is based on Aengus, the god of love, having a tower of glass, but see notes on 'The Harp of Aengus', p. 531   *Wood-of-Wonders . . . dawn*: in Douglas Hyde's edition of the tale of the 'Adventures of the Children of the King of Norway', *Irish Texts Society* (1899), 128–9, the hero Cod meets in the Forest of Wonders a wondrous ox with 'two gold horns on him and a horn trumpet in his mouth' which he kills. Later Cod sees 'a fair bevy of women' coming towards him, 'a high-headed sensible queen' at the head of the band and a golden bier borne by four before her. The Queen addresses him as Son of the King of Norway and tells him that they have the ox for him in the bier   *Branwen*: from Lady Charlotte Guest's translation of the *Mabinogion*, the daughter of Llyr and wife of Matholwch, King of Ireland   *Guinevere*: Arthur's queen   *Niamh*: see notes on *WO*, p. 486   *Laban*: (Irish, *Li Ban*, woman's beauty) was changed to an otter by her magic well when she neglected it. She was a sister of Fand, wife of Manannan MacLir, god of the sea. Fand was loved by Cuchulain (see notes on 'The Secret Rose, p. 518) but he returned to his mortal life after a time with her   *woodwoman*: Cod, in the 'Adventures of the Children of the King of Norway' met her before he entered the Forest of Wonders; she told him that her lover was turned into a blue-eyed hawk by the vindictive daughter of the King of Greece   *hunter's moon*: the full moon next after the harvest moon. The moon full within a fortnight of the autumn equinox (22/23 Sept.), which rises nearly at the same time for several nights at points successively further north on the eastern horizon

p. 135, 'The Ragged Wood'   *fp*: untitled in the story 'The Twisting of the Rope', *Stories of Red Hanrahan* (1904). It was entitled 'The Hollow Wood' in *CW*   *silver-proud . . . golden hood*: for the juxtaposition of silver and gold imagery, cf. 'The Man who Dreamed of Faeryland', p. 79, and 'The Song of Wandering Aengus', p. 93

p. 135, 'O Do Not Love Too Long'   *dc*: before 23 Feb. 1905   *fp*: *The Acorn*, Oct. 1905, entitled 'Do Not Love Too Long'   *so much at one*: Yeats is referring to his close friendship with Maud Gonne. Cf. 'Among School Children', p. 323: '. . . it seemed that our two natures blent/Into a sphere from youthful sympathy'   *in a minute she changed*: probably a reference to Maud Gonne's unexpected marriage to John MacBride in 1903

p. 136, 'The Players ask for a Blessing on the Psalteries and on Themselves'   *dc*: probably June 1902, *fp*: *ISW* (1903)   *Title*: the psaltery, similar to a lyre but with a trapezoidal sounding-board, originated in the Near East and was popular in Europe in the Middle Ages. Arnold Dolmetsch made one for Yeats and Florence Farr (Florence Farr Emery (1869–1917), an actress and student of the occult. A member of the Order of the Golden Dawn, she met Yeats in 1890. She gave recitals of Yeats's poetry to this instrument, which contained all the chromatic intervals within the range of the speaking voice.) See 'Speaking to the Psaltery' (*E & I*, 13–27)   *O masters*: These may be the seven archangels, for Yeats wrote to Arnold Dolmetsch on 3 June 1902 to say he was writing a 'Prayer to the Seven Archangels to bless the Seven Notes'   *kinsmen of the Three in One*: the 'masters' or archangels are related to the Christian Trinity

p. 137, 'The Happy Townland'   *fp: The Weekly Critical Review*, 4 June 1903. Entitled 'The Rider from the North' in *ISW*, its original title was restored in editions from *P* (1899–1905) onward. Yeats said that the poem symbolised striving after an impossible idea (radio talk, 1932)   *the townland*: Paradise   *golden and silver wood*: see notes on 'The Man who Dreamed of Faeryland', p. 503, and 'The Song of Wandering Aengus', p. 511   *The little fox*: Sheila O'Sullivan (*YUIT*) suggests that the fox is based on a song 'An Maidrin Rua' (Irish, the little red fox)   *the world's bane*: cf. 'bane' as used by Blake in 'Jerusalem', where God '. . . told me that all I wrote should prove/The bane of all that on earth I love'. Yeats and Ellis, *The Works of William Blake*, stressed that Blake had his own career in mind in 'The Monk' and *Milton* when he used 'bane'; they drew attention to lines Blake wrote at Felpham, sent in a letter to Mr Butts: 'Must my wife live in my sister's bane/And my sister survive on my love's pain?' See also Grace Jackson, *Mysticism in AE and Yeats in relation to Oriental and American Thought* (1932), 162   *golden and silver boughs*: see note on *golden or silver wood* above   *Michael*: the archangel   *Gabriel . . . fish-tail . . . old horn*: Yeats described him as 'the angel of the Moon' in the Cabbala and thought he might 'command the waters at a pinch'. *EPY*, 83, links Gabriel with Bertrand, *La Réligion des Gaulois*, with its figures who have human heads and fish-tails, and the 'old horn' with one of hammered silver in the National Museum of Ireland in Dublin

THE SHADOWY WATERS

dc: probably finished towards the end of 1899; Sept. 1900 appended to text (*P* (1949))   *fp*: '[Introductory Lines]' *TS*, 1 Dec. 1900; 'The Harp of Aengus', *North American Review*, May 1900; these two poems and the text of the play *P* (1899–1905). There are several versions of the text (see *VE*, 745 ff.) in *CP & CPl* (the latter an acting version used at the Abbey Theatre and published by Bullen in 1907). Yeats's note of 1922 read:

I published in 1902 a version of *The Shadowy Waters*, which, as I had no stage experience whatever, was unsuitable for stage representation, though it had some little success when played during my absence in America in 1904, with very unrealistic scenery before a very small audience of cultivated people. On my return I rewrote the play in its present form, but found it still too profuse in speech for stage representation. In 1906 I made a stage version, which was played in Dublin in that year. The present version must be considered as a poem only.

Dedication: Augusta, Lady Gregory (1852–1932), Irish playwright, translator and Director of the Abbey Theatre. See notes on 'He hears the Cry of the Sedge', p. 518. She helped Yeats to create an Irish theatre; she got him to help her in collecting folklore; she lent him money enabling him to give up journalism; and she provided him with conditions at Coole Park in which he was able to work very efficiently

p. 143, '[Introductory Lines]'   *Coole*: see 'Coole Park, 1929', p. 357, and 'Coole and Ballylee, 1931', p. 358   *Shan-walla*: Old Wall (Irish, *Sean bhalla*; PNE suggests *Sean bhealach*, Old Road)   *Kyle-dortha*: Dark Wood (Irish, *coill* (kyle), a wood; *dortha, dorracha*, dark, destroyed by fire)   *Kyle-na-no*: the Wood of the Nuts (Irish, *Coill na Gno*)   *Pairc-na-lee*: the Park or Field of the Calves (Irish, *Pairc na Laoigh*)   *Pairc-na-carraig*: the Park or Field of the Rock (Irish, *Pairc na Carraig*; PNE suggests *Pairc na gCarraig*, Field of Stones)   *Pairc-na-tarav*: Park or Field of the Bulls (Irish, *Pairc na d Tarbh*)   *Inchy wood*: Wood of the Islands or Wood of the Water Meadows (Irish, [*Coill na*] *nInsi*)   *Biddy Early*: a famous witch who lived in Co. Clare (cf. *A*, 401)   *Forgael and Dectora*: the main characters in *The Shadowy Waters*

p. 145, 'The Harp of Aengus'   *Edain*: see notes on *WO*, p. 485   *Midhir's hill*: (Irish, *Sliabh Golry*) near Ardagh, Co. Longford   *Aengus . . . tower of glass*: in the legend, Aengus, god of love, carried Edain about in a glass cage or 'sun-booth'. See notes on *WO*, p. 485   *Druid*: see note on *WO*, p. 486   *chrysolite*: a gemstone, brown or yellowish-green in colour, of magnesium iron silicate   *Midhir's wife*: his first wife, Fuamnach, a 'jealous woman', turned Edain into a purple fly which was carried by the wind to the house of Aengus (the great tumulus of Newgrange in the Boyne Valley). Fuamnach discovered where Edain was hidden and called up (by druid spells) another wind to blow her out of the house. Aengus killed Fuamnach. Edain, however, was blown through Ireland for seven years. Then Etar drank her down in a glass of wine and bore her as a reincarnated Edain. Yeats first read the stories in 'poor translations' but then in Lady Gregory's *COM* and *GFM*, which he greatly admired

p. 147, 'The Shadowy Waters'   *Red Moll*: an invented character   *A beautiful young man and girl*: Aengus and Edain. See notes on 'The Harp of Aengus' above   *the Ever-living*: the Irish gods and goddesses   *tower of glass*: see notes on 'The Harp of Aengus' above   *man-headed birds*: spirits of the dead   *Seaghan the fool*: invented character   *Druids*: see note on *WO*, p. 486   *hurley*: an Irish ball game of some antiquity, played with wooden hurley sticks (or hurleys)   *chryso-prase, Or chrysoberyl, or beryl, or chrysolite*: all gemstones, respectively an apple-green variety of chalcedony; a greenish-yellow mineral of beryllium aluminate in orthorhombic crystalline form (used in the form of cat's eye and alexandrite); a green, blue, yellow or white mineral of beryllium aluminium silicate (emerald and aquamarine are transparent varieties of it); a brown or yellowish green olivine of magnesium iron silicate   *opoponax*: a firm resin formerly used in medicine and in perfumery   *to wake*: to hold a vigil over a dead body   *keen*: see notes on 'The Ballad of Father O'Hart', p. 494   *Iollan*: either Iollan, son of Fergus Mac Roy (see notes on *WO*, p. 484), or, more likely, Finn's uncle, Iollan Eachtach, a chief of the Fianna (see notes on *WO*, p. 487) who left Uchtdealb of the Sidhe for Finn's aunt Tuireann, whom Uchtdealb then turned into a hound (see notes on *WO*, p. 484). When Iollan promised to return to her she turned Tuireann back into a human being   *Shape-changers*: here identified with the Ever-laughing Ones, the Immortal Mockers. Frequent changes of shape occur in Gaelic mythology; see D. E. S. Maxwell, 'The Shape-Changers', *Yeats, Sligo and Ireland* (ed. Jeffares, 1976), 153–69   *ancient worm*: probably change and decay. In *CK* Yeats mentions 'the old worm of the world', but there may be a hint of the materialism of the devil since the 'Dragon' could refer to Satan, the Old Serpent

FROM 'THE GREEN HELMET AND OTHER POEMS'

An edition was published by the Cuala Press in 1910; the 1912 edition, published by Macmillan, contained six additional poems.

p. 183, 'His Dream'   *dc*: 3 July [?1908]   *fp*: N, 11 July 1908 with the title 'A Dream'. This poem, like those that follow it up to and including 'Against Unworthy Praise', p. 187, were originally grouped under the general title 'Raymond Lully and his wife Pernella' in *TGH* (1910 and 1911 (a New York edition)). Lully (*c.* 1232–1315) was a Spanish theologian and philosopher. An erratum slip in *TGH* (1910) points out that Yeats put Raymond Lully's name by a slip of the pen 'in the room of the later alchemist Nicolas Flamel'. A note after the title of the poem in the first printing reads:

a few days ago I dreamed that I was steering a very gay and elaborate ship upon some narrow water with many people upon its banks, and that there was a figure upon a bed in the middle of the ship. The people were pointing to the figure and questioning, and in my dream I sang verses which faded as I awoke, all but this fragmentary thought, 'we call it, it has such dignity of limb, by the sweet name of Death'. I have made my poem out of my dream and the sentiment of my dream, and can almost say, as Blake did, 'The Authors are in Eternity' [Blake, letter, 6 July 1803, to Thomas Butts about *Milton*; cf. *The Works of William Blake*, ed. Ellis and Yeats (1893), I, vii]

p. 184, 'A Woman Homer Sung'   dc: between 5 and 15 April 1910   fp: TGH (1910) with the title 'Raymond Lully and his wife Pernella/A Woman Homer Sung'; see notes on 'His Dream', p. 532   her: Maud Gonne   being grey: Yeats was nearly forty-five when he wrote the poem   shadowed in a glass: Maud Gonne seemed to Yeats to hate her own beauty's image in the mirror (A, 365)   what thing her body was: this may reflect St Augustine's Confessions, 10:5, and I Corinthians 13:12: 'we see now through a glass darkly but then face to face. Now I know in part but then I shall know even as I am then'   A woman Homer sung: see notes on 'The Rose of the World', p. 498. Maud is associated with Helen of Troy in several poems

p. 184, 'Words'   dc: 22 Jan. [1909], with revised verses added on 23 Jan.   fp: TGH (1910) with the title 'Raymond Lully and his wife Pernella/The Consolation'; see notes on 'His Dream', p. 532   The prose version of the poem in Yeats's diary reads:

> Today the thought came to me that P.I.A.L. [Maud Gonne's motto in the Order of the Golden Dawn, Per Ignem ad Lucem, Through Fire to Light] never really understands my plans, or nature or ideas. Then came the thought – what matter? How much of the best I have done and still do is but the attempt to explain myself to her? If she understood I should lack a reason for writing and one can never have too many reasons for doing what is so laborious

cannot understand: Maud Gonne thought Yeats's art was not sufficiently propagandist: by introducing him to Arthur Griffith of the Sinn Fein political movement she hoped – after she and Yeats had left the IRB (the Irish Republican Brotherhood, a secret revolutionary organisation) – that the literary movement would take a more nationalist political line

p. 185, 'No Second Troy'   dc: Dec. 1908   fp: TGH (1910) with the title 'Raymond Lully to his wife Pernella/No Second Troy'; see notes on 'His Dream', p. 532   her: Maud Gonne   With misery: by not agreeing to marry him and marrying John MacBride   of late: after Maud Gonne's marriage broke up she withdrew from public life until about 1918   most violent ways . . . little streets: Maud Gonne became increasingly involved in anti-British activities. In 1898 Yeats dissuaded her from a plan to incite tenants in Mayo to violence. She had linked the IRB (Irish Republican Brotherhood) with French military intelligence; she offered a Boer agent in Brussels a plan to plant bombs in British troopships bound for South Africa. Yeats may here have been thinking of the street riots in Dublin in 1897   courage equal to desire: see Conor Cruise O'Brien, 'Passion and Cunning: an Essay on the Politics of W. B. Yeats', IER, 223, who draws attention to Yeats's portrayal of his political associates of the 1890s as men who 'had risen above the traditions of the countryman, without learning those of cultivated life, or even educating themselves and who because of their poverty, their ignorance, their superstitious piety, are much subject to all kinds of fear'   *tightened bow*: sexual symbolism in Blake. See note on 'The Arrow', p. 525   *not natural in an age like this*: Maud Gonne looked as if she 'lived in an ancient civilisation'. See notes on 'Old Memory', p. 526. Elsewhere he described her as a classical impersonation of the spring; Virgil's phrase, 'she walks like a goddess', seemed 'made for her alone' (*A*, 123)   *high and solitary and most stern*: see notes on 'Old Memory', p. 526   *Troy for her to burn*: again she is compared to Helen of Troy (see notes on 'The Rose of the World', p. 498). There may be an echo here of Dryden's 'Alexander's Feast': 'And like another *Helen*, fired another Troy'

p. 185, 'Reconciliation'   *dc*: included in the portion of Yeats's diary which can be dated 26–7 Feb. 1909. He 'made the following poem about six months ago and write it here that it may not be lost'. Ellmann dated it Sept. 1908 (*IY*, 288)   *fp*: TGH (1910) with the title 'Raymond Lully and his wife Pernella/Reconciliation'; see notes on 'His Dream', p. 532   *you took*: Maud Gonne   *on the day . . . you went from me*: on 21 Feb. 1903 Yeats heard the unexpected news of Maud Gonne's marriage to John MacBride   *a song . . . kings, Helmets, and swords*: probably a reference to Yeats's heroic plays *The King's Threshold* and *On Baile's Strand*   *pit*: grave (not theatre pit)   *barren thoughts*: another version of the poem written in the diary between Aug. 1910 and Nov. 1911 contained these lines:

> But every powerful life goes on its way
> Too blinded by the sight of the mind's eye
> Too deafened by the cries of the heart
> Not to have staggering feet and hands

p. 186, 'King and No King'   *dc*: 7 Dec. 1909   *fp*: TGH (1910) with the title 'Raymond Lully and his wife Pernella/King and No King'; see notes on 'His Dream', p. 532   *but merely voice*: the poem is based upon the Beaumont and Fletcher play *A King and No King* (staged 1611; published 1619), in which King Arbaces falls in love with his supposed sister; he could destroy the words 'brother and sister' were they anything but words: 'Let 'em be anything but merely voice'   *Old Romance being kind*: Arbaces turns out to be an adopted child, hence 'No King'; finally he is able to marry Panthea and become king   *that pledge . . . In momentary anger*: possibly some vow Maud Gonne took not to marry in view of her relationship with a Frenchman, Lucien Millevoye, a married journalist and Boulangist, by whom she had two children (Georges, *d*. 1891, and Iseult, *b*. 1895). When Yeats first proposed to her in 1891 she told him there were reasons she could never marry. For her 'spiritual' marriage with Yeats in 1898 and its later renewal, see *MGLE*, 157–8, 164–7, 258–63   *your faith*:

Maud Gonne was formally received into the Roman Catholic Church in Feb. 1903 before her marriage to John MacBride

p. 186, 'Peace'   *dc*: May 1910   *fp*: *TGH* (1910) with the title 'Raymond Lully and his wife Pernella/Peace'; see notes on 'His Dream', p. 532   *Homer's age*: see notes on 'The Rose of the World', p. 498   *a hero's wage*: the Trojan hero Paris ran away with Helen, wife of the king of Sparta, Menelaus. Maud married Major John MacBride who had fought for the Boers in the South African war   *sternness . . . strength*: Yeats was troubled by apparent contradictions and complexities in Maud Gonne's character. Cf. 'The labyrinth of her days' in 'Against Unworthy Praise', p. 187, and her 'great labyrinth' in 'The Tower', II, p. 302

p. 187, 'Against Unworthy Praise'   *dc*: 11 May 1910   *fp*: *TGH* (1910) with the title 'Raymond Lully and his wife Pernella/Against Unworthy Praise'; see notes on 'His Dream', p. 532   *Nor knave nor dolt*: possibly a reflection upon theatre audiences in Dublin, who did not seem to appreciate the great art being offered them   *for a woman's sake*: an undated entry in Yeats's diary: 'How much of the best that I have done and still is but the attempt to explain myself to her'   *labyrinth*: see notes on 'Peace' above   *slander, ingratitude*: on 20 Oct. 1906 Maud Gonne, escorted by Yeats, went to a performance at the Abbey and was hissed by the audience, expressing disapproval of her official separation from her husband. She had sought a divorce because of his drunkenness and his assaulting her half-sister, but a French court ruled this out because MacBride was resident in Ireland, granting a separation instead

p. 188, 'The Fascination of What's Difficult'   *dc*: probably between Sept. 1909 and March 1910   *fp*: *TGH* (1910) under the general title of 'Momentary Thoughts/The Fascination of What's Difficult'   *The fascination*: the prose draft of the poem in Yeats's diary reads:

> Subject: To complain at the fascination of what's difficult. It spoils spontaneity and pleasure, and wastes time. Repeat the line ending difficult three times and rhyme on bolt, exalt, coalt [*sic*], jolt. One could use the thought that the winged and unbroken coalt must drag a cart of stones out of pride because it is difficult, and end by denouncing drama, accounts, public contests and all that's merely difficult

our colt: Pegasus, the winged horse of Greek mythology, sprang from the blood of Medusa the Gorgon and flew to heaven. The Latin poet Ovid (43 BC–AD 17) related a legend in which Pegasus lived on Mount Helicon, sacred to the Muses; by striking it with his hoof he created the fountain of Hippocrene, after which the Muses made him their favourite   *Olympus*: Greece's highest mountain; the home of the gods   *road metal*: here there may be an echo of T. Sturge Moore's *Art and Life* (1910), 76:

Swift as a rule used his Pegasus for a cart-horse, since it was strong, and he sorely
importuned by the press of men and notions in need of condign punishment; but
even when plodding in the ruts, its motion betrays the mettle in which it here
revels

Heinrich Heine, *Atta Troll* III (1876), 9, also used the image. Pegasus,
prancing in the land of fable, is '. . . no useful, safely virtuous/Cart-horse
of your citizen.'

p. 188, 'A Drinking Song'   dc: 17 Feb. 1910   fp: *TGH* (1910)
under the general title 'Momentary Thoughts/A Drinking Song'   The
poem was written for *Mirandolina*, Lady Gregory's adaptation of *La
Locandiera* by Carlo Goldoni (1707–93), the prolific Venetian writer of
comedies   *I lift . . . I sigh*: the speaker is Mirandolina, an innkeeper; she
is flirting with a captain who is a misogynist

p. 188, 'The Coming of Wisdom with Time'   dc: 21/22 Mar.
1909   fp: *MCM*, Dec. 1910, with the title 'Youth and Age'. In *TGH*
(1910) it was entitled 'Momentary Thoughts/The Coming of Wisdom
with Time'

p. 189, 'On hearing that the Students of our New University have
joined the Agitation against Immoral Literature'   dc: 3 April
1912   fp: *TGH* (1912) with the title 'On hearing that the Students of our
New University having joined the Ancient Order of Hibernians are taking
part in the Agitation against Immoral Literature'   *Title*: the New
University was originally named the Royal University of Ireland. It was
founded on a federal basis (1908) and became the National University of
Ireland, composed of colleges in Dublin, Cork, Galway and Maynooth. It
is 'new' compared to the University of Dublin (Trinity College, Dublin)
founded in 1591 by Queen Elizabeth I

p. 189, 'To a Poet, who would have me Praise certain Bad Poets,
Imitators of His and Mine'   dc: between 23 and 26 April 1909   fp:
TGH (1910) with the title 'Momentary Thoughts/To a Poet . . . and of
Mine'   *You*: Yeats's friend George Russell ('A.E.', 1867–1935), who
had a literary circle in Dublin. Yeats thought he overpraised his disciples,
who were still writing in the mode of the Celtic Twilight

p. 189, 'The Mask'   dc: between 8 Aug. 1910 and May 1911   fp:
TGH (1910) with the title 'Momentary Thoughts/A Lyric from an
Unpublished Play'. It comes from *The Player Queen* (1922) in which the
parts are clearly allocated to man and woman, the man speaking ll. 1–2,
6–7, 11–12   *that mask*: 'an emotional antithesis' to all that comes out of
the internal nature of subjective men (*A*, 189)

p. 190, 'Upon a House shaken by the Land Agitation'   *dc*: 7 Aug.
1909   *fp*: *MCM*, Dec. 1910, with the title 'To a Certain Country House
in Time of Change'. This became in *TGH* (1910) 'Momentary Thoughts/
Upon a Threatened House'. The prose draft read:

> Subject for a poem. A Shaken House. How should the world gain if this house
> failed, even though a hundred little houses were the better for it, for here power
> has gone forth, or lingered giving energy, precision; it gives to a far people
> beneficent rule; and still under its roof loving intellect is sweetened by old
> memories of its descents from far off; how should the world be better if the wren's
> nest flourish and the eagle's house is scattered

this house: Lady Gregory's house, Coole Park, near Gort, Co. Galway.
Yeats wrote the poem on hearing that the courts had reduced the rents to be
paid by tenants, and explained in his diary:

> One feels that when all must make their living they will live not for life's sake but
> the work's and all be the poorer. My work is very near to life itself and my father's
> very near to life itself but I am always feeling a lack of life's own values behind my
> thought. They should have been there before the stream began, before it became
> necessary to let the work create its values. This house has enriched my soul out of
> measure because here life moves within restraint through gracious forms. Here
> there has been no compelled labour, no poverty-thwarted impulse.

the lidless eye: a reference to a belief that only an eagle can stare into the sun
without blinking. Cf. Blake's line in 'King Edward the Third': 'The Eagle,
that doth gaze upon the sun' and his query '[Ask] the winged eagle why he
loves the sun?' Yeats uses the eagle as a symbol for an active, objective
person   *eagle thoughts*: it is possible Yeats had in mind Blake's eagle
imagery in 'An Imitation of Spenser' and in 'Visions of the Daughters of
Albion'   *Mean roof-trees*: the cottages, whose inhabitants rented land
from the Coole estate   *The gifts that govern men*: Lady Gregory's
husband, Sir William Gregory, had been Governor of Ceylon; the first
Gregory to own Coole (in 1768) had been a Director of the East India
Company   *a written speech*: Lady Gregory's books of Irish legend, *Gods
and Fighting Men* and *Cuchulain of Muirthemne*, and her plays for the Abbey
Theatre

p. 190, 'At the Abbey Theatre'   *dc*: May 1911   *fp*: *TGH*
(1912)   *Title*: the Abbey Theatre was established in Dublin in 1904.
Subtitle: the poem sticks closely to Ronsard's sonnet:

> Tyard, on me blasmoit, à mon commencement,
> Dequoy j'estois obscur au simple populaire,
> Mais on dit aujourd'huy que je suis au contraire,
> Et que je me démens, parlant trop bassement.
>   Toy de qui le labeur enfante doctement
> Des livres immortels, dy-moy, que doy-je faire?

Dy-moi, car tu sçais tout, comme doy-je complaire
A ce monstre testu, divers en jugement?
Quand je tonne en mes vers, il a peur de me lire;
Quand ma voix se desenfle, il ne fait qu'en mesdire.
Dy-moy de quel lien, force, tenaille, ou clous
   Tiendray-je ce Proté qui se change à tous coups?
Tyard, je t'enten bien, il le faut laisser dire,
Et nous rire du luy, comme il se rit de nous.
                    [*Œuvres complètes* (1950), I, 116]

Craoibhin Aoibhin: the pen-name (Irish, the Little Pleasant Branch) of Dr Douglas Hyde (1860–1949), poet, folklorist, translator, creator of the Gaelic League, first President of Eire   *high and airy . . . they'll leave*: the heroic verse plays staged in the Abbey Theatre did not attract large audiences; realistic plays about Ireland were more popular   *common things*: realistic plays and 'cottage comedies'   *dandled them . . . to the bone*: the Gaelic League under Hyde's chairmanship was very successful. Lady Gregory commented that through the Gaelic League:

> country people were gathered together in the Irish speaking places to give the songs and poems, old and new, kept in their memory. This discovery, this disclosure of folk learning, the folk poetry, the ancient tradition, was the small beginning of a weighty change. It was an upsetting of the table of values, an astonishing excitement. The imagination of Ireland had found a new homing place. . . . [*The Kiltartan Books* (1972), 19]

Proteus: the old man of the sea in Greek legend, in charge of the flocks of Poseidon, god of the sea

p. 191, 'These are the Clouds'   *dc*: May 1910   *fp*: TGH (1910) with the title 'Momentary Thoughts/These are the Clouds'   *weak lay hand*: cf. 'Upon a House shaken by the Land Agitation', p. 190   *lifted high*: originally 'builded'; the poem was originally intended to refer to Coole Park   *friend*: Lady Gregory. The poem praises her achievement, her 'great race', and 'greatness', her companion   *for children*: she held the Coole estate in trust for her son Robert, living frugally to clear off debts and charges on the estate. After Robert was killed in Jan. 1918 (see 'In Memory of Major Robert Gregory', p. 234), she continued to run the estate, hoping to hand it on in a good state to her grandson Richard (*b.* 6 Jan. 1909)

p. 191, 'At Galway Races'   *dc*: either summer 1908 (*WBY*, 225) or 21 Oct. 1908 (*IY*, 288)   *fp*: *ER*, Feb. 1909, with the title 'Galway Races', altered to 'Momentary Thoughts/At Galway Races', *TGH* (1910)   *the course*: at Galway in the west of Ireland, where horse races are held annually   *We, too*: poets. In his diary Yeats compared poets to the aristocracy of birth   *horsemen*: elsewhere, simple, violent, passionate men; here presumably aristocratic patrons of poets in an imagined pre-middle-class world which may return when 'the whole earth' changes its tune (l. 12). Cf. 'The Gyres', p. 411   *hearteners*: an appreciation of the support of aristocratic patronage of poets

p. 192, 'A Friend's Illness'   *dc*: Feb. 1909   *fp*: *TGH* (1910) with the title 'Momentary Thoughts/A Friend's Illness'   *Sickness*: Lady Gregory was seriously ill in late Jan. 1909, probably from a cerebral haemorrhage. Yeats realised when he first heard of her illness (4 Feb. 1909) that she had been to him 'mother, friend, sister and brother'. More than kin was at stake; the thought of losing her was 'like a conflagration in the rafters' (*MS*, 160–1)

p. 192, 'All Things can Tempt me'   *dc*: summer 1908   *fp*: *ER*, Feb. 1909. In *TGH* (1910) the title was 'Momentary Thoughts/All Things can Tempt me'   *All things*: Yeats wrote little poetry while manager of the Abbey Theatre (1904–10)   *woman's face*: Maud Gonne's

p. 193, 'Brown Penny'   *fp*: *TGH* (1910) with the title 'Momentary Thoughts/The Young Man's Song'

RESPONSIBILITIES

Some of the poems in this volume appeared in *TGH* (1912), *PWD* (1913) and *RPP* (1914). The last included 'The Two Kings' and the play *The Hour-Glass*. *RPP* (1916) omitted the play but added 'The Well and the Tree' (from the play *At the Hawk's Well*)   *First epigraph*: not yet identified   *Second epigraph*: from Confucius (*c*. 557–*c*. 479 BC), *Analects* VII, v. Legge's translation reads 'Extreme is my decay. For a long time I have not dreamed as I was wont to, that I saw the Duke of Chau.' (Chau-Kung (*d*. 1105 BC), Chinese author and statesman)

p. 197, '[Introductory Rhymes]'   *dc* 1912–14 in *R* (1916); Jan. 1914 in *P* (1949). Ellmann (*IY*, 288) suggests Dec. 1913   *fp*: *RPP*   *old fathers*: Yeats's ancestors. The poem was provoked by George Moore's mocking remarks in portions of *Vale* (published in *ER*, 1914) on Yeats's 'own class: millers and shipowners on one side and on the other a portrait-painter of distinction'. At the time Yeats had become interested in his family's history   *Old Dublin merchant*: probably Benjamin Yeats (1750–95), Yeats's great-great-grandfather, a wholesale linen merchant (the first of the Yeats family to live in Ireland was Jervis Yeats (*d*. 1712), a linen merchant of Yorkshire stock)   *ten and four*: Yeats's note of 1914 reads:

'Free of the ten and four' is an error I cannot now correct without more rewriting than I have a mind for. Some merchant in Villon, I forget the reference, was 'free of the ten and four' [Francois Villon (1531–?) wrote, in 'Epistre a ses amis', 'nobles hommes, francs de quart et de dix' (Noblemen free of the quarter and the tenth), a reference to different taxes]. Irish merchants exempted from certain duties by the Irish Parliament were, unless memory deceives me again, for I am writing away from books, 'free of the eight and six'.

Irish merchants originally were not required to pay import duties until their merchandise was sold to retailers; under a new system in the 18th century merchants who had been wholesalers under the earlier system had allowances of 10 per cent on all wine and tobacco and 6 per cent on all other goods. Benjamin Yeats was listed in a Dublin directory as 'free of the six and ten per cent tax at Custom-house, Dublin' from 1783 to 1794   *country scholar . . . Emmet's friend*: Yeats's great-grandfather, the Rev. John Yeats (1774–1846), Rector of Drumcliff, Co. Sligo (1805–46), was a friend of Robert Emmet (1778–1803), who led a rebellion in 1803. It failed and he was hanged. John Yeats, suspected of supporting it, was imprisoned for a few hours   *to the poor*: he was known for his charity   *Merchant and scholar*: Benjamin and the Rev. John Yeats   *huckster's loin*: Yeats is drawing a difference between his ancestors – 'merchants' – and the new middle-class of Ireland – 'huckster', a contemptuous word   *Soldiers . . . A Butler or an Armstrong*: in 1773 Benjamin Yeats married Mary Butler (1751–1834), a member of the great Ormonde family, which came to Ireland in the 12th century. The Yeatses set great store by his connection, frequently using Butler as a Christian name. Grace Armstrong (1774–1864) married William Corbet (1757–1824); their daughter Jane Grace Corbet (1811–76) married the Rev. William Butler Yeats (1806–62), the poet's grandfather. Both Butler and Armstrong families had strong military traditions   *Boyne*: on 12 July 1690, in the Battle of the Boyne (a river flowing into the sea at Drogheda, about 40 miles north of Dublin), James II (1633–1701) was defeated by William of Orange, William III (1650–1702)   *Old merchant skipper*: William Middleton (1770–1832), Yeats's maternal great-grandfather, sea captain and smuggler, who had a depot in the Channel Islands, traded to South America and developed cargo traffic between Sligo and the Iberian peninsula   *silent and fierce old man*: William Pollexfen (1811–92), the poet's maternal grandfather, a sea captain and merchant, who married Elizabeth Middleton, daughter of his cousin Elizabeth (born a Pollexfen, she had married William Middleton). Yeats gives an account of his Pollexfen grandfather in *A*, 6 ff.   *wasteful virtues*: possibly an implicit contrast between the Middleton relatives in Sligo and the Pollexfens; the former 'had not the pride and reserve, the sense of decorum and order, the instinctive playing before themselves that belongs to those who strike the popular imagination' (*A*, 17)   *barren passion's sake*: Yeats's unrequited love for Maud Gonne   *forty-nine*: Yeats was born on 13 June 1865; the poem was first published on 25 May 1914

p. 199, 'The Grey Rock'   *dc*: before 1913   *fp*: *P*(Ch), April 1913; *TBR*, April 1913   *Title*: the Grey Rock (see Glossary) is near Killaloe, Co. Clare, the home of Aoibhell in Irish fairy legend. She offered Dubhlaing O'Hartagan 200 years with her on condition he did not join his friend Murchad (Murrough) son of King Brian Boru, in the Battle of Clontarf, north of Dublin, where the Danes were defeated in 1014. O'Hartagan refused her offer and was killed in the battle. Yeats may have drawn on Nicholas O'Kearney's 'The Festivities at the House of Conan', *Transactions of the Ossianic Society* (1856), II, 98–102, though it is included in Lady Gregory's *GFM*, which he read and praised   *Poets . . . Cheshire Cheese*: a group of poets calling themselves the Rhymers' Club (organised by Yeats and Ernest Rhys) used to meet in the Cheshire Cheese, a chop house in Fleet Street, London   *Goban*: Gobniu, the Celtic god, a smith and mason, famous for his ale, which conferred immortality on those who drank it   *Slievenamon*: mountain in Co. Tipperary (see Glossary), where the Bodb Derg, a king of the Tuatha de Danaan, had his palace   *one . . . like woman made*: see note below on *Aoife*   *a dead man*: O'Hartagan   *a woman*: Maud Gonne   *lout*: a word used in 'Easter 1916', p. 287, to describe John MacBride, Maud Gonne's husband   *wine or women*: possibly references to Lionel Johnson (1867–1902) and Ernest Dowson (1867–1900), described by Yeats as 'the one a drunkard, the other a drunkard and mad about women' (*M*, 331), who are mentioned in l. 62, see *NC*, 122   *The Danish troop . . . King of Ireland's dead*: Brian Boru and his son Murchad died in the battle which destroyed the power of the Norsemen, who had begun to invade the British Isles from about AD 800 onwards, virtually controlling Ireland by 977   *an unseen man*: O'Hartagan   *a young man*: O'Hartagan   *Aoife*: a Scottish warrior queen, mother of Cuchulain's son; but the Aoife of this poem is a woman of the Sidhe (see Glossary), probably Aoibhell of Craig Liath, the fairy mistress, elsewhere described by Yeats as a 'malignant phantom'   *that rock-born, rock-wandering foot*: Maud Gonne is being compared to this fairy   *loud host*: possibly a reference to Yeats's unpopularity with Irish nationalists because of, *inter alia*, his accepting a British Civil List pension of £150 a year in 1910 (he was sneeringly dubbed 'Pensioner Yeats') and his stance in the controversies over *The Playboy of the Western World* and Lane's pictures

p. 202, 'The Two Kings'   *dc*: Oct. 1912   *fp*: *P*(Ch), Oct. 1913, and *BR*, Oct. 1913   Likely basic sources are *The Yellow Book of Lecan*, *The Book of the Dun Cow* and *The Voyage of Bran*. D. M. Hoare translated the saga in *The Works of Morris and Yeats in Relation to Early Saga Literature* (1937), 124–7 and 151 ff.   *Eochaid . . . Tara*: Eochaid the Ploughman (Irish, *Eochaid Airem*) was High King of Ireland. Yeats remarked in a note of 1913 that 'Eochaid is pronounced "Yohee" '. The seat of the High Kings was Tara, Co. Meath   *his queen*: Edain. In the original tale she married

Eochaid when re-born; but Midhir (Midir), by winning a board-game (of chess) in play with Eochaid, wins the right to kiss her. He and she then fly out of the smoke-hole of the king's house and return to the fairy mounds, which Eochaid digs up to get her back. He is tricked into accepting her (identical) daughter as his wife, but Edain remains with Midhir. See notes on *WO*, p. 485, and 'The Harp of Aengus', p. 531   *African Mountains of the Moon*: the Ruwenzori, in Ruanda   *Ardan*: he is called Ailill Anguba in the original tale, to be found in *The Yellow Book of Lecan* and *The Book of the Dun Cow*. Yeats may have read it in R. I. Best's translation of H. Arbois de Jubainville, *The Irish Mythological Cycle and Celtic Mythology* (1903)   *Ogham*: see notes on *WO*, p. 487   *Loughlan waters*: Norse waters   *man . . . unnatural majesty*: Midhir, King of the Sidhe   *your husband . . . being betrayed*: see notes on 'The Harp of Aengus', p. 531, and on *his queen* above   *Thrust him away*: in the original tale she returns to Midhir and the Land of Faery

p. 208, 'To a Wealthy Man who promised a Second Subscription to the Dublin Municipal Gallery if it were proved the People wanted Pictures'   *dc*: Dec. 1912 (appended to text *P* (1949)). Yeats gave 8 Jan. 1913 in the first printing; Ellmann (*IY*, 288) dated it 24 Dec. 1912   *fp*: *IT*, 11 Jan. 1913, with the title 'The gift/To a friend who promises a bigger subscription than his first to the Dublin Municipal Gallery if the amount collected proves that there is a considerable "popular demand" for the pictures'   Yeats wrote this general note, dated 1922, to the poems beginning with 'To a Wealthy Man . . .' and ending with 'To a Shade', p. 212:

> In the thirty years or so during which I have been reading Irish newspapers, three public controversies have stirred my imagination. The first was the Parnell controversy. There were reasons to justify a man's joining either party, but there were none to justify, on one side or on the other, lying accusations forgetful of past service, a frenzy of detraction. And another was the dispute over *The Playboy [of the Western World]*. There may have been reasons for opposing as for supporting that violent, laughing thing, though I can see the one side only, but there cannot have been any for the lies, for the unscrupulous rhetoric spread against it in Ireland, and from Ireland to America. The third prepared for the Corporation's refusal of a building for Sir Hugh Lane's famous collection of pictures. . . .

Title: Sir Hugh Lane (1874–1915), Lady Gregory's nephew, offered his collection of French paintings to Dublin provided they would be properly housed. He himself liked a design by Sir Edward Lutyens for a bridge-gallery over the River Liffey. Disgusted by Dublin Corporation's reaction to his proposed gift, he placed the pictures in the National Gallery, London, leaving them to London in his will; but he added a pencilled codicil (which was not properly witnessed) to this will leaving them to Dublin. He died when the *Lusitania* was torpedoed by a German submarine. The pictures were retained in the Tate Gallery in London until

1959, when a compromise agreement was reached by the British and Irish governments through which the pictures are shared between London and Dublin. For Yeats's notes, see *NC*, 105–7   *You*: Lord Ardilaun   *Paudeen's . . . Biddy's*: Paudeen, a diminutive for Patrick; Biddy, for Bridget; the names are used contemptuously for common people   *blind and ignorant*: in the controversy over the proposed gallery Yeats particularly disliked philistine attacks on Lane in *II*. This poem was itself, as Yeats wrote to Lane, part of the controversy, being published in *IT*, to counter political (anti-Home Rule) objections to supporting the gallery and still more to meet the 'argument of people like Ardilaun that they should not give unless there is a public demand'   *Duke Ercole*: Ercole de l'Este (1431–1505), Duke of Ferrara, a generous, discriminating patron of the arts   *his Plautus*: the Duke had five plays by Plautus (*c.* 254–184 BC), the Latin comic dramatist, performed at his son Alphonso's wedding in 1502   *Guidobaldo*: Guidobaldo di Montefeltro (1472–1508), Duke of Urbino   *That grammar school*: the Duke's court was cultivated, elegant and refined. Yeats read about it in the Italian humanist Baldassare Castiglione's (1478–1529) *Il Cortegiano* [*The Courtier*] (1528) in the translations by Sir Thomas Hoby (1561) and L. E. Opdycke (1902). In 1907 he also visited Urbino, finely situated on the slopes of the Apennines   *Cosimo*: Cosimo de Medici (1389–1464), member of the Florentine family who began its glorious epoch, encouraging art, literature and providing splendid buildings at Florence; he was exiled for a year in Venice (1433–4)   *Michelozzo*: Michelozzo de Bartolommeo Michelozzi (1396–1472), Italian sculptor and court architect to Cosimo de Medici, responsible for the San Marco Library in Florence   *Greece*: presumably because of the influence of classical Greek culture upon the Italian Renaissance   *the sun's eye*: cf. notes on 'Upon a House Shaken by the Land Agitation', p. 537

p. 210, 'September 1913'   *dc*: 7 Sept. 1913   *fp*: *IT*, 8 Sept. 1913, with the title 'Romance in Ireland (On reading much of the correspondence against the Art Gallery)'. In *Nine Poems* (1914) the title became 'Romantic Ireland (September 1913)'. The present title was first used in *RPP*   *you*: the people of Ireland   *greasy till*: an image reflecting Yeats's dislike of contemporary Ireland's materialism; 'a little greasy huxtering nation', if 'the present intellectual movement failed'   *O'Leary*: John O'Leary (1830–1907), influenced by the Young Ireland movement, became identified with the Fenian movement which succeeded it. Arrested in 1865, he was condemned to twenty years' penal servitude but released after four years on condition that he kept out of Ireland for fifteen years. He lived in Paris, returning to Dublin in 1885; he lent Yeats books by Irish authors and translations of Irish literature, influencing his moving from his father's Home Rule views to more nationalist attitudes. Yeats saw him as belonging to the traditions of an older Irish nationalism, that of Henry

Grattan (1746–1820), based on the reading of Homer and Virgil, and that of Thomas Davis (1814–45), influenced by the idealism of the Italian idealist and patriot Giuseppe Mazzini (1805–72)   *the wild geese*: Irishmen who served in the armies of France (which had an Irish Brigade up to the Revolution), Spain and Austria, being excluded from holding commissions in the British Army as a result of the Penal Laws passed after 1691   *Edward Fitzgerald*: Lord Edward Fitzgerald (1763–98), a romantic figure who served in America, became an Irish MP, then joined the United Irishmen in 1796, was president of its military committee and died of wounds received when he resisted arrest   *Emmet*: see notes on '[Introductory Rhymes]', p. 539   *Tone*: Theobald Wolfe Tone (1763–98), called to the Irish Bar in 1789, founded the United Irish Club. He and his friends turned to France for help. He was appointed adjutant-general in the French army and sailed with the French fleet in a fruitless expedition to Ireland in 1796; in 1798 he was captured when a small French fleet was defeated at Lough Swilly. Sentenced by a court martial in Dublin to be hanged, he committed suicide in prison   *delirium*: Yeats contrasts the 'delirium' of his past heroes with the uncultured excitement of his own time, probably using the word as a counter to Swinburne's use of it, attacking Yeats indirectly in *William Blake* (1906). See *NC*, 111   *You'd cry*: the modern middle-classes of Ireland cannot understand the love these past heroes had for their country   *Some woman's . . . hair*: 'We Irish', Yeats thought, 'had never served any abstract cause except that of Ireland', and that 'we personified by a woman'. The woman was Cathleen ni Houlihan

p. 211, 'To a Friend whose Work has come to Nothing'   *dc*: 16 Sept. [1913]   *fp*: *PWD*   *Title*: the friend was Lady Gregory, who had supported her nephew Hugh Lane's proposals for a Dublin Municipal Gallery of Art   *defeat*: the final decision of Dublin Corporation about the Lane pictures. See notes on 'To a Wealthy Man . . .', p. 542   *one Who*: William Martin Murphy (1844–1919), proprietor of two Dublin-based newspapers, the *II* and the *EH*, a highly successful businessman whom Yeats disliked as typical of commercial middle-class Ireland. See 'old foul mouth' in 'To a Shade', p. 212. The *II* attacked Lane's proposals for the gallery

p. 211, 'Paudeen'   *dc*: 16 Sept. 1913   *fp*: *PWD*   *Title*: Paudeen; see notes on 'To a Wealthy Man . . .', p. 542   *fumbling wits, the obscure spite*: probably a reference to William Martin Murphy's attack on 'To a Wealthy Man . . .' with its reference to 'Paudeen's pence' (see notes on 'To a Friend . . . Nothing' above). Murphy wrote, in *II*, 17 Jan. 1913, and *IT*, 18 Jan. 1913, that if 'Paudeen's pennies, so contemptuously poetised a few days ago in the press by Mr. W. B. Yeats, are to be abstracted from Paudeen's pockets, at least give him an opportunity of saying whether he

approves of the process or not. . . .'   *our old Paudeen*: in a note of 1914
Yeats wrote:

> The first serious opposition [to Lane's gallery] began in the 'Irish Catholic', the
> chief Dublin clerical paper, and Mr. William Murphy the organiser of the recent
> lock-out [The Dublin lock-out of 1913 was organised by Murphy against the
> Unionising activities of James Larkin (1876–1947) and caused great hardship,
> against which Yeats protested publicly] and Mr. Healy's financial supporter in his
> attack upon Parnell, a man of great influence, brought to its support a few days
> later his newspapers 'The Evening Herald' and 'The Irish Independent', the most
> popular of Irish daily papers. He replied to my poem 'To a Wealthy Man' (I was
> thinking of a very different wealthy man) [Lord Ardilaun] from what he
> described as 'Paudeen's point of view' and 'Paudeen's point of view' it was.

God's eye: Yeats described experiencing an emotion which seemed to him
what a devout Christian must feel when he surrenders his will to God. He
woke next day to hear a voice saying 'The Love of God is infinite for every
human soul because every human soul is unique; no other can satisfy the
same need in God'. Cf. *M*, 68

  p. 212, 'To a Shade'   *dc*: 29 Sept. 1913 (appended to text *P*
(1949))   *fp*: *PWD*   *the town*: Dublin   *thin Shade*: the ghost of
Charles Stewart Parnell, leader of the Irish Parliamentary Party, repudiated by the English Prime Minister Gladstone and by many of the Irish
party because of the disclosure of his affair with Mrs O'Shea. See notes on
'Come Gather Round Me, Parnellites', p. 626   *monument*: the Parnell
monument at the northern end of O'Connell Street, Dublin   *gaunt
houses*: of Dublin   *a man*: Sir Hugh Lane   *what*: the gift of French
Impressionist paintings he offered to Dublin (see notes on 'To a Wealthy
Man . . .', p. 542)   *an old foul mouth*: William Martin Murphy; see notes
on 'Paudeen', p. 544   *set the pack*: a reference to the influence of
Murphy's two popular papers, *II* and *EH*, and probably an echo of
Goethe's description of the Irish as 'like a pack of hounds, always dragging
down some noble stag', quoted in *A*, 316   *Glasnevin coverlet*: Parnell
was buried in Glasnevin cemetery, in north Co. Dublin, on 11 Oct. 1891.
See 'Parnell's Funeral', p. 395

  p. 213, 'When Helen Lived'   *dc*: between 20 and 29 Sept. 1913   *fp*:
P(Ch), May 1914   *Title*: Helen of Troy. See notes on 'The Rose of the
World', p. 498   *topless towers*: cf. Christopher Marlowe, *Doctor Faustus*,
act 5, scene 1, 94–5: 'Was this the face that launched a thousand ships/And
burnt the topless towers of Ilium?'   *a word and a jest*: cf. Yeats's thought
on 6 July 1909: 'Why should we complain if men ill-treat our Muses, when
all that they gave to Helen while she still lived was a song and a jest?'
(*A*, 521)

  p. 213, 'On those that hated "The Playboy of the Western World",

1907'   *dc*: 5 April [1910]   *fp*: *TIR*, Dec. 1911, with the title 'On those who Dislike the Playboy'   *Title*: the production at the Abbey Theatre, Dublin, of *The Playboy of the Western World* by John Millington Synge was greeted by riots in the theatre. Arthur Griffith (1872–1922), founder and editor of the *United Irishman* and *Sinn Fein*, attacked Synge's plays in these journals, arguing that literature should be subordinate to politics. Yeats was comparing 'Griffith and his like' to the eunuchs in Charles Ricketts's (1866–1931) paintings of eunuchs watching Don Juan riding through hell; he thought the sterility of much Irish writing was due to sexual abstinence   *great Juan*: Don Juan, the legendary Spanish libertine, delivered to devils by the statue of the father of a girl he attempted to ravish

p. 214, 'The Three Beggars'   *fp*: *HW*, 15 Nov. 1913   *lebeen-lone*: probably minnow's food (Irish, *libin leamham*, a small fish, a minnow; *libin*, a minnow; *lon*, food)   *cranes*: herons   *Gort*: a market town in Co. Galway (see Glossary); the entrance to Coole Park is 2 miles to the north   *King Guare*: Guaire Aidne (*d.* 663), King of Connaught, famous for his generous hospitality

p. 216, 'The Three Hermits'   *dc*: 5 March 1913   *fp*: *TSS*, Sept. 1913   *Pass the Door of Birth again*: the poem presents different views about reincarnation (notably in ll. 22–8), which Yeats would have met in A. P. Sinnett, *Esoteric Buddhism* (1915), 205–6, and in H. P. Blavatsky, *Isis Unveiled* (1900), I, 179

p. 217, 'Beggar to Beggar Cried'   *dc*: 5 March 1913   *fp*: *P*(Ch) May 1914   *make my soul*: a common expression in Ireland meaning to prepare for death; cf. 'The Tower', III, p. 307

p. 217, 'Running to Paradise'   *dc*: 20 Sept. 1913   *fp*: *P*(Ch), May 1914   *Windy Gap*: possibly the one in Co. Sligo opposite Carraroe Church or the valley among hills south of Galway Bay (see Glossary). See W. B. Yeats, *The Speckled Bird: with variant Versions*, ed. William H. O'Donnell (1977), 41; cf. also *M*, 243. Sheila O'Sullivan (*YUIT*, 276) thinks that the poem continues the theme of 'The Happy Townland', p. 137, the two opening lines echoing a popular riddle: 'As I was going through Slippery Gap/I met a little man with a red cap'   *running to Paradise*: possibly from Lady Gregory, *A Book of Saints and Wonders* (1906), which gives a version of a tale from *The Book of Leinster* (tr. Whitley Stokes in *Anecdota Oxoniensis, Lives of the Saints from the Book of Lismore* (1890), 194) about St Brigit, who sees Nindid the scholar running past her; he tells her he is going to Heaven. See *YUIT*, 277   *And there the king . . . beggar*: the refrain may come, Sheila O'Sullivan suggests (*YUIT*, 277), from Lady Gregory's translation (*Kiltartan Poetry Book* (1918), 57–8) of Douglas Hyde's poem 'He meditates on the Life of a Rich Man': 'A golden cradle under you . . . means herds and flocks . . . at the end of your days death . . . what one better after tonight than Ned the beggar or Seaghan the fool?' *skelping*: beating *a bare heel*: as a young man in London Yeats inked his heels so that the holes in his socks would not be noticeable; here, however, a clever but poor (barefoot) child is probably indicated, seen to grow dull when wealth ('an old sock full [of money]') has been achieved

p. 218, 'The Hour before Dawn' *dc*: 19 Oct. 1913 *fp*: RPP *Cruachan*: the capital of Connacht (Connaught) in Co. Roscommon. See notes on *The Old Age of Queen Maeve*, p. 523 *Maeve's nine Maines*: Queen of Connaught, she had nine sons, the Maines, by Ailill (see l. 36). In tradition there were seven or eight sons *Hell Mouth*: the Cave of Cruachan, known as the Hell Gate of Ireland *Goban's mountain-top*: see notes on 'The Grey Rock', p. 541 *Midsummer Day*: 24 June, the Feast of John the Baptist *It's plain . . . shift a point*: Louis MacNeice, *The Poetry of W. B. Yeats* (1941), 113, thought these lines echoed the tramp's speech in Synge's *The Shadow of the Glen*:

> We'll be going now, I'm telling you, and the time you'll be feeling the cold, and the frost, and the great rain and the sun again, and the south wind blowing in the glens, you'll not be sitting up in a wet ditch, the way you're after sitting in this place making yourself old with looking on each day, and it passing you by. You'll be saying one time, 'It's a good evening, by the grace of God,' and another time 'It's a wild night, God help us; but it'll pass surely'

a good Easter wind: the date of the celebration of Easter shifts between 22 March and 25 April. In Ireland March winds can be notoriously cold *Michael's trumpet*: to be sounded on the Day of Judgement

p. 222, 'A Song from "The Player Queen"' *fp*: P(Ch), May 1914, with the title 'The Player Queen'/*Song from an Unfinished Play* *The Player Queen* (1922), on the writing of which Yeats spent many years, was first produced in 1919. In the play Decima, an actress, introduces this song made by her husband Septimus the poet:

> It is the song of the mad singing daughter of a harlot. The only song she had. Her father was a drunken sailor waiting for the full tide, and yet she thought her mother had foretold that she would marry a prince and become a great queen

p. 222, 'The Realists' *fp*: P(Ch), Dec. 1912

p. 223, 'The Witch' *dc*: 24 May 1912 *fp*: P(Ch), May 1914. This printing did not number this poem 'I' (nor 'The Peacock', p. 223, 'II') *rich*: Yeats's financial position had begun to improve after 1910 because of his British Civil List pension of £150 per year, funds from his American lecture tours and increased royalties

p. 223, 'The Peacock' *fp*: P(Ch), May 1914 *What's riches to him*:

cf. 'The Grey Rock', p. 199, where the poet's friends of the Rhymers' Club (see notes on 'The Grey Rock', p. 541) are praised because they 'never made a poorer song' in order to 'have a heavier purse'   *Three Rock*: probably the Three Rock Mountain which overlooks Dublin

p. 223, 'The Mountain Tomb'   *dc*: Aug. 1912   *fp*: *P*(Ch), Dec. 1912   *Father Rosicross*: Father Christian Rosencrux reputedly founded the Rosicrucian Order in 1484. Yeats tells of the tradition that his followers wrapped his

> imperishable body in noble raiment and laid it under the house of their Order, in a tomb containing the symbols of all things in heaven and earth, and in the waters under the earth, and set about him inextinguishable magical lamps, which burnt on generation after generation, until other students of the Order came upon the tomb by chance . . .'

his tomb: the poem probably uses the tomb as an image of the contemporary period as Yeats draws a parallel between the situation of the imagination, during 'the last two hundred years' laid in 'a great tomb of criticism' where 'inextinguishable magical lamps of wisdom and romance' have been set over it (*E & I*, 196 ff.)

p. 224, 'To a Child Dancing in the Wind'   *dc*: Dec. [?1912 (*IY*, 289)/ 1910]   *fp*: *P*(Ch), Dec. 1912, with the title 'To a Child dancing upon the Shore'   *you*: Iseult Gonne (1895–1954), Maud Gonne's daughter by Lucien Millevoye (see notes on 'King and No King', p. 534)   *The fool's triumph*: probably William Martin Murphy's campaign against Lane's pictures. See notes on 'To a Wealthy Man . . .' p. 542   *Love lost as soon as won*: probably Yeats's relationship with Maud Gonne in 1907–8. See *MGLE*, 157–8, 164–7, 258–63, for the 'spiritual marriage' of Yeats and Maud Gonne of 1898, for a sexual relationship between them in 1907–8 and the renewal of the 'spiritual marriage' after that. See also 'His Memories', p. 331   *the best labourer*: probably John Millington Synge (1871–1909). See notes on 'In Memory of Major Robert Gregory', p. 552

p. 225, 'Two Years Later'   *dc*: 3 Dec. 1912 or 1913   *fp*: *P*(Ch), May 1914, with the title 'To a Child Dancing in the Wind'   *you*: Iseult Gonne; see notes on 'To a Child Dancing in the Wind' above   *your mother*: Maud Gonne   *suffered*: a reference to Maud Gonne's unhappy marriage to John MacBride

p. 225, 'A Memory of Youth'   *dc*: [?13 Aug. 1912]   *fp*: *P*(Ch), Dec. 1912, with the title 'Love and the Bird'   *her praise*: the poem was written to Maud Gonne   *silent as a stone*: cf. the image of the 'stone of the heart' in 'Easter 1916', p. 287, where coldness is indicated as well as the effect of single-minded political ruthlessness

p. 226, 'Fallen Majesty' *dc*: 1912 *fp*: *P*(Ch), Dec. 1912 *crowds gathered . . . she*: a reference to Maud Gonne's effect on crowds: 'when men and women did her bidding they did it not only because she was beautiful, but because that beauty suggested joy and freedom' (*A*, 364) *even old men's eyes*: this suggests the admiration the old people in Troy felt for Helen (see 'When Helen Lived', p. 213); 'even' implies that though older Irish nationalists felt a certain disapproval of Maud's attitude to and encouragement of violence in the 1890s they nonetheless responded to her charisma *lineaments*: a word used by Blake, which Yeats obviously found very effective *what's gone. A crowd*: Yeats is contrasting the present, a time when Maud Gonne was not involved in public affairs (having withdrawn from them after her marriage broke up in 1905) with the past, particularly the period when Yeats was president of the '98 Centennial Association in Great Britain and France and travelled with her to various public meetings which she addressed with such panache

p. 226, 'Friends' *dc*: Jan. 1911 *fp*: *TGH* *One*: Olivia Shakespear (1867–1938), a married woman and cousin of Lionel Johnson, whom Yeats first met in 1894 in London. He wrote that for more than forty years she was the centre of his life in London, and during that time they never had a quarrel, 'sadness sometimes, but never a difference' *fifteen . . . years*: they had a love affair in 1896. See *WBY*, 123–5, *Y:M & P*, 100–3, and *YANB*, 82–4, 295 *And one*: Lady Gregory. See notes on 'He hears the Cry of the Sedge', p. 518, and 'The Shadowy Waters', p. 531 *changed me*: by creating conditions at Coole Park which suited his health, by helping his work in many ways, by enabling him to give up journalism *Labouring in ecstasy*: possibly a reference to Yeats's first tour in Italy in 1907 with Lady Gregory and her son Robert, which introduced him to the achievements of Italian Renaissance art and architecture; the summers at Coole afforded an Irish parallel to Urbino's court. See notes on 'The People', p. 560 *her that took*: Maud Gonne *eagle look*: Yeats associated this with active rather than contemplative people. Maud Gonne said to him that she hated talking about herself

p. 227, 'The Cold Heaven' *fp*: *TGH* (1912) Yeats told Maud Gonne that the poem was an attempt to describe the feelings aroused in him by the cold, detached sky in winter, when he felt responsible in his loneliness for all the past mistakes that were disturbing and indeed tormenting his peace of mind. He believed that after death men live their lives backwards (*A*, 378) *love crossed long ago*: his for Maud Gonne *out of all sense and reason*: Henn (*LT*, 94) commented that the ambiguous Irish expression 'out of all sense' means both far beyond what commonsense could justify *and* beyond the reach of sensation

p. 228, 'That the Night Come'   fp: TGH (1912)   She: the poem is about Maud Gonne

p. 228, 'An Appointment'   dc: 1907 or 1908   fp: ER, Feb. 1909, with the title 'On a Recent Government Appointment in Ireland'   government: Yeats was enraged that the position of Curator of the National Museum in Dublin had been given to Count Plunkett rather than Sir Hugh Lane   the tame will, nor timid brain: Yeats thought it a great crime, Lady Gregory recorded in Hugh Lane's Life and Achievement (1921), 85, not to use 'the best man, the man of genius, in place of the timid obedient official . . . when walking in the woods [at Coole], the sight of a squirrel had given him a thought for some verses . . .'

p. 229, 'The Magi'   dc: 20 Sept. 1913   fp: P(Ch), May 1914, with the title 'I/The Magi'   Yeats's note of 1914 on 'The Dolls', p. 229, reveals that

> The fable for this poem ['The Dolls'] came into my head while I was giving some lectures in Dublin. I had noticed once again how all thought among us is frozen into 'something other than human life'. After I had made the poem I looked up one day into the blue of the sky, and suddenly imagined, as if lost in the blue of the sky, stiff figures in procession. I remembered that they were the habitual image suggested by blue sky, and looking for a second fable called them 'The Magi', complementary forms of those enraged dolls.

unsatisfied ones: the Magi, the three wise men from the East who came to see the Christ child, have not been satisfied by Christ's death on the Cross at Calvary, outside Jerusalem   hoping to find . . . mystery: they express Yeats's belief that the Christian revelation was not final, that history occurs in alternating movements (cf. 'The Second Coming', p. 294, and 'The Gyres', p. 411). They are searching again for an incarnation which, because it will overthrow the world, is uncontrollable   turbulence: Yeats thought the Christian era overthrew preceding eras. The birth of Jesus Christ was a sign of an antithetical revelation   the bestial floor: of the stable in which Christ was born

p. 229, 'The Dolls'   dc: 20 Sept. 1913   fp: RPP, with the title 'II/The Dolls'   Yeats's note on this poem is quoted in notes on 'The Magi' above   That: the baby the woman has brought into the house

p. 230, 'A Coat'   dc: 1912   fp: P(Ch), May 1914. The poem emphasises Yeats's rejection of his early style   my song a coat: the (ambiguous) line means 'I made a coat for my song'   old mythologies: the Gaelic legends Yeats had read in translations, such as those of O'Grady, O'Donovan, O'Curry, O'Looney, Mangan, Sir Samuel Ferguson and others   the fools: a slighting reference to the circle of poets gathered about George Russell ('A.E.'), particularly James Starkey, who wrote as Seumas O'Sullivan. Cf. 'To a Poet . . . and Mine', p. 189

p. 230, '[Closing Rhymes]'   dc: 1914   fp: NS, 7 Feb. 1914, with the title 'Notoriety/*Suggested by a recent magazine article*'   The poem was provoked by an article by George Moore in ER   *the dull ass's hoof . . .* *Jonson's phrase*: see Ben Jonson's (1572–1637) 'An Ode to Himself', *Underwoods* (1640), and the Epilogue to *The Poetaster* (staged 1601, published 1602), in both of which Jonson used the phrase:

> Leave me. There's something come into my thought
> That must and shall be sung high and aloof,
> Safe from the wolf's black jaw, and the dull ass's hoof

Kyle-na-no: see notes on '[Introductory Lines]', p. 531   *that ancient roof*: Coole Park   *a post*: in his diary Yeats wrote that he would adapt a metaphor from Erasmus 'to make myself a post for dogs and journalists to defile'

THE WILD SWANS AT COOLE

This volume, first published by the Cuala Press in 1917, contained the play *At the Hawk's Well*. The Macmillan edition of 1919 contained seventeen more poems. Most of the poems in *The Wild Swans at Coole* were written between 1915 and 1918. Yeats deliberately arranged them out of chronological order.

p. 233, 'The Wild Swans at Coole'   dc: 1918   fp: TLR, June 1917. In the first printing ll. 25–30 were placed between ll. 12 and 13   *The trees . . . paths . . . water*: the lake and its surroundings at Coole Park, Co. Galway. They are well described in Lady Gregory, C   *nine-and-fifty*: there *were* fifty-nine swans there when Yeats wrote the poem, in a mood of intense depression   *nineteenth autumn*: not a reference to Yeats's first brief visit to Coole in the summer of 1896, but to 1897 when he stayed from summer to autumn there. He was fifty-one when he wrote the poem   *Trod with a lighter tread*: Yeats regarded 1897 as a crucial year in his life; he was then thirty-two and involved in his

> miserable love affair, that had but for one brief interruption absorbed my thoughts for years past and would for some years yet. My devotion [to Maud Gonne] might as well have been offered to an image in a milliner's window, or to a statue in a museum, but romantic doctrine had reached its extreme development. [*A*, 399 ff.]

His health was undermined, his nerves wrecked, but Lady Gregory had set him to work again   *Their hearts . . . old*: Yeats was troubled by the death of his love for Maud Gonne. He had proposed to her in 1916, after her husband was executed, but was refused again. He may also have felt that Maud's daughter Iseult, to whom he proposed marriage in 1916 and 1917, would regard him as too old   *Among what rushes*: in 1928 Yeats recorded that, for the first time in his thirty years' knowledge of the lake, swans had built a nest at Coole

p. 234, 'In Memory of Major Robert Gregory'   *dc*: completed by 14 June 1918   *fp*: *ER*, Aug. 1918, with the title 'In Memory of Robert Gregory'. The first printing had this note after the title: '(Major Robert Gregory, R.F.C., M.C., Legion of Honour, was killed in action on the Italian Front, January 23, 1918)'   This is one of four poems – the others are 'Shepherd and Goatherd', p. 244, 'An Irish Airman Foresees his Death', p. 237, and 'Reprisals' (see notes on 'An Irish Airman Foresees his Death', p. 553) – that Yeats wrote in memory of Lady Gregory's only child, Major Robert Gregory, who was killed in action on the Italian front, 23 Jan. 1918. It was later learned that he had been shot down in error by an Italian pilot   *almost settled in our house*: the poem was written when Yeats and his wife (he married Georgie Hyde Lees on 20 Oct. 1917) were staying at Ballinamantane House, lent to them by Lady Gregory while they were supervising alterations to 'our house', Ballylee Castle, the Norman tower and two adjoining cottages which Yeats bought for £35 in 1917 (and later called Thoor Ballylee, *thoor* being Irish for tower), in which he and his family spent their summers until 1929   *turf*: peat   *ancient tower*: the tower became a potent symbol in Yeats's poetry   *narrow winding stair*: the stone staircase, associated in Yeats's mind with the spiral of the gyres   *Discoverers of forgotten truth*: those interested in the occult tradition   *Lionel Johnson*: Yeats met him in 1888 or 1889; see notes on 'The Grey Rock', p. 541   *his learning*: he had a large library and impressed Yeats by his 'knowledge of tongues and books'   *courteous*: Yeats envied Johnson his social poise; he did not discover till much later that Johnson invented many of the conversations he reported that he had had with famous men   *falling . . . sanctity*: the 'falling' may be ambiguous; it may refer to his excessive drinking, or to his theological outlook – 'I am one of those who fall', he wrote in his poem 'Mystic and Cavalier' – or to both. See *L(W)*, 548, and *E & I*, 491–5   *John Synge*: John Millington Synge (1871–1909), Irish dramatist, poet and essayist, studied Irish and Hebrew at Trinity College, Dublin, then music in Germany. His plays include *In the Shadow of the Glen*, *Riders to the Sea*, *The Well of the Saints* and *The Tinkers' Wedding*; see notes on 'On those that hated "The Playboy of the Western World"', 1907', p. 545   *dying*: Synge died of Hodgkin's Disease. Yeats thought some of his poems were written in expectation of early death (*E & I*, 307)   *long travelling*: perhaps 'into the world beyond himself' (*A*, 344)   *desolate stony place*: the Aran Isles off Co. Galway, which Synge visited in 1898, 1899, 1900 and 1901. He wrote *The Aran Islands* (1906); and his plays *Riders to the Sea* and *The Playboy of the Western*

World (1907) owe much to his stays there   *Passionate and simple*: the islands were remote, the inhabitants Irish-speaking, believers in the miraculous and supernatural, often near to sudden death in their battles with the elements, and possessed of a wildness Synge found very appealing   *George Pollexfen*: Yeats's maternal uncle (1839–1910), who lived in Sligo, a pessimistic hypochondriac   *muscular youth*: he had been a successful rider in steeplechases   *Mayo men*: Co. Mayo, south of Co. Sligo   *By opposition, square and trine*: astrological terms for heavenly bodies, respectively separated by 180°, 90° and 120°   *sluggish and contemplative*: George Pollexfen became interested in astrology and symbolism   *Our Sidney*: Sir Philip Sidney (1554–86), the Elizabethan courtier, soldier and author of a pastoral romance, *Arcadia* (1590; 1598), *Apologie for Poetrie* (1591) and the sonnets and songs of *Astrophel and Stella* (1591). He died in battle near Zutphen in Holland. The parallels between his versatile life and Gregory's are continued in succeeding stanzas   *all things*: Robert Gregory had encouraged Yeats to buy the tower and had made several drawings of it   *When . . . feet*: these lines were added at the request of Gregory's widow   *Galway*: Co. Galway, in the west of Ireland   *Castle Taylor*: an early 19th-century big house belonging to the Persse family, incorporating a former Norman keep   *Roxborough*: between Loughrea and Gort, Co. Galway, where Lady Gregory (*née* Persse) was brought up   *Esserkelly*: near Ardrahan, Co. Galway; see Glossary   *Mooneen*: near Esserkelly; see Glossary   *a great painter*: some of his work is reproduced in *Robert Gregory 1881–1981*, ed. Colin Smythe (1981)   *Clare*: county, south of Co. Galway   *dried straw*: 'a fire of straw', Yeats wrote, consumes in a few minutes the nervous vitality, and is useless in the arts (*A*, 318). Yeats envied Gregory his lack of introspection

    p. 237, 'An Irish Airman Foresees his Death'   *dc*: 1918   *fp*: WSC (1919)   *I*: Robert Gregory   *Those that I fight*: the Germans   *Those that I guard*: the English   *Kiltartan Cross*: a crossroads in the Barony of Kiltartan near Coole, Co. Galway. Lady Gregory used it as part of the title in her series of Kiltartan books; her style in her translations is sometimes known as Kiltartan.
    A later poem, 'Reprisals' (*dc*: 1921   *fp*: *Rann An Ulster Quarterly of Poetry*, autumn 1948), was intended for *TN*(L) but withheld from publication. See *Y: M & P*, 328.

Reprisals

Some nineteen German planes, they say,
You had brought down before you died.
We called it a good death. Today
Can ghost or man be satisfied?

> Although your last exciting year
> Outweighed all other years, you said,
> Though battle joy may be so dear
> A memory, even to the dead,
> It chases other thought away,
> Yet rise from your Italian tomb,
> Flit to Kiltartan cross and stay
> Till certain second thoughts have come
> Upon the cause you served, that we
> Imagined such a fine affair:
> Half-drunk or whole-mad soldiery
> Are murdering your tenants there.
> Men that revere your father yet
> Are shot at on the open plain.
> Where may new-married women sit
> And suckle children now? Armed men
> May murder them in passing by
> Nor law nor parliament take heed.
> Then close your ears with dust and lie
> Among the other cheated dead.

German planes: see notes on 'In Memory of Major Robert Gregory', p. 552   *the cause*: of the Allies against the Germans   *a fine affair*: the defence of small nations, the German invasion of Belgium having led to Britain's entry into the war   *Half drunk . . . soldiery*: a reference to atrocities in Co. Galway in the 1920s

p. 238, 'Men Improve with the Years'   *dc*: 19 July 1916   *fp*: *TLR*, June 1917   *worn out with dreams*: the poem treats the effect of Maud Gonne's daughter Iseult's youth and beauty on Yeats, who endeavours to persuade himself that the wisdom he has won compensates for his age, which prevents him loving her as he might have in his 'burning youth'. See notes on 'The Living Beauty', p. 555   *triton*: Tritons in Greek legend were a race of sea deities, usually represented in semi-human form, as bearded men with the hindquarters of fish holding a trident or a shell

p. 238, 'The Collar-Bone of a Hare'   *dc*: 5 July 1916   *fp*: *TLR*, June 1917   *the lawn . . . and the dancing*: this Edenic picture may derive from Blake, in whose 'boys and girls walking or dancing on smooth grass and in golden light, as on pastoral scenes cut upon wood or copper by his disciples Palmer and Calvert, one notices the peaceful Swedenborgian heaven' (*E*, 44). Cf. 'Under Ben Bulben', p. 449: 'Calvert and Wilson,

Blake and Claude,/Prepared a rest for the people of God . . .' *collar-bone of a hare*: this may come from a peasant story. Cf. the character in Yeats's story 'The Three O'Byrnes and the Evil Faeries', who found the shin-bone of a hare lying on the grass (*M*, 87) *marry in churches*: the prospect of marriage may have seemed daunting at times to a bachelor of fifty-one; the poem was written when Lady Gregory and Mrs Shakespear (see notes on 'Friends', p. 549) were advising Yeats to marry

   p. 239, 'Under the Round Tower' *dc*: March 1918 *fp*: *TLR*, Oct. 1918 *Billy Byrne*: the name was probably suggested by that of William Byrne of Ballymanus, Co. Wicklow, a member of the Leinster Directory of the United Irishmen, captured and hanged in 1798. He was a legendary figure in Glendalough, Co. Wicklow (see Glossary), where Yeats and his wife stayed at the Royal Hotel in March 1918 *great-grandfather's battered tomb*: in the graveyard at Glendalough, where a pencil-shaped round tower is situated, as well as stone crosses and ruined churches, part of the monastery established by St Kevin (*d.* 618), later a monastic school and place of pilgrimage. Many Byrnes and O'Byrnes are buried in the graveyard *sun and moon*: the 'golden king and silver lady', cf. the next stanza; they echo the imagery of 'The Man who Dreamed of Faeryland', p. 79; here they symbolise the continuous oscillation which in *AV* is representative of the horizontal movement of the historical cones (see Book V of *AV*(B)) *the round tower*: one of many pencil-shaped stone towers originally built in Ireland as a defence against Scandinavian raiders from about the 9th century *wild lady*: the moon is wild in 'Solomon and the Witch', p. 283, and becomes 'wilder'; the word has sexual implications; cf. the link between sun and moon 'the man and the girl' in one of Yeats's 'Stories of Red Hanrahan' (*M*, 227–8)

   p. 240, 'Solomon to Sheba' *dc*: [?]March 1918 *fp*: *TLR*, Oct. 1918 *Solomon to Sheba*: Solomon (*c*. 972–32 BC), King of the Hebrews. See I Kings 10:1–13 for Sheba's visit to him. She was a ruler in Arabia, in the Yemen. Here Solomon and Sheba are also symbols of the poet and his wife *theme of love*: Yeats wrote that true love seemed to him a discipline:

   . . . it needs so much wisdom that the love of Solomon and Sheba must have lasted, for all the silence of the Scriptures. Each divines the secret self of the other, and refusing to believe in the mere daily self, creates a mirror where the lover or the beloved sees an image to copy in daily life; for love also creates the Mask [*A*, 464]

   p. 241, 'The Living Beauty' *dc*: 1917 *fp*: *TLR*, Oct. 1918 *Title*: refers to Iseult Gonne, Maud's daughter. Yeats proposed to her in 1916 but was rejected. He spent the summer of 1917 at Maud

Gonne's house, 'Les Mouettes', at Colville, Calvados; he renewed his proposal of marriage to Iseult, and was finally refused, when Maud and her family arrived in London in September accompanied by Yeats

p. 241, 'A Song' *dc*: probably 1915 *fp*: *TLR*, Oct. 1918 *dumb-bell and foil*: Yeats did Sandow exercises and Ezra Pound, when acting as his secretary, taught him fencing at Stone Cottage, Ashdown Forest, Sussex, in the winter of 1912–13 *heart grows old*: cf. an early poem, 'Ephemera', p. 50

p. 242, 'To a Young Beauty' *dc*: [probably autumn] 1918 *fp*: *Nine Poems* [Oct.] 1918 *Dear fellow-artist*: the poem was written to Iseult Gonne. See notes on 'The Living Beauty', p. 555 *every Jack and Jill*: Yeats disliked Iseult's bohemian friends in London and Dublin *Ezekiel's cherubim*: see Ezekiel 9:3; 10:2, 6, 7, 14, 16, 19; 11:22; 28:16; 41:18. Ezekiel the prophet lived in the 6th century BC *Beauvarlet*: Jacques Firmin Beauvarlet (1751–97), a mediocre French painter and engraver *Landor and with Donne*: 'I shall dine late; but the dining-room will be well lighted, the guests few and selected' ('XXXV Archdeacon Hare and Walter Landor', in Landor, *Words* (1876)). Walter Savage Landor (1775–1864), a polished minor poet, whom Yeats read between 1914 and 1916; John Donne (1571/2–1631), the metaphysical poet, whom Yeats read in Professor Grierson's edition of 1912. He appreciated how 'the more precise and learned the thought the greater the beauty, the passion' of Donne's poetry. In Landor he appreciated the metaphysical paradox of 'the most violent of men' using his intellect to disengage a 'visionary image of perfect sanity'

p. 242, 'To a Young Girl' *dc*: May 1915 *fp*: *TLR*, Oct. 1918 *My dear*: Iseult Gonne. In 1915 she proposed to Yeats and was refused by him because there was too much Mars in her horoscope (see *Y: M & P*, 190). He did not think himself in love with her until 1916 (see notes on 'The Living Beauty', p. 555) *your own mother*: Maud Gonne

p. 243, 'The Scholars' *dc*: April 1915 (Ellmann (*IY*, 289) gives 1914 and April 1915); the latter date is on an MS) *fp*: *CA* (1915) *Catullus*: the Roman love poet Caius Valerius Catullus (?84–?54 BC)

p. 243, 'Tom O'Roughley' *dc*: 16 Feb. 1918 *fp*: *TLR*, Oct. 1918 *logic-choppers*: Yeats probably had in mind Newton, Hobbes and Locke. Cf. *W & B*, 76–7 *An aimless joy*: in 'Bishop Berkeley', Yeats quoted from paragraph 639 of Berkeley's *Commonplace Book*, 'Complacency seems rather to . . . constitute the essence of volition', which seemed to him what an Irish poet meant who sang to some girl 'A joy within guides you' and what he himself meant when he wrote 'An aimless joy is a pure joy' (*E & I*, 408)   *Tom O'Roughley*: a fool of the kind Yeats described in *AV*; his thoughts are 'an aimless reverie, his acts are aimless like his thoughts, and it is in this aimlessness that he finds his joy' (*AV*(B), 182)   *wisdom . . . bird of prey*: '. . . I have a ring with a hawk and a butterfly upon it, to symbolise the straight road of logic, and so of mechanism, and the crooked road of intuition: "For wisdom is a butterfly and not a gloomy bird of prey" ' (Yeats's note, 1928)   *trumpeter Michael*: see note on 'The Hour before Dawn', p. 547. Here Yeats gives the archangel the role of trumpeter of the Last Judgement

p. 244, 'Shepherd and Goatherd'   *dc*: *c.* 22 Feb.–19 March 1918   *fp*: *WSC* (1919) with the title 'The Sad Shepherd'; this was altered in *CP* (1933) to the present title   *Title*: the poem is a pastoral elegy for Major Robert Gregory (see 'In Memory of Major Robert Gregory', p. 234, and notes, p. 552). Yeats told Lady Gregory that he was deliberately echoing Spenser's 'A pastoral Aeglogue upon the death of Sir Philip Sidney Knight etc'; later he announced that he had finished the poem 'modelled on what Virgil wrote for some friend of his [The Fifth Eclogue; itself probably an imitation of Theocritus's Elegy on Daphnis] and on what Spenser wrote of Sidney' (*L*(W), 646, 647)   *He that was best . . . Is dead*: Robert Gregory was an excellent athlete   *thrown the crook away*: see notes on 'In Memory of Major Robert Gregory', p. 552   *their loneliness*: Yeats thought Gregory's paintings captured the nature of the Galway countryside   *neither goat nor grazing*: a gracious mention of Lady Gregory's friendship (and presumably her lending Yeats money so that he could give up journalism). She imposed a routine on him when he stayed at Coole for long periods in the summers from 1897 on, and he did a great deal of writing there   *New welcome and old wisdom*: his summer visits to Coole; 'old wisdom' may refer to his collecting folklore with her   *his children and his wife*: Gregory married in 1907. He and his wife Margaret had three children   *speckled bird*: *The Speckled Bird* was the title of Yeats's unfinished autobiographical novel, posthumously published in 1977, ed. W. H. O'Donnell   *lost companions*: possibly the friends lamented in 'In Memory of Major Robert Gregory', p. 234   *the road that the soul treads*: a reference to Yeats's interest in the occult   *He grows younger*: Gregory, growing younger, is living his life backwards, an idea later set out in terms of Indian belief in which the dead travel back through events to their source and 'seem to live backwards through time' (*E*, 366). An essay of 1914 suggested that 'after death every man grows upward or downward to the likeness of thirty years' (*E*, 39). See *Y & T*, 201 ff. for likely sources for the idea   *Jaunting, journeying*: taking a jaunt for pleasure (jaunting cars, horse drawn, were in common use in Ireland at the time)   *dayspring*: probably derived from Swedenborg. See *A*, 311, 541   *the loaded pern*: Yeats's note of 1919 read:

When I was a child at Sligo I could see above my grandfather's trees a little column of smoke from 'the pern-mill,' and was told that 'pern' was another name for the spool, as I was accustomed to call it, on which thread was wound. One could not see the chimney for the trees, and the smoke looked as if it came from the mountain, and one day a foreign sea-captain asked me if that was a burning mountain.

the close-cropped grass: see Yeats's comment that Swedenborg felt horror amid rocky, uninhabited places, associated evil with them but thought that 'the good are amid smooth grass and garden walks and the clear sunlight of Claude Lorraine' (pseudonym of Claude Gelée, French landscape painter (1600–82)) (*E*, 37). Cf. 'Under Ben Bulben', p. 449

p. 249, 'Lines Written in Dejection'   *dc*: [probably Oct.] 1915   *fp*: WSC   *the moon . . . embittered sun*: the moon symbolises subjectivity in this poem, the sun objectivity, cf. 'The Man Who Dreamed of Faeryland', p. 79, and 'Men Improve with the Years', p. 238, 'The Living Beauty', p. 241, and 'A Song', p. 241   *the holy centaurs*: in Greek mythology centaurs usually have the head, arms and torso of a man joined to a lower body with the four legs of a horse. Yeats thought all art should be 'a Centaur finding in the popular lore its back and its strong legs' (*A*, 191)   *embittered sun*: objective life could be considered as destroying creative. Here Yeats is probably thinking of how 'the heterogeneous labour' of recent years, especially his work for the Abbey Theatre, had diminished his inner life (*A*, 484)

p. 249, 'The Dawn'   *that old queen*: Emain   *a town*: Emain Macha or Armagh (see Glossary). Macha, the horse goddess, was the mother of twins, which may be the two hills in Armagh. Emain claimed to rule in her father's right after his death (he was Hugh Roe); she defeated his brother Dihorba in battle, and compelled his five sons, captured by a stratagem, to build her a palace at Armagh, which became the capital of Ulster in the Irish legends   *pin of a brooch*: she marked out the site of her palace with the pin or bodkin of her cloak, hence the name of her palace, Emania in Latinised form. (See Standish James O'Grady, *History of Ireland: Critical and Philosophical* (1881), I, 181)   *withered men . . . Babylon*: Babylon, famous for astronomy and astrology, was the chief city of ancient Mesopotamia, first settled in 3000 BC. The Babylonian Empire flourished from *c.* 2200–538 BC   *glittering coach*: presumably the chariot of Phœbus, the sun. But 'the dawn' may suggest the particular dawn on which, according to Greek myth, Phæton, son of Phœbus, made his disastrous attempt to drive the chariot; he was killed by a thunderbolt Zeus hurled at him because he was likely, through his erratic driving, to set the earth on fire. The dawn may be 'Ignorant and wanton' because it just looked on detachedly

p. 250, 'On Woman'   *dc*: 25 May 1914   *fp*: *P*(Ch), Feb. 1916   *Solomon*: see notes on 'Solomon to Sheba', p. 555; his wisdom was proverbial   *shuddered in the water*: this is a sexual symbol; cf. 'Leda and the Swan', p. 322   *yawn*: cf. 'Three Things', p. 379   *Pestle of the moon*: Yeats is qualifying belief in rebirth. An entry in the Maud Gonne Manuscript Book read:

> O God grant me for my gift not in this life for I begin to grow [old] but somewhere that I shall love some woman, so that every passion, pity, cruel desire, the affection that is full of tears to abasement as before an image

p. 251, 'The Fisherman'   *dc*: 4 June 1914   *fp*: *P*(Ch), Feb. 1916   *him*: the ideal man   *Connemara clothes*: homespun tweed from the west of Ireland   *All day . . . the reality*: these lines refer to the ideal audience ('what I had hoped it would be') and the actual audience (the reality), so unlike that of his hopes   *The living men . . . beating down*: a description of the 'reality'   *the dead man*: probably John Millington Synge. See notes on 'In Memory of Major Robert Gregory', p. 552   *Art beaten down*: possibly the rejection by Dublin Corporation of the proposals for the Lane Gallery (see notes on 'To a Wealthy Man . . .', p. 542)   *a twelvemonth since*: an entry in the Maud Gonne Manuscript Book dated between 18 and 25 May 1913 was headed 'subject for a poem':

> Who is this by the edge of the stream
> That walks in a good homespun coat
> And carries a fishing [rod] in his hand
> We singers have nothing of our own.
> All our hopes, our loves, our dreams
> Are for the young, for those whom
> We stir into life. But [there is] one
> That I can see always though he is not yet born
> He walks by the edge of the stream
> In a good homespun coat
> And carries a fishing rod in his hand.

down-turn of his wrist: a description of skilled casting; Yeats was a good fisherman   *cold And passionate as the dawn*: the phrase came from a letter of Yeats's father, the artist John Butler Yeats

p. 252, 'The Hawk'   *fp*: *P*(Ch), Feb. 1916   *the hawk*: see notes on 'Tom O'Roughley', p. 556. Yeats added the first six lines of this poem to a discussion of his belief that in man and race there is something he called Unity of Being: he thought abstraction (the isolation of occupation, or class, or faculty) was the enemy of this Unity (*A*, 189 ff.)

p. 253, 'Memory'   *dc*: [?]1915–16   *fp*: P(Ch), Feb. 1916   *a lovely face*: Olivia Shakespear. See notes on 'Friends', p. 549   *form*: where a hare crouches   *the mountain hare*: probably a reference to Iseult Gonne. See note on 'Two Songs of a Fool', p. 567

p. 253, 'Her Praise'   *dc*: 27 Jan. 1915   *fp*: P(Ch), Feb. 1916   *She is foremost*: Maud Gonne   *the long war*: the First World War (1914–18), which many had at first expected to be over very quickly   *Manage the talk*: an Irish phrase which Yeats liked

p. 254, 'The People'   *dc*: 10 Jan. 1915   *fp*: P(Ch), Feb. 1916, with the title 'The Phoenix'. The poem records a conversation with Maud Gonne, the Phoenix in this poem and in 'His Phoenix', p. 255   *all that I have done*: for the Irish literary movement, for various political movements and for the Abbey Theatre   *this unmannerly town*: Dublin, which had failed to appreciate the plays of Synge and Hugh Lane's generous offer of his pictures (see notes on 'To a Wealthy Man', p. 542)   *most defamed*: Dublin's often vicious journalism, its gossip, and probably George Moore's malice in *Hail and Farewell* (see notes on '[Introductory Rhymes]', p. 539, and '[Closing Rhymes]', p. 551)   *Ferrara*: Yeats visited it in 1907. Cf. praise of its Duke Ercole in 'To a Wealthy Man . . .', p. 542   *Urbino . . . dawn*: a reference to an occasion described in Castiglione's *The Book of the Courtier*, which Yeats read in both Hoby's translation and that of Opdycke. How Elisabetta Gonzaga (1471–1526) and her courtiers talked till dawn is told in Opdycke's translation, *The Courtier* (1902), 308   *my phoenix*: Maud Gonne   *pilferers of public funds*: possibly a reference to Frank Hugh O'Donnell's mishandling of money obtained by Maud Gonne from the Boers. (See *YANB*, pp. 129–30)   *my luck changed*: an oblique reference to the break-up of Maud's marriage. A French court granted her a legal separation (not the divorce she sought, as her husband was an Irish resident); see notes on 'Against Unworthy Praise', p. 535   *After nine years*: this could place the conversation in 1906

p. 255, 'His Phoenix'   *dc*: Jan. 1915   *fp*: P(Ch), Feb. 1916   *that sprightly girl*: Leda. See 'Leda and the Swan', p. 322; in Greek mythology Zeus in the shape of a swan coupled with her   *Gaby's laughing eye*: Gaby Deslys (1884–1920), French actress and dancer   *Ruth St. Denis*: American dancer (1878/9–1968)   *Pavlova*: Anna Matreyevna Pavlova (1885–1931), famous Russian ballerina   *player in the States*: Julia Marlowe (1866–1950), known for her Shakespearian roles; Yeats saw her act during his lecture tour in the USA in 1930–4   *Margaret . . . Mary*: a list of Ezra Pound's girlfriends. In April 1914 Pound married Dorothy, Olivia Shakespear's daughter. (See notes on 'Friends', p. 549)   *the simplicity of a child*: cf. 'Against Unworthy Praise', p. 187, where Maud is 'Half lion, half child', and 'Long-legged Fly', p. 463, where she is 'part woman, three parts a child'   *proud look . . . sun*: see notes on 'Upon a House Shaken by the Land Agitation', p. 537

p. 256, 'A Thought from Propertius'   *dc*: probably before Nov. 1915   *fp*: WSC   Title: Sextus Propertius (*c*. 50–16 BC), a Roman love poet   *She*: Maud Gonne   *noble . . . wine*: a description very close to the second poem in the second book of Propertius; for instance 'fit spoil for a centaur' echoes the 'Centaurs' welcome spoil in the revels' midst'   *Pallas Athene*: in 'Beautiful Lofty Things', p. 421, Maud Gonne is like 'Pallas Athene in that straight back and arrogant head'. Pallas Athene, in Greek mythology, was the virgin goddess of wisdom, practical skills, the arts of peace and prudent warfare. The image of her as goddess was used in *A*, 123, to describe Yeats's first impressions of Maud Gonne in 1889

p. 256, 'Broken Dreams'   *dc*: 24 Oct. 1915   *fp*: TLR, Nov. 1915   *your hair*: the poem is written to Maud Gonne   *The poet stubborn with his passion*: Yeats   *chilled his blood*: he was fifty when he wrote the poem   *a flaw*: in an essay 'The Tragic Theatre', written five years earlier than this poem, Yeats praised the attractiveness of the unusual in a beloved; this emphasised the quality of uniqueness

p. 258, 'A Deep-sworn Vow'   *dc*: 17 Oct. 1915   *fp*: TLR, June 1917   *you did not keep That . . . vow*: Maud Gonne's vow not to marry

p. 258, 'Presences'   *dc*: Nov. 1915   *fp*: TLR, June 1917   *my creaking stair*: in Woburn Buildings, London, where Yeats had rooms from Feb. 1896–June 1919   *harlot*: Mabel Dickinson. See *WBY*, 301   *a child*: Iseult Gonne. See notes on 'To a Child Dancing in the Wind', p. 548, 'Men Improve with the Years', p. 554, and 'The Living Beauty', p. 555   *a queen*: Maud Gonne

p. 258, 'The Balloon of the Mind'   *dc*: before 1917   *fp*: NS, 29 Sept. 1917   *balloon*: cf. Yeats's description of his English schooldays, when he had to:

> . . . give the whole evening to one lesson if I was to know it. My thoughts were a great excitement, but when I tried to do anything with them, it was like trying to pack a balloon into a shed in a high wind [*A*, 41]

p. 259, 'To a Squirrel at Kyle-na-no'   *dc*: Sept. 1912   *fp*: NS, 29 Sept. 1917   Title: Kyle-na-no: one of the seven woods at Coole Park, Co. Galway; see notes on '[Introductory Lines]', p. 531   *I'd a gun*: Yeats 'shot at birds with a muzzle-pistol until somebody shot a rabbit and I heard it squeal. From that day on I would kill nothing but the dumb fish' (*A*, 55)

p. 259, 'On being asked for a War Poem'   dc: 6 Feb. 1915   fp: The
Book of the Homeless, ed. Edith Wharton (1916), with the title 'A Reason for
Keeping Silent'   I think it better: Yeats told Henry James that it was the
only thing he had written of the war,

> . . . or will write, so I hope it may not seem unfitting. I shall keep the
> neighbourhood of the seven sleepers of Ephesus, hoping to catch their comfort-
> able snores till bloody frivolity is over [L(W), 600]

p. 259, 'In Memory of Alfred Pollexfen'   dc: Aug. 1916   fp: TLR,
June 1917, with the title 'In Memory'   Five-and-twenty: William Pollexfen (Yeats's maternal grandfather) died in 1892. See '[Introductory
Rhymes]', p. 197   strong bones: perhaps an echo of Yeats's grandfather's
use of the word; he decided not to be buried beside his wife's relatives, the
Middletons: 'I am not going to lie with those old bones'. The Middletons
had settled in Sligo earlier; he was the first male Pollexfen to settle there. He
used to walk to St John's Church every day to superintend the making of
his tomb   his wife Elizabeth: she, née Middleton (1819–92), was 'gentle
and patient'   George: George Pollexfen (1839–1910), Yeats's uncle,
with whom he stayed in Sligo in the late 1880s and early 1890s   Masons
drove: Yeats described his 'very touching' funeral to Lady Gregory: 'the
church full of the working people, Catholics who had never been in a
Protestant church before. . . . The Masons (there were 80 of them) had
their own service and one by one threw acacia leaves into the grave with
the traditional Masonic goodbye "Alas my brother so mote it be" '   a
melancholy man: George Pollexfen was a hypochondriac. See L(W),
551   Many a son and daughter: cf. A, 10   The Mall . . . grammar school:
a street in Sligo; the school still flourishes   the sailor John: John Pollexfen
(1845–1900), who died in Liverpool   the youngest son: Alfred Pollexfen
(1854–1916), 'stout and humorous'   journey home . . . fiftieth year:
Alfred returned to Sligo from Liverpool, where he had worked in the
family firm, W. & G. T. Pollexfen & Co., at the age of fifty to take
George's place in it in Sligo. He died ten years later   fiftieth: he actually
returned in 1910   'Mr. Alfred': Yeats wrote to his sister Lily to say this
poem was simply 'an expansion of the end of your letter', in which she
probably described her uncle's last years in Sligo in the terms she had used
in writing to her father that her uncle had become 'Mr. Alfred' in a place
where he was known, which had 'known and respected his people before
him'   visionary . . . bird: Yeats wrote that a sea-bird is the omen that
announces the death or danger of a Pollexfen (A, 10); he wrote to Lady
Gregory to say that his sister Lily and the nurse had heard the Banshee the
night before George Pollexfen died. (Lily had dreamt she held a wingless
sea-bird in her arms and later heard that another Pollexfen uncle had died in
his madhouse)

p. 261, 'Upon a Dying Lady'   *dc*: between Jan. 1912 and July 1914
(I probably in Jan. 1913, II in Jan. 1912 and VII in July 1914)   *fp*:
TLR, Aug. 1917, with the general title 'Seven Poems', the fourth, fifth
and sixth being given numerical subtitles
I   *Title*: the subject of the poem is Mabel Beardsley (1871–1916), sister
of the painter Aubrey Beardsley; she had married an actor, George Bealby
Wright, and was dying of cancer   *a wicked tale*: Yeats wrote to Lady
Gregory about her courage. A palmist had told her that her life would take
a turn for the better when she was forty-two:

> 'and now I shall spend my forty second year in Heaven . . . Oh yes, I shall go to
> heaven. Papists do.' She told improper stories and at times shook with laughter
> [*L*(W), 573–5]

Petronius Arbiter: Gaius Petronius (*d.* AD 66), thought to be the author of
Satirae, a satirical romance; described by the historian Tacitus as the *arbiter
elegentiae* at Nero's court, he aroused the jealousy of Tigellenius, who
procured his disgrace; he was ordered to commit suicide
II   *new . . . doll*: the artist Charles Ricketts (1866–1931) made her dolls
dressed like people out of her brother's drawings   *Turkish fashion . . .
boy's*: Yeats described the dolls as 'women with loose trousers and boys
that looked like women'
III   *Title*: see note on *new . . . doll* above   *Longhi*: Pietro Longhi
(1702–62), a Venetian painter   *our Beauty*: see note on *Turkish fashion
. . . boy's* above   *dog his day*: probably an echo of the French poet Paul
Fort's (*b.* 1872) lines, included in one of Yeats's brother Jack B. Yeats's
Broadsides (hand-coloured prints and poetry): 'And they came back so
merrily: all at the dawn of day;/A singing all so merrily: '*The dog must have
his day!*'
IV   *but half done*: because she was only forty-two
V   *dead brother's valour*: Aubrey Beardsley (1872–98), artist and art
editor of *The Yellow Book*, died of TB at the age of twenty-six
VI   *Grania . . . Diarmuid*: see notes on *WO*, p. 488   *Giorgione*: a
famous Venetian painter (*c.* 1478–1510)   *Achilles*: in Greek mythology
the son of Peleus and Thetis (see 'News for the Delphic Oracle', p. 461); he
was mortally wounded in his heel (the rest of his body was invulnerable)
by Paris, son of Priam, King of Troy, and Queen Hecuba (see notes on
'The Rose of the World', p. 498)   *Timor*: Tamerlaine (1336–1405),
Mongol conqueror, the ruler of Samarkand 1369–1405   *Babar*: Zahir-
ud-din-Mohammed (?1480–1530), the founder of the Moghul Empire in
India   *Barhaim*: probably Bahrám Gur, called Bahram of the Wild Ass
from his skill in hunting this animal, the 'Great Hunter' of Edward
Fitzgerald's *Rubaiyat of Omar Khayyam* (1859)
VII   *Title*: see Yeats's letter to Lady Gregory (*L*(W), 573–5); the
Christmas tree was brought by 'Mr Davis – Ricketts' patron – I daresay it
was Ricketts's idea'

p. 264, 'Ego Dominus Tuus'   *dc*: completed by 5 Oct. 1915 (a second MS is dated Dec. 1915)   *fp*: P(Ch), Oct. 1917   *Title*: from Dante Alighieri's (1265–1321) *Vita Nuova* (?1292–3), which Yeats read in a translation of 1861 by Dante Gabriel Rossetti and in that by C. L. Shadwell. Dante sees a 'Lord of terrible aspect' who says to him 'Ego dominus tuus' (Latin, I am your master). The poem takes the form of a dialogue between *Hic* and *Ille*, Latin pronouns meaning in this case 'the one', 'the other'. *Hic* defends objective views, *Ille* subjective; the poem embodies Yeats's theories of the anti-self, developed in the prose of *Per Amica Silentia Lunae* (Latin, through the friendly silences of the moon; the phrase comes from Virgil's *Aeneid*, II, 255) (*M*, 319–67) and in *AV*   *wind-beaten tower*: Yeats's tower, Thoor Ballylee, often buffeted by westerly winds coming in off the Atlantic   *Michael Robartes*: an invented character. See notes on 'The Lover Tells of the Rose in his Heart', p. 509   *Magical shapes*: in *AV*(A) Robartes traces on Arabian sands diagrams – those of *AV* – 'whose gyres and circles grew out of one another . . . there was a large diagram . . . where lunar phases and zodiacal symbols were mixed with various unintelligible symbols'. Cf. *M*, 343, and notes on 'The Gift of Harun al-Rashid', p. 592   *I call to my own opposite*: see *A*, 503:

> all happiness depends on the energy to assume the mask of some other self. . . .
> We put on a grotesque or solemn painted face to hide us from the terrors of
> judgement, invent an imaginative Saturnalia where one forgets reality, a game
> like that of a child, where one loses the infinite pain of self-realisation.

This phrase in the poem cannot be fully understood until expanded in *Ille*'s final speech, 'I call to the mysterious one . . .', answered by *Hic*'s query, which, in effect, asks why pursue unreality?   *gentle, sensitive mind . . . the old nonchalance*: modern work, *Ille* replies, lacks inspiration; modern culture is passive, self-analytical, but men of the Middle Ages and the Renaissance 'made themselves overmastering creative persons by turning from the mirror to meditation on a mask' (*M*, 333)   *that hollow face . . . the hunger*: Yeats saw Dante not only moved by the purity of Beatrice and Divine Justice, her death and his own banishment from Florence, but also because he had to struggle in his own heart with unjust anger and his lust. (See *NC*, 168–77, and *M*, 329–31)   *Lapo and that Guido*: probably Lapo Gianni (*c*. 1270–*c*. 1330) and Guido Calvalcanti (*c*. 1230–1300), Italian poets, friends of Dante   *Bedouin's horse-hair roof*: some Bedouins (Arabic, tent-dwellers) are still nomadic, inhabiting the deserts of Arabia   *doored and windowed cliff*: probably suggested by Petra, in Jordan

p. 267, 'A Prayer on going into my House'   *dc*: 1918   *fp*: TLR, Oct. 1918   *this tower and cottage*: Ballylee Castle, Co. Galway, which Yeats owned from 1917. See M. Hanley, *Thoor Ballylee – Home of William Butler Yeats* (1965); *TCA*, 29–46, and Sheelagh Kirby, *The Yeats Country* (1962)   *No table . . . stool*: local craftsmen made heavy furniture out of a

local elm tree   *Galilee*: in Palestine, the scene of Christ's early
ministry   *the Loadstone Mountain*: the story 'Sinbad the Sailor' is
included in the *Arabian Nights' Entertainment*, tr. Sir Richard Burton (1821–
90). Sinbad's ship was wrecked on a loadstone mountain on his sixth
voyage. Yeats first 'walked upon Sinbad's yellow shore' in 1872
(*A*, 52)   *limb of the Devil*: expression in common use in Ireland

p. 267, 'The Phases of the Moon'   *dc*: 1918   *fp*: WSC   Title:
this poem presents one of the central ideas later expressed in *AV* in a similar
manner to that of 'Ego Dominus Tuus', p. 264. Here Michael Robartes
and Owen Aherne are speaking, Aherne being another invented character.
Yeats's note of 1922, reads

> Years ago I wrote three stories in which occur the names of Michael Robartes and
> Owen Aherne. I now consider that I used the actual names of two friends, and that
> one of these friends, Michael Robartes, has but lately returned from
> Mesopotamia, where he has partly found and partly thought out much philo-
> sophy. I consider that Aherne and Robartes, men to whose namesakes I had
> attributed a turbulent life or death, have quarrelled with me. They take their place
> in a phantasmagoria in which I endeavour to explain my philosophy of life and
> death. To some extent I wrote these poems as a text for exposition.

a bridge: over the river flowing past one of the tower's walls   *Connemara
cloth*: see notes on 'The Fisherman', p. 559   *he is reading*: Yeats   *Mere
images*: Milton's Platonist derives from Milton's *Il Penseroso* (1632):

> Or let my lamp, at midnight hour,
> Be seen in some high lonely tower,
> Where I may oft outwatch the *Bear*,
> With thrice great *Hermes*, or unsphere
> The spirit of *Plato*, to unfold
> What worlds, or what vast regions hold
> The immortal mind that hath forsook
> Her mansion in the fleshly nook; . . .

This lamp is 'the lonely light' in 'The Lonely Tower', an illustration by the
artist Samuel Palmer (1805–81) in *The Shorter Poems of John Milton* (1889).
Shelley's 'visionary prince' is the title character of *Prince Athanase* (1817),
whose soul sat apart from men 'as in a lonely tower' which has affinities
with Milton's poem, in the lamp in Laian's turret:

> The Balearic fisher, driven from shore,
> Hanging upon the peaked wave afar,
> Then saw their lamp from Laian's turret gleam,
> Piercing the stormy darkness, like a star . . .

Other parallels are drawn in *NC*, 205–6   *extravagant style . . . Pater*:
Walter Pater (1839–94), the academic critic whose involuted style affected
Yeats's prose in the 1890s, particularly in *TSR*   *Said I was dead*: in 'Rosa

Alchemica' (*M*, 267–92); his death is also mentioned in *M*, 'The Adoration of the Magi'   *Twenty-and-eight*: see diagram from *A V*, p. 696; the phrases are linked to the relevant parts of *A V* in *NC*, 175–8   *Athene*: see notes on 'A Thought from Propertius', p. 561   *Achilles . . . dust*: in Greek mythology, the son of Peleus and Thetis; he killed Hector, eldest son of Priam, King of Troy, and Queen Hecuba; this is described in Homer's *Iliad*, I, 197, and XXII, 30. Achilles was killed by Paris; see notes on 'Upon a Dying Lady', p. 563   *Nietzsche*: Friedrich Nietzsche (1844–1900), the German philosopher, whom Yeats began reading in 1902   *Sinai's top*: Mount Sinai, where Moses received the Ten Commandments (see Exodus 19 and 20), on the Sinai peninsula, between the Mediterranean and the Red Sea   *the man within*: Yeats

p. 273, 'The Cat and the Moon'   *dc*: 1917   *fp*: *Nine Poems* (1918)   *Title*: 'The Cat' was Minnaloushe, a black Persian cat in Maud Gonne MacBride's household in Normandy; Yeats wrote the poem when staying there. In his Introduction to *The Cat and the Moon*, a play performed in the Abbey Theatre in 1926, Yeats mentioned this 'little poem where a cat is disturbed by the moon, and in the changing pupils of its eyes seems to repeat the movement of the moon's changes'. As he wrote the poem he allowed himself to think of the cat 'as the normal man and of the moon as the opposite he seeks perpetually or as having any meaning I have conferred upon the moon elsewhere'   *his pupils*: Mrs Robert Felkin, a clairvoyant, wrote to Yeats that her animal was 'the cat whose dilating pupils correspond to the waxing and waning moon' (*LWBY*, 206)

p. 274, 'The Saint and the Hunchback'   *dc*: 1918   *fp*: *WSC* (1919)   This poem epitomises two phases of *A V*, the Hunchback being of phase twenty-six, the Saint of phase twenty-seven   *A Roman Caesar*: title given to Roman Emperors from Augustus to Hadrian; the name derives from Caius Julius Caesar (?102–44 BC), the Roman general, statesman and historian   *a different plan*: possibly a reference to the twenty-eight phases of the moon in *A V*   *the taws*: a form of birch   *I may thrash*: in *A V* the Saint is described as substituting for emulation

> an emotion of renunciation, and for the old toil of judgment and discovery of sin, a beating upon his breast and an ecstatical crying out that he must do penance, that he is even the worst of men. . . . His joy is to be nothing, to do nothing, to think nothing; but to permit the total life, expressed in its humanity, to flow in upon him and to express itself through his acts and thoughts [*A V* (B), 180]

Greek Alexander: Alexander the Great (356–323 BC), King of Macedon, conqueror of Greece, Egypt and the Persian Empire, and founder of Alexandria   *Augustus Caesar*: Caius Julius Caesar Octavianus (63 BC–AD 14); first Emperor of Rome, he adopted the title Augustus in 27 BC   *Alcibiades*: an Athenian statesman and general (450–404 BC), both brilliant and unstable

p. 274, 'Two Songs of a Fool'   *dc*: between July and Sept. 1918   *fp*: WSC (1919)   *A speckled cat*: Mrs Yeats. Cf. another personal joke: 'Who can keep company with the goddess Astraea if his eyes are on the brindled cat?' (*Essays 1931–1936*, 3)   *a tame hare*: Iseult Gonne, for whom Yeats had a great feeling of responsibility after his marriage in 1917. Cf. 'To a Young Beauty', p. 242   *Providence*: God, in his protection and care of his creatures

p. 275, 'Another Song of a Fool'   *fp*: WSC (1919)   *butterfly*: in 'Tom O'Roughley', p. 243, the butterfly symbolises the wisdom of wideranging thought. The poem is related to Mrs Yeats's automatic writing. See *MYAV*, 2, 198–201

p. 276, 'The Double Vision of Michael Robartes'   *dc*: completed by July 1918   *fp*: WSC (1919)   *Title*: see notes on 'Ego Dominus Tuus', p. 564. For connections between the poem and Mrs Yeats's automatic writing, see *MYAV*, 2, 198–201   *rock of Cashel*: the Rock of Cashel, Co. Tipperary, has several ecclesiastical ruins on it, including the chapel Cormac MacCarthy constructed in the 12th century, mentioned in the last stanza   *the cold spirits*: from the later phases of the moon in *AV*   *Constrained*: in the last gyre, in *AV*, decadence is predicted; it may 'suggest bubbles in a frozen pond – mathematical Babylonian starlight'. The new era will bring 'its stream of irrational force'. The eight lines beginning 'Constrained' were quoted by Yeats in an essay to conclude a passage distinguishing between the arts and 'visible history, the discoveries of science, the discussions of politics' (*E*, 258–9)   *A Sphinx*: the 'introspective knowledge of the mind's self-begotten unity'; in Greek mythology a sphinx usually has the head and bust of a woman, the body of a lion, and wings. It was originally a monster, later a messenger of the gods   *A Buddha*: 'the outward-looking mind'. Both Buddha and Sphinx guard the mystery of the fifteenth phase of *AV*. Gautama Buddha (*c*. 563–*c*. 483 BC) was the Indian founder of Buddhism   *between these two a girl*: the girl represents art; she dances between the intellect (the Sphinx) and the heart, the emotions (the Buddha), art being a balance between, a combination of intellect and emotion   *Homer's Paragon*: Helen of Troy, a symbol usually suggesting Maud Gonne   *Cormac's ruined house*: see note on *rock of Cashel* above. See also Yeats's reference to the Church of Ireland bishop who took the lead roof from the Gothic church to save his legs (*E*, 266) (Archbishop Price used the roof for a new cathedral on the plain)

MICHAEL ROBARTES AND THE DANCER

The Preface alludes to Michael Robartes's exposition of the *Speculum Angelorum et Hominum* of Giraldus, part of the background Yeats invented for *A Vision* (see 'Ego Dominus Tuus', p. 264, and 'The Phases of the Moon', p. 267); there are several notes on the poems which deal with this material. See *VE*, 821–5; the Preface is reprinted on 853

p. 281, 'Michael Robartes and the Dancer'   *dc*: 1918   *fp*: *DL*, Nov. 1920   *Title*: for Michael Robartes see notes on 'The Lover tells of the Rose in his Heart', p. 509, and 'The Phases of the Moon', p. 565   *He*: probably represents Yeats's views, *She* Iseult Gonne's. See notes on 'Men Improve with the Years', p. 554, 'The Living Beauty', p. 555, and 'To a Young Beauty', p. 556   *this altar-piece*: probably 'Saint George and the Dragon' in the National Gallery, Dublin, ascribed to Bordone (*c.* 1500–71)   *Athene*: Pallas Athene, Greek goddess, patron of arts and crafts   *Paul Veronese*: cognomen of Paolo Cagliari (1528–88), Venetian painter; he settled in Venice in 1535   *lagoon*: at Venice   *Michael Angelo's Sistine roof*: Michelangelo Buonarroti (1475–1564), Italian artist who painted the roof of the Sistine Chapel in the Vatican in Rome from 1508–12   *this Latin text*: Joseph M. Hassett, *Yeats and the Politics of Hate* (1986), 88, suggests Ficino's Latin translation of Plotinus

p. 283, 'Solomon and the Witch'   *dc*: 1918   *fp*: *MRD*   *that Arab lady*: the Queen of Sheba, who came from Arabia to visit Solomon, King of the Hebrews (*c.* 972–932 BC). See I Kings 10:1–13. The poem, about Yeats and his wife, deals with a possible annihilation of time through the occurrence of a perfect union of lovers   *Solomon*: Yeats   *A cockerel*: possibly the Hermetic cock, the harbinger of the cycles, in the Tree of Life (see 'The Two Trees', p. 83). The cockerel thinks that eternity has returned: it has not; the lovers try again   *the Fall*: the Fall of Man brought about when Adam and Eve ate the forbidden fruit (the 'brigand apple') of the Tree of Knowledge in the Garden of Eden   *Choice and Chance*: Yeats's long note on Chance and Choice in *Four Plays for Dancers* (1921) is quoted in *NC*, 218–20

p. 285, 'An Image from a Past Life'   *dc*: Sept. 1919   *fp*: *TN*(L), 6 Nov. 1920   *He*: represents Yeats, *She* Mrs Yeats. F. F. Farag, *YCE*, 43, sees the poem's inspiration in Rabindranath Tagore's 'In the Dusky Path of a Dream', where the lover seeks 'the love who was mine in a former life'   *that scream*: associated with moments of revelation, as when Juno's peacock screams in 'Meditations in Time of Civil War', p. 308, and when the 'miraculous strange bird' of 'Her Triumph' shrieks, p. 386   *Image*: Yeats's note in *MRD* (see *NC*, 187–9) concluded that no mind's contents are necessarily shut off from another, 'and in moments of excitement images pass from one mind to another with extraordinary ease, perhaps most easily from that portion of the mind which for the time being is out of consciousness'   *its lesson*: that happiness is not unalloyed. Other women have been loved by the poet   *A sweetheart*: with the exception of the word 'arrogance', this stanza employs language used in Yeats's early love poetry   *the hovering thing*: Yeats's note in *MRD* (see *NC*, 188–9) describes 'Over Shadowers', forms the lover has loved in some past earthly life and sees in sleep: 'Souls that are once linked by emotion never cease till the last drop of that emotion is exhausted – call it desire, hate, or what you will – to affect one another, remaining always as it were on contact.'

p. 286, 'Under Saturn'   *dc*: Nov. 1919 (appended to text *P* (1949))   *fp*: *DL*, Nov. 1920   *saturnine*: gloomy, taciturn, born under the influence of the planet Saturn   *lost love*: for Maud Gonne   *the wisdom that you brought*: probably a reference to Mrs Yeats's share in *AV*. She began automatic writing shortly after their marriage; the scripts were a basis for *AV*. See 'Introduction' to *AV*(B) 8–25, *YANB*, ch. 13, and *MYAV*, X–XIV   *The comfort*: Yeats enjoyed living in a house (now demolished) on Broad Street, Oxford, after his marriage. The Yeatses bought 82 Merrion Square, Dublin, in Feb. 1922   *an old cross Pollexfen*: William Pollexfen, Yeats's maternal grandfather. See notes on '[Introductory Rhymes]', p. 539   *a Middleton*: one of Yeats's maternal grandmother's relatives, living in Sligo – possibly, Mrs Yeats suggested, William Middleton (1806–62), Yeats's great-uncle (probably not the William Middleton (1770–1832) of '[Introductory Rhymes]')   *a red-haired Yeats*: the Rev. William Butler Yeats (1806–62), Rector of Tullylish, Co. Down, son of the Rev. John Yeats, rector of Drumcliffe, Co. Sligo (see notes on '[Introductory Rhymes]', p. 539

p. 287, 'Easter 1916'   *dc*: 25 Sept. 1916 (appended to text *P* (1949))   *fp*: *Easter, 1916* (1916), privately printed; later in *NS*, 23 Oct. 1920   This poem records Yeats's reactions, when staying with Maud Gonne MacBride at her house in Normandy, to the Easter Rising of 1916. The centre of Dublin was occupied on 24 April by about 700 republicans (members of the Irish Volunteers and the Irish Citizen Army), who held out until 29 April against British troops. After a series of courts martial from 3–12 May, fifteen of the leaders were executed. From l. 17 onwards Yeats names some of them   *them*: the revolutionaries   *Eighteenth-century houses*: Dublin has many houses built of granite from the hills, others of limestone from the plains   *the club*: probably the Arts Club, founded in Dublin in 1907   *That woman's days*: Countess Constance Markievicz, born a Gore-Booth of Lissadell, Co. Sligo; cf. 'In Memory of Eva Gore-Booth and Con Markiewicz', p. 347. When they were both art students in Paris she married Casimir Dunin-Markievicz, a Polish land-owner with estates in the Ukraine; she became an Irish nationalist in 1908, founded the Fianna, a nationalist boys' organisation, joined the Citizen Army, was a staff officer in the Rising and was sentenced to death. Her sentence commuted to life imprisonment, she was released in an amnesty in 1917. Imprisoned again in 1918, she was the first woman elected to the

Westminster Parliament; she did not take her seat, but became Shadow Minister of Labour in Dail Eireann in 1919. She served gaol sentences in 1919, 1920 and 1923, having opposed the Treaty. She joined the Fianna Fail party and was elected to the Dail in 1927   *rode to harriers*: cf. 'On a Political Prisoner', p. 290   *This man*: Patrick Pearse (1879–1916), founder of St Enda's School, a member of the Irish Bar, an orator, who published poetry and prose in Irish and English. A leader of the IRB section in the Irish Volunteers, he was in charge of the General Post Office in the Easter Rising in 1916. See notes on 'The Rose Tree' below   *This other*: Thomas MacDonagh (1878–1916), poet, dramatist and critic who taught at University College, Dublin   *This other man*: Major John MacBride (1865–1916), who had fought against England in the Boer War; he married Maud Gonne in 1903   *most bitter wrong*: a reference to his behaviour after his marriage   *near my heart*: Maud Gonne and her daughter Iseult   *a stone*: a symbol for those who devote themselves to some cause without thought of life or love. The 'stone of the heart' (l. 58) refers to Maud Gonne's devoting herself to revolutionary ideals   *needless death*: there was initially little welcome for the Rising in Ireland, but the execution of the leaders altered this   *may keep faith*: the Bill creating Home Rule for Ireland had been passed by Westminster in 1913, but suspended on the outbreak of war in 1914; it was promised that it would be introduced after the war was over   *their dream*: of an independent Ireland   *Connolly*: James Connolly (1870–1916), trade union organiser who founded the *Irish Worker*, organised the Citizen Army, and was Commandant General of the insurgent forces (the Citizen Army and Irish Volunteers combined as the Irish Republican Army) in Dublin in the 1916 Rising

p. 289, 'Sixteen Dead Men'   *dc*: 17 Dec. 1916/17   *fp*: DL, Nov. 1920   *Title*: Yeats is presumably adding Sir Roger Casement (1864–1916) to the fifteen leaders shot by firing squad in 1916. Casement, a member of the British Consular Service (1875–1912), joined the Sinn Fein movement in 1914, went to Germany, returned in a German U-boat to Ireland and was arrested in the south-west. Tried for High Treason in London, he was hanged on 3 Aug. 1916; his remains were returned to Ireland on 23 Feb. 1965   *stir the boiling pot*: Yeats explains the effect of the executions, of making those executed into martyrs   *Pearse . . . MacDonogh's*: see notes on 'Easter 1916', p. 569   *Lord Edward and Wolfe Tone*: Lord Edward Fitzgerald (1763–98) and Wolfe Tone (1763–98), Irish leaders of the 1798 Revolution; see notes on 'September 1913', p. 543

p. 290, 'The Rose Tree'   *dc*: 7 April 1917   *fp*: DL, Nov. 1920   *Pearse to Connolly*: see notes on 'Easter 1916', p. 569   *our Rose Tree*: Ireland   *our own red blood*: Pearse believed that 'the blood of the sons of Ireland' was needed for Ireland's redemption. This poem may have been influenced by a ballad, 'Ireland's Liberty Tree' (deriving from the '*arbres de la liberté*' planted in France in 1790 to celebrate Revolution and Liberty), the tree 'watered with tears of the brave' which also celebrates the martyr cult: 'The pure blood of Ireland's Martyrs/gave it strength and it [the tree] shall never die'. Another possible source is Aubrey De Vere's poem, 'The Little Black Rose shall be red at last'

p. 290, 'On a Political Prisoner'   *dc*: between 10 and 29 Jan. 1919   *fp*: *DL*, Nov. 1920   *She*: Countess Markievicz, then imprisoned for the second time in Holloway Gaol (May 1918–March 1919) for being a Sinn Fein leader and having made 'seditious speeches'. See notes on 'Easter 1916', p. 569   *under Ben Bulben*: Ben Bulben, mountain north of Sligo where Conall Gulban, a son of Nial of the Nine Hostages, was fostered (see Glossary). Yeats admired Constance Gore-Booth's arrogance when 'young and beautiful/She rode to harriers' (see 'Easter 1916', p. 287); he told an anecdote of a hunt which reinforced this (BBC, April 1932). She was renowned as a dashing horsewoman   *lonely wildness*: Constance and her sister Eva grew up in Lissadell House, Co. Sligo, but were not satisfied with the conventional life of a 'big house'

p. 291, 'The Leaders of the Crowd'   *dc*: 1918   *fp*: *MRD*   to *keep their certainty*: Yeats wrote that the political movement with which Maud Gonne was associated, finding it hard to build up any fine lasting thing, 'became content to attack little persons and little things' (*E & I*, 249–50). He thought all movements were held together more by what they hate than by what they love   *gutter . . . Helicon*: this line contrasts gutter-press journalism and poetry. Yeats particularly disliked *Sinn Fein*, edited by Arthur Griffith; see notes on 'On those that hated "The Playboy of the Western World", 1907', p. 545   *Helicon*: see notes on 'The Fascination of What's Difficult', p. 535   *student's lamp . . . no solitude*: the lamp is the image in 'Ego Dominus Tuus', p. 264, and 'The Phases of the Moon', p. 267, of 'mysterious wisdom won by toil'. See also 'Meditations in Time of Civil War', II, with the 'candle and written page', p. 309; 'that lamp' may link the Miltonic, Shelleyan and Yeatsian images of solitary study with the 'everlasting taper' in 'The Mountain Tomb', p. 223. The 'crowd' necessarily has none of the solitude essential for achieving wisdom

p. 292, 'Towards Break of Day'   *dc*: Jan. 1918   *fp*: *DL*, Nov. 1920   The poem records two dreams experienced by the poet and his wife on the same night when they were staying at the Powerscourt Arms Hotel, Enniskerry, Co. Wicklow, in Jan. 1918   *The woman that by me lay*: Mrs Yeats   *a waterfall*: possibly suggested by the waterfall in the grounds of Powerscourt, which the Yeatses went to see on this visit; it resembled one at Glen-Car, Co. Sligo, possibly 'The Stream against the Cliff' (Irish, *Strith-in-naghaidh-an-Aird*). See 'The Stolen Child', p. 53: 'Where the wandering water gushes/From the hills above Glen-

Car'   *the marvellous stag*: in 'The Tale of King Arthur', *The Works of Sir Thomas Malory*, III, v, the stag appears at the marriage feast of Arthur and Guinevere; it is pursued by a white bratchet and thirty couple of running hounds. Yeats alluded to the white stag that flits in and out of the tales of Arthur (*CT* (1902), 109) but here, according to Mrs Yeats, he had in mind the passage in Malory

p. 293, 'Demon and Beast'   *dc*: 23 Nov. 1918   *fp*: *DL*, Nov. 1920   *Title:* see *The Lausiac History* of Palladius, tr. W. K. Lowther Clarke (1918), 164: 'Intelligence . . . separated from the thought of God becomes either a demon or a brute beast'. The poem describes a momentary state of aimless joy   *perned in the gyre*: to pern is to move in a circular spinning movement. See Yeats's note, notes on 'Shepherd and Goatherd', p. 557. Gyre is used to describe a whirling spiral or circular motion:

> A line is the symbol of time and it expresses a movement . . . [it] symbolises the emotional subjective mind. . . . A plane cutting the line at right angles constitutes, in combination with the moving line, a space of three or more dimensions, and is the symbol of all that is objective, and so . . . of intellect as opposed to emotion. Line and plane are combined in a gyre, and as one tendency or the other must always be stronger, the gyre is always expanding or contracting. For simplicity of representation the gyre is drawn as a cone. Sometimes this cone represents the individual soul . . . sometimes general life . . . understanding that neither the soul of man nor the soul of nature can be suppressed without conflict . . . we substitute for this cone two cones. [*AV* (A), 129]

There are thus four gyres, two expanding, two narrowing, the apex of each cone coinciding with the base of the other:

> When, however, a narrowing and widening gyre reach their limit, the one the utmost contraction the other the utmost expansion, they change places, point to circle, circle to point, for this system conceives the world as catastrophic, and continue as before, one always narrowing, one always expanding, and yet bound for ever to one another. [*AV* (1925), 131]

In a note included in *MRD*, Yeats wrote

> The figure while the soul is in the body, or suffering from the consequences of that life, is frequently drawn as a double cone, the narrow end of each cone being in the centre of the broad end of the other.

It had its origin from a straight line which represents, now time, now emotion, now subjective life, and a plane at right angles to this line which represents, now space, now intellect, now objective life; while it is marked out by two gyres which represent the conflict, as it were, of plane and line, by two movements, which circle about a centre because a movement outward on the plane is checked by and in turn checks a movement onward upon the line; & the circling is always narrowing or spreading, because one movement or other is always the stronger. In other words, the human soul is always moving outward into the objective world or inward into itself; & this movement is double because the human soul would not be conscious were it not suspended between contraries, the greater the contrast the more intense the consciousness. The man, in whom the movement inward is stronger than the movement outward, the man who sees all reflected within himself, the subjective man, reaches the narrow end of a gyre at death, for death is always, they contend, even when it seems the result of accident, preceded by an intensification of the subjective life; and has a moment of revelation immediately after death, a revelation which they describe as his being carried into the presence of all his dead kindred, a moment whose objectivity is exactly equal to the subjectivity of death. The objective man on the other hand, whose gyre moves outward, receives at this moment the revelation, not of himself seen from within, for that is impossible to objective man, but of himself as if he were somebody else. This figure is true also of history, for the end of an age, which always receives the revelation of the character of the next age, is represented by the coming of one gyre to its place of greatest expansion and of the other to that of its greatest contraction. At the present moment the life gyre is sweeping outward, unlike that before the birth of Christ which was narrowing, and has almost reached its greatest expansion. The revelation which approaches will however take its character from the contrary movement of the interior gyre. All our scientific, democratic, fact-accumulating, heterogeneous civilization belongs to the outward gyre and prepares not the continuance of itself but the revelation as in a lightning flash, though in a flash that will not strike only in one place, and will for a time be constantly repeated, of the civilisation that must slowly take its place. This is too simple a statement, for much detail is possible.

Their symbolic meaning can be seen best in 'The Second Coming', p. 294. In 'Demon and Beast' the gyre can be explained in *AV*'s terminology as being between hatred and desire, but in the third stanza it seems to be used merely to describe the movement of the seagull. For a fuller discussion see *TCA*, 103–14   *Luke Wadding*: an Irish Franciscan (1588–1657), president of the Irish College at Salamanca; the portrait by the Spanish painter Jose Ribera (1588–1652) is in the National Gallery of Ireland, Merrion Square, Dublin   *Ormondes*: portraits of titled members of the Butler family, in the National Gallery. Yeats was proud of his family's link with the Butler family; see notes on '[Introductory Rhymes]', p. 539   *Strafford*: Sir Thomas Wentworth, 1st Earl of Strafford (1593–1641), Lord Deputy of Ireland (1632–40) and Lord Lieutenant (1640–1), whose portrait hangs in the National Gallery   *the little lake*: in St Stephen's Green, Dublin. When he wrote the poem Yeats and his wife were living in 73 St Stephen's Green, Maud Gonne MacBride's house   *absurd . . . bird*: one of the many ducks on the lake   *barren*

Thebaid: in upper Egypt, where Egyptian monasticism flourished; its barren nature was emphasised in two books on early Christian monasticism by Rev. J. O. Hannay, which Yeats had read   *Mareotic sea*: one of the five regions known for monasticism. Shelley's witch of Atlas glided down the Nile 'By Moeris and the Mareotid lakes'   *exultant Anthony*: St Anthony of Coma (AD ?240–*c*. 345), whose enthusiasm Hannay described in *The Spirit and Origin of Christian Monasticism* (1903), 101. Other sources were Flaubert's *La Tentation de St Antoine* (1874) and *The Lausiac History* of Palladius   *twice a thousand more*: monasticism spread rapidly under St Anthony's influence   *the Caesars . . . thrones*: the Caesars, emperors of Rome; the name was taken from Caius Julius Caesar (?102–44 BC). Yeats had read in the German historian Theodor Mommsen (1817–1903) the theory that from Julius Caesar onwards the Roman State became a dead thing, a mere mechanism. Cf. 'The hand and lash that beat down frigid Rome' in 'Whence had they come?', p. 406.

p. 294, 'The Second Coming'   *dc*: Jan. 1919   *fp*: DL, Nov. 1920   This poem deals with Christ's prediction of the Second Coming in Matthew 24 and St John's description of the Beast of the Apocalypse in Revelation. Yeats is, however, predicting the arrival of a rough beast in Bethlehem (see l. 22), traditionally associated with the gentle innocence of infancy   *the widening gyre*: see notes on 'Demon and Beast', p. 572   *The falcon . . . the falconer*: the falcon presumably represents modern civilisation, out of touch with Christ, the falconer   *Mere anarchy*: Yeats was disturbed by the effects of the Russian Revolution, regarding Marxism as 'the spear-head of materialism and leading to inevitable murder'. He was also worried by a breakdown in respect for the law in Ireland after the Civil War   *some revelation*: Christ's birth had been the revelation of the Christian era   *the Second Coming*: the new era seemed likely to be one of irrational force. See notes on 'The Double Vision of Michael Robartes', p. 567   *Spiritus Mundi*: in a note of 1921 Yeats glossed this as 'a general storehouse of images which have ceased to be a property of any personality or spirit'   *A shape with lion body*: in a note to *The Resurrection*, Yeats wrote of imagining 'a brazen winged beast' that he associated with 'laughing ecstatic destruction'

p. 295, 'A Prayer for my Daughter'   *dc*: between Feb. and June 1919 (June 1919 appended to text P (1949))   *fp*: Poetry, Nov. 1919 and *The Irish Statesman*, 8 Nov. 1919   *Title*: Yeats's daughter, Anne Butler Yeats, was born in Dublin on 26 Feb. 1919; this poem was begun shortly after and finished at Yeats's tower, Thoor Ballylee, in June 1919   *Gregory's wood*: Yeats's tower was near Lady Gregory's estate, Coole Park   *Atlantic*: to the west of the tower   *Helen*: Helen of Troy, associated earlier with Maud Gonne. See notes on 'The Rose of the World', p. 498   *great Queen*: Aphrodite, goddess of love; born of the sea (Greek, *aphros,* foam), hence fatherless   *bandy-leggèd smith*: Aphrodite's husband was Hephaestus, the lame god of fire   *Horn of Plenty*: Zeus, chief of the Greek gods, was suckled by the goat, Amalthea. Her horns flowed with nectar and ambrosia and she gave one which broke off to him. The cornucopia is an image of plenty   *played the fool . . . beauty's very self*: probably a reference to Yeats's love for Maud Gonne   *a poor man . . . glad kindness*: the poor man is Yeats; the glad kindness a reference to his marriage   *Prosper but little*: Maud Gonne and Constance Markiewicz had been imprisoned in Holloway Gaol in May 1918. See notes on 'Easter 1916', p. 569   *the loveliest woman born*: Maud Gonne, hinted at in the fourth stanza; the parallels are implicit between Helen's, Aphrodite's and Maud's choice of partners

p. 297, 'A Meditation in Time of War'   *dc*: 9 Nov. 1914   *fp*: DL, Nov. 1920, with the title 'A Mediation [probably a misprint] in Time of War'; *TN*(L), 13 Nov. 1920   *artery*: cf. Blake's poem 'Time' with its 'pulsation of the artery'. Cf. also this prose passage:

> When all sequence comes to an end, time comes to an end, and the soul puts on the rhythmic or spiritual body or luminous body and contemplates all the events of its memory and every possible impulse in an eternal possession of itself in one single moment. That condition is alone animate, all the rest is fantasy, and from thence come all the passions, and, some have held, the very heat of the body. [*M*, 357]

p. 298, 'To be Carved on a Stone at Thoor Ballylee'   *dc*: 1918 (probably between May and July)   *fp*: MRD   *Gort*: the tower was about 4 miles from the village of Gort, Co. Galway (see Glossary)   *George*: Bertha Georgie Hyde Lees (1894–1968), whom Yeats married on 20 October 1917   *all is ruin*: the tower fell into disrepair after Yeats's death but has been restored

THE TOWER

The poems in this volume were previously published in *SPF*, *CATM* and *OB*. Poems included in these volumes were brought together in *The Tower* (1928). 'Fragments' was added to *The Tower* in *CP*, a volume in which the order of the poems was altered and 'The Hero, the Girl, and the Fool' replaced by 'The Fool by the Roadside' (see Appendix Six, note 19)

p. 301, 'Sailing to Byzantium'   *dc*: autumn 1926 (probably Sept.; two TSS are dated 26 Sept. (1927 appended to text after *TSR* (1927). There are seventeen other MS sheets)   *fp*: OB   Yeats said that he was trying to write about the state of his soul:

> . . . for it is right for an old man to make his soul, and some of my thoughts upon that subject I have put into a poem called 'Sailing to Byzantium'. When Irishmen

were illuminating the Book of Kells [in the 8th century] and making the jewelled croziers in the National Museum, Byzantium was the centre of European civilisation and the source of its spiritual philosophy, so I symbolise the search for the spiritual life by a journey to that city. [BBC, 8 Sept. 1921]

That . . . country: Ireland   *salmon-falls, the mackerel-crowded seas:* Yeats took a delight in salmon going upstream to spawn, particularly at the Salmon Leap at Leixlip, Co. Dublin, and at the salmon-weir at Galway. The Irish hero Cuchulain was famous for his 'salmon-leap'. Shoals of mackerel 'come in', in great profusion, to Irish shores. Both images reinforce the vigorous 'sensual music' of l. 7   *Byzantium:* the Roman emperor Constantine (AD ?287–337), a convert to Christianity in AD 312, chose Byzantium as his capital, inaugurating it under the name Constantinople in 330. Yeats wrote of it thus in *A V*(A), 190–2, and *A V*(B), 279–81:

> I think if I could be given a month of Antiquity and leave to spend it where I chose, I would spend it in Byzantium, a little before Justinian opened St. Sophia and closed the Academy of Plato. I think I could find in some little wine-shop some philosophical worker in mosaic who could answer all my questions, the supernatural descending nearer to him than to Plotinus even, for the pride of his delicate skill would make what was an instrument of power to princes and clerics, a murderous madness in the mob, show as a lovely flexible presence like that of a perfect human body.
>
> I think that in early Byzantium, maybe never before or since in recorded history, religious, aesthetic and practical life were one, that architect and artificers – though not, it may be, poets, for language had been the instrument of controversy and must have grown abstract – spoke to the multitude and the few alike. The painter, the mosaic worker, the worker in gold and silver, the illuminator of sacred books, were almost impersonal, almost perhaps without the consciousness of individual design, absorbed in their subject-matter and that the vision of a whole people. They could copy out of old gospel books those pictures that seemed as sacred as the text, and yet weave all into a vast design, the work of many that seemed the work of one, that made building, picture, pattern, metalwork of rail and lamp, seem but a single image; and this vision, this proclamation of their invisible master, had the Greek nobility, Satan always the still half-divine Serpent, never the horned scarecrow of the didactic Middle Ages.
>
> The ascetic, called in Alexandria 'God's Athlete', has taken the place of those Greek athletes whose statues have been melted or broken up or stand deserted in the midst of cornfields, but all about him is an incredible splendour like that which we see pass under our closed eyelids as we lie between sleep and waking, no representation of a living world but the dream of a somnambulist. Even the drilled pupil of the eye, when the drill is in the hand of some Byzantine worker in ivory, undergoes a somnambulistic change, for its deep shadow among the faint lines of the tablet, its mechanical circle, where all else is rhythmical and flowing, give to Saint or Angel a look of some great bird staring at a miracle. Could any visionary of those days, passing through the Church named with so untheological a grace 'The Holy Wisdom', can even a visionary of today wandering among the mosaics at Ravenna or in Sicily, fail to recognise some one image seen under his closed eyelids? To me it seems that He, who among the first Christian communities was little but a ghostly exorcist, had in His assent to a full Divinity

made possible this sinking-in upon a supernatural splendour, these walls with their little glimmering cubes of blue and green and gold.

sages . . . gold mosaic: the martyrs in the frieze at S. Apollinare Nuova, Ravenna, which Yeats saw in 1907. His memories of that visit may have been aroused by a visit he made to Sicily in 1924 where he saw Byzantine mosaics   *perne in a gyre*: see notes on 'Shepherd and Goatherd', p. 557, and 'Demon and Beast', p. 572   *such a form*: Yeats's note states that he had read 'somewhere' that in the Emperor's palace at Byzantium was 'a tree made of gold and silver, and artificial birds that sang'. He probably remembered being read Hans Andersen's tale 'The Emperor's Nightingale' as a child, possibly from the edition which had for cover an illustration of the Emperor and his court listening to the artificial bird. Other sources, however, have been suggested; see *NC*, 257

p. 302, 'The Tower'   *dc*: 1925 (the MS of the last section is dated 7 Oct. 1925; 1924 appended to *OB*; 1926 in *P* (1949))   *fp*: *TNR*, 29 June 1927; *TC*, June 1927   Yeats's general note, dated 1928, reads:

> The persons mentioned are associated by legend, story and tradition with the neighbourhood of Thoor Ballylee or Ballylee Castle, where the poem was written. Mrs. French lived at Peterswell in the eighteenth century and was related to Sir Jonah Barrington, who described the incident of the ears and the trouble that came of it. The peasant beauty and the blind poet are Mary Hynes and Raftery, and the incident of the man drowned in Cloone Bog is recorded in my *Celtic Twilight*. Hanrahan's pursuit of the phantom hare and hounds is from my *Stories of Red Hanrahan*. The ghosts have been seen at their game of dice in what is now my bedroom, and the old bankrupt man lived about a hundred years ago. According to one legend he could only leave the Castle upon a Sunday because of his creditors, and according to another he hid in the secret passage.

I   *Decrepit age*: he was sixty; he had been seriously ill in the autumn of 1924   *Ben Bulben's back*: mountain north of Sligo (see Glossary)   *the Muse*: presumably of poetry; one of the nine muses in Greek mythology   *Plato and Plotinus*: Yeats's note (*CP*, 533) read:

> When I wrote the lines about Plato and Plotinus I forgot that it is something in our own eyes that makes us see them as all transcendence. Has not Plotinus written: 'Let every soul recall, then, at the outset the truth that soul is that author of all living things, that it has breathed the life into them all, whatever is nourished by earth and sea, all the creatures of the air, the divine stars in the sky; it is the maker of the sun; itself formed and ordered this vast heaven and conducts all that rhythmic motion – and it is a principle distinct from all these to which it gives law and movement and life, and it must of necessity be more honourable than they, for they gather or dissolve as soul brings them life or abandons them, but soul, since it never can abandon itself, is of eternal being?'

Plato (*c*. 429–347 BC), the Athenian philosopher (see notes on 'Mad as the Mist and Snow', p. 608), developed the theory of ideas or forms: these are the true objects of knowledge, timeless, unchanging, universal examples of transient finite particulars or objects of the impressions of sense. Unphilosophical man at the mercy of his sense impressions is like a prisoner in a cave who mistakes shadows on the wall for reality. Plotinus (?205–70), one of the first Neoplatonic philosophers, probably born in Egypt; he settled in Rome in 244, and died at Minturnae. His pupil Porphyry arranged his fifty-four books in six groups of nine books or *Enneads*

II   *the battlements*: of Yeats's tower   *Mrs. French*: see Sir Jonah Barrington's (1760–1834) *Personal Sketches of his own Time* (2 vols, 1827, 1832)   *when I was young A peasant girl*: in an essay of 1900 Yeats wrote of Mary Hynes, whose memory was 'still a wonder by turf fires' (*M*, 22–30); she died sixty years before he wrote the essay (she was found dead in Mooneen, the little bog, near Esserkelly, Co. Galway)   *a song*: the Irish folk poet and travelling fiddler Antony Raftery (*c.* 1784–1835), who spent most of his life in the Gort and Loughrea districts of Galway; his poems were edited by Douglas Hyde in 1903. Yeats gives Lady Gregory's translation of the poem Raftery wrote on Mary Hynes in *M*, 24–5 (see *NC*, 262–3)   *that rocky place*: it is a limestone area   *certain men . . . bog of Cloone*: Yeats reported the old weaver's memories in his essay:

> There was a lot of men up beyond Kilbecanty one night sitting together drinking, and talking of her, and one of them got up and set out to go to Ballylee and see her; but Cloone Bog was open then, and when he came to it he fell into the water, and they found him dead there in the morning.

Homer: the connection is a double one. Raftery was blind; so was Homer. Each sang of a woman who was spoken of similarly by the old; Yeats wrote in *BS* of speaking to old people who remembered Mary Hynes: 'they spoke of her as the old men upon the wall of Troy spoke of Helen, nor did man and woman differ in their praise' (*A*, 561)   *Helen*: Mary Hynes resembled her; and Helen is a symbol for Maud Gonne. This leads on to the poet himself in ll. 56ff. See notes on 'The Sorrow of Love', p. 501   *moon and sunlight*: cf. 'The Man who Dreamed of Faeryland', p. 79   *Hanrahan*: see notes on 'He reproves the Curlew', p. 514. Ll. 57–73 retell the story 'Red Hanrahan', with some omissions   *bawn*: usually a fortified enclosure   *a man . . . so harried*: this bankrupt owner of the tower lived about 100 years earlier. Yeats's note adds that 'According to one legend he could only leave the castle upon a Sunday because of his creditors, and according to another he hid in the secret passage' (*CP*, 532)   *for centuries*: Yeats's tower was a medieval building owned by the de Burgo family, mentioned in 1385 as Islandmore Castle, the property of Edward Ulrick de Burgo   *images . . . wooden dice*: 'The ghosts have been seen', Yeats commented, 'at their game of dice in what is now my bedroom'   *Great Memory*: this contained archetypal images, transmitted from generation to generation. See *M*, 343–66   *half-mounted*: the bankrupt owner of the

tower; the phrase implies his lack of social standing   *beauty's* . . .
celebrant: the poet Raftery   *the red man*: Hanrahan   *an ear*: that of
Dennis Bodkin, the 'insolent farmer' (l. 31), who lost both his ears in Sir
Jonah Barrington's account   *The man drowned*: the man of l. 48   *Old
lecher*: Hanrahan   *woman lost*: presumably Maud Gonne

III   *spat on . . . spat*: a private joke, referring to friends of Yeats, whom
he called 'Spit, spat, and spat on'   *The people of Burke and Grattan*:
Edmund Burke (1729–97), Irish author, politician, and orator who fought
for the freedom of the House of Commons from the control of George III;
for the emancipation of the American Colonies; of India from the mis-
government of the East India Company; of Irish trade, the Irish parliament
and Irish Catholics; and against the atheistical Jacobin excesses of the
French Revolution. Henry Grattan (1746–1820), Irish patriot, parliamen-
tarian and orator; a Protestant who fought for Catholic Emancipation, he
was unable to persuade the Irish parliament to share his own largeness of
vision. He carried an address demanding legislative independence for
Ireland (1782); the parliament known as 'Grattan's Parliament' sat during
one of Ireland's brief spells of prosperity. He opposed the Union in
1800   *fabulous horn*: see notes on 'A Prayer for my Daughter',
p. 574   *when the swan*: Yeats's note reads:

> In the passage about the Swan in Part III I have unconsciously echoed one of the
> loveliest lyrics of our time – Mr Sturge Moore's 'Dying Swan'. I often recited it
> during an American lecturing tour, which explains the theft.

THE DYING SWAN

> O silver-throated Swan
> Struck, struck! A golden dart
> Clean through thy breast has gone
> Home to thy heart.
> Thrill, thrill, O silver throat!
> O silver trumpet, pour
> Love for defiance back
> On him who smote!
> And brim, brim o'er
> With love; and ruby-dye thy track
> Down thy last living reach
> Of river, sail the golden light –
> Enter the sun's heart – even teach,
> O wondrous-gifted Pain, teach thou
> The god to love, let him learn how.

Plotinus' thought . . . Plato's teeth: Yeats's note of 1928 reads:

> When I wrote the lines about Plato and Plotinus I forgot that it is something in our
> own eyes that makes us see them as all transcendence. Has not Plotinus written:
> 'Let every soul recall, then, at the outset the truth that soul is the author of all
> living things, that it has breathed the life into them all, whatever is nourished by

earth and sea, all the creatures of the air, the divine stars in the sky; it is the maker of the sun; itself formed and ordered this vast heaven and conducts all that rhythmic motion – and it is a principle distinct from all these to which it gives law and movement and life, and it must of necessity be more honourable than they, for they gather or dissolve as soul brings them life or abandons them, but soul, since it never can abandon itself, is of eternal being'?

learned Italian things: such as the writings of Dante and Castiglione, the work of the Italian painters and sculptors he had seen on his visits to Italy. Cf. 'To a Wealthy Man . . .', p. 208, and 'The People', p. 254, and notes on 'The People', p. 560   *stones of Greece*: particularly the sculptures in the British Museum   *loophole*: in the tower   *make my soul*: expression in common use in Ireland, to prepare for death

p. 308, 'Meditations in Time of Civil War'   *dc*: the first poem was written in England in 1921, the others mainly at Thoor Ballylee during the Irish Civil War of 1922–3 (1923 appended to text)   *fp*: DL, Jan. 1923; LM, Jan. 1923   The 'civil war' is the Irish Civil War, 1922–3, between the newly established Irish Free State Government and those Republicans who rejected the Anglo-Irish Treaty, signed in London on 6 Dec. 1921, ratified by the Irish parliament on 7 Jan. 1922
I   *The abounding . . . jet*: a symbol used by Yeats for delight in living   *gardens . . . the peacock strays*: peacocks, symbols of immortality, were sacred to Juno and usually accompanied her; here Yeats remembers Lady Ottoline Morrell's house and gardens at Garsington, near Oxford   *Juno*: Queen of the Gods in Roman mythology
II   This poem describes Yeats's tower, Thoor Ballylee, Co. Galway   *symbolic rose*: see notes on 'To the Rose upon the Rood of Time', p. 496   *chamber arched with stone*: Yeats's bedroom on the first floor of the castle, also used as a study   *Il Penseroso's Platonist*: see notes on 'The Phases of the Moon', p. 565   *Benighted travellers*: possibly a memory of Samuel Palmer's illustration to Milton's poem, and of Shelley's *Prince Athanase*. See notes on 'The Phases of the Moon', p. 565   *My bodily heirs*: Anne Butler Yeats, born 26 Feb. 1919, and Michael Butler Yeats, born 22 Aug. 1921
III   *Sato's gift*: Junzo Sato, then Japanese Consul at Portland, Oregon, met Yeats there in 1920. He had read Yeats's poetry in Japan and heard his lecture in Portland:

He had something in his hand wrapped up in embroidered silk. He said it was a present for me. He untied the silk cord that bound it and brought out a sword which had been for 500 years in his family. It had been made 550 years ago and he showed me the maker's name upon the hilt. I was greatly embarrassed at the thought of such a gift and went to fetch George [Mrs Yeats], thinking that we might find some way of refusing it. When she came I said 'But surely this ought always to remain in your family?' He answered 'My family have many swords.' But later he brought back my embarrassment by speaking of having given me 'his sword'. I had to accept it but I have written him a letter saying that I 'put him under a vow' to write and tell me when his first child is born – he is not yet married – that I may leave the sword back to his family in my will. [*L* (W), 662]

Chaucer . . . forged: Geoffrey Chaucer (?1340/5–1400), the poet, *had* drawn breath if the sword was made 500 years before, but the figure is a round one   *Juno's peacock*: see note above on l. 25, p. 580. In *AV* a peacock's scream symbolises the end of a civilisation. See *AV*(B), 268

IV   *fathers*: probably Yeats's father, grandfather and great-grand-father, all educated at Trinity College, Dublin, which gave Yeats an honorary degree in 1922   *a woman and a man*: his children, Anne and Michael   *Primum Mobile*: in the Ptolemaic system, the outermost sphere, supposed to revolve around the earth from east to west in twenty-four hours, carrying with it the contained spheres of fixed stars and planets – a prime source of motion   *an old neighbour's friendship*: that of Lady Gregory, Yeats's tower being near Coole Park   *a girl's love*: that of Mrs Yeats

V   *Irregular*: a member of the Irish Republican Army, which was opposed to the signing of the Treaty. Yeats's note read:

> These poems were written at Thoor Ballylee in 1922, during the civil war. Before they were finished the Republicans blew up our 'ancient bridge' one midnight. They forbade us to leave the house, but were otherwise polite, even saying at last 'Goodnight, thank you', as though we had given them the bridge.

Falstaffian: from Sir John Falstaff, the comic fat knight in several of Shakespeare's plays   *Lieutenant . . . Half dressed*: 'Free Staters', members of the new national army loyal to the Provisional Government; their green uniforms had not yet been issued

VI   *The stare's nest . . . window*: Yeats's note in BS reads

> I was in my Galway house during the first months of civil war, the railway bridges blown up and the roads blocked with stones and trees. For the first week there were no newspapers, no reliable news, we did not know who had won nor who had lost, and even after newspapers came, one never knew what was happening on the other side of the hill or of the line of trees. Ford cars passed the house from time to time with coffins standing upon end between the seats, and sometimes at night we heard an explosion, and once by day saw the smoke made by the burning of a great neighbouring house. Men must have lived so through many tumultuous centuries. One felt an overmastering desire not to grow unhappy or embittered, not to lose all sense of the beauty of nature. A stare (our West of Ireland name for a starling) had built in a hole beside my window and I made these verses out of the feeling of the moment . . . [quotes from 'The bees build in the crevices' to 'Yet no clear fact to be discerned:/Come build in the empty house of the stare.'] . . . That is only the beginning but it runs on in the same mood. Presently a strange thing happened. I began to smell honey in places where honey could not be, at the end of a stone passage or at some windy turn of the road, and it came always with certain thoughts. When I got back to Dublin I was with angry people who argued over everything or were eager to know the exact facts: in the midst of the mood that makes realistic drama.

VII   *Jacques Molay*: Jacques de Molay (1244–1314), Grand Master of the Templars, was arrested for heresy in 1307 and burned alive in Paris. Yeats's explanation of the line is:

> A cry for vengeance because of the murder of the Grand Master of the Templars seems to me fit symbol for those who labour from hatred, and so for sterility in various kinds. It is said to have been incorporated in the ritual of certain Masonic societies of the eighteenth century, and to have fed class-hatred.

Magical unicorns bear ladies: probably a memory of Gustave Moreau's (1825–99) painting, *Ladies and Unicorns*, a copy of which hung in Yeats's house in Dublin   *brazen hawks*: Yeats's note of 1928 explained that

> I suppose that I must have put hawks into the fourth stanza because I have a ring with a hawk and a butterfly upon it, to symbolise the straight road of logic, and so of mechanism, and the crooked road of intuition: 'For wisdom is a butterfly and not a gloomy bird of prey.'

p. 314, 'Nineteen Hundred and Nineteen'   *fp: DL*, Sept. 1921. In *LM*, Nov. 1921, the title was 'Thoughts upon the Present State of the World'; the title 'Nineteen Hundred and Nineteen' was first used in *The Tower* (1928). This poem arose out of 'some horrors at Gort', Co. Galway (see Glossary), during the period when guerrilla warfare waged by the Irish Republican Army was countered by the activities of the British forces, notably the Auxiliaries and the Black-and-Tans   *An ancient image*: the olive-wood statue of the goddess of Athene in the Erechtheum on the Acropolis in Athens   *Phidias' famous ivories*: Phidias (c. 490–423 BC), famous Athenian sculptor commissioned by Pericles to execute the main statues in Athens   *golden grasshoppers and bees*: Yeats's sources were probably the Greek historian Thucydides (c. 460–c. 400 BC), who describes golden grasshoppers used as brooches, and Walter Pater, who mentions the 'golden honeycomb' of Daedalus in *Greek Studies: a Series of Essays* (1895)   *We thought*: in a speech of 2 Aug. 1924 Yeats described a belief current in the 1880s that the world was growing better   *no cannon*: cf. Isaiah 2:4: 'And they shall beat their swords into plowshares and their spears into pruning hooks: nation shall not lift up sword against nation neither shall they learn war any more.' Cf. Micah 4:3 and Joel 3:19 (where the plowshares are beaten into swords)   *unless a little powder burned*: a reference to parades and reviews before the First World War. '"There will never be another war"', that was our opium dream' (speech, 2 Aug. 1924)   *dragon-ridden . . . scot-free*: a reference to atrocities committed in the pre-Treaty fighting in Ireland by Auxiliaries and Black-and-Tans in the Gort area of Co. Galway, when a Mrs Ellen Quinn was killed and the Loughnane brothers murdered and mutilated. See *Lady Gregory's Journals 1916–1930* (1946), 129–46   *That country round*: a linkage of the burning of 'big' houses in Ireland, unthinkable before the fighting between the IRA and the British Army, with the destruction of the artefacts in

Athens   *Loie Fuller's Chinese dancers*: Loie Fuller (1862–1928), an American dancer, had a troupe of Japanese dancers; she danced 'in a whirl of draperies manipulated on sticks' at the Folies Bergère in the 1890s   *Platonic Year*: discussed at length by Yeats in *AV*(B), 245–54; see also *AV*(A), 154–5, where he based his ideas on Pierre Duhem, *Le Système de Monde* (1913) and used Cicero's (see notes on 'Mad as the Mist and Snow', p. 608) definition of the Great Year when the whole of the constellations return to the positions from which they once began, 'thus after a long interval remaking the first map of the heavens'   *mythological poet*: probably Shelley, in *Prometheus Unbound* (1820), II, 5, 72–4: 'My soul is like an enchanted boat,/Which, like a sleeping swan, doth float/Upon the silver waves of thy sweet singing'   *Some Platonist affirms*: possibly Thomas Taylor (1758–1835), 'The Platonist', who in his translation of Porphyry's *De Antro Nympharum* (*The Cave of the Nymphs*) alluded to departed souls being ignorant of their earthly lives once they have crossed the River Styx, but added that they recognise material forms, and recollect their pristine condition on the earth'   *Some few . . . are garlanded*: Yeats's note, dated 21 May, read:

> The countrypeople see at times certain apparitions whom they name now 'fallen angels', now 'ancient inhabitants of the country', and describe as riding at whiles 'with flowers upon the heads of the horses'. I have assumed in the sixth poem that these horsemen, now that the times worsen, give way to worse. My last symbol, Robert Artisson, was an evil spirit much run after in Kilkenny at the start of the fourteenth century. Are not those who travel in the whirling dust also in the Platonic Year?

Herodias' daughters: see notes on 'The Hosting of the Sidhe', p. 506   *Robert Artisson . . . Lady Kyteler*: see note on *Some few* above. Yeats read the *History of the Diocese of Ossory* and MS accounts in the British Library of the trial of Dame Alice Kyteler for witchcraft. Of a good family, settled in the city of Kilkenny for many years, she had been married four times – she was supposed to have poisoned her first three husbands – and was charged with being the head of a band of sorcerers and with having an incubus, a demon named Robin, son of Art. The sacrifice to an evil spirit is said to have consisted of nine red cocks and nine peacocks' eyes

p. 318, 'The Wheel'   *dc*: 13 Sept. 1921   *fp*: SPF. The poem was written directly on to a sheet of notepaper in the Euston Hotel when Yeats was waiting to board the Irish mail train

p. 318, 'Youth and Age'   *dc*: 1924 (appended to text)   *fp*: CATM

p. 318, 'The New Faces'   *dc*: Dec. 1912   *fp*: SPF   *you*: Lady Gregory, whom Yeats first met in London in 1894; he visited Coole briefly in 1896 (he was then thirty-one, she forty-five), making his first long summer visit there in 1897   *catalpa tree*: in the garden at Coole   *tread Where*: Coole Park   *the new faces*: Robert Gregory and his wife. See notes on 'In Memory of Major Robert Gregory', p. 552

p. 319, 'A Prayer for my Son'   *dc*: Dec. 1921   *fp*: SPF   *my Michael*: Yeats's son, registered as Michael William Yeats but christened Michael Butler Yeats, was born in August 1921 at Castlebrook House, Thame, Oxfordshire   *Some there are*: in *AV* Yeats described how he was told that frustrators would attack his health and that of his children. See *AV*(B), 16   *You*: Jesus Christ   *Your enemy*: King Herod. See Matthew 2:19–23   *the Holy Writings*: see Matthew 2

p. 320, 'Two Songs from a Play'   *dc*: 1926 (except for the latter stanza of II, probably written in 1930–1)   *fp*: I and the first stanza of II, *The Adelphi*, June 1927. The fuller version of II first appeared in *Stories of Michael Robartes and His Friends* (1931). There are marked differences between the text of the play in *The Adelphi* and subsequent printings. See *VPl*, 900–36   These are two songs sung by the chorus of musicians in *The Resurrection* (1931), the theme of which is Christ's first appearance to the Apostles after the Crucifixion; the play puts Yeats's view that Christianity terminated a 2000-year period of history, ushering in the beginning of another era with radical violence. See Yeats's Introduction to the play in *W&B*, and *E*, 392–8, quoted *NC*, 285–9. This poem can be linked with 'The Second Coming', p. 294   *a staring virgin . . . play*: this stanza draws a parallel with the myth of Dionysus, born of a mortal, Persephone, and Zeus. He was torn to pieces by the Titans, but Athene, the 'staring virgin' goddess, snatched his heart from his body and brought it to Zeus, who swallowed it, killed the Titans, and begat Dionysus again upon another mortal, Semele   *Magnus Annus . . . but a play*: see notes on 'Nineteen Hundred and Nineteen', p. 582, and see *NC*, 232–3 and 238–42. The Muses sing of it as a play because they regarded the ritual death and rebirth of the god as recurring, part of the cycles of history. Yeats wrote that:

> Ptolemy thought the precession of the equinoxes moved at the rate of a degree every hundred years, and that somewhere about the time of Christ and Caesar the equinoctial sun had returned to its original place in the constellations, completing and recommencing the thirty-six thousand years, of three hundred and sixty incarnations of a year apiece, of Plato's man of Ur. Hitherto almost every philosopher had some different measure for the Greatest Year, but this Platonic Year, as it was called, soon displaced all others. [*E&I*, 395]

Another Troy: see Virgil's (70–19 BC) *Eclogue* IV (40 BC) which tells how Astraea, daughter of Jupiter and Themis, is the last to leave Earth at the end of the Golden Age and becomes the constellation Virgo, but will return again bringing back the Golden Age:

> Yet shall some few traces of olden sin lurk behind, to call men to essay the sea in

ships, to gird towns with walls, and to cleave the earth with furrows. A second Tiphys shall then arise, and a second Argo to carry chosen heroes; a second warfare, too, shall there be, and again shall a great Achilles be sent to Troy.

Virgil's prophecy was later taken by Christians to foretell the coming of the Virgin Mary (equated with Astraea in Virgo) and Christ, the Star of Bethlehem (equated with Spica, the main star in the constellation Virgo)   *Another Argo's painted prow . . . flashier bauble*: a further echo of Virgil. Jason with his Argonauts stole the Golden Fleece (the 'flashy bauble') from Colchis with the aid of Medea, daughter of the King of Colchis. The prow of the ship *Argo*, made of oak from Dodona (the seat of a famous oracle), could prophesy (see William Morris, *The Life and Death of Jason*, IV)   *Roman Empire . . . called*: because the Empire would be destroyed by Christianity. A parallel is drawn here between Astraea and Spica, Athene and Dionysus, Mary and Christ   *fabulous darkness*: Yeats wrote in *AV* of '"that fabulous formless darkness" as it seemed to a philosopher of the fourth century', a description of Christianity taken either from Proclus (a 4th-century philosopher whom Yeats read in Thomas Taylor's translation of 1816) or from Eunapius (*c*. AD 347–420), paraphrased by E. R. Dodds, *Select Passages Illustrating Neo Platonism* (1923), 8, as describing the church as 'a fabulous and formless darkness mastering the loveliness of the world'   *that room*: presumably (as in *The Resurrection*) where the Last Supper was eaten   *Galilean turbulence*: Christ's ministry was chiefly in Galilee, in Palestine   *Babylonian starlight*: this is referred to in *AV*(A), 181 and 213. Yeats thought the development of astrology (which he associated with science) in Babylon reduced man's status (see notes on 'The Dawn', p. 558)   *Platonic . . . Doric*: Plato's philosophy and the Doric style of architecture symbolise the classical world replaced by Christianity   *The painter's brush . . . dreams*: Yeats wrote that no school of painting outlasts its founders, 'every strike of the brush exhausts the impulse, Pre-Raphaelitism had some twenty years; Impressionism thirty perhaps' (*A*, 315)

p. 321, 'Fragments'   *dc*: probably 1931   *fp*: *DM*, Oct.–Dec. 1931, the first stanza as part of Yeats's commentary on *WWP*; the second was included in *CP* (1933)
I   *Locke*: John Locke (1632–1784), English empirical philosopher whose ideas Yeats, probably influenced by Blake, hated. He wrote that: 'Descartes, Locke and Newton took away the world and gave us its excrement instead' (*E*, 325)   *The Garden died . . . Out of his side*: a parody of the account of Eve's coming into the world in Genesis 2:18–23   *the spinning-jenny*: Yeats wrote that he could see in a sort of nightmare the 'primary qualities' torn from the side of Locke . . . some obscure person [James Hargreaves (*d*. 1778)] somewhere inventing the spinning jenny (*E*, 358–9). The spinning jenny symbolises the Industrial

Revolution, which Yeats saw as a consequence of Locke's 'mechanical' philosophy
11   This poem discusses the nature of poetic inspiration, returning to Yeats's youthful belief that the nearest one would get to an authoritative religion was what great poets had affirmed in their finest moments of inspiration. Cf. *WBY*, 47   *The crowns of Nineveh*: Nineveh, capital of the Assyrian Empire, at its height in the 8th and 7th centuries BC, was destroyed by the Medes and Babylonians in 612 BC. Yeats thought that a little lyric evokes an emotion

> and this emotion gathers others about it and melts into their being in the making of some great epic; and at last, needing always a less delicate body, or symbol, as it grows more powerful, it flows out, with all it has gathered, among the blind instincts of daily life, where it moves a power within powers, as one sees ring within ring in the stem of an old tree. This is maybe what Arthur O'Shaughnessy meant when he made his poets say they had built Nineveh with their sighing [*E&I*, 157–9]

O'Shaughnessy wrote of Nineveh in his *Ode*, in *Music and Moonlight*, 2:

> We in the ages lying
> In the buried part of the earth
> Built Nineveh itself with our sighing
> And Babel itself with our mirth;
> And o'erthrew them with prophesying
> To the old of the new world's worth . . .

Yeats misquoted the poem in *E*, 337, and wrote four lines on the theme in *W&B* (see *E*, 401)

p. 321, 'Wisdom'   *dc*: uncertain; probably 1926, about the same time as 'Two Songs from a Play', p. 320   *fp*: OB   *sawdust . . . carpenter*: probably founded upon Pre-Raphaelite paintings, such as *Christ in the House of His Parents* by John Everett Millais (1829–96)   *working-carpenter*: Joseph   *Chryselphantine*: a Greek term used for statues overlaid with gold and ivory   *His majestic Mother*: the Virgin Mary   *Babylon*: see notes on 'Two Songs from a Play', p. 584   *Noah's freshet*: the flood, described in Genesis 6:5–7, 19, as covering the whole world   *King Abundance . . . Innocence*: allegorical account of God's creation of Christ through the Virgin Mary

p. 322, 'Leda and the Swan'   *dc*: 18 Sept. 1923 (1923 appended to most texts after 1928)   *fp*: DL, June 1924   Yeats was asked for a poem for the *Irish Statesman* by the editor, his friend George Russell, and thought that

> after the individualist, demagogic movement, founded by Hobbes [Thomas Hobbes (1588–1679), English philosopher] and popularised by the Encyclopaed-

ists [the authors of the French *Encyclopedie* (1751–72), which helped to bring about the French Revolution in 1789] and the French Revolution, we have a soil so exhausted that it cannot grow that crop again for centuries. Then I thought 'Nothing is now possible but some movement, or birth from above, preceded by some violent annunciation'. My fancy began to play with Leda and the Swan for metaphor and I began this poem; but as I wrote, bird and lady took such possession of the scene that all politics went out of it, and my friend tells me that 'his conservative readers would misunderstand the poem'.

In the Greek myth Leda, wife of Tyndareus, King of Sparta, was seen bathing in the river Eurotas by Zeus, who coupled with her in the form of a swan; of this union Castor and Pollux were born, and Helen. (See notes on the 'Ledean body' of Maud Gonne, 'Among School Children', p. 588.) Yeats had a copy of Michelangelo's painting of *Leda and the Swan* in Venice, and there was a copy of a statuette of the union of Zeus and Leda at the Coopers' house, Markree Castle, Co. Sligo. Poems on the subject by Yeats's friend Oliver St John Gogarty (1878–1957) may also have influenced the poem, which echoes the language – the swan's 'rush' – of Spenser's *Faerie Queene*, III, xi, 32   *Agamemnon dead*: Agamemnon led the army of the Greeks to Troy to get back Helen, wife of his brother Menelaus (see notes on 'The Rose of the World', p. 498). On his return from the successful destruction of Troy ('the broken wall') Agamemnon was murdered by Clytaemnestra (a daughter of Leda by her husband Tyndareus) and her lover Aegisthus   *his knowledge*: Zeus's divine knowledge. Yeats saw the union of Leda and Zeus, the human and divine, as the annunciation of Greek civilisation

p. 323, 'On a Picture of a Black Centaur by Edmund Dulac'   *dc*: Sept. 1920   *fp*: SPF with the title 'Suggested by a Picture of a Black Centaur'   *Title*: Edmund Dulac (1882–1953), English artist, designer of masks and costumes for Yeats's *At the Hawk's Well* (1916), illustrated several of Yeats's books and set several of his poems to music. WS is dedicated to him. This poem was begun in relation to a picture by him but altered in relation to one by Cecil Salkeld. See WBY, 326–8   *mummy wheat*: Yeats implies hidden wisdom, ripened centuries after its sowing. This poem, like 'All Souls' Night', p. 340, was written when Yeats was full of the ideas of *A Vision*, which, he felt, were revelations of hidden truth he was bringing into the light out of the darkness where it had been concealed. He had been reading of discoveries in Egyptian tombs (cf. 'The Gyres', p. 411)   *seven Ephesian topers*: the seven sleepers of Ephesus, who reputedly slept for two centuries in a cave near Ephesus, from the persecution of the Christians by the Emperor Decius (*c.* AD 200–51) to the time of the Emperor Theodosius II (407–50), whose faith was confirmed when they were brought to him after their awakening   *Alexander's empire*: Alexander the Great (356–23 BC) pacified Ephesus and lived there in 334 BC   *Saturnian sleep*: the reign of Saturn, an ancient Italian god of

agriculture (later associated with the Greek god Cronos), was so beneficent
that it was regarded as the Golden Age

p. 323, 'Among School Children'   *dc*: 14 June 1926   *fp*: *DL*, Aug.
1927; *LM*, Aug. 1927, with the title 'Among Schoolchildren'   A prose
draft written about 14 March 1926 reads

> . . . Topic for poem – School children and the thought that live [life] will waste
> them perhaps that no possible life can fulfil our dreams or even their teacher's
> hope. Bring in the old thought that life prepares for what never happens.

the long schoolroom: St Otteran's School, Waterford, visited by Yeats in
February 1926, was run on principles suggested by Maria Montessori
(1870–1952), Italian doctor and educationist, author of *The Montessori
Method* (1912; rev. edn 1919), to create spontaneity and neatness in
children   *A kind old nun*: the Mistress of Schools, Rev. Mother
Philomena   *public man*: Yeats, Senator of the Irish Free State and Nobel
Prize winner   *Ledaean body*: Maud Gonne's (the link is that by which
Yeats symbolised her, through Leda's daughter Helen; see notes on 'Leda
and the Swan', p. 586, and 'The Rose of the World', p. 498). Leda suggests
the story of the eggs, cited in *A V*(A):

> . . . I imagine the annunciation that founded Greece as made to Leda, remember-
> ing that they showed in a Spartan temple, strung up to the roof as a holy relic, an
> unhatched egg of hers; and that from one of her eggs came Love and from the
> other War.

This leads to Plato's *Symposium*, 190, in which Aristophanes (*c*. 450–385
BC), the Greek playwright, argues that man was originally double in a
nearly spherical shape until Zeus divided him in two, like a cooked egg cut
in half. Love is an attempt to regain the unity   *Her present image*: Maud
Gonne's appearance at the time of the poem   *Quattrocento finger*: a 15th-
century Italian artist; Yeats probably had Leonardo da Vinci (1452–1519) in
mind; a version of the poem printed in *LM*, 1927, had 'Da Vinci
finger'   *Honey of generation*: Yeats's note states that he had taken the
phrase from Porphyry's essay on 'The Cave of the Nymphs' but that he
found 'no warrant in Porphyry for considering it the drug that destroys the
"recollection" of pre-natal freedom. He blamed a cup of oblivion given
in the zodiacal sign of cancer'. See notes on 'Nineteen Hundred and
Nineteen', p. 582. Porphyry's work is a commentary on the symbolism of
Homer's *Odyssey*, and the 'honey' was stored by bees in a cave (in Book 13)
via which Odysseus had to return to Ithaca   *Plato . . . scare a bird*: for
Plato, see notes on 'The Tower', p. 577. Yeats described this stanza as a
fragment of his last curse on old age:

> It means that even the greatest men are owls, scarecrows, by the time their fame
> has come. Aristotle, remember, was Alexander's tutor, hence the taws (form of
> birch) . . . Pythagoras made some measurements of the intervals between notes
> on a stretched string [*L*(W), 719]

paradigm was a word used by Thomas Taylor for an archetype, for the Platonic idea of essence   *king of kings*: Alexander the Great was tutored by the philosopher Aristotle, a pupil of Plato   *Pythagoras*: another Greek philosopher (*fl.* 6th century BC), to whom the doctrine of the transmigration of souls is attributed; he and his school at Crotona were known for their investigations into the relations of numbers

    p. 326, 'Colonus' Praise (From "Oedipus at Colonus")'   *dc*: 24 March (approx.) 1927   *fp*: *The Tower* (1928)   Yeats used Paul Masqueray's French translation when writing *Oedipus at Colonus*, which was produced at the Abbey Theatre, Dublin, on 12 Sept. 1927 and first appeared in *CPl*   *Colonus*: an Attic deme or district (Greek, Κολωνὸς Ἵππιος, Colonus of the Horses), the birthplace of Sophocles (495-406 BC), a hill a mile north of Athens, given its name because Poseidon, the god who gave the gift of horses to men, was worshipped there   *Semele's lad*: Dionysus, son of Zeus and Semele, a daughter of Cadmus. Hera, Zeus's consort, jealous of Semele's association with Zeus, disguised herself and advised Semele to test the divinity of her lover by asking him to come to her in his true shape. Semele did so and was killed by the fire of his thunderbolts. Zeus put her unborn child in his thigh; he was born at full time, went to Hades and brought up Semele, who became an Olympian goddess   *the gymnasts' garden*: the Lycaeum in Athens, situated on the banks of the River Cephisus, a grove sacred to the hero Admetus, the site of the Academy founded by Plato about 386 BC   *olive-tree*: Athene gave the olive as a gift to man; the original olive tree was on the Acropolis in Athens; the olive tree at the Academy was reputed to be the next tree to grow   *grey-eyed Athene*: Athene was the patron goddess of Athens, 'grey-eyed' one of her standard epithets; she had produced the olive tree in a struggle with Poseidon for ownership of the land in Attica   *Great Mother*: Demeter (or Ceres), a corn goddess mourning for her daughter Persephone (or Proserpine), carried to the Underworld by Pluto (or Hades), the brother of Zeus and Poseidon. Zeus granted Persephone permission to spend half the year with her mother, half with Pluto   *Cephisus*: river in Attica   *Poseidon . . . bit and oar*: god of horses and of the sea, Poseidon taught men to manage boats as well as horses

    p. 327, 'The Fool by the Roadside'   *dc*: uncertain   *fp*: *SPF*. It then formed ll. 18-29 of 'The Hero, the Girl, and the Fool'. It was first published as a separate poem in *AV*(A), then appeared in *CP* entitled 'The Fool by the Roadside'   *upon a spool*: imagery reminiscent of Plato's spindle in *The Republic* as well as Yeats's memories of the pern mill in Sligo. Cf. notes on 'Shepherd and Goatherd', p. 557, and on 'Demon and Beast', p. 572

    p. 327, 'Owen Aherne and his Dancers'   *dc*: first section 24 Oct. 1917, second section 27 Oct. 1917   *fp*: *DL*, June 1924, the first section entitled 'The Lover Speaks', the second 'The Heart Replies'   *Title*: Owen Aherne is an invented persona, described in Yeats's 'The Tables of the Law' (*M*, 293–4); see notes on 'The Phases of the Moon', p. 565. Here, however, he is used as a disguise for Yeats himself   *unsought . . . Norman upland*: the poem describes Yeats's feelings of love for Iseult Gonne in the summer of 1917. See notes on 'The Living Beauty', p. 555.   *run from that young child*: Iseult was born in 1895. Yeats tried to persuade her to marry him, finally giving her an ultimatum in Sept. 1917 that she must give him a definite answer within a week: if she did not marry him he had a friend who would, 'a girl strikingly beautiful in a barbaric manner'. Iseult met him at an ABC tearoom in London and refused him. On 20 Oct. he married Georgie Hyde-Lees. Warwick Gould has suggested an echo here of an old sheet ballad, 'Johnny, I hardly knew ye'. See Yeats, *A Book of Irish Verse* (1895), 238: 'When my poor heart you first beguiled/Why did you run from me and the child?'   *cage bird*: this image may have been suggested by a letter from Yeats's father: 'It is easy to cage the poet bird. Tennyson was caught and as for Browning he was born in a cage.' (*WBY*, 251)   *the woman at my side*: Mrs Yeats, whose automatic writing began *A Vision* and released much of the poet's tension and unhappiness

p. 328, 'A Man Young and Old'   *dc*: 1926 and 1927 (IV on 3 Jan. 1926, V in Dec. 1926, VII on 2 July 1926, XI on or before 13 March 1927)   *fp*: *LM*, April 1926 (VI, VII and VIII, with the general title 'More Songs of an Old Countryman'); *LM*, May 1927 (I, II, III & IV, with the title 'Four Songs from the Young Countryman'; V & IX, with the title 'Two Songs from the Old Countryman'); *OB* (XI)

I   *Title*: the poem encapsulates Yeats's love for Maud Gonne   *heart of stone*: Yeats used this image to portray those who devoted themselves to a cause without thought of life or love. Cf. 'a stone of the heart', 'Easter 1916', p. 287

II   *her kindness*: this poem also describes his love for Maud Gonne   *no comprehension*: Yeats wrote that Maud Gonne 'never understands' his plans, nature or ideas. But then he thought

> What matter? – How much of the best I have done and still do is but the attempt to explain myself to her? If she understood I should lack a reason for writing, and one can never have too many reasons for doing what is so laborious [*WBY*, 228]

Cf. 'Words', p. 184   *if I shrieked*: Yeats described himself in 1897 as being 'tortured with sexual desire and disappointed love'. Often, as he walked in the woods at Coole, 'it would have been a relief to have screamed aloud' (*M*, 125)

III   *mermaid*: this refers to Yeats's brief affair with Olivia Shakespear in 1896 (see notes below on part V). Warwick Gould comments that the imagery may come from George Moore's *Evelyn Innes* (1898), 294, where

Ulick Dean (a character based on Yeats) kisses Evelyn Innes, who 'threw her arms about his neck and drew him down as a mermaiden draws her mortal lover into the depths. . . . '

IV   *hare*: Iseult Gonne (see notes on 'The Living Beauty', p. 555). Yeats commented to Maurice Wollman that the poem 'means that the lover may, while loving, feel sympathy with his beloved's dread of captivity' (*L*(W), 840–1)   *death*: possibly a reference to her marriage in 1920 to Francis Stuart (*b*. 1902). See Stuart's fictionalised account of their marriage in *Black List Section H* (1971)

V   *A crazy man*: Yeats   *cup*: the poem is about Yeats's affair of 1896 with Olivia Shakespear, to whom he wrote on 6 Dec. 1926, 'One looks back to one's youth as to [a] cup that a mad man dying of thirst left half tasted. I wonder if you feel like that.' (*L*(W), 721–2)   *moon-accursed*: the affair lasted only a year; cf. 'First Love', p. 328, 'Human Dignity', p. 329, and, especially, 'The Lover mourns for the Loss of Love', p. 95. See *YANB*, 295

VI   *Hector*: see notes on 'The Phases of the Moon', p. 565   *She*: Helen of Troy. Virginia Moore, *The Unicorn* (1954), 202, and Richard Ellmann, *Golden Codgers* (1973), 108, think the poem indicates that Yeats slept with Maud Gonne

VII   *King of the Peacocks*: a peacock symbolises pride, possibly because of its strutting walk and ostentatious display of its tail

VIII   *halved a soul*: cf. 'Among School Children', ll. 13–17, p. 323

IX   *straw . . . down*: possibly an antithesis of cottage and great house

X   *Paris' love . . . so straight a back*: a description of Helen of Troy, hence of Maud Gonne, whose 'straight back' is praised in 'Beautiful Lofty Things', p. 421. See notes on 'The Rose of the World', p. 498

XI   *wandering beggar*: Œdipus, who blinded himself after he discovered that he had killed his father Laius and married his mother Jocasta   *God-hated children*: Antigone and Ismene, the daughters of Œdipus and Jocasta

p. 334, 'The Three Monuments'   *dc*: 11 June 1925   *fp*: OB   *re-nownèd patriots stand*: the statues in Dublin of Daniel O'Connell (1745–1833), Charles Stewart Parnell (1846–91) and Horatio, Lord Nelson (1758–1805)   *One . . . stumpier*: Nelson, whose statue was on a column, Nelson's Pillar, higher than the other two monuments (to Parnell at the northern end of O'Connell Street, to O'Connell at the southern) which are stumpier; Nelson's column was blown up in 1966; its place is at present taken by a fountain   *The three old rascals*: the private lives of all three were not regarded as regular: Yeats alluded elsewhere to the saying that you could not throw a stick over a workhouse wall in O'Connell's day without hitting one of his children; Parnell's affair with Mrs O'Shea led to his political downfall; and Nelson's relationship with Lady Hamilton was well known

p. 334, 'The Gift of Harun Al-Rashid'   *dc*: 1923 (appended to text *P* (1949))   *fp*: *English Life and the Illustrated Review*, Jan. 1924   This poem is a tribute to Mrs Yeats, to be understood through a flippant note (in *CATM*, 38ff.) in which Yeats tells how Harun Al-Rashid has presented Kusta (symbolising Yeats) with a new bride:

> According to one tradition of the desert, she had, to the great surprise of her friends, fallen in love with the elderly philosopher, but according to another Harun bought her from a passing merchant. Kusta, a Christian like the Caliph's own physician, had planned, one version of the story says, to end his days in a monastery at Nisibis [the Syrian residence of Armenian kings], while another story has it that he was deep in a violent love affair that he had arranged for himself. The only thing on which there is general agreement is that he was warned by a dream to accept the gift of the Caliph, and that his wife a few days after the marriage began to talk in her sleep, and that she told him all those things which he had searched for vainly all his life in the great library of the Caliph and in the conversation of wise men.

This refers to the automatic writing and the material of *AV*. Cf. *AV*(B), 8–15, particularly the references to his wife 'in the broken speech of some quite ordinary dream' and to 'an unnatural story of an Arabian traveller which I must amend and find a place for some day because I was fool enough to write half a dozen poems [*Michael Robartes and his Friends*] that are unintelligible without it' (*AV*(B), 19)   *Title*: Harun Al-Rashid (766–809), Caliph from 786–809   *Kusta Ben Luka*: a doctor and translator who lived from 820 to [?]892. In his note Yeats writes that these stories seem a confused recollection of a 'little old book lost many years ago with Kusta-ben-Luka's longer book. . . . This little book was discovered . . . between the pages of a Greek book which had once been in the Caliph's library . . .'. He continues that he has elaborated in his poem but does not think it

> too great a poetical licence to describe Kusta as hesitating between the poems of Sappho [Greek poetess (*c*. 612 BC) who lived in Lesbos] and the treatise of Parmenides as hiding places. Gibbon [Edward Gibbon (1737–94)] says the poems of Sappho were still extant in the twelfth century [Gibbon, *The History of the Decline and Fall of the Roman Empire*, ed. J. B. Berry (1909–14), VII, 111]. And it does not seem impossible that a great philosophical work of which we possess only fragments, may have found its way into an Arab library of the eighth century. Certainly there are passages of Parmenides that for instance numbered one hundred and thirty by Burkitt [Yeats read John Burnet, *Early Greek Philosophy* (1892), and *PNE* remarks that he marked in his copy, opposite the marginal number 130 (p. 188) a passage from Parmenides] and still more in his immediate predecessors which Kusta would have recognised as his own thought. This from Herakleitus [Heracleitus (*c*. 535–475 BC) Greek philosopher who held that fire is the primordial substance and that all things are in perpetual flux] for instance, 'Mortals are immortals and immortals are Mortals, the one living the other's death and dying the other's life (*VPl*, 828–9). [This passage was also marked in Yeats's copy of Burnet's *Early Greek Philosophy*, p. 138.]

Treatise of Parmenides: Parmenides (*b.* 513 BC) founded the Eleatic School of Philosophy (after Elea in Italy) and rejected the theories of Heracleitus, regarding the universe as an unchanging, continuous, indivisible whole   *Vizir Jaffer*: Vizier from 786 to 803, when he was imprisoned by the Caliph   *shirt . . . knew . . . tear*: Warwick Gould suggests as source Powys Mathers's 1923 translation of the *Arabian Nights*, 4, 712: 'If I thought my shirt knew I would tear my shirt in pieces'   *her sleeping form . . .*: this relates the experiences that went to the making of *A V*   *Djinn*: a supernatural being   *All, all those . . . things*: Yeats's footnote read, 'This refers to the geometrical forms which Robartes describes the Judwali Arabs as making upon the sand (*DL*, June 1924). The source was 'King Wird Khan, his Women and his Wazirs' in Burton's translation of the *Arabian Nights*. See Warwick Gould, 'A Lesson for the Circumspect', *The Arabian Nights in English Literature*, ed. Peter L. Carraciolo (1988), 264–73, for the influence of the *Arabian Nights* on *A V*, 'Ego Dominus Tuus' and this poem. Yeats invented the Judwalis. See *A V*(A), xix, and *A V*(B)

p. 340, 'All Souls' Night'   *dc*: Nov. 1920 (Oxford, autumn, 1920, appended to text in *A V* (A); Oxford 1920 to text in *P* (1949))   *fp*: *NR*, 9 March 1921; *LM*, 1921   *Christ Church Bell*: Christ Church, Oxford. Yeats was living in Broad Street, Oxford, when he wrote the poem. All Souls' Night is the feast on which the Roman Catholic Church on earth prays for the souls of the departed who are still in Purgatory; the poem, Yeats said, was written in a moment of exaltation   *Horton's the first*: William Thomas Horton (1864–1919), mystical painter and illustrator, an Irvingite, for whose *A Book of Images* (1898) Yeats wrote a pre-face   *platonic love . . . his lady died*: Amy Audrey Locke (1881–1916), with whom Horton lived platonically   *of her or God*: in *A V*(A), x, Yeats remarked that Horton survived Audrey Locke 'but a little time during which he saw her in apparition and attained through her certain of the traditional experiences of the saint'   *companionable ghost*: Yeats wrote to Horton after Miss Locke's death 'the dead are not far from us . . . they cling in some strange way to what is most deep and still in us'   *Florence Emery*: Florence Farr Emery (1869–1917) produced Yeats's *The Land of Heart's Desire* in 1984, and acted Aleel in his *The Countess Cathleen* in 1899. She recited Yeats's poems to the psaltery; see notes on 'The Players ask for a Blessing . . .', p. 529   *teach a school . . . dark skins*: she left England in 1912 to teach at Ramanathan College, Ceylon   *foul years*: she died of cancer in 1917   *some learned Indian*: probably Sir Ponnambalam Raman-athan, who founded the college where she taught   *Chance and Choice*: see notes on 'Solomon and the Witch', p. 568   *MacGregor*: MacGregor Mather (1854–1918), originally Samuel Liddle Mathers, who studied occultism in London from 1885. Yeats met him possibly in 1887 (see *A*, 182–3), certainly not later than 1890. He married Moina, sister of Henri Bergson, the philosopher, and for a time was Curator of the Horniman

Museum in London. When he left to live in Paris, Annie Horniman continued to give him a subsidy for some years   *estranged*: he was a founder of the Order of the Golden Dawn; Yeats and he quarrelled over matters connected with the Order in 1900

THE WINDING STAIR AND OTHER POEMS

The Winding Stair was published by the Fountain Press, New York, in 1929; it contained five poems and those of *A Woman Young and Old*; in the Macmillan edition of 1933 the poems of *WMP* were included   *Dedication*: for Dulac, see notes on 'On a Picture of a Black Centaur by Edmund Dulac', p. 587. In his notes Yeats included a letter he wrote as dedication for the Macmillan edition:

> I saw my *Hawk's Well* played by students of our Schools of Dancing and of Acting a couple of years ago in a beautiful little theatre called 'The Peacock', which shares a roof with the Abbey Theatre. Watching Cuchulain in his lovely mask and costume, that ragged old masked man also seems hundreds of years old, that Guardian of the Well, with your great golden wings and dancing to your music, I had one of those moments of excitement that are the dramatist's reward and decided there and then to dedicate to you my next book of verse.

He commented in this note on the symbolism of the volume:

> In this book and elsewhere I have used towers, and one tower in particular, as symbols and have compared their winding stairs to the philosophical gyres, but it is hardly necessary to interpret what comes from the main track of thought and expression. Shelley uses towers constantly as symbols, and there are gyres in Swedenborg, and in Thomas Aquinas and certain classical authors.

p. 347, 'In Memory of Eva Gore-Booth and Con Markiewicz'   *dc*: 21 Sept.–Nov. 1927   *fp*: *WS* (1929)   *Lissadell*: the Gore-Booth house in Sligo, where Yeats visited the Gore-Booth sisters in the winter of 1894–5   *one a gazelle*: Eva (1870–1926), who wrote poetry, worked for the women's suffrage movement and was strongly committed to social work   *The older . . . death*: for her part in the 1916 Rising. Constance was born in 1868. See notes on 'Easter 1916', p. 569, and 'On a Political Prisoner', p. 571, for details of her political career   *lonely years*: her friend James Connolly was shot after the Easter Rising; her husband Casimir had left Dublin for his estates in the Ukraine in 1913 and never lived in Dublin again; her stepson Stasko left to join his father in 1915; her daughter Maeve Alys was estranged from her (they met again in America in 1922). Her husband and Stasko arrived from Warsaw to see her a few days before her death in Dublin in 1927   *old Georgian mansion*: Lissadell, built in 1832 to the design of Francis Goodwin (1784–1835)   *shadows*: as they were both dead   *gazebo*: three possible meanings are: a summer-house; to make a gazebo of yourself (in Hiberno-English) is to make yourself ridiculous; and a place to look from

p. 348, 'Death'   dc: 13/17 Sept. 1927   fp: WS: (1929)   Yeats said in a note of 1933 that he was roused to write this poem, like 'Blood and the Moon', by the assassination of Kevin O'Higgins (1892–1927), Minister of Justice in the Irish Free State, 'the finest intellect in Irish public life, and, I think I may add, my friend'. O'Higgins was convinced that the Irish Civil War could only be ended by the execution of anyone captured carrying arms. It was thought that he was shot on 10 July 1927 on his way to mass at Booterstown, Dublin, as an act of revenge   knows death: Yeats wrote to Olivia Shakespear in April 1933 that he remembered a saying of O'Higgins to his wife: 'Nobody can expect to live who has done what I have.'

p. 348, 'A Dialogue of Self and Soul'   dc: between July and Dec. 1927 (Yeats, however, described it in his notes as written (by which he may have mean 'completed') in the spring of 1928, 'during a long illness, indeed finished the day before a Cannes doctor told me to stop writing'   fp: WS: (1929)
I   ancient stair: of Thoor Ballylee, Yeats's tower in Co. Galway   the star: Ursa Minor, the Pole Star   Sato's ancient blade: see notes on 'Meditations in Time of Civil War', p. 580   Montashigi: Bishu Osafune Motoshigi lived in the period of Oei (1394–1428)
II   blind man's ditch . . . men: see Matthew 15:14 and Luke 6:39 for the blind leading the blind and falling into the ditch   A proud woman: a reference, no doubt, to his own passion for Maud Gonne   So great a sweetness: the creative joy of the artist. Cf. E&I, 322

p. 351, 'Blood and the Moon'   dc: Aug. 1927   fp: The Exile, spring 1928; WS (1929)
I   this place: Thoor Ballylee, Yeats's tower in Co. Galway   cottages: two cottages adjoining the tower   Half dead at the top: the tower was never completely restored; one room remained empty at the top. The phrase probably derives from Swift's remark made when gazing 'at a noble tree, which in its uppermost branches was much withered and decayed. Pointing at it, he said "I shall be like that tree, I shall die at [the] top."' (cited by Edward Young, Works (1798), III, 196)
II   Alexandria's . . . beacon tower: the Pharos, the lighthouse built by King Ptolemy Philadelphus on the island of Pharos), one of the Seven Wonders of the world   Babylon's: see notes on 'The Dawn', p. 558, and 'Two Songs from a Play', p. 584   Shelley . . . towers: Shelley referred to thought's crowned powers in Prometheus Unbound (1820), IV, 103   Goldsmith: Oliver Goldsmith (1728–74), Irish writer, author of 'The Deserted Village', The Vicar of Wakefield and She Stoops to Conquer   the Dean: Jonathan Swift (1667–1745), Irish writer and Dean of St Patrick's Cathedral, Dublin, author of A Tale of a Tub and Gulliver's Travels   Berkeley: George Berkeley (1685–1753), Irish philosopher, Bishop of Cloyne, Co. Cork   Burke: Edmund Burke (1729–97), Irish

politician, author and orator. See notes on 'The Tower', p. 577   *honey-pot*: probably a reference to Goldsmith's essays and humorous verse in *The Bee* (1759)   *the State a tree*: Yeats thought Burke the first to say (in *Reflections, Works*, II, 357) that a nation is a tree, Berkeley the first to say the world is a vision   *pragmatical . . . pig*: the phrase may reflect upon Yeats's experiences when chairing the Commission responsible for Ireland's coinage; the artist was asked to alter the shape of the pig on the halfpenny coin to a shape, better for merchandising 'but less living' ('What We Did or Tried to Do', *Coinage of Saorstat Eireann* (1928), 1-7)   *Saeva Indignatio*: Latin, fierce or savage indignation, from the epitaph Swift wrote for his own tomb in St Patrick's Cathedral, translated by Yeats as 'savage indignation' in 'Swift's Epitaph', p. 361   *Tortoiseshell butterflies, peacock butterflies*: Yeats remarked in a note that part of the symbolism of the poem was suggested by the fact that Thoor Ballylee had a waste room at the top and that butterflies came in through the loopholes and died against the window-panes   *Half dead*: see note above on *Half dead . . . top*, p. 595

   p. 353, 'Oil and Blood'   *dc*: probably Dec. 1927, but reworked in 1928 and 1929   *fp*: WS (1929)   *Miraculous oil*: Yeats read several books on St Teresa (1515-82), the Spanish Carmelite nun. Lady Lovat, *The Life of Saint Teresa* (1911), 606, wrote that

> the body of the Saint was intact, her flesh white and soft, as flexible as when she was buried, and still emitted the same delicious and penetrating smell. Moreover the limbs exuded a miraculous oil which bore a similar perfume and embalmed the air and everything with which it came in contact

the vampires: Yeats had read *Dracula* (1897), the novel about vampires by the Irish writer Bram (Abraham) Stoker (1847-1912)

   p. 353, 'Veronica's Napkin'   *dc*: 1929   *fp*: WMP   *Title*: Yeats's source is not known. The legend is that the Veronica, a veil or handkerchief, has impressed upon it the likeness of the face of Jesus Christ. A holy woman, Veronica, gave him this handkerchief or towel to wipe his face when he was carrying his Cross to Calvary; he gave it back to her having impressed his image on it   *The Heavenly Circuit*: title of an essay by Plotinus (AD ?205-?270), the philosopher who regarded God as the centre of a perfect circle; he thought the heavenly bodies rotated around God, the planets at a fixed distance from him. He also thought that the human soul rotated around him   *Berenice's Hair*: Berenice II, daughter of King Magas of Cyrene and Apama, daughter of Antiochus I, was betrothed to Ptolemy III. When her father died her mother tried to marry her to Demetrius; she rebelled and ordered his death. She then married Ptolemy III. He named a constellation, 'Berenice's Curls', after her, she having offered her hair for his safe return from war. After her husband's death her son Ptolemy IV murdered her   *Tent-pole of Eden*: probably the

Pole Star, or the pole of the heavens. See notes on 'He hears the Cry of the Sedge', p. 518   *a different pole*: the Cross on which Jesus was crucified   *napkin*: the handkerchief Veronica offered to Jesus

p. 354, 'Symbols'   *dc*: Oct. 1927   *fp*: *WMP*   *watch-tower* . . . *hermit*: a passage in 'Discoveries' records an experience which probably prompted these lines. See *E & I*, 290–1   *silk on the sword-blade*: the image is probably prompted by Junzo Sato's sword (see 'Meditations in Time of Civil War', III, p. 310, and 'A Dialogue of Self and Soul', p. 348). The sword was wrapped in a piece of silk from a Japanese lady's court dress. The sword and its silk covering are symbols of life

p. 354, 'Spilt Milk'   *dc*: 8 Nov. 1930   *fp*: *WMP*   The poem was based upon 'the upshot of my talk upon a metaphor of Lady Ottoline's'. Yeats and the poet Walter de la Mare had visited Lady Ottoline Morrell on 7 Nov. 1930, as Virginia Woolf records in her diary

p. 354, 'The Nineteenth Century and After'   *dc*: between Jan. and 2 March 1929   *fp*: *WMP*   The poem expresses Yeats's thought, after he had turned from reading Browning to reading William Morris's *Defence of Guinevere*, that the world's last great poetical period was over. (See *L*(W) 759)

p. 354, 'Statistics'   *dc*: 1931   *fp*: *WMP*   *Platonists*: followers of the Greek philosopher Plato; see notes on 'The Tower', p. 577

p. 355, 'Three Movements'   *dc*: 26 Jan. 1932 (a prose draft is dated 20 Jan. 1932)   *fp*: *WMP*   *Shakespearean fish*: the prose draft read 'Passion in Shakespeare was a great fish in the sea, but from Goethe to the end of the Romantic movement the fish was in the net. It will soon be dead upon the shore.' In an essay on Bishop Berkeley, Yeats wrote that imagination sank after the death of Shakespeare (*E & I*, 396)   *Romantic fish*: Yeats regarded Lady Gregory and himself as 'the last romantics', part of a literary movement that had begun in the latter part of the 18th century

p. 355, 'The Seven Sages'   *dc*: 30 Jan. 1931   *fp*: *WMP*   *Title*: Solon, Chilo, Thales, Bias, Cleobolus, Pittochus, and Periander   *My great-grandfather . . . great-grandfather's father*: Yeats is involved in a search for his intellectual ancestry among the Anglo-Irish of the 18th century. Cf. these remarks in his 1930 diary:

> How much of my reading is to discover the English and Irish originals of my thought, its first language, and, where no such originals exist, its relation to what original did. I seek more than idioms, for thoughts become more vivid when I find they were thought out in historical circumstances which affect those in which I live, or, which is perhaps the same thing, were thought first by men my

ancestors may have known. Some of my ancestors may have been Swift, and probably my Huguenot grandmother who asked burial near Bishop King spoke both to Swift and Berkeley. [*E*, 293]

Edmund Burke . . . Grattan: see notes on 'The Tower', p. 577   *Oliver Goldsmith*: see notes on 'Blood and the Moon', p. 595   *Bishop of Cloyne*: George Berkeley (see notes on 'Blood and the Moon', p. 595) believed strongly in the medicinal properties of tar-water, extolled in his *Siris* (1744)   *Stella*: Swift's (see notes on 'Blood and the Moon', p. 595) name for Esther Johnson, whom he first met at Moor Park, Sir William Temple's house in England. His *Journal to Stella* consists of the letters he wrote to her and her friend Rebecca Dingley during 1710–13. Their close Platonic friendship lasted till Stella's death. The best account of her is Swift's, written at the time of her death. She is buried near Swift in St Patrick's Cathedral, Dublin   *Burke was a Whig*: so, initially, was Swift; both men had a strong conservative sense. Swift aided the Tory Ministry in London till its collapse; Burke, disturbed by the violent excesses of the French Revolution, sided with the Tories   *great melody*: see notes on 'The Tower', p. 577   *Roads full of beggars, cattle . . .*: Goldsmith's poem 'The Deserted Village' depicts the evil effects of rural depopulation

p. 357, 'The Crazed Moon'   *dc*: April 1923   *fp*: WMP   *much child-bearing*: Henn suggested that Cornelius Agrippa, *Occult Philosophy*, II, xxxii, may be a source for this idea that the moon is the wife of all the stars; she is the mistress of all generation (*LT*, 174). But Yeats may also be alluding to the fact that Diana, an Italian divinity (regarded as identical with the Greek Artemis), daughter of Jupiter and Latona and sister of Apollo, and the virgin moon goddess (Luna), was, in addition to being the patroness of virginity, the presider over child-birth (in which character she was called Lucina)

p. 357, 'Coole Park, 1929'   *dc*: 7 Sept. 1928   *fp*: Lady Gregory, C A prose draft of the poem reads:

Describe house in first stanza. Here Synge came, Hugh Lane, Shaw[e] Taylor, many names. I too in my timid youth. Coming and going like migratory birds. Then address the swallows fluttering in their dream like circles. Speak of the rarity of circumstances that bring together such concords of men. Each man more than himself through whom an unknown life speaks. A circle ever returning into itself.

an aged woman: Lady Gregory (1852–1932). See notes on 'Friends', p. 549   *her house*: Coole Park near Gort, Co. Galway (see Glossary)   *Hyde*: Dr Douglas Hyde (1860–1949), Irish poet, translator and scholar, founder of the Gaelic League, first President of Ireland (1938–45). Yeats remarked in *Dramatis Personae* that Hyde had given up verse writing because it affected his lungs or his heart (see *A*, 439–40)   *one that ruffled*: Yeats himself   *slow man . . . Synge*: John

Millington Synge; see notes on 'In Memory of Major Robert Gregory', p. 552   *Shawe-Taylor and Hugh Lane*: both nephews of Lady Gregory. Shawe-Taylor (1866–1911) seemed to have 'the energy of swift decision, a power of sudden action'. He called a Land Conference, which, in effect, settled the land question (see *E&I*, 343–5). For Lane, see notes on 'To a Wealthy Man . . .', p. 542   *compass-point*: swallows often fly around a turning-point, such as a steeple or high building   *rooms and passages are gone*: the Forestry Department took over the estate during Lady Gregory's life; she rented the house from the Department, which sold it after her death; the purchaser demolished it

p. 358, 'Coole and Ballylee, 1931'   *dc*: Feb. 1931   *fp*: *WMP* with the title 'Coole Park and Ballylee 1932'; this became 'Coole and Ballylee 1932' from *TWSOP* on; the present title was used in *CP* (1950)   *my window-ledge*: at Thoor Ballylee, Yeats's castle in Co. Galway   *'dark' Raftery's 'cellar'*: Eoghan O'Rahilly (1670–1726), Irish poet; 'dark' because he was blind. See notes on 'The Tower', p. 577. The 'cellar' is where the river goes underground in a shallow hole   *the generated soul*: water was used as a symbol of generation by the Neoplatonics. Yeats probably had a passage from *On the Cave of the Nymphs* by Porphyry (233–304), who studied in Athens under Longinus and in Rome under Plotinus, the Neoplatonic philosopher whose life he wrote and whose works he edited   *buskin*: the cothurnus, a high, thick-skinned boot worn in Athenian tragedy (opposed to the soccus, or low shoe worn in comedy)   *sudden . . . mounting swan*: intended as a symbol of inspiration   *murdered with a spot of ink*: an allusion to *M. Triboulat Bonhomet* (1887), a novel by the French symbolist writer Comte Auguste de Villiers de l'Isle Adam (1838–89), in which Dr Bonhomet is a hunter of swans   *somebody*: Lady Gregory. See notes on 'Friends', p. 549   In *C* she describes the contents of the house and its surroundings well; see also Yeats, *A*, 388–91, cited *NC*, 289–90)   *a last inheritor*: her only child Robert was killed in 1918; see notes on 'In Memory of Major Robert Gregory', p. 552   *that high horse*: Pegasus. See notes on 'The Fascination of What's Difficult', p. 535

p. 360, 'For Anne Gregory'   *dc*: Sept. 1930   *fp*: *WMP*   *Title*: Anne Gregory (*b.* 1911), second grandchild of Lady Gregory

p. 361, 'Swift's Epitaph'   *dc*: completed Sept. 1930   *fp*: *Dublin Magazine*, Oct.–Dec. 1931 (untitled in first printings)   This is a translation of the Latin epigraph in St Patrick's Cathedral, Dublin, where Jonathan Swift, Dean of the Cathedral, is buried. Yeats's addition to the epitaph is the epithet 'World-besotted'; he altered the first line ('Here is laid the body [of Jonathan Swift]') to 'Swift has sailed into his rest'. The Latin reads:

Hic depositum est Corpus
JONATHAN SWIFT S.T.D.
Hujus Ecclesiae Cathedralis
Decani,
Ubi saeva indignatio
Ulterius
Cor lacerare nequit.
Abi Viator
Et imitare, si poteris,
Strenuum pro virili
Libertatis Vindicatorem
Obiit 19° Die Mensis Octobris
A.D. 1745 Anno Aetatis 78.

p. 361, 'At Algeciras – A Meditation upon Death'   *dc*: Nov. 1927   *fp*: *PEP*, 4 Feb. 1929, appended to text (*PEP*); Nov. 28 *P* (1949), with the title 'Meditations upon Death, I' (the companion poem being 'Mohini Chatterjee, p. 362)   *cattle-birds*: Yeats watched them flying in to roost near the Hotel Reina Cristina at Algeciras in Southern Spain in 1927   *Newton's metaphor*: Sir Isaac Newton's words were:

> I do not know how I may appear to the world; but to myself I seem to have been only like a boy, playing on the seashore, and diverting myself, in now and then finding another pebble or prettier shell than ordinary, while the great ocean of truth lay all undiscovered before me. [David Brewster, *Memoirs . . . of Sir Isaac Newton* (1855), 11, 407]

Rosses' level shore: district near Sligo   *Great Questioner*: Yeats, seriously ill with congestion of the lungs in October 1927, had been sent to Spain in search of sunshine

p. 362, 'The Choice'   *dc*: Feb. 1931   *fp*: *WMP* untitled (it was originally the penultimate stanza of 'Coole Park and Ballylee 1932', p. 358)   *A heavenly mansion*: probably an echo of Christ's saying 'In my Father's house are many mansions; if it were not so, I would not have told you; for I go to prepare a place for you.' John 14:2

p. 362, 'Mohini Chatterjee'   *dc*: between 23 Jan. and 9 Feb. 1929 (February 9th appended to text *PEP*; 1928 in *P* (1949))   *fp*: *PEP*   *Title*: he was a Bengali Brahmin (1858–1936), one of the earliest members of the Theosophical Society in India, whom Yeats and his friends in the Hermetic Society invited to Dublin to lecture to them   *Pray for nothing*: Mohini Chatterjee thought prayer was 'too full of hope, of desire of life, to have any part in that acquiescence that was his beginning of wisdom'   *these, or words like these*: an early poem 'Kanva on Himself' in *TWO* also gave the Brahmin's reply in verse which Yeats put in a note:

One should say, before sleeping 'I have lived many lives, I have been a slave and a prince. Many a beloved has sat upon my knees and I have sat upon the knees of many a beloved. Everything that has been shall be again'

p. 363, 'Byzantium'   *dc*: Sept. 1930 (1930 appended to text)   *fp*: WMP   The prose draft is in Yeats's 1930 diary:

Subject for a poem. Death of a friend. . . . Describe Byzantium as it is in the system towards the end of the first Christian millennium. A walking mummy. Flames at the street corners where the soul is purified, birds of hammered gold singing in the golden trees, in the harbour [dolphins] offering their backs to the wailing dead that they may carry them to Paradise.

In the MS of 'Modern Ireland' (*Massachusetts Review*, winter 1964), Yeats wrote that in his later poems he

called it Byzantium ['it' being 'an example of magnificence: and style, whether in literature or life, comes, I think, from excess, from that something over and above utility, which wrings the heart'], that city where the Saints showed their wasted forms upon a background of gold mosaic, and an artificial bird sang upon a tree of gold in the presence of the Emperor; and in one poem I have pictured the ghosts swimming, mounted upon dolphins, through the sensual seas, that they may dance upon its pavements

cathedral gong: the great *semantron*, a board suspended in the porch of churches, beaten by mallets   *dome*: of Santa Sophia   *image, man or shade*: Yeats wrote in a note that

the world wide belief that the dead dream back for a certain time, through the more personal thoughts and deeds of life. The wicked, according to Cornelius Agrippa, dream themselves to be consumed by flames and persecuted by demons. . . . The Shade is said to fade out at last, but the Spiritual Being does not fade, passing on to other states of existence after it has attained a spiritual state, of which the surroundings and aptitudes of early life are a correspondence.

Hades' bobbin: probably taken from the spindle in Plato's myth of Er (*The Republic*, 820). Hades, son of Kronos, was a lord of the lower world in Greek mythology   *Emperor's pavement*: an open space, an extension of the Forum of Constantinople, called the pavement from its finished marble floor. Yeats got this from W. G. Holmes, *The Age of Justinian and Theodora* (2nd edn 1912), I, 69   *blood-begotten spirits*: Ellmann, *IY*, 221, quoted notes Yeats made two years before writing 'Byzantium':

At first we are subject to Destiny . . . but the point in the Zodiac where the whirl becomes a sphere once reached, we may escape from the constraint of our nature and from that of external things, entering upon a state where all fuel has become flame, where there is nothing but the state itself, nothing to constrain it or end it. We attain it always in the creation or enjoyment of a work of art, but that moment though eternal in the Daimon passes from us because it is not an attainment of our whole being. . . .

complexities . . . leave: after purgation   *dolphin's mire and blood*: dolphins carried dead men or their souls in transit to the Isles of the Blessed. Yeats's information came from Mrs A. Strong, *Apotheosis and After Life* (1915), 153, 195, 215, 266   *Marbles . . . floor*: see note above on *Emperor's pavement*, p. 601   *golden smithies*: also derived from W. G. Holmes, *The Age of Justinian and Theodora*, 69

p. 364, 'The Mother of God'   *dc*: 3 Sept. 1931; finally revised 12 Sept. 1931   *fp*: *WMP*   *a fallen flare*: Yeats's note reads

> In 'The Mother of God' the words 'A fallen flare through the hollow of an ear' are I am told, obscure. I had in my memory Byzantine mosaic pictures of the Annunciation, which show a line drawn from a star to the ear of the Virgin. She received the word through the ear, a star fell and a star was born

p. 365, 'Vacillation'   *dc*: during 1931 and 1932 (I in Dec. 1931; IV in Nov. 1931; VI between Jan. and 5 March 1932; VII on 3 and 4 Jan. 1932; VIII on 3 Jan. 1932); 1932 appended to text *P* (1949)   *fp*: *WMP*. In this printing the titles of the sections were: I, 'What is Joy'; II, 'The Burning Tree' (this included the stanza II & III of later printings); III (subsequently IV), 'Happiness'; IV (subsequently V), 'Conscience'; V (subsequently VI), 'Conquerors'; VI (subsequently VII), 'A Dialogue'; VII (subsequently VIII), 'Von Hugel'

I   Yeats sent the first section to Olivia Shakespear in late November 1931:

> . . . I went for a walk after dark and there among some great trees became absorbed in the most lofty philosophical conception I have found while writing *A Vision*. I suddenly seemed to understand at last and then I smelt roses. I now realised the timeless nature of the timeless spirit. Then I began to walk and with my excitement came – how shall I say? – that old glow so beautiful with its autumnal tint. The longing to touch it was almost unendurable. The next night I was walking in the same path and now the two excitements came together. The autumnal image, remote, incredibly spiritual, erect, delicate featured, and mixed with it the violent physical image, the black mass of Eden. Yesterday I put my thoughts into a poem which I enclose, but it seems to me a poor shadow of the intensity of the experience. [*L*(W), 785]

extremities: this relates to Blake's ideas about contraries, which Yeats dealt with in his and Edwin Ellis's 1893 edition of Blake. He marked the following passage in Denis Saurat, *Blake and Modern Thought* (1929):

> With contraries there is no progression. Attraction and Repulsion, Love and Hate, are necessary to Human existence. From these contraries spring what the religious call Good and Evil. Good is the passive that obeys Reason. Evil is the active springing from Energy. Good is Heaven – Evil is Hell.

II   *A tree there is*: this derives from Lady Charlotte Guest's translation of the *Mabinogion* (1877), 109: 'A tall tree by the side of the river, one half of

which was in flames from the root to the top, and the other half was green
and in full leaf'   *Attis*: Attis was a vegetation god in Greek legend; to
prevent him marrying someone else Cybele, the earth mother, drove him
to frenzy and he castrated himself. Yeats read Sir James Frazer's *The Golden
Bough* (1890), I, 297–9, and *Attis, Adonis and Osiris*, 219–49, in which the
effigy of Attis was hung on a sacred pine tree as an image of his coming to
life again in the form of a tree

III   *trivial days*: possibly refers to Yeats's administrative work at the
Abbey Theatre   *Lethean foliage*: Lethe meant oblivion in Greek. The
waters of Lethe, a river in Hades, were drunk by souls about to be
reincarnated so that they forgot their past lives   *fortieth winter*: Yeats
was forty in 1905, by which time he had settled into his new bare style of
poetry

IV   *fiftieth year*: Yeats was fifty in 1915–16; his 'fiftieth year' probably
means 13 June 1914–12 June 1915. In 'Anima Mundi' he wrote

> At certain moments, always unforeseen, I become happy, most commonly when
> at hazard I have opened some book of verse. Sometimes it is my own verse when,
> instead of discovering new technical flaws, I read with all the excitement of the
> first writing. Perhaps I am sitting in some crowded restaurant, the open book
> beside me, or closed, my excitement having over-brimmed the page. I look at the
> strangers near as if I had known them all my life, and it seems strange that I cannot
> speak to them: everything fills me with affection, I have no longer any fears or any
> needs; I do not even remember that this happy mood must come to an end. It
> seems as if the vehicle had suddenly grown pure and far extended and so luminous
> that the images from *Anima Mundi*, embodied there and drunk with that
> sweetness, would, like a country drunkard who has thrown a wisp into his own
> thatch, burn up time.
>
> It may be an hour before the mood passes, but latterly I seem to understand that
> I enter upon it the moment I cease to hate. I think the common condition of our
> life is hatred – I know that this is so with me – irritation with public or private
> events or persons. [*M*, 364–5]

VI   *Chou*: probably the Chinese statesman and author Chou-Kung (*d.*
1105 BC), known as the Duke of Chou   *Babylon*: see notes on 'The
Dawn', p. 558, and on 'Two Songs from a Play', p. 584   *Nineveh*:
capital of the Assyrian Empire; see notes on 'Fragments', p. 585

VII   *Isaiah's coal*: in Isaiah, 6:6–7, the prophet Isaiah is purified by an
angel who applies a live coal taken from the altar to his lips

VIII   *Von Hügel*: Baron Friedrich von Hügel (1852–1925), whose *The
Mystical Element in Religion* (1908) Yeats had been reading   *Saint Teresa*:
St Teresa, a Carmelite nun. See notes on 'Oil and Blood', p. 596   *self-
same hands*: of the embalmers who embalmed St Teresa (a modern
saint)   *Pharaoh's mummy*: the bodies of the Pharaohs of Egypt were
mummified   *The lion and the honeycomb . . . Scripture*: in Judges 14:5–18,
Samson kills a lion and gets honey from its carcass. He made up a riddle,
'Out of the eater came forth what is eaten and out of the strong what is

sweet'. He told the answer to his wife, who was exposed by revealing it

p. 368, 'Quarrel in Old Age'   *dc*: Nov. 1931   *fp*: *WMP*   *her sweetness*: Maud Gonne's. The poem records a quarrel with her, probably over the treatment of women prisoners on a hunger strike   *blind bitter town*: Dublin, 'the blind and ignorant town' of 'To a Wealthy Man . . .', p. 208, this 'blind bitter land' of 'Words', p. 184   *All lives*: Yeats found consolation at times in the idea of reincarnation   *Targeted*: protected as with a round shield or targe   *like Spring*: Maud Gonne seemed to Yeats like 'a classical impersonation of the spring' as he recalled her in *A*, 123

p. 369, 'The Results of Thought'   *dc*: between 18 and 25 Aug. 1931 (August 1931 appended to text *P* (1949))   *fp*: *WMP*   *companion*: Olivia Shakespear; see notes on 'Friends', p. 549   *dear brilliant woman*: Lady Gregory

p. 369, 'Gratitude to the Unknown Instructors'   *dc*: unknown   *fp*: *WMP*   *they*: the communicators of *A Vision*. See *AV*(B), 8 and 9

p. 370, 'Remorse for Intemperate Speech'   *dc*: 28 Aug. 1931 (appended to text)   *fp*: *WMP*   *knave and fool*: probably a reference to Yeats's youthful work as a nationalist   *Fit audience found*: possibly friends Yeats made from 1897 onwards, Lady Gregory and various friends in England   *fanatic*: Yeats commented that he pronounced the word in what he supposed the older and more Irish way, 'so that the last line of each stanza contains but two beats'   *hatred*: Yeats thought hatred a common-place in Ireland, where it found in his class rather than in the mass of the people 'a more complicated and determined conscience to prey upon' (letter to Olivia Shakespear, 7 Sept. 1927)

p. 370, 'Stream and Sun at Glendalough'   *dc*: 23 June 1932 (June 1932 appended to text *P* (1949))   *fp*: *WMP*   *Title*: for Glendalough, see notes on 'Under the Round Tower', p. 555. Yeats had been visiting Iseult Gonne and her husband Francis Stuart; they lived at Laragh Castle, near Glendalough, Co. Wicklow

'Words for Music Perhaps'

On 2 March 1929 Yeats wrote to Olivia Shakespear that he was writing *Twelve Poems for Music*, not so much that they might be sung as that he might define their kind of emotion to himself. He wanted them to be 'all emotion and all impersonal' (*L*(W), 758). By September he was telling her that he hoped to finish the book of thirty poems for music. The poems, written between 1929 and 1932, include the Crazy Jane poems, founded on the sayings of an old woman, 'Cracked Mary', who lived near Gort in Co.

Galway and was 'the local satirist and a really terrible one'; she had 'an amazing power of audacious speech'. In his notes of 1933 Yeats told how

> in the spring of 1929 life returned to me as an impression of the uncontrollable energy and daring of the great creators; it seemed that but for journalism and criticism, all that evasion and explanation, the world would be torn in pieces. I wrote *Mad as the Mist and Snow*, a mechanical little song, and after that almost all that group of poems, called in memory of those exultant weeks *Words for Music Perhaps*. Then ill again, I warmed myself back into life with 'Byzantium' and 'Veronica's Napkin', looking for a theme that might befit my years. Since then I have added a few poems to *Words for Music Perhaps*, but always keeping the mood and plan of the first poems.

p. 371, 'Crazy Jane and the Bishop'   *dc*: 2 March 1929   *fp*: *NR*, 12 Nov. 1930; *LM*, Nov. 1930. The title in *NR* was 'Four Poems/Cracked Mary and the Bishop'   *Jack the Journeyman*: a character in Yeats's play *The Pot of Broth* (1903); the name was also used by Lady Gregory in her play *The Losing Game* (1902)

p. 372, 'Crazy Jane Reproved'   *dc*: 27 March 1929   *fp*: *NR*, 12 Nov. 1930, with the title 'Four Poems/Cracked Mary Reproved'   *Heaven yawns . . . To round that shell's elaborate whorl*: cf. a passage in which Yeats asked rhetorically 'Is it not certain that the Creator yawns in earthquake and thunder and other popular displays, but toils in rounding the delicate spiral of a shell' (*A*, 249)   *Europa*: the daughter of Agenor, King of Tyre. Zeus fell in love with her, assumed the shape of a bull and carried her off to Crete, where she became the mother of Minos, Sarpedon and Rhadamathus

p. 372, 'Crazy Jane on the Day of Judgment'   *dc*: Oct. 1930   *fp*: *WMP* with the title 'Words/Crazy Jane on the Day of Judgment'   *the whole Body and soul*: both Sir William Rothenstein, *Since Fifty*, 242, and John Sparrow (*Y: M & P*, 257) quoted Yeats's remark that 'the tragedy of sexual intercourse is the perpetual virginity of the soul'

p. 373, 'Crazy Jane and Jack the Journeyman'   *dc*: Nov. 1931   *fp*: *WMP* with the title 'Words/Crazy Jane and Jack the Journeyman'   *Title*: see notes on 'Crazy Jane and the Bishop' above   *A lonely ghost*: for some of Yeats's ideas on ghosts and their relationships see *M*, 355–6

p. 374, 'Crazy Jane on God'   *dc*: 18 July 1931   *fp*: *WMP* with the title 'Words/Crazy Jane on God'   *Men come, men go*: this stanza puts Crazy Jane's realisation that sexual love is transitory, as well as her awareness of some permanence   *Banners . . . horses*: the reliving of a battle, or of passionate moments is discussed by Yeats in *E*, 368–9, and *M*,

354. The stanza may have been inspired by talk of 'Cracked Mary', who saw 'unearthly riders on white horses', or of Mary Battle, George Pollexfen's servant in Sligo, who saw ghostly figures on the mountain (*A*, 266)   *a house . . . lit up*: probably Castle Dargan, in Co. Sligo (referred to in *E*, 388–9), seen by an Irish countrywoman as 'lit up'. It is described in Yeats's play, *The King of the Great Clock Tower*. See also *A*, 53, 77. The image is also used in *Purgatory* and in 'The Curse of Cromwell', p. 422

p. 374, 'Crazy Jane talks with the Bishop'   *dc*: Nov. 1931   *fp*: *TWSOP   Those breasts*: possibly an echo of Synge's translation of Villon's 'An Old Woman's Lamentation', *Poems and Translations*, 44   *The place of excrement*: probably prompted by Blake's line in *Jerusalem*, 'For I will make their place of love and joy excrementitious'

p. 375, 'Crazy Jane Grown Old looks at the Dancers'   *dc*: 6 March 1929   *fp*: *NR*, 12 Nov. 1930 with the title 'Four Poems/Cracked Mary and the Dancers'   *that ivory image*: the source of the poem is a dream:

> Last night I saw in a dream strange ragged excited people singing in a crowd. The most visible were a man and a woman who were I think dancing. The man was swinging around his head a weight at the end of a rope or leather thong, and I knew that he did not know whether he would strike her dead or not, and both had their eyes fixed on each other, and both sang their love for one another. I suppose it was Blake's old thought 'sexual love is founded on spiritual hate' – I will probably find I have written a poem in a few days – though my remembering my dream may prevent that – by making my criticism work upon it (at least there is evidence to that effect) [L(W), 758]

Cared not a thraneen: an Irish phrase meaning not to care (Irish, *traithnin*, a dry stalk of grass, a straw)

p. 376, 'Girl's Song'   *dc*: 29 March 1929   *fp*: *NR*, 22 Oct. 1930 with the title 'Seven Poems/Girl's Song'   *an old man young Or young man old*: this is very reminiscent of Blake

p. 376, 'Young Man's Song'   *dc*: after 29 March 1929   *fp*: *NR*, 22 Oct. 1930 with the title 'Seven Poems/Young Man's Song'   *Before the world was made*: cf. 'Before the World was Made', p. 385   *bend the knee*: a phrase much used in 19th-century Irish political rhetoric

p. 377, 'Her Anxiety'   *dc*: after 17 April 1929   *fp*: *NR*, 22 Oct. 1930 with the title 'Seven Poems/Her Anxiety'

p. 377, 'His Confidence'   *dc*: after 29 March 1929   *fp*: *NR*, 22 Oct. 1970 with the title 'Seven Poems/His Confidence'   *wrote . . . corners . . . eye*: Warwick Gould suggests as source the Powys Mathers translation of *The Book of the Thousand Nights and One Night* (1923), III, 75: 'written with needles on the corner of an eye'

p. 378, 'Love's Loneliness'   *dc*: 17 April 1929   *fp*: *NR*, 22 Oct. 1930 with the title 'Seven Poems/Love's Loneliness'

p. 378, 'Her Dream'   *dc*: after 29 March 1929   *fp*: *NR*, 22 Oct. 1930 with the title 'Seven Poems/Her Dream'   *I dreamed*: Yeats wrote that 'Everybody has some story or some experience of the sudden knowledge in sleep or waking of some event, a misfortune for the most part, happening to some friend far off' (*M*, 358)   *Berenice's burning hair*: Yeats's dream links him with Berenice's devotion to her betrothed. See notes on 'Veronica's Napkin', p. 596

p. 378, 'His Bargain'   *dc*: after 29 March 1929   *fp*: *NR*, 22 Oct. 1930 with the title 'Seven Poems/His Bargain'. The first printing included, probably through error, six lines, the last stanza of 'Young Man's Song' (p. 376)   *Plato's spindle*: this probably derives from Plato's myth of Er (see *NC*, 314–15). The individual soul chooses its lot, is despatched by Lachesis, passes beneath the 'whirling distaff' of Clotho, thence to Atropos, its doom then irreversible   *Before the thread began*: cf. 'Before the World was Made', p. 385. Yeats quoted Miss Radford's lines, 'The love within my heart for thee/Before the world had its birth' (*L*(K), 253 and *n*.); cf. *E & I*, 290, and *E*, 301   *A bargain*: Warwick Gould suggests lyric LXVIII of Hafiz of Shiraz: 'From time without beginning my heart made covenant with thy tresses: to time without end, my promise shall not be broken' (*Ghazels . . . Hafiz*, tr. Justin McCarthy (1893), 77). Cf. *E & I*, 290

p. 379, 'Three Things'   *dc*: March 1929   *fp*: *NR*, 2 Oct. 1929   *stretch and yawn*: David R. Clark, *YASAC*, 44–50, suggests the phrase means sexual arousal rather than consummation and he thinks that Pound's translation of Arnault Daniel's 'Doutz brais e critz' is a literary source: '. . . I yawn and stretch because of that fair who surpasseth all others . . .', *The Spirit of Romance* (1910)

p. 379, 'Lullaby'   *dc*: 20/27 March 1929   *fp*: *The New Keepsake* (1931) with the title 'Words/Lullaby'. Yeats described the poem to Olivia Shakespear as 'A mother sings to her child' (*L*(W), 760–1)   *Paris . . . Helen's arms*: son of Priam, King of Troy, and his wife Hecuba. Exposed as an infant on Mount Ida because it was prophesied he would bring ruin on his country, he was brought up by shepherds, lived with Oenone, a nymph, and was appointed to award the prize for beauty to one of the three goddesses Hera, Athene and Aphrodite. Aphrodite offered him the fairest mortal woman if she was awarded the prize; as a result Paris visited Sparta and persuaded Helen, wife of King Menelaus, to elope with him. This caused the Trojan War, the Greeks besieging Troy for ten years before taking it by the stratagem of the wooden horse. Paris was mortally wounded in the siege; he was brought to Oenone too late for her to cure

him and she committed suicide   *Tristram*: Malory in *Le Morte d'Arthur*
tells how Tristram, son of the King of Lyonesse, sent to Ireland to be cured
of a wound, falls in love with La Beale Isoud, the King's daughter. When
he returns to Cornwall, King Mark sends him back to Ireland to ask La
Beale Isoud to marry King Mark. She does so but remains in love with
Tristram (unwittingly they drank a love potion); they are betrayed to
Mark. Tristram leaves Mark's court. There are two versions of his
death   *the potion's work*: the love potion which caused Tristram and La
Beale Isoud to fall in love   *Eurotas' grassy bank*: the Eurotas is the main
river of Sparta   *the holy bird*: Zeus in the form of a swan. Cf. 'Leda and
the Swan', p. 322   *Leda*: see notes on 'Leda and the Swan', p. 586, and
'Among School Children', p. 588

     p. 380, 'After Long Silence'   *dc*: Nov. 1929   *fp*: *WMP* with the
title 'Words/After Long Silence'   *We loved each other*: the poem is about
Yeats's relationship with Olivia Shakespear. See notes on 'Friends', p. 549

     p. 380, 'Mad as the Mist and Snow',   *dc*: 12 Feb. 1929   *fp*: *WMP*
with the title 'Words/Mad as the Mist and Snow'. Yeats wrote in *OTB* that
when he grew old he could no longer spend all his time 'amid masterpieces
and trying to make the like'. He gave part of each day to mere entertainment, 'and it seemed when I was ill that great genius was "mad as the mist
and snow" ' (*E*, 436)   *Horace*: Quintus Horatius Flaccus (65–8 BC),
Roman poet, pardoned after fighting on the losing side at Philippi, became
a friend of Maecenas who gave him a Sabine farm   *Homer*: Greek epic
poet (?born between 1950–850 BC), whom the ancients regarded as the
author of the *Iliad* and the *Odyssey*; seven cities claimed to be his birthplace
and tradition represents him as blind and poor in his old age   *Plato*:
Greek philosopher (427–348 BC), born in Athens or Aegina   *Tully's
open page*: Marcus Tullius Cicero (106–43 BC) became Consul in 63 BC. He
was pardoned by Caesar after Pharsalia, having fought on Pompey's side.
He attacked Mark Antony in his Phillipic orations, was proscribed by the
Triumvirate and put to death in 43 BC. He wrote on rhetoric, political and
moral philosophy, and his letters give an account of his life and times

     p. 381, 'Those Dancing Days are Gone'   *dc*: 8 March 1929   *fp*:
NR, 12 Nov. 1930 with the title 'Four Poems/A Song for Music'   *Title*:
owed to 'Johnny, I hardly knew ye: /Indeed, your dancing days are done!',
A Book of Irish Verse (1895), 239   *the sun in a golden cup, The moon in a
silver bag*: the first line of this refrain is taken from Ezra Pound's *Canto
XXIII*, which, Yeats said in his notes, he read in *A Draft of the Cantos 17–27*
(1928), 33. Cf. also the golden and silver imagery in 'The Man who
Dreamed of Faeryland', p. 79, and other poems

     p. 382, ' "I am of Ireland" '   *dc*: Aug. 1928   *fp*: *WMP* with the
title 'Words/"I am of Ireland"', Yeats's note describes the poem as

'developed from three or four lines of an Irish fourteenth-century dance song somebody repeated to me a few years ago'. Frank O'Connor (penname of Michael O'Donovan, 1903–66) read Yeats this version from J. E. Wells, *Manual of The Writings in Middle English 1050–1400*, 492:

> Icham of Irlande
> Aut of the holy lande of Irlande
> Gode sir pray ich ye
> For of saynte charite
> Come and daunce wyt me,
> In Irlaunde

Mrs Yeats said the source was St John D. Seymour, *Anglo-Irish Literature, 1200–1582* (1929), who thought the lines 'placed in the mouth of an Irish girl, and so presumably . . . composed by an Anglo-Irish minstrel'

p. 383, 'The Dancer at Cruachan and Cro-Patrick'   *dc*: Aug. 1931   *fp*: *WMP* with the title 'Words/The Dancer at Cruachan and Croagh Patrick'   Yeats's footnote to *Cruachan* read 'Pronounced in modern Gaelic as if spelt "Crockan" '   *Title*: for Cruachan, see notes on '*The Old Age of Queen Maeve*', p. 523. Cro-Patrick, or Croagh Patrick (see Glossary), a mountain in Connemara, near Westport, Co. Mayo, is known for its Christian pilgrimage on the last Sunday in July   *I, proclaiming*: St Cellach, Cellach Mac Aodh, Archbishop of Armagh from 1105–29, known as St Celsus. See Standish Hayes O'Grady, 'The Life of Cellach of Killala', *Silva Gadelica*, II, 50–69. Cf. also Yeats's remark about an Irish saint, whose name he had forgotten, singing 'There is one among the birds that is so perfect one among the fish, one perfect among men' (*E & I*, 431). See also *E & I*, 291

p. 383, 'Tom the Lunatic'   *dc*: 27 July 1931   *fp*: *WMP* with the title 'Words/Tom the Lunatic'   *Title*: Tom O'Bedlam was a name applied to inmates of Bedlam (the hospital of St Mary of Bethlehem, a London lunatic asylum). Tom Fool is another traditional name for a fool or buffoon. (Cf. Shakespeare's 'Poor Tom' in *King Lear*, act 3, scene 4, 123–34)   *Huddon and Duddon and Daniel O'Leary*: Yeats put these characters in a poem in *A V*(B), 32; in a footnote he remarked that as a child he pronounced 'O'Leary' as though it rhymed with 'dairy'. O'Leary explains himself in *A V*(B), 33–55. The characters may echo the 'Hudden and Dudden and Donald O'Nery' from 'Donald and His Neighbours', *FFT*, 299–303. Yeats's source is *The Royal Hibernian Tales* (n.d.)   *Holy Joe*: presumably an invented character. The term is used in Ireland (often contemptuously) for excessively religious persons

p. 384, 'Tom at Cruachan'   *dc*: 29 July 1931   *fp*: *WMP* with the title 'Words/Tom at Cruachan'   *Cruachan's plain*: see notes on *The Old Age of Queen Maeve*, p. 523

p. 384, 'Old Tom Again'   *dc*: Oct. 1931   *fp*: WMP with the title 'Words/Old Tom Again'   Yeats described the poem to his wife as a reply to 'the Dancer's Song' (presumably 'The Dancer at Cruachan and Cro-Patrick', p. 383)

p. 384, 'The Delphic Oracle upon Plotinus'   *dc*: 19 Aug. 1931 (appended to text *P* (1949))   *fp*: WMP with the title 'Words/The Delphic Oracle upon Plotinus'   *Title*: the oracle at Delphi (in a rocky cleft on the south-western slopes of Mount Parnassus) was the chief Greek oracle, its greatest point of influence being between the 8th and 5th centuries BC   *Plotinus*: see notes on 'The Tower', p. 577. The poem is based upon the oracle given to Amelius, who consulted Delphi to find out where the soul of Plotinus had gone after his death. See Porphyry's *Life of Plotinus*, which Yeats read both in Thomas Taylor's translation and in Stephen MacKenna's translation of 1917:

> . . . the bonds of human necessity are loosed for you and, strong of heart, you beat your eager way from out the roaring tumult of the fleshy life to the shores of that wave-washed coast free from the thronging of the guilty, thence to take the grateful path of the sinless soul: /where glows the splendour of God, where Right is throned in the stainless place, far from the wrong that mocks at law. /Oft-times as you strove to rise above the bitter waves of this blood-drenched life, above the sickening whirl, toiling in the mid-most of the rushing flood and the unimaginable turmoil, oft-times, from the Ever-Blessed, there was shown to you the Term still close at hand: /Oft-times, when your mind thrust out awry and was like to be rapt down unsanctioned paths, the Immortals themselves prevented, guiding you on the straightgoing way to the celestial spheres, pouring down before you a dense shaft of light that your eyes might see from amid the mournful gloom. /Sleep never closed those eyes: high above the heavy murk of the mist you held them; tossed in the welter, you still had vision; still you saw sights many and fair not granted to all that labour in wisdom's quest. /But now that you have cast the screen aside, quitted the tomb that held your lofty soul, you enter at once the heavenly consort; /where fragrant breezes play, where all is unison and winning tenderness and guileless joy and the place is lavish of the nectar streams the unfailing Gods bestow, with the blandishments of the Loves, and delicious airs, and tranquil sky: /where Minos and Rhadamanthus dwell, great brethren of the golden race of mighty Zeus; where dwells the just Aeacus, and Plato, consecrated power, and stately Pythagoras and all else that form the choir of Immortal Love, there where the heart is ever lifted in joyous festival.
>
> O Blessed One, you have fought your many fights; now crowned with unfading life, your days are with the Ever-Holy./
>
> Rejoicing Muses, let us stay our song and the subtle windings of our dance; thus much I could but tell, to my golden lyre, of Plotinus, the hallowed soul.
>
> [S. MacKenna, *Plotinus*, 'Porphyry's Life of Plotinus', 22–4; revd edn (1946), 16]

Rhadamanthus: in Greek mythology, a son of Zeus and Europa, a judge of souls in the Underworld, in Elysium, the place to which favoured heroes exempt from death were sent by the gods   *Golden Race*: either the immortals, or, more likely, from MacKenna's translation, 'the great brethren of the golden race of Zeus', Rhadamanthus and Minos (see l. 8). Porphyry also adds Aeacus as the third enthroned judge of souls   *dim*: they looked dim to Plotinus, but poured down a dense shaft of light so that he could see 'amid the mournful gloom'   *salt blood*: Plotinus was struggling to free himself, to rise above 'the bitter waves of this blood-drenched life'   *Plato . . . Minos . . . choir of Love*: this is very close to MacKenna's translation, one of Yeats's favourite quotations

'A Woman Young and Old'

This series of poems was written between 1926 and 1929; in them 'the woman speaks first in youth, then in age' (*WBY*, 374). The series was written before the publication of *The Tower*, but was, Yeats said in a note of 1933, left out for some reason he could not recall

p. 385, 'Father and Child'   *dc*: 1926/1927   *fp*: WS (1929)   *She*: Anne Butler Yeats, Yeats's daughter   *strike the board*: an echo of George Herbert's 'The Collar': 'I struck the board, and cry'd no more'   *a man*: the poem records an incident when Anne Yeats, then a child, praised the appearance of a youthful friend, Fergus Fitzgerald

p. 385, 'Before the World was Made'   *dc*: Feb. 1928   *fp*: WS (1929)   *the face I had*: the woman is searching for her archetypal face; this may reflect Plato's ideas in the *Republic*, 597, *Timaeus*, 28, and *Phaedrus*, 250. God, Plato argued, was the creator of the models of all things; in making the world he looked to his created pattern; and earthly things are copies of higher ideas. See notes on 'The Tower', p. 577

p. 386, 'A First Confession'   *dc*: June 1927   *fp*: WS (1929)   *that I pull back*: in his note on this poem in *TWS* (NY, 1929) Yeats said he had 'symbolised a woman's love as the struggle of the darkness to keep the sun from rising from its earthly bed'   *Zodiac*: see notes on 'Chosen', p. 612

p. 386, 'Her Triumph'   *dc*: 29 Nov. 1926   *fp*: WS (1929)   *the dragon's will*: possibly Yeats had in mind the picture described in 'Michael Robartes and the Dancer' (*Saint George and the Dragon*, ascribed to Bordone, in the National Gallery of Ireland, Dublin). Another possible source is Cosimo Tura's *St George and the Dragon*, which Yeats saw in Ferrara Cathedral in 1907   *Saint George or else a pagan Perseus*: Yeats had a reproduction of Perino del Vaga's *Andromeda and Perseus*, which may have been in his mind when he wrote this poem. Perseus was a son of Zeus and Danae (whom Zeus visited in a shower of gold), daughter of Acrisius, King of Argos, whom Perseus later killed by mistake. Perseus, who killed Medusa the Gorgon, rescued Andromeda, the daughter of Cepheus, King of Ethiopia and Cassiopeia, from a dragon   *strange bird*: possibly the source is William Morris, 'The Doom of King Acrisius', in *The Earthly Paradise*

p. 387, 'Consolation'   *dc*: probably June 1927   *fp*: *WS* (1929)   *crime of being born*: cf. 'the crime of death and birth' in 'A Dialogue of Self and Soul', p. 348

p. 387, 'Chosen'   *dc*: probably early in 1926   *fp*: *WS* 1929 with the title 'VI/The Choice'   *chosen*: possibly a reflection of Plato's myth of Er in which the souls of men and women in heaven choose the lots which represent their future destinies   *the whirling Zodiac*: Yeats's note in *WS* (1929) reads:

> I have symbolised a woman's love as the struggle of the darkness to keep the sun from rising from its earthly bed. In the last stanza of the Choice [the original title of 'Chosen'] I change the symbol to that of the souls of man and woman ascending through the Zodiac. In some Neoplatonist or Hermatist – whose name I forget – the whorl changes into a sphere at one of the points where the Milky Way crosses the Zodiac

The note was expanded in *TWSOP*:

> The 'learned astrologer' in *Chosen* was Macrobius [Ambrosius Theodosius Macrobius, a fifth-century Neoplatonist], and the particular passage was found for me by Dr. Sturm [Dr F. P. Sturm, a doctor who practised in Lancashire; he published three books of poems and was interested in the occult] that too little known poet and mystic. It is from Macrobius's comment upon 'Scipio's Dream' (Lib. I, Cap. XII, Sec. 5): '. . . when the sun is in Aquarius, we sacrifice to the Shades, for it is in the sign inimical to human life; and from thence, the meeting-place of Zodiac and Milky Way, the descending soul by its defluction is drawn out of the spherical, the sole divine form, into the cone'. [Cf. a note on l. 28 of 'Byzantium' (*NC*, 298) and see *Frank Pearce Sturm: His Life, Letters and Collected Work*, ed. Richard Taylor (1969), 92]

both adrift on the miraculous stream: the Milky Way, a symbol used for the abode of the soul before birth   *wrote a learned astrologer*: Wilson (*Y & T*, 210) quotes a passage from Macrobius:

> Since those who are about to descend are yet in Cancer, and have not left the Milky Way, they rank in the order of the gods. . . . From the confine, therefore, in which the zodiac and galaxy touch one another, the soul, descending from a round figure which is the only divine form, is produced into a cone [T. Taylor, *Porphyry*, 187]

Wilson points out that Cancer is 'the confine in which the zodiac and galaxy touch one another', where Milky Way and zodiac meet, and Cancer is therefore 'the gate'. The soul passes through it, loses its spherical shape. It descends through the signs; after death it returns through the gate of

Capricorn, eventually returning to its source. Cf. Yeats's explanation of the thirteenth cycle or thirteenth cone:

> It is that cycle which may deliver us from the twelve cycles of time and space. The cone which intersects ours is a cone in so far as we think of it as the antithesis to our thesis, but if the time has come for our deliverance it is the phaseless sphere, sometimes called the Thirteenth Sphere, for every lesser cycle contains within itself a sphere that is, as it were, the reflection or messenger of the final deliverance. Within it live all souls that have been set free and every *Daimon* and *Ghostly Self;* our expanding cone seems to cut through its gyre; spiritual influx is from its circumference, animate life from its centre. 'Eternity also', says Hermes in the Aeslepius dialogue, 'though motionless itself, appears to be in motion'. When Shelley's Demogorgon – eternity – comes from the centre of the earth it may so come because Shelley substituted the earth for such a sphere. [*AV*(B), 210–11. Yeats's footnote read: 'Shelley, who had more philosophy than men thought when I was young, probably knew that Parmenides represented reality as a motionless sphere. Mrs Shelley speaks of the "mystic meanings" of *Prometheus Unbound* as only intelligible to a "mind as subtle as his own" ']

Yeats also commented on it as follows:

> The *Thirteenth Cone* is a sphere because sufficient to itself; but as seen by Man it is a cone. It becomes even conscious of itself as so seen, like some great dancer, the perfect flower of modern culture, dancing some primitive dance and conscious of his or her own life and of the dance. There is a mediaeval story of a man persecuted by his Guardian Angel because it was jealous of his sweetheart, and such stories seem closer to reality than our abstract theology. All imaginable relations may arise between a man and his God. I only speak of the *Thirteenth Cone* as a sphere and yet I might say that the gyre or cone of the *Principles* is in reality a sphere, though to Man, bound to birth and death, it can never seem so, and that it is the antinomies that force us to find it a cone. Only one symbol exists, though the reflecting mirrors make many appear and all different. [*AV*(B), 240]

p. 388, 'Parting'   *dc*: Aug. 1926   *fp*: *WS* (1929)   *his loud song*: Hone (*WBY*, 433) suggested that there is an echo here of *Romeo and Juliet*, act 3, scene 5:

> No, night's bird and love's
> Bids all true lovers rest,
> While his loud song reproves
> The murderous stealth of day.

p. 388, 'Her Vision in the Wood'   *dc*: Aug. 1926   *fp*: *WS* (1929)   *a wounded man*: probably the Adonis legend (see notes on 'Vacillation', p. 602) is suggested here, though Henn (*TLT*, 246) thought Diarmid (Diarmuid), the Irish hero killed on Ben Bulben, a Sligo mountain, by a boar, may have been intended   *the beast*: in Greek legend a wild boar killed Adonis, a beautiful young man beloved by Aphrodite; the anemone flower was said to have sprung from his blood. Persephone restored him to life on condition that he spent six months of the year with her and six with Aphrodite (this implying a winter–summer symbol). His death and revival were celebrated in many festivals   *Quattrocento*: (Italian) fifteenth century; see also 'Among School Children', p. 323   *Mantegna*: Andrea Mantegna (1431–1506), Italian painter born near Vicenza

p. 389, 'A Last Confession'   *dc*: June, 23 and 24 July and Aug. 1926   *fp*: WS (1929)   *bird of day*: Henn (*LT*, 59) remarks that the bird (cf. 'the most ridiculous little bird' of 'A Memory of Youth', p. 225, and the 'miraculous strange bird' of 'Parting', p. 388) has an eternalising function; not only is it a link with daytime and the dissipation of the lovers' ecstasies but a 'half malicious, half mystical symbol' suggesting a supernatural and eternal commentary on the act

p. 390, 'Meeting'   *dc*: possibly 1926   *fp*: WS (1929)

p. 391, 'From the "Antigone" '   *dc*: probably completed by Dec. 1927   *fp*: WS (1929). Yeats knew the translations by Richard Jebb, Lewis Campbell and Paul Masqueray (whose French version he used when writing this poem)   *Parnassus*: a mountain some miles from Adelphi, sacred to the Muses in Greek mythology, one peak sacred to Apollo, the other to Dionysus   *Empyrean*: the highest part of the supposedly spherical heavens, thought in classical cosmology to contain the element of fire. Early Christians considered it the abode of God and the angels   *Brother and brother*: Antigone's brothers, Eteocles and Polyneices, who killed each other   *Œdipus' child*: in Sophocles' *Antigone*, Antigone, daughter of Œdipus (see notes on XI ('From "Œdipus at Colonus" '), p. 591) commits suicide, having been buried alive by Creon, King of Thebes. His son Haemon, who loved her, killed himself on her grave

FROM 'A FULL MOON IN MARCH'

p. 395, 'Parnell's Funeral'   *dc*: April 1933   *fp*: ll. 16–23 appeared untitled in 'Introduction to "Fighting the Waves" ', *DM*, April–June 1932, and in *W & B*. The whole poem, sections I and II, first appeared in *SP*, 19 Oct. 1934, with the titles: I, 'A Parnellite at Parnell's Funeral', and, II, 'Forty Years Later'. The first appearance of the whole poem with its title 'Parnell's Funeral' was in *FMM* (1935)   *Title*: funeral of Charles Stewart Parnell (1846–91); see notes on 'To a Shade', p. 545, and 'Come Gather Round Me, Parnellites', p. 626   *Great Comedian*: Daniel O'Connell (1775–1847), Irish politician responsible for Catholic Emancipation in 1929: he is a great comedian in contrast to the tragedian

Parnell   *a brighter star*: the star of which Maud Gonne told Yeats, which fell as Parnell's body was lowered into the grave at Glasnevin cemetery, Dublin   *the Cretan barb*: explained by Yeats (*A*, 372–5; quoted *NC*, 406) in a very fully annotated passage. He described a vision he had of a galloping centaur, and a moment later a naked woman standing on a pedestal shooting an arrow at a star; he interpreted it as akin to the mother goddess (the 'Great Mother', see l. 13), whose priestess shot an arrow at a child whose death symbolised the death and resurrection of the tree-spirit of Apollo. She was depicted on some 5th-century BC Cretan coins sitting in the heart of a branching tree   *Sicilian coin*: presumably derived from the Cretan coins mentioned to Yeats by Vacher Burch, who directed him to G. F. Hill, *A Handbook of Greek and Roman Coins* (1899), 163, which illustrates the coin showing the Cretan goddess in the tree   *strangers murdered Emmet, Fitzgerald, Tone*: those who killed them were not Irish people. See comment on them in notes on 'September 1913', p. 543   *popular rage*: the difference is that now Irish people themselves have attacked their own leader, Parnell   *Hysterica passio*: hysteria; from Shakespeare's *King Lear*, act 2, scene 4, l. 56, 'Hysterica passio, down, thou climbing sorrow'   *dragged this quarry down*: Parnell, whose leadership of the Irish party was repudiated after his adulterous relationship with Mrs O'Shea became known (see notes on 'To a Shade', p. 545). A contemporary cartoon showed Parnell defending himself against a pack of wolves   *devoured his heart*: Parnell is envisaged as the sacrificial victim, the god devoured in a ritual   *Come, fix*: Yeats is presumably challenging those nationalists who spurned Parnell   *the rhyme rats hear*: possibly a reflection of the belief that Irish poets could rhyme rats to death, or make them migrate by the power of their poetry. The poet Seanchan Torpest killed ten rats in King Guare's palace at Gort, Co. Galway, by speaking poetry against them   *de Valéra*: Eamonn de Valera (1882–1975), sentenced to death in 1916, released in 1917; opposed the Treaty of 1922; President of the Executive Council of the Irish Free State after 1932 election until 1948, re-elected 1951–4, 1957–9; President of Ireland, 1959–73   *Cosgrave*: William T. Cosgrave (1880–1965), sentenced to death in 1916, released in 1917; President of the Executive Council of the Irish Free State (1922–32), member of Dail Eireann (1922–44)   *O'Higgins*: Kevin O'Higgins (1892–1927); see notes on 'Death', p. 595   *O'Duffy*: Eoin O'Duffy (1892–1944), joined IRA in 1917, first Commissioner of the Civic Guard in 1922, dismissed in 1933, leader of the Blue Shirt organisation July 1933; in 1936 organised an Irish Brigade to fight for the Nationalists in the Spanish Civil War   *Jonathan Swift*: see notes on 'Blood and the Moon', p. 595   *bitter wisdom*: possibly a reference to Swift's *Discourse of the Contests and Dissentions between the Nobles and the Commons in Athens and Rome* (1701). Yeats thought Swift argued that the health of all states depends upon a right balance between the one, the few and the many. See *E*, 357, quoted *NC*, 413–14; see also *NC*, 332–8

p. 396, 'Three Songs to the Same Tune'   *dc:* between 30 Nov. 1933 and Feb. 1934   *fp: SP*, 23 Feb. 1934. They were revised as 'Three Marching Songs' in *LPTP*   Yeats's note after the title in the *SP* printing read:

> In politics I have but one passion and one thought, rancour against all who, except under the most dire necessity, disturb public order, a conviction that public order cannot long persist without the rule of educated and able men. . . . Some months ago that passion laid hold upon me with the violence which unfits the poet for all politics but his own. While the mood lasted, it seemed that our growing disorder, the fanaticism that inflamed it like some old bullet embedded in the flesh, was about to turn our noble history into an ignoble farce. For the first time in my life I wanted to write what some crowd in the street might understand and sing; I asked my friends for a tune; they recommended that old march, 'O'Donnell Abu'. I first got my chorus, 'Down the fanatic, down the clown,' then the rest of the first song. But I soon tired of its rhetorical vehemence, thought that others would tire of it unless I found some gay playing upon its theme, some half-serious exaggeration and defence of its rancorous chorus, and therefore I made the second version. Then I put into a simple song a commendation of the rule of the able and educated, man's old delight in submission; I wrote round the line 'The soldier takes pride in saluting his captain,' thinking the while of a Gaelic poet's lament for his lost masters: 'My fathers served their fathers before Christ was crucified.' I read my songs to friends, they talked to others, those others talked, and now companies march to the words 'Blueshirt Abu,' and a song that is all about shamrocks and harps or seems all about them, because its words have the particular variation upon the cadence of 'Yankee Doodle' Young Ireland reserved for that theme. I did not write that song; I could not if I tried. Here are my songs. Anybody may sing them, choosing 'clown' and 'fanatic' for himself, if they are singable – musicians say they are, but may flatter – and worth singing.

The 'Commentary on Three Songs' Yeats appended to the printing in *P(Ch)*, Dec. 1934, is quoted with annotations in *NC* 498–500; see also *VE*, 835–8.

I   *the tune of O'Donnell Abu:* 'O'Domhnaill Abu' by Michael Joseph McCann (?1824–83), a Young Irelander, was meant to be sung to the tune 'Roderick Vick Alpine Dhu', the 'Boat Song' in Sir Walter Scott's *Lady of the Lake*, but another tune composed by Joseph Halliday (1775–1846) proved more popular   *out of pride:* Saul, *PYP*, 156, has suggested an echo of the 18th-century ballad 'The Night before Larry was stretched': 'He kicked too – but was all pride'

II   *Drown all the dogs:* this is based on the behaviour of Yeats's neighbours in Rathfarnham, Co. Dublin. See *YM & P*, 279, *L(W)*, 820, and Frank O'Connor, *The Backward Look*, 181–2   *O'Donnell:* possibly Red Hugh O'Donnell (*c.* 1571–1602), chief of the O'Donnells, who shared victory with Hugh O'Neill in the Battle of the Yellow Ford (1598). He went seeking aid in Spain and was reputedly poisoned there, dying in 1602. His younger brother, Rory O'Donnell (1575–1665), succeeded him and was created an Earl in 1603. He attempted to raise the Catholic Lords to rebel, but when their plot was discovered he fled to Rome with the eldest son of the Earl of Tyrone   *both O'Neills*: possibly Shane O'Neill 'the Proud', The O'Neill (*c.* 1530–1567); he submitted to Elizabeth I in London in 1562 but invaded the Pale (the English controlled area of Ireland) and burned Antrim in 1566, and was killed by the MacDonnells in 1567. Yeats is probably also thinking of Hugh O'Neill (*b. c.* 1540), the 2nd Earl of Tyrone, elected The O'Neill in 1591. He marched to relieve a Spanish force at Kinsale, but his territory was largely taken by Elizabeth's forces. When he thought a plot was laid to trap him, he and O'Donnell left Ireland in 1607 to settle in Rome. This 'Flight of the Earls' effectively marked the end of Gaelic civilisation in Ireland   *Emmet*: see notes on 'September 1913', p. 543   *Parnell*: see notes on 'To a Shade', p. 545   III   *Troy backed its Helen*: see notes on 'His Memories', p. 591   *empty up there at the top*: probably derived from Swift's remarks; see notes on 'Blood and the Moon', p. 595

p. 399, 'Alternative Song for the Severed Head in "The King of the Great Clock Tower" '   *dc*: probably 1934   *fp*: *LL*, Nov. 1934 ('Tune by Arthur Duff' appended to text)   *Ben Bulben and Knocknarea*: mountains overlooking Sligo. See Glossary   *Rosses' crawling tide*: Rosses, sea coast and a village near Sligo   *Cuchulain . . . foam*: cf. 'Cuchulain's Fight with the Sea', p. 68   *Niamh that rode on it*: Niamh, the fairy princess who sought Oisin; see notes on *WO*, p. 486   *lad and lass . . . the chess*: Naoise and Deirdre, captured by Conchubar on their return under safeguard to Ireland. In *Deirdre*, Deirdre and Naoise re-enact the situation of Lugaidh Redstripe, a warrior in the Red Branch cycle of tales, when Fergus, their safe conduct, has been tricked away to a feast and they realise they can expect no mercy from Conchubar. See notes on 'The Rose of the World', p. 498   *Aleel, his Countess*: a reference to Yeats's play *The Countess Cathleen*, in which Aleel (originally Kevin) is the poet, Cathleen the heroine. See notes on 'The Countess Cathleen in Paradise', p. 502   *Hanrahan*: see notes on 'He reproves the Curlew', p. 514   *King . . . feathers*: in Yeats's story 'The Wisdom of the King', the child of the High Queen of Ireland is visited by the crones of the grey hawk (the Sidhe: see notes on 'The Hosting of the Sidhe', p. 506), one of whom lets a drop of blood fall on the child's lips. The King dies two years later, the child grows very wise, but the grey hawk's feathers grow in his hair. The child is deceived by the poets and men of law about them, being told that everyone has feathers too (because of a law that no one with a bodily blemish could sit on the throne). The child, become King, eventually discovers the truth, orders that Eochaid should rule in his stead and vanishes

p. 400, 'Two Songs Rewritten for the Tune's Sake'   *fp*: *PPV* (untitled, I, *LC*, 1–4, 7–10 and 13–16 in *The Pot of Broth* and untitled, II, *LC*, 1 and 6–12 in *The Player Queen*. The second song appeared in *DL*,

Nov. 1922, subsequently in *PPV* ('From the Pot of Broth. Tune: Paistin
Finn' appended to text of I; 'From *The Player Queen*' to text of II)
I   *Paistin Finn*: a Munster folk tune, possibly a version of a song from
the Ossianic cycle, since the title can mean 'Little Child of Fionn' as well as
'Fair-haired little child'
II   *dreepy*: an Irish dialect word meaning dreary, doleful, droopy

p. 401, 'A Prayer for Old Age'   *dc*: 1934   *fp*: *SP*, 2 Nov. 1934 with
the title 'Old Age'   The poem was provoked by Ezra Pound's condemnation of Yeats's play *The King of the Great Clock Tower*; it expresses
Yeats's dislike of 'intellectual' poetry. See *NC*, 349

p. 401, 'Church and State'   *dc*: Aug. 1934 (appended to text)   *fp*:
SP, 23 Nov. 1934 with the title 'A Vain Hope'   *wine . . . Bread*: a
reflection of the bread and wine of the communion service

'Supernatural Songs'

Yeats wrote a general comment on these poems, included in *KGCT*; this is
quoted and annotated in *NC*, 350

p. 402, 'Ribh at the Tomb of Baile and Aillinn'   *dc*: completed by 24
July 1934   *fp*: *P*(Ch) Dec. 1934; *LM*, Dec. 1934, with the title
'Supernatural Songs/Ribh . . . Aillinn'   *Title*: Ribh is an invented
character, an old hermit, described by Yeats as 'an imaginary critic of St
Patrick. His Christianity, come perhaps from Egypt, like much early Irish
Christianity, echoes pre-Christian thought' (Preface to *FMM*). For Baile
and Aillinn, see notes on *Baile and Aillinn*, p. 524, and 'The Withering of
the Boughs', p. 527   *me*: Ribh   *apple and the yew*: when Aengus, god
of love, gave each lover false news of the other's death they died of broken
hearts and were changed into swans linked with a golden chain (see notes
on 'The Withering of the Boughs', p. 527). A yew tree grew where Baile's
body lay, an apple over Aillinn's; their love stories were written on boards
made of yew and apple   *the intercourse of angels*: derived from
Swedenborg's saying 'that the sexual intercourse of angels is a conflagration of the whole being' (*L*(W), 805); another letter of 9 March (*L*(W), 807)
echoed this, and there is a reference to it in 'Anima Mundi'   *circle*: this
indicates the perfect harmony achieved by the lovers. Yeats's comments
suggest that this poem may owe something to the Noh play *Nishikigi* (see
E & I, 232 and 234)

p. 403, 'Ribh denounces Patrick'   *dc*: late July 1934   *fp*: *P*(Ch),
Dec. 1934, *LM*, Dec. 1934, both with the title 'Supernatural Songs/Ribh
Prefers an Older Theology'; numbered 2 in *LM*   The point of the poem
is that 'we beget and bear because of the incompleteness of our love' (*L*(W),

824)   *the man*: St Patrick   *Great Smaragdine Tablet*: a medieval Latin work on alchemy, published in 1541, attributed to the Egyptian Hermes Trismegistus (cf. notes on title of 'Ribh at the Tomb of Baile and Aillinn', p. 618)   *her coil*: Yeats thought 'the line of Nature is crooked, that, though we dig the canal-beds as straight as we can, the rivers run hither and thither in their wildness' (*E & I*, 5)   *mirror-scalèd serpent*: cf. Yeats's argument that the poet must not seek for what is still and fixed (*E & I*, 287—8)

p. 403, 'Ribh in Ecstasy'   *dc*: probably late 1934   *fp*: *FMM*   *you understood*: possibly Maud Gonne, or, more likely, Frank O'Connor who said, when Yeats asked him if he understood 'Ribh denounces Patrick', he 'didn't understand a word of it' (*IY*, 282)   *Those amorous cries*: the poem generally describes Yeats's feeling of unity or happiness after finishing a philosophical poem, a feeling interrupted by 'the common round of day'

p. 404, 'There'   *dc*: probably late 1934 or early 1935   *fp*: *FMM*   *Title*: 'There' is perfection, the sphere of *AV*'s thirteenth cone

p. 404, 'Ribh considers Christian Love Insufficient'   *dc*: probably 1934   *fp*: *P*(Ch), Dec. 1934; *LM*, Dec. 1934, with the title 'Supernatural Songs/Ribh . . . Insufficient'. Numbered 3 in *LM*   *I study hatred*: Ellmann (*IY*, 283) suggested the idea came from some of Mrs Yeats's automatic writing; a communicator, Yeats recorded, had said 'hate God . . . always he repeated "hatred, hatred" or "hatred of God" . . . said, "I think about hatred" '. Yeats saw this as the growing hatred among men which had 'long been a problem with me'   *stroke of midnight*: the end of life. Cf. the final couplet of 'The Four Ages of Man', p. 406

p. 405, 'He and She'   *dc*: before 25 Aug. 1934   *fp*: *P*(Ch), Dec. 1934; *LM*, Dec. 1934, with the title 'Supernatural Songs/He and She'. Numbered 4 in *LM*   Yeats described it as being on the soul: 'It is, of course, my central myth' (*L*(W), 829)

p. 405, 'What Magic Drum?'   *dc*: probably 1934   *fp*: *FMM*   The poem deals with the union of some god or hero with perhaps a human mother (cf. 'Leda and the Swan', p. 322)   *beast*: cf. the 'rough beast' of 'The Second Coming', p. 294

p. 405, 'Whence had they Come?'   *dc*: probably 1934   *fp*: *FMM*   This poem asks what imponderables lie behind personal love or general history, behind *AV*'s interpretation of both. There are some resemblances to the Platonic Idea here   *Dramatis Personae*: the characters in the play   *Charlemagne*: Charlemagne (742–814), King of the Franks, crowned Emperor of the Holy Roman Empire in 800

p. 406, 'The Four Ages of Man'   *dc*: 6 Aug. 1934   *fp*: P(Ch) Dec. 1934; *LM*, Dec. 1934, with the title 'Supernatural Songs/The Four . . . Man'. Numbered 5 in *LM*   Yeats wrote that these are the four ages of individual man but also 'the four ages of civilization' (*L*(W), 826). Earlier (in a letter of 24 July 1934) he had written to Olivia Shakespear:

The Earth	=	Every early nature-dominated civilization
The Water	=	An armed sexual age, chivalry, Froissart's Chronicles
The Air	=	From the Renaissance to the end of the 19th century
The Fire	=	The purging away of our civilisation by our hatred

p. 406, 'Conjunctions'   *dc*: before 25 Aug. 1934   *fp*: P(Ch), Dec. 1934; *LM*, Dec. 1934, with the title 'Supernatural Songs/Conjunctions'. Numbered 6 in *LM*. Yeats wrote to Mrs Shakespear that he was told (presumably by the 'Communicators') his two children would be respectively Mars conjunctive Venus (Anne) and Saturn conjunctive Jupiter (Michael), that he could study in them the alternating dispositions, the Christian or objective, then the Antithetical or subjective. The Christian, he went on, 'is the Mars–Venus – it is democratic. The Jupiter–Saturn civilisation is born free among the most cultivated, out of tradition, out of rule' (*L*(W), 828)

p. 406, 'A Needle's Eye'   *dc*: uncertain   *fp*: P(Ch), Dec. 1934; *LM*, Dec. 1934, with the title 'Supernatural Songs/A Needle's Eye'. Numbered 7 in *LM*

p. 407, 'Meru'   *dc*: probably between August 1933 and June 1934   *fp*: P(Ch), Dec. 1934; *LM*, Dec. 1934, with the title 'Supernatural Songs/Meru'   Yeats was about to begin his Introduction to Shri Purohit Swami's translation of Bhagwan Shri Hamsa's *The Holy Mountain* (1934) in Aug. 1933 (see Yeats's *E & I*, 448–73). This poem envisages man as a destroyer of what he creates and the hermits learn the truth of the succession of civilisations   *Meru or Everest*: a friend of the Swami had been ordered in meditation to seek *Turiya*, the greater or conscious Samadhi at Mount Kailas, the twin of the legendary Meru, the centre of Paradise in Hindu mythology. Everest, the highest mountain in the world, is in the Himalayas, on the borders of Tibet and Nepal   *Caverned*: cf. the mysterious sage of 'The Gyres', p. 411, who speaks 'Out of cavern'

NEW POEMS

Yeats's *New Poems* were published by the Cuala Press in 1938; they were included with other poems (posthumously published) in *LPTP* (also published by the Cuala Press) and *LPP*. See 'A Note on the Text', p. 633

p. 411, 'The Gyres' *dc*: probably between July 1936 and Jan. 1937 *fp*: NP *The gyres*: see notes on 'Demon and Beast', p. 572, and see 'The Second Coming', p. 294 *Old Rocky Face*: some seer, possibly akin to Shelley's Ahasuerus, the cavern-dwelling Jew, 'master of human knowledge' in *Hellas* (MSS versions refer to the 'old cavern man') *Empedocles*: Empedocles (*c*. 490–430 BC), Greek philosopher, who thought all things were composed of earth, air, fire and water, mingled by love or separated by strife *Hector . . . Troy*: see notes on 'The Phases of the Moon', p. 565 *tragic joy*: Yeats held this attitude strongly:

> There is in the creative joy of acceptance of what life brings, because we have understood the beauty of what it brings, or a hatred of death for what it takes away, which arouses within us, through some sympathy perhaps with all other men, an energy so noble, so powerful that we laugh aloud and mock, in the terror or the sweetness of our exaltation, at death and oblivion. [*E & I*, 322]

p. 412, 'Lapis Lazuli' *dc*: July 1936 (completed 25 July) *fp*: LM, March 1938 *Title*: Yeats was given by Henry (Harry) Clifton a lapis lazuli carving as a seventieth birthday present *nothing drastic . . . and Zeppelin*: a reflection of mounting political tension in the 1930s. Italy invaded Abyssinia in 1935; Germany reoccupied the Rhineland in 1936; there was a general fear of war and air raids. German Zeppelins, rigid-frame airships named after their designer Graf Von Zeppelin (1838–1917), had raided London in the First World War *King Billy*: King William III (William of Orange), an echo of a ballad 'The Battle of the Boyne':

> King James he pitched his tents between
> The lines for to retire;
> But King William threw his bomb-balls in
> And set them all on fire

Hamlet . . . their lines: Shakespeare's tragic heroes and heroines (Cordelia and Ophelia are implicitly contrasted with the contemporary 'hysterical women') convey through their looks, or through the metaphorical patterns of their speech, 'the sudden enlargement of their vision, their ecstasy at the approach of death' *Gaiety . . . dread*: Yeats remarked: 'I have heard Lady Gregory say, rejecting some play in the modern manner . . . "Tragedy must be a joy to the man who dies" ' (*E & I*, 523) *Callimachus*: Greek sculptor of the late 5th century BC who invented the running drill but was thought to have ruined his art by over-elaboration. He made a golden lamp (in the shape of a palm tree with a long bronze chimney) for the Erechtheum at Athens *Two Chinamen . . . instrument*: these lines describe the lapis lazuli carved

> into the semblance of a mountain with temple, trees, paths and an ascetic and pupil about to climb the mountain. Ascetic, pupil, hard stone, eternal theme of

the sensual east. But no, I am wrong, the east has its solutions always and therefore knows nothing of tragedy. It is we, not the east, that must raise the heroic cry. [L(W), 837]

p. 413, 'Imitated from the Japanese'   *dc*: towards the end of Dec. 1936 (final version dated 30 Oct. 1937)   *fp*: NP   Yeats wrote to his friend Dorothy Wellesley (1889–1956), a minor English poet, that he had made this poem 'out of a prose translation of a Japanese Hokku in praise of Spring' (*DWL*, 116). A hokku is a poem of seventeen syllables, in three lines of five, seven and five syllables. *PNE* suggests as source Gekkyo (1745–1824), 'My longing after the departed Spring/Is not the same every year', *An Anthology of Haiku Ancient and Modern*, tr. Asatoro Mijamori (1932)

p. 414, 'Sweet Dancer'   *dc*: Jan. 1937   *fp*: *LM*, April 1938   *The girl*: Margot Ruddock. This was her maiden name; divorced from Jack Collis, she had married Raymond Lovell in 1932. When Yeats met her she was twenty-seven; she asked him to help her in creating a poet's theatre. He wrote her several poems (the unpublished 'Margot' is included in *YANB*, 324) and wrote an Introduction to her poems in *The Lemon Tree* (1937). She took part in some BBC broadcasts of poetry arranged by Yeats. See *Ah, Sweet Dancer, W. B. Yeats, Margot Ruddock. A Correspondence*, ed. Roger McHugh (1970). For the happenings described in this poem and 'A Crazed Girl', p. 421, see L(W), 856

p. 414, 'The Three Bushes'   *dc*: July 1936   *fp*: *LM*, Jan. 1937   The source of this subtitle is invented, though Olivia Shakespear referred Yeats to Pierre de Bourdeilles (?1527/40–1614), abbot, Lord of Brantôme, and author of *Vies des dames galantes* (see *Yeats Annual No. 6* (1988), 81. The poem derived from a ballad by Dorothy Wellesley; for its elaboration see Yeats's correspondence with her, 2 July, 1936, *DWL*

p. 416, 'The Lady's First Song'   *dc*: completed by Nov. 1936   *fp*: NP   *No better than a beast*: cf. 'A Last Confession', p. 389: 'And laughed upon his breast to think/Beast gave beast as much'

p. 417, 'The Lady's Second Song'   *dc*: July 1936   *fp*: NP   *The Lord have mercy upon us*: this liturgical refrain leads forward not only to the Chambermaid's final confession to the priest (when old and dying in the penultimate stanza of 'The Three Bushes', p. 416) but is 'a counterparted gesture, as by some bystander, on the "heresy" that the Lady propounds' (*LT*, 332)

p. 418, 'The Lady's Third Song'   *dc*: July 1936   *fp*: NP   *contrapuntal serpent*: contrapuntal because of the soul–body conflict, the serpent is a symbol of the Fall of Man (Genesis 3:1–6), hence here equated with sex (the post-Fall covering of themselves with leaves by Adam and Eve marks their departure from innocence)

p. 418, 'The Lover's Song'   *dc*: 9 Nov. 1936   *fp*: *NP*

p. 418, 'The Chambermaid's First Song'   *dc*: Nov. 1936   *fp*: *NP*   *Weak as a worm*: see the discussion in letters of 15, 20 and 28 Nov. 1936 about the adjective (*DWL*, 103–8)

p. 419, 'The Chambermaid's Second Song'   *dc*: Nov. 1936   *fp*: *NP*

p. 419, 'An Acre of Grass'   *dc*: Nov. 1936   *fp*: *AM*, April 1938; *LM*, April 1938   *acre of green grass . . . old house*: Riversdale, Rathfarnham, Co. Dublin, a 'little creeper-covered farmhouse', which Yeats leased for thirteen years in 1932   *Timon*: known as the Misanthrope, an Athenian contemporary of Socrates (*d*. 399 BC), he was attacked by the comic writers for his disgust with mankind (caused by the ingratitude of his early friends). Shakespeare's *Timon of Athens* follows the story told in William Painter's *Palace of Pleasure* (1566–7)   *William Blake*: English poet and engraver (1757–1827). Yeats edited his *Works* (3 vols., 1893) with Edwin Ellis, and a selection of his poems (1893)   *Michael Angelo*: see notes on 'Michael Robartes and the Dancer', p. 568   *eagle mind*: Yeats was rereading the German philosopher Friedrich Wilhelm Nietzsche in 1936–7 and this idea may come from his *The Dawn of Day*, 347, where minds of men of genius are 'but loosely linked to their character and temperament, like winged beings which easily separate themselves from them, and then rise far above them'

p. 420, 'What Then?'   *dc*: probably 1936   *fp*: *The Erasmian*, April 1936   Yeats described it as 'a melancholy biographical poem' (*L(W)*, 895); like 'An Acre of Grass', p. 419, it was inspired by a rereading of Nietzsche   *comrades thought at school*: at the High School, Dublin, an Erasmus Smith foundation, it was recognised that Yeats was unusual in his gifts, 'a white blackbird among the others'   *A small old house*: Riversdale, Rathfarnham. See notes on 'An Acre of Grass' above.

p. 421, 'Beautiful Lofty Things'   *dc*: possibly 1937   *fp*: *NP*   *O'Leary's noble head*: see notes on 'September 1913', p. 543   *my father*: John Butler Yeats (1839–1922) attended the 1907 debate in the Abbey Theatre on the issues arising out of the riots about J. M. Synge's *The Playboy of the Western World*. His account of the incident, *Letters to His Son W. B. Yeats and Others* (1944), 214, is somewhat different but no less vivid   *Standish O'Grady . . . drunken audience*: Standish James O'Grady

(1866–1928), Irish historian and novelist, sometimes called the father of the Irish literary revival, speaking at a dinner in honour of the Irish Literary Theatre, 11 May 1899, described by Yeats in *A*, 423–4   *Augusta Gregory . . . blinds drawn up*: on being threatened in 1922 by one of her tenants, Lady Gregory showed him how easy it would be to shoot her through her unshuttered window if he wanted to use violence. See *Lady Gregory's Journals* (1978), I, 337   *Maud Gonne at Howth station*: a memory going back to their walks at Howth (see notes on 'The Ballad of Moll Magee', p. 495), possibly to the first occasion when Yeats proposed to her, 4 Aug. 1891   *Pallas Athene*: see notes on 'A Thought from Propertius', p. 561 and *A*, 123, 364, for her walking 'like a goddess'   *the Olympians*: in Greek mythology the gods, who dwelt upon Mount Olympus

p. 421, 'A Crazed Girl'   *dc*: May 1936   *fp*: *The Lemon Tree* (1937) with the title 'At Barcelona'   *That crazed girl*: Margot Ruddock. See notes on 'Sweet Dancer', p. 622   *O sea-starved, hungry sea*: from a song in her essay, 'Almost I tasted ecstasy', *The Lemon Tree*, 9

p. 422, 'To Dorothy Wellesley'   *dc*: Aug. 1936   *fp*: *LM*, March 1938, with the title 'To a Friend'   (*For since the horizon's bought strange dogs are still*): a comma after 'bought' would have clarified the sense. Dorothy Wellesley bought a ridge opposite Penns in The Rocks, her home in Sussex (see *DWL*, 53). No newcomers would now build there, therefore no 'strange dogs' would come to make a noise   *Great Dane*: Brutus, Dorothy Wellesley's dog   *Proud Furies*: a letter to Dorothy Wellesley conveys the poem's intention:

> We all have something within ourselves to batter down and get our power from this fighting. I have never 'produced' a play in verse without showing the actors that the passion of the verse comes from the fact that the speakers are holding down violence or madness – 'down Hysterica passio'. All depends on the completeness of the holding down, on the stirring of the beast underneath. Even my poem 'To D. W.' should give this impression. The moon, the moonless night, the dark velvet, the sensual silence, the silent room and the violent bright Furies. Without this conflict we have no passion only sentiment and thought. . . . [*DWL*, 86–7]

The Furies are the Erinyes or Eumenides (a euphemism, the Kindly Ones), avenging spirits in Greek mythology who execute curses pronounced on criminals, or inflict famines or pestilences

p. 422, 'The Curse of Cromwell'   *dc*: between Nov. 1936 and 8 Jan. 1937   *fp*: *AB*, No. 8 (New Series), Aug. 1937   *Cromwell's . . . into the clay*: Yeats regarded Cromwell as 'the Lenin of his day'. After the execution of Charles I, Oliver Cromwell (1599–1658) spent nine months in Ireland, sacked Drogheda and Wexford, and left bitter memories of the cruelty of his campaign and the ruthlessness of his settlement, which, through an Act of 1652, brought almost every Irish landlord under condemnation. They were ordered to move to Clare or Connaught to make way for new settlers from England. In 1641 the majority of landlords had been Roman Catholics; after the Cromwellian Settlement the majority were Protestants. In this poem the lovers, dancers, tall men, swordsmen and horsemen are presumably those who suffered from Cromwell's activities. The phrase 'beaten into the clay' comes from a translation by Frank O'Connor (Michael O'Donovan, 1903–66) of the Irish poem 'Kilcash': 'the earls, the lady, the people beaten into the clay'   *an old beggar . . . crucified*: Yeats echoes Egan O'Rahilly's (1670–1726) 'Last Lines', tr. Frank O'Connor, *The Wild Birds Nest: Poems from the Irish* (1932), 23   *He that's mounting up*: a reference to the ebb and flow of civilisations (cf. 'The Gyres', p. 411)   *the Spartan boy's*: in Plutarch's (*c.* AD 46–*c.* 120) life of Lycurgus the story is told of a Spartan stealing a fox, concealing it under his clothes and, when apprehended, letting it gnaw him to death rather than be detected in theft   *great house . . . ruin*: cf. notes on 'Crazy Jane on God', p. 605

p. 423, 'Roger Casement'   *dc*: Nov. 1936   *fp*: IP, 2 Feb. 1937   The ballad was meant to be sung to the tune of 'The Glen of Aherlow'. Yeats wrote letters about it to Ethel Mannin on 15 Nov. 1936 (*L(W)*, 867–8) and to Dorothy Wellesley on 4, 7 and 10 Dec. 1936 (*DWL*, 108–9; 110 and 111)   *Subtitle*: William J. Maloney claimed in his book *The Forged Casement Diaries* (1936) that diaries written by Casement showing him to be a homosexual (then a criminal offence) were forgeries   *Roger Casement*: Sir Roger Casement, KCMG (1864–1916), knighted for public services, a British consular official (1895–1913) who joined the Irish National Volunteers in 1913, went to seek armed aid for Ireland in Germany in 1914, returned to Ireland in a German U-Boat and was arrested in south-west Ireland. Tried in London on a charge of High Treason, he was hanged in 1916   *a trick by forgery*: Yeats means a slander based on the forged diaries was spread throughout the world. Casement's diaries, circulated at the time of his trial to show him 'a degenerate', are now thought by Rene MacColl and Brian Inglis, his biographers, to have been genuine. See Brian Inglis, *Roger Casement* (1973), 377–81   *Spring-Rice*: Sir Cecil Arthur Spring-Rice (1859–1918), British Ambassador to the USA from 1912   *Come Tom and Dick, come all the troop*: originally Yeats had inserted 'Come Alfred Noyes and all the troop' (Maloney had quoted Noyes, then a Professor at Princeton, as describing Casement's confessions in 1916 as 'filthy beyond all description'). This was altered to 'Come Gilbert Murray, Alfred Noyes' when Noyes wrote a disclaimer (*IP*, 12 Feb. 1937). Yeats then revised the ballad and wrote to accept Noyes's explanation (*IP*, 13 Feb. 1937)   *in quicklime laid*: bodies of those hanged were buried in quicklime in British prisons. (In 1965 Casement's remains were returned to Ireland and reburied in Dublin with military honours)

p. 424, 'The Ghost of Roger Casement'   *dc*: Oct. 1936 (MS date)   *fp*: *NP*   This poem is complementary to 'Roger Casement', p. 423. It was meant to be sung to the tune of 'The Church's One Foundation'   *John Bull . . . India*: John Bull, popular name for the English nation. Dominion status for India (declared part of the British Empire when Victoria became Queen Empress in 1877) was not agreed until 1947   *a village church . . . family tomb*: an echo of Thomas Gray's (1716–71) 'Elegy Written in a Country Churchyard'; the MSS versions of Yeats's poem echoed the Hampden and Milton (though not the Crom-well!) of Gray's poem. Casement had told his cousin, Gertrude Bannister, that he wanted to be buried at Murlough Bay

p. 425, 'The O'Rahilly'   *dc*: Jan. 1937   *fp*: *NP*. The original refrain was *'Praise the Proud'*   Title: 'The' is a hereditary title in Ireland, denoting the head of a clan   *Pearse and Connolly*: see notes on 'Easter 1916', p. 569   *to great expense . . . Kerry men*: he was head of the O'Rahilly clan in Kerry; he had tried to stop the plans for the 1916 Rising by arguing vainly with Pearse and then by persuading Professor Eoin MacNeill (1867–1945), elected chairman of the council forming the Irish Volunteers in 1913, and later chief of staff, to countermand the orders for the Rising (initially given without MacNeill's knowledge to the Irish Volunteers by the secret IRB membership of the movement, and with the support of Connolly and his Citizen Army). The Rising, after Casement had been made captive and the German ship *Aud* bringing arms had been scuttled off the Irish coast, seemed doomed to fail   *That he might be there*: The O'Rahilly took part in the fighting in the General Post Office in Dublin and was killed in Henry Street

p. 427, 'Come Gather Round Me, Parnellites'   *dc*: 8 Sept. 1936   *fp*: *AB*, No. 1 (New Series), Jan. 1937. The title omits comma between 'me' and 'Parnellites' in this printing and in *NP*   *Parnellites*: those who supported Charles Stewart Parnell (see note on 'To a Shade', p. 545) after the O'Shea divorce case and the consequent split in the Irish Party. See *A*, 356–7   *fought the might of England*: Parnell, a Protestant Irish landlord, leader of the Irish Parliamentary Party 1880, imprisoned 1881, threw out the Liberal Party 1885 and supported the Conservatives. He held the balance of power in the Westminster parliament in 1886, and converted Gladstone to Home Rule   *brought it all to pass*: Parnell was first President of the Land League; the land war of 1879–82 led to the eventual creation of a system of peasant proprietorship in Ireland. He reached the summit of his career after a special commission found that letters accusing him of complicity in murder and outrage in the land war were forgeries   *a lass*: Mrs Kathleen (Kitty) O'Shea. Parnell was co-respondent in the divorce case brought in 1890 by her husband Captain William Henry O'Shea (1840–1905)   *a proud man*: see *AV*(B), 124   *The Bishops and the Party . . . betrayed*: Parnell was repudiated by Gladstone and the Irish hierarchy. Yeats, influenced by Henry Harrison, *Parnell Vindicated: The Lifting of the Veil* (1931), published his views in 'Parnell', *Essays 1931–1936* (1937), 2:

> Captain O'Shea knew of their liaison from the first . . . he sold his wife for money . . . for £20,000 could Parnell have raised that sum, he was ready to let the divorce proceedings go, not against Parnell, but himself

p. 428, 'The Wild Old Wicked Man'   *dc*: 1937   *fp*: *AM*, April 1938   At the time he wrote the poem Yeats was considering going to India with Lady Elizabeth Pelham, a friend of Shri Purohit Swami, as indicated by his letters to Shri Bhagwan Hamsa (12 March 1937) and to Shri Purohit Swami (21 March and 15 May 1937). See Shankar Mokashi-Punekar, *The Later Phase in the Development of William Butler Yeats* (1966), 264–5   *Girls down on the seashore*: probably memories of stories told by a boy in Sligo. See *A*, 75   *warty lads*: Yeats wrote to Laura Riding to tell her that poets were 'good liars who never forgot that the Muses were women who liked the embraces of gay warty lads'. He added in a letter to Dorothy Wellesley, 'I wonder if she knows that warts are considered by the Irish peasantry a sign of sexual power?' (*LDW*, 63)

p. 430, 'The Great Day'   *dc*: Jan. 1937   *fp*: *LM*, March 1938, with the title 'Fragments/The Great Day'

p. 430, 'Parnell'   *dc*: Jan. 1937   *fp*: *LM*, March 1938, with the title 'Fragments/Parnell'   See Yeats's commentary on 'Parnell's Funeral' in *KGCT*, quoted *NC*, 332–5

p. 430, 'What Was Lost'   *dc*: Jan. 1937   *fp*: *LM*, March 1938, with the title 'Fragments/What was Lost'   The poem relates to *AV*'s thought:

> Even our best histories treat men as function. Why must I think the victorious cause the better? Why should Mommsen [Theodore Mommsen (1817–1903), German historian, known particularly for his *History of Rome* (3 vols., 1854–5)] think the less of Cicero [see notes on 'Mad as the Mist and Snow', p. 608] because Caesar [see notes on 'The Saint and the Hunchback', p. 566] beat him? I am satisfied, the Platonic Year in my head, to find but drama. I prefer that the defeated cause should be more vividly described than that which has the advertisement of victory. No battle has been finally won or lost; 'to Garret or Cellar a wheel I send' [*E*, 398]

p. 430, 'The Spur'   *dc*: 7 Oct. 1936   *fp*: *LM*, March 1938, with the

title 'Fragments/The Spur'   Yeats called the poem his 'final apology'
(*DWL*, 110)

p. 431, 'A Drunken Man's Praise of Sobriety'   *dc*: uncertain   *fp*:
NP   *dancing like a wave*: cf. 'The Fiddler of Dooney', p. 109: 'dance like
a wave of the sea'

p. 431, 'The Pilgrim'   *dc*: uncertain   *fp*: *AB*, No. 10 (New Series),
Oct. 1937   *Lough Derg's holy island*: the poem deals with one of Ireland's
main pilgrimages, to Lough Derg, on the borders of Co. Fermanagh and
Co. Donegal (see Glossary). St Patrick's Purgatory is situated on an island
there; its cave of vision is where the saint (see notes on *WO*, p. 484, and see
'The Dancer at Cruachan and Cro-Patrick', p. 383) is reputed to have
fasted and received a vision of the next world   *Stations*: the Stations of
the Cross, usually fourteen stages representing Christ's Passion and
Crucifixion   *Purgatory*: state after death where, in Roman Catholic
belief, the soul is purified before going to Heaven   *black ragged bird*:
Yeats had read several accounts of the history of the pilgrimage, in which a
mysterious black bird, thought to be an evil spirit, probably an old heron,
terrified pilgrims

p. 432, 'Colonel Martin'   *dc*: 10 Aug. 1937   *fp*: *AB*, No. 12 (New
Series), Dec. 1937, with a refrain (suggested to Yeats by the Irish poet F. R.
Higgins) 'Lullabulloo, buloo, buloo, lullabulloo, buloo'. In a lecture in
1910 Yeats had argued that countrymen in Ireland, as everywhere in the
world, had kept simplicity. He told the poem's story, which he had heard
from a Galway shepherd. It showed that the people delighted in a striking
personality (*IY*, 205–6). Torchiana argues (*Y & GI*, 335) that the poem is
nearer to a version in Lady Gregory, *Kiltartan History Book* (1926), that the
factual source was a report of a case that came before Lord Kenyon at
the Guildhall; it was reported in the *Connaught Telegraph*, 22 Dec.
1791   *The Colonel*: Richard Martin (1754–1834), MP for Galway, JP
and High Sheriff of Co. Galway, and Colonel of the Galway Volunteers,
married in 1777 and again in 1796. He was a well-known duellist   *the
rich man*: John Petrie of Soho, London   *Assize Court*: in Galway (possibly a preliminary hearing: the case was tried at the Guildhall in London
in 1797)   *damages*: the Colonel was awarded £10,000 damages   *From
the seaweed*: by gathering it to sell. It is used in the production of edible
material and is still spread on fields in the west of Ireland as a form of
manure

p. 435, 'A Model for the Laureate'   *dc*: July 1937   *fp*:
NP   *Title*: the lifetime office of Poet Laureate, the Court Poet of
Britain, expected to write poems on official occasions. Yeats entitled the
poem 'A Marriage Ode' (*DWL*, 141); it was written on the occasion of

Edward VIII's abdication   *from China to Peru*: an echo of the opening of Samuel Johnson's *The Vanity of Human Wishes*: 'Let observation with extensive view/Survey mankind, from China to Peru'

p. 435, 'The Old Stone Cross'   *dc*: between April and June 1937   *fp*: *TN*, 12 March 1938; *LM*, March 1938   *man . . . old stone Cross*: possibly Denadhach (*d.* 871), buried at Drumcliffe, Co. Sligo, whom Yeats described as a pious soldier of the race of Conn in *CT* (*M*, 92–3); he lies under hazel crosses, watching over the graveyard in his armour   *unearthly stuff*: Yeats disliked actors reading poetry. See *DWL*, 145, his comments on the way Heron Allen and Florence Farr read poetry (*A*, 120–1) and his notes to *KGCT* (quoted *NC*, 396)

p. 436, 'The Spirit Medium'   *dc*: uncertain. The poem was written during a visit to Penns in The Rocks, Sussex, Dorothy Wellesley's home)   *fp*: *NP   Confusion of the bed*: cf. 'The Cold Heaven', p. 227   *Perning*: see notes on 'Shepherd and Goatherd', p. 557, and 'Demon and Beast', p. 572   *my body to the spade*: the refrain is a composite picture of Mrs Yeats and Dorothy Wellesley, both gardeners

p. 437, 'Those Images'   *dc*: on or before 10 Aug. 1937   *fp*: *LM*, March 1938   This poem was inspired by dislike of C. E. M. Joad's talk on politics when both men were visiting Penns in The Rocks, Sussex. Yeats told Dorothy Wellesley he had always worked with the idea of keeping the 30 millions of Irish (the Irish at home and abroad) 'one people from New Zealand to California', but was 'as anarchic as a sparrow'. He quoted Blake: 'Kings and Parliaments seem to me something other than human life', and Hugo: 'they are not worth one blade of grass that God gives for the nest of the linnet'. The poem followed and it 'says what I have just said' (*DWL*, 142–3)   *The cavern of the mind*: pure intellect   *those images*: 'I recall an Indian tale: certain men said to the greatest of sages "Who are your Masters?" And he replied, "The wind and the harlot, the virgin and the child, the lion and the eagle" ' (*E & I*, 530)   *Call the Muses home*: an allusion to the epigraph of Walter Savage Landor's *Hellenics* (1859)

p. 438, 'The Municipal Gallery Revisited'   *dc*: between Aug. and early Sept. 1937   *fp*: *ASTP*. In *ASTP* Yeats described a visit he made in Aug. 1937 to the Municipal Gallery of Modern Art in Dublin:

For a long time I had not visited the Municipal Gallery. I went there a week ago and was restored to many friends. I sat down, after a few minutes, overwhelmed with emotion. There were pictures painted by men, now dead, who were once my intimate friends. There were the portraits of my fellow-workers; there was that portrait of Lady Gregory, by Mancini, which John Synge thought the greatest portrait since Rembrandt; there was John Synge himself; there, too, were portraits of our Statesmen; the events of the last thirty years in fine pictures: a peasant ambush, the trial of Roger Casement, a pilgrimage to Lough Derg, event after event: Ireland not as she is displayed in guide book or history, but, Ireland seen because of the magnificent vitality of her painters, in the glory of her passions.

For the moment I could think of nothing but that Ireland: that great pictured song. The next time I go, I shall stand once more in veneration before the work of the great Frenchmen. It is said that an Indian ascetic, when he has taken a certain initiation on a mountain in Tibet, is visited by all the Gods. In those rooms of the Municipal Gallery I saw Ireland in spiritual freedom, and the Corots, the Rodins, the Rousseaus were the visiting gods.

An ambush; pilgrims: the first a painting by Sean Keating (1889–1977), *The Men of the West*; the second *St Patrick's Purgatory* (see notes on 'The Pilgrim', p. 628) by Sir John Lavery (1856–1941)   *Casement upon trial:* Lavery's *The Court of Criminal Appeal*; see notes on 'Roger Casement', p. 625   *Griffith:* Lavery's *Arthur Griffith*; see notes on 'On those that hated "The Playboy of the Western World", 1907', p. 545   *Kevin O'Higgins:* Lavery's *Kevin O'Higgins*; see notes on 'Death', p. 595   *soldier . . . Tricolour:* Lavery's *The Blessing of the Colours*   *a woman's portrait:* probably *Lady Charles Beresford* by John Singer Sargent (1856–1925); she was the wife of Baron Beresford of Metemmeh and Curraghmore, Co. Waterford   *Heart-smitten . . . My heart recovering:* at the time of the visit Yeats was suffering from heart trouble   *Augusta Gregory's son: Robert Gregory* by Charles Shannon (1863–1937)   *Hugh Lane:* probably Sargent's *Sir Hugh Lane*. He was 'the onlie begetter' phrase from the Dedication to Shakespeare's Sonnets) because of his dedication to great art and his gift of paintings to Dublin (see notes on 'To a Wealthy Man . . .', p. 542)   *Hazel Lavery living and dying:* the 'living' may be Lavery's *Portrait of Lady Lavery*, but two other paintings of her by Lavery could have been intended – *Hazel Lavery at Her Easel* is the most likely. The 'dying' portrait is *It is finished – The Unfinished Harmony* by Lavery. Lady Lavery died in 1935   *Mancini's portrait: Lady Gregory* by Antonio Mancini (1852–1930), an Italian artist. For Lady Gregory see notes on 'Friends', p. 549   *Rembrandt:* the famous Dutch painter and etcher, Rembrandt van Rijn (1606–69); for Synge, see notes on 'In Memory of Major Robert Gregory', p. 552   *My mediaeval knees:* a note in *P* (1949), written by Thomas Mark of Macmillan, reads

It will be noticed that the fifth stanza has only seven lines instead of eight. In the original version of the poem, this stanza ran as follows:—

My mediaeval knees lack health until they bend,
But in that woman, in that household, where
Honour had lived so long, their health I found.
Childless, I thought, 'my children may learn here
What deep roots are,' and never foresaw the end
Of all that scholarly generations had held dear;
But now that end has come I have not wept;
No fox can foul the lair the badger swept:

Yeats was pleased that the Swedish Royal Family thought (when he visited Stockholm to receive the Nobel Prize in 1923) that he had the manners of a courtier   *that woman, in that household*: Lady Gregory, Coole Park   *its end*: Lady Gregory thought of preserving the place for her grandson once her son Robert was killed; but his family moved to England   *No fox . . . Spenser*: from 'The Ruins of Time' by Edmund Spenser (?1552–99), part of which Yeats had included in his 1906 edition of *Poems of Spenser*: 'He [the Earl of Leicester] is now gone, the whiles the Foxe is crept/Into the hole, the which the badger swept'   *John Synge . . . I . . . Gregory*: linked by their work for the Abbey Theatre, as writers and directors, and by their delight in history and tradition   *Antaeus-like*: the giant Antaeus, son of Poseidon and Earth, in Greek mythology, grew stronger whenever he came into contact with the earth   *noble and beggar-man*: Yeats mentions Lady Gregory quoting from Aristotle, 'to think like a wise man, but express oneself like the common people'   *here's John Synge*: *John M. Synge* by Yeats's father, John Butler Yeats. See notes on 'In Memory of Major Robert Gregory', p. 552

p. 440, 'Are you Content?'   *dc*: uncertain (probably 1937)   *fp*: *AM*, April 1938; *LM*, April 1938   *He that in Sligo . . . stone Cross*: Rev. John Yeats, Rector of Drumcliff, Co. Sligo, from 1805 to 1846. See notes on '[Introductory Rhymes]', p. 539. The old stone cross still stands in the churchyard; the three-storeyed rectory, now demolished, was on the opposite side of the road   *That red-headed rector*: Rev. William Butler Yeats, curate at Moira, Co. Down, later Rector of Tullylish, near Porta-down. On retirement he lived at Sandymount   *Sandymount Corbets*: Yeats's great-uncle Robert Corbet (*d.* 1872) lived at Sandymount Castle, outside Dublin, on the south side of Dublin Bay   *William Pollexfen . . . Butlers far back*: see notes on '[Introductory Rhymes]', p. 539   *an old hunter talking with Gods*: the words come from *Pauline* (1833) by Robert Browning (1812–89)

[POEMS FROM 'ON THE BOILER']

p. 443, '[Why Should not Old Men be Mad?]'   *dc*: Jan. 1936   *fp*: *OTB*   *a drunken journalist*: probably R. M. (Bertie) Smylie (1894–1954), editor of *IT* from 1924, who wrote under the name 'Nichevo' and held court in the Palace Bar, Fleet Street, Dublin   *A girl . . . Dante once*: Iseult Gonne. See notes on 'Michael Robartes and the Dancer', p. 568   *a dunce*: Francis Stuart. See notes on IV ('The Death of the Hare'), p. 591. Yeats changed his mind about him from time to time. In 1932 he thought 'If luck comes to his aid he will be our great writer' (*L(W)*, 799–80); he regarded Stuart as 'typical of the new Ireland'   *A Helen . . .*: possibly Maud Gonne, though Constance Markiewicz may also have been on Yeats's mind (see notes on 'The Rose of the World', p. 498, and 'Easter 1916', p. 569

p. 443, '[Crazy Jane on the Mountain]'   dc: July 1938   fp: OTB   Bishop . . . Crazy Jane: see notes on WMP, p. 604   King . . . throne: George V (1865–1936), King of England, whose cousins were Nicholas II (1868–1918), last Tsar of Russia, and his family, brutally murdered at Ekaterinburg in July 1918. Yeats wrote that King George V asked that the Russian Royal Family should be brought to England but the Prime Minister refused, fearing the effect on the working class. He added that the story might have been 'no more true than other stories spoken by word of mouth' (E, 422–3). See Kenneth Rose, King George V (1983)   Great-bladdered Emer: Emer, Cuchulain's wife (see notes on 'Cuchulain's Fight with the Sea', p. 497. Yeats alluded to an early version of the Irish story 'The Courting of Emer', in which Emer was chosen for the strength and volume of her bladder, a sign of vigour

p. 444, '[The Statesman's Holiday]'   dc: completed in April 1938   fp: OTB   No Oscar: probably Oscar Wilde (1854–1900), Irish author and wit, whom Yeats regarded as 'the greatest talker of his time'   Avalon: see notes on 'Under the Moon', p. 528   Lord Chancellor . . . Sack: the Lord Chancellor sits upon a wool sack in the House of Lords. Here Yeats probably means F. E. Smith (1872–1930), Earl of Birkenhead, who was Lord Chancellor from 1919–22; a brilliant orator, he supported Lord Carson's (there may be a link here with Wilde, whom Carson cross-examined brilliantly in Wilde's action of 1895 against the Marquis of Queensberry) resistance to Home Rule in 1914; he appeared for the Crown in the Roger Casement trial (see notes on 'Roger Casement', p. 625); and played a major part in the Irish settlement of 1921   Commanding officer: Sir Hubert Gough (1870–1963), commanding officer of the Third Cavalry Brigade based on the Curragh, Co. Kildare, was leader of the 'Curragh Mutiny'; refusing to promise to fight against the Ulster Volunteers, he resigned his commission   de Valéra: see notes on 'Parnell's Funeral', p. 614   the King of Greece: George II (1890–1947), who returned to Greece in 1925   made the motors: probably William Richard Morris (1887–1963), created Lord Nuffield, who manufactured Morris cars at Cowley, Oxford   Montenegrin: Montenegro, a state in what became Yugoslavia after the First World War

[LAST POEMS]

These poems are arranged in the order Yeats indicated on a list

p. 449, 'Under Ben Bulben'   dc: 4 Sept. 1938 (appended to text P (1949))   fp: IT, IP [Part II only] and II, 3 Feb. 1939   Ben Bulben:

see notes on 'The Tower', p. 577   *Mareotic Lake . . . Witch of Atlas*: see
notes on 'Demon and Beast', p. 572. Shelley's 'Witch of Atlas' passed
along the Nile 'by Moeris and the Mareotid Lakes'   *those horsemen . . .
form*: possibly the visionary beings described to Yeats by Mary Battle, his
uncle George Pollexfen's servant, as coming from Knocknarea:

> 'Some of them have their hair down, but they look quite different, more like the
> sleepy-looking ladies one sees in the papers. Those with their hair up are like this
> one ['the finest woman you ever saw', described earlier]. The others have long
> white dresses, but those with their hair up have short dresses, so that you can see
> their legs right up to the calf.' And when I questioned her, I found that they wore
> what might well be some kind of buskin. 'They are fine and dashing-looking, like
> the men one sees riding their horses in twos and threes on the slopes of the
> mountains with their swords swinging. There is no such race living now, none so
> finely proportioned' [*A*, 266]

Ben Bulben sets the scene: probably because some events in the Fenian cycle
of tales take place there, notably the death of Diarmuid (see notes on 'Her
Vision in the Wood', p. 613)   *Mitchel's prayer*: John Mitchel (1815–75),
the Irish nationalist, parodied the prayer 'Give us peace in our time,
O Lord' in his *Jail Journal* (1854) with 'Give us war in our time, O
Lord'   *Phidias*: see notes on 'Nineteen Hundred and Nineteen',
p. 582   *Michael Angelo*: see notes on 'Michael Robartes and the Dancer',
p. 568, and on 'Long-legged Fly', p. 638   *Quattrocento*: see notes
on 'Among School Children', p. 588   *Gyres*: see notes on 'Demon
and Beast', p. 572   *Calvert*: Edward Calvert (1799–1883), English
visionary artist   *Wilson*: Richard Wilson (1714–82) landscape
painter   *Claude*: see notes on 'Shepherd and Goatherd', p. 557; he was
a master of the Picturesque style   *Palmer's phrase*: see notes on 'The
Phases of the Moon', p. 565. Yeats quoted Palmer's comments on Blake's
illustrations to Thornton's *Virgil* as 'the drawing aside of the fleshy
curtain, and the glimpse which all the most holy, studious saints and sages
have enjoyed, of that rest which remaineth to the people of God' (*E & I*,
125; the quotation is from A. H. Palmer, *The Life and Letters of Samuel
Palmer* (1892), 15–16)   *the lords and ladies gay*: a phrase from *Kilcash*;
see notes on 'The Curse of Cromwell', p. 624   *An ancestor*: Rev.
John Yeats; see notes on '[Introductory Rhymes]', p. 539   *Cast a cold
eye . . .*: Yeats's tombstone has this epitaph cut on it; his remains
were reinterred in the churchyard on 17 Sept. 1948

    p. 452, 'Three Songs to the One Burden'   *dc*: uncertain   *fp*: *SP*, 25
May 1939
I   *From mountain . . . fierce horsemen*: possibly the supernatural beings
seen by Mary Battle; see notes on 'Under Ben Bulben', p. 632, and *A*, 266.
There may be a memory of Blake in the refrain too, for Yeats wrote to
Ethel Mannin on 11 Dec. 1936 that he used as a young man to repeat
Blake's lines, 'And he his seventy disciples sent,/Against religion and

government', that he hated more than she could, for his hatred could have no expression in action. 'I am', he added, 'a forerunner of that horde that will some day come down the mountain'   *Manannan*: Manannan Mac-Lir, the Gaelic god of the sea   *Crazy Jane*: an invented character. See notes on *WPM*, p. 604   *likely couples*: Yeats was interested in eugenics at the time; see his quotation in *OTB* from Burton's *The Anatomy of Melancholy* (*E*, 418) and his giving the Old Man in *Purgatory* the words that states are justified by 'the best born of the best'

II   *Henry Middleton*: a cousin of the poet, a recluse   *small forgotten house*: Elsinore, near Rosses Point, Co. Sligo, reputedly a smuggler's house and haunted   *keys to my old gate*: Hone (*WBY*, 22) describes how Yeats and Mrs Yeats visited Henry Middleton in 1919 and found the gate locked. Yeats climbed the wall; his cousin was in a white suit in the sitting room surrounded by cheap novels. In 1930 Michael and Anne Yeats climbed the wall but were turned away by the garden boy when they reached the hall door   *the Green Lands*: a desolate area running inland from Deadman's Point at Rosses Point in Co. Sligo

III   *Nineteen-Sixteen*: the Easter Rising of 1916. See notes on 'Easter 1916', p. 569. This poem was originally entitled 'An Abbey Player – I meditate upon 1916', which became 'An Abbey Player and his Song'   *Post Office*: the General Post Office in the centre of Dublin, north of the Liffey in O'Connell (then Sackville) Street, occupied by the insurgents in 1916   *City Hall*: on Cork Hill, south of the Liffey; built by Thomas Cooley (1769–79) as the Royal Exchange, it was taken over by Dublin Corporation in 1850   *the player Connolly*: an actor shot in the fighting on Easter Monday (not to be confused with the labour leader James Connolly (see notes on 'Easter 1916', p. 569), military commander at the General Post Office, who was shot after a court martial   *Patrick Pearse*: see notes on 'Easter 1916', p. 569. Yeats described him as 'preaching the blood sacrifice', saying that blood must be shed in every generation. See 'The Rose Tree', p. 290

p. 455, 'The Black Tower'   *dc*: 21 Jan. 1939   *fp*: LP & TP (1939)   *the old black tower*: this may derive from Browning, but see Patrick Diskin, 'O'Grady's Finn and his companions. Source for Yeats's "The Black Tower" ', *N & Q*, March 1961, 107–8   *banners*: of political propaganda   *the dead upright*: see notes on *WO*, p. 485   *the king's great horn*: W. J. Keith, 'Yeats's Arthurian Black Tower', *MLN*, lxxv, Feb. 1960, suggests that this imagery derives from the Arthurian legend that Arthur, Guinevere, his court and a pack of hounds sleep in a vault beneath the Castle of Servingshields in Northumberland. The King waits for someone to blow the horn lying on a table and to cut a garter laid beside it with a sword of stone. A farmer found the vault, cut the garter and Arthur woke, only to sleep again as the sword was sheathed, saying:

A woe betide that evil day
On which the witless might was born
Who drew the sword – the garter cut
But never blew the bugle horn

p. 456, 'Cuchulain Comforted'   *dc*: 13 Jan. 1939 (appended to text
P (1949)). The prose draft was dictated on 7 Jan. 1939   *fp*:
LPTP   The poem is related to Yeats's play *The Death of Cuchulain*   *a
man had six mortal wounds*: Cuchulain. See notes on 'To the Rose upon the
Rood of Time', p. 496. The six who gave him the fatal wounds were
themselves killed by Conall Caernach   *Shrouds*: *PNE* suggests this is
reminiscent of Plato's myth of Er, in which unborn souls have lots and
samples of life put before them. See Plato, *Republic* (tr. Jowett 1875), III,
515–17

p. 457, 'Three Marching Songs'   *dc*: between 3 Nov. 1933 and 27
Feb. 1934, rewritten Dec. 1938 (later versions of 'Three Songs to the Same
Tune', p. 396)   *fp*: *LPTP*
I   *Fled to far countries*: see notes on 'September 1913', p. 543   *O'Don-
nell . . . both O'Neills*: see notes on 'Three Songs to the Same
Tune', p. 616   *Emmet*: see notes on '[Introductory Rhymes]',
p. 539   *Parnell*: see notes on 'To a Shade', p. 545
II   *Troy . . . Helen*: see notes on 'When Helen Lived', p. 545, and 'The
Rose of the World', p. 498   *airy*: Yeats wrote in a footnote that 'airy'
may be 'an old pronunciation of "eerie" often heard in Galway and Sligo'.
It may echo William Allingham's poem 'The Faeries': 'Up the airy
mountain . . .'   *nothing up there at the top*: cf. 'Blood and the Moon',
p. 351: 'time/Half dead at the top' and its query: 'Is every modern nation
like the tower,/Half dead at the top?' Cf. also 'Three Songs to the Same
Tune', p. 396
III   *he kicked*: cf. notes on 'Three Songs to the Same Tune', p. 616

p. 460, 'In Tara's Halls'   *dc*: June 1938   *fp*: *LPTP*   *A man*: in
the MS 'A certain king in the great house at Tara'   *Tara's halls*: the Hill
of Tara, Co. Meath, once the seat of the High Kings of Ireland

p. 460, 'The Statues'   *dc*: 9 April 1938   *fp*: *LM*, March 1939; *NR*,
22 March 1939   A passage in *OTB* clarifies some of the poem's
meanings:

> There are moments when I am certain that arts must once again accept those
> Greek proportions which carry into plastic art the Pythagorean numbers, those
> faces which are divine because all there is empty and measured. Europe was not
> born when Greek galleys defeated the Persian hordes at Salamis; but when the
> Doric studios sent out those broad-backed marble statues against the multiform,
> vague, expressive Asiatic sea, they gave to the sexual instinct of Europe its goal,
> its fixed type. [*E*, 451]

Pythagoras . . . numbers: Pythagoras (*c.* 582–507 BC) developed a theory of numbers and this paved the way for the art of Greek sculptors, who carved their statues by exact proportions and measurements ('plummet-measured' of l. 8)   *All Asiatic vague immensities . . . Phidias*: cf. *AV*(A), 182, and *AV*(B), 270:

> Side by side with Ionic elegance there comes after the Persian wars a Doric vigour, and the light-limbed dandy of the potters, the Parisian-looking young woman of the sculptors, her hair elaborately curled, give place to the athlete. One suspects a deliberate turning away from all that is Eastern, or a moral propaganda like that which turned the poets out of Plato's Republic, and yet it may be that the preparation for the final systematisation had for its apparent cause the destruction, let us say, of Ionic studios by the Persian invaders, and that all came from the resistance of the *Body of Fate* to the growing solitude of the soul. Then in Phidias Ionic and Doric influence unite – one remembers Titian – and all is transformed by the full moon, and all abounds and flows.

For Phidias the Athenian sculptor, see notes on 'Nineteen Hundred and Nineteen', p. 582; see also 'Under Ben Bulben', p. 449   *Salamis*: in the naval battle of Salamis, 480 BC, the Greeks defeated the Persians. Yeats is saying that Greek intellect was the real force that defeated the Persians   *No Hamlet . . . flies*: Yeats's comments on William Morris, a 'dreamer of the Middle Ages', as possessing 'a mind that has no need of the intellect to remain sane, though it gives itself to every fantasy'. It is

> 'the fool of Faery . . . wide and wild as a hill', the resolute European image that yet half remembers Buddha's motionless meditation, and has no trait in common with the wavering, lean image of hungry speculation, that cannot but because of certain famous Hamlets of our stage fill the mind's eye. Shakespeare himself foreshadowed a symbolic change, that is, a change in the whole temperament of the world, for though he called his Hamlet 'fat' and even 'scant of breath', he thrust between his fingers agile rapier and dagger. [*A*, 141–2]

One image . . . Dreamer of the Middle Ages: Yeats commented:

> In reading the third stanza remember the influence on modern sculpture and on the great seated Buddha of the sculptors who followed Alexander. Cuchulain is in the last stanza because Pearse and some of his followers had a cult of him. The Government has put a statue of Cuchulain in the rebuilt post office to commemorate this. [*L*(W), 911]

See next stanza   Empty eyeballs: in *AV*(B), 275–7, Yeats discusses the decay of Roman civilisation at about AD 1–250:

> . . . Roman sculpture – sculpture made under Roman influence whatever the sculptor's blood – did not, for instance, reach its full vigour, if we consider what it had for Roman as distinct from Greek, until the Christian Era. It even made a discovery which affected all sculpture to come. The Greeks painted the eyes of marble statues and made out of enamel or glass or precious stones those of their bronze statues, but the Roman was the first to drill a round hole to represent the

pupil, and because, as I think, of a preoccupation with the glance characteristic of a civilisation in its final phase. The colours must have already faded from the marbles of the great period, and a shadow and a spot of light, especially where there is much sunlight, are more vivid than paint, enamel, coloured glass or precious stone. They could now express in stone a perfect composure. The administrative mind, alert attention had driven out rhythm, exaltation of the body, uncommitted energy. May it not have been precisely a talent for this alert attention that had enabled Rome and not Greece to express those final *primary* phases? One sees on the pediments troops of marble Senators, officials serene and watchful as befits men who know that all the power of the world moves before their eyes, and needs, that it may not dash itself to pieces, their unhurried, unanxious, never-ceasing care. Those riders upon the Parthenon had all the world's power in their moving bodies, and in a movement that seemed, so were the hearts of man and beast set upon it, that of a dance; but presently all would change and measurement succeed to pleasure, the dancing-master outlive the dance. What need had those young lads for careful eyes? But in Rome of the first and second centuries, where the dancing-master himself has died, the delineation of character as shown in face and head, as with us of recent years, is all in all, the sculptors, seeking the custom of occupied officials, stock in their workshops toga'd marble bodies upon which can be screwed with the least possible delay heads modelled from the sitters with the most scrupulous realism. When I think of Rome I see always these heads with their world-considering eyes, and those bodies as conventional as the metaphors in a leading article, and compare in my imagination vague Grecian eyes gazing at nothing, Byzantine eyes of drilled ivory staring upon a vision, and those eyelids of China and of India, those veiled or half-veiled eyes weary of world and vision alike.

Grimalkin: a name for a cat. The description of Hamlet thin with eating flies may have suggested the introduction of Grimalkin, as cats are often supposed to grow thin by eating flies   *When Pearse summoned Cuchulain . . . Post Office*: Pearse is envisioned as calling intellectual and aesthetic forces into being (by an appeal to the Irish heroic past) as well as skills of measuring and numbering so that the Irish can return to their Pythagorean proportions, their 'Greek' proportions. Pearse (see notes on 'Easter 1916', p. 569) fought in the General Post Office, Dublin, in 1916; he had 'a cult' of Cuchulain, the Irish hero in the *Tain Bo Cualgne*

p. 461, 'News for the Delphic Oracle'   *dc*: probably in 1938   *fp*: *LM*, March 1939; *NR*, 22 March 1939   *the golden codgers*: the immortals, viewed ironically. See notes on 'The Delphic Oracle upon Plotinus', p. 610 *silver dew*: F. A. C. Wilson, *Yeats and Tradition* (1958), 219, suggests this relates to the nectar described in the oracle   *Man-picker . . . Oisin*: Yeats is blending Irish mythology with Greek. Niamh, daughter of Aengus and Edain, chose Oisin to accompany her to the magic islands, described in *WO*   *Pythagoras*: for Pythagoras, see notes on 'Among School Children', p. 588; for Plotinus, see notes on 'The Tower', p. 577, and on 'The Delphic Oracle upon Plotinus', p. 610   *a dolphin's back*: the poem refers to pictures in Rome (School of Raphael in the Papal

Apartments at Castel S. Angelo) which include nymphs, satyrs and dolphins. See also notes on 'Byzantium', p. 601   *Those Innocents*: possibly the Holy Innocents (male children under two whom Herod had killed, in an attempt to eliminate Jesus Christ. See Matthew 2:16–18). Yeats knew Raphael Santi's (1483–1520) statue of the dolphin carrying one of the Holy Innocents to Heaven   *the choir of love*: see notes on 'The Delphic Oracle upon Plotinus', p. 610   *Peleus on Thetis stares*: a reference to Nicolas Poussin's (1594–1665) *The Marriage of Peleus and Thetis* (now entitled *Acis and Galatea*) in the National Gallery of Ireland, Dublin. In Greek mythology the marriage of Peleus, son of Aeacus and Endeis, to Thetis, a Nereid, daughter of Nereus and Doris, was celebrated on Mount Pelion. Their surviving son was the hero Achilles   *Pan's cavern*: Pan, a fertility god in classical mythology, usually represented with small horns in his human head and with the legs, thighs and tail of a goat, was thought to have invented the flute and was reputed to delight in caverns

p. 463, 'Long-legged Fly'   *dc*: between Nov. 1937 and April 1938 (probably completed by 11 April)   *fp*: *LM*, March 1937   *Caesar*: presumably Gaius Julius Caesar (?102–44 BC) Roman general, orator, author and statesman, who transformed the Roman Republic into a government under a single ruler   *the topless towers . . . She*: an echo of Christopher Marlowe's (1564–93) *Doctor Faustus* (1604), act 5, scene 1, ll. 94–5: 'Was this the face that launched a thousand ships/And burnt the topless towers of Ilium?' The face is that of Helen of Troy (see notes on 'The Rose of the World', p. 498); the thought moves via her to Maud Gonne, whose feet 'practise a tinker shuffle'   *the first Adam . . . Michael Angelo*: a description of Michelangelo's painting of Adam about to be wakened into life by God (see notes on 'Michael Robartes and the Dancer', p. 568) in the Sistine Chapel, Rome

p. 464, 'A Bronze Head'   *dc*: probably 1937 or 1938   *fp*: *LM*, March 1939; *NR*, 22 March 1939   The poem was prompted by a plaster-cast painted bronze by Laurence Campbell, RHA, in the right of the entrance to the Municipal Gallery of Modern Art, Dublin   *Hysterica passio*: see notes on 'Parnell's Funeral', p. 614   *great tomb-haunter*: Maud Gonne MacBride had a habit of attending funerals (on political occasions). In old age she constantly wore long black flowing clothes and a veil   *Profound McTaggart*: J. McT. E. McTaggart (1866–1925), Cambridge philosopher, author of *Studies in Hegelian Cosmology* (1901), which Yeats read in 1928. This poem probably draws on his [*Human*] *Immortality and Pre-existence* (1915), which Yeats also read, as well as his *The Nature of Existence* (1921). The last, based on McTaggart's Hegelian studies, argues for the compound nature of all substances. The supernatural dimensions of the bronze head in the poem may come from McTaggart's remarks in [*Human*] *Immortality and Pre-existence*, that when science says a material object ceases to exist it does not mean anything is annihilated, but that units formerly combined in a certain way are combined differently. Yeats cited McTaggart as thinking that Hegel believed in the rebirth of the soul, and called this 'the foundation of McTaggart's own philosophical system' (*E*, 396–7)

p. 465, 'A Stick of Incense' *dc*: probably 1938 *fp*: *LPTP* *empty tomb*: the tomb where Christ's body was placed *Virgin . . . Saint Joseph*: the Virgin Mary, mother of Jesus Christ, and her husband Joseph

p. 465, 'Hound Voice' *dc*: probably summer 1938 *fp*: *LM*, Dec. 1938; *TN*, 16 Dec. 1938

p. 466, 'John Kinsella's Lament for Mrs. Mary Moore' *dc*: 21 or 29 July 1938. *fp*: *LM*, Dec. 1938. It was originally entitled 'A Strong Farmer's Complaint about Death', but this was not used in printed versions. Yeats wrote to Edith Shackleton Heald to say that he had just thought of a chorus for a ballad: 'A strong farmer is mourning over the shortness of life and changing times, and every stanza ends "What shall I do for pretty girls now my old bawd is dead?"' (*L(W)*, 912) *Title*: John Kinsella and Mary Moore are invented characters *a skin*: an Irish phrase, to put a skin on a story, to polish it, make it more effective *Adam's sin*: see note on 'Adam's Curse', p. 527

p. 467, 'High Talk' *dc*: between 29 July and Aug. 1938 *fp*: *LM*, Dec. 1938; *TN*, 10 Dec. 1938 *high stilts*: Yeats commented that when the 1890s were over 'we all got down off our stilts'; he may be referring to his own poetic mythology of the 1890s. In this case his 'great-granddad' with a pair of stilts 20 feet high might stand for the Romantics; his were 15 feet and were stolen: the theft may relate to the poets who were writing in the Celtic Twilight style after Yeats had left it behind. (See 'A Coat', p. 230) *piebald ponies*: the poem is reminiscent of some paintings by Jack Butler Yeats, Yeats's brother (cf. 'The Circus Animals' Desertion', p. 471) *women in the upper storeys . . . patching old heels*: presumably the women in the upper storeys of the houses are darning old socks and stockings *Malachi Stilt-Jack*: Malachi was a minor Hebrew prophet, the supposed author of the last book of the Old Testament: the name here may be that of an invented character or of someone remembered from Yeats's youth in Sligo

p. 467, 'The Apparitions' *dc*: March and April 1938 *fp*: *LM*, Dec. 1938 *Title*: a series of death dreams, some of which Yeats experienced after his illness in Jan. 1938, others earlier *Fifteen apparitions*:

Yeats wrote on 11 Nov. 1933 to Olivia Shakespear that his apparition had come a seventh time:

> As I awoke I saw a child's hand and arm and head – faintly self luminous – holding above – I was lying on my back – a five of diamonds or hearts I was [not] sure which. It was held as if the child was standing at the head of the bed. Is the meaning some fortune teller's meaning attached to the card or does it promise me five months or five years. Five years would be about long enough to finish my autobiography and bring out *A Vision.* [Yeats lived just a little over five years from Nov. 1933]

Sheila O'Sullivan (*YUIT*, 277–8) links this poem to a story told to Lady Gregory, *Poets and Dreamers* (1903), 26–7, about the blind Irish poet Raftery being ill in Galway and seeing his coat on the wall in the night; in the morning he asked his wife where the coat was and she told him 'and that was the very place he saw it'   *coat upon a coat-hanger*: in a manuscript book Yeats wrote, about the time of this poem's composition, 'The first apparition was the passage of a coat upon a coathanger slowly across [the] room – it was extraordinarily terrifying'   *increasing Night*: an image of death, 'that great night' in 'Man and the Echo', p. 469

p. 468, 'A Nativity'   *dc*: probably Aug. 1936   *fp*: LM, Dec. 1938   *What woman . . . Another star*: see notes on 'The Mother of God', p. 602   *Delacroix*: the French painter Ferdinand Victor Eugene Delacroix (1798–1863)   *Landor's tarpaulin*: an obscure image. Henn suggested this was a temporary cover against popular ridicule. See notes on 'To a Young Beauty', p. 556   *Irving and his plume of pride*: Sir Henry Irving (1838–1905), *né* Jonathan Henry Broadribb, famous for his characterisation of Mephistopheles, whom Yeats had seen acting and met in his teens. Yeats admired his 'intellectual pride' (*A*, 125, and *Plays and Controversies*, 215)   *Talma*: François Joseph Talma (1763–1826), French tragic actor   *the woman*: the woman of ll. 1–2, to whom the Annunciation is made

p. 469, 'Man and the Echo'   *dc*: July 1938, but revised up to Oct. 1938   *fp*: AM, Jan. 1939; LM, Jan. 1939, with the title 'Man and the Echo' (altered to 'The Man and the Echo' in *LPTP*)   *Alt*: a steep rocky glen at Knocknarea, a mountain in Sligo (see Glossary)   *play of mine . . . shot*: *Cathleen ni Houlihan* (1902), in which Maud Gonne performed the title role, first produced in Dublin, 2 April 1902. See Stephen Gwynn (1864–1950), *Irish Literature and Drama in the English Language* (1936), 158:

> The effect of Cathleen ni Houlihan on me was that I went home asking myself if such plays should be produced unless one was prepared for people to go out to shoot and be shot. Yeats was not alone responsible; no doubt but Lady Gregory had helped him to get the peasant speech so perfect; but above all Miss Gonne's impersonation had stirred the audience as I have never seen another audience stirred.

Certain men: presumably the leaders of the 1916 Rising. See 'Easter 1916', p. 287   *reeling brain*: Margot Collis or Ruddock, whom Yeats befriended. She became temporarily insane in Barcelona and Yeats paid her return fare to England (see *L(W)*, 856). *Ah, Sweet Dancer* (1970) contains the correspondence between Yeats and Margot Ruddock   *house lay wrecked*: probably Coole Park. See notes on 'Upon a House shaken by the Land Agitation', p. 537   *bodkin*: symbol of suicide. Cf. *Hamlet*, act 3, scene 1, 'When he himself might his quietus make/With a bare bodkin'   *rocky voice*: cf. notes on 'The Gyres', p. 621   *great night*: death

p. 471, 'The Circus Animals' Desertion'   *dc*: probably between Nov. 1937 and Sept. 1938   *fp*: *AM*, Jan. 1939; *LM*, Jan. 1939   *Winter and summer*: circuses, unlike the poet, usually worked a half-year season   *My circus animals . . . Lord knows what*: the poet's work: the stilted boys may be the larger-than-life heroes of his early poems and plays, the chariot may be Cuchulain's; the lion and woman may refer to Maud Gonne, 'half lion, half child' in 'Against Unworthy Praise', p. 187   *old themes*: probably the chivalrous poetry written in the 1880s and 1890s, in particular *The Wanderings of Oisin* (1889)   *Oisin led by the nose*: see *WO*, which tells how the immortal Niamh, 'his faery bride', fell in love with Oisin and brought him to fairyland with her (while preferring the form 'faery', Yeats's spelling was not always consistent and he also used 'fairy')   *three enchanted islands, allegorical dreams*: symbolising infinite feeling, infinite battle and infinite repose, the 'three incompatible things which man is always seeking'. Yeats described the poem in 1888 as 'full of symbols'   *The Countess Cathleen*: the play Yeats wrote for Maud Gonne, published in 1892   *given her soul away*: in the play two agents of the Devil come to Ireland in a famine, offering to buy the souls of the starving peasants for gold. The Countess sacrifices her goods to buy food for her people and is about to sell her soul when the poet tries, in vain, to stop her. The Countess symbolises all those who lose their peace or fineness of soul or beauty of spirit in political service, and Maud Gonne seemed to Yeats at the time to have an unduly restless soul. See notes on 'The Countess Cathleen in Paradise', p. 502   *my dear*: Maud Gonne   *Fool and Blind Man*: characters in Yeats's play *On Baile's Strand* (1903), in which Cuchulain dies fighting the sea. Cf. also 'Cuchulain's Fight with the Sea', p. 68   *Heart-mysteries there*: possibly a reference to John MacBride's marrying Maud Gonne in 1903   *Players . . . stage*: Yeats was deeply involved in the work of the Abbey Theatre as manager from 1904–10. Cf. 'The Fascination of What's Difficult', p. 188, and 'All Things can Tempt me', p. 192

p. 472, 'Politics'   *dc*: 23 May 1938   *fp*: *AM*, Jan. 1939; *LM*, Jan. 1939   *Epigraph*: the first printings correctly read 'meanings' not 'meaning'. The poem was stimulated by Archibald MacLeish (1892–1982), whose article 'Public Speech and Private Speech in Poetry', *Yale Review*, spring 1938 (containing the quotation from Mann used as this poem's epigraph), was described by Yeats as the only article on the subject 'which has not bored me for years'. He liked its commendation of his language as 'public' and told Dorothy Wellesley that the article had gone on to say that, owing to his age and his relation to Ireland, he was unable to use this 'public' language 'on what it obviously considered the right public material, politics'. The poem was his reply: 'It is not a real incident, but a moment of meditation.' He added a P.S.: 'In part my poem is a comment on ——'s panic-stricken conversation' (*DWL*, 163)

Textual Notes

A NOTE ON THE TEXT

The copy text for this edition is *The Poems of W. B. Yeats* (2 vols., 1949). It is described by Warwick Gould in Appendix Six. Where emendations have been made they are listed below under the heading 'Corrections of Misprints or Other Alterations Made to the Copy Text'. Under the heading 'Possible Emendations of the Copy Text', alternative readings are given, with their sources.

The poems placed under the heading 'Last Poems' in the copy text have here been placed under the heading 'New Poems', a section which contains the poems of the Cuala Press edition, *New Poems* (1938), the proofs of which Yeats saw, '[Poems from *On the Boiler*]' and '[Last Poems (1938–1939)]', a section containing the poems Yeats wrote in the last year of his life.

The order of 'Last Poems' in the copy text was arranged by Thomas Mark of Macmillan, responsible for many years for the editing of Yeats's writings, in agreement with the poet's widow. This Papermac edition follows the order which Yeats planned for what turned out to be a posthumous volume. It is also the order in which the poems appeared in the Cuala Press edition of *Last Poems and Two Plays* (1939). The order of the poems in the copy text follows that of the Macmillan edition *Last Poems and Plays* (1940); it is the order subsequently followed in *The Collected Poems of W. B. Yeats* (1950, and subsequent printings). The case for the order in this Papermac edition was first made by the late Professor Curtis Bradford, and the reader is referred to his 'Chronology of Composition' and 'The Order of Yeats's Last Poems' in *Yeats's 'Last Poems' Again, Dolmen Press Yeats Centenary Papers* (1966), VIII, ed. Liam Miller, 285–6, 287–8, respectively.

Under the heading '[Poems from *On the Boiler*]' have been added three poems included in Yeats's *On the Boiler* (1939) and in the copy text's section 'Last Poems'. (These three poems were not included in the list Yeats drew up for a projected volume of poems – which, because of his death in January 1939, became his 'Last' poems – but were included in the Cuala Press edition, *Last Poems and Two Plays*.)

The copy text section entitled 'Last Poems' presents some textual problems because in it Thomas Mark carried out the editorial processes he normally undertook and submitted to Yeats for approval when the poet was alive. Yeats usually deferred to Mark's suggestions, particularly about punctuation and hyphenation, but the complete text of the copy text 'Last Poems' was not approved by Yeats. It is, however, in line with what he would probably have approved and presents his last poems in a way which is generally consistent with the rest of the poems (but not always) in the two volumes of the copy text (the texts of which the poet had overseen). Where emendation could be made in the light of the Cuala Press *New Poems* and of magazine or newspaper publication of particular poems, or the Cuala Press *Last Poems and Two Plays* (1939), these have been listed under the heading 'Possible Emendations of the Copy Text' and sources are given for them. This heading also includes possible alternatives for other parts of the copy text, the sources for which are given with their first occurrence and alternatives in other volumes approved by Yeats after he had concluded work on the copy text in 1932.

Printed sources only are cited as authority for corrections or alterations in the copy text, or for suggested possible emendations of it. Thus the last alterations Yeats made to 'Brown Penny' (four new lines substituted), to 'Two Songs Rewritten for the Tune's Sake' (a line altered) and to 'Ribh denounces Patrick' (second line altered) for the projected but unpublished American edition, the 'Dublin Edition' to be published by Charles Scribner's Sons (these alterations are in material at the Humanities Research Center, University of Texas, Austin), are given in a separate section after the section entitled 'Possible Emendations of the Copy Text'.

The dates appended to some poems in the copy text have been removed from the text; they are included in the Notes to this edition where dates of composition and first printings are given (as *dc* and *fp* respectively), for all poems where these are known. Footnotes have been removed from the text and are included in the Notes.

CORRECTIONS OF MISPRINTS OR OTHER ALTERATIONS MADE TO THE COPY TEXT

The copy text version is given in the left-hand column, the correction or alteration in the middle column, and the source or reason for the change in the right-hand column. The abbreviations used in it are listed on p. 475. Where *CP* is used, it indicates both the London and New York editions of the *Collected Poems* (1933) and, for interest, the London edition (1950) and the New York edition (1951) of the volume. Brackets after *CP* indicate which of the editions is cited when they vary: (L) is the London edition of 1933, (NY) the New York edition of 1933, and (1950) covers the later edition published in both London and New York. Where any of the editions of the *Collected Poems* reverts to an earlier version, the first instance of that version is given. Changes in successive printings are listed in the *Variorum Edition*. The texts of the *Collected Poems* are referred to as Yeats corrected proofs of the copy text in 1932 and the *Collected Poems* texts give later versions approved by him. He was an inveterate alterer of his texts, writing characteristically (to Olivia Shakespear on 27 Dec. 1930) of his getting material ready for the *Edition de Luxe* (of which the copy text was to be part): 'Months of re-writing. What happiness!'

	Copy text	*Correction or emendation*	*Source or reason*
p. 8	gently,t 'I	gently, 'It	misprint
p. 16	cold	cold,	*P* (1895); *CP*
p. 16	love	love,	*P* (1895); *CP*
p. 47	swear to her love	swear to love her	misprint
p. 51	Inver Amergin	Invar Amargin	*P* (1895); *CP*(L; NY)
p. 56	Coloney	Coloony	*P* (1895); *CP*(L; NY)
p. 67	king,	king	*EPS*; *CP*
p. 72	*dew*	*dew,*	*CK*; *CP*(L; 1950)
p. 79	Dromahair	Drumahair	*P* (1895); *CP*(L; NY)
p. 81	tree	tree,	*EPS*; *CP*(L; 1950)
p. 90	remade,	re-made,	*SBRC* re-made (*CP*: re-made,)
p. 115	break between ll. 84–5	no break	*P:SS* (1909); *CP*(L)
p. 121	Uladh	Ulad	*MR*, July 1902; *CP*(L;NY)
p. 123	Uladh	Ulad	*MR*, July 1902; *CP*(L; NY)
p. 130	seem	seems	*CP*
p. 134	Uladh	Ulad	*ISW*; *CP*(L; NY)
p. 136	TOGETHER	[TOGETHER]	*ISW*; *CP*
p. 137	TOGETHER	[TOGETHER]	*ISW*; *CP*
p. 143	no title	[Introductory Lines]	'Introductory Rhymes' contents list, *Later Poems* (1922); 'Introductory Lines' contents list, *CP*
p. 146	DRAMATIC POEM	POEM	*CP*
p. 170	generosity,	generosity;	*P* (1899–1905); *CP*
p. 188	road-metal	road metal	*TGH* (1910); *CP*(L; NY)
p. 193	young.	young,	*TGH* (1910); *CP*(L; 1950)
p. 197	no title	[Introductory Rhymes]	contents list, *ROP*; *CP*(L; 1950); (*CP*(NY) gives: Rhyme)
p. 197	of ten	of the ten	*CP*
p. 199	remade	re-made	*RPP*; *CP*(L; NY)

Copy text	*Correction or emendation*	*Source or reason*
p. 202	beech-trees	beech trees	*ROP*; *CP*(L; NY)
p. 207	wandering	whirling	*P*(Ch), Oct. 1913; *CP*(L; NY)
p. 207	away'?	away'.	*P*(Ch), Oct. 1913; *CP*(L; NY)
p. 208	beech-tree	beech tree	*P*(Ch), Oct. 1913; *CP*(L; NY)
p. 230	no title	[Closing Rhymes]	contents list, *ROP*; (*CP*: Rhyme)
p. 240	feather bed.	feather-bed.	*CP*(L; NY) (*Nine Poems* (1918) gives: feather-bed,)
p. 312	pear-tree	pear tree	*DL*, Jan. 1923; *CP*(L; NY)
p. 318	catalpa-tree	catalpa tree	*TT* (1928); *CP*; (*SPF* gives: Catalpa tree)
p. 325	chestnut-tree	chestnut tree	*DL*, Aug. 1927; *LM*, Aug. 1927; *CP*(L; NY)
p. 325	great-rooted	great rooted	*DL*, Aug. 1927; *LM*, Aug. 1927; *CP*(L; NY)
p. 327	The Hero, the Girl, and the Fool given in full (ll. 1–29). (Lines 1–17 given on page 665.)	The Fool by the Roadside (ll. 18–29 of The Hero, the Girl, and the Fool)	See Appendix Six, note 19; ll. 18–29 only given in *AV*(A) and *CP*
p. 341	wine,	wine.	*NR*, 9 March 1921; *LM*, March 1921; *CP*
p. 343	ecstasy	ecstasy.	*CP*(L; NY)
p. 347	stanzas numbered	stanzas unnumbered	*TWSOP*; *CP*
p. 358	*Coole Park and*	*Coole and*	*TWSOP*; *CP*(L; NY)
p. 365	ambition, animate	ambition, or animate	*TWSOP*; *CP*(L; NY)
p. 369	these,	these	*WMP*; *CP*
p. 369	time's	Time's	*TWSOP*; *CP*
p. 374	go,	go:	*TWSOP* (*CP*: go;)
p. 374	on;	on:	*TWSOP*; *CP*
p. 379	*shore,*	*shore;*	*WMP*; *CP*(NY; 1950)
p. 391	gods	Gods	*TWS*; *CP*

	Copy text	Correction or emendation	Source or reason
p. 415	chastity?	chastity?'	*LM*, Jan. 1937; *NP*
p. 424	Spring Rice	Spring-Rice	*IP*, 2 Feb. 1937; *NP*
p. 427	mind.	mind,	*B* (No. 1), Jan. 1937; *E* (1937) (*NP*: mind)
pp. 431–2	ll. 5, 10, 15, 20, 25 italicised	these lines unitalicised	*B* (No. 10), Oct. 1937; *NP*
pp. 436–7	ll. 7–8, 15–16, 23–4 italicised	these lines unitalicised	*NP*
p. 443	*Why should not Old Men be Mad?*	[Why should not Old Men be Mad?]	untitled in *OTB*
p. 443	*Crazy Jane on the Mountain*	[Crazy Jane on the Mountain]	untitled in *OTB*
p. 444	*The Statesman's Holiday*	[The Statesman's Holiday]	untitled in *OTB*
p. 449	no break between ll. 20–1	break between these lines	*IT*, 3 Feb. 1939; *II*, 3 Feb. 1939
p. 450	no break between ll. 44–5	break between these lines	*IT*, 3 Feb. 1939; *II*, 3 Feb. 1939
p. 452	no break between ll. 8–9, 17–18, 26–7 in each section of the poem	break between these lines in each section of the poem	*SP*, 26 May 1939; *LPTP*
p. 458	Were we	We were	*LPTP*
p. 458	gain?	gain.	*LPTP*.
p. 463	no break between ll. 8–9, 18–19, 28–9	a break between these lines	*LM*, March 1939; *LPTP*
p. 463	ll. 9–10, 19–20, 29–30 italicised	these lines unitalicised	*LM*, March 1939; *TN(NY)*, 15 April 1939
p. 466	ll. 11–12, 23–4, 35–6 italicised	these lines unitalicised	*LM*, Dec. 1938; *NR*, 15 Feb. 1939
p. 467	loose;	loose.	*LPTP*
p. 469	*The Man and the Echo*	*Man and the Echo*	*AM*, Jan. 1939; *LM*, Jan. 1939
p. 472	*meaning*	*meanings*	misprint; correct in *AM*, Jan. 1939, *LM*, Jan. 1939, and *LPTP*
p. 472	arms!	arms.	*AM*, Jan. 1939; *LPTP*

POSSIBLE EMENDATIONS OF THE COPY TEXT

The copy text version is given in the left-hand column, the possible emendation in the middle column and the source or reason for considering it in the right-hand column (which also gives its first appearance, for interest). Obvious misprints or mistakes in possible sources have not been included. Abbreviations are listed on pp. 475–82.

	Copy text	*Possible alternative*	*Source*
p. 32	And because I	And before I	CP
p. 44	O may	O, may	P (1895); CP
p. 81	tyranny,	tyranny;	EPS; CP(L; NY)
p. 122	*wind,*	*wind;*	PW, I (1906); CP(L; NY)
p. 129	Pairc-na-lee	Parc-na-lee	CP(L; NY)
p. 131	their dances	dancing	CP(L; NY)
p. 132	said:	said,	CP
p. 132	Replied:	Replied,	CP
p. 132	said:	said,	MR; CP
p. 143	*Coole:*	Coole,	TS, 1 Dec. 1900; CP(L; NY)
p. 162	huge	huge,	P (1899–1905); CP(L; NY)
p. 174	O I	O, I	P (1899–1905); CP
p. 210	bone?	bone;	PWD; CP(L; NY)
pp. 214–15	Guaire (also ll. 19, 26, 54)	Guare (also ll. 19, 26, 54)	CP(L; NY)
p. 225	North	north	RPP; CP(L; NY)
p. 230	hoof –	hoof,	ROP; CP(L; NY)
p. 235	him:	him;	ER, Aug. 1918; CP(L; NY)
p. 239	gimlet,	gimlet	LR; CP(L; NY)
p. 240	Sang	Said	CP
p. 245	wife?	wife.	WSC (1919); CP(L; NY)
p. 246	milking-shed	milking shed	WSC (1919); CP(L; NY)
p. 254	Duchess	duchess	P(Ch), Feb. 1916; CP(L; NY)
p. 256	Athene's	Athena's	CP(L; NY)
p. 257	sake's	sakes'	WSC (1917); CP(L; NY)

	Copy text	Possible alternative	Source
p. 264	And,	And	*P*(Ch), Oct. 1917; *CP*(L; NY)
p. 264	life,	life	*P*(Ch), Oct. 1917; *CP*(L; NY)
p. 264	hope,	hope	*WSC* (1917); *CP*(L; NY)
p. 266	And,	And	*P*(Ch), Oct. 1917; *CP*(L; NY)
p. 266	characters,	characters	*P*(Ch), Oct. 1917; *CP*(L; NY)
p. 267	Devil	devil	*TLR*, Oct. 1918; *CP*(L; NY)
p. 267	late-risen	late risen	*WSC* (1919); *AV*(B)
p. 268	learnt	learned	*AV*(A); *AV*(B)
p. 269	Athene	Athena	*AV*(A); *CP*(L; NY)
p. 269	hero's	heroes'	*WSC* (1919); *CP*(L; NY)
p. 269	after,	after	*WSC* (1919); *CP*(L up to 1949 printing; NY)
p. 269	moon,	moon	*WSC* (1919); *CP*(L; NY)
p. 270	countrymen	country men	*WSC* (1919); *CP*(L; NY)
p. 270	thought;	thought,	*WSC* (1919); *CP*(NY)
p. 271	moon.	moon:	*AV*(A); *AV*(B)
p. 271	changed,	changed.	*AV*(B)
p. 271	Deformed	Deformed,	*AV*(B)
p. 271	And	But	*AV*(B)
p. 272	fancies	fancies,	*AV*(B)
p. 272	Saint	saint	*WSC* (1919); *CP*(L; NY)
p. 272	Fool	fool	*WSC* (1919); *CP*(L; NY)
p. 272	countryman	country man	*WSC* (1919); *CP*(L; NY)
p. 272	Saint	saint	*WSC* (1919); *CP*(L)
p. 272	Fool	fool	*WSC* (1919); *CP*(L)
p. 282	Athene	Athena	*DL*, Nov. 1920; *CP*(L; NY)

	Copy text	*Possible alternative*	*Source*
p. 282	Devil	devil	*DL*, Nov. 1920; *CP*(L; NY)
p. 285	starlight	star-light	*TN*(L), 6 Nov. 1920; *CP*(L; NY)
p. 287	Easter	Easter,	*Easter, 1916* (1916); *CP*(L; NY)
p. 291	fantasy	phantasy	*MRD*; *CP*(L; NY)
p. 292	wild,	wild	*TN*(L), 13 Nov. 1920; *CP*(L; NY)
p. 301	trees	trees,	*TT* (1928); *CP*(L; NY)
p. 304	cottages.	cottages:	*CP*(L)
p. 305	Muses	muses	*NR*, 29 June 1927; *TC*, June 1927; *CP*(L; NY)
p. 307	mountain-side	mountain side	*NR*, 29 June 1927; *CP*(L; NY)
p. 307	fades,	fades;	*TC*, 29 June 1927; *CP*
p. 314	young:	young;	*DL*, Sept. 1921; *CP*(L; NY)
p. 326	Athene	Athena	*CP*(L; NY)
pp. 320–7	'Two Songs from a Play', 'Fragments', 'Wisdom', 'Leda and the Swan', 'On a Picture . . . Dulac', 'Among School Children', 'Colonus' Praise', 'The Hero, the Girl, and the Fool'	'Two Songs from a Play', 'Fragments', 'Leda and the Swan', 'On a Picture . . . Dulac', 'Among School Children', 'Colonus' Praise', 'Wisdom', 'The Fool by the Roadside'	*CP*
p. 336	break between ll. 48–9	no break between these lines	*English Life and the Illustrated Review*, Jan. 1924 *CP*(L; NY)
p. 341	And knowing that the future would be vexed	And by foreknowledge of the future vexed;	*AV*(B)
p. 341	With 'minished beauty, multiplied commonplace,	Diminished beauty, multiplied commonplace;	*AV*(B)
p. 341	about,	about	*NR*, 9 March 1921; *AV*(B)

	Copy text	*Possible alternative*	*Source*
p. 342	And I call up MacGregor	I call MacGregor Mathers	*AV*(B)
p. 342	the grave,	his grave,	*AV*(B)
p. 342	springtime	spring-time	*AV*(A); *AV*(B)
p. 350	source	source,	*CP*(L; NY)
p. 352	pure,	pure;	*TWS*
p. 352	butterflies,	butterflies:	*TWSOP*(L) (*TWSOP*(NY): butterflies.)
p. 361	rest;	rest:	*WWP*; *W & B*
p. 364	threefold	three-fold	*WMP*; *CP*(NY)
p. 366	faith,	faith	*TWSOP*
p. 373	must	would	*WMP*; *CP*(L; NY)
p. 373	walk when	walk, being	*WMP*; *CP*(L; NY)
p. 378	tomb;	tomb:	*WMP*; *CP*
p. 382	*charity*,	*charity*	*WMP*
p. 382	*charity*, (also l. 30)	*charity* (also l. 30)	*WMP*; *CP*
p. 383	canopy:	canopy;	*WMP*; *CP*(L; NY)
pp. 396–9	'Three Songs to the Same Tune'	omit whole poem	Yeats probably intended to replace this poem with the later 'Three Marching Songs'. The final versions of both poems, 'on the whole, so similar', were included in the copy text after Mrs Yeats discussed the matter with various poets and communicated her decision to Thomas Mark in April 1939
p. 399	mountain-side	mountain side	*LL*, Nov. 1934; *CP*(L; NY)
p. 403	mirror-scalèd	mirror scalèd	*P*(Ch), Dec. 1934; *CP*(L; NY)
p. 404	wit.	wit;	*P*(Ch), Dec. 1934; *CP*(L; NY)
p. 405	tongue.	tongue,	*FMM*
p. 411	Face, look	Face look	*NP*
p. 411	thought,	thought	*NP*

Copy text	Possible alternative	Source
p. 411	top,	top	NP
p. 411	cavern	Cavern	NP
p. 411	voice,	voice	NP
p. 411	Rejoice!	Rejoice.	NP
p. 411	matter?	matter!	NP
p. 411	shall,	shall	NP
p. 411	sepulchre,	sepulchre	NP
p. 412	drop-scenes	drop scenes	NR, 13 April 1938; NP
p. 412	Callimachus,	Callimachus	NR, 13 April 1938; NP
p. 413	lamp-chimney	lamp chimney	LM, March 1938; NP
p. 413	again,	again	LM, March 1938; NP
p. 413	lapis lazuli	Lapis Lazuli	LM, March 1938; NP
p. 413	bird,	bird	NP
p. 413	dent,	dent	LM, March 1938; NP
p. 413	stare.	stare;	LM, March 1938; NP
p. 413	play.	play;	LM, March 1938; NP
p. 413	thing—	thing	NP
p. 413	beggar-man	beggar man	NP
p. 414	Escaped from bitter youth,	lacking	NP
p. 414	*Ah, dancer, ah, sweet dancer!* (also l. 14)	*Ah dancer, ah sweet dancer!* (also l. 14)	LM April 1938; NP
p. 414	away,	away	NP
p. 414	man.	man.'	LM, Jan. 1937; NP
p. 415	she.	she,	LM, Jan. 1937; NP
p. 415	chastity?	chastity?'	LM, Jan. 1937; NP
p. 415	barked,	barked	LM, Jan. 1937; NP
p. 415	mine,	mine	LM, Jan. 1937; NP
p. 416	rabbit-hole	rabbit hole	LM, Jan. 1937; NP
p. 416	O	O,	LM, Jan. 1937; NP
p. 416	grave,	grave.	LM, Jan. 1937; NP
p. 416	can,	can	LM, Jan. 1937; NP
p. 416	there,	there	LM, Jan. 1937; NP
p. 416	matter, we	matter we	NP

	Copy text	Possible alternative	Source
p. 417	fragrance,	fragrance	NP
p. 417	beast.	breast.	NP
p. 417	touch,	touch	NP
p. 418	whole,	whole	NP
p. 418	breast?	breast.	NP
p. 419	for?	for,	NP
p. 419	goes;	goes,	AM, April 1938; NP
p. 420	frenzy,	frenzy.	NP
p. 420	Truth	truth	NP
p. 420	clouds,	clouds	AM; NP
p. 420	shrouds;	shrouds,	AM; NP
p. 420	mankind,	mankind;	LM, April 1938
p. 420	*ghost.* 'What (also ll. 10 & 15)	*ghost,* 'what (also ll. 10 & 15)	NP
p. 420	*ghost,* 'What	*ghost* 'What	NP
p. 421	things:	things;	NP
p. 421	crowd:	crowd.	NP
p. 421	table,	table	NP
p. 421	approaching:	approaching;	NP
p. 421	life.	life,	NP
p. 421	table,	table	NP
p. 421	steamship,	steamship	TLT; NP
p. 421	wound,	wound	NP
p. 421	sea-starved,	sea-starved	TLT; NP
p. 422	trees,	trees	TN(NY), 12 March 1938; LM, March 1938; NP
p. 422	knee,	knee	TN(NY), 12 March 1938; LM, March 1938; NP
p. 422	Great Dane	great dane	TN(NY), 12 March 1938; NP
p. 422	found,	found	NP
p. 422	go:	go,	B (No. 8), Aug. 1937; NP
p. 422	horsemen,	horsemen	B (No. 8), Aug. 1937; NP
p. 422	pride—	pride,	B (No. 8), Aug. 1937; (NP: pride)
p. 422	*that,*	*that*	B (No. 8), Aug. 1937; NP

	Copy text	Possible alternative	Source
p. 422	gone,	gone	*B* (No. 8), Aug. 1937; *NP*
p. 422	on.	on,	*B* (No. 8), Aug. 1937; *NP*
p. 423	mount,	mount	*B* (No. 8), Aug. 1937; *NP*
p. 423	own,	own	*B* (No. 8), Aug. 1937; *NP*
p. 423	*that*, (also ll. 23 & 31)	*that* (also ll. 23 & 31)	*NP*
p. 423	destroys,	destroys	*B* (No. 8), Aug. 1937; *NP*
p. 423	boy's,	boy's	*NP*
p. 423	company,	company;	*NP*
p. 423	night,	night	*B* (No. 8) Aug. 1937; *NP*
p. 423	do.	do,	*IP*, 2 Feb. 1937; *NP*
p. 423	gallows,	gallows	*NP*
p. 423	Time,	Time	*NP*
p. 424	world,	world	*NP* (*IP*: world –)
p. 424	it,	it	*NP*
p. 424	quicklime	quick-lime	*IP*, 2 Feb. 1937; *NP*
p. 424	him,	him	*NP*
p. 424	say,	say	*NP*
p. 425	heed,	heed	*NP*
p. 425	round,	round	*NP*
p. 425	O'Rahilly,	O'Rahilly	*NP*
p. 426	sense	sense,	*NP*
p. 426	look:	look,	*NP*
p. 426	Street;	Street,	*NP*
p. 427	*Me, Parnellites*	*Me Parnellites*	*B* (No. 1), Jan. 1937; *NP*
p. 427	me,	me	*B* (No. 1), Jan. 1937; *NP*
p. 427	Parnellites,	Parnellites	*B* (No. 1), Jan. 1937; *NP*
p. 427	man;	man,	*NP*
p. 427	laid,	laid	*B* (No. 1), Jan. 1937; *NP*
p. 427	reason,	reason	*NP*
p. 427	man,	man	*B* (No. 1), Jan. 1937; *NP*
p. 427	country,	country	*NP*

	Copy text	*Possible alternative*	*Source*
p. 427	his lass	a lass.	*B* (No. 1), Jan. 1937; *E* (1937)
p. 428	skies.	skies.'	*AM*, April 1938; *NP*
p. 428	*candle-end* (also ll. 18, 27, 36, 45, 54, 63)	*candle end* (also ll. 18, 27, 36, 45, 54, 63)	*LM*, April 1938; *NP*
p. 428	withhold.	withhold,	*AM*, April 1938; *NP*
p. 428	cold?	cold.	*AM*, April 1938; *NP*
p. 428	man,	man	*AM*, April 1938; (*NP* gives: man)
p. 428	man:	man,	*AM*, April 1938; (*NP* gives: man)
p. 428	ways,	ways	*LM*, April 1938; *NP*
p. 429	fishermen;	fishermen,	*AM*, April 1938; (*NP* gives: fishermen)
p. 429	fisher-lads	fisher lads	*AM*, April 1938; *NP*
p. 429	beds.	beds.'	*AM*, April 1938; *NP*
p. 429	I,	I	*AM*, April 1938; *NP*
p. 429	light,	light	*NP*
p. 429	marrow-bones	marrow bones	*NP* (*AM* & *LM* give: marrowbones)
p. 429	bodies lay.	bodies lay.'	*AM*, April 1938; *NP*
p. 429	suffering,	suffering	*AM*, April 1938; *NP*
p. 429	womb.	womb.'	*AM*, April 1938; *NP*
p. 429	right-taught	right taught	*AM*, April 1938; *NP*
p. 430	cannon-shot!	cannon shot;	*LM*, March 1938; *NP*
p. 430	on foot.	upon foot;	*LM*, March 1938; *NP*
p. 430	again!	again,	*LM*, March 1938; *NP*
p. 430	places,	places	*LM*, March 1938; *NP*

Copy text	Possible alternative	Source
p. 430	man:	man;	NP
p. 430	run,	run	NP
p. 430	attention	attendance	NP
p. 431	around,	around	NP
p. 431	punk,	punk	NP
p. 431	pretty	Pretty	NP
p. 431	man,	man	NP
p. 431	buttermilk,	buttermilk	B (No. 10), Oct. 1937; NP
p. 431	women,	women	NP
p. 431	marrow-bones	marrow bones	B (No. 10), Oct. 1937; NP
p. 431	man,	man	NP
p. 432	stuck,	stuck	NP
p. 432	them,	them	NP
p. 432	display,	display	B (No. 10), Oct. 1937; NP
p. 432	public-house	public house	NP
p. 432	may,	may	NP
p. 432	Jew,	Jew	B (No. 12), Dec. 1937; NP
p. 432	Infidel,	Infidel	B (No. 12), Dec. 1937; NP
p. 432	he,	he	B (No. 12), Dec. 1937; NP
p. 432	town.	town,	B (No. 12), Dec. 1937; NP
p. 433	there,	there	B (No. 12), Dec. 1937; NP
p. 433	say?'	say,'	B (No. 12), Dec. 1937; NP
p. 433	maid,	maid	B (No. 12), Dec. 1937; NP
p. 433	things,	things	B (No. 12), Dec. 1937; NP
p. 433	abed,	abed	B (No. 12), Dec. 1937; NP
p. 433	man,	man	B (No. 12), Dec. 1937; NP
p. 433	wore.	wore,	B (No. 12), Dec. 1937; NP
p. 434	Court,	Court	B (No. 12), Dec. 1937; NP

	Copy text	Possible alternative	Source
p. 434	told,	told	*B* (No. 12), Dec. 1937; *NP*
p. 434	man,	man	*B* (No. 12), Dec. 1937; *NP*
p. 434	street-corners	street corners	*B* (No. 12), Dec. 1937; *NP*
p. 434	Sir.'	Sir;'	*B* (No. 12), Dec. 1937; *NP*
p. 434	grand-dad	grand-dad,	*NP*
p. 434	seaweed	sea-weed	*B* (No. 12), Dec. 1937; *NP*
p. 435	waiting?	waiting.	*NP*
p. 435	sold,	sold	*NP*
p. 435	signature,	signature.	*NP*
p. 436	wretch;	wretch,	*TN* (NY), 12 Mar. 1938; *NP*
p. 436	scene,	scene.	*TN* (NY), 12 Mar. 1938; *NP*
p. 436	unbegotten,	unbegotten.	*NP*
p. 437	action,	action	*NP*
p. 437	sand,	sand	*NP*
p. 437	lightning,	lightning	*NP*
p. 437	Rome.	Rome,	*LM*, March 1938; *NP*
p. 438	years:	years;	*NP*
p. 438	blessed;	blessed.	*ASTP*; *NP*
p. 438	not,' I	not' I	*NP*
p. 438	stand,	stand;	*ASTP*; *NP*
p. 438	Heart-smitten	Heart smitten	*NP*
p. 438	down,	down	*NP*
p. 438	images:	images;	*NP*
p. 438	ballad-singer	ballad singer	*ASTP*; *NP*
p. 438	all;	all.	*ASTP*; *NP*
p. 438	humility?	humility,	*NP*
p. 439	'My	'my	*ASTP*; *NP*
p. 439	swept—	swept.	*NP*; (*ASTP*: swept:)
p. 439	tongue).	tongue)	*ASTP*; *NP*
p. 439	Gregory,	Gregory	*ASTP*; *NP*
p. 439	beggar-man.	beggarman	*ASTP*; *NP*
p. 439	man,	man	*NP*
p. 439	me,	me	*ASTP*; *NP*
p. 440	ends,	ends	*NP*
p. 440	great-aunts,	great-aunts	*NP*

	Copy text	Possible alternative	Source
p. 440	Drumcliff	Drumcliffe	*AM*, April 1938; *NP*
p. 440	Down,	Down	*AM*, April 1938; *NP*
p. 443	fly-fisher's	fly fisher's	*OTB*
p. 443	dream,	dream	*OTB*
p. 443	a matter	matter	*OTB*
p. 443	tell,	tell	*OTB*
p. 443	Bishop,	Bishop	*OTB*
p. 444	cousins,	cousins	*OTB*
p. 444	cellar,	cellar	*OTB*
p. 444	mountain,	mountain	*OTB*
p. 444	two-horsed	two horsed	*OTB*
p. 444	Great-bladdered	Great bladdered	*OTB*
p. 444	Cuchulain	Cuchulain,	*OTB*
p. 444	side;	side,	*OTB*
p. 444	thing,	thing	*OTB*
pp. 444–5	*grass-green* (also in ll. 26 & 39)	*grass green* (also in ll. 26 & 39)	*OTB*
p. 445	lute,	lute	*OTB*
p. 449	women	women,	*IT*, 3 Feb. 1939; *II*, 3 Feb. 1939; *LPTP*
p. 449	long-visaged	long visaged	*IT*, 3 Feb. 1939; *II*, 3 Feb. 1939; *LPTP*
p. 449	air in	airs in	*IT*, 3 Feb. 1939; *LPTP* (*II*, 3 Feb. 1939: airs an)
p. 449	eternities,	eternities	*IT*, 3 Feb. 1939
p. 449	soul,	soul	*IT*, 3 Feb. 1939
p. 449	muscles	muscle	*IT*, 3 Feb. 1939; *II*, 3 Feb. 1939
p. 450	heard,	heard	*IT*, 3 Feb. 1939; *LPTP*
p. 450	blind,	blind	*IT*, 3 Feb. 1939; *LPTP*
p. 450	peace.	peace,	*IT*, 3 Feb. 1939; *II*, 3 Feb. 1939; *LPTP*
p. 450	sculptor,	sculptor	*IT*, 3 Feb. 1939; *II*, 3 Feb. 1939
p. 450	work,	work	*IT*, 3 Feb. 1939
p. 450	paint	paint,	*IT*, 3 Feb. 1939; *II*, 3 Feb. 1939; *LPTP*

	Copy text	Possible alternative	Source
p. 450	Saint	Saint,	*IT*, 3 Feb. 1939; *II*, 3 Feb. 1939; *LPTP*
p. 450	eye,	eye	*IT*, 3 Feb. 1939
p. 450	sky,	sky	*IT*, 3 Feb. 1939
p. 451	are or	are, or	*IT*, 3 Feb. 1939; *II*, 3 Feb. 1939
p. 451	heavens	Heavens	*IT*, 3 Feb. 1939; *II*, 3 Feb. 1939
p. 451	Calvert and Wilson, Blake and Claude	And Wilson, Blake and Calvert, Claude	*IT*, 3 Feb. 1939; *II*, 3 Feb. 1939
p. 451	Drumcliff	Drumcliffe	*IT*, 3 Feb. 1939; *II*, 3 Feb. 1939; *IP*, 3 Feb. 1939; *LPTP*
p. 451	churchyard	Churchyard	*IT*, 3 Feb. 1939
p. 451	laid.	laid,	*IT*, 3 Feb. 1939; *II*, 3 Feb. 1939
p. 451	ago,	ago;	*IT*, 3 Feb. 1939; *II*, 3 Feb. 1939; *IP*, 3 Feb. 1939
p. 453	Middleton,	Middleton	*LPTP*
p. 453	green.	green,	*SP*, 26 May 1939; *LPTP*
p. 453	them,	them	*SP*, 26 May 1939; *LPTP*
p. 453	pitch-and-toss	pitch and toss	*SP*, 26 May 1939; *LPTP*
p. 453	henwives	hen wives	*SP*, 26 May 1939
p. 454	me,	me	*SP*, 26 May 1939; *LPTP*
p. 454	skill,	skill	*LPTP*
p. 454	greater,	greater	*SP*, 26 May 1939; *LPTP*
p. 454	come?	come,	*SP*, 26 May 1939; *LPTP*
p. 455	tower,	tower	*LPTP*
p. 455	men:	men;	*LPTP*
p. 455	*shore*: (also ll. 18 & 28)	*shore*, (also ll. 18 & 28)	*LPTP*
p. 455	morn	morn,	*LPTP*
p. 455	hound:	hound;	*LPTP*
p. 456	came,	came	*LPTP*
p. 456	still.	still;	*LPTP*
p. 456	shroud;	shroud.	*LPTP*

	Copy text	Possible alternative	Source
p. 456	eyes,	eyes	*LPTP*
p. 456	can,	can	*LPTP*
p. 456	all,	all	*LPTP*
p. 456	'Or	Or	*LPTP*
p. 456	before;	before	*LPTP*
p. 457	crevice,	crevice	*LPTP*
p. 457	*that is*	*that's*	*LPTP*
p. 457	those	these	*LPTP*
p. 458	Helen;	Helen,	*LPTP*
p. 458	*son, not* (also ll. 18 & 28)	*son not* (also ll. 18 & 28)	*LPTP*
p. 458	*spot,* (also ll. 19 & 29)	*spot* (also ll. 19 & 29)	*LPTP*
p. 458	the wind	wind	*LPTP*
p. 458	tune,	tune	*LPTP*
p. 458	run?	run.	*LPTP*
p. 459	gallows:	gallows,	*LPTP*
p. 459	*tambourine,* (also l. 27)	*tambourine* (also l. 27)	*LPTP*
p. 459	had, and	had and	*LPTP*
p. 459	had,	had	*LPTP*
p. 459	tune:	tune,	*LPTP*
p. 460	still.	still,	*LPTP*
p. 460	said, "Lie	said 'lie	*LPTP*
p. 460	that,	that	*LPTP*
p. 460	hear.	hear:	*LPTP*
p. 460	numbers,	numbers	*TN* (NY), 15 April 1939
p. 460	girls,	girls	*LM*, March 1939; *TN*, 15 April 1939
p. 460	beds,	beds	*TN* (NY), 15 April 1939
p. 460	enough,	enough;	*LM*, March 1939; *TN*, 15 April 1939
p. 461	No! Greater	No; greater	*TN* (NY), 15 April 1939
p. 461	looking-glass	looking glass	*LPTP*
p. 461	Middle Ages	Middle-Ages	*LPTP*
p. 461	eyeballs	eye-balls	*LPTP*
p. 461	bless	bless,	*LPTP*
p. 461	side,	side	*LPTP*
p. 461	formless	formless,	*LM*, March 1939; *TN* (NY), 15 April 1939

	Copy text	Possible alternative	Source
p. 461	spawning	spawning,	*LM*, March 1939; *LPTP*
p. 461	love,	love	*LM*, March 1939; *LPTP*
p. 462	salt-flakes	salt flakes	*LM*, March 1939; *LPTP*
p. 462	fin,	fin	*LM*, March 1939; *LPTP*
p. 462	Until,	Until	*LM*, March 1939; *LPTP*
p. 462	stares.	stares,	*LM*, March 1939; *LPTP*
p. 463	sink,	sink	*LM*, March 1939; *TN* (NY), 15 April 1939
p. 463	post;	post.	*LM*, March 1939; *TN* (NY), 15 April 1939
p. 463	a street	the street	*LM*, March 1939; *TN* (NY), 15 April 1939
p. 464	superhuman	super-human	*LM*, March 1939; *LPTP*
p. 464	sky	sky;	*NR*, 22 March 1939; *LM*, March 1939
p. 464	die;)	die)	*NR*, 22 March 1939; *LPTP*
p. 464	*Hysterica passio*	*Hysterico-passio*	*NR*, 22 March 1939; *LPTP*
p. 464	light,	light	*NR* 22 March 1939; *LPTP*
p. 464	right?	right,	*NR*, 22 March 1939; *LM*, March 1939
p. 464	maybe	may be	*LM*, March 1939; *LPTP*
p. 464	held	hold	*NR*, 22 March 1939; *LM*, March 1939
p. 464	itself:	itself.	*NR*, 22 March 1939; *LM*, March 1939
p. 464	everywhere, 'My	everywhere 'my	*NR*, 22 March 1939; *LM*, March 1939
p. 464	supernatural:	supernatural,	*LPTP*

	Copy text	Possible alternative	Source
p. 465	melt	melt,	*LPTP*
p. 465	slumber-bound	slumber bound	*LM*, Dec. 1938; *LPTP*
p. 465	name—'Hound	name: 'Hound	*LPTP* (*LM*, Dec. 1938, & *TM*, 10 Dec. 1938 give: 'hound voice'.
p. 465	Then	That	*LM*, Dec. 1938; *TN* (NY), 10 Dec. 1938
p. 466	Death	death	*LM*, Dec. 1938; *LPTP*
p. 466	sister,	sister	*LM*, Dec. 1938; *NR*, 15 Feb. 1939
p. 466	score,	score.	*NR*, 15 Feb. 1939
p. 466	bargain,	bargain	*LM*, Dec. 1938; *NR*, 15 Feb. 1939
p. 466	stories,	stories	*LM*, Dec. 1938; *LPTP*
p. 466	alive,	alive	*LM*, Dec. 1938; *LPTP*
p. 466	there,	there	*LM*, Dec. 1938; *LPTP*
p. 467	storeys	stories	*LM*, Dec. 1938; *LPTP*
p. 467	pane,	pane	*LM*, Dec. 1938; *TN* (NY), 10 Dec. 1938
p. 468	length,	length	*LM*, Dec. 1938; *NR*, 15 Feb. 1939
p. 469	work,	work	*AM*, Jan. 1939; *LPTP*
p. 470	be work	be a work	*AM*, Jan. 1939; *LPTP*
p. 470	more,	more	*AM*, Jan. 1939; *LM*, Jan. 1939
p. 470	view,	view	*AM*, Jan. 1939; *LM*, Jan. 1939
p. 470	Rocky Voice,	rocky voice,	*AM*, Jan. 1939; *LPTP* (*LM*, Jan. 1939, & *LPTP* omit comma after voice)
p. 470	theme,	theme	*LM*, Jan. 1939
p. 470	struck,	struck	*LM*, Jan. 1939

	Copy text	Possible alternative	Source
p. 470	out,	out	*AM*, Jan. 1939; *LPTP*
p. 471	*Animals'*	*Animal's*	*AM*, Jan. 1939; *LPTP*
p. 471	last,	last	*LM*, Jan. 1939
p. 471	man,	man	*LM*, Jan. 1939
p. 471	themes?	themes,	*AM*, Jan. 1939; *LPTP*
p. 471	faery	fairy	*AM*, Jan. 1939; *LPTP*
p. 471	*The Countess Cathleen*	'The Countess Cathleen'	*AM*, Jan. 1939; *LPTP*
p. 471	it;	it,	*LM*, Jan. 1939; *LPTP*
p. 471	away,	away	*AM*, Jan. 1939; *LPTP*
p. 471	destroy,	destroy	*AM*, Jan. 1939; *LPTP*
p. 471	Heart-mysteries	Heart mysteries	*AM*, Jan. 1939; *LPTP*
p. 472	love,	love	*AM*, Jan. 1939; *LPTP*
p. 472	mind,	mind	*LM*, Jan. 1939; *LPTP*
p. 472	a street	the street	*LPTP*
p. 472	gone,	gone	*AM*, Jan. 1939; *LPTP*
p. 472	start,	start	*AM*, Jan. 1939; *LPTP*
p. 472	rag-and-bone	rag and bone	*AM*, Jan. 1939; *LPTP*
p. 472	politics?	politics,	*AM*, Jan. 1939; *LM*, Jan. 1939
p. 472	has read	has both read	*LM*, Jan. 1939; *LPTP*

POSSIBLE EMENDATIONS FROM COPY SUBMITTED FOR
THE PROPOSED DUBLIN EDITION

	Copy text	*Possible alternative*	*Source*
p. 193	O love is the crooked thing,	And the penny sang up in my face	*CDE*, HRCAT
p. 193	There	'There	*CDE*, HRCAT
p. 193	Till the stars had run away	That is looped in the loops of her hair,	*CDE*, HRCAT
p. 193	And the shadows eaten the moon.	Till the loops of time had run.'	*CDE*, HRCAT
p. 400	My Paistin Finn is my sole desire,	A brighthaired slut is my heart's desire,	*CDE*, HRCAT; *FMIM* reads: 'That blonde girl there is my heart's desire'
p. 403	man—	man,	*CDE*, HRCAT
p. 403	Recall that masculine Trinity. Man, woman, child (a daughter or a son),	A Trinity that is wholly masculine. Man, woman, child (daughter or son),	*CDE*, HRCAT

TEXT OF LINES 1–17 OF 'THE HERO, THE GIRL, AND THE FOOL' GIVEN IN THE COPY TEXT

The Hero, the Girl, and the Fool

THE GIRL

I rage at my own image in the glass
That's so unlike myself that when you praise it
It is as though you praised another, or even
Mocked me with praise of my mere opposite;
And when I wake towards morn I dread myself,
For the heart cries that what deception wins
Cruelty must keep; therefore be warned and go
If you have seen that image and not the woman.

THE HERO

I have raged at my own strength because you have loved it.

THE GIRL

If you are no more strength than I am beauty
I had better find a convent and turn nun;
A nun at least has all men's reverence
And needs no cruelty.

THE HERO

     I have heard one say
That men have reverence for their holiness
And not themselves.

THE GIRL

     Say on and say
That only God has loved us for ourselves,
But what care I that long for a man's love?

Appendix One
Biographical Summary

WILLIAM BUTLER YEATS 1865–1939

1865   William Butler Yeats, the son of John Butler Yeats and his wife, Susan (*née* Pollexfen), born at 1 George's Ville, Sandymount Avenue, Dublin, 13 June.

1867   John Butler Yeats moves with his family to 23 Fitzroy Road, Regent's Park, London. Robert (*d.* 1873), John Butler (Jack), Elizabeth Corbet (Lolly) were born here. Susan Mary (Lily), the elder daughter, was born at Enniscrone (1866). Frequent visits were made to Sligo to Mrs Yeats's parents, the Pollexfens.

1874   The family moves to 14 Edith Villas, West Kensington.

1876   The family moves to 8 Woodstock Road, Bedford Park.

1877   Yeats goes to the Godolphin School, Hammersmith. Holidays spent in Sligo.

1880   John Butler Yeats's income declines because of Land War and decline in economy.

1881   Family returns to Ireland, is lent Balscaddan Cottage, Howth, Dublin. W. B. Yeats goes to the High School, Harcourt Street, Dublin (until 1883).

1882   Family moves to Island View, small house overlooking Howth Harbour. Yeats thinks himself in love with his cousin Laura Armstrong.

1884   W. B. Yeats enters School of Art, Dublin.

1885   Family moves to 10 Ashfield Terrace, off Harold's Cross Road, Dublin. First published poems (and Charles Johnston's article on esoteric Buddhism) appear in *Dublin University Review*. Founder member of Dublin Hermetic Society. Becomes friend of Katharine Tynan and John O'Leary.

1886   First experience of seance. Attacks Anglo-Irish, begins to read Irish poets who wrote in English and translations of Gaelic sagas.

1887   Family moves to 58 Eardley Crescent, Earls Court, London. Mrs Yeats has two strokes. W. B. Yeats visits William Morris at Kelmscott House. Joins London Lodge of Theosophists.

1888   Family installed in 3 Blenheim Road, Bedford Park (J. B. Yeats's home until 1902). Last of Yeats family land sold in accordance with Ashbourne Act (1888). Contributions to American journals. Visits Oxford to work in Bodleian. Joins esoteric section of Theosophists.

1889   Mild collapse. Prepares selections for Walter Scott. *The Wanderings of Oisin and Other Poems*. Maud Gonne visits Bedford Park; he falls in love with her; offers to write *The Countess Cathleen* for her. Visits W. E. Henley, meets Oscar Wilde, John Todhunter, York Powell, John Nettleship and Edwin Ellis (with whom he decides to edit Blake's poems). Edits *Fairy and Folk Tales of the Irish Peasantry*.

1890　'The Lake Isle of Innisfree'. Asked to resign from Theosophists. Meets Florence Farr, who was acting in John Todhunter's *A Sicilian Idyll*. Initiated into the Hermetic Order of the Golden Dawn. Founds the Rhymers' Club in London with Rhys and Rolleston.

1891　*Representative Irish Tales*. Friendship with Johnson and Dowson. Asks Maud Gonne to marry him. She goes to France. He meets her on her return on ship with Parnell's body. Writes poems on Parnell. Founds London–Irish Literary Society with T. W. Rolleston. Founds National Literary Society in Dublin with John O'Leary as President. *John Sherman and Dhoya*.

1892　*The Countess Kathleen and Various Legends and Lyrics*. *Irish Fairy Tales*. Irish literary societies established in London and Dublin.

1893　*The Celtic Twilight*. *The Works of William Blake* (ed. Ellis and Yeats, 3 vols.).

1894　First visit to Paris; stays with MacGregor Mathers and proposes to Maud Gonne again. Sees *Axel*. Meets Mrs Shakespear ('Diana Vernon'). Revises *The Countess Cathleen* in Sligo while staying with George Pollexfen and conducting experiments with symbols. *The Land of Heart's Desire* produced. Visits Gore-Booths at Lissadell.

1895　*Poems*. Not on good terms with Dowden and Mahaffy. Lionel Johnson drinking heavily. Shares rooms in the Temple with Arthur Symons for a few months (between early October 1895 and 1896).

1896　Takes rooms in Woburn Buildings; affair with 'Diana Vernon' lasts a year. Visits Edward Martyn with Arthur Symons, meets Lady Gregory, visits Aran Islands. Meets Synge in Paris, when there to found order of Celtic Mysteries. Member of IRB; forms idea of uniting Irish political parties.

1897　*The Secret Rose*. *The Tables of the Law: Adoration of the Magi*. Disturbed by effects of Jubilee Riots in Dublin. Visits Coole; collects folklore there with Lady Gregory; writing *The Speckled Bird* (posthumously published novel).

1898　Accompanies Maud Gonne on tour of Irish in England and Scotland. Forms idea of creating Irish Theatre with Lady Gregory and Edward Martyn. 'Spiritual marriage' with Maud Gonne.

1899　*The Wind Among the Reeds*. In Paris, again proposes marriage to Maud Gonne. *The Countess Cathleen* and Martyn's *Heather Field* produced in Antient Concert Rooms, Dublin, as programme of Irish Literary Theatre.

1900　Proposes marriage to Maud Gonne in London. Leaves IRB (probably in 1900). Forms new Order of Golden Dawn after trouble with

Mathers and Aleister Crowley. Helps George Moore to rewrite Martyn's *The Tale of a Town*, which became *The Bending of the Bough*.

1901   Proposes marriage to Maud Gonne again. Sees the Fays acting.

1902   Lectures on the psalteries. *Diarmid and Grania* written in collaboration with George Moore. Becomes President of Irish National Dramatic Society. *Cathleen ni Houlihan* performed in Dublin with Maud Gonne in title role.

1903   Maud Gonne marries John MacBride. *The Countess Cathleen, The Pot of Broth* and *The Hour Glass* produced in visit of Irish National Dramatic Company to London. First lecture tour in US, arranged by John Quinn.

1904   Abbey Theatre opens with Yeats as producer-manager. *The King's Threshold* and *On Baile's Strand*.

1905   Limited company replaces National Theatre. Co-director with Lady Gregory and Synge. *Stories of Red Hanrahan*.

1906   *Poems 1895–1905*.

1907   Crisis over Synge's *The Playboy of the Western World*. Visits Italy with Lady Gregory and her son. Works on *The Player Queen*. Father goes to New York.

1908   *Collected Works* (in 8 vols.). Stays with Maud Gonne in Paris. Meets Ezra Pound. Affair with Mabel Dickinson begins.

1909   Synge dies. Yeats quarrels with John Quinn.

1910   Receives Civil List pension of £150 p.a.

1911   Accompanies Abbey players to US. Meets Georgie Hyde Lees.

1912   Stays with Maud Gonne in Normandy.

1913   Visits Mabel Beardsley in hospital. *Poems Written in Discouragement* (dealing with Lane Gallery controversy). Stays at Stone Cottage, Coleman's Hatch, Sussex, in autumn with Ezra Pound.

1914   Visits US (January). Returns for Ezra Pound's marriage to Mrs Shakespear's daughter. Investigates miracle at Mirebeau with Maud Gonne MacBride and the Hon. Everard Feilding (May). *Responsibilities: Poems and a Play*. Becomes interested in family history; finishes *Reveries* (first part of *Autobiographies*).

1915   Hugh Lane goes down with *Lusitania*. Yeats refuses knighthood.

1916   With the Pounds (winter). First of the *Plays for Dancers* produced in Lady Cunard's house, London (March). Easter Rising, writes 'Easter, 1916'. In Normandy proposes marriage to Maud Gonne. Reads French poets with Iseult Gonne, discusses marriage with her.

1917   Buys Castle at Ballylee. Proposes to Iseult Gonne. Marries Georgie Hyde Lees on 20 October. *The Wild Swans at Coole*.

1918   They stay at Oxford, then Glendalough, then visit Sligo; stay at Coole (and supervise restoration of tower), later at 73 St Stephen's Green (Maud Gonne's house) until December. *Per Amica Silentia Lunae*.

1919   Anne Butler Yeats born (26 February) in Dublin. Summer at Ballylee. Winter spent in Oxford in Broad Street.

1920   American lecture tour until May. Yeats in Ireland in autumn.

1921   Michael Butler Yeats born (22 August). *Michael Robartes and the Dancer. Four Plays for Dancers.*

1922   Buys Georgian house, 82 Merrion Square, Dublin. J. B. Yeats dies in New York. DLitt. of Dublin University. Spends summer at Ballylee. *The Trembling of the Veil. Later Poems. The Player Queen.* Becomes Senator of Irish Free State.

1923   Nobel Prize for Literature. Visits Stockholm in December for award of Nobel Prize.

1924   *Essays. The Cat and the Moon and Certain Poems.* Year mainly spent in final work on *A Vision.* Reading history and philosophy. High blood pressure. Visits Sicily (November).

1925   Visits Capri, Rome, Milan (February). May at Ballylee. Reading Burke and Berkeley. Speech on divorce in Senate. *A Vision* (dated 1925, published January 1926).

1926   *Estrangement.* Chairman of Coinage Committee in Senate. Visits St Otteran's School in Waterford ('Among School Children').

1927   Ballylee in summer. *October Blast.* Congestion of lungs (October). Algeciras, Seville (lung bleeding). Cannes.

1928   Cannes (till February). *The Tower.* Rapallo (April). Dublin house sold. Ballylee (June). Furnished house at Howth (July). Last Senate Speech (July).

1929   Rapallo (winter). Summer in Ireland, in flat (Fitzwilliam Square, Dublin), at Coole and Ballylee, then at Howth. *A Packet for Ezra Pound* (August). *The Winding Stair* (October). Rapallo. Malta fever (December). Ezra Pound and George Antheil at Rapallo.

1930   Portofino (April). Writes 'Byzantium'. Renvyle, Connemara (June). Coole. *Words upon the Window-pane* produced at Abbey Theatre (November). Visits Masefield at Boar's Hill, Oxford, thirtieth anniversary of their first meeting. Spends winter in Dublin, in furnished house on Killiney Hill.

1931   Writes 'The Seven Sages'. DLitt. at Oxford (May). Delivers most of MS for proposed *Edition de Luxe* to Harold Macmillan. Writes much verse at Coole in summer. Broadcast BBC Belfast (September). Spends winter at Coole, reading Balzac; Lady Gregory dying.

1932   Works on 'Coole and Ballylee, 1931'. Winter and spring at Coole. Lady Gregory dies. Leases Riversdale, Rathfarnham, Co. Dublin. Foundation of Irish Academy of Letters (September). Last American tour (October). *Words for Music Perhaps and Other Poems* (November).

1933   Interested in O'Duffy's blueshirt movement. *The Winding Stair and Other Poems* (September), *Collected Poems* (November).

1934   Steinach operation. Rapallo (June). Rome (autumn). *Wheels and Butterflies. Collected Plays. The King of the Great Clock Tower.*

1935 Attacks of congestion of the lungs. Stays with Dorothy Wellesley at Penns in The Rocks, Sussex. Majorca (winter). Shri Purohit Swami collaborates in translation of *Upanishads*. *Dramatis Personae*. *A Full Moon in March* (November).

1936 Seriously ill; heart missing beat (January); nephritis. Returns to Riversdale. Broadcasts on modern poetry, BBC, London (summer). *Oxford Book of Modern Verse (1892–1935)*.

1937 Elected member Athenaeum. Broadcasts BBC London (April, July, September). *A Speech and Two Poems* (August). Begins friendship with Edith Shackleton Heald. Visits Dorothy Wellesley. *A Vision* (October). *Essays 1931–1936* (December).

1938 *The Herne's Egg* (January). Spends January–March in south of France. Visits Sussex, stays with Dorothy Wellesley, and with Edith Shackleton Heald. *New Poems* (May). Sussex (June). Last public appearance at Abbey Theatre for performance of *Purgatory* (August). Maud Gonne visits him at Riversdale (late summer). Sussex (September). Leaves for south of France (late November).

1939 Dies 28 January, buried at Roquebrune. *Last Poems and Two Plays* (June). *On the Boiler*.

1948 Body reinterred at Drumcliffe Churchyard, Sligo.

Appendix Two
Maps

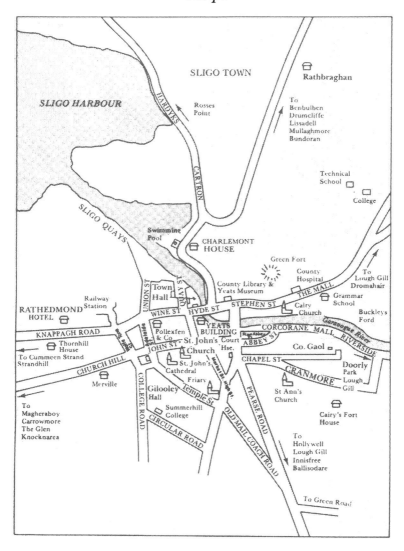

The Town of Sligo

Ballylee (*W. B. Yeats*)
Sandymount (*Yeats's birthplace*)
Rathfarnham (*Yeats's last Irish residence*)
Aran Islands (*J. M. Synge*)
Coole Park (*Lady Gregory*)
French Park (*Douglas Hyde*)

Tulira (*Edward Martyn*)
Lissoy (? *The Deserted Village*)
Moore Hall (*George Moore*)
Elphin (*Oliver Goldsmith*)
Cloyne (*Bishop Berkeley*)
Ballyshannon (*Wm. Allingham*)

Yeats's Ireland

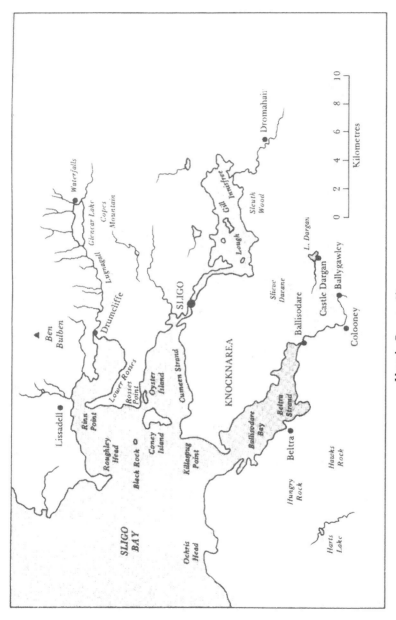

Yeats's County Sligo

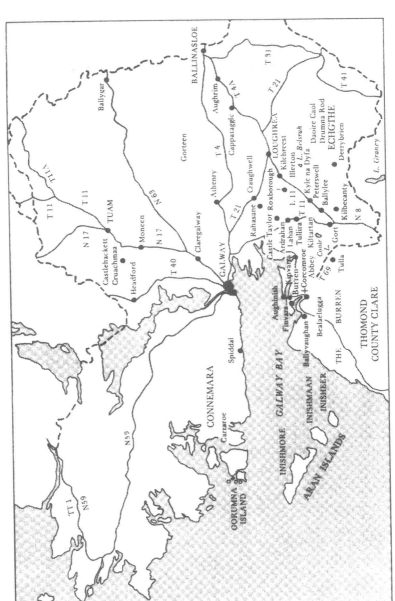

Yeats's County Galway

Appendix Three
Diagrams from 'A Vision'

THE GREAT WHEEL OF THE LUNAR PHASES

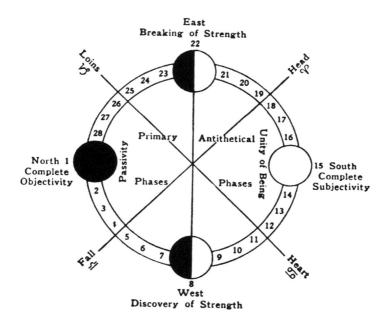

THE HISTORICAL CONES

The numbers in brackets refer to phases, and the other numbers to dates AD. The line cutting the cones a little below 250, 900, 1180 and 1927 shows four historical *Faculties* related to the present moment, May 1925.

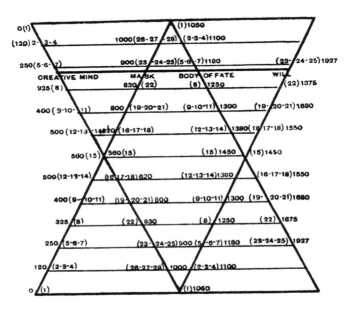

THE GYRES

According to Simplicius,[1] a late commentator upon Aristotle, the Concord of Empedocles fabricates all things into 'an homogenous sphere', and then Discord separates the elements and so makes the world we inhabit, but even the sphere formed by Concord is not the changeless eternity, for Concord or Love but offers us the image of that which is changeless.

If we think of the vortex attributed to Discord as formed by circles diminishing until they are nothing, and of the opposing sphere attributed

[1]quoted by Pierre Duhem in *Le système du monde*, vol. 1, p. 75.

to Concord as forming from itself an opposing vortex, the apex of each vortex in the middle of the other's base, we have the fundamental symbol of my instructors.

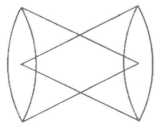 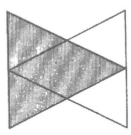

If I call the unshaded cone 'Discord' and the other 'Concord' and think of each as the bound of a gyre, I see that the gyre of 'Concord' diminishes as that of 'Discord' increases, and can imagine after that the gyre of 'Concord' increasing while that of 'Discord' diminishes, and so on, one gyre within the other always. Here the thought of Heraclitus dominates all: 'Dying each other's life, living each other's death'.

Appendix Four
Glossary

IRISH PEOPLE AND PLACES IN THE POEMS

This glossary has frequently drawn on an admirable reference work by James P. McGarry, *Place Names in the Writings of W. B. Yeats* (1976), for information on the original Irish names of places mentioned in the poems. The names of Irish persons mentioned are also included. Other names and places are explained in the Notes.

Abbey Theatre	The Abbey Theatre, Dublin, opened in 1904
Aedh [Aodh]	Irish form of Hugh; but also the Irish for fire. Aedh was a personage in Yeats's *The Secret Rose* (1897)
Aengus	Yeats's spelling of Aonghus (modern Oengus), the 'Master of Love', also known as Angus Og. He was Niamh's father, the lover of Caer, and lived at Brughna-Boinne
Aherne, Owen	an invented character
Aibric	a character in *The Shadowy Waters* who had served Forgael since childhood
Ailell	husband of Maeve, queen of Connacht
Aillinn	legendary lover of Baile; they were turned into swans by Aengus. *See under* Baile below
Aleel	name given to a poet (originally called Kevin) in *The Countess Cathleen*
Almhuin	Sid Almhain, the Hill of Allen, Co. Kildare, site of Finn MacCool's palace; one of the three residences of the Kings of Leinster
Alt	a glen on Knocknarea, mountain in Co. Sligo
Aodh	Aodh, Hugh
Aoife	(i) a Scottish warrior-queen, mother of Cuchulain's son, whom he killed not knowing who he was (ii) 'Rock nurtured' Aoife, a woman of the Sidhe, a 'malignant phantom', probably Aoibhell of Craigh Liath, the Grey Rock, Killaloe, Co. Clare
Aoibhill/Aoibhell	see Aoife
Ardan	(i) brother of King Eochaid (Ailell Anguba in the original tale) (ii) brother of Naoise, one of the sons of Usna/Usnach
Armstrong, an	Yeats's grandfather, the Rev. William Butler Yeats,

	married Jane Grace Corbet in 1835: she was the daughter of William Corbet and Grace Armstrong; both Corbet and Armstrong families had military traditions
Artisson, Robert	Robert, son of Art, an evil spirit in Kilkenny, who was the incubus of Dame Alice Kyteler in the 14th century
Aslauga Shee	an Sluagh Sidhe, the fairy host of the mound
Baile	(i) Baile, son of Buan, the lover of Aillinn, the daughter and heir of Lugaidh (Lugaidh was the son of Curaoi MacDaire, a King of Munster). He was known as Baile Honey-Mouth or Baile Little-Land (ii) Traigh mbaile, Baile's Strand, near Dundalk, Co. Louth, near Cuchulain's fort
Ballinafad	village in Aughanagh, on the Sligo road, near Boyle
Ballygawley Hill	Baile Dhalaigh, Ballydawley, O'Daly's townland, about 5 miles from Sligo
Ballylee	Baile an Liagh, Baile ui Laoi, the townland of Ballylee, Co. Galway, about 3 miles from Gort, Co. Galway. Yeats's tower, Thoor, is situated in it
Balor	a Fomorian king who led the hosts of darkness at the battle of Moytura (Magh Tuiridh, the plain of the pillars, or Magh Turach, the towered plain) near Sligo. The battle marked the final overthrow of the Firbolgs by the Tuatha de Danaan
Barach	a Red Branch warrior who, at Conchubar's instigation, asked Fergus to a feast when he was in charge of Deirdre, Naoise and his brothers. The absence of Fergus, the safe conduct, led to the murder of the men
bawn	a fortified enclosure
bell-branch	a legendary branch, the shaking of which 'cast all men into a gentle sleep'
Ben Bulben	Beann Ghulben, Binn Gulbain, Gulban's peak, mountain in Co. Sligo
Bera of Ships	Beare Island, Bantry Bay, Co. Cork
Berkeley	George Berkeley (1685–1753), Bishop of Cloyne and distinguished philosopher
Biddy	pet form of Bridget, sometimes used contemptuously
Billy, King	William of Orange, William III (1650–1702)
Blanid/Blanaid	a daughter of the Lord of Manainn, she was claimed as a prize by Curaoi Mac Daire who helped Cuchulain in the sacking of Manainn. She was killed by Curaoi's harper Feircheirtne in revenge for conspiring with Cuchulain to kill Curaoi
boreen	boirin, a lane

Boyne	an Bhoinn, the River Boyne, which enters the sea near Drogheda, Co. Louth. The river's goddess Boann and her husband Dagda lived at Bruigh na Boinne, New Grange. The Battle of the Boyne, at which James II was defeated, took place in 1690
Bran	one of Finn's cousins; his aunt Uirne was transformed when pregnant; Finn's other hound cousin was Sceolan, their third whelp was Lomair
Bride's well	Tober Bride/Tubberbride, a townland in Collooney, Co. Sligo, named after a holy well dedicated to St Brigid
Bridget	newly married bride of O'Driscoll, character in 'The Host of the Air', founded on a ballad
Bruen, Paddy	imagined character
Bual	probably Ethal (or Etal) Anbuail (or Anbual), father of Caer
Bual's hill	Anbual's hill, probably the residence of Anbuail, Sid Uamain, the fairy mount of Uaman in Connacht
Buan's son	Buan was an Ulster goddess, the wife of Megesdra, a King of Leinster
Bull, brown and bull, white-horned	the brown bull of Cooley, coveted by Maeve to replace her own white-horned bull which went to her husband's herds. The *Tain Bo Cualgne* arose from the seizure of this bull
Burke	Edmund Burke (1729–97), Irish statesman, author and orator
Butler	*see* Ormondes
Byrne, Billy	William Byrne (?–1798) a member of the Leinster Directorate of the United Irishmen.
Byrnes	a Wicklow family
Caer	the daughter of Ethal Anbual from the Sidhe of Connaught
Caoilte	Caoilte MacRonain (Ronan), Finn's favourite warrior and a friend of Finn's son Oisin. He drove the gods out of their liss or fort at Ossory (or Asseroe) and he appears as a 'flaming man' in 'The Hosting of the Sidhe'
Casement	Sir Roger Casement (1864–1916) retired from the British Colonial Service in 1912, joined the Irish National Volunteers in 1913, tried to enlist Irish prisoners in Germany for an Irish rising, landed in Ireland from German submarine, was arrested and hanged in 1916
Cashel/the Rock of Cashel	Caiseal, Cashel of the Kings, Cashel of the Steps, Co. Tipperary, at one time capital of Munster, an imposing

	rock site with a round tower, Cormac's chapel and a ruined cathedral on it
Castle Dargan	Caiseal Locha Deargain, the stone fort of Loch Dargain, near Ballygawley, Co. Sligo
Castle, the	Ballylee Castle, Co. Galway, bought by Yeats in 1917; he called it Thoor Ballylee
Castle Taylor	in Co. Galway, near Craughwell, incorporated into a mansion by the Taylor family in 1802
Cathleen ni Houlihan	a female figure who traditionally symbolises Ireland
City Hall	south of the Liffey on Cork Hill, Dublin; originally the Royal Exchange, it was taken over by Dublin Corporation in 1850
Clare	an clar, the stone (corner) of contention, name of Irish county taken from small village, now Clarecastle
Clare-Galway	Baile an Chlair, the townland of the Plain, Co. Galway
Cloone, Bog of	near Gort, Co. Galway, where one of the country beauty Mary Hynes's admirers accidentally drowned himself on his way to see her
Clooth na Bare	Cailleach Beare, the old woman Bare. The Cailleach Beare's house is an ancient monument on Ballygawley Mountain, Co. Sligo. Yeats describes her seeking a lake deep enough to drown her fairy life and finding it in Lough Ia (Lough Dagea, the Lake of the Two Geese) on Sliabh da-En, Slieve Daene, the Mountain of the Two Birds, Co. Sligo
Cloyne	Cluain-uamha (or Cluain more), the Meadow of the Cave, Co. Cork, name of diocese of which George Berkeley was bishop
Colooney/ Coloony	Collooney, Cuil Maoile or Cuil Mhuine, a village south of Sligo
Comedian, the Great	Yeats's term for Daniel O'Connell (1775–1847), Irish political leader who won Catholic emancipation in 1829
Conall Carnach	one of Conchubar's twelve chief heroes, known as the Victorious
Conan	Conan Maol, Conan the Baldheaded, a braggart Fenian warrior, described by Yeats as the Thersites of the Red Branch cycle of tales
Conchubar	Conor MacNessa, King of Ulster in the Red Branch cycle of tales
Connacht	Coicid Connacht, fifth of Connacht, one of the fifths into which the legendary Firbolgs divided Ireland. The name may derive from the descendants of Conn the Hundred Fighter who settled there, or from a tribe called Olnechacht who were aboriginal dwellers there

	called Olnechacht who were aboriginal dwellers there
Connemara	Conmaicne Mara, an area in Co. Galway named after the descendants of Conmac, one of the sons of Maeve and Fergus MacRoy. He was known as Conmaicne, and a branch of his family as Conmaicne Mara, the Hounds of the Sea
Connolly, James	(i) James Connolly (1868–1916), socialist leader, organiser of the Citizen Army, executed by firing squad for his part in the 1916 Rising (ii) 'the player Connolly', an Abbey actor, shot in the fighting on Easter Monday, 1916
Coole/Coole Park	an cuil, the corner, near Gort, Co. Galway. The Gregory estate of Coole Park was purchased in 1768; the house was pulled down in 1941
Corbets, Sandymount	Robert Corbet, an uncle of Yeats's father, who lived at Sandymount Castle, Dublin
Cormac	Cormac MacCarthy, King of Desmond or South Munster, who had a chapel constructed in the 12th century on the Rock of Cashel
Cormac's ruined house	the 12th-century chapel on the Rock of Cashel, Co. Tipperary
Cosgrave	William T. Cosgrave (1880–1966), Sinn Fein MP who became first President of Dail Eireann (1922–32); he was a member of the Dail from 1922 to 1944
County of the Young	*see* Tir-na-nOg
Craoibhin Aoibhin	pen-name of Dr Douglas Hyde (1860–1947) poet, translator, creator of the Gaelic League and first President of Eire
Crazy Jane	invented character, based on a real person, 'Cracked Mary', who lived near Gort, Co. Galway
Crevroe	Craobh Ruadh, a building at Emain Macha, in which the Red Branch heroes lived
Cromlech	a neolithic construction of stones, usually with one large horizontal stone resting upon three or four smaller vertical stones
Cro-Patrick	Croagh Patrick, Patrick's Heap, a mountain near Westport, Co. Mayo, site of an annual pilgrimage. St Patrick is reputed to have fasted on its summit and when there to have banished snakes from Ireland
Cruachan	Cruacha, Uaimh Cruacha, near Tulsk, Co. Roscommon, named after Cruacha, mother of Maeve. It was the capital of Connacht, a royal site and the burial ground associated with the *Tain Bo Cualgne*
Cuchulain	Cu Culann, the Hound of Culain, a name given to the

	Red Branch hero, also called the Hound of Ulster. He was the son of Sualtim and Dechtire (Conor Mac-Nessa's (Conchubar's) sister); at the age of seven he made his way to Conchubar's palace at Emain Macha and later in self-defence killed the hound of Culain the Smith. In compensation the boy offered to protect Culain's possessions and his herds and was consequently called Cuchulain by Cathbad the Druid
Cullinan, Shemus	imagined character
Cumhal	invented character in 'The Blessed'; in early versions 'Cumhal the King'
Cummen/ Cummen Strand	Cuimin, the little common, between Strandhill and Sligo Town, Co. Sligo
Dan [?Lout]	imagined character
Danaan/ de Danaan	of the Tuatha de Danaan, see Sidhe and Tuatha de Danaan
Dargan, Castle	see Castle Dargan
Dathi	character in 'The Blessed'; in early versions 'Dathi the Blessed'
Davis	Thomas Davis (1814–45), Irish poet and nationalist, founded The Nation newspaper in 1842 and led the Young Ireland Party
Dean, the	see Swift
Dectora	a queen whose husband Iollan is killed by Forgael's crew in The Shadowy Waters
Derg, Lough	a small lake on the borders of Co. Donegal and Co. Fermanagh; an island in it is known as St Patrick's Purgatory. (He was alleged to have fasted there and had a vision of the next world in a cave.) It is the site of a famous annual pilgrimage
de Valéra	Eamon de Valéra (1882–1975), revolutionary, scholar, politician, and President of Ireland
Diarmuid/ Diarmid/ Dermot	Diarmuid eloped with Grania, daughter of Cormac MacArt (she was betrothed to the ageing widower Finn, who pursued the lovers). Diarmuid was killed by a boar on Ben Bulben in Co. Sligo
Doe, Paddy	invented character
Dooney/Dooney Rock	Dun Aodh, Aodh's (Hugh's) Fort, on the shore of Lough Gill, Co. Sligo, a place where, in Yeats's youth, James Howley, a blind fiddler, played the music for outdoor dancing
Down, County	Irish county; the poet's grandfather, Rev. William Butler Yeats, was curate at Moira and Rector at

	Tullylish in that county
Druid	wise man, magician, soothsayer
Drumahair/	Drom-dha-eithiar, the Ridge of the Two Demons,
Dromohair/	Co. Leitrim, at the Leitrim end of Lough Gill, the site
Dromahair	of O'Rorke's Castle and banqueting hall
Drumcliff/	Druim Chliach, the Ridge of the Hazels, Co. Sligo, at
Drumcliffe	the foot of Ben Bulben near the mouth of the Glencar Valley. It was the site of a monastery founded by St Columkille in 575. There remain part of a round tower, a high cross and the shaft of an older cross in the churchyard where Yeats is buried along with his grandfather, Rev. John Yeats (1774–1846) who was rector of the parish
Drunken vainglorious lout	Major John MacBride (1865–1916) who married Maud Gonne in 1903. He was shot after a court martial in 1916
Dublin merchant	Yeats's paternal great-great-grandfather Benjamin Yeats (1750–95), who married Mary Butler (1751–1834)
Duddon	a fictional character
Dun	a fort
Eade's Grammar School	Sligo Grammar School
Early, Biddy	a famous witch who lived in County Clare
Echtge	Sliabh [Sleev] Echte (Aughty), a mountain range running from Loughrea, Co. Galway, to near Lough Derg, Co. Clare; it was named after Echte of the Tuatha de Danaan, whose marriage dowry it was
Edain	Edain (Etain) Echraide, whom Midhir (already married to Fuamnach) took to wife. She was driven out of Bri Leith by a druid's spells at Fuamnach's request, and Aengus (Angus Og) looked after her; Fuamnach turned her into a fly. Aengus struck off Fuamnach's head and searched for Etain who was blown about for seven years before being drunk in wine by Etar's wife, who bore her as a daughter nine months later. She was again called Etain, and married Eochaid Fiedlech (later Airem) the High King. Midhir, King of the Sidhe, appeared to her when Eochaid's brother Ailell was ill, and appealed to her to return to him. He played chess with Eochaid, won a kiss from Etain in the third game, and took her away. Eventually she was brought back to Tara after Eochaid had besieged and dug into Midhir's mound at Bri Leith (called after Leith, son of

	Celtchar of Cualir, a young man of the Sidhe)
Eire	Irish for Ireland. It was originally the name of a queen of the Tuatha de Danaan
Emain/Emain Macha	Emain Macha, Macha's Height, the capital of Uladh (Ulster) near modern Armagh, founded by Macha of the Golden Hair, Queen of Cimbaeth, King of Ulster. For more than six hundred years it continued to be the residence of the Ulster kings
Emer	Cuchulain's wife, daughter of Forgall Manach
Emmet	Robert Emmet (1778–1803), United Irishman, who was publicly hanged after the failure of the rebellion he led in 1803
Emmet's friend	Rev. John Yeats (1774–1846), Yeats's great-grandfather, rector of Drumcliff, Co. Sligo
Enniscrone	Inis Crabhann, the promontory of Crone, a seacoast village in Co. Sligo, where Yeats's sister Susan Mary 'Lily' (1866–1949) was born
Eochaid, King	Eochaid Airem, a High King of Ireland (Yeats's note gives the pronunciation of his name as 'Yohee'). He was called Airem ('of the plough') because he taught his people to yoke their oxen by the neck and shoulder as the Sidhe did. *See also* Edain
Esserkelly plain	Esirtkelly/Dysert Cheallagh/Disert Ceallagh, Ceallagh's hermitage near Ardrahan, Co. Galway, named after St Ceallagh, eldest son of Eoghan Bel (see Knocknarea)
Falias	one of the four mysterious cities whence the Tuatha de Danaan came to Ireland
Fand	Fand was the daughter of Aedh Abratane, wife of Manannan MacLir, god of the sea. She was loved for a time by Cuchulain after she had enchanted him. She returned to Manannan and the druids made Cuchulain and his wife Emer forget the affair
father, my	John Butler Yeats (1839–1922), barrister, artist and conversationalist
Fenians, the	Yeats explained them as 'the great military order of which Finn was chief'. Their deeds are collected in the Fenian or Ossianic cycle of tales
Fergus	Fergus MacRoigh (MacRoy), King of Ulster, married to Ness/Nessa, renounced his kingdom for a year in favour of his stepson Conor MacNessa (Conchubar) but did not regain it. He later became Maeve's lover
Ferguson	Sir Samuel Ferguson (1810–86) Irish poet, translator, antiquarian

Fierce old man	William Pollexfen (1811–92), sea captain and merchant who settled in Sligo; Yeats's maternal grandfather
Findrias	one of the four mysterious cities whence the Tuatha de Danaan came to Ireland
findrinny	findruine, an alloy (white bronze)
Finn	Finn MacCumhail (MacCool) leader of the Fenians, killed on the Boyne AD 283
Firbolgs	legendary invaders of Ireland (fir, man; builg, god of lightning) who partitioned Ireland into five provinces ruled by the five sons of Dela who led them to Ireland from the Mediterranean. They were at the peak of their power *c.* 300 BC, and were defeated at the Battle of Moytura
Fitzgerald	Lord Edward Fitzgerald (1763–98), soldier in British army, served in US and Canada, joined United Irishmen, headed a military committee planning 1798 Rising, died of wounds incurred when resisting arrest
Forgael	main character in *The Shadowy Waters*; he is searching for an unearthly kind of beauty
French	Mrs French (*née* O'Brien) lived at Peterswell, Co. Galway, in the 18th century
Gabhra	site of battle, near Garristown, north Co. Dublin, in which the Fenians were heavily defeated
Gallery, the	the National Gallery of Ireland, Merrion Square, Dublin
Galway	Cathair na Gaillimh [Gol-yiv]: Galway, the City of the Tribes; west coast city and seaport
Gap of the Wind	*see* Windy Gap
Gill, Lough	Loch Gile, the Bright Lake, in Co. Sligo
Gill, Michael	invented character
Glasnevin coverlet	Glas-Naeidhen, Naeidhe's little stream, Glasnevin, Co. Dublin, site of Dublin's main cemetery, where Parnell was buried
Glen-Car/ Glencar Lough	An Chairthe, Gleann-an Chairthe, the Glen of the Standing Stone, Co. Sligo
Glendalough	Glendalocha, the Glen or Valley of the Two Lakes, Co. Wicklow; site of St Kevin's hermitage, with ruined churches, crosses and a round tower
Goban	Goibniu/Goibhniu, the god of the smiths, who made and repaired weapons for the Tuatha de Danaan before the battle of Moytura
Goban's mountain top	Sliagh Anieran, the Iron Mountain, Co. Leitrim
Goldsmith	Oliver Goldsmith (1728–74), Irish author
Gonne	Maud Gonne (1866–1953), revolutionary, met Yeats

	in 1889, had two children by Lucien Millevoye, married John MacBride 1903; their son Sean was born 1904; separated from MacBride 1905; arrested 1918, in Holloway gaol six months; later lived in Dublin
Gorias	one of the four mysterious cities whence the Tuatha de Danaan came to Ireland
Gore-Booth	the Gore-Booth family owned Lissadell, Co. Sligo, from early in the 18th century. In 1894–5 Yeats visited the Gore-Booth sisters, Constance (1868–1927), who married Casimir de Markievicz, and Eva (1870–1926)
Gort	Gort-Innse-Guaire: the Island Field of Guaire (*see* Guaire), a market town in Co. Galway, 2 miles south of Coole Park
Grania	she fled with Diarmid (Diarmuid/Dermot) to escape the love of Finn, then aged; in Standish O'Grady's version of the tale she returns to Finn after Diarmid is killed in Sligo
Grattan	Henry Grattan (1746–1820), Irish parliamentarian and orator, after whom 'Grattan's Parliament' was named
Great Plain, the	the Great Plain of the other world, the Land of the Dead and Happy
Green Lands	the Greenlands, unfenced part of Rosses Point, Co. Sligo, sandhills stretching inland from Deadman's Point
Gregory, Anne	Anne Gregory (*b.* 1911) daughter of Robert and granddaughter of Lady Gregory
Gregory, Lady Augusta	Lady Isabella Augusta Gregory (1852–1932), Irish authoress and friend of Yeats, co-director of the Abbey Theatre with Yeats and Synge
Gregory, Robert	Robert Gregory (1881–1918), RFC pilot, only child of Lady Gregory, killed in action over Italy
Grey Rock, the	Craig Liath, the Grey Stone, near Killaloe, Co. Clare, the house of Aoibheal (whom Yeats called Aoife in 'The Grey Rock') of the Sidhe
Griffith	Arthur Griffith (1871–1922), Irish political leader and journalist, led plenipotentiaries to negotiations which resulted in the Anglo-Irish Treaty of December 1921
Guaire/Guare	a 6th-century King of Connacht, who lived at Gort, Co. Galway
Hanrahan	Red Hanrahan, an invented character in Yeats's *Stories of Red Hanrahan*, a poet probably founded on Eoghan Ruadh O'Suilleabhain (1748–84), a lyric and satiric Irish poet
Hart Lake	originally Loch Minnaun, called Hart Lake after the

	family living near it, in the Ox Mountains, Co. Sligo
Hart, Peter	imagined character
Heber	one of the sons of Miled; he gained the two provinces of Munster, his brother Leinster and Connacht, Ulster being given to Eimher, the son of Ir, another son of Miled
Henry Street	Dublin street running at right angles to Sackville (now O'Connell) Street
Houlihan	father of Cathleen (see Cathleen ni Houlihan)
House, an old/A small old	Riversdale, Rathfarnham, Co. Dublin
Howth	the name (pronounced Hōth) is derived from Danish Hovud, the Irish name being Ben Eadair, Eadar's peak. Howth is a peninsula forming the northern arm of Dublin Bay
Huddon	a fictional character
Hyde	Douglas Hyde (1860–1949), poet, translator, founder of the Gaelic League and first President of Ireland
Inchy wood	*see* Seven Woods
Innisfree	Inisfraoich/Inisfree, the heathery island, in Lough Gill, Co. Sligo
Invar Amargin	the mouth of the River Avoca, Co. Wicklow; landing place of the druid Amergin who came to Ireland with the Milesians
Ith	Magh Itha, the valley of the Lagan river, Co. Donegal; named after Ith, a Milesian, the 'first of the Gael to get his death in Ireland'
Keeners	those who raise the keen, an Irish form of mourning
Kerry	Ciarraighe, Kerry, Irish county, named after the Lady Ceasair, an invader, who landed at Dunmore, Co. Kerry
Kiltartan/ Kiltartan Cross	townland near Gort, Co. Galway, after which some of Lady Gregory's books (and her prose style) are named
Kilvarnet	Cill Bhearnais, the Church in the Gap, a townland near Ballinacarrow, Co. Sligo, which contains the ruins of a church
Kinsale	Cionntsaile, the head of the sea, seaport in Co. Cork
Kinsella, John	an invented character, a 'strong farmer'
Knockfefin	Sliabh na mban Feimhinn, the Mountain of the Women of the Feimhenn (Femen), Co. Tipperary, a fairy place called Sid ar Femen, the home of Bodb Derg, son of Dagda, where the Sidhe enchanted Finn MacCool. It is now known as Slievenamahon. The women, Fe and Men, were wives of two bards of the Tuatha de Danaan

Knocknarea	Cnoc na Riaghadh, Cnoc na Riogh, the Hill of the King (or, less likely, the Hill of the Execution). A mountain in Co. Sligo. A cairn on its summit is reputedly the burial place of Queen Maeve, but more likely to have been that of Eoghan Bel, the last pagan King of Connacht, whose body was later buried by his enemies face down near Sligo. Maeve is more likely to have been buried at Cruachan, at Reilig na Riogh, the royal burial place
Knocknashee	probably Knocknashee Common in the Barony of Leyney, Co. Sligo (there is another Knocknashee near Boyle, Co. Roscommon)
Kyle dortha	*see* Seven Woods
Kyle-na-no	*see* Seven Woods
Kyteler, Lady	Lady Alice Kyteler, member of an Anglo-Norman family in Kilkenny, four times married, and accused of sorcery, and of having relations with an incubus, Robin, son of Art
Laban	a sister of Fand, the wife of Manannan MacLir; she was changed into an otter by her magic well when she neglected it
Laighen	a hill fort, seat of the Kings of Leinster, on the Co. Kildare–Co. Dublin borders
Land of the Tower	possibly the tower or house of glass belonging to Aengus. It may be Toraigh, Tory Island, a Place of Towers, Co. Donegal
Lane-under-wave	Tir-fa-thon, an enchanted underworld beneath the sea
Lane	Sir Hugh Lane (1875–1915), art collector and critic, who offered his collection of modern paintings to Dublin
Lavery, Hazel	Sir John Lavery's (1856–1941) second wife, who died in 1935
Liss	a fort
Lissadell	lis-a-doill, the Fort of the Blind Man, Co. Sligo; the house owned by the Gore-Booth family was built there in 1832
Lomair	one of Oisin's hounds, named in *The Wanderings of Oisin* with Bran and Sceolan, one of their three whelps. Bran and Sceolan were Finn's cousins
Loughlann waters	Lochlann, Norse/Scandinavian waters, the North Sea
Lout, Jerry	imagined character
Lugaidh	Lugaidh, son of Curoi (Curaoi) MacDaire, was a King of Munster
Lugnagall	Lug na nGall, the Hollow of the Strangers (not, as

	Yeats translates it, the 'steep place' of the strangers) a townland in Glen-Car Valley, Co. Sligo, at the foot of Cope's mountain
Lavery	Lady Hazel Lavery (*d.* 1935) an American painter, 2nd wife of Sir John Lavery; her portrait appeared on Irish banknotes from 1923. Sir John Lavery (1856–1941), successful painter, famous for his conversation pieces
MacBride	John MacBride (1865–1916) fought in Boer War against the British, married Maud Gonne in 1903, executed for taking part in 1916 Rising
MacBride	Maud Gonne MacBride, *see* Maud Gonne
MacDonagh	Thomas MacDonagh (1878–1916), poet and critic; executed in 1916 for taking part in the Rising
MacNessa	Conor MacNessa (Conchubar) King of Ulster, leader of the Red Branch knights
Maeve	Queen of Connacht, married to Ailill; had love affair with Fergus. Her wish to outdo Ailill led her to want the Brown Bull of Cooley and this led to the war celebrated in the *Tain Bo Cualgne*
Magh Ai	Machaire Connacht, the great plain dominated by Cruachan in Co. Roscommon
Magee, Moll	invented character
Maines	Maeve's son, married to Ferbe, killed by Conchubar
Maines, the children of the	usually considered the children of Maeve and Ailill, but they could be the children of Maeve's son Maines and Ferbe
Malachi (Stilt Jack)	biblical name; Malachi was a 5th-century Hebrew prophet. Yeats uses the name for a circus clown
The Mall	street in Sligo
Mancini	Antonio Mancini (1852–1930), an Italian artist who worked in Dublin
Mangan	James Clarence Mangan (1803–49), Irish poet
Manannan	Manannan MacLir, god of the sea, husband of Fand
Mannion	invented character, the 'Roaring Tinker'
Markiewicz, Constance	*see* Gore-Booth
Martin, Colonel	Richard Martin (1754–1834), MP, JP, High Sheriff of Galway and Colonel of the Galway Volunteers
Mayo	Mayo, the Plain of the Yew Trees, a western Irish county which derives its name from a village where St Colman founded a monastery in the 7th century
Middleton, a	one of Yeats's Middleton relatives in Sligo
Middleton, Henry	a cousin of the poet, a recluse who lived in Elsinore, Rosses Point, Sligo

Middleton, the smuggler	William Middleton (?1770–1832), Yeats's maternal great-grandfather
Midhir/Midir	a King of the Sidhe, who was in love with Edain, King Eochaid's wife
Midhir's wife	(i) Fuamnach, killed by Aengus for her treatment of Etaine/Edain (ii) *see* Edain
Mitchel	John Mitchel (1815–75) wrote for *The Nation*, founded the *United Irishmen*, arrested in 1848, sentenced to fourteen years' transportation, escaped from Van Dieman's Land (Tasmania)
Mocharabuiee	Machaire Bui, Magheraboy, the Yellow Plain, south-west of Sligo town
Mooneen	Moneen, moinin; the Little Bog, near Esserkelly, by Ardrahan, Co. Galway
Moore, Mary	invented character
Mourteen	Irish name
Moytura	Magh Tuireadh, the Plain of the Pillars (or Magh Turach, the Towered Plain), Co. Sligo, site of defeat of Firbolgs by Tuatha de Danaan
Muirthemne	a plain in Co. Louth, site of the main fight in the *Tain Bo Cualgne*. Cuchulain came from there
Municipal Gallery, the	situated in the former Charlemont House, Parnell Square, Dublin
Munster	the southern of Ireland's four provinces
Murias	one of the four mysterious cities whence the Tuatha de Danaan came to Ireland
Murrough	Murrough (Murchad), son of King Brian Boru, who killed Earl Sigurd in the Battle of Clontarf (1014) but was himself mortally wounded by Anrad the Dane
Naoise	Naoise, the son of Usna, ran away with Deirdre whom Conor intended to marry: accompanied by his brothers Ainnle and Ardan they went to Scotland; returned under Fergus's safe conduct. The sons of Usna were killed treacherously by Conchubar
Nessa	Ness/Nessa; mother of Conchubar/Conor, she cheated Fergus her husband into giving up the kingdom to his stepson Conor
Niam/Niamh	the fairy princess who brought Oisin to the underworld where he stayed three hundred years. She was the daughter of Aengus
O'Byrnes	a Co. Wicklow family
O'Donnells	(1) Red Hugh O'Donnell (c. 1571–1602), chief of the O'Donnells; he went to Spain for aid and was reputedly poisoned there

	(2) Rory O'Donnell (1575–1665), younger brother of Red Hugh, created Earl (1603); fled to Rome with the Earl of Tyrone
O'Driscoll	an invented character, in 'The Host of the Air', a poem founded on an old ballad; he lost his wife Bridget to the fairies
O'Duffy	Eoin O'Duffy (1892–1944), first commissioner of the Garda Siochana (1922–33); he led an Irish Brigade to fight for Franco in the Spanish Civil War
Ogham	an ancient alphabet of twenty characters
O'Grady	Standish James O'Grady (1846–1928), historian and novelist, whose writings awakened a sense of the epic past of Ireland
O'Higgins	Kevin O'Higgins (1892–1927), Minister of Justice in the Irish Free State, took a strong line against the Republicans in the Civil War and was assassinated in 1927
Oisin	son of Finn, leader of the Fenians, and Saeve of the Sidhe. Yeats described him as the poet of the Fenian cycle. In *The Wanderings of Oisin* he spent three hundred years visiting the other world with Niamh, a fairy princess
old country scholar	Rev. John Yeats (1774–1846), Rector of Drumcliffe, Co. Sligo, Yeats's great-grandfather
old Dublin merchant	probably Benjamin Yeats (1750–95), a wholesale linen merchant in Dublin, Yeats's great-great-grandfather
old merchant skipper	William Middleton (1770–1892), Yeats's maternal great-grandfather, a sea captain and smuggler
old queen	Macha, who measured the circumference of Emain Macha, the town she was founding, with the pin of her brooch, enclosing 18 acres of land
old stone cross	at Drumcliffe, Co. Sligo
O'Leary	John O'Leary (1830–1907), a Fenian, sentenced to twenty years' imprisonment, who was released after serving four on condition he did not return to Ireland, spent his exile in Paris, returned to Dublin in 1885
O'Leary, Daniel	a fictional character
ollave	ollamh, ollave, a learned person; the equivalent of the holder of a doctorate; there were ollaves of the different professions; their courses lasted twelve years
O'Neills, both	probably (1) Shane O'Neill the Proud (*c.* 1530–67), The O'Neill; he submitted to Elizabeth (1562), supported Mary Queen of Scots, burned Armagh (1566); killed by the MacDonnells at Cushendun (2) Hugh O'Neill (*b. c.* 1540–1616), 2nd Earl of

	Tyrone, elected The O'Neill (1591), submitted to Elizabeth, was received by James I; he left for Rome with Hugh Roe O'Donnell in 1607
O'Rahilly	The O'Rahilly (1875–1910), head of a Co. Kerry clan, was shot in the fighting during the 1916 Rising
Orchil	a Fomorian sorceress
Ormondes	members of the ducal family of the Butlers, descended from Theobald Walter ('Le Botiller', butler to Prince John), who was the first of the family to settle in Ireland. Benjamin Yeats married Mary Butler (1751–1834)
O'Roughley, Tom	invented character
Oscar	son of Oisin; he was killed at the Battle of Gabhra near Garristown, Co. Dublin, in 824
Oscar	Oscar Wilde (1854–1900), Irish dramatist, poet, critic and wit
Pairc-na-carraig	*see* Seven Woods
Pairc-na-lee	Pairc na laoi/laoigh the park or field of the calves at Coole, Co. Galway
Pairc-na-Tarav	*see* Seven Woods
Paistin Finn	Little Child of Finn (Oisin's father) or Fair-haired Child, the subject of a Munster folk-tune
Parnell	Charles Stewart Parnell (1846–91) Protestant Irish landowner and statesman who led the Irish Party at Westminster most successfully; it split when he was named co-respondent in the O'Shea divorce case of 1890, and married Mrs O'Shea in 1891
Parnellites	followers of Charles Stewart Parnell
Patrick	St Patrick (*c.* 385–*c.* 461), a native of Roman Britain, captured by Irish raiders, who escaped from slavery in Antrim and subsequently returned to begin the conversion of Ireland to Christianity. 17 March is annually celebrated as his and the national festival
Paudeen	diminutive of Padhraig, Patrick; a contemptuous name
Pearse	Patrick (Padraig) Henry Pearse (1879–1916) educationist, writer and revolutionary, condemned to death by court martial and executed for leading the Easter 1916 Rising
Place of the Strangers, the Steep Plain	*see* Steep Place . . . Strangers
Plain, the Great	*see* Great Plain, the
Pollexfens,	Alfred Pollexfen (1854–1916), worked in the family

Alfred, Elizabeth, George, John, William	shipping firm in Liverpool, returning to Sligo in 1910; Elizabeth, *née* Middleton (1819–92), born in Sligo, married Yeats's grandfather, William Pollexfen; George Pollexfen (1839–1910), Yeats's maternal uncle, a hypochondriac who lived in Sligo, interested in horses and occultism; John Pollexfen (1845–1900), was a sailor; 'An old cross Pollexfen' probably William Pollexfen (1811–92), the 'silent and fierce old man' of '[Introductory Rhymes]', Yeats's maternal grandfather, a sea captain and merchant, who lived in Sligo
Post Office, the	the General Post Office, Sackville (now O'Connell) Street, Dublin, seized by insurgents and ruined in the fighting of Easter 1916
Rachlin	Reachlainn/Rechru, Rathlin Island, off the coast of Co. Antrim
Raftery, 'dark'	Antoine/Anthony Raftery (*c.* 1784–1835), a blind (hence 'dark') folk poet born in Co. Mayo, who lived mostly in Co. Galway in the Gort and Loughrea areas
Raftery's cellar	an soilear, a swallow hole; the river that runs by Yeats's tower forms a deep pool and runs underground not far from the tower, the local limestone being porous
rann	Irish, a verse of a poem
Red Branch, the	the knights/heroes of the Red Branch were a kind of militia for the defence of the throne of Ulster, notably under Conor MacNessa (Conchubar), who lived in Emain Macha. The Red Branch cycle of tales deals with them, the best known being the *Tain Bo Cualgne*
redheaded rector	Rev. W. B. Yeats (1806–62), rector of Tullylish, Co. Down, the poet's grandfather
Ribh	Irish name: it occurs in Lady Gregory's 'Angus Og', *Gods and Fighting Men* (1904; 1970)
Robartes, Michael	an invented character
Rosses/Rosses Point	Ros Ceite, Co. Sligo, a seaside village about 5 miles from Sligo, where the Yeats family spent summer holidays with relatives
Round Tower, the	at Glendalough, Co. Wicklow
Roxborough	Craig-a-Roiste, Roche's Rock, Co. Galway; the name was changed to Roxborough in 1707. It was the Persse estate, on which Lady Gregory (*née* Persse) grew up
Rury	Baile was of the race of Rudraige, a term used for Ulster heroes other than Cuchulain who were traced back to Ir, the son of Mil

Salley Gardens
willow gardens, probably those on the bank of the Ballisodare river, Co. Sligo, near the mills at Ballisodare

Sandymount
Corbets
Sandymount Castle, Sandymount Green, in south Dublin, was owned by Robert Corbet, great-uncle of Yeats, who lived there with his mother and an aunt. Yeats's paternal grandfather, the Rev. William Butler Yeats, had a small house near it after he retired from Tullylish parish

Scanavin
tober sceanmhan, the well of Scanavin, the well of fine shingle; a small village a mile from Collooney, Co. Sligo

Sceolan
one of Oisin's hounds, a cousin of his, Uirne his aunt, having been transformed when pregnant

Seaghan the Fool
character mentioned in *The Shadowy Waters*

Sennachies
storytellers

Seven Hazel
Trees, the
possibly equivalent to the Nine Hazel Trees of Wisdom of the Tuatha de Danaan. Yeats placed them in 'the midst of Ireland'

Seven Woods,
the
the seven woods of Coole. Yeats listed them in 'In the Seven Woods' as Shan walla (either Sean balla, Old Wall, or sean bealach, Old Road); Kyle-dortha (Coill dorracha, the Dark Wood); Kyle-na-no (Coill na gno, the Wood of the Nuts); Pairc-na-lee (Pairc na Laoigh, the Field of the Calves); Pairc-na-carraig (Pairc na Carraig, the Field of the Rock, but known locally as the Fox Rock); Pairc-na-Tarav (Pairc na tara, the Bull Field or Park); and Inchy Wood (Incha Wood)

Shan walla
see Seven Woods

Shawe-Taylor
John Shawe-Taylor (1866–1911), a landowner, nephew of Lady Gregory, who called a crucial conference to settle the land question

Shoneen
an upstart, someone affecting stylish ways, a 'big' farmer aping the rank of a gentleman

Sidhe
the gods of ancient Ireland, the Tuatha de Danaan or tribes of the goddess Danu or the Sidhe, from Aes Sidhe or Sluagh Sidhe, the People of the Faery Hills. Sidhe also means whirling winds as well as the People of Faery

Slieveen
an Irish word for a rogue

Sleuth Wood
from Sliu, a slope. The wood, known usually as Slish Wood, from Slios, inclined or sloped, is situated on the Killery mountains at the edge of Lough Gill, Co. Sligo

Slievenamahon
Slievenamon, slieve-na-man, sliabh na mban Feimhenn, the Mountain of the Two Women (Fe and

	Men, wives of two Tuatha de Danaan poets), Co. Tipperary
Sligo	Sligeach, the Shelly River (or the Place of Shells), a reference to the Garavogue River which drains Lough Gill, Co. Sligo, and reaches the sea at Sligo
Steep Place of the Strangers, the	Lug na nGall, the hollow of the strangers, Co. Sligo; it is situated in a townland in Glencar Valley at the foot of Cope's Mountain
Strafford	Sir Thomas Wentworth, 1st Earl of Strafford (1593–1641), Lord Deputy of Ireland 1632–40
Swift	Jonathan Swift (1667–1745), author and Dean of St Patrick's Cathedral, Dublin
Synge	John Millington Synge (1871–1909), Irish author; the name is pronounced sing
Tara	Temair/Temhair, a Place with a View, near Navan, Co. Meath, the seat of the High King of Ireland. The kings were inaugurated there on the Lia Fail, the Stone of Destiny
that woman's days	a reference to Constance Markiewicz, *née* Gore-Booth (1868–1927)
thin Shade	the ghost of Charles Stewart Parnell (1846–91), Irish Parliamentarian and political leader
This man	Padraic Pearse (1879–1916), poet, schoolmaster, revolutionary leader, President of Provisional Government, 1916; shot after court martial
thraneen	Irish word meaning a dry stalk of grass or straw
Tiraragh	probably teeraree (Irish, *Tire a rig*), a townland in Kilmorgan Parish, Co. Sligo
Tir-nan-Oge	Tir-na-nOg, the Country of the Young, the Gaelic Other World
Thoor Ballylee	*see* Ballylee
Three Rock	mountain in Co. Dublin, one part of which is the Three Rock Mountain, the other the Two Rock Mountain
Tom the Lunatic	invented character
Tone	Theobald Wolfe Tone (1764–98), one of the founders of the United Irishmen; left Ireland for US, went to Paris, sailed as French adjutant-general in abortive expedition of 1796; then was in expedition of 1798 to Lough Swilly; captured and sentenced to be hanged, he committed suicide in prison
Tower of Glass	created by Aengus to hold Edain after Fuamnach had turned her into a purple fly (*see* Edain)
Tower, the/this	Thoor Ballylee, Yeats's tower in Co. Galway, *see* Ballylee

town, the	Dublin
Tuatha de Danaan	*see* Sidhe
Ulad/Uladh	Ulster, the northern province of Ireland. Ster is a northern addition to the name Ulaid. Yeats means the territory ruled from Emain Macha, which was destroyed in AD 450.
Usheen	*see* Oisin
Usna/Usnach	Uisnech, a Place of Fawns, Co. Westmeath. The Hill of Uisneach was regarded as the centre of Ireland, the meeting place of the original five provinces. Naoise, Ainnle and Ardan were the sons of Usna/Usnach
Wadding	Luke Wadding (1588–1657), an Irish Franciscan, founder of the college of St Isodore at Rome; his picture by José Ribera is in the National Gallery, Dublin
Wealthy Man, a	Lord Ardilaun
Well of Bride	*see* Bride's Well
Windy Gap	Bearna na Gaoithe, possibly the Windy Gap in the townland of Carrickhenny, Co. Sligo, opposite Carraroe Church
Wood of Wonders	a place described in the tale of the *Adventures of the King of Norway*
Wood-woman	a woman who tells Cod in the Wood of Wonders that the daughter of the King of Greece had turned her lover into a blue-eyed hawk
Yeats	a 'red-haired Yeats', probably Yeats's paternal grandfather, Rev. William Butler Yeats (1806–62), curate of Moira, later Rector of Tullylish, Co. Down
Yeats	William Butler Yeats (1865–1939), the poet, buried in Drumcliffe Churchyard, Co. Sligo
Young man, a	Dubhlaing O'Hartagan, killed in the Battle of Clontarf (AD 1014); in 'The Grey Rock' he refused the aid of Aoife, who offered him a magic pin which would make him invisible

YEATS'S NOTE OF 1938 ON THE SPELLING OF GAELIC NAMES

In this edition of my poems I have adopted Lady Gregory's spelling of Gaelic names, with, I think, two exceptions. The 'd' of 'Edain' ran too well in my verse for me to adopt her perhaps more correct 'Etain', and for some reason unknown to me I have always preferred 'Aengus' to her 'Angus'. In her *Gods and Fighting Men* and *Cuchulain of Muirthemne* she went as close to the Gaelic spelling as she could without making the names unpronounceable to the average reader.

Appendix Five
Pronunciation

Loreto Todd

IRISH WORDS IN THE POEMS

Modern Irish has three main dialects and three acceptable pronunciations of most items. Dr Loreto Todd has kindly provided the most widely accepted pronunciation of each of the words in Yeats, but where common variants occur, these are given.

She has also provided simple phonetic equivalents of all names and an approximate pronunciation using the orthographic conventions of Standard English. The pronunciations given in square brackets are those of Lady Gregory, which would have been known to Yeats. The phonetic system used is as follows:

VOWELS ( ) Sounds in parentheses are optionally pronounced, cf. the 't' in 'often'.

Short Vowels

i	the sound of the vowel in 'bit'
e	'get'
a	'hat'
o	'got'
u	'put'
ʌ	'but'
ə	unstressed first vowel in 'ago'

Long Vowels

i:	the sound of the vowel in 'bee'
e:	French 'the'
a:	the BBC pronunciation of 'path'
ɔ:	'saw'
o:	French 'peau'
u:	'who'
ə:	the BBC pronunciation of 'church'

Diphthongs

ei	the sound of the vowel in the BBC pronunciation of 'day'
ou	'go'
au	'house'
ai	'high'
oi	'boy'

CONSONANTS

Consonants have their normal Standard English values but the following should be noted:

x   is used to represent the final sound of the Scottish pronunciation of 'Loch'
k   is always used for the initial sound in words like 'cat'
t   is pronounced like the initial sound in French 'tant'
d   'dans'
θ   'thought'
ð   'then'
j   is always used for the initial sound in words like 'June'
ly is one sound, roughly the equivalent of a rapid pronunciation of 'will+you'
ny is one sound, roughly the equivalent of the British pronunciation of 'n' in 'news'
'   prefixes the syllable with the strongest stress

Name in Yeats	Phonetic Equivalent	English Approximation
Aedh/Aodh	e:	'Ay' as in 'day' [Ae, rhyming to 'day']
Aengus	'engis	'Engus' like Genghis
Agallamh na Senorach	'agalu: na 'Seno:rax	aggaloo na shen+ore+rach
Aherne	a'hərn	a+hern
Aibric	'abrik	a+brick
Ailell	'ɔlyil/ailyil	All+yill/Aisle+yill
Aillinn	'ɔlyin	All+yin
Aleel	'alyi:l/'ə:lyi:l	Al+yeel/All+yeel
Almhuin	'ɔluin/lwin	All+oo+in/All+win [All-oon or Alvin]
Anbual	an'bual	An+boo+ull
Alt	olt	Ollt
Aoibhell	'i:vəl	Eevel[Evill]
Aoife	'i:fə	Eefa[Eefa]
Ardan	'a:rda:n/a:rdan	Arrdawn/Arrdan
Aslauga Shee	a(n)'slua'shi:	A(n)sloo+a Shee
Baile	'bolyə	Boll+ye
Ballinafad	'balina'fad	Bal+in+a+fad
Ballygawley Hill	bali'g:li:hil	Ballygawlee Hill
Ballylee	bali'li:	Ballylee
Balor	'ba:lor/be:lor	Barlor/Baylor
Barach	'barax	Barach
bawn	bɔ:n	bawn

Name in Yeats	*Phonetic Equivalent*	*English Approximation*
bell-branch	'bel braːnsh	bell-branch
Ben Bulben	ben bʌlbin	Ben Bulben
Bera of Ships	bera av ships	Bera of Ships
Biddy	biddi	Biddy
Biddy Early	'bidiː'ərliː	Bidee earlee
Blanid	'blanid/blanij	Blan+id/Blan+idj
boreen	boəriːn	bore+een
Boyne	boin	
Bran	bran	
Bride's well	'braidz wel	
Bual	'buəl	Boo+el
Bual's hill	buəlz hill	
Buan	'buːən	Boo+un
Bull (brown)	bul (braun)	
white-horned	wait hɔrnd	
Byrne, Billy	bəːrn, bili	
Byrnes	bəːrnz	
Caer	kyar/kyer	Kyarr/Kyair
Caoilte	'kiːltshə	Keel+chih [Cweeltia]
Cashel/the Rock of	'kashəl/ðə rok əv	
Cashel	'kashəl	
Castle Dargan	kasəl daːrgon	
Cathleen-ni-Houlihan	'kotshliːn niː 'huːləhan	Cotchleen nee Hool+i+hawn
Clare	'kleːər on klɔːr	
Clare-Galway	'kleːr-'gɔːlwei bolye on hlɔːr	
Cloone, bog of	kluːn, bog əv	
Clooth na Bare	kluː(x) nə baːr	
Cloyne	kloin kluən ua	
Colooney	kol 'uːniː	Col:ooney
Conall Cearnach	'konəl 'kyarnax	Conal Cyarnach
Conan	'konan	
Conchubar	'konər	Conor [Conachoor]
Connacht	'konət	
Connemara	konə'mara	
Coole/Coole Park	kuːl/kuːl paːrk	
Cormac	'kormak	
Cormac's ruined house	'kormaks ruind haus	
Craoibhin Aoibhin	'kriːviːn 'iːviːn	Creeveen Eeveen
Crevroe	'krivro/'kriəv'ruə	Kree+iv roo+a
Cromlech	'kromlex	
Cro-Patrick	kro(x)'patrik	

Name in Yeats	*Phonetic Equivalent*	*English Approximation*
Cruachan	'kruəxən	
Cuchulain	ku'hʌlən	Koo+hullin
		[Cuhoolin,
		or Cu-hullin]
Cullinan, Shemus	'kʌlənən, she:mis	Shame+us
Cumhal	'ku:əl	Coo+ull
Danaan	da'neən	Da:nayan
Dathi	'daxi	Dah+hee
Dectora	'dektərə	Deck+tor+rah
Derg, Lough	lox'də:rg	
de Valera	'deva'le:ra	Dev+alaira
Diarmuid	'di:ərmid/dermat	Deer+mid/Dermot
Doe, Paddy	do: padi	
Dooney/Dooney Rock	'duni/'duni rok	
Down, County	daun, kaunti	
Dromahair	ɖrʌma'heər	Drumahairr
Druid	'druəd	
Drumcliff	ɖrvm'klif	
Dun	ɖu:n	Dhoon [Doon]
Echte	'extgyə	Echt+gyeh [Acht-ga]
Edain	'e:di:n	Aydheen
Eire	'e:ərə	Ayera
Emain	'e:wən	Aywin]Avvin]
Emain Macha	'e:wan moxə	Aywin Moh+ha
Emer	'e:mər/e:vər	Aymir/Ayvir
Enniscrone	inish'kro:n	Innishcrone
Eochaid	'yɔ:xi:/'ɔ:xi	Yawhee/Awe+hee
		[Eohee]
Esserkelly Plain	'esərkeli 'plein	
Falias	'fali:əs	Fal+ee+uss
Fand	fan(d)	Fan(dh)
Fenians, the	'fi:nyinz	Feen+yans
Fergus	'fə:rgəs	
Ferguson	'fə:rg sən	
Findrias	fin'dr:əs	Finn+dree+uss
findrinny	fin'drini:	
Finn	fin	
Firbolgs	fir'bologz	Firr bollogs
Forgael	'fo:rge:l	Four+gale
Gabhra	'gaura/gauvra	Gowra/Gow+vra
Galway	gɔ:lwei	
Gap of the Wind	'gap əv 'ɓ'a 'wind	
Geaghan	'ge:gin	Gay+gen
Glasnevin coverlet	glas'nevin 'kʌvərlət	

Name in Yeats	*Phonetic Equivalent*	*English Approximation*
Glencar	glen'ka:r	
Glencar Lough	'glenka:r 'lox	
Glendalough	'glendalox	
Goban	'gauwan/'gʌbən	Gowan/Gubbin
Goban's mountain top	gauwanz mauntin top	
Goldsmith	'go:l(d)smiθ	
Gorias	'go:riəs	Goree+uss
Gort	gʌrt	Guh+rt
Grania	grɔ:ny/gra:ny	Grawnya
Green Lands	'gri:n landz	
Gregory	'gregəri	
Grey Rock	'gre: rok	
Guaire	'guairə/guərə	Gwai+ra/Goo+ir+eh
Hanrahan	'hanrəhan	
Hart Lake	'hart 'leik	
Hart, Peter	'hart 'pi:tər	
Heber	'(h)e:vər	(H)ayver
Houlihan	'hu:ləhan	
Howth	ho:θ	Hoe+th
Inchy Wood	'inSi:'wu:d	Inch+ee+wood
Innisfree	'inish'fri	Innishfree
Innish murray	'iniS'mʌri:	Inn+ish murry
Invar Amargin	'invər 'amərgin	
Iollan	'yolan	Yoll+lan
Ir	i:r	Ear
Ith	i:x	Eech/Ech
Kiltartan Cross	kil:tartən	
Kerry	'keri	
Kilvarnet	kil'varnət	
Kinsale	kin'seil	
Knockfefin	nok'fefin	Knock feffin
Knocknarea	'noknar'i/noknare:	Knock+na+ree
Kyle-dortha	kail'dorxa	Kile dor+cha
Kyle-na-no	'kailnə'no	Kile+na+no
Laban	'lavan/'laban	Lavan/Laban
Land of the Tower	'land əv ðə 'tauər	
Land-under-Wave	'land ʌndər 'weiv	
Leighin	'laiən	Lie+in
Leyney	'le:ni:/laini:	Lay+nee/Line+ee
Liss	lis	
Lomair	'lʌmər	Lummer
Loughlann waters	'loxlən 'wɔtərz	
Lugaid	'lʌgəd/lu	Lud+ud/Loo
Lugnagall	'lʌgnə'gɔ:l	

Name in Yeats	*Phonetic Equivalent*	*English Approximation*
MacDonagh	mak'dʌna	
MacNessa	mak'nesa	
Maeve	me:v	May+iv
Magee, Moll	mə'gi:, mol	
Magh Ai	mox'ai/mai ai	Moch Aye/My+eye
Maines	'mainis/mwi:nis	Minus/Mween+us
Malachi (Stilt Jack)	'maləkai	
Manannan	'mananən	Man+an+an
		[Mānănuan]
Mayo	'me:o	May+o[Muigheo]
Midhir	'miḏər/mi:r	Meedher/Meer
Midhir's wife	'mi:ḏərz waif/	
	mi:rz waif	
Mil	mil	Mill
Mocharabuiee	'moxəra 'bwi:	Moh+her+abwee
Mooneen	'muəni:n	Moo+ineen
Mourteen	'mu:rti:n	Moor+teen
Moytura	'moiturə/moichu:rə	[Moytirra]
Murias	'mʌri:as	Muh+ree+uss
Muirthemne	'mwiremnə	Mwir+rim+neh
Murrough	'murxu:	Moor+uh+oo
Naoise	'ni:shə	Neesha
Niam	'ni:əv	Nee+iv[Nee-av]
Nessa	'nesa	
O'Byrnes	o:'bə:rnz	
O'Duffy	o:'dʌfi:	
Ogham	'ogom	Oh+gomm
Oisin	'oshi:n	Osheen
ollave	'olu:/oləv	olloo/ollave
O'Rahilly	o:'rahili	
O'Roughley	o:'roxli:	O+Roch+lee
Orchil	'orxil	Orh+hill
Oscar	'oskər	
Pairc-na-carraig	'pɔ:rknə'korig	Paw+irk na corrig
Pairc-na-lee	'pɔ:rknə'li:	Paw+irk nalee
Pairc-na-Tarav	'pɔ:rknətar v	Paw+irk na tarav
Patrick	'patrik	
Paudeen	'pɔ:di:n/pɔ:ji:n	Paw+jean
Place of the Strangers	'pleis əv ðə 'streinjarz	
Rachlin	'raθlin	Rath+linn
Raftery, 'dark'	'raftəri, 'da:rk	
Raftery's cellar	'raftəriz 'selər	
rann	ran	rannnn
Ribh	ri:v	Reeve

Name in Yeats	Phonetic Equivalent	English Approximation
Rosses/Point	'rosiz/point	
Roxborough	roksbʌrə	
Rury	'ru:əri:	Roo+er+ree
Sandymount Corbets	'sandimaunt 'kɔ:rbəts	
Scanavin	'skanavin	
Sceolan	sko'lɔ:n	Sco+lawn [Skolaun]
Sennachies	'shanaxi:z	Shanaheez
Seven Woods	'sev(e)n 'wudz	
Shan walla	'Sanwala	Shann+walla
Shoneen	'So:ni:n	Shown+een
Sidhe	shi:	Shee [Shee]
Sleuth Wood	'slux wud	Slooh
Slievenamon	'sli:vnə'mɔ:n/ 'shli:vnə'maən	
Sligo	'slaigo:	
Tain Bo Cualgne	'taə bo:cu:əlnyə	Ta+in bo Coo+ull+nyen
Tara	'tyauər/tara	T+yower [T'yower or Tavvir]
Thoor Ballylee	'tu:r bali'li:	Thoor Ballylee
Thraneen	'trɔ:nyi:n	Thraw+nyeen
Tireragh	'ti:rərax	Teer+rerach
Tir-nan-Oge	'ti:r nə'no:g	Theer na nogue
Tone	to:n	
Tuatha de Danaan	'tuəxə'dədə'neən	Thoo aha da danayan [Too-ă-hă-dae Donnan]
Uladh	'ʌlə	Ulla
Usna	'ushna	Ooshna
Windy Gap	'windi 'gap	

Appendix Six
The Definitive Edition: a History of the Final Arrangements of Yeats's Work

Warwick Gould

THE PRESENT VOLUME

The Poems of W. B. Yeats (London, Macmillan, 1949; henceforth *P* (1949)) was published in a signed, two-volume edition of 375 sets of which 350 were for sale. It sold out on the day of publication and was not reprinted. Seen through the press by the poet's widow, George Yeats, his publisher, Harold Macmillan (later the first Earl of Stockton), and his publisher's reader, Thomas Mark, it proposed final texts, a canon of poems and a preferred arrangement of the volumes of poetry Yeats had published in his lifetime.

P (1949) was the outcome of a project Yeats himself had initiated in 1930 when Macmillan agreed to plan an *Edition de Luxe* of the works. Increasingly Yeats came to think, as it was postponed because of poor market conditions and other factors during the 1930s, that it would appear only after his death. Throughout that decade, he began to delegate many aspects of the production of his books to his wife, Macmillan and Mark, while of course always retaining, through the approval of lists of contents and proof materials, direct personal control of his publications.

For many years after Yeats's death, the knowledge of his intentions and preferences vested in these three people went unchallenged. In recent years, however, the text, canon and arrangement of *P* (1949) have all been questioned, chiefly by the work of Yeats's most recent editor, Professor Richard J. Finneran. In *Editing Yeats's Poems* (London, Macmillan, 1983; hereafter *EYP*) he sought to justify the textual choices he made for *The Poems: a New Edition* (New York, Macmillan Publishing Co., 1983; London, Macmillan, 1984; henceforth *PNE*), which, despite its title, was *not* a new edition of *P* (1949), but the first volume in a newly conceived *Collected Edition of the Works of W. B. Yeats*. *PNE* based its fundamental choice of copy text upon *The Collected Poems* (London, Macmillan, 1933; hereafter *CP*), a popular one-volume edition Yeats had suggested to his publisher while the *Edition de Luxe* was delayed by the Depression. *CP* employed a two-part arrangement of 'Lyrical' and 'Narrative and Dramatic' sections, expressly to encourage new readers browsing in bookshops. This way, they would first of all confront Yeats's early, short and well-loved lyrics, rather than 'The Wanderings of Oisin', which Yeats had placed first in his *œuvre* in the *Edition de Luxe* arrangements.

PNE was greeted with much criticism[1] of its choices of arrangement and of text, but has recently gone into a second edition as *The Poems Revised* (New York, Macmillan Publishing Company, 1989; hereafter *PR*), and *EYP* has been largely rewritten as *Editing Yeats's Poems: a Reconsideration* (London, Macmillan, 1989; hereafter *EYPR*) to cope with archival[2] material which came to light during and after the controversy of 1984, and to bolster the rebuttal of criticism of its chosen arrangement.

It is against the challenge that *EYPR* and *PR* pose to *P* (1949) that A. Norman Jeffares embarked upon this new edition. He has corrected misprints and made other alterations to *P* (1949), proposing – largely from printed sources – further possible emendations to the texts which Mrs Yeats and Thomas Mark prepared from the proofs on which Yeats had worked, and from his later MSS and publications (see 'Textual Notes' above, pp. 643–65). Jeffares has redivided the section entitled 'Last Poems 1936–1939' in *P* (1949) to give 'New Poems' (the title of the Cuala Press volume of 1938), '[Poems from *On the Boiler* (1939)]', and '[Last Poems (1938–1939)]'. The poems in the last of these sections are arranged according to the volume-order prepared by Yeats himself for the Cuala Press collection which became after his death *Last Poems and Two Plays* (1939).

A fresh judgment, too, has been used on the matter of canon. But, except in one or two respects, Jeffares has not sought to emend the texts by removing decisions agreed by Mrs Yeats and Thomas Mark. The result is an edition which shows exactly where current scholarship can confront the work of Yeats and his delegates, his wife (who was also his executrix) and his trusted editor, and helps us to recover clearly the point at which Yeats's work broke off. It does not overturn the *textual* decisions inevitably left by the dead poet to be settled by his widow and his editor.

An alternative mode of enquiry dictated the text and arrangement of *PNE* and *PR*. Finneran chose not to trust Yeats's delegation. The copy texts for most of the poems are taken from *CP*. For poems from *The Winding Stair and Other Poems* (1933) to the end of Yeats's life, Finneran uses a multitude of sources, published and unpublished. While he has uncovered instances where Mrs Yeats and Thomas Mark did not replace earlier with later readings in their updating of the *Edition de Luxe* proofs, he has provided no collation of their work against his own, and has implicitly dismissed[3] many of their decisions.

DEFINITIVES: *THE POEMS* (1949) AND ITS CLAIM TO BE 'COMPLETE AND DEFINITIVE'

As *P* (1949)'s most determined critic, Finneran has said it was 'probably as accurate an edition as would [*sic*] have been produced'. This is no concession, because it is qualified by the apparently devastating 'given the prevailing editorial standards of the time'.[4] But *P* (1949) was something rather different: it was the best embodiment of Yeats's work possible at the time. Since an ingrained assumption of *EYP* and *EYPR* is that Yeats's intentions are usually clear and that the editorial work which was done on his texts after his death was a 'process . . . of . . . corrupting the texts which he had worked so hard to perfect' (*EYP*, 30; *EYPR*, 39), it needs to be said at once that when he died Yeats left a large body of material which needed much work. Crucial decisions remained to be taken before it could be put into any publishable form, let alone a 'final' form.

Editors do not always appreciate the extent to which they fulfill the demands of *Zeitgeist*.[5] Certain of the decisions to which Mrs Yeats gave her assent, such as that of re-ordering the 'Last Poems' so that they concluded with 'Under Ben Bulben', or endeavouring to include both the 'Three Marching Songs' and 'Three Songs to the Same Tune' out of which the former had been revised, were decisions made in accordance with invisible conventions, based upon the prevailing assumptions of readers of memorial editions. In its broad outlines, in its overall contents and arrangement, however, *P* (1949) retains an authority which time has not conferred on any other edition of Yeats's poems (except, of course, its derivative, the *Variorum Edition*[6]).

The *Edition de Luxe* in seven volumes which Yeats and Harold Macmillan began to plan in 1930 had been an obligation on the firm since they had signed a contract with Yeats in 1916. It had been held over throughout the 1920s because the firm had judged it an uneconomic proposition. By 1930 Yeats had built up an excellent working relation with Thomas Mark (1890–1963) and in that year described him in a letter to Sir Frederick Macmillan as 'the best reader for the press I have ever come across' (*VSR*, xviii; *B. L. Add. MS* 55003, f. 119). Similar tributes were to follow throughout the 1930s, and to Mark alone Yeats confided some of his 'metrical tricks': admiring Mark's suggested punctuation he evidently felt that his editor deserved an explanation of how he had arrived at his versification, presumably in part to help Mark in his work. Mark's practice was to indicate suggestions on proofs with a question mark: Yeats could accept the emendation by deleting the question mark or could, of course, reject the suggestion. In time, Yeats was to delegate to Mark a very great deal of responsibility for the final form and arrangement of his work. The 'admirable scholar', as Yeats called him, was responsible for checking the final revise of *The Winding Stair and Other Poems* (1933). He was to complete the revision of the page proofs of *Mythologies* which Yeats, in mid-1932, judged he 'need not see again' because Mark could 'complete [it] . . . better than I could'. By September 1932 Yeats was to suggest that 'in the remaining volumes [of the *Edition de Luxe*] you do not query your own corrections' (*VSR*, xix–xx).

In 1980, Harold Macmillan told me[7] that Thomas Mark had also been given the task of writing to Yeats, his wife and agent, on the firm's behalf. The office codes on many letters signed by Harold Macmillan bear this out. Macmillan, after all, had something of a political career to pursue. He recalled the shrewd business arrangement he had worked out with Yeats for the plural presentation of his poems to suit different markets. The chief result of a flair which Mark and Macmillan shared for maximising the returns of their poet was that while the *Edition de Luxe* was in active abeyance[8] during the Depression, *CP*, with its new arrangement designed to win new readers, enjoyed a good sale and went through several reissues.[9] For ventures such as this one (which owed its rearranged contents to a suggestion of Mark's[10]), Mark deferred to the commercial judgment of Harold Macmillan. Yeats responded as actively to the acumen of his publisher – although he must have chafed at the perpetual postponement of his *Edition de Luxe* – as he did to the editorial skills of his reader.

Though worked at on and off for nearly twenty years under the titles *Edition de Luxe*, 'Coole Edition' (Mrs Yeats's chosen title for the resumed project in eleven volumes, announced for publication in September 1939) and finally *Poems* (1949), the texts published in 1949 and later were essentially the outgrowth of the project for which Yeats had corrected proofs in 1932.[11] By 1939, all that he had written, or revised, or published in single-volume form since that date posed problems for his widow, publisher and reader as they tried to bring the edition to completion in the difficult circumstances of that year. Textual changes made to poems for *CP* had to be incorporated on to newer states of the *Edition de Luxe* proofs. There was not only Yeats's newer work to be considered, including that which he had been writing at the time of his death, but there was also (had Macmillan known it) the matter of textual changes to three poems[12] which Yeats had made in the copy he had consigned to Charles Scribner's Sons for the 'Dublin Edition'. This was another *de luxe*, signed, limited edition in 750 sets which Macmillan (New York) had sublet for a 'one-off' venture to be sold 'house-to-house' in the United States only. Yeats had also written three prefaces for this edition.[13]

The *Edition de Luxe* had been held over since the autumn of 1932 because of the Depression, and even in 1935–6, when Harold Macmillan judged the rest of the book trade to have recovered from the slump, it did not seem, in his view, an appropriate moment to issue an *Edition de Luxe* for the collectors' market: indeed, the parallel edition of the works of the recently deceased Kipling was agreed to only under the most stringent conditions which would not have been appropriate to an author as given to revision as Yeats.[14] Macmillan had welcomed the offer from Scribner's Sons in late 1935 as a relief from a certain embarrassment they inevitably felt about having to postpone the *Edition de Luxe* (*VSR*, xxiii; *B. L. Add. MS* 55774, ff. 153–4, 27 November 1935). Although during the latter months of Yeats's life it must have seemed likely that the Scribner's Sons project would finally get under way, they too found reason to put it to the back of their own queue, behind a Keats venture and an Ellen Glasgow edition. Yeats's death spurred both firms into action.

Mrs Yeats was to remark rather drily in reply to Harold Macmillan's condolence letter that Yeats had 'always said' that Macmillan 'would only bring out [the *Edition de Luxe*] after his death . . .'. Heavy weather has been made with this comment, especially with its trailing ellipsis, but overstating its undoubted irony as 'exasperation' (*EYPR*, 171, n. 27), Finneran selectively omits what precedes it. Mrs Yeats says that she hopes that Macmillan will remain Yeats's publishers 'as long as his family owns the copyright of his work. He would most certainly wish this' (*NLI* 30248, 13 February 1939). It can be assumed, therefore, that in his wife, publisher and publisher's reader Yeats had felt for some time that he had a team to which he could assign the very different task of preparing a memorial edition with some claims to definitiveness.

While Yeats was alive he could overrule suggestions made on his proofs. Without him, the editorial team split between London and Dublin had to produce something which was not just the latest in a series of increasingly stable but always provisional 'final' arrangements (which is what Yeats's canon could only ever amount to while he was alive). It had also to be, in words first used by Harold Macmillan in a letter to Mrs Yeats of 8 February 1939, 'complete and definitive' (*NLI* 30248; *B. L. Add. MS* 55819, ff. 189–90). The words were also used in a 'Preliminary Notice'[15] headed 'The Collected Edition of the Works of W. B. Yeats' which was released to the trade press in late March 1939, and those words have had a vexatious history.

Two imperatives shaped what Mrs Yeats, Harold Macmillan and Thomas Mark set out to do. First they were committed to producing a distinctive and handsome set for collectors, to sell in a market perceived as a very narrow one. Uniformity and finish were important, and Macmillan knew that they had a rival in the Dublin Edition, which, since 1935, had made them even more aware of the importance of 'special features' (including, doubtless, the chronological arrangement) which could make 'so much difference to the success of such an edition' (*VSR*, xxiii; *B. L. Add. MS* 55787, ff. 444–5). Neither the Coole nor the Dublin Edition was large, at 350 and 750 sets respectively, and the two firms agreed to divide the potential market between them.[16]

The second imperative was that the *Edition de Luxe* had now become a memorial edition, just as Yeats had foreseen. It was immediately enhanced from seven to eleven volumes (a decision later echoed in New York). Charles Scribner's Sons' London officer, Charles Kingsley, at once feared that Macmillan 'had put a fast one over us'.[17] The Macmillan rearrangement was submitted to George Yeats, but Scribner's Sons did not bother to consult her about their rearrangement.

There were two reasons for Macmillan's enhancement. One was 'completeness and definitiveness' (as a publisher thought a buyer or collector would understand such a term). Yeats had written a lot since the edition had last been in production, and the contract had always called for the inclusion of all his newest work (*EYPR*, 8). Another reason was a more spacious layout. The edition was being brought into being at last in a nervous and difficult year to fulfill a longstanding contractual obligation, because of the brief market Yeats's death provided. It was to be a handsome and accurate memorial, and it was to establish a canon. A similar attitude to sales (though an indifference to text) prevailed across the Atlantic.

'Complete and definitive' – the phrase as it was then understood by publisher, estate and book trade has caused widespread confusion for recent scholars, accustomed to think and to judge by different and not wholly appropriate criteria. But neither the Coole nor the Dublin Edition – and while both firms and Mrs Yeats made uncoordinated attempts to harmonise their contents, no one after Yeats himself[18] sought to make their respective arrangements of contents uniform – set out to be *exhaustive* records of Yeats's writings. Macmillan wanted a canon for a limited edition. Other editions of his works for other markets could follow. Early versions of poems (with the exception of 'Three Songs to the Same Tune', and 'The Hero, the Girl, and the Fool' which was included in error[19]) and other abandoned writings were not to be included. Nor were poems which Yeats had published only in the context of prose, stories or plays to be dislodged and dragged into the volumes of poems, nor his uncollected writings as book editor, except as chosen by Yeats to stand in his works. The eleventh volume, originally entitled *Essays and Reviews* by Macmillan, was left vague, with a mention of 'miscellaneous later and unpublished papers', presumably to account for *Essays 1931 to 1936* (Cuala Press, 1937) and other pieces. The early proof sent to Mrs Yeats was returned by her with the title changed to *Essays and Introductions* and she indicated firmly that 'no REVIEWS' would ever be republished in her lifetime (*B. L. Add. MS* 54904, f. 171, 17 April 1939).

The canon was not, however, to be closed entirely by these two limited editions. Mrs Yeats and Harold Macmillan thought of adding a twelfth volume – of autobiographical writings – at some future date, and Mrs Yeats certainly thought of extending the idea to Scribner's Sons as well (*NLI* 30248, 14, 15, 24 April 1939; *B. L. Add. MS* 54904, f. 171, 17 April 1939). So neither the Yeats estate nor the publisher had in mind a *Complete Works*, and Scribner's Sons were in no position to do anything but proceed with what copy they had in hand while looking nervously at Macmillan's latest plans to see if they had everything to which they were entitled. Scribner's Sons banked on making their set unique, with distinctive plates (apparently unaware that Yeats initially had wanted the plates to be uniform in both sets[20]) and with three prefaces which he had written especially for the Dublin Edition.

Macmillan, in delaying their *Edition de Luxe* until after the Dublin Edition, naturally planned that their own edition would incorporate any new materials and had asked Yeats's agent, A. P. Watt and Son, to make it a condition of the agreement with Scribner's Sons that Macmillan be supplied with a set of the Dublin Edition (*VSR*, xxiii). In 1940, Scribner's Sons were happy to agree to supply Macmillan with the special prefaces once they had been set into proof form, by which time Scribner's Sons would have been committed to publication. Such an arrangement was a natural consequence of the two firms' gentlemen's agreement to sell in different markets.[21]

But in the spring of 1939, with much of the Coole Edition in type, Harold Macmillan rejected Scribner's Sons' offer of electros of their setting, shared costs *and* the prefaces. His reasons were that costs had already been incurred on those volumes by now in type, and that the Macmillan arrangement of contents was clearly superior to that of the Dublin Edition. So he decided for the moment to dispense with the prefaces, sight unseen, telling Mrs Yeats (and himself) that they would probably contain some sense of the occasion for which they had been written. This was a hasty decision, as Scribner's Sons had given Macmillan a clear hint of the size and significance of 'A General Introduction for my Work', and Mrs Yeats was prepared to be persuaded to allow Macmillan to use it.[22] In the end, the Coole and Dublin Editions having been abandoned, Macmillan did indeed first publish all three prefaces, in the 1961 *Essays and Introductions*.

Surely, then, everyone involved in both editions in 1939 knew that this was not the moment for a scholarly *Complete Works*. To finish off long-planned collectors' editions in the shadow of the war was ambitious enough. What then might 'complete and definitive' have meant to those collectors, or, indeed, to Yeats himself? Since canonicity has recently been so misunderstood, it is worth pausing over this question.

DEPARTURES – REMADE SELVES AND A PERMANENT SELF: THE IDEA OF A CANON

i. *The plural presentation of the 1930s*

To Yeats, who all his life had faced the stark realities of being published, and who therefore was accustomed to seeing his work in different arrangements to suit different audiences or occasions, the insistence of the first generation of his scholarly editors on finding a 'definitive' final textual arrangement would have been understandable. He had, after all, laboured to edit a poet himself.[23] His happiness with plural conceptions of his own work in the 1930s (and earlier) did not mean, however, that he did not entertain clear hierarchies of textual arrangements, even while constantly revising the texts of poems and writing new ones. For the

1908 *Collected Works in Verse and Prose* (hereafter *CW*), he wrote two well-known occasional verses:

> *The friends that have it I do wrong*
> *When ever I remake a song,*
> *Should know what issue is at stake:*
> *It is myself that I remake.*
>
> *Accursed who brings to light of day*
> *The writings I have cast away!*
> *But blessed he that stirs them not*
> *And lets the kind worm take the lot!*
>   [*VE*, 778–9]

Books are not easily or cheaply remade. Rewriting a poem had its own labours: reshaping an edition was not, however, a matter entirely within the poet's control. Chronological arrangements, to a publisher, had much to commend them, since they could be augmented easily. Yeats, however, must have been a fairly tiresome author because he rewrote and frequently rearranged. With chronologically arranged volumes, costly resetting was held to a minimum. Some such basic economics underlay the fact that Yeats kept *Poems* (1899) in print (and in the same overall arrangement) through so many new editions, until it had come, by 1927, to represent a discarded (though still popular) self. Accommodating himself to economic realities led to the pattern whereby major reassessments of self, such as in the 1908 *CW*, and the uniform edition of the 1920s and the *Edition de Luxe*, were rather rare and important events in his life.

The remade self and the abandoned text of Yeats's occasional verses are only apparently antithetical. There are certain continuities. After all, each abandoned self had had to seem in its time a permanent self. Yet while many self-conceptions changed and passed, not all proved ephemeral, and clear hierarchies of text were increasingly stable aspects of Yeats's mature personality as a poet.

He had come to hope by 1927 that he had virtually completed the revision of his youthful work. When planning the *Edition de Luxe* he became more and more interested in allowing much of his work to settle into a canon, in what he called a 'chronological' arrangement. The archives suggest that the idea of what he had many years before called his 'permanent self' (*L*(W), 576), the image of the man in his writings, took on this chronological form for a number of reasons. Chiefly this arrangement showed his continually updated, subjective sense of development. It was *not* a record of composition, nor was it wholly a record of dates of publication: neither in strict accuracy could do justice to that sense of self-development and self-reconstruction which is so familiar a feature of his work (*VE*, 778).

It also had its practical side: the chronological arrangement was built upon the best, latest editions of his poems in *Early Poems and Stories* (1925) and *Later Poems* (1922). It was the easiest way for Macmillan to cope with a writer who continued to produce. In all likelihood the initial arrangement of the *Edition de Luxe* was a mutual decision between Yeats and Mark.

While the *Edition de Luxe* was temporarily held up during the Depression, Yeats, in search of another money-spinner, proposed what became *CP* at a meeting in London with Harold Macmillan on 19 October 1932. *Poems* (1899), in its sixth edition, was languishing. The rights in the book had passed from T. Fisher Unwin to Ernest Benn, who had published a couple of editions of it by 1929. Yeats recorded in a copy in his library that while under Unwin's control, *Poems* had brought him for nearly thirty years 'twenty or thirty times as much as all my other books put together' (*Wade*, item 154, 156–7). In Benn's hands, sales fell within twelve months to just half of what they had been, and another year saw them drop to one-tenth.

The original suggestion of a replacement for the Benn *Poems* (1929) might have come from Sir John Squire, for Yeats, when sending him a copy of *CP*, inscribed it to the 'only begetter'²⁴ Macmillan and Watt negotiated successfully with Benn for the rights to *Poems*,²⁵ and then Yeats turned his thoughts to its contents. Certain letters between Yeats and Harold Macmillan in late 1932 suggest that both men thought of *CP* as an edition of Yeats's '*lyric* [emphasis added] poems in one volume' (*B. L. Add. MSS* 55003, f. 139, 22 December 1932; 55736, f. 105, 5 January 1933), and by 17 March Yeats wrote asking Macmillan or Mark to advise whether 'The Shadowy Waters' (dramatic-poem version) should be omitted, and leaving the decision up to them (*B. L. Add. MS* 55003, f. 140). On 30 March, Mark drafted a response for Macmillan to sign which suggested that it would be 'a pity' to omit 'The Shadowy Waters', but which went on to suggest

one departure from the arrangement of the Edition de Luxe volume which I should like to put before you, as it has been suggested by more than one person [? including Sir John Squire]. We think it possible that the book would be more attractive to the potential purchaser who glances through it in a bookshop if what first caught his eye were the shorter lyrical poems contained in 'Crossways', 'The Rose', 'The Wind among the Reeds', etc., rather than a lengthy work like 'The Wanderings of Oisin'. Our impression is that we might move the longer narrative and dramatic pieces to the end of the volume, where they would make a group more or less related in style, subject, and length, and I wonder if you would agree to our taking this course with the following longer works:–
  'The Wanderings of Oisin'
  'The Old Age of Queen Maeve'
  'Baille and Aillinn'
  'The Shadowy Waters'
and 'The Two Kings['].²⁶

If this arrangement commends itself to you, and if you could think of some general title we could use to cover this particular group, I will instruct the printers to proceed. . . . Needless to say, however, the suggestion is quite tentative, and we should not wish to do anything of the kind without your full approval. [*B. L. Add. MS* 55738, ff. 460–2; *NLI* 30248]

Yeats's reply of 2 April was unambiguous:

I am delighted with your suggestion to put long poems in a section at the end. I wish I had thought of it before.

You could call this group 'longer poems' & the rest of the book 'shorter poems', or you could call this group 'Narrative and dramatic poetry['], & the rest of the book 'lyrical poetry.' [*B. L. Add. MS* 55003, f. 141, received 8 April]

On 10 April Mark agreed to using the second set of suggested group titles (*B. L. Add. MS* 55739, ff. 55–6; *NLI* 30248) in a letter which also concerned the signing of sheets for the *Edition de Luxe*. Both projects were mentioned in the same letter, but there was no suggestion in anyone's mind that the rearrangement to attract 'potential purchasers' of *CP* should be extended to the *Edition de Luxe*.

While *CP* in this new arrangement was passing through the press, and Yeats was preoccupied with *its* offspring, separate volume publication of *The Winding Stair and Other Poems* (1933), he wrote to reassure Macmillan: 'The *Edition De Luxe* will not lack new work for I am constantly writing essays & poems & what I write will be added at the end of the various volumes' (*B. L. Add. MS* 55003, ff. 145–6, 13 August 1933). Harold Macmillan replied on 17 August that 'by the time the edition de luxe appears' the 'new material . . . can be added at the end of the various volumes' (*B. L. Add. MS* 55743, f. 194–5).

It is essential to realise that these letters are unambiguous evidence that between Yeats and his publisher there was no possibility of a misunderstanding. The two projects involved two different arrangements of the poems, and *CP* was seen by both men as a one-off 'departure' from the chronological arrangement for a specific publishing purpose. The archive exactly bears out the information given to me by Harold Macmillan in the interview of 12 August 1980. To add new material at the back of *CP* with its two-part generic division would have been absurd unless Yeats had written nothing but new narrative or dramatic verse. To add new lyrics at the end of the 'Lyrical' section would have involved renumbering the pages of the rest of the book, not to mention the havoc it would cause with tables of contents and other necessary resetting. Such problems were as likely to have been on the poet's mind as they would have been on that of his publisher.[27]

The whole error on which the arrangement of *PNE* and *PR* has been built began with the overlooking of these letters, and subsequently the archive has been largely misconstrued by their editor. The crucial sentence quoted above was also quoted in the preface of Jeffares's *New Commentary* (p. ix) and was thus in the public domain before the controversy of 1984.

Yet it is still maintained that Yeats's expression of 'delight' at Mark's suggested rearrangement for *CP* is 'his only documented comment on the matter' (*EYPR*, 171), when it is clear from this subsequent letter that, as he had two arrangements in mind at the time, his 'delight' must have been directed at the appropriateness of the revised arrangement for its particular popular purpose. And as he never (in a remarkably full archive) wrote, or instructed his wife or agent to write, to his publisher to extend the new scheme to the *Edition de Luxe*, it follows that he was happy with *that* arrangement for its intended purpose.

Other fundamental misreadings of the archive which follow on from the basic failure to understand this plural conception of Yeats's work in the 1930s will be addressed in due course. When Finneran comments that 'it is . . . difficult to believe that a writer who had been arranging and re-arranging his poems at least since the 1895 *Poems* should have "not thought of" the generic division before it was suggested to him' (*EYP*, 15), he labours under the misapprehension that the remark was of general applicability. But with two conceptions of his poems in being at the same time, Yeats meant the comment to indicate that he wished he had thought of the two-part arrangement for *CP* when it was being planned.

Naturally, he would have been 'delighted' by the suggestion. With its prominent positioning of 'Crossways' and 'The Rose' thrust before the 'potential purchaser who glance[d] through it in a bookshop', the new arrangement would have recalled to Yeats (and to many of those pur-chasers) the successful presentation of his early (and much-loved) work in *Poems* (1899) and its six subsequent editions. A canonical arrangement or rearrangement was quite simply not under discussion.

In order to see just how experienced and sophisticated an arranger of his own work Yeats had become by 1933, it is worth looking back over some of his prior arrangements – popular and periodically 'definitive' alike.

ii. Yeats and the arrangement of his poems: a synopsis

Any collector or reader with an overview of Yeats's collections in 1939 when the Coole Edition was first advertised as a 'complete and definitive' edition to build on the 1920s *Collected Works*. While Yeats's *œuvre* was by its nature constantly in a state of becoming rather than being a stable entity, it had become by the 1920s recognisably and chronologically shaped. We have seen some of the practical aspects of this array; it remains to see how it had come about.

The chronological arrangement of the *Edition de Luxe* and its derivatives has been almost wilfully misunderstood in the attempt to destabilise it in *EYP* and *EYPR*. The volume-section THE SHADOWY WATERS (1906),[28] for instance, is placed between IN THE SEVEN WOODS (1904) and FROM THE GREEN HELMET AND OTHER POEMS (1912) in *Later Poems* (1922). This placement reflects neither the genesis of the play (which stretches back to about 1883[29]), nor its style and preoccupations, which associate it with *The Wind Among the Reeds* (1899), but the moment of 1906 when the dramatic poem (as distinct from the acting version, first played that year and published in 1907) had reached its own apogee of development.

It might be appropriate to see the subjectivity of Yeats's sense of chronology by suggesting for it the metaphor of geological layering. He had always been aware that his published work contributed to an order of self in print. The self he built up, the rewritten text and remade self, formed a continuously updated personality, one designed to prepare his audience for his latest work. Thus it is absurd to suggest that an 'obvious problem with a chronological scheme is Yeats's constant revision of his poetry' (*EYPR*, 158). It was no more of a problem in such a scheme than in any other, and it was certainly no problem to Yeats, as any examination of the patterns of his revisions will show. He certainly felt that '[w]hatever changes I have made are but an attempt to express better what I thought and felt when I was a very young man' (*VE*, 842): the image of the man in the work had to be constantly retouched.

In particular, library or *de luxe* editions prepared his audience to confront the newer stages of their poet's development. He wrote to A. H. Bullen in 1907 when preparing his *Collected Works*:

> This edition ought to prepare the way for an ordinary edition at a moderate price. . . . Why I have been so insistent upon my revisions etc. in this expensive edition is that I must get my general personality and the total weight of my work into people's minds, as a preliminary to new work. I know that I have just reached a time when I can give up constant revisions but not till the old is right. I used to revise my lyrics as I now do my plays. [*L(W)*, 497–8]

Revision and new work were interdependent aspects of that slowly evolving 'general personality' or 'permanent self' (*L(W)*, 576). How could they not be? Impermanent work could be suppressed: no discerning collector in 1939 would have expected to find in a 'complete and definitive' edition such works as *Mosada: a Dramatic Poem* (1886), which Yeats had suppressed since 1889.

Yeats had come to decide that his real work had begun with, and that his poetic personality was based on, 'The Wanderings of Oisin' in which 'my subject-matter became Irish' (*VE*, 841), despite the fact that many of the lyrics of the 1889 volume of that title had been written and had appeared before the epic (*Wade*, item 2). The process of building up a self in collected volumes began with *Poems* (1895). There, a prefatory note apologised that it contained 'all the writer cares to preserve out of his previous volumes of verse' (*VE*, 845). The arrangement of that volume was determined by the desire to put his major work first in chronological array: thus 'The Wanderings of Oisin' is followed by *The Countess Cathleen* and *The Land of Heart's Desire*. Then came the lyrics, with later work placed first. Those from *The Countess Kathleen and Various Legends and Lyrics* (1892) are grouped as *The Rose*, while those from *The Wanderings of Oisin and Other Poems* (1889) are grouped as *Crossways* with a couple of ballads from the later collection (*Wade*, item 15). Various imperatives, then, were compromised into a representative self, which like all selves contained its own arranged view of its own past. No distinction between narratives, lyrics and dramas is admitted by the title of the book. When the poems were removed for separate publication in *The Poetical Works of William B. Yeats*, Vol. I: *Lyrical Poems* (New York, Macmillan Company, 1906 (*Wade*, item 65)), Yeats tried a more strictly chronological arrangement for them, and he did so too for the plays in the companion volume, *Dramatical Poems* (1907 (*Wade*, item 71)). He did so for an unspecified 'special reason' (*L(W)*, 485), probably intent on establishing in America (where he was less well known) a self on which his subsequent publications might build. He was content to try out various masks of selves for various publishing purposes, as other arrangements show.[30]

Above all – scholars tend to forget it – Yeats had to try to make money to live. When it seemed likely that the first season of the Irish Literary Theatre in 1899 would help to sell that second edition of *Poems* (*Wade*, item 17), he placed the play of that season, the rewritten *Countess Cathleen*, first in the book, followed by the lyrics from the 1892 volume of that title, *The Land of Heart's Desire* (1894), *Crossways* and finally 'The Wanderings of Oisin'. The imperative was to keep the newer work to the fore, as fit accompaniment for *The Wind Among the Reeds*, just out.

Yeats's organic sense of canon can, however, best be seen in the periodic updatings of the 'permanent self', such as the chronologically arranged *Poems* (1899–1905) (1906 (*Wade*, item 64)). *The Collected Works in Verse and Prose* of 1908 (*Wade*, items 75–82) made special demands in the balancing of imperatives. There the poems began with a run of new work in what was to be its final chronological arrangement: *The Wind Among the Reeds*, 'The Old Age of Queen Maeve', 'Baile and Aillinn', *In the Seven Woods* and two added poems. This was followed by a new array of the early work: *Ballads and Lyrics* (including 'The Fiddler of Dooney' from *The Wind Among the Reeds*, and *Crossways*); *The Rose*; 'The Wanderings of Oisin'. The 1906 version of 'The Shadowy Waters' is treated as a drama and placed in a volume of plays, while its acting version appears in an appendix of that volume too. By 1909 *Poems Second Series* has reintegrated 'The Shadowy Waters' into the chronological arrangement of the poems, which there begins with *The Wind Among the Reeds*.

Although the Collected Edition of the 1920s was a compromise (see *VSR*, xviii) between the *Edition de Luxe* specified in Yeats's 1916 contract and the publishing conditions of the time, it allowed reasonably spacious arrangements. In the issuing of the six volumes Yeats was able both to arrange his poems chronologically *and* to put his later work first: that is, *Later Poems* was issued first, in 1922, with its section titles in uniform upper case. This printing style made volumes, sections and longer poems typographically indistinguishable, and the titles appeared as follows: THE WIND AMONG THE REEDS (1899), THE OLD AGE OF QUEEN MAEVE (1903), BAILE AND AILLINN (1903), IN THE SEVEN WOODS (1904), THE SHADOWY WATERS (1906), FROM THE GREEN HELMET AND OTHER POEMS (1912), RESPONSIBILITIES (1914), THE WILD SWANS AT COOLE (1919), MICHAEL ROBARTES AND THE DANCER (1921) in that arrangement. The same style was adopted in *Early Poems and Stories* (1925), where THE WANDERINGS OF OISIN (1889) was followed by CROSSWAYS (1889), THE ROSE (1893)[31] and the volumes of stories beginning with THE CELTIC TWILIGHT (1893). *Later Poems* was prefaced with a note explaining that 'The Shadowy Waters' was 'a long poem in dramatic form, of which a much shortened version, intended for stage representation, is in my book of plays'.[32] A clear demarcation had been drawn between early and later work, yet in each of the two volumes which contained poems a chronological arrangement had been established. It was an edition with which the Yeatses were delighted (*L*(W), 691), and it provided the basis on which the plans for the *Edition de Luxe* were laid.

DIVERGENCES: THE *EDITION DE LUXE* AND DUBLIN EDITION PROJECTS IN THE MID-1930s

Late in 1935, Charles Scribner proposed to George P. Brett of the Macmillan Company, New York (Yeats's American publishers), that his firm be allowed to produce a subscription set of Yeats's works to be 'sold solely by mail order and house to house canvas' (*Callan*, 90, 8 November 1935). Brett anticipated that Yeats stood to earn some $3500–4600 from the issue. Yeats's agent accepted the offer by 3 December 1935 (*Callan*, 91), but not before negotiation with Harold Macmillan, who wrote to Watt after Yeats had written on 18 November:[33]

> . . . you and he [Yeats] will realise that the publication of our edition, a great deal of which is now in type, had better be postponed until we judge that the general situation will justify the publication of another collected edition. Although I do not suppose that many of the American sets will reach this country, some of them will; and it is therefore important that we should be allowed to judge as to the moment when it may be possible to produce our edition. Since, however, we have, quite frankly, felt difficulty in pursuing our edition with any vigour, in the present state of the market, I am very glad that this American proposal has come along, which will give Mr. Yeats a substantial profit and will not impede the publication of an English edition.
>   By the way, I shall be glad if a condition can be made that we shall have a set of the American edition. It will be useful to us for many purposes. [*B. L. Add. MS* 55774, ff. 153–4, 27 November 1935; *VSR*, xxiii]

One of those purposes, we may be sure, would have been that of checking their own text in standing type against the revisions Yeats would inevitably make in proof for the Scribner's Sons' edition. Appreciating the 'one-off' nature of the venture, out of the normal line of book production for his American market, Yeats evidently thought it a simple matter to consign copy from in-print texts and to correct proof. Through Watt he insisted that Scribner's Sons 'must print from the latest London text of my work'. He knew that the New York editions of his work were frequently badly misprinted,[34] and so stipulated that *CP* and *Collected Plays* (London, Macmillan, 1934; hereafter *CPl*) be used. These created problems which he anticipated: *CPl* had been designed like *CP* for a popular market and lacked notes.[35] They were, of course, desirable in a collected edition, and were to be taken, said Yeats, from *Plays in Prose and Verse* (London, Macmillan, 1922), which would also if necessary provide the prose version of *The Hour-Glass*. It was left up to Scribner's Sons to decide if they wanted *Fighting the Waves*. Yeats concluded, 'I must see final proofs' (*Callan*, 91, 3 December 1935).

Ten months later a contract was made between Macmillan (New York) and Charles Scribner's Sons. The delay was caused by Scribner's Sons' uncertainty about the viability of the venture, unless Yeats would contribute prefaces and possibly unpublished materials to make it more attractive. At the time he was unwilling to do so and put them off throughout the summer of 1936, eventually agreeing to write three prefaces but not to supply any more unpublished writings.[36]

On 30 September, Charles Scribner informed George P. Brett that Yeats had agreed to their terms. The contract, which had initially stipulated that the prefaces were not to exceed three pages each, was changed to allow 'whatever prefatory material' Yeats might provide (*Callan*, 93). Scribner wrote to Brett, 'I do not think that any of them will exceed three pages but if the boy should be inspired to write five or six pages in any instance, I do not think you would complain. After all, the material will be yours except for use in this limited edition' (*Princeton*, 7 October 1936). The contract was signed on 9 October (*Princeton*, 15 October 1936).

Yeats, 'overwhelmed with work' on *The Oxford Book of Modern Verse*, was not ready to turn his mind to the prefaces, submission of copy, or even a title for the set (*Princeton*, 31 December 1936). He was also being forced to think again about the Macmillan *Edition de Luxe*. As he grew more enthusiastic about the Scribner's Sons' project, he obviously wondered if they could not use the *Edition de Luxe* proofs instead of his current in-prints and volumes from the 1920s *Collected Works*. Through Watt, he asked Macmillan for up-to-date lists of contents of the *Edition de Luxe* (*B. L. Add. MS* 54903, f. 133; 23 October 1936), which were supplied in duplicate through Watt by 29 October (*B. L. Add. MS* 54903, f. 136). Yeats kept one annotated copy of these lists (now *NLI* 30202) and returned the other to Macmillan via Watt by 12 November (*B. L. Add. MS* 55787, f. 362). With the lists, he sent the following question:

Are Messrs. Macmillan going ahead at once with the de luxe edition? The list of contents I propose to send to Scribner is exactly the same as that which I have sent to Messrs. Macmillan, *though slightly different in form* [emphasis added]. I shall send it to you in a couple of days, this applies to the portraits also. If Messrs. Macmillan were going on with their edition at once would it not be possible to make some arrangement both about contents and portraits. Could I not send the sheets or corrected proofs of the Macmillan edition to Scribner? If Messrs. Macmillan are not going on at once the process might be reversed. Of course if it is desirable to have the two editions completely different, I could make some rearrangement, though not much.

On consideration I will delay sending you my list for Scribner until I get an answer on this point. [*B. L. Add. MS* 54903, f. 148, 10 November 1936]

That slight difference in form[37] and the opened possibility of 'some rearrangement' indicate that Yeats had to the forefront of his mind the plural arrangements of his text. He was well aware that the *Edition de Luxe* volume of poems was in a chronological arrangement, while he had, as we have seen, quickly proposed to send Scribner's Sons his latest in-prints, including *CP*. He had rearranged his plays into a chronological series of plays and volume-sections on the Macmillan lists, too, and naturally saw the desirability of superseding his provisional instruction to Scribner's Sons to print from *CP*.[38] So it is clear that had Yeats had his way, the two *de luxe* editions would have been identical, and would ideally have been edited from London and set by Macmillan's printers (R. & R. Clark, Edinburgh). Thomas Mark would have overseen the proofing and both sets would use the same portraits. Doubtless, too, an agreement between the two firms to sell in separate markets (similar to that which they eventually concluded after Yeats's death) would have resulted in the use of the prefaces in the Macmillan *Edition de Luxe* also. Scribner's Sons, for the moment, would have taken over the role usually taken by Macmillan (New York).

It was Macmillan (New York) who would, of course, have been losers by this arrangement. They had, after all, issued the various volumes of the Collected Edition in the 1920s, including a signed limited edition for the American collectors' market. Nothing had been agreed with Macmillan in London over American publication of the *Edition de Luxe*, but had it ever come close to publication the question would have arisen. Macmillan (New York), therefore, also had an investment in delay to allow the Scribner's Sons' venture its market: they too, it would seem, were gambling that Yeats would live long enough to permit a later collected edition of their own. In any event, Watt, normally a very discreet man, was to agree with Harold Macmillan that it was simply not in Yeats's interest for both the Macmillan and Scribner's Sons editions to appear simultaneously and in the same format.[39]

What is notable about the episode is Yeats's entire openness and practicality, his desire to get on with the job, and his willingness to be advised by his agent and publisher. He was happy if necessary to entertain 'some rearrangement' if it were to be judged on his behalf that to do so would be in his interests. He was prepared to accept that if Macmillan could not 'go on' with their plans, that they then might receive 'sheets or proofs' from Scribner's Sons, which would of course have embodied corrections and revisions.

Macmillan's reply was clear and yet rather canny. Again, it makes clear that so far as the firm and Yeats were concerned there were two arrangements of his poems in play, with the later, that of *CP*, still seen as a 'departure' from the former:

> On the whole I think it would be judicious for us to hold over our edition for the time being, as we want to make it a very fine piece of work and to see that it has the special features that makes [*sic*] so much difference to the success of such an edition. In the circumstances, if Mr. Yeats does not mind, we should prefer not to let Scribners have the sheets or corrected proofs of our own edition. For one thing, we want to put the revises of two or three of the volumes in hand, now that we have the further instructions Mr. Yeats has given on our lists, and for another, I think that the more divergence there could be between our edition and Scribners, the better it would be in the interests of the former.
>
> My own suggestion would be that Scribners should be told to follow the text of our two volumes of Collected Plays and Collected Poems for those works – it is, after all, the latest text in both cases – and that of the Uniform (10/6d.) Edition for the prose works; but we should not wish to oppose Mr. Yeats' own wishes in this matter. Perhaps you will kindly put these observations before him. . . . [*B. L. Add. MS* 55787, ff. 444–5; *VSR*, xxiii–iv]

Yeats's reply does not appear to have survived, but we know that he concurred with the plan.[40] He could hardly do otherwise, given that he must have been urged by his agent to follow Macmillan's suggestion. So it was that *CP* became the basic copy text for the Dublin Edition. As he was to write to Watt on a subsequent occasion: 'Macmillan's interest and mine should not clash' (*B. L. Add. MSS* 54904, f. 45, 28 July; 55798, f. 127, 4 August 1937).

The lists show the 'present extent' of each volume in the *Edition de Luxe* and the arrangement of their contents, and on them Mark asked certain questions about the arrangement of plays and about the placement of newer material. In the case of the volume of poems, 470 pages were in standing type, and they ended with the poems of *The Winding Stair and Other Poems*. Mark asked no questions about the arrangement of this volume, since its augmentation at the end had been agreed in August 1933, but he was concerned about newer material. He assured Yeats that the proofs now contained everything which had been in the subsequent *CP*, except 'Fragments' (which Yeats had added to *The Tower* section of *CP*) and 'The Fool by the Roadside'. (In the case of the latter, Mark was dozing: that poem was of course the last twelve lines of 'The Hero, the Girl, and the

Fool' which was in the *Edition de Luxe* proofs in its entirety. Yeats had decided to drop lines 1–17 for *CP* and to retitle the piece. The change had not been incorporated into the *Edition de Luxe* proofs.) The other apparently absent poem from the proofs was 'The Choice', but it was in the proofs which Yeats had seen in 1932 in a different form,[41] as the sixth stanza of 'Coole Park and Ballylee', whereas it had been removed and printed as a poem in its own right in *The Winding Stair and Other Poems* and in *CP*.

Mark's simple request was, 'Are we to add the following', followed by a list of these titles. Yeats's reply was just as simple, 'Yes'. Naturally, had the volume gone a stage further at this point, Mark would have realised, and Yeats would have had to confront, the problems of volume-order in the sections for *The Tower* and *The Winding Stair and Other Poems*, but it did not. The unsatisfactory question and incomplete answer remained unresolved until after Yeats's death, when Mrs Yeats and Thomas Mark did what they could, printing 'The Hero, the Girl, and the Fool' rather than just 'The Fool by the Roadside',[42] printing 'The Choice' as a separate poem, and inserting 'Fragments' correctly after the four-stanza version of 'Two Songs from a Play'. However, they did not take account of Yeats's later volume-order for *The Tower* in *CP* – naturally, since it had been created in part by the removal of the narrative poem 'The Gift of Harun Al-Rashid' to the 'Narrative and Dramatic' section at the rear of that volume – and their decisions have been criticised by Finneran, who chooses to think that their dismissal of the later *CP* order of that volume must be an affront to Yeats's wishes.[43]

The lists of contents which Yeats sent to Watt to be forwarded to Scribner's Sons on 28 January 1937 were in essence preliminary, and more detailed thinking was to follow.[44] That for the volume of poems specified that it should be Volume 1 of the set, should 'contain everything that is in the one-volume "Collected Poems"', plus a section to be entitled 'Poems from "A FULL MOON IN MARCH"', to contain 'Parnell's Funeral', 'Three Songs to the Same Tune', 'Alternative Song for the Severed Head', 'Two Songs re-written for the Tune's Sake', 'A Prayer for Old Age', 'Church and State', 'Supernatural Songs', in that order. The list, typed on Mrs Yeats's typewriter, is based on the Macmillan list discussed above. She had typed from it Yeats's holograph addition: 'I have seven or eight new poems'. He then updated it further in his own hand to read 'eighteen or nineteen' new poems, and added the comment: 'The edition used must be that published by Macmillan & Co London. The New York edition has many misprints'.

This list has been seized upon[45] in pursuit of the idea that either the Macmillan list and this Scribner's Sons' list are identical or, if they are not (for indeed they are not), then Yeats must have read the Macmillan list in a way which suggests that he thought it referred to the *CP* arrangement.[46] Therefore, this new list is said to represent Yeats's latest preference for that arrangement. The first claim ignores the whole plural conception of text between Yeats and his publisher in the 1930s, as well as the fact that the list clearly refers to 470 pages *in standing type*, of which Yeats had seen (and retained) proofs. The second claim also ignores the plural conception, one of the virtues of which, we recall, was expressed by Yeats when he pointed out how easily the delayed *Edition de Luxe* could be augmented by adding new work at the end of the book. Both cases have been contrived to make Yeats seem either inexperienced in book production, or rather foolish about its processes, when the very difficulty which he had foreseen in 1933 about the two-part arrangement of the popular edition was one he himself had experienced before, and rather painfully. In 1899 he had augmented *A Book of Irish Verse* (1895) for Methuen's second edition of 1900. He wanted to catch the market created by Rolleston and Brooke's *A Treasury of Irish Poetry* (1900), but his publisher was unwilling to spend on the amount of resetting which the book's two-part structure demanded if new poems by young Irish poets were to be added at the end of the first section, before the second, 'Anonymous' section. The result was that Yeats, embarrassingly, had to add the new poems in a signature numbered 'pp. 225A, 226A', etc., in order to preserve the setting of the second section.[47]

On 5 June 1937, Yeats was asked by Macmillan if he had 'any further material for the volume of your Poems in the De Luxe Edition of your Works, which at present ends with "From the 'Antigone'"', the last poem in *The Winding Stair*' (*B. L. Add. MS* 55795, f. 298). Again, such a letter unambiguously shows that the plural conception of Yeats's texts was in both men's minds.[48] Yeats came to London on 8 June, and by 22 June had a long discussion with Harold Macmillan at which it must have been made clear to him that while the firm wished to bring their proofs of the *Edition de Luxe* up to date, they had no immediate plans to issue it. This was in accordance with their policy of allowing the Dublin Edition to appear first. The meeting was occasioned by Macmillan's desire to reprint *CP* again, and the problem that book's format caused when augmentation of it with newer work was to be considered. It seemed to them that it was not worth the 'good deal of dislocation of type, alterations to the two Indexes etc.' just to insert the poems from *A Full Moon in March* before the 'Narrative and Dramatic' section (*B. L. Add. MS* 55796, f. 128–9, 21 June 1937).

Macmillan's suggestion was to reprint the book as it stood and to wait for sufficient new work to accrue to justify 'dislocation' on such a scale. At the same time, Macmillan asked if Yeats had enough new verse for 'a new volume for this year'. At the meeting, the new volume of lyrics was projected for 'the spring of 1938' (it would have been the trade edition of *New Poems* (Cuala Press, May 1938), but not separately published by Macmillan); it was agreed that *CP* would be reprinted, but not augmented until 'a later reprint, which will probably be required in about two years time';[49] and other ventures were agreed (*B. L. Add. MS* 54904, ff. 16–18, 23 June 1937).

While the *Edition de Luxe* was still postponed, it is clear that Macmillan and Mark, who on 5 June had been asking for more copy for Volume 1 in order to set in hand an update of its contents, would have been in no position to turn down a request from Yeats had he then indicated that he wished to rearrange that volume to conform to the *CP* arrangement, or that he would wish it when new poems were to be added. But he did not, and in this case one can be quite clear about negative evidence, for Harold Macmillan's working notes of the meeting survive to show that no rearrangement was discussed (*B. L. Add. MS* 54904, ff. 14–15).

COMPLICATIONS

i. *The two projects until Yeats's death*

When Watt had forwarded the preliminary lists to Scribner's Sons, the question of a name for their edition had not been agreed, nor had the number of prefaces been settled. The firm had suggested 'Dublin Edition'. Watt added a postscript, '"copy" per book post' (*Princeton*, 28 January 1937) which caused immense confusion, for it came to seem to John Hall Wheelock of Scribner's Sons that Yeats had already consigned volumes to him (*Princeton*, 9 February 1937). Yeats's rather more pertinently local suggestions for the title, 'Rathfarnham Edition' and 'Coole Edition' (despite its 'thin sound') were to meet with opposition in New York, but Yeats was prepared to allow 'Dublin', and the Dublin Edition it became (*Princeton*, 2, 10 March). Sheets were despatched to Yeats to sign, and Scribner's Sons for the moment still fancied they would receive four prefaces.[50]

But, despite letters and cables to Watt, no 'copy' turned up in New York, and on 8 June Wheelock wrote to Charles Kingsley in the firm's London office to 'stir up Mr. William Butler Yeats', who was suspected of revising his texts and holding things up. Indeed he was, and both Kingsley and Wheelock had purchased sets of the Macmillan volumes in the hope that they could begin setting from unrevised copy. Wheelock was enough of a poet himself, or through his friendship with Padraic Colum was well enough aware of Yeats's habits of composition by revision, to let himself be restrained from such an unwise course (*Princeton*, 8 June 1937).

In order to understand the confused circumstances which followed, involving Mrs Yeats in Dublin trying to pack off copy and lists, Kingsley in London and Wheelock in New York, it is necessary to remember that Yeats himself was in England from 8 June onwards. The resultant confusion – he was not, apparently, answering letters – has left its mark on the surviving archive of letters, and on the lists which had been prepared by *Macmillan* in October 1936, which Mrs Yeats now annotated.

Yeats *had* been slow in preparing copy, and left its despatch to his wife as he departed for London. According to those new annotations she made on the Macmillan lists, she sent to A. P. Watt Yeats's marked-up copy of *CP* and other material on 11 June – materials which Yeats had promised 'within the week' on 10 May, according to the archive (*Princeton*, Kingsley to Wheelock, 15 June). At some date Mrs Yeats marked the despatch of the other volumes: 2–4 were sent on 14 June.[51] The Macmillan lists were being used as her file copies of what she had done, which included sending her copies of the Scribner's Sons' copy lists to Yeats in London, and sending further copies of each list with the volumes she was packing off to Watt (*Princeton*, Kingsley to Wheelock, 24 June).

While her letters are not entirely free from error – she calls Volume 2 *Autobiographies* at one point, rather than *Mythologies*, thus compounding confusion at Watt and at Scribner's Sons – it seems likely that it was Watt who confused Kingsley into thinking that the marked copy of *CP* for the volume of poems had been lost when it had in fact already been forwarded.[52] The Scribner's Sons' internal memos are surprisingly crass about Yeats and his wife,[53] but by 21 June the missing material, which was the second volume of plays, had come to light. Mrs Yeats had been deliberating with Yeats about its arrangement and the placement of the introductions to the plays from *Wheels and Butterflies* (now *More Plays for Dancers*): the volume of *Essays* had seemed a likely place for these introductions but on the whole she urged that plays and prefaces be kept together. On 12 June she had written to Yeats:

> I hope you will not dislike the re-arrangement I made in 'Plays II' as the result of your wire. I think it makes a better sequence while preserving *the chronological order* [emphasis added]. Each *set* of plays for dancers comes together under the date of the Macmillan & Co first edition, each play dated separately. Perhaps you will not think it necessary to give each play its own date, but students of your work may be glad of it. Cat and Moon for instance obviously belongs to the earlier sequence of dance plays allthough in a different mood. I have checked all the dates by *your own signed* dates on final versions! Also the two Oedipusses follow each other which pleases me. IF YOU WANT TO MAKE SOME OTHER ARRANGEMENT TELEPHONE TO WATT AT ONCE AS I POST THE COPY ON MONDAY. It is all packed up ready to go. [SB 2401982]

What George Yeats had effected was a chronological sequence of volumes and units of plays, with plays ordered chronologically within the two units, headed 'FOUR PLAYS FOR DANCERS 1921' (*At the Hawk's Well*. 1917, *The Dreaming of the Bones*. 1919, *The Only Jealousy of Emer*. 1919, *Calvary*. 1920) and 'WHEELS AND BUTTERFLIES (More Plays for Dancers) 1934' (*The Cat and the Moon*. 1917, *Fighting the Waves*. 1929, *The Words upon the Window-pane*. 1930, *The Resurrection*. 1931). The notes for the plays were to be included in a separate section,[54] as was the music. But, instead of sending the copy to Watt as she indicated on the Macmillan (file) list, she sent it to Yeats himself with the following note, written on his birthday, 13 June:

I am posting you the material for PLAYS II. I was re-reading the 'Introductions' to the Wheels and Butterflies plays, and I grew more and more discontented at the thought of separating the 'Introductions' from the plays, The Cat and Moon, Fighting the Waves, and Resurrection especially. I had at one time numbered them as NOTES, and then when going through the material for Essays I saw that you had put them in that list. If you want to keep them for ESSAYS please return them to me, (they are pinned together separately). The copy for PLAYS II to go direct to Watt of course. [*SB* 2401995]

Yeats finally sent the copy, complete with the Notes, to Watt, who received it on 21 June (*Princeton*, Watt to Kingsley, 21 June). The evidence of Yeats's annotation to those Macmillan lists shows that he wanted a chronological array of volumes, and a chronological order of plays within those volumes.[55] This is what George Yeats had effected, and there seems little doubt that it represents a development of the preferred arrangement of the poems. By keeping to the spirit of Macmillan's wishes in the matter of not supplying Scribner's Sons with *Edition de Luxe* proofs, Yeats and his wife clearly felt free to exploit the opportunity provided by the fact that *CPl* lacked notes and music. Overhauling that volume for a *de luxe* edition, they could also get the plays into the preferred arrangement.

There was a further problem with the volume of *Autobiographies*. Chronological arrangement in terms of the dates of the events described was irreconcilable with the chronology of composition and publication. *Dramatis Personae* (1896–1902) had not been published until 1935, well after the 1909 diary passages published as *Estrangement* in 1926 and as *The Death of Synge* in 1928. *The Bounty of Sweden* had been published in 1925 and related to events of 1923. Mrs Yeats's clear decision in favour of the chronology of the life over dates of composition and publication reinforces the view that the Yeatses shared, for all of these volumes, a preference for arrangements which reconstructed a life in the text.[56] Yeats was, in these later volumes of the Dublin Edition copy, clearly revising plans expressed on both the Macmillan and Scribner's Sons (preliminary) lists. In all volumes apart from the volume of poems the differences that remain between Macmillan and Scribner's Sons arrangements are, so far as one can tell, slight.[57]

Why then do the poems remain in the *CP* arrangement? It seems likely that Yeats was compelled by the advice of Watt[58] to abide by the spirit of Macmillan's wish for 'divergence' between the two editions in order to preserve as one of its 'special features' the superior chronological arrangement of the poems. The other volumes, less important than the volume of poems, could meanwhile be overhauled. Watt would have had to point out the *commercial* advantage of such a course of action to Yeats.

George Yeats's use of the Macmillan list as her own record of despatch of the copy to Watt has compounded the problem of assessing the evidence of these papers. Yeats wanted to see his latest London *text* used, and Macmillan were unwilling that their commercial edge should be blunted by an American publisher's 'one-off' project. It is claimed that Yeats himself must naturally have expected Macmillan to have adopted automatically the *CP* arrangement for the *Edition de Luxe* (*OYP*, 169; *EYPR*, 164), but that claim is worthless because it ignores the plural scheme of 1933. George Yeats sent to Scribner's Sons her own top copy of the list for the volume of poems. It included Yeats's own annotation that 'from "A Full Moon in March"' should be used as a subsection title for the poems from 'Parnell's Funeral' to the last of the 'Supernatural Songs'. These were the first group of poems to come under a general rubric 'POEMS 1933–37'.[59] Marking her file (Macmillan) list with the words 'Poems 1933–37', she crossed out the item typed into the list by Macmillan, 'Poems from "A Full Moon in March"'. That item had been listed before Macmillan knew of any subsequent poems: her cancellation of the section heading does not indicate an overall preference for the title 'Poems 1933–37', which would only ever have had any point had either *de luxe* edition been issued that year. Her decision subsequently to insert 'From "A Full Moon in March"' into the Coole Edition was surely correct in that it accorded with the Yeatses' usual practice of allowing section titles to have some relation to volume titles. Neither *PNE* nor *PR* has adopted 'From "A Full Moon in March"'.

Sometime around 11 June when she marked this list, Mrs Yeats also deleted Yeats's own comment from the previous November: 'I have seven or eight new poems' (in reply, as we have seen, to Macmillan's query), and replaced it with 'All new poems'.[60] By 23 July, Wheelock in New York had everything the Yeatses had submitted, and had been comparing the 28 January list with the various new lists and, where discrepancies existed, deciding in favour of the latter.

Yeats was still being pressed for four prefaces, and by 15 October had supplied three and was to supply no more. *A Vision*, delayed because it was in the press with Macmillan, was forwarded on that date, when he also forwarded copy for *Essays*, also delayed, pending proof of *Essays 1931 to 1936* (Cuala Press). Copy was in New York by 8 November, and by February 1938 Scribner's Sons admitted that they now saw no reason to bring out the Dublin Edition before February 1939 (*Princeton*, 23 February 1938). In fact, once the bulk of the material for the edition was in their hands, they were remarkably less eager to proceed than Yeats had been led to believe. Apart from sending him proof of the illustrations, no further work was done on the edition before his death. 'No great rush', 'no great hurry', the archive reiterates (*Princeton*, 29 August, 20 September 1938). Publication was now planned for the autumn of 1939.

If the Macmillan *A Vision* had delayed Scribner's Sons in 1937, then their plans, at least from Yeats's point of view, caused postponement to the Macmillan *Edition de Luxe*. On 29 September 1937, Daniel Macmillan and Thomas Mark wrote to ask where to put the rest of the prefaces to the plays in *Wheels and Butterflies* (now *More Plays for Dancers*), given that Yeats had wanted the preface to *The Words upon the Window-pane* to be placed in *Essays* under the title 'Swift' (*B. L. Add. MS* 55800, ff. 125–6). That volume too was incomplete. Yeats's reply crossed with a further letter from Mark (12 October 1937) pointing out that the plays and introductions were, after all, 'in type' (*NLI* 30248). Yeats simply asked Macmillan to hold up the volumes of plays and essays until he got proof from Scribner's Sons (*B. L. Add. MS* 55003, f. 229, 13 October 1937). Macmillan were not about to print, however, but only in the middle of obtaining 'clean revises' (*B. L. Add. MS* 55800, f. 447, 13 October 1937). Yeats also wrote to Mark, 'My wife & I arranged the contents of the American edition, & she was very urgent about the placing of the introductions to the *Wheels & Butterflies* plays. I am not quite certain what we did, or if we did right. I would like your opinion' (*B. L. Add. MS* 55003, f. 174, 15 October 1937).

Two things are notable about this episode.[61] The first is the interdependent nature of the two projects. Yeats, on receiving a gentle hint from Mark that it would be costly to rearrange *More Plays for Dancers* to separate the plays from their prefaces and augment *Essays*, was prepared to postpone the *Edition de Luxe* in order to have Mark review the chronological-by-volume arrangement as finalised for the Dublin Edition by George Yeats. But Yeats did not suggest that the volume of poems should similarly be delayed to await proof of the Dublin Edition arrangement. In other words, he was maintaining the plural scheme, and was evidently convinced that such textual changes as he had made to the Scribner's Sons copy could be incorporated on to the *Edition de Luxe* proofs in due course, without any major disturbance to its preferable arrangement. It is one further indication that Yeats had no intention of cancelling this major distinction between his two projects. It must have seemed to him that the additions and alterations to *The Tower* were unlikely to involve major resetting.

ii. The two projects after Yeats's death

Between October 1937 and Yeats's death on 28 January 1939, neither project advanced materially. So far as the volume of poems was concerned, Scribner's Sons had their 'copy', submitted in June 1937, while Macmillan had the rather less tidy file of the *Edition de Luxe* proofs, *CP* and Yeats's annotated lists. We have already seen how Macmillan and Scribner's Sons considered and rejected the idea of printing from the same plates, Macmillan having seen the lists of volume arrangements for the Dublin Edition and having decided in favour of their own superior arrangement (*Princeton*, 19 May 1939). Temporarily, too, at this time, they decided to dispense with the prefaces. In mid-1939, Mrs Yeats and Thomas Mark began to work intensively on the text and proofs of what was now the Coole Edition, which, with the setting of Yeats's newer work and the vexing questions of what from his unpublished essays was to be included, was a considerable task for the widow, especially as she was moving house and coping with other matters consequent on Yeats's death.

The arrangement of volumes in the first volume of the Coole Edition was, however, never queried. Why? Mrs Yeats was, with Thomas Mark and Harold Macmillan, fully aware that the Dublin Edition was in a very different arrangement. It would be possible to argue that the publisher, with one eye on costs, wanted to avoid the resetting that would have been necessary had she wanted to adopt the *CP* arrangement. The *CP* and *Edition de Luxe* had very different typefaces and formats, and the former would have been even more costly to adapt and update than the latter. It is, according to such a hypothesis, even likely that Harold Macmillan would have succeeded in persuading Mrs Yeats to stick with the *Edition de Luxe* arrangement. Haste and cost would have prevailed with her. But there is simply no evidence in the very full archive that such a course was even considered. Therefore, one must accept that Mrs Yeats, with or without her husband's agreement, preferred the *Edition de Luxe* arrangement. And there is already plenty of evidence that a preference for volumes in the reconstructed life-order was a preference they shared and developed. There is, therefore, no reason to think that either through design or error she was responsible for a volume which went against his wishes.

In mid-1939, George Yeats and Thomas Mark began to work intensively on problems in the proofs. New material, in the form of *New Poems* and 'Last Poems', was added by 17 April and she had returned proofs of the two volumes of poems by 16 June. The edition was put 'on ice' by 19 October, seven weeks into the war, but proof materials were still being prepared for possible despatch to Mrs Yeats in January and February 1940 (*B. L. Add. MSS* 55830, f. 334; 55833, f. 223; 55834, ff. 522–3). However, by 20 February 1940, Lovat Dickson of Macmillan had told Charles Kingsley of Scribner's Sons that the Coole Edition had been indefinitely postponed. None the less, on 7 March 1940 Harold Macmillan was still trying to get proofs of the 'Introduction to the Collected Edition' from Scribner's Sons while informing them that 'war-time conditions' were preventing his firm from 'proceed[ing] with our original plans for our own . . . Edition'. A follow-up letter on 7 August 1940 elicited the reply that Macmillan could indeed have the 'General Introduction' in proof but that the Dublin Edition was also postponed and that proofs would not be available 'for many months to come' (*Princeton*, 23 August 1940). By 28 March Mrs Yeats was not replying about proofs of *On the Boiler* and other parts of the last volume in the set. The Cuala Press publication of *If I were Four and Twenty* in September 1940 prompted Daniel Macmillan to write to Watt seeking the contents for the Coole Edition, but Mrs Yeats did not respond (*Basingstoke*, Box 469, f. 197, 22 November 1940).

By 29 July 1947, Harold Macmillan was prepared to abandon the whole idea of the Coole Edition because of the 'staggeringly high' costs and the absence of a market 'for this kind of limited edition', as he wrote to Watt

(*Basingstoke*, Letter Book 498, f. 392). He suggested the idea of the two-volume *Poems* incorporating the signed sheet. Watt agreed with this 'excellent idea' by 14 August. By December 1948 both an expanded *Collected Poems* and the two-volume *Poems* were under way (*Basingstoke*, Letter Book 507, f. 150, 13, 16 December 1948). Shortly after 1 April 1949, Mark wrote that Macmillan were to announce the limited edition *Poems* for the autumn, with second editions of *CP* and *CPl* to follow. A contract holding royalties to 10 per cent and a likely price of £4 or 4 guineas was proposed by Harold Macmillan to Watt on 2 June 1949; the set was published on 25 November 1949 and sold out that day (*Basingstoke*, Letter Book 509, f. 567; 51, f. 114).

The Scribner's Sons project never came to fruition, but did not die until 1953. On the exchange of contents lists in early 1939 the two firms, as we have seen, agreed to sell in separate markets, an arrangement which had given Macmillan every reason to feel they had a right to press for the prefaces. Scribner's Sons had failed in their attempt to tie the release of the prefaces to an agreement that Macmillan would print from (and contribute to the cost of setting) Scribner's Sons' text. Scribner's Sons, on sight of the Macmillan 'Preliminary Notice', realised that they did not have 'Last Poems', *Purgatory*, *The Death of Cuchulain* and *On the Boiler* (*Princeton*, Wheelock to Macmillan, 8 April 1939). Mrs Yeats supplied the extra copy for Volume 1 in time for Watt to forward it to Kingsley on 23 May. All the copy for the edition, including *On the Boiler*, was in New York by 19 September. By 22 January 1940, Scribner's Sons were beginning to wonder if the Coole Edition had appeared after all, but Lovat Dickson's letter of 20 February told them of its indefinite postponement, probably 'until after the war'. For the moment, Macmillan's difficulty seemed to Scribner's Sons to be their own opportunity and they hoped to have their first volume out in November 1940 (*Princeton*, Wheelock to Kingsley, 27 March 1940).

By 22 March they had expanded the set from eight to eleven volumes and were endeavouring to match the Macmillan venture volume for volume. Without reference to Mrs Yeats or A. P. Watt, the contents of Volumes 1 and 2 (as they now were) were rearranged. The Scribner's Sons editor, known only by his initials 'B.S.', worked without any clear idea of what he was doing, but, following blindly the Macmillan 'Preliminary List', he was able, for the most part, to put the two volumes back into the chronological arrangement of the Coole Edition on new lists drawn up at this time and now in the Scribner's Sons archive in the Humanities Research Center, University of Texas, Austin. Thus he began with 'The Wanderings of Oisin', and put 'The Old Age of Queen Maeve' and 'Baile and Aillinn' and 'The Shadowy Waters' into their correct positions, but he was puzzled over what to do with 'The Two Kings' and 'The Gift of Harun Al-Rashid'. The reason is clear. Whereas the other narratives were listed as separate 'volume-units' in the 'Preliminary List', these two poems, being simply longer poems in *Responsibilities* and *The Tower* respectively, were not named in that list. Unfamiliar with Yeats's work, he could not reinsert them in their correct volumes, and so provisionally inserted them after 'The Wanderings of Oisin'. Noting carefully their dates from their half-titles in *CP*, he inserted with each the query, 'Vol II?'. By itself this query would not have yielded a correct solution to the problem, and the episode demonstrates little more than Scribner's Sons' faith that the Macmillan arrangement was bound to represent Yeats's preference. In this they were right, though for the wrong reason.

The Scribner's Sons archive provides corroborating evidence that the use of the term 'definitive' in the book trade at that time meant something rather less than it does now in scholarly contexts. They felt that it was 'quite hopeless' to try 'to get into this Edition everything written by Yeats . . . the material we now have . . . is enough to warrant our calling it a "definitive edition"' (*Princeton*, 13 June 1940).

Scribner's Sons did not formally abandon their project until 5 January 1953. Thereafter they tried to sell the signed sheets, plates, and prefaces to the Macmillan Company of New York for $4000, but without success. Photostats of the prefaces were, however, supplied to Macmillan by 14 September 1953 and the original typescripts were sold through the Scribner Book Store to Cyril I. Nelson of the E. P. Dutton Company. The 850 signed leaves were turned over to the Macmillan Company in 1954 for $800. They were eventually used in the limited edition of *VE* (*Princeton*, 12 March, 22 April 1954).

SACRED BOOKS: *P* (1949) – CHANGING CLAIMS FOR 'THE DEFINITIVE EDITION'

P (1949) came to be referred to as 'the definitive edition', and on that claim Allt and Alspach based their copy text for the 'canonical' first part of *VE*. As early as 1955 the arrangement of *P* (1949) had been declared 'sacred',[62] but by 1983 it was being attacked as a sacred cow, and the whole idea of 'the definitive edition' had been denounced as a 'myth' (*EYP*, 1–4, 15). To see how this was accomplished is instructive.

i. The 'Prospectus' of 1949, its pedigree and influence
P (1949) had been advertised with a prospectus,[63] a bifolium the first page of which was a mock-up of the title page, including, as a virtual subtitle, the following words which surmounted a facsimile of the author's signature:

A DEFINITIVE EDITION
LIMITED TO 350 SETS
SIGNED BY THE AUTHOR

When the two-volume set was published it made no such claim for itself on either title page or colophon, but the description stuck. Words initially chosen for an advertisement to attract collectors came to have an entirely different authority for bibliographers, and via their own efforts. Allan Wade, in the first edition of his *A Bibliography of the Writings of W. B. Yeats* (London, Rupert Hart-Davis, 1951), used the phrase 'THE DEFINITIVE EDITION' to preface his description of *P* (1949) and the description is repeated in items 209 and 210 of the two subsequent editions of that work. Nowhere is it pointed out that the words come not from the volumes themselves, but from their prospectus.

Allan Wade was greatly familiar with Yeats's methods of literary production, and was in contact with George Yeats after *P* (1949) had been published, when he was working on the 1951 *Wade*, and on his edition of Yeats's *Letters* (1954). His application of the word 'definitive' to *P* (1949) shows a profound knowledge of how Yeats had come to depend on his wife and his editor at Macmillan. Had anyone at the time asserted that the term was inaccurate precisely *because* of that delegation, it would have seemed to Wade an absurd charge.

In 1957, Allt and Alspach relied on the word 'definitive' when justifying their choice of copy text (*VE*, 641), resting their case on *Wade*, and on the *P* (1949) 'Prospectus', which had claimed:

> For some time before his death, W. B. Yeats was engaged in revising the text of this edition of his poems, of which he had corrected the proofs, and for which he had signed the special page to appear at the beginning of Volume I. The outbreak of the Second World War, however, came at a crucial stage in the production of the work, and Messrs. Macmillan & Co. Ltd. had to consider the effects of austere conditions on a publication which had been projected on a lavish scale and which, after the untimely death of this great writer, would have formed a worthy monument to him. It was finally decided that production should be discontinued until after the war, and it is only now, a decade later, that it has become possible to offer the work as it was originally planned. ['Prospectus', p. 2; *VE*, xxix–xxx]

Comparison with the 1939 'Preliminary Notice', the source of the 'Prospectus', shows that the edition's claims had shifted:

> Messrs. Macmillan have for some time past had in preparation a complete and definitive edition of the works of WILLIAM BUTLER YEATS. The author had made a careful and extensive revision of his writings for this purpose, and almost up to the date of his lamented death he was constantly adding to the remarkable group of poems and plays which had given lustre to his latter years. It now remains for his publishers to proceed with the undertaking in which he had shown so keen an interest, and they therefore announce that *the new edition will appear in September 1939*, in eleven volumes, provisionally arranged as detailed overleaf. The first volume of each set has been signed by Mr. Yeats.[64]

This 1939 document makes qualified claims for completeness and definitiveness; the claim for Yeats's revision appears in the context of a fair but alluring statement of his last new work. Potential buyers in 1939 had the chance to see that new work could not be carefully revised work, but buyers in 1949 might have casually assumed that Yeats had corrected *all* of the proof of the entire edition.

Even so, it is hard to see how a Yeats scholar such as Colonel Alspach could have made such an assumption. Both he and Peter Allt must have known from the dates on *Last Poems and Two Plays* (Dublin, Cuala Press, 1939) and *On the Boiler* (Dublin, Cuala Press, 1939) that Yeats had not corrected proofs of those books, at least. What evidently mattered to Allt and Alspach, faced with the monumental task of collation of a variorum edition, was that here in *P* (1949) (on offer, as it were) was a copy text which had George Yeats's authority.

P (1949) is easily criticised only if one retains an absolute, or monolithic, conception of what 'definitive' might mean. It is perfectly clear from Finneran's dismissal of what he calls 'the myth of the "definitive edition"' (*EYP, EYPR*, 1–4) that the word has changed meaning since it was first used by Thomas Mark and Harold Macmillan in their 1939 letters to Mrs Yeats and in their 'Preliminary Notice'. Its most recent connotation is scholarly (and hence anachronistic). The meaning of 'definitive' by which the 1939 claims are dismissed is something like 'the state of the text as approved by, or last seen by, the author himself, and meeting with what we can infer to be his fullest satisfaction, or reconstructed to be as like such a text as we can now manage'.[65] But, as this history has been at some pains to point out, such a view is extraordinarily simplistic, because it omits the overwhelming evidence that for Yeats the textual process involved the interposition of others with delegated powers and responsibilities to get his work into 'the final form he wished', in Mrs Yeats's comment.

ii. 'Definitive' arrangement and 'definitive' order
One feature of Finneran's textual enquiry in *EYP* and *EYPR* is that for all the evidence that it so usefully opened up of the practical problems of editing late Yeats, and for all of its vaunted rejection of 'any single editorial policy' (*EYP, EYPR*, ix), it is built on a monolithic conception of the main copy text. Whether one is to choose *P* (1949) or *CP*, 'order' or 'arrangement' (the terms are, to Finneran, synonymous – see *EYPR*, 169) will be determined by that choice, which, to him, is a choice between 'not merely two different "arrangements"', but two different incarnations of the archetypal "Sacred Book" of the poems', one of which must be 'in fact Yeats's "final intention"' (*EYP*, 15).

But in fact order and arrangement are very different matters. There is in *P* (1949) a 'chronological' *arrangement* of volumes, sections – such as 'THE ROSE' – seen for a long time as volume-units by Yeats, and long poems which are typographically indistinguishable from volumes or volume-units in the table of contents. Then there is *order*, the order of the individual poems (or groups of poems) in those volumes or volume-units, sometimes in this work referred to as volume-order to avoid ambiguity. Finally there is *sequence*: Yeats frequently put individual poems into sequences (such as 'Words for Music Perhaps'). It is apparent from his correspondence with his editor and publisher that even while he was 'delighted' with the popular arrangement they had suggested to bring *CP* into the hands of a new audience, he remained adamant about matters of volume-order and sequence, and the publisher respected this.[66]

For Yeats, therefore, matters of arrangement were to be distinguished from matters of volume-order and sequence, even though any particular rearrangement, such as that performed for *CP*, had implications for volume-order.[67] As we know that he was happy to entertain plural ideas about arrangement according to publishing purpose, it follows that matters of *text* and matters of arrangement are not simply different aspects of the same monolithic copy text, but separate problems for the modern editor.[68]

Any pure editorial theory, undoubtedly, will fail to do justice to the almost complete record of practical decisions faced and taken (or postponed, or delegated) by this working writer. We have seen this from Yeats's annotation to the 1936–7 lists, which left further questions which Thomas Mark would undoubtedly have posed, and Yeats answered, had he lived to see the proofs taken a step further. An intelligently incomplete, step-at-a-time approach was simply how Yeats worked. And so, adopting a 'later and correct' text,[69] or having to accommodate a new placement for a poem in a revised volume-order were problems which, for poet, widow and publisher's reader did not automatically imply a major change in overall arrangement.

It will be objected of the approach here advocated that it inherently 'privileges' the arrangement of the *Edition de Luxe*, Coole Edition and *P* (1949), putting it beyond question. But we have seen that Yeats had a plural arrangement in 1933 which conceded for a popular edition an arrangement suggested by his editor to attract sales. We have seen that when he suggested that Scribner's Sons be asked to follow the 'latest London text' (*CP*), his concern was with the fact that the American texts of his works contained misprints. Finally, we have seen that at no time did Yeats, his wife, agent, publisher or publisher's reader ever question the overall arrangement of the *Edition de Luxe* or its status, and that after his death that status was enhanced because of the memorial nature of the Coole Edition project. Mrs Yeats and Thomas Mark had no reason to overturn it because of Yeats's decision to use the *CP* arrangement for the Dublin Edition, or because of any other subsequent decision. To 'privilege' *CP* over the *Edition de Luxe* arrangement (as Finneran did at the outset of his enquiry) and thereafter to assume that 'later' *is* 'correct' opens the question which Finneran nowhere addresses, viz. how and why

Mrs Yeats, A. P. Watt, Thomas Mark and Harold Macmillan came to get it all so wrong after Yeats died.

In his research for *PNE*, Richard Finneran sought the advice of the late Colonel Alspach, who wrote that George Yeats had '"assured me in conversation that the 1949 two-volume edition fully warranted the word 'definitive': that WBY had corrected the proof and arranged the poems in the order he wanted. She clearly implied that his were the final corrections"' (*EYP*, 3, *EYPR*, 4). These remarks were made in 1976 and we are not offered the questions to which they are Alspach's reply. It is not therefore possible to tell whether Alspach conflated order and arrangement – as the quoted words seem to suggest – or whether he was simply answering an awkwardly worded question which did not distinguish between the problems. Of course, Alspach by then had the colossal labour of *VE* to defend, and the quoted words are the only grounds of his defence of its copy text which Finneran chooses to give us. Faced with Alspach's memories on the one hand, and on the other with the evidence provided by Curtis Bradford that Mrs Yeats and Thomas Mark had changed the volume-order of *Last Poems and Two Plays* for both *P* (1949) and the Macmillan *Last Poems & Plays* (1940), Finneran chose to topple *P* (1949) wholly and to invest *CP* with a new kind of authority, making the first part of *PNE* conform to that arrangement and calling it 'a hypothetical reconstruction of the contents *and* order [emphasis added] of an expanded "Collected Poems" had Yeats authorized such an edition as of 28 January, 1939'.[70]

Finneran does not speculate whether by 'order' Mrs Yeats (in Alspach's recollection) meant the overall arrangement of volumes and volume-units in *P* (1949) or the order of the poems in that set. Nor does he tell us whether Alspach had any misgivings about saying that 'WBY had corrected *the* proof [emphasis added]', which would be a very different matter from saying that Yeats had corrected proof (i.e. some of the proof), which indeed he had. We have no way of knowing how carefully Colonel Alspach questioned Mrs Yeats, and it does not really matter, since it is clear from Finneran's line of enquiry that the expectations of a later generation of scholars were more absolute, more naive because more purist in their expectations of textual transmission, than were those of the earlier scholars who had known the poet, his wife, his editor and the conditions of 1939.

Of Alspach's few quoted remarks about what Mrs Yeats is supposed to have said to him many years before, Finneran writes, 'Sadly, this was something less than the full truth, *and Mrs Yeats knew that it was* [emphasis added]'.[71] An extraordinarily graceless, not to say hostile, attitude to her, and a simplistic, not to say unrealistic, grasp of the practicalities of her life as Yeats's widow and executrix are revealed by the remark, to say nothing of Finneran's grasp of the rules of hearsay. He simply chooses to adopt Alspach's credibility, while declining to do the same for Harold Macmillan's, or for Professor Jeffares's memories.

Neither is it a particularly self-conscious approach to the history of modern editing. At the time Allt and Alspach began their labours, editors of modern literary texts were accustomed to think (in terms more appropriate to Renaissance texts on which the theories of editing at the time had been developed) of editing as a process of conjectural emendation towards an ideal text, corrupted by time and irregular transmission. It is a model which clearly has influenced the labours of Finneran himself.[72] Allt and Alspach might perhaps have been more ready in the early 1950s than Alspach might have cared to admit in 1976 to seek assurance from the poet's widow that a seamless process of textual evolution had occurred between 1932 and 1949, the poet's death and a world war notwithstanding. Mrs Yeats's comments (whatever they were) gave them the start they needed for their main concern – collation of variant texts. They weren't looking for fissures in their copy text: indeed, when Colonel Alspach began work on *The Variorum Edition of the Plays* he lamented that, unlike for the poems, there was not '[r]eady to hand . . . an authoritative basic text'.[73] By that time, too, the saga of *P* (1949) had receded or telescoped in Alspach's mind to 'shortly before his death Yeats had revised his poetry and signed pages for a de luxe edition'.[74]

In short, the first generation of academic editors was not in quest of the perfect, re-scrutinised copy text. Their aim was to recover and display the full panoply of abandoned texts. Mrs Yeats might have expected that what she said about the 'definitive edition' would offer certain certainties to editors with such a purpose. She cannot have envisaged that her (reported) remarks would have been used, as they have been in recent years, to undermine her authority and her work in so wholesale a fashion. The first generation of bibliographers and scholars evidently did not feel that they had the right to question Yeats's delegation to his wife and publisher's reader: to them it was, as far as they knew, part of the process by which his texts had been externalised. Now that the question has been opened, and by so unsubtle a procedure as that adopted by Finneran, it is possible to appreciate how much care and editorial 'negative capability' is required now to recover that humane sense of Mrs Yeats's work which Wade, Allt and Alspach must have had.

On 14 June 1939, Mrs Yeats had acceded to a suggestion of Thomas Mark's, writing 'Certainly put "Under Ben Bulben" at the end of the volume. Its present position was WBY's, but I t[h]ink now it should undoubtedly be at the end as you suggest' (*NLI* 30248). George Yeats and Thomas Mark were opting for a closure which was surely a convention for a memorial edition. Their action went unnoticed until Curtis Bradford took up the problem of the volume-order of *Last Poems & Plays* (1940). In 1961 he was able to demonstrate that the order of the Cuala

Last Poems and Two Plays (1939) had indeed been Yeats's own.[75] Later he showed that the eighteen poems and two plays which follow 'Under Ben Bulben' are articulated, as it were, from beyond the grave.[76] Finneran and other modern editors who follow Bradford in adopting the volume-order Yeats had sketched out for a volume he did not live to see[77] are right to do so, but Mrs Yeats's action has not been without stout defence.[78] It remains important to be able to see just where Yeats 'broke off'.

Bradford also alerted Yeats's readers to discrepancies between the Cuala and posthumous *texts* of the 'Last Poems', and with that began the process whereby *P* (1949) became destabilised. But that process is a story in itself, taken up in my *Yeats's Permanent Self: Canon, Arrangement and Order in the Collected Works* (forthcoming).

NOTES

1. See my own 'The Editor takes Possession' in the *Times Literary Supplement*, 29 June 1984, 731–3, and the following replies, all headed 'Editing Yeats' in the *TLS* controversy: 20 July, 811 (Denis Donoghue, Mary FitzGerald); 3 August, 868–9 (Richard J. Finneran); 10 August, 893 (A. Norman Jeffares, Warwick Gould); 31 August, 969 (Richard J. Finneran); 21 September, 1055 (Warwick Gould). For a restatement of Finneran's position compiled probably before the last-named item, see 'The Order of Yeats's Poems', *Irish University Review*, 14:2 (autumn 1984), 165–76 (hereafter cited as *OYP*). For an extended consideration of the problems of the new edition, including its relation to *VE*, see Michael J. Sidnell, 'Unacceptable Hypotheses: the New Edition of Yeats's Poems and its Making', in Warwick Gould (ed.), *Yeats Annual No. 3* (London, Macmillan Press, 1985), 225–43. For a reassessment of the problems facing editors of the 'Last Poems', see Phillip L. Marcus, 'Yeats's "Last Poems": A Reconsideration' in Warwick Gould (ed.) *Yeats Annual No. 5* (London, Macmillan Press, 1987), 3–14.

2. Frequently mentioned archives are cited in the text using the following abbreviations: correspondence of Yeats and his agents A. P. Watt & Son with Thomas Mark and Harold Macmillan (British Library, Dept of Western MSS) is cited after the symbol *B. L. Add. MS*, followed by folio no.; papers formerly in the collection of Mr Michael Yeats and now in the National Library of Ireland are cited using the abbreviation *NLI* before a MS no. and date if known; '*Basingstoke*' will signify the archive of the Macmillan Group, including papers formerly in the Birch Grove collection of Lord Stockton. '*Princeton*' signifies the Charles Scribner's Sons archive of correspondence relating to the Dublin Edition (Author Files I, Box 174, II, Box 37) now in the Rare Books Library, Princeton University; *HRHRC* will signify the copy submitted for the Dublin Edition now held in the Harry Ransom Humanities Research Center, University of Texas at Austin. *SB*, followed by an image number, will signify the W. B.

Yeats microfilmed archives at the State University of New York at Stony Brook, where certain original documents now unnumbered at the National Library of Ireland or in the collection of Mr Michael B. Yeats can be traced.

3. See *PNE*, 711–13; *PR*, 714–17. Although brief reasons for the emending of copy texts are given, no indication is shown of whether those emended texts differ from those of *P* (1949). Occasionally the information is in *EYPR*.

4. *EYPR*, 3. *EYP* was a little more generous: 'given the prevailing attitudes of the time, the 1949 *Poems* was probably as accurate an edition as could have been produced' (p. 2). Neither assessment is useful, since neither names (nor attempts to measure) scholarly editions 'of the time'. Memorial editions produced shortly after an author's death, then – as now – simply did not have 'scholarly' priorities. By such standards, George Yeats and Thomas Mark faced difficult problems at a difficult time with admirable care and insight.

5. The guiding preference for Richard Finneran's attempts to 'restore' Yeats's texts after the posthumous 'corruption' he feels they have undergone at the hands of Mrs Yeats and Thomas Mark has been his adoption of 'what Curtis Bradford has termed "rhetorical as opposed to grammatical punctuation"' (*EYP*, 74; *EYPR*, 93–4), but the proceeding is quite without historical sense and may have parallels with the zealous over-cleaning of pictures, including the removal of glazes. If this parallel is correct, a preference for lightly or under-punctuated texts might be a preference for texts which, to a reader of fifty years ago, would seem uncompleted texts. It therefore would be nothing more than a prejudice against the habitual punctuation of an earlier era. Mrs Yeats on 17 April 1939 wrote to Thomas Mark, 'WBY wrote to you in September (or October) 1932 about punctuation and generally asking your help, *without which he knew he could never get his work into the final form he wished* [emphasis added]. There are, however, a few metrical "tricks" as he called them, and tricks of repetition of words and phrases, deliberately used, which we should, I think, carefully preserve' (*NLI* 30248). The letter had been enclosed in one to Harold Macmillan of 8 September 1932 (*B. L. Add. MS* 55003, f. 136). See also Phillip L. Marcus, Warwick Gould and Michael J. Sidnell, eds., *The Secret Rose, Stories by W. B. Yeats: a Variorum Edition* (Ithaca and London, Cornell University Press, 1981; hereafter cited in text as *VSR*), xix.

6. *The Variorum Edition of the Poems of W. B. Yeats*, edited by Peter Allt and Russell K. Alspach (New York, The Macmillan Co., 1957, cited from the corrected printing of 1966, hereafter cited as *VE*).

7. Interview at Birch Grove, Chelwood Gate, West Sussex, 12 August 1980. I am very grateful to the present Earl of Stockton for facilitating my work among his grandfather's papers, then stored in an apple barn in Birch Grove but now in *Basingstoke*.

8. Yeats had been 'counting on some substantial gain from the edition de

luxe', as he wrote in a draft letter to A. P. Watt probably in 1931 (*SB* 0302220). It is likely that the success of *CP* helped to assuage his frustration with financial circumstances unfavourable to the publication of the *Edition de Luxe*. The Memorandum of Agreement for the *Edition de Luxe* is dated 17 April 1931. A marginal addition to the clause calling for a publication date not later than 30 September 1932 includes the words 'unless prevented by circumstances over which they [the publishers] have no control'. See *EYPR*, 7–9, for an account of how 'the publication of the project had been tied to economic conditions'.

9. Published 28 November 1933; reprinted 1934, 1935, 1937 and November 1939. See Allan Wade, *A Bibliography of the Writings of W. B. Yeats*, 3rd edn, revised and edited by Russell K. Alspach (London, Rupert Hart-Davis, 1968). Hereafter cited in text as *Wade* followed by item no. and page.

10. *B. L. Add. MS* 55738, ff. 460–2, 30 March 1933. The letter's code 'TM/MHM/MFE' shows it to have been drafted by Mark. See above pp. 714–15.

11. See below n. 41.

12. See 'Textual Notes', pp. 643–65. Only two of these changes are accepted in *PR*, viz., that to 'Brown Penny' and that to 'Ribh denounces Patrick', see *PR*, 714–15; *EYPR*, 57; also Finneran, 'A Note on the Scribner Archive at the Humanities Research Center' in Finneran (ed.), *Yeats: An Annual of Critical and Textual Studies* (Ithaca, Cornell University Press), 2, 1984, 227–32. However, he does not discuss the fact that a change to only *one* of the two appearances of a lyric in *The Land of Heart's Desire*, viz., '[The wind blows out of the gates of the day]' (A36 in *PR* [p. 536]) creates two different, simultaneous texts of that poem. The problem demonstrates how difficult it is to lift a 'poem' from its context in a play unless the poet has done so first. But see *EYPR*, 132. Also discountenanced is the Dublin Edition emendation to 'Two Songs Rewritten for the Tune's Sake'. The poem's revisions are discussed in *EYPR*, 55–7. A marked-up page from *A Full Moon in March* offers as the first line: 'A bright haired slut is my heart's desire', which might be a preferable reading. It is subsequent to the version found in *Nine One Act Plays* (1937), which began 'My pretty Paistin is my heart's desire,' and which included further changes. As a book for amateur performers, *Nine One Act Plays* offered this rather tame first line perhaps to avoid offence. But that version was further emended to the version in *P* (1949) which begins 'My Paistin Finn is my sole desire'; the sole copy text Finneran accepts from *P* (1949), (*EYPR*, 57, n. 4). Yet with a bifurcated stemma of texts, the problem might not be wholly solved. Yeats doubtless had Frank O'Connor to advise him on the Irish, but 'a bright haired slut' is more characteristic of late Yeats.

13. On the Dublin Edition, see Edward Callan, *Yeats on Yeats: The Last Introductions and the 'Dublin' Edition* (Dublin, Dolmen Press, New Yeats Papers Series XX, 1981, hereafter cited as *Callan*). See also *EYPR*, 12–23.

14. *B. L. Add. MS* 55779, f. 154, 31 March 1936. A. P. Watt, who was also Kipling's agent, was asked to undertake that the Sussex Edition would be complete, final and definitive, including all that the executors of Kipling would ever agree to publish and all works ever published by Kipling. It is no wonder that Yeats came to think that Macmillan would only ever bring out the *Edition de Luxe* after his death.

15. The copy sent to John Hall Wheelock by Charles Kingsley, of Scribner's London office, together with a clipping from the *Bookseller* (30 March 1939, 501) is filed at *Princeton*, 4 April 1939. An early proof of this prospectus, leaving a blank space where the word 'Collected' would appear, was sent to George Yeats on 28 February 1939 (*B. L. Add. MS* 55820, ff. 203–5) and returned with her annotations and is now filed at *B. L. Add. MS* 55890. See above p. 733.

16. See *Princeton*, Wheelock/Macmillan letters, 27 March, 8 April, 21 April, 28 April; *B. L. Add. MS* 55823, f. 457, 9 May 1939. By the terms of their agreement, the two firms were to refer buyers from the British market to the Coole Edition and buyers in the American market to the Dublin Edition. 750 sets in the Dublin Edition were for sale, plus thirty for presentation, in the earliest plan. The number was later increased, and Yeats signed 850 leaves (*Princeton*, 14 March 1954).

17. *Princeton*, 4 April 1939, a letter accompanying the 'Preliminary Notice' and press cutting. But in fact Macmillan had already sent a courtesy copy of the prospectus direct to the New York office on 27 March 1939.

18. See above p. 721.

19. When George Yeats rearranged and provided corrections for *CP* (New York, Macmillan Company, 1956) to conform to the *P* (1949) arrangement, she did not admit 'The Hero, the Girl, and the Fool' but included 'The Fool by the Roadside'. This suggests that she accepted it as the later and preferable text. That edition was dubbed the 'definitive edition with the author's final corrections' (*Wade*, item 211A, 209). 'The Fool by the Roadside' has been adopted in this edition.

20. *B. L. Add. MS* 54903, f. 148, H. Watt to Harold Macmillan, 10 November 1936.

21. Following Yeats's instructions, Macmillan in 1937 had delayed the *Edition de Luxe* pending Dublin Edition proofs, which Yeats hoped to work on before submitting revised copy to Macmillan (*B. L. Add. MSS* 55003, f. 229; 55800, f. 447, both 13 October 1937). After Yeats's death, Macmillan asked Scribner's Sons for proof (*Princeton*, 28 February 1939) when seeking a list of Dublin Edition contents, and were told on 16 March that galleys would be sent when composition had begun. By 27 March, having seen a list of the Dublin Edition contents and judged their own to be the fuller and the more recent, Macmillan felt that they 'need not trouble' Scribner's Sons for duplicate galleys (*Princeton*, 27 March 1939). By 8 April Scribner's Sons realised that while they had the prefaces which Macmillan

did not have, Macmillan had 'Last Poems' and other vital items of Yeats's late work which they now had to seek from the Yeats estate. George Yeats was very slow to provide such material, doubtless because she was waiting for Macmillan to get it into proof for the Coole Edition before supplying Scribner's Sons with corrected copy in that form (*Princeton*, 21, 28 April, 2, 9, 23 May 1939). By 12 May, with the two editions apparently converging, Scribner's Sons offered Macmillan a deal. If Macmillan would take electrotypes of the Dublin Edition, in order to make the two editions uniform and give Scribner's Sons some vital Macmillan assistance on 'various problems' which would appear at proof stage, Macmillan could have the 'General Introduction' and other prefaces. On 19 May Harold Macmillan declined the offer, stating that 'the whole of our Coole Edition is in type and will shortly be passed for press', and asked for proof of 'the general introduction and the three prefaces' (*B. L. Add. MS* 55824, f. 179). On the later history of Macmillan's negotiations over the prefaces, see above p. 730.

22. *B. L. Add. MS* 55825, ff. 301–2, 13 June 1939; *NLI* 30248. Harold Macmillan had heard from Scribner's Sons in a letter of 12 May that the 'General Introduction' was of 'about 28 pages' and that there were also 'three [in fact two] prefaces of about seven or eight pages' and that these prefaces were 'of very great value as casting light upon his theory of poetry and his methods of composition' (*Princeton*; *B. L. Add. MS* 55824, ff. 586–8, 2 June 1939). He had already enquired of George Yeats about them on 21 April (*B. L. Add. MS* 55822, f. 550), having been alerted to their existence by Scribner's Sons' letter of 8 April (*Princeton*). She replied to his letter of 2 June on 7 June that the prefaces and 'General Introduction' '*were* written by WBY for the exclusive use of the Scribner edition; I do not know if they would allow Macmillans to use them. Perhaps you or Mr. Watt would ask them? I am not sure that the *short* prefeaces [*sic*] are very essential; I think they would hardly "separate" from the particular purpose for which they were written' (*Basingstoke*). Thomas Mark has written 'No' into the margin which suggests that A. P. Watt & Son were consulted and advised against it. But see above p. 730.

23. Though in *The Works of William Blake Poetic, Symbolic and Critical etc.* (London, Bernard Quaritch, 1893) Yeats and Edwin Ellis had focused on interpretation, they also did pioneering work on Blake's texts, including unpublished MSS, e.g. 'Vala'.

24. *HRHRC* inscribed copy, PR 5900 A3 1933b. 'To the only begetter J. Squire from WBY Dec 1933' is on the recto of the front free endpaper. Sir John Collings Squire (1884–1958) was editor of the *London Mercury* and a reader for Macmillan at this stage. It is not yet known just how Squire involved himself – with Yeats or Macmillan – in respect of *CP*, but it seems possible that Yeats, frustrated at the delays to the *Edition de Luxe*, asked Squire to prepare Harold Macmillan for the idea of taking over Benn's rights in *Poems*, thus clearing the way for a new popular edition. Alter-

nately, Squire might perhaps have suggested putting the longer poems at the back for this edition.

25. *B. L. Add. MSS* 55733, ff. 424, 589; 54902, f. 4; 55737, f. 291. The matter was settled by 1 March 1933. Negotiations were needed for the *Edition de Luxe*. Benn's agreement with Yeats was due to expire in May 1933 (*B. L. Add. MS* 54902, f. 4).

26. When published, *CP* included 'The Gift of Harun Al-Rashid' in the 'Narrative and Dramatic' section. It is not known who included it, since it is not related in 'style' or 'subject' to the above group of Irish mythological poems. It is quite likely that Yeats consigned it to this section while reading proof and re-ordering the 'Tower' section of the book.

27. See above p. 724.

28. It is claimed by Finneran that 1906 is merely 'the date of one of its revisions' in *OYP*, 166–7.

29. See Michael J. Sidnell, George P. Mayhew, David R. Clark (eds.), *Druid Craft: The Writing of 'The Shadowy Waters'* (Amherst, University of Massachusetts Press, 1971), 4. The acting version of the play took up its position in both *Plays in Prose and Verse* (London, Macmillan, 1922) and *The Collected Plays* (London, Macmillan, 1934) as a play of 1907 (i.e. before *Deirdre*), even though the 1911 revision of that version is printed in both contexts. However, in lists prepared for the *Edition de Luxe* in 1936 (see pp. 722–3) on which Yeats had added comments at the request of Thomas Mark, he specifically requested *The Shadowy Waters* (acting version) to be 'left where it is', as a play of 1911, succeeding *The Green Helmet* (*NLI* 30202).

30. For example, *Selected Poems Lyrical and Narrative* (London, Macmillan, 1929; *Wade*, item 165), in which he wrote 'I have arranged in chronological order whatever lyrical and narrative poems of mine best please my friends or myself. . . . Though I have often in those thirty years corrected the earliest, I leave all, even two in "The Rose" that are almost wholly new, in their original context, for all belong in thought and sentiment to the time when they were first written' (*VE*, 855).

31. An odd date: *The Countess Kathleen and Various Legends and Lyrics* had been published in 1892.

32. *Later Poems* (London, Macmillan, 1922), v. The volume of plays is *Plays in Prose and Verse written for an Irish Theatre and generally with the help of a friend* (London, Macmillan, 1922).

33. 'I dont want to do anything unfair' (*B. L. Add. MS* 55003, f. 193; *NLI* 30248). He left it to Watt and Macmillan to negotiate, instructing Watt on the same day that while he was 'not legally bound' to consider his English publisher in the matter, he knew that Macmillan had their *Edition de Luxe* in type. The two editions 'would not clash in any way' and '[s]hould Macmillan ask me to refuse the American offer I would expect him to say at what date he can bring out the English edition . . . [which] has been put off from year to year' (*NLI* 30248).

34. *Princeton*, list accompanying letter from A. P. Watt to Wheelock, 28 January 1937, with Yeats's annotation informing him that the American edition of *CP* had 'many misprints'. This point has however been misunderstood by Finneran, see *EYPR*, 169.

35. It was an ordinary trade edition, neither for collectors nor for 'the possible producer', but as Macmillan wrote, 'intended for the ordinary reader' (*B. L. Add. MS* 55750, ff. 287–90; 6 March 1934). Once again Yeats departed from the arrangement of the *Edition de Luxe* and provided a list of plays in 'not entirely chronological [arrangement] as I think it better to put the plays of the Irish Heroic Age in the order in which the events are supposed to have happened', and offered to 'explain this classification in a preface' (*B. L. Add. MS* 55003, ff. 160–2).

36. As early as 17 December 1935, internal office memos mention details of the edition, which C. B. Merritt of Scribner's Sons wanted to be 'definitive' and to contain new material. Scribner's own doubts led him to write to George P. Brett to say that 'the least [Yeats] could do' to help sales would be to write 'three short forewords for the three natural divisions of the set – namely, Poems, Plays, and Essays – also some of his admirers and friends . . . feel certain that he would be able to dig up a little unpublished material that would tend to make the set more definitive as well as more of a collector's item. Please do not think for a moment that I am trying to encroach on your preserve as his publisher, and anything in our set you would naturally be perfectly free to use, but it is important to the success of the project that we get his cooperation in making it as attractive as possible' (*Princeton*, 27 December 1935). Yeats agreed to write 'a brief introduction to the set', but thought further new writing 'unnecessary' (*Princeton*, Watt to Wheelock, 9 June 1936). Wheelock, claiming he had met Yeats once and putting pressure on him via Padraic Colum, pressed Scribner's Sons' case for the prefaces (*Princeton*, 24 February, 17 June 1936), while Yeats put him off due to pressure of work (*Princeton*, Watt to Wheelock, 25 August 1936). By 28 January 1937, when Yeats did forward lists of contents, he again protested that he did 'not promise a preface for every volume', adding that further prefatory material to *A Vision* might 'look ridiculous'. Wheelock's reply of 9 February requested a General Introduction and three prefaces to Poems, Plays and Essays, making four in all (*Princeton*). See also above p. 725 and note 50.

37. The remark might also envisage the projected prefaces for the Scribner's Sons edition, as yet unwritten.

38. Mark had asked of Vol. 3, Plays Vol. I, whether the 'chronological order' was 'correct, and are we to follow it? It is different from the one originally supplied us, in which "The Pot of Broth" preceded "The Hour Glass", and "The Shadowy Waters" preceded "Deirdre"'. Yeats's reply was to cancel all after 'follow it?', having annotated two plays followed by their dates in the chronological list 'correct'. He also added '"Pot of Broth" should precede "Hour Glass" [prose version of 1904]. But *The Shadowy*

Waters left where it is as this is the acting version the other is in Vol. I'. He then cancelled the comment. He wanted Vol. 4, Plays II, to begin with *Four Plays for Dancers* (1917) – the verse version of *The Hour Glass* being moved to Vol. 3, Plays I – and for the rest of his plays to follow in chronological order until the *Wheels and Butterflies* plays of 1934 which were to be regrouped chronologically within that volume, according to composition date, and retitled *More Plays for Dancers*. His reply to Mark's question, 'Is this the correct order as in the separate volume? It is not chronological' was 'Print them chronologically.' Later plays were to be added (*NLI* 30202).

39. Watt told Harold Macmillan, 'As you know, I entirely share your opinion that the more divergence between this edition and that of Messrs. Scribner the better it will be' (*B. L. Add. MS* 54903, f. 151, 10 November 1936).

40. Because when he did submit contents lists to Scribner's Sons on 28 January 1937 (*Princeton*), the directions suggested by Macmillan were largely followed, except with regard to the volumes of plays, for which he took notes, music, etc., from the Collected Edition of the 1920s. His compliance has illogically been read as preference, see *EYPR*, 168–9. It is possible he did not reply at all, given that Watt sent no remarks on to Macmillan.

41. Complete marked proofs of Vol. 1 had been sent to Yeats on 17 June 1932 (*B. L. Add. MS* 55729, f. 477), and returned by Yeats on 5 July with a request for a revise (*B. L. Add. MS* 55003, f. 129). The *Edition de Luxe* project was temporarily shelved after 11 August 1932 (*B. L. Add. MS* 55731, ff. 405–7) but Yeats's further request for the revise on 13 August (*B. L. Add. MS* 55003, f. 135) was answered by the despatch of pp. 1–384 on 23 August 1932 (*B. L. Add. MS* 55731, f. 569). The remainder were sent to Yeats on 16 September and returned on 28 September (*B. L. Add. MSS* 55732, f. 366; 55003, f. 138). A further revise of pp. 385 ff. was sent later. It bears the date stamp 4 October 1932, and is now in *NLI* 30262. See *EYP*, 10–11; *EYPR*, 10–11.

42. See above n. 19.

43. See *EYPR*, 159–63. The argument illogically assumes that the contents and order of *The Tower* in *CP* because *later* must be *better*. It also presumes that one must choose *either* the *Edition de Luxe or* the *CP* order and contents, and blames Mrs Yeats and Mark for not sharing Finneran's monolithic conception of copy text.

44. Yeats had always intended to 'arrange the volumes to suit himself' (*Princeton*, 7 October 1936), but this wish was overtaken by the advice of Macmillan and Watt. On the later lists see above pp. 726–7.

45. *EYPR*, 17–18, 163–5. The first argument relies on an unpublished essay by David R. Clark. The second, 'Yeats's response [to Mark's questions] only makes sense if he assumed the publishers were now going to adopt the arrangement of the Collected Poems [for the *Edition de Luxe*]'

(*EYPR*, 164), ignores the unsatisfactory nature of both the question and the answer.

46. In fact both the Macmillan and Scribner's Sons lists are concerned with contents, not with arrangement; the Macmillan one because arrangement of the volume to which it referred was already fully determined, and the Scribner's Sons one because it was merely a preliminary list. In its second state, as completed by Mrs Yeats in June 1937 (see above p. 728), it is indeed tied to the arrangement of *CP*. Such is however not clear from this preliminary list. It would have made no sense to have added the poems from *A Full Moon in March*, etc., after the end of the 'Narrative and Dramatic' section.

47. Unpublished letters of 1899.

48. The letter has been absurdly misinterpreted. See *EYPR*, 164–5.

49. The comment has been used to justify Part I of *PR* (see p. xxv).

50. An illusion they preserved for a long time after they had received the typescripts themselves. Wheelock never could make up his mind whether there were three or four prefaces, wondering, for example, on 31 December 1940 if a preface to *Autobiographies* had gone missing from the file. On 16 January 1953, however, he conceded to George P. Brett that Yeats 'never did the fourth' (*Princeton*).

51. *NLI* 30202. 'Sent to Watt', she wrote, followed by the date and her initials. In fact, Vol. 4 was sent to Yeats at the Athenæum, as we shall see below.

52. *Princeton*, Watt to Kingsley, 15 June 1937. George Yeats had posted three parcels on 14 June, Watt already had a further parcel containing the copy for Vol. 1 (posted by Mrs Yeats on 11 June) and he forwarded four parcels on 15 June to Kingsley, who persisted in thinking they represented Vols. 2, 3, 4 and 6 rather than 1–3, 6.

53. For example, Kingsley to Wheelock, on 22 June, refers to Mrs Yeats possibly 'stir[ring] up more trouble', and on the 24th writes '[w]hat between W. B. Yeats somewhere up in the clouds, Mrs Yeats, who apparently deals with him largely by correspondence (for she claims in her letter to Watt [22 June] that he won't answer her letters) this Yeats business seems to be pretty badly confused'.

54. On the 28 January lists Yeats had wanted to displace the commentaries to the *Wheels and Butterflies* plays to Vol. 5, *Essays*. This was a development of his revised plan for the *Edition de Luxe* Vol. 5, in which he had decided to put the preface to *The Words upon the Window-pane* retitled 'Swift' (*NLI* 30202). Other minor discrepancies between the lists show the developing nature of his conception of his *œuvre*, and reinforce the view that the only major anomaly between the two editions would have been the use of *CP* for the Scribner's Sons' project.

55. This is clear from his deletions to Mark's questions on Vol. 3, Plays I, in his instruction 'Print them chronologically' beside the list of plays from *Wheels and Butterflies* in Vol. 4, Plays II. For the misunderstanding of this

matter of arrangement and order see Finneran, 'Editing Yeats', the *Times Literary Supplement*, 31 August 1984, 969; see also my 'Editing Yeats' in the same journal, 10 August and 21 September 1984, 893 and 1055.

56. H. Watt wrote to Kingsley on 15 June about the problem of *Autobiographies*, having heard that '"Mr. Yeats wants to keep Dramatis Personae with the other biographical fragments in the same order as in the Macmillan book"' [i.e. *Dramatis Personae 1896–1902 Estrangement The Death of Synge The Bounty of Sweden* (London, Macmillan, 1936)]. George Yeats had therefore '"given each of these sections their true date of first publication (Cuala Press)"'. This decision reversed that of the 28 January preliminary list, in which *Dramatis Personae* had been placed last (*Princeton*).

57. In the 28 January lists, Yeats had indicated that Vol. 2 should be called not *Mythologies and the Irish Dramatic Movement* but *Mythical Stories and The Irish Dramatic Movement*. However, subsequently the Yeatses or George Yeats reverted to *Mythologies and The Irish Dramatic Movement* in the 'third carbon copy' list sent to Watt by George Yeats on 22 June 1937. It must be assumed that Yeats, who had seen copies of the lists as despatched by Mrs Yeats, approved of the restoration of *Mythologies* to the title. *Mythical Stories* was never submitted as a title to Macmillan. Just why Yeats temporarily entertained the weaker *Mythical Stories* for the American edition is not known.

58. Watt's letters to Yeats and Yeats's to Watt are not available in an otherwise complete archive, but many of Yeats's to Watt are substantially quoted *verbatim* in the Watt letters to Macmillan and to Kingsley. But we know how Watt and Macmillan agreed on this issue, and there can be no doubt how Yeats was advised (*B. L. Add. MS* 54903, f. 151, 10 November 1936).

59. This sheet is preserved in *Princeton* with a copy of George Yeats's letter to Watt of 22 June 1937. It seems likely that it should have been returned (copy letter, Watt to Kingsley, 23 June 1937).

60. Finneran suggests that Yeats 'dictated' the changes in response to Macmillan's 5 June letter (*B. L. Add. MS* 55795, f. 298) calling for 'further material' for the *Edition de Luxe* (*EYPR*, 19). This could well be the case; however, George Yeats *was* marking the Macmillan list as a file copy.

61. Which has been misconstrued in *EYPR*, 167, n. 18.

62. In Hugh Kenner's influential article, 'The Sacred Book of the Arts', *Irish Writing* (W. B. Yeats: A Special Number), 31 (summer 1955), 24–35; also *Sewannee Review*, 64:4 (Oct.–Dec. 1956), 574–90. Reprinted in Kenner: *Gnomon: Essays on Contemporary Literature* (New York, Obolensky, 1958), 9–29.

63. The prospectus is rare and does not have a separate entry in *Wade*. Remarks from it are quoted in *Wade*, items 209, 210, which add to the confusion over the (unattributed) headnote 'THE DEFINITIVE EDITION' in those two items. Copies of the prospectus can be found in the British Library (tipped in to their set of *P* (1949) (Cup. 402 L. 2) and in the

library of Wake Forest University, Winston Salem, North Carolina. 64. *B. L. Add. MS* 55890, f. 1; *Princeton*, 4 April 1939. A second state of the notice was prepared after Mrs Yeats had settled on the name 'Coole Edition'. It was printed on the ivory paper chosen for the volumes themselves. A fragment of it (the first half of a bifolium, printed on both sides) is filed at *B. L. Add. MS* 55890, f. 2. It might actually have been issued. Its blurb ran: THE *COOLE* EDITION / OF / THE WORKS OF / W. B. YEATS/ MESSRS. MACMILLAN will have ready for publication this autumn a complete and definitive edition of the writings of WILLIAM BUTLER YEATS to be known as THE *COOLE* EDITION. Mr. YEATS had corrected and revised the text of his *published* [emphasis added] works for this purpose, and had autographed the first volume of each set of the edition. The later poems, plays, essays, introductions, and other material which remained unpublished at the time of his lamented death have now been added to the appropriate volumes, and the arrangement is given in detail overleaf' [arrangement page is missing]. This version, if published, was as honest a statement of the extent of Yeats's involvement as could have been expected in a brief compass. The force of the word 'published' has been quite missed in *EYPR*, 1–2.

65. As with such other controversial terms as 'arrangement' and 'order', Finneran offers no definition of 'definitive'. Holding these matters to be self-evident, he usually prefers some such formulation as 'the proper text' (*EYP*, 22).

66. Yeats wrote to Harold Macmillan while preparing proof of *The Winding Stair and Other Poems*, 'Please leave the section called "Words for Music Perhaps" as I have arranged every poem with its number. It is a series of poems related one to another & leads up to a quotation from The Delphic oracle, as the two other series "A Man Young & Old" and "A Woman Young & Old" lead up to quotations from Sophocles. The poems in "Words for Music Perhaps" describe first wild loves, then the normal love of boy & girl, then follow poems about love but not love poems, then poems of impersonal ecstasy & all have certain themes in common' (*B. L. Add. MS* 55003, f. 147). Yeats added his permission in advance for the publisher to leave the word 'Perhaps' out of running titles 'after the first naming' if the title were to prove 'inconveniently long', and delegated the inspection of revised proof to 'your admirable reader' who 'seems to be able to read my difficult handwriting'. Harold Macmillan's reply on 9 August 1939 was that the 'explanation of the scheme' had been 'very interesting' and that 'the numbering will make the arrangements clear' (*NLI* 30248; *B. L. Add. MS* 55743, f. 19).

67. 'The Two Kings' was removed from *Responsibilities*, and 'The Gift of Harun Al-Rashid' from *The Tower*. Both displacements had implications for the readers of those collections, but the disruption to *Responsibilities* was if anything worse than that to *The Tower*. *EYPR*, 160, ignores this problem of *Responsibilities*.

68. The point was made during the controversy over *PNE* and *EYP*. See my own reply, 'Editing Yeats' (*Times Literary Supplement*, 21 September 1984, 1055), to Finneran's rejoinder (31 August 1984, 969) which misapprehends the evidence of the 1936–7 lists and confuses *Edition de Luxe* and Dublin Edition materials.

69. The comment is Thomas Mark's, made on p. 411 of the 4 October 1932 proofs of the *Edition de Luxe*, in reply to a question of George Yeats's about the *text* of 'The Choice' and of 'Coole Park and Ballylee'. See *EYP*, 34, and *EYPR*, 43, where Finneran conflates questions of text and arrangement, apparently sure that both Mrs Yeats and Mark ought to have considered that 'the two-part division of the *Collected Poems* into "Lyrical" and "Narrative and Dramatic"' was likewise both "later and correct"'.

70. *PNE*, xxiii, cf. the revised comment in *PR*, 'a reconstruction of the expanded version of *The Collected Poems* (1933) which as of 22 June 1937 Yeats had planned to publish "in about two years time"' (p. xxv). No distinction is made here between 'contents' and 'order'. The new date given refers to the meeting between Harold Macmillan and Yeats discussed above p. 724.

71. *EYP*, 3. The comment has been muted in *EYPR*, 4, to 'Sadly, this was less than the full truth.'

72. Yeats 'had not been long in his temporary resting-place at Roquebrune before the process began of – not to put too fine a point on it – corrupting the texts which he had worked so hard to perfect' (*EYP*, 30; *EYPR*, 39).

73. *The Variorum Edition of the Plays of W. B. Yeats*, ed. Russell K. Alspach, assisted by Catherine C. Alspach (London, Macmillan, 1966), xi.

74. Ibid. Having already edited *VE*, Alspach must have known that this was an oversimplification of the claims of the 'Prospectus'.

75. 'The Order of Yeats's *Last Poems*', *Modern Language Notes*, 76:6 (June 1961), 515–16.

76. In 'Yeats's *Last Poems* Again' in Liam Miller (ed.), *Dolmen Press Yeats Centenary Papers*, No. 8 (Dublin, Dolmen Press, 1966), 259–88, at p. 261. Even Bradford refers to *P* (1949) as 'the *Definitive Edition*' as though it were its title (p. 283). Tempting as it is to suggest that 'Politics' wishes the poet back to 'The Wanderings of Oisin' in its last line, giving a circular, reincarnative shape to the 'book' of Yeats's poems, such a suggestion also seems too neat to accord with Yeats's last days.

77. Nor to provide a title for. For Yeats's own list see Plate 1 in Warwick Gould (ed.), *Yeats Annual No. 5* (London, Macmillan Press, 1987).

78. Phillip L. Marcus, 'Yeats's "Last Poems": A Reconsideration', *loc. cit.* (see above n. 1).

Appendix Seven
Yeats's Notes

THE NOTES IN *THE POEMS OF W. B. YEATS* (1949)

The Wanderings of Oisin

(page 5)

The poem is founded upon the Middle Irish dialogues of Saint Patrick and Oisin and a certain Gaelic poem of the last century. The events it describes, like the events in most of the poems in this volume, are supposed to have taken place rather in the indefinite period, made up of many periods, described by the folk-tales, than in any particular century; it therefore, like the later Fenian stories themselves, mixes much that is mediaeval with much that is ancient. The Gaelic poems do not make Oisin go to more than one island, but a story in *Silva Gadelica* describes 'four paradises,' an island to the north, an island to the west, an island to the south, and Adam's paradise in the east. – 1912.

Crossways. The Rose

(pages 37, 61)

Many of the poems in *Crossways*, certainly those upon Indian subjects or upon shepherds and fauns, must have been written before I was twenty, for from the moment when I began *The Wanderings of Oisin*, which I did at that age, I believe, my subject-matter became Irish. Every time I have reprinted them I have considered the leaving out of most, and then remembered an old school friend who has some of them by heart, for no better reason, as I think, than that they remind him of his own youth. The little Indian dramatic scene was meant to be the first scene of a play about a man loved by two women, who had the one soul between them, the one woman waking when the other slept, and knowing but daylight as the other only night. It came into my head when I saw a man at Rosses Point carrying two salmon. 'One man with two souls,' I said, and added, 'O no, two people with one soul.' I am now once more in *A Vision* busy with that thought, the antitheses of day and of night and of moon and of sun. *The Rose* was part of my second book, *The Countess Kathleen and Various Legends and Lyrics*, 1892, and I notice upon reading these poems for the first time for several years that the quality symbolised as The Rose differs from the Intellectual Beauty of Shelley and of Spenser in that I have imagined it as suffering with man and not as something pursued and seen from afar. It must have been a thought of my generation, for I remember the mystical painter Horton, whose work had little of his personal charm and real strangeness, writing me these words, 'I met your beloved in Russell Square, and she was weeping,' by which he meant that he had seen a vision of my neglected soul. – 1925.

THE HOSTING OF THE SIDHE
(page 89)

The gods of ancient Ireland, the Tuatha de Danaan, or the Tribes of the goddess Dana, or the Sidhe, from Aes Sidhe, or Sluagh Sidhe, the people of the Faery Hills, as these words are usually explained, still ride the country as of old. Sidhe is also Gaelic for wind, and certainly the Sidhe have much to do with the wind. They journey in whirling wind, the winds that were called the dance of the daughters of Herodias in the Middle Ages, Herodias doubtless taking the place of some old goddess. When old countrypeople see the leaves whirling on the road they bless themselves, because they believe the Sidhe to be passing by. Knocknarea is in Sligo, and the countrypeople say that Maeve, still a great queen of the western Sidhe, is buried in the cairn of stones upon it. I have written of Clooth-na-Bare in *The Celtic Twilight*. She 'went all over the world, seeking a lake deep enough to drown her faery life, of which she had grown weary, leaping from hill to hill, and setting up a cairn of stones wherever her feet lighted, until, at last, she found the deepest water in the world in little Lough Ia, on the top of the bird mountain, in Sligo.' I forget, now, where I heard this story, but it may have been from a priest at Coloney. Clooth-na-Bare is evidently a corruption of Cailleac Beare, the old woman of Beare, who, under the names Beare, and Berah, and Beri, and Verah, and Dera, and Dhira, appears in the legends of many places. – 1899–1906.

THE HOST OF THE AIR
(page 90)

This poem is founded on an old Gaelic ballad that was sung and translated for me by a woman at Ballisodare in County Sligo; but in the ballad the husband found the keeners keening his wife when he got to his house. – 1899.

HE MOURNS FOR THE CHANGE THAT HAS COME UPON HIM AND HIS BELOVED, AND LONGS FOR THE END OF THE WORLD
(page 95)

My deer and hound are properly related to the deer and hound that flicker in and out of the various tellings of the Arthurian legends, leading different knights upon adventures, and to the hounds and to the hornless deer at the beginning of, I think, all tellings of Oisin's journey to the country of the young. The hound is certainly related to the Hounds of Annwoyn or of Hades, who are white, and have red ears, and were heard, and are, perhaps, still heard by Welsh peasants, following some flying thing in the night winds; and is probably related to the hounds that Irish countrypeople believe will awake and seize the souls of the dead if you lament them too loudly or too soon. An old woman told a friend and myself that she saw what she thought were white birds, flying over an enchanted place, but found, when she got near, that they had dogs' heads; and I do not doubt that my hound and these dog-headed birds are of the same family. I got my hound and deer out of a last-century Gaelic poem about Oisin's journey to the country of the young. After the hunting of the hornless deer, that leads him to the seashore, and while he is riding over the sea with Niamh, he sees amid the waters – I have not the Gaelic poem by me, and describe it from memory – a young man following a girl who has a golden apple, and afterwards a hound with one red ear following a deer with no horns. This hound and this deer seem plain images of the desire of the man 'which is for the woman,' and 'the desire of the woman which is for the desire of the man,' and of all desires that are as these. I have read them in this way in *The Wanderings of Oisin*, and have made my lover sigh because he has seen in their faces 'the immortal desire of Immortals.'

The man in my poem who has a hazel wand may have been Aengus, Master of Love; and I have made the Boar without bristles come out of the West, because the place of sunset was in Ireland, as in other countries, a place of symbolic darkness and death. – 1899.

THE CAP AND BELLS

(page 99)

I dreamed this story exactly as I have written it, and dreamed another long dream after it, trying to make out its meaning, and whether I was to write it in prose or verse. The first dream was more a vision than a dream, for it was beautiful and coherent, and gave me the sense of illumination and exaltation that one gets from visions, while the second dream was confused and meaningless. The poem has always meant a great deal to me, though, as is the way with symbolic poems, it has not always meant quite the same thing. Blake would have said, 'The authors are in eternity,' and I am quite sure they can only be questioned in dreams. – 1899.

THE VALLEY OF THE BLACK PIG

(page 100)

All over Ireland there are prophecies of the coming rout of the enemies of Ireland, in a certain Valley of the Black Pig, and these prophecies are, no doubt, now, as they were in the Fenian days, a political force. I have heard of one man who would not give any money to the Land League, because the Battle could not be until the close of the century; but, as a rule, periods of trouble bring prophecies of its near coming. A few years before my time, an old man who lived at Lissadell, in Sligo, used to fall down in a fit and rave out descriptions of the Battle; and a man in Sligo has told me that it will be so great a battle that the horses shall go up to their fetlocks in blood, and that their girths, when it is over, will rot from their bellies for lack of a hand to unbuckle them. If one reads Rhys' *Celtic Heathendom* by the light of Frazer's *Golden Bough*, and puts together what one finds there about the boar that killed Diarmuid, and other old Celtic boars and sows, one sees that the Battle is mythological, and that the Pig it is named from must be a type of cold and winter doing battle with the summer, or of death battling with life. – 1899–1906.

THE SECRET ROSE

(page 104)

I find that I have unintentionally changed the old story of Conchubar's death. He did not see the Crucifixion in a vision but was told of it. He had been struck by a ball made out of the dried brains of an enemy and hurled out of a sling; and this ball had been left in his head, and his head had been mended, the *Book of Leinster* says, with thread of gold because his hair was like gold. Keating, a writer of the time of Elizabeth, says: 'In that state did he remain seven years, until the Friday on which Christ was crucified, according to some historians; and when he saw the unusual changes of the creation and the eclipse of the sun and the moon at its full, he asked of Bucrach, a Leinster Druid, who was along with him, what was it that brought that unusual change upon the planets of Heaven and Earth. "Jesus Christ, the Son of God," said the Druid, "who is now being crucified by the Jews." "That is a pity," said Conchubar; "were I in his presence I would kill those who were putting him to death." And with that he brought out his sword, and rushed at a woody grove which was convenient to him, and began to cut and fell it; and what he said was, that if he were among the Jews, that was the usage he would give them, and from the excessiveness of his fury which seized upon him, the ball started out of his head, and some of the brain came after it, and in that way he died. The wood of Lanshraigh, in Feara Rois, is the name by which that shrubby wood is called.'

I have imagined Cuchulain meeting Fand 'walking among flaming dew,' because, I think, of something in Mr. Standish O'Grady's books.

I have founded the man 'who drove the gods out of their liss,' or fort, upon something I have read about Caoilte after the battle of Gabhra, when almost all his companions were killed, driving the gods out of their liss, either at Osraige, now Ossory, or at Ess Ruadh, now Assaroe, a water-fall at Ballyshannon, where Ilbrec, one of the children of the goddess

Dana, had a liss. But maybe I only read it in Mr. Standish O'Grady, who has a fine imagination, for I find no such story in Lady Gregory's book.

I have founded 'the proud dreaming king' upon Fergus, the son of Rogh, but when I wrote my poem here, and in the song in my early book, *Who goes with Fergus?*, I only knew him in Mr. Standish O'Grady, and my imagination dealt more freely with what I did know than I would approve of to-day.

I have founded him 'who sold tillage, and house, and goods,' upon something in *The Red Pony*, a folk-tale in Mr. Larminie's *West Irish Folk Tales*. A young man 'saw a light before him on the high road. When he came as far, there was an open box on the road, and a light coming up out of it. He took up the box. There was a lock of hair in it. Presently he had to go to become the servant of a king for his living. There were eleven boys. When they were going out into the stable at ten o'clock, each of them took a light but he. He took no candle at all with him. Each of them went into his own stable. When he went into his stable he opened the box. He left it in a hole in the wall. The light was great. It was twice as much as in the other stables.' The king hears of it, and makes him show him the box. The king says, 'You must go and bring me the woman to whom the hair belongs.' In the end, the young man, and not the king, marries the woman. – 1899–1906.

THE SHADOWY WATERS

(page 139)

I published in 1902 a version of *The Shadowy Waters*, which, as I had no stage experience whatever, was unsuitable for stage representation, though it had some little success when played during my absence in America in 1904, with very unrealistic scenery before a very small audience of cultivated people. On my return I rewrote the play in its present form, but found it still too profuse in speech for stage representation. In 1906 I made a stage version, which was played in Dublin in that year. The present version must be considered as a poem only. – 1922.

RESPONSIBILITIES

PREFATORY POEM

(page 197)

'Free of ten and four' is an error I cannot now correct, without more rewriting than I have a mind for. Some merchant in Villon, I forget the reference, was 'free of the ten and four.' Irish merchants exempted from certain duties by the Irish Parliament were, unless memory deceives me again, for I am writing away from books, 'free of the eight and six.' – 1914.

POEMS BEGINNING WITH THAT 'TO A WEALTHY MAN'
AND ENDING WITH THAT 'TO A SHADE'

(pages 208–212)

In the thirty years or so during which I have been reading Irish newspapers, three public controversies have stirred my imagination. The first was the Parnell controversy. There were reasons to justify a man's joining either party, but there were none to justify, on one side or on the other, lying accusations forgetful of past service, a frenzy of detraction. And another was the dispute over *The Playboy*. There may have been reasons for opposing as for supporting that violent, laughing thing, though I can see the one side only, but there cannot have been any for the lies, for the unscrupulous rhetoric spread against it in Ireland, and from Ireland to America. The third prepared for the Corporation's refusal of a building for Sir Hugh Lane's famous collection of pictures. . . .

[*Note.* – I leave out two long paragraphs which have been published in earlier editions of these poems. There is no need now to defend Sir Hugh Lane's pictures against Dublin newspapers. The trustees of the London National Gallery, through his leaving a codicil to his will unwitnessed, have claimed the pictures for London, and propose to build a wing to the Tate Gallery to contain them. Some that were hostile are now contrite, and doing what they can, or letting others do unhindered what they can, to persuade Parliament to such action as may restore the collection to Ireland. – Jan. 1917.]

These controversies, political, literary, and artistic, have showed that neither religion nor politics can of itself create minds with enough receptivity to become wise, or just and generous enough to make a nation. Other cities have been as stupid – Samuel Butler laughs at shocked Montreal for hiding the Discobolus in a lumber-room – but Dublin is the capital of a nation, and an ancient race has nowhere else to look for an education. Goethe in *Wilhelm Meister* describes a saintly and naturally gracious woman, who, getting into a quarrel over some trumpery detail of religious observance, grows – she and all her little religious community – angry and vindictive. In Ireland I am constantly reminded of that fable of the futility of all discipline that is not of the whole being. Religious Ireland – and the pious Protestants of my childhood were signal examples – thinks of divine things as a round of duties separated from life and not as an element that may be discovered in all circumstance and emotion, while political Ireland sees the good citizen but as a man who holds to certain opinions and not as a man of good will. Against all this we have but a few educated men and the remnants of an old traditional culture among the poor. Both were stronger forty years ago, before the rise of our new middle class which made its first public display during the nine years of the Parnellite split, showing how base at moments of excitement are minds without culture. – 1914.

Lady Gregory in her Life of Sir Hugh Lane assumes that the poem which begins 'Now all the truth is out' (p. 211) was addressed to him. It was not; it was addressed to herself. – 1922.

THE DOLLS
(page 229)

The fable for this poem came into my head while I was giving some lectures in Dublin. I had noticed once again how all thought among us is frozen into 'something other than human life.' After I had made the poem, I looked up one day into the blue of the sky, and suddenly imagined, as if lost in the blue of the sky, stiff figures in procession. I remembered that they were the habitual image suggested by blue sky, and looking for a second fable called them 'The Magi' (p. 229), complementary forms of those enraged dolls. – 1914.

THE WILD SWANS AT COOLE
SHEPHERD AND GOATHERD
(page 244)

'Unpacks the loaded pern': When I was a child at Sligo I could see above my grandfather's trees a little column of smoke from 'the pern-mill,' and was told that 'pern' was another name for the spool, as I was accustomed to call it, on which thread was wound. One could not see the chimney for the trees, and the smoke looked as if it came from the mountain, and one day a foreign sea-captain asked me if that was a burning mountain. – 1919.

THE PHASES OF THE MOON
(page 267)

THE DOUBLE VISION OF MICHAEL ROBARTES
(page 276)

MICHAEL ROBARTES AND THE DANCER
(page 281)

Years ago I wrote three stories in which occur the names of Michael Robartes and Owen Aherne. I now consider that I used the actual names of two friends, and that one of these friends, Michael Robartes, has but lately returned from Mesopotamia, where he has partly found and partly thought out much philosohpy. I consider that Aherne and Robartes, men to whose namesakes I had attributed a turbulent life or death, have quarrelled with me. They take their place in a phantasmagoria in which I endeavour to explain my philosophy of life and death. To some extent I wrote these poems as a text for exposition. – 1922.

The Tower

SAILING TO BYZANTIUM

(Stanza IV, page 302)

I have read somewhere that in the Emperor's palace at Byzantium was a tree made of gold and silver, and artificial birds that sang.

THE TOWER

(page 302)

The persons mentioned are associated by legend, story and tradition with the neighbourhood of Thoor Ballylee or Ballylee Castle, where the poem was written. Mrs. French lived at Peterswell in the eighteenth century and was related to Sir Jonah Barrington, who described the incident of the ears and the trouble that came of it. The peasant beauty and the blind poet are Mary Hynes and Raftery, and the incident of the man drowned in Cloone Bog is recorded in my *Celtic Twilight*. Hanrahan's pursuit of the phantom hare and hounds is from my *Stories of Red Hanrahan*. The ghosts have been seen at their game of dice in what is now my bedroom, and the old bankrupt man lived about a hundred years ago. According to one legend he could only leave the Castle upon a Sunday because of his creditors, and according to another he hid in the secret passage.

In the passage about the Swan in Part III I have unconsciously echoed one of the loveliest lyrics of our time – Mr. Sturge Moore's *Dying Swan*. I often recited it during an American lecturing tour, which explains the theft.

THE DYING SWAN

O silver-throated Swan
Struck, struck! A golden dart
Clean through thy breast has gone
Home to thy heart.
Thrill, thrill, O silver throat!
O silver trumpet, pour
Love for defiance back
On him who smote!
And brim, brim o'er
With love; and ruby-dye thy track
Down thy last living reach
Of river, sail the golden light –
Enter the sun's heart – even teach,
O wondrous-gifted Pain, teach thou
The god to love, let him learn how.

When I wrote the lines about Plato and Plotinus I forgot that it is something in our own eyes that makes us see them as all transcendence. Has not Plotinus written: 'Let every soul recall, then, at the outset the truth that soul is the author of all living things, that it has breathed the life into them all, whatever is nourished by earth and sea, all the creatures of the air, the divine stars in the sky; it is the maker of the sun; itself formed and ordered this vast heaven and conducts all that rhythmic motion – and it is a principle distinct from all these to which it gives law and movement and life, and it must of necessity be more honourable than they, for they gather or dissolve as soul brings them life or abandons them, but soul, since it never can abandon itself, is of eternal being'? – 1928.

MEDITATIONS IN TIME OF CIVIL WAR

(page 308)

These poems were written at Thoor Ballylee in 1922, during the civil war. Before they were finished the Republicans blew up our 'ancient bridge' one midnight. They forbade us to leave the house, but were otherwise polite, even saying at last 'Good-night, thank you,' as though we had given them the bridge.

The sixth poem is called *The Stare's Nest by my Window*. In the west of Ireland we call a starling a stare, and during the civil war one built in a hole in the masonry by my bedroom window.

In the second stanza of the seventh poem occur the words, 'Vengeance upon the murderers, vengeance for Jacques Molay.' A cry for vengeance because of the murder of the Grand Master of the Templars seems to me fit symbol for those who labour from hatred, and so for sterility in various kinds. It is said to have been incorporated in the ritual of certain Masonic societies of the eighteenth century, and to have fed class hatred.

I suppose that I must have put hawks into the fourth stanza because I have a ring with a hawk and a butterfly upon it, to symbolise the straight road of logic, and so of mechanism, and the crooked road of intuition: 'For wisdom is a butterfly and not a gloomy bird of prey.' – 1928.

NINETEEN HUNDRED AND NINETEEN

(Sixth poem, page 317)

The countrypeople see at times certain apparitions whom they name now 'fallen angels,' now 'ancient inhabitants of the country,' and describe as riding at whiles 'with flowers upon the heads of the horses.' I have assumed in the sixth poem that these horsemen, now that the times worsen, give way to worse. My last symbol, Robert Artisson, was an evil spirit much run after in Kilkenny at the start of the fourteenth century. Are not those who travel in the whirling dust also in the Platonic Year?

TWO SONGS FROM A PLAY

(page 320)

These songs are sung by the Chorus in *The Resurrection*.

AMONG SCHOOL CHILDREN

(Stanza V, page 324)

I have taken the 'honey of generation' from Porphyry's essay on 'The Cave of the Nymphs,' but find no warrant in Porphyry for considering it the 'drug' that destroys the 'recollection' of pre-natal freedom. He blamed a cup of oblivion given in the zodiacal sign of Cancer.

THE WINDING STAIR AND OTHER POEMS

(page 345)

I am of Ireland (page 382) is developed from three or four lines of an Irish fourteenth-century dance song somebody repeated to me a few years ago. 'The sun in a golden cup' in the poem that precedes it, though not 'The moon in a silver bag,' is a quotation from the last of Mr. Ezra Pound's *Cantos*. In this book and elsewhere I have used towers, and one tower in particular, as symbols and have compared their winding stairs to the philosophical gyres, but it is hardly necessary to interpret what comes from the main track of thought and expression. Shelley uses towers constantly as symbols, and there are gyres in Swedenborg, and in Thomas Aquinas and certain classical authors. Part of the symbolism of *Blood and the Moon* (page 351) was suggested by the fact that Thoor Ballylee has a waste room at the top and that butterflies come in through the loopholes and die against the window-panes. The 'learned astrologer' in *Chosen* (page 387) was Macrobius, and the particular passage was found for me by Dr. Sturm, that too little known poet and mystic. It is from Macrobius's comment upon 'Scipio's Dream' (Lib. I. Cap. XII. Sec. 5): '. . . when the sun is in Aquarius, we sacrifice to the Shades, for it is in the sign inimical to human life; and from thence the meeting-place of Zodiac and Milky Way, the descending soul by its defluction is drawn out of the spherical, the sole divine form, into the cone.'

When *The Winding Stair* was published separately by Macmillan & Co. it was introduced by the following dedication:

DEAR DULAC,

I saw my *Hawk's Well* played by students of our Schools of Dancing and of Acting a couple of years ago in a beautiful little theatre called 'The Peacock,' which shares a roof with the Abbey Theatre. Watching Cuchulain in his lovely mask and costume, that old masked man who seems hundreds of years old, that Guardian of the Well, with your great golden wings and dancing to your music, I had one of those moments of excitement that are the dramatist's reward and decided there and then to dedicate to you my next book of verse.

A Woman Young and Old was written before the publication of *The Tower*, but left out for some reason I cannot recall. I think that I was roused to write *Death* and *Blood and the Moon* by the assassination of Kevin O'Higgins, the finest intellect in Irish public life, and, I think I may add, to some extent, my friend. *A Dialogue of Self and Soul* was written in the spring of 1928 during a long illness, indeed finished the day before a Cannes doctor told me to stop writing. Then in the spring of 1929 life returned to me as an impression of the uncontrollable energy and daring of the great creators; it seemed to me that but for journalism and criticism, all that evasion and explanation, the world would be torn in pieces. I wrote *Mad as the Mist and Snow*, a mechanical little song, and after that almost all that group of poems, called in memory of those exultant weeks *Words for Music Perhaps*. Then ill again, I warmed myself back into life with *Byzantium* and *Veronica's Napkin*, looking for a theme that might befit my years. Since then I have added a few poems to *Words for Music Perhaps*, but always keeping the mood and plan of the first poems.

1933

Last Poems

THE MUNICIPAL GALLERY REVISITED

(Stanza V, page 439)

It will be noticed that the fifth stanza has only seven lines instead of eight. In the original version of the poem, this stanza ran as follows:–

> My mediaeval knees lack health until they bend,
> But in that woman, in that household, where
> Honour had lived so long, their health I found.
> Childless, I thought, 'my children may learn here
> What deep roots are,' and never foresaw the end
> Of all that scholarly generations had held dear;
> But now that end has come I have not wept;
> No fox can foul the lair the badger swept:

[This note was added to *Poems* (1949) by Thomas Mark and Mrs Yeats.]

Bibliography

I. SELECT BIBLIOGRAPHY OF WRITING ON YEATS'S POETRY

Ellmann, Richard, *The Identity of Yeats* (London, Faber & Faber, 1954)

Jeffares, A. Norman, *The Poetry of W. B. Yeats* (London, Edward Arnold, 1961)

—, *W. B. Yeats*, Profiles in Literature Series (London, Routledge & Kegan Paul, 1971)

—, *A New Commentary on the Poems of W. B. Yeats* (London, Macmillan, 1984)

Melchiori, Giorgio, *The Whole Mystery of Art: Pattern into Poetry in the Work of W. B. Yeats* (London, Routledge & Kegan Paul, 1960)

Stock, A. G., *W. B. Yeats. His Poetry and Thoughts* (Cambridge, Cambridge University Press, 1961)

Unterecker, John, *A Reader's Guide to W. B. Yeats* (London, Thames and Hudson, 1959)

Ure, Peter, *Towards a Mythology: Studies in the Poetry of W. B. Yeats* (Liverpool, Liverpool University Press, 1946)

II. SELECT BIBLIOGRAPHY OF OTHER WORKS ON YEATS

Cosgrave, Patrick, 'Yeats, Fascism and Conor O'Brien', *London Magazine*, 7, No. 4 (July 1967), 22–41

Donoghue, Denis, *Yeats*, Fontana Modern Masters (London, Collins, 1971)

Ellmann, Richard, *Yeats: The Man and the Masks* (London, Faber & Faber, 1948; New York, W. N. Norton, 1979)

Finneran, Richard J., *Editing Yeats's Poems* (London, Macmillan, 1983; rev. edn 1989)

Flannery, Mary Catherine, *Yeats and Magic: the Earlier Works* (Gerrards Cross, Colin Smythe, 1977)

Harper, George Mills (ed.), *Yeats and the Occult* (Toronto, Macmillan of Canada; Maclean-Hunter Press, 1975)

—, *The Making of Yeats's 'A Vision'. A Study of the Automatic Script* (London, Macmillan, 2 vols., 1987)

Henn, T. R., *The Lonely Tower* (London, Methuen, 1950; rev. edn 1965)

Hone, Joseph, *W. B. Yeats 1865–1939* (London, Macmillan, 1942; rev. edn, 1962)

Hough, Graham, *The Mystery Religion of W. B. Yeats* (Sussex, The Harvester Press, 1984)

Jeffares, A. Norman, *Yeats: man and poet* (London, Routledge & Kegan Paul, 1949; 1962)

—, *The Circus Animals. Essays on W. B. Yeats* (London, Macmillan, 1970)

—, *W. B. Yeats: A New Biography* (London, Hutchinson, 1988)

Longenbach, James, *Stone Cottage: Pound, Yeats and Modernism* (Oxford, Oxford University Press, 1988)

McGarry, James, *Place Names in the Writings of William Butler Yeats* (Gerrards Cross, Colin Smythe, 1976)

MacLiammóir, Micheál, and Boland, Eavan, *W. B. Yeats and His World* (London, Thames and Hudson, 1971)

Malins, Edward, *A Preface to Yeats* (New York, Charles Scribner's Sons, 1974)

Martin, Augustine, *W. B. Yeats* (Dublin, Gill & Macmillan, 1983)

Moore, Virginia, *The Unicorn: William Butler Yeats's Search for Reality* (New York, Macmillan, 1954)

Rajan, B., *W. B. Yeats. A Critical Introduction* (London, Hutchinson, 1965)

Ronsley, Joseph, *Yeats's Autobiography: Life as symbolic pattern* (London, Oxford University Press, 1968)

Saul, George Brandon, *Prolegomena to the Study of Yeats's Poems* (Philadelphia, University of Pennsylvania Press, 1957)

Torchiana, Donald T., *Yeats and Georgian Ireland* (Evanston, Northwestern Press, 1966)

Tuohy, Frank, *Yeats* (London, Macmillan, 1976)

Ure, Peter, *Yeats* (Edinburgh and London, Oliver and Boyd, 1963)

Wilson, F. A. C., *W. B. Yeats and Tradition* (London, Gollancz, 1958)

—, *Yeats's Iconography* (London, Gollancz, 1960)

III.   SELECT BIBLIOGRAPHY OF WORKS ON YEATS'S METHODS OF WORK

Bradford, Curtis, *Yeats at Work* (Illinois, Southern Illinois University Press, 1965)

Clark, David R., *Yeats At Songs and Choruses* (Gerrard's Cross, Colin Smythe, 1983)

Jeffares, A. Norman, 'Yeats's Technique as a Poet', Appendix I, *Poems of W. B. Yeats. A New Selection* (Basingstoke and London, Macmillan Education Ltd, 2nd edn, 1988)

Stallworthy, Jon, *Between the Lines. Yeats's Poetry in the Making* (Oxford, Clarendon Press, 1963)

—, *Vision and Revision in Yeats's Last Poems* (Oxford, Clarendon Press, 1963)

IV. COLLECTIONS OF CRITICAL COMMENT

Donoghue, Denis, and Mulryne, J. R. (eds.), *An Honoured Guest. New Essays on W. B. Yeats* (London, Edward Arnold, 1965)

Hall, James, and Steinmann, Martin (eds.), *The Permanence of Yeats* (New York, Macmillan, 1950; New York, Collier Books, 1961)

Jeffares, A. Norman (ed.), *W. B. Yeats: the critical heritage* (London, Henley and Boston, Routledge & Kegan Paul, 1977)

—, (ed.), *Yeats the European* (Gerrard's Cross, Colin Smythe, 1989)

Jeffares, A. Norman, and Cross, K. G. W. (eds.), *In Excited Reverie. A Centenary Tribute to W. B. Yeats 1865–1939* (London, Macmillan; New York, St Martin's Press, 1965)

Maxwell, D. E. S., and Bushrui, S. B. (eds.), *W. B. Yeats 1865–1965. Centenary Essays* (Ibadan, Ibadan University Press, 1965)

Pritchard, William H. (ed.), *W. B. Yeats. A Critical Anthology* (Harmondsworth, Penguin Books, 1972)

Unterecker, John (ed.), *Yeats: a collection of critical essays* (Englewood Cliffs, New Jersey, Prentice-Hall, 1963)

Index to Titles

Index to First Lines